Kaplan Publishing are constantly finding difference to your studies and our excit offer something different to students lc

C000126902

This book comes with free MyKaplan or study anytime, anywhere. **This free on**....... **separately and is included in the price of the book.**

Having purchased this book, you have access to the following online study materials:

CONTENT		ACCA (including FBT, FMA, FFA)		FIA (excluding FBT, FMA, FFA)	
		Text	Kit	Text	Kit
Electronic version of the book		✓	✓	✓	✓
Check Your Understanding Test with instant answers		✓			
Material updates		✓	✓	✓	✓
Latest official ACCA exam questions*			✓		
Extra question assistance using the signpost icon**			✓		
Timed questions with an online tutor debrief using clock icon***			✓		
Interim assessment including questions and answers		✓		✓	
Technical answers		✓	✓	✓	✓

* Excludes BT, MA, FA, FBT, FMA, FFA; for all other papers includes a selection of questions, as released by ACCA
** For ACCA SBL, SBR, AFM, APM, ATX, AAA only
*** Excludes BT, MA, FA, LW, FBT, FMA and FFA

How to access your online resources

Kaplan Financial students will already have a MyKaplan account and these extra resources will be available to you online. You do not need to register again, as this process was completed when you enrolled. If you are having problems accessing online materials, please ask your course administrator.

If you are not studying with Kaplan and did not purchase your book via a Kaplan website, to unlock your extra online resources please go to www.mykaplan.co.uk/addabook (even if you have set up an account and registered books previously). You will then need to enter the ISBN number (on the title page and back cover) and the unique pass key number contained in the scratch panel below to gain access. You will also be required to enter additional information during this process to set up or confirm your account details.

If you purchased through the Kaplan Publishing website you will automatically receive an e-mail invitation to MyKaplan. Please register your details using this email to gain access to your content. If you do not receive the e-mail or book content, please contact Kaplan Publishing.

Your Code and Information

This code can only be used once for the registration of one book online. This registration and your online content will expire when the final sittings for the examinations covered by this book have taken place. Please allow one hour from the time you submit your book details for us to process your request.

Please scratch the film to access your unique code.

Please be aware that this code is case-sensitive and you will need to include the dashes within the passcode, but not when entering the ISBN.

KAPLAN

PUBLISHING

ACCA

Applied Skills

Audit and Assurance (AA)

EXAM KIT

British Library Cataloguing-in-Publication Data

A catalogue record for this book is available from the British Library.

Published by:

Kaplan Publishing UK
Unit 2 The Business Centre
Molly Millar's Lane
Wokingham
Berkshire
RG41 2QZ

ISBN: 978-1-78740-622-3

Acknowledgements

These materials are reviewed by the ACCA examining team. The objective of the review is to ensure that the material properly covers the syllabus and study guide outcomes, used by the examining team in setting the exams, in the appropriate breadth and depth. The review does not ensure that every eventuality, combination or application of examinable topics is addressed by the ACCA Approved Content. Nor does the review comprise a detailed technical check of the content as the Approved Content Provider has its own quality assurance processes in place in this respect.

This product contains material that is ©Financial Reporting Council Ltd (FRC). Adapted and reproduced with the kind permission of the Financial Reporting Council. All rights reserved. For further information, please visit www.frc.org.uk or call +44 (0)20 7492 2300.

This Product includes propriety content of the International Accounting Standards Board which is overseen by the IFRS Foundation, and is used with the express permission of the IFRS Foundation under licence. All rights reserved. No part of this publication may be reproduced, stored in a retrieval system, or transmitted in any form or by any means, electronic, mechanical, photocopying, recording, or otherwise, without prior written permission of Kaplan Publishing and the IFRS Foundation.

The IFRS Foundation logo, the IASB logo, the IFRS for SMEs logo, the "Hexagon Device", "IFRS Foundation", "eIFRS", "IAS", "IASB", "IFRS for SMEs", "IFRS", "IASs", "IFRSs", "International Accounting Standards" and "International Financial Reporting Standards", "IFRIC" and "IFRS Taxonomy" are **Trade Marks** of the IFRS Foundation.

Trade Marks

The IFRS Foundation logo, the IASB logo, the IFRS for SMEs logo, the "Hexagon Device", "IFRS Foundation", "eIFRS", "IAS", "IASB", "IFRS for SMEs", "NIIF" IASs" "IFRS", "IFRSs", "International Accounting Standards", "International Financial Reporting Standards", "IFRIC", "SIC" and "IFRS Taxonomy".

Further details of the Trade Marks including details of countries where the Trade Marks are registered or applied for are available from the Foundation on request.

CONTENTS

Section

This document references IFRS® Standards and IAS® Standards, which are authored by the International Accounting Standards Board (the Board), and published in the 2019 IFRS Standards Red Book.

Features in this edition

In addition to providing a wide ranging bank of real past exam questions, we have also included in this edition:

- An analysis of all of the recent new syllabus examinations.

- Subject specific information and advice on exam technique.

- Our recommended approach to make your revision for this particular subject as effective as possible.

  This includes step by step guidance on how best to use our Kaplan material (Study text, pocket notes and exam kit) at this stage in your studies.

- Enhanced tutorial answers packed with specific key answer tips, technical tutorial notes and exam technique tips from our experienced tutors.

- Complementary online resources including full tutor debriefs and question assistance to point you in the right direction when you get stuck.

You will find a wealth of other resources to help you with your studies on the following sites:

www.MyKaplan.co.uk

www.accaglobal.com/students/

Quality and accuracy are of the utmost importance to us so if you spot an error in any of our products, please send an email to mykaplanreporting@kaplan.com with full details.

Our Quality Co-ordinator will work with our technical team to verify the error and take action to ensure it is corrected in future editions.

INDEX TO QUESTIONS AND ANSWERS

INTRODUCTION

The majority of the questions within the kit are past ACCA exam questions, the more recent questions are labelled as such in the index. Where changes have been made to the syllabus, the old ACCA questions within this kit have been adapted to reflect the new style of exam and the new guidance. If changed in any way from the original version, this is indicated in the end column of the index below with the mark *(A)*.

Note that

The specimen exam is included at the end of the kit.

KEY TO THE INDEX

EXAM KIT ENHANCEMENTS

We have added the following enhancements to the answers in this exam kit:

Key answer tips

All answers include key answer tips to help your understanding of each question.

Tutorial note

All answers include more tutorial notes to explain some of the technical points in more detail.

Top tutor tips

For selected questions, we walk through the answer giving guidance on how to approach the questions with helpful 'tips from a top tutor', together with technical tutor notes.

These answers are indicated with the 'footsteps' icon in the index.

ONLINE ENHANCEMENTS

 Timed question with Online tutor debrief

For selected questions, we recommend that they are to be completed under full exam conditions (i.e. properly timed in a closed book environment).

In addition to the examiner's technical answer, enhanced with key answer tips and tutorial notes in this exam kit, you can find an answer debrief online by a top tutor that:

- works through the question in full

- discusses how to approach the question

- discusses how to ensure that the easy marks are obtained as quickly as possible

- emphasises how to tackle exam questions and exam technique.

These questions are indicated with the 'clock' icon in the index.

Online answer debriefs will be available on MyKaplan at:

www.MyKaplan.co.uk

SECTION A-TYPE QUESTIONS

SECTION B-TYPE QUESTIONS

Planning and risk assessment

Internal controls

221	Caterpillar		111	319	Dec 16
222	Heraklion		112	325	Sep 16
223	Lemon Quartz		113	333	M16/J16
224	Bronze		114	337	S15/D15 (A)
225	Trombone		116	345	Jun 14
226	Oregano		117	353	Dec 13
227	Fox Industries		118	358	Jun 13
228	Lily Window Glass		119	365	Dec 12
229	Pear International		121	373	Jun 12

Substantive procedures, completion and reporting

230	Spadefish		122	378	S19/D19
231	Hyacinth		123	383	M19/J19
232	Jasmine		125	389	S18/D18
233	Gooseberry		126	395	M18/J18
234	Dashing		127	400	S17/D17
235	Airsoft		128	405	M17/J17
236	Insects4U		129	410	Dec 16
237	Elounda		130	414	Sep 16
238	Andromeda		131	419	S15/D15
239	Hawthorn		132	423	Jun 15
240	Pineapple Beach Hotel		134	428	Jun 12

Additional questions

241	Saxophone Enterprises		135	432	June 14
242	Orange Financials		136	435	Jun 12
243	Violet & Co		137	438	Dec 12

ANALYSIS OF PAST EXAMS

The table below summarises the key topics that have been tested in the new syllabus examinations to date.

	Specimen	M/J 17	S/D 17	M/J 18	S/D 18	M/J 19	S/D 19
Audit Framework							
Audit vs. assurance engagements							
Statutory audits							
Benefits/limitations of an audit							
Elements of assurance							
Corporate governance						✓	
Audit committee							
Ethics	✓	✓	✓				
Acceptance			✓				
Engagement letter							
Limited assurance engagements	✓						
Planning and risk assessment							
Audit risk	✓	✓	✓	✓	✓	✓	✓
Analytical procedures	✓				✓		✓
Understanding the entity							
Materiality						✓	
Fraud & error				✓			✓
Laws & regulations							
Audit strategy & plan	✓		✓				
Interim & final	✓						
Audit documentation							
Quality control							

	Specimen	M/J 17	S/D 17	M/J 18	S/D 18	M/J 19	S/D 19
Internal control							
Components		✓					
Systems/tests of controls:							
– Revenue system	✓	✓				✓	✓
– Purchases system	✓		✓			✓	
– Payroll system		✓		✓		✓	
– Capital system	✓						
– Inventory system		✓				✓	
– Cash system		✓			✓		
Systems documentation	✓		✓			✓	
IT controls	✓						
Internal Audit							
Scope/limitations	✓						
Contrast with external audit	✓						
Outsourcing internal audit							
IA assignments				✓			
Audit Evidence							
ISA 500 Audit procedures							
Assertions	✓						
Audit sampling							
Sufficient appropriate evidence	✓						
Use of experts	✓						
Use of internal audit							
Service organisations							
Automated tools and techniques		✓					
The audit of specific items:							
– Revenue					✓		
– Purchases			✓				
– Payroll				✓			
– Tangible non-current assets	✓			✓			✓
- Research & development				✓		✓	

	Specimen	M/J 17	S/D 17	M/J 18	S/D 18	M/J 19	S/D 19
– Trade receivables	✓		✓		✓		✓
– Inventory					✓	✓	
– Bank		✓			✓		
– Trade payables / accruals		✓				✓	
– Provisions	✓		✓				
– Equity							
– Directors' remuneration		✓		✓			
Completion & reporting							
Misstatements	✓						
Final review							
Subsequent events	✓					✓	
Going concern	✓				✓		✓
Written representations							
Auditor's reports/opinions	✓		✓	✓	✓	✓	
Key audit matters		✓					
Reporting to those charged with governance					✓		

EXAM TECHNIQUE

GENERAL COMMENTS

- Read the questions and examination requirements **carefully**.

- **Divide the time** you spend on questions in proportion to the marks on offer:

  - there are 1.8 minutes available per mark in the computer based examinations so a 20 mark question should be completed in approximately 36 minutes

  - within that, try to allow time at the end of each question to review your answer and address any obvious issues

  Whatever happens, always keep your eye on the clock and **do not over run on any part of any question.**

- **Objective test case questions:**

  - Don't leave any questions unanswered. If in doubt, guess.

  - Try and identify the correct answer.

  - If you can't identify the correct answer, try and rule out the wrong answers.

- Spend the last **five minutes** of the examination:

  - reading through your answers, and

  - **making any additions or corrections**.

- If you **get completely stuck**, flag the question for review and **return to it later.**

- Stick to the question and **tailor your answer** to what you are asked.

  - Pay particular attention to the verbs in the question.

  - Apply your comments to the scenario.

- If you do not understand what a question is asking, **state your assumptions**.

  Even if you do not answer in precisely the way the examiner hoped, you may be given some credit, if your assumptions are reasonable.

- You should do everything you can to make things easy for the marker.

  The marker will find it easier to identify the points you have made if your **answers are understandable, well-spaced out and clearly referenced to the requirement being answered.**

OBJECTIVE TEST QUESTIONS

- Decide whether you want to attempt these at the start of the exam or at the end.

- No credit for working will be given in these questions, the answers will either be correct (2 marks) or incorrect (0 marks).

- Read the question carefully, as any alternative answer choices will be given based on common mistakes that could be made in attempting the question.

- If a question looks particularly difficult or time consuming, then miss it out first time through (make sure you flag it) and come back to it later.

CONSTRUCTED RESPONSE (LONG) QUESTIONS

- **Written elements**:

  Your answer should:

  - Have a clear structure

  - Be concise: get to the point!

  - Address a broad range of points: it is usually better to write a little about a lot of different points than a great deal about one or two points.

- **Reports, memos and other documents**:

  Some questions ask you to present your answer in the form of a report, a memo, a letter or other document.

  Make sure that you use the correct format – there could be easy marks to gain here.

COMPUTER-BASED EXAMS – ADDITIONAL TIPS

- Do not attempt a CBE until you have **completed all study material** relating to it.

- On the ACCA website there is a CBE demonstration. It is **ESSENTIAL** that you attempt this before your real CBE. You will become familiar with how to move around the CBE screens and the way that questions are formatted, increasing your confidence and speed in the actual exam.

- Be sure you understand how to use the **software** before you start the exam. If in doubt, ask the assessment centre staff to explain it to you.

- Questions are **displayed on the screen** and answers are entered using keyboard and mouse.

- In addition to the traditional multiple choice question type, CBEs will also contain other types of questions, such as multiple response (select two or more), drop down list, drag and drop, hot spots and hot areas.

- You need to be sure you **know how to answer questions** of these types before you sit the exam, through practice.

SUBJECT SPECIFIC INFORMATION

THE EXAM

FORMAT OF THE EXAM

The exam will be in **TWO** sections

All questions are compulsory

		Number of marks
Section A:	3 objective test case questions	
	5 questions worth 2 marks per case	30
Section B:	3 constructed response questions	
	2 × 20 mark questions (mainly scenario based)	40
	1 × 30 mark question (mainly scenario based)	30
		_____
		100
		_____

Time allowed: 3 hours.

In the AA exam the 'current' date will be 1 July 20X5. Year-end dates will then be flexed around this depending on the nature of the question. For example, a question set at the planning stage of the audit may have a year-end of 30 June 20X5 or 31 July 20X5. A question set at the completion stage of the audit may have a year-end of 31 January 20X5 or 31 March 20X5.

PASS MARK

The pass mark for all ACCA Qualification exams is 50%.

APPROACH TO THIS EXAM

Audit and Assurance is a computer based exam.

Any part of the syllabus can be tested in any section.

Section A

- The objective test case questions will be based around a short scenario and you will have to choose the correct answer(s) from the options given.

- You should begin by reading the OT questions that relate to the case, so that when you read through the information for the first time, you know what is required.

- Each OT question is worth two marks. Therefore you have 18 minutes (1.8 minutes per mark) to answer the five OT questions relating to each case.

- It is likely that all of the cases will take the same length of time to answer, although some of the OT questions within a case may be quicker than other OT questions within that same case.

- Work steadily. Rushing leads to careless mistakes and the OT questions are designed to include 'plausible distractors' i.e. answers which result from careless mistakes.

- If you don't know the answer, eliminate those options you know are incorrect and see if the answer becomes more obvious.

- After you have eliminated the options that you know to be wrong, if you are still unsure, guess.

Section B

- The constructed response questions will require a written response rather than being OT questions.

- Each question will contain some knowledge based requirements. Knowledge of ISAs may be required in this section.

- The other requirements will require application of knowledge to the scenario provided. For these requirements it is important you relate your answers to the scenario rather than just regurgitate rote-learned knowledge.

- For the scenario based questions it is important to read the information carefully and only use this information to generate your answers. There are unlikely to be any marks awarded to students creating their own scenario and generating answers from that.

- **For each question**, read the requirements and then the detail of the question carefully.

  Always read the requirement first as this enables you to **focus on the detail of the question with the specific task in mind**.

- Take notice of the format required (e.g. letter, memo, notes) and identify the recipient of the answer . You need to do this to judge the level of sophistication required in your answer and whether the use of a formal reply or informal bullet points would be satisfactory.

- There are times when you are instructed to use tables to present your answer. This is the case when you are asked to link answers together. Pre-formatted tables will usually be set up in the workspace for you to use.

- Spot the easy marks to be gained in a question. Make sure that you do these parts first when you tackle the question.

- **Highlight questions for review if you are not sure and want to check your answers before you end your exam**.

The three questions in section B will usually focus on planning and audit risk assessment, internal controls and audit evidence.

Audit risks

Candidates need explain audit risks by stating the specific area of the financial statements impacted with an assertion (for example cut off, valuation etc.), or, a reference to over/under/misstated, or a reference to inherent/ control/ detection risk. Credit is only awarded for misstated when it is clear that a balance could be either over or understated. Credit is not given for misstated if it is clear that a balance could only be overstated or could only be understated.

Control deficiencies and recommendations

Internal control deficiency questions typically require internal control deficiencies to be identified (½ mark each), explained (½ mark each) which must cover the implication of the deficiency to the company and a relevant recommendation to address the deficiency (1 mark). Candidates are required to explain the implication to the business to be awarded credit, for example that 'loss of revenue or loss of customer goodwill'. Recommendations must be described in sufficient detail.

Key controls and tests of control

Questions typically require the key control to be identified (½ mark each), explained as to why it is a key control (½ mark each) and a test of control provided (1 mark). To explain why the control is key, candidates must explain how the control will prevent or detect and correct a misstatement.

Audit evidence

Audit procedures must be clearly described. A well described substantive procedure will clearly detail the source of the evidence, clearly detail the purpose of the test, and state exactly 'how' the procedure should be performed.

All sections

- Don't skip parts of the syllabus. The AA exam has 18 different questions, each with multiple requirements, so the examination can cover a very broad selection of the syllabus each sitting.

- Practice plenty of questions to improve your ability to apply the techniques.

- Spend the last five minutes reading through your answers and making any additions or corrections.

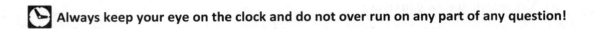 **Always keep your eye on the clock and do not over run on any part of any question!**

DETAILED SYLLABUS

The detailed syllabus and study guide written by the ACCA can be found at:

www.accaglobal.com/students/

KAPLAN'S RECOMMENDED REVISION APPROACH

QUESTION PRACTICE IS THE KEY TO SUCCESS

Success in professional examinations relies upon you acquiring a firm grasp of the required knowledge at the tuition phase. In order to be able to do the questions, knowledge is essential.

However, the difference between success and failure often hinges on your exam technique on the day and making the most of the revision phase of your studies.

The **Kaplan study text** is the starting point, designed to provide the underpinning knowledge to tackle all questions. However, in the revision phase, pouring over text books is not the answer.

Kaplan online tests help you consolidate your knowledge and understanding and are a useful tool to check whether you can remember key topic areas.

Kaplan pocket notes are designed to help you quickly revise a topic area, however you then need to practice questions. There is a need to progress to full exam standard questions as soon as possible, and to tie your exam technique and technical knowledge together.

The importance of question practice cannot be over-emphasised.

The recommended approach below is designed by expert tutors in the field, in conjunction with their knowledge of the examiner and their recent real exams.

The approach taken for the applied skills exams is to revise by topic area. However, with the professional stage exams, a multi topic approach is required to answer the scenario based questions.

You need to practice as many questions as possible in the time you have left.

OUR AIM

Our aim is to get you to the stage where you can attempt exam standard questions confidently, to time, in a closed book environment, with no supplementary help (i.e. to simulate the real examination experience).

Practising your exam technique on real past examination questions, in timed conditions, is also vitally important for you to assess your progress and identify areas of weakness that may need more attention in the final run up to the examination.

In order to achieve this we recognise that initially you may feel the need to practice some questions with open book help and exceed the required time.

The approach below shows you which questions you should use to build up to coping with exam standard question practice, and references to the sources of information available should you need to revisit a topic area in more detail.

Remember that in the real examination, all you have to do is:

- attempt all questions required by the exam

- only spend the allotted time on each question, and

- get them at least 50% right!

Try and practice this approach on every question you attempt from now to the real exam.

EXAMINER COMMENTS

We have included the examiners comments to the specific new syllabus examination questions in this kit for you to see the main pitfalls that students fall into with regard to technical content.

However, too many times in the general section of the report, the examiner comments that students had failed due to:

- lack of knowledge or exam preparation

- candidates not adequately explaining audit risks

- candidates not clearly understanding/explaining the implication of control deficiencies

- audit procedures not clearly described

- substantive procedures being too generic and not related to the scenario given

- candidates re-writing the question requirement at the start of each question which is unnecessary and not an efficient use of time.

Good exam technique is vital.

ACCA SUPPORT

For additional support with your studies please also refer to the ACCA Global website.

KAPLAN PUBLISHING

THE KAPLAN AA REVISION PLAN

Stage 1: Assess areas of strengths and weaknesses

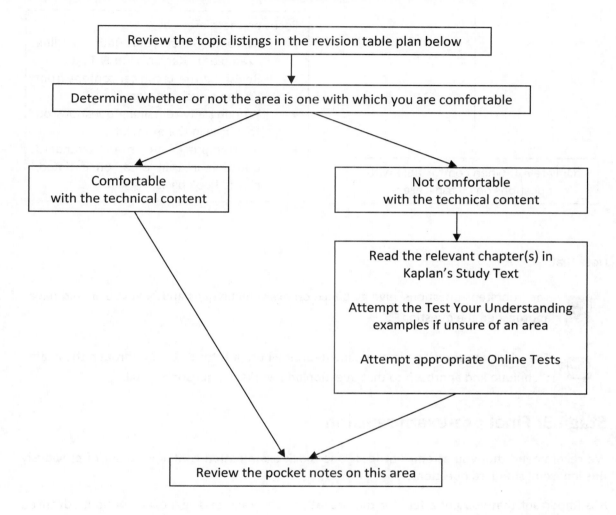

Stage 2: Practice questions

Follow the order of revision of topics as recommended in the revision table plan below and attempt the questions in the order suggested.

Try to avoid referring to text books and notes and the model answer until you have completed your attempt.

Try to answer the question in the allotted time.

Review your attempt with the model answer and assess how much of the answer you achieved in the allocated exam time.

Fill in the self-assessment box below and decide on your best course of action.

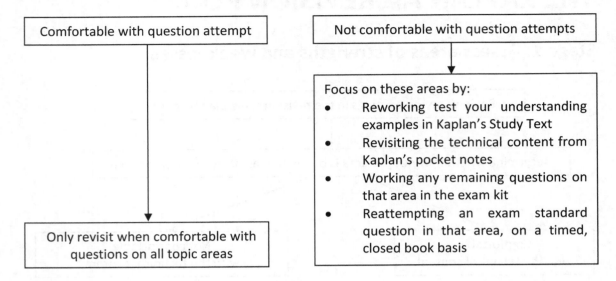

Note that :

 The 'footsteps questions' give guidance on exam techniques and how you should have approached the question.

 The 'clock questions' have an online debrief where a tutor talks you through the exam technique and approach to that question and works the question in full.

Stage 3: Final pre-exam revision

We recommend that you **attempt at least one mock examination** containing a set of previously unseen exam standard questions.

It is important that you get a feel for the breadth of coverage of a real exam without advanced knowledge of the topic areas covered – just as you will expect to see on the real exam day.

Ideally this mock should be sat in timed, closed book, real exam conditions and could be:

- a mock examination offered by your tuition provider, and/or

- the specimen exam in the back of this exam kit, and/or

- the last real examination.

KAPLAN'S DETAILED REVISION PLAN

In addition to the questions below, you should practise a selection of OT case questions from Section A of the exam kit.

	Topics	Study Text (and Pocket Note) Chapter	Questions to attempt	Tutor guidance	Date attempted	Self-assessment
1	Audit framework and regulation	1, 2, 3, 4	Hurling Freesia Saxophone Enterprises Orange Financials OT cases 1 – 50	You must also be able to discuss the purpose of assurance and the levels of assurance offered by accountants. Make sure that you can define the elements of the Code of Ethics and that you practice applying the concepts to specific scenarios. You need to be able to identify and explain the main requirements of corporate governance regulations (e.g. UK Corporate Governance Code) and be able to identify when a company is not compliant with best practise.		
2	Planning and risk assessment	5 & 6	Harlem Peony Darjeeling Prancer Hurling Centipede Sitia Sparkle	Audit risk is a vital concept. You need to be able to: discuss what it is, including materiality; perform risk assessment for a client; and discuss its impact on audit strategy.		

KAPLAN PUBLISHING

Topics	Study Text (and Pocket Note) Chapter	Questions to attempt	Tutor guidance	Date attempted	Self-assessment
3 Internal controls	8, 9	Amberjack Freesia Camomile Raspberry Comet Equestrian Lemon Quartz	You need to know how a simple financial control system (e.g. sales, purchases, payroll etc.) operates. You may be asked to identify deficiencies in control systems and provide recommendations. You need to be able to state how those systems and controls should be tested.		
4 Audit evidence	7 & 10	Spadefish Hyacinth Jasmine Gooseberry Dashing Airsoft	It is vital that you are able to identify **specifically** what procedures are required (e.g. tests of control, analytical procedures) and what assertions are being tested (e.g. completeness, existence, accuracy) for a particular balance or issue given.		
5 Review and reporting	11 & 12	Spadefish Hyacinth Jasmine Gooseberry Dashing Airsoft Violet & Co OT cases 141 – 200	There are a wide range of issues that need to be considered at the completion stage of an audit. Typical examples include: subsequent events, going concern, written representations and evaluation of misstatements. It is important that you are able to assess a scenario and identify how it might impact upon the auditor's report and opinion. You also need to be able to discuss the content and purpose of the sections of an auditor's report. In addition, you should be able to identify matters which should be reported to those charged with governance.		

KAPLAN PUBLISHING

Section 1

OBJECTIVE TEST CASE QUESTIONS

AUDIT FRAMEWORK

The following scenario relates to questions 1 – 5

The board of directors of Sistar Co are concerned that they are not currently applying best practice in terms of corporate governance and are seeking to make improvements.

The company currently has three non-executive directors (NEDs) on the board, who are paid a fee which changes annually depending on company performance. The NEDs all sit on the audit, nomination and remuneration committees. There is currently no reference to the work of these committees in the annual report.

At present, Sistar Co does not have an internal audit function but the directors are establishing a team which will be responsible for a range of internal audit assignments.

The following is the current proposed structure for the internal audit (IA) department

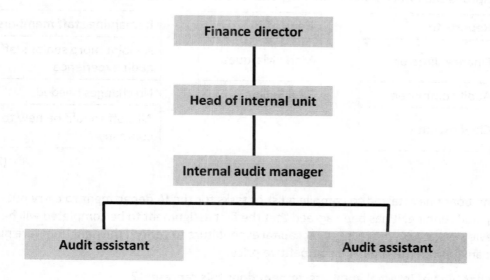

The only role still to be filled is the Head of internal audit. There are two potential candidates: Paul Belling a consultant who helped design and implement the company's current control system, and Maria Marquez who is currently an audit manager at Rossi & Bell, an audit firm which has never been used by Sistar Co.

Out of the other three members of the proposed IA department, two of them have moved from other departments in Sistar Co and one of the audit assistants has audit experience.

1   **Which of the following should be included in the annual report regarding the work of the audit committee?**

o   Responsibility for preparing the annual report and financial statements

o   Significant issues considered relating to the financial statements

o   A description of the principal risks the company faces

o   The process used to make appointments to the board   **(2 marks)**

2   **Which of the following options correctly describes the deficiency relating to NEDs' remuneration and makes a valid recommendation for improvement?**

Deficiency	*Recommendation*
o Compromises NED independence	NEDs should be remunerated on the same basis as the executive team
o Compromises the motivation of NEDs	NEDs' remuneration should be tied to profit targets
o Compromises NED independence	NEDs' remuneration should be a set amount based on time committed
o Compromises the motivation of NEDs	NEDs' remuneration should be linked to individual performance **(2 marks)**

3   The board is in the final stages of establishing the IA department.

Select one option from each column which provides appropriate recommendations to improve the effectiveness and independence of the IA department.

Reports to	**Head of IA**	**Remaining staff members**
Finance director	Maria Marquez	Appoint more senior staff with audit experience
Audit committee	Paul Belling	No changes needed
Chief executive		All staff should be new to the company

(2 marks)

4   The board has started to compile a list of tasks for the IA department to carry out once it is up and running. It has been agreed that the first assignment to be completed will be for IA to review Sistar Co's processes over capital expenditure to verify if the right items are purchased at an appropriate time and competitive price.

What type of internal audit assignment does this represent?

o   A value for money audit

o   A management audit

o   A financial audit

o   An IT audit   **(2 marks)**

5   When deciding on the role of the IA department in undertaking operational audits, which TWO of the following should the team NOT be involved in?

    O   Observing procedures carried out by Sistar Co's staff

    O   Reperforming procedures documented in procedures manuals

    O   Designing and implementing internal control procedures to address deficiencies

    O   Reporting findings directly to the board of directors

    O   Authorising transactions and performing reconciliations   **(2 marks)**

The following scenario relates to questions 6 – 10

You are an audit manager in Bark & Co and have been assigned to the audit of Foliage Co for the first time this year. Foliage Co is a listed company which specialises in manufacturing musical instruments. You will be taking over from Kim Baum, the audit manager who has been in charge of the audit for the last three years. Kim has just announced that he is leaving Bark & Co to join Foliage Co as the financial controller. Kim has recently completed the planning for the current year audit in preparation for the final audit which is due to commence next month.

Jane Leaf has been the audit engagement partner since Foliage Co became an audit client almost eight years ago. As she has completed seven years as the audit engagement partner, Jane has recently been rotated off the audit engagement. The new audit engagement partner, Chang Petiole, has suggested that in order to maintain a close relationship with Foliage Co, Jane Leaf should undertake the role of Engagement Quality Control Reviewer this year.

The total fees received by Bark & Co from Foliage Co in respect of all services provided in the last year amounted to 16% of the firm's total fee income. The current year's total fee income for audit, tax and other audit-related services is expected to be greater than last year.

---

6   What is the most appropriate response to the suggestion that Jane Leaf takes on the role of Engagement Quality Control Reviewer?

    O   Jane Leaf could take the review role immediately

    O   Jane Leaf could take the review role immediately but additional safeguards will be required

    O   Jane Leaf should not serve as the Engagement Quality Control Reviewer for a period of at least five years

    O   Bark & Co will need to consider resigning as auditor of Foliage Co   **(2 marks)**

7   Which of the following is the LEAST appropriate response in relation to fee income received by Bark & Co from Foliage Co?

    O   Bark & Co should assess whether audit and non-audit fees would represent more than 15% of gross practice income for two consecutive years

    O   If the recurring fees are likely to exceed 15% of annual practice income this year Bark will need to resign as auditors of Foliage Co

    O   If the recurring fees are likely to exceed 15% of annual practice income this year, additional consideration should be given as to whether the taxation and audit-related services should be undertaken by the firm

    O   If the fees do exceed 15% this should be disclosed to those charged with governance at Foliage Co   **(2 marks)**

8   **What action should Kim Baum have taken when the possibility of employment with Foliage Co arose?**

○   Kim should have notified Bark & Co of the potential employment so he could be removed from the audit team

○   Kim should have declined the offer of employment

○   Kim should not have applied for employment with an audit client while employed by Bark & Co

○   Kim should have asked for permission from Bark & Co before applying for a job with Foliage Co

(2 marks)

9   **Which ethical threat will be created when Kim Baum commences employment with the client and what action should be taken to manage the threat?**

	Threat	Action
A	Intimidation	The manager should not be allowed to take the role of financial controller
B	Familiarity	The composition of the audit team must be reviewed and changed as appropriate
C	Confidentiality	The manager should not be allowed to take the role of financial controller
D	Self-review	The composition of the audit team must be reviewed and changed as appropriate

○   Option A

○   Option B

○   Option C

○   Option D

(2 marks)

10   **Select whether the following statements describe a rulebook approach or a conceptual framework approach to ethics.**

Clearly defined laws for the auditor to follow	Rule book approach	Conceptual framework approach
Useful in a dynamic profession	Rule book approach	Conceptual framework approach
A set of guidelines with which the auditor uses judgment to apply to specific circumstances	Rule book approach	Conceptual framework approach
Easy to know what is allowed and not allowed	Rule book approach	Conceptual framework approach

(2 marks)

The following scenario relates to questions 11 – 15

You are an audit manager in Miranda & Co and you are planning the audit of Milberry Co which manufactures luxury handbags and other fashion accessories. Milberry Co has been an audit client of your firm for four years.

From a review of the correspondence file you note that the audit engagement partner and the finance director have known each other socially for many years and in fact went on holiday together last summer with their families. As a result of this friendship the partner has not yet spoken to the client about the fee for last year's audit, 20% of which is still outstanding.

The financial controller of Milberry Co was appointed two months ago. Prior to this appointment the financial controller was an audit senior at Miranda & Co and was a member of the audit team for Milberry Co.

Employees of Milberry Co are entitled to purchase handbags at a discount of 40% and during the planning meeting with the finance director he offers you and your audit team the same level of staff discount.

The finance director has asked if your firm will prepare the company's tax return and provide tax advice to minimise the amount of tax payable.

11   **Select which threat to objectivity is created by the information obtained from the review of the correspondence file.**

	Advocacy	Familiarity	Self-interest
The partner and the finance director have known each other socially for many years		✓	
20% of the fee for last year's audit is still outstanding			✓

(2 marks)

12   **Which is the MOST appropriate response to the outstanding fees from Milberry Co?**

○   The auditor should resign from the client

○   The auditor should report the client to the ACCA

✗   The auditor can continue working for the client but should ensure that the audit firm's credit control department are informed of the outstanding fees

○   The auditor's report for this year should not be issued until the fees have been paid

(2 marks)

13 Which of the following statements in respect of the relationship between the new financial controller and the audit firm are TRUE?

    ○   The audit approach should be revised to ensure procedures and items to be tested are not predictable

    ○   The audit team should comprise people who know the audit senior as this will make the audit run more smoothly and increase efficiency

    ○   The firm must resign as auditor as the threat to objectivity is too significant to safeguard

    ○   The audit senior should not be allowed to be the financial controller and should resign

    (2 marks)

14 Which is the MOST appropriate response with respect to the discount offered by Milberry Co to the audit team?

    ○   The discount may be accepted as it is the same as that offered to the client's employees

    ○   The discount should be rejected as it is unlikely to be a trivial monetary amount

    ○   The discount should be rejected as gifts or hospitality are not acceptable per the ACCA Code of Ethics

    ○   Audit manager approval must be obtained before the discount is accepted   **(2 marks)**

15 Select the option which correctly identifies whether or not a self-review threat is likely to arise in relation to the tax services requested.

	Tax return	Tax advice
A	Yes	Yes
B	No	No
C	Yes	No
D	No	Yes

    ○   Option A

    ○   Option B

    ○   Option C

    ○   Option D

    (2 marks)

The following scenario relates to questions 16 – 20

You are an audit manager in Tigger & Co, a large audit firm which specialises in the car manufacturing industry. Details of three companies operating in this industry are given below.

Winnie Co

Tigger & Co has audited Winnie Co for many years. The audit engagement partner for Winnie Co has been responsible for the audit for six years. The board of directors has asked if Tigger & Co will provide payroll and bookkeeping services, including providing advice on appropriate accounting policies, in addition to the external audit this year. They have also suggested that the external audit fee should be renegotiated with at least 20% of the fee being based on the company's profit after tax as they feel that this will align the interests of Tigger & Co and Winnie Co.

Eeyore Co

Eeyore Co is a subsidiary of a major global car manufacturer. During the current year audit, the audit team discovered that Eeyore Co had developed and used a device which gave false readings during government tests which are required for all cars. The false readings enabled cars to meet government restrictions on carbon emissions which would otherwise have failed and therefore could not have been sold. The audit engagement partner has discussed the matter with senior management of Eeyore Co and advised them to report the matter to the industry regulator. Senior management has refused and reminded the engagement partner that the audit firm has a duty of confidentiality towards the company.

Piglet Co

Piglet Co has recently approached Tigger & Co to act as auditor due to the firm's expertise in the car manufacturing industry. Piglet Co is the main competitor of Winnie Co.

16   **Which TWO of the following statements are TRUE in respect of the conflict of interest between Winnie Co and Piglet Co?**

   o   Tigger & Co must decline the audit engagement of Piglet Co

   o   Winnie Co and Piglet Co may be concerned that commercially sensitive information may be disclosed by Tigger & Co to their competitor

   o   Tigger & Co must ask permission of ACCA before accepting the audit of Piglet Co

   o   Tigger & Co must obtain consent of both clients before continuing with the engagements   **(2 marks)**

17   **Which of the following is NOT an action that your firm should take to manage the conflict of interest between Winnie Co and Piglet Co?**

   o   Regular monitoring of safeguards by an engagement quality control reviewer

   o   Require every employee of Tigger & Co to sign a confidentiality agreement

   o   Use separate engagement teams and engagement partners for each client

   o   Operate secure data filing of all audit information   **(2 marks)**

18 **Which of the following statements is TRUE in respect of the audit of Winnie Co?**

○   The audit engagement partner must be rotated

○   Providing the additional services for Winnie Co will create a confidentiality threat

○   Payroll and bookkeeping services cannot be provided to an external audit client

○   Providing advice on accounting policies is acceptable as long as the client is responsible for choosing the specific policies used   **(2 marks)**

19 **In relation to the proposal that 20% of the audit fee is based on the profit after tax of the company, which of the following statements is TRUE?**

○   This will lead to fee-dependency which is a self-interest threat. The proposal should be rejected.

○   This is a contingent fee arrangement which creates an advocacy threat. The proposal should only be accepted if no more than 15% of the audit fee is based on profit before tax

○   This is a contingent fee arrangement which creates a self-interest threat. The proposal should be rejected.

○   This will lead to fee-dependency which is a self-interest threat. The proposal should only be accepted if no more than 15% of the audit fee is based on profit before tax   **(2 marks)**

20 **Select whether the following statements are true or false in respect of the issue with Eeyore Co?**

Senior management is correct that reporting the company will constitute a breach of confidentiality	True	False
Tigger & Co must report the breach of laws and regulations to the appropriate authority if the client refuses	True	False
Tigger & Co must report the breach of laws and regulations as it is a public interest matter	True	False
Tigger & Co must report the matter to the parent company and the audit firm responsible for the parent company audit	True	False

     (2 marks)

The following scenario relates to questions 21 – 25

Cameron Co has recently become a listed company. Cameron Co is required to comply with corporate governance principles in order to maintain its listed status. The finance director, Lindsay Lewis has undertaken a review of compliance with corporate governance regulations.

Board composition

Cameron Co's board of directors comprises six members:

Name	Role(s)	Length of service at Cameron Co
Ola Osbourne	Chief executive and chair	5 years
Lindsay Lewis	Finance director	10 years
Hayden Huq	Sales director	5 years
Karie Khan	Human resources director	7 years
Jules Jardine	Independent non-executive	10 years
Taylor Tahir	Independent non-executive	3 years

Directors were last subject to re-election three years ago.

Ola Osbourne has been the chief executive of Cameron Co for five years and has recently been appointed the board chair. Ola Osbourne is considering appointing one of her close friends as a non-executive director.

Directors' remuneration

Executive directors are paid a fixed salary which increases annually in line with inflation. There is no performance related pay or bonus awarded to the executive directors as the company does not want to provide incentive for financial results to be manipulated.

Audit committee

The company does not have an audit committee as the board of directors did not consider it necessary due to the experience of Lindsay Lewis. They are aware that an audit committee is now required and have proposed that one is established comprising the two independent non-executive directors, Lindsay Lewis and Ola Osbourne.

21   Select whether the following matters in respect of board composition represent a corporate governance strength or deficiency.

Ola Osbourne is the chair and chief executive	**Strength**	**Deficiency**
All of the current NEDs are independent	**Strength**	**Deficiency**
Ola Osbourne is considering appointing her friend as a non-executive director	**Strength**	**Deficiency**

(2 marks)

22   **Which of the following can be a member of the audit committee once it is established?**

1   Lindsay Lewis

2   Ola Osbourne

o   1 only

o   1 and 2

o   2 only

o   Neither 1 nor 2   **(2 marks)**

23   **Match the two issues given to the most appropriate response.**

Issue	
1	The board is not balanced
2	Executive directors are paid a fixed salary which increases annually in line with inflation

Response	
A	An audit committee should be set up immediately
B	Establish specific criteria to assess candidates to ensure appointments are based on merit and relevant skills and experience
C	Introduce share options to align the remuneration of executive directors with the long-term success of the company
D	Appoint two more independent non-executive directors
E	Reduce the number of executive directors on the board

(2 marks)

24   **Which of the following would NOT ensure Cameron Co is compliant with corporate governance principles?**

o   Jules Jardine should replace Ola Osbourne as chair

o   All directors should be subject to re-election this year

o   A Nomination Committee should be established

o   Directors contracts should be reviewed to ensure notice periods are one year or less

(2 marks)

25 **Select whether the following statements in relation to directors' remuneration are true or false.**

Remuneration of directors should be set by the Nomination Committee	**True**	**False**
Workforce remuneration should be taken into consideration when setting the remuneration of executive directors	**True**	**False**
The company should be able to withhold bonuses and share awards from directors whose performance is not acceptable	**True**	**False**

(2 marks)

The following scenario relates to questions 26 – 30

Sycamore & Co is the auditor of Fir Co, a listed company operating in the computer software industry. The audit team comprises an engagement partner, a recently appointed audit manager, an audit senior and a number of audit assistants. The audit engagement partner has only been appointed this year due to the rotation of the previous partner who had been involved in the audit for seven years. Only the audit senior has experience of auditing a company in this specialised industry. The previous audit manager left the firm before the completion of the prior year audit and is now the finance director of Fir Co. The finance director and new audit manager are good friends.

The board of Fir Co has asked if Sycamore & Co can take on some additional work and have asked if the following additional non-audit services can be provided:

(1)   Routine maintenance of payroll records

(2)   Assistance with the selection of a new non-executive director

(3)   Tax services whereby Sycamore & Co would liaise with the tax authority on Fir Co's behalf.

Sycamore & Co has identified that the current year fees to be received from Fir Co for audit and other services will represent 16% of the firm's total fee income and totalled 15.5% in the prior year. The audit engagement partner has asked you to consider what can be done in relation to this self-interest threat.

26 **In relation to the composition of the current audit team, select which of the fundamental principles is at risk and select an appropriate safeguard.**

Fundamental principle			Safeguard	
1	Integrity		A	Reinstate previous partner
2	Professional competence and due care		B	Resign from the engagement
3	Confidentiality		C	Assign a completely new audit team
4	Objectivity		D	Provide industry training for team members

(2 marks)

27 Select the type of threat which could arise as a result of the finance director's relationship with the audit manager and select an appropriate safeguard.

Type of threat		Safeguard	
1	Self-review	A	The finance director must not have contact with the audit manager whilst the audit is ongoing
2	Familiarity	B	The firm should resign from the engagement
3	Advocacy	C	A different audit manager should be appointed

(2 marks)

28 Ignoring the potential effect on total fee levels, identify the threats to independence from providing the non-audit services.

	Self-review	Self-interest	Advocacy
Routine maintenance of payroll records			
Assistance with the selection of a new non-executive director			
Tax services whereby Sycamore & Co would liaise with the tax authority on Fir Co's behalf			

(2 marks)

29 Which of the following safeguards would NOT be relevant in mitigating the threat identified in relation to fees?

o   Disclosure to those charged with governance that fees from Fir Co represent more than 15% of Sycamore & Co's total fee income

o   A pre-issuance review to be conducted by an external accountant

o   The use of separate teams to provide the audit and non-audit services

o   Assign an engagement quality control reviewer

(2 marks)

30   During the course of the audit of Fir Co, a suspicious cash transfer has been identified. The audit team has reported this to the relevant firm representative as a potential money-laundering transaction.

Which of the following statements is TRUE regarding the confidentiality of this information?

○   Details of the transaction can only be disclosed with the permission of Fir Co

○   If there is a legal requirement to report money laundering, this overrides the principle of confidentiality

○   Sycamore & Co is not permitted to disclose details of the suspicious transaction as the information has been obtained during the course of the audit

○   In order to maintain confidentiality, Sycamore & Co should report their concerns anonymously

(2 marks)

The following scenario relates to questions 31–35

You are an audit manager at Horti & Co and you are considering a number of ethical issues which have arisen on some of the firm's long-standing audit clients.

Tree Co

Horti & Co is planning its external audit of Tree Co. Yesterday, the audit engagement partner, Charlie Thrower, discovered that a significant fee for information security services, which were provided to Tree Co by Horti & Co, is overdue. Charlie hopes to be able to resolve the dispute amicably and has confirmed that he will discuss the matter with the finance director, Percy Marsh, at the weekend, as they are both attending a party to celebrate the engagement of Charlie's daughter and Percy's son.

Bush Co

Horti & Co is the external auditor of Bush Co and also provides other non-audit services to the company. While performing the audit for the year ended 31 October 20X8, the audit engagement partner was taken ill and took an indefinite leave of absence from the firm. The ethics partner has identified the following potential replacements and is keen that independence is maintained to the highest level:

Brian Smith	who is also the partner in charge of the tax services provided to Bush Co
Monty Nod	who was the audit engagement partner for the ten years ended 31 October 20X7
Cassie Dixon	who introduced Bush Co as a client when she joined the firm as an audit partner five years ago
Pete Russo	who is also the partner in charge of the payroll services provided to Bush Co

Plant Co

Plant Co is a large private company, with a financial year to 30 June, and has been an audit client of Horti & Co for several years. Alan Marshlow, a partner of Horti & Co, has acted as the engagement quality control reviewer (EQCR) on the last two audits to the year ended 30 June 20X8. At a recent meeting, he advised that he can no longer be EQCR on the engagement as he is considering accepting appointment as a non-executive director and will sit on the audit committee of Plant Co.

The board of directors has also asked Horti & Co if they would be able to provide internal audit services to the company.

Weed Co

Weed Co, a listed company, is one of Horti & Co's largest clients. Last year the fee for audit and other services was $1.2m and this year it is expected to be $1.3m which represents 16.6% and 18.1% of Horti & Co's total income respectively.

31 **Which of the following statements correctly explains the possible threats to Horti & Co's independence and recommends an appropriate safeguard in relation to their audit of Tree Co?**

    1   An intimidation threat exists due to the overdue fee and Tree Co should be advised that all fees must be paid prior to the auditor's report being signed

    2   A self-review threat exists due to the nature of the non-audit work which has been performed and an engagement quality control review should be carried out

    3   A self-interest threat exists due to the relationship between Charlie and Percy and Charlie should be removed as audit partner

    o   1, 2 and 3

    o   1 and 2 only

    o   2 only

    o   3 only   **(2 marks)**

32 **Taking into account the concern of the ethics partner, which of the partners identified as potential replacements should take over the audit of Bush Co for the year ended 31 October 20X8?**

    o   Brian Smith

    o   Monty Nod

    o   Cassie Dixon

    o   Pete Russo   **(2 marks)**

33 **Which of the following correctly identifies the threats to Horti & Co's independence and proposes an appropriate course of action for the firm if Alan Marshlow accepts appointment as a non-executive director of Plant Co?**

	Threats	Course of action
o	Self-interest and familiarity	Can continue with appropriate safeguards
o	Self-interest and self-review	Must resign as auditor
o	Self-review and familiarity	Must resign as auditor
o	Familiarity only	Can continue with appropriate safeguards

                                                      (2 marks)

34 You are separately considering Plant Co's request to provide internal audit services and the remit of these services if they are accepted.

Which of the following would result in Horti & Co assuming a management responsibility in relation to the internal audit services?

1 Taking responsibility for designing and maintaining internal control systems

2 Determining which recommendations should take priority and be implemented

3 Determining the reliance which can be placed on the work of internal audit for the external audit

4 Setting the scope of the internal audit work to be carried out

○ 1 and 3

○ 2, 3 and 4

○ 1, 2 and 4

○ 3 and 4 only **(2 marks)**

35 Which of the following actions should Horti & Co take to maintain their objectivity in relation to the level of fee income from Weed Co?

1 The level of fee income should be communicated to those charged with governance

2 Separate teams should be used for the audit and non-audit work

3 Request payment of the current year's audit fee in advance of any work being performed

4 Request a pre-issuance review be conducted by an external accountant

○ 1 and 4 only

○ 3 and 4 only

○ 2 and 3 only

○ 1, 2, 3 and 4 **(2 marks)**

The following scenario relates to questions 36–40

You are an audit manager in CL & Co, an accountancy firm with six offices and 15 partners.

You are planning the audit of LV Fones Co, which has been an audit client for four years and specialises in manufacturing luxury mobile phones. During the planning stage of the audit you have obtained the following information.

The audit team of LV Fones Co are entitled to purchase mobile phone accessories at a discount of 10%. The finance director has commented that this is to encourage the audit team to be more favourable towards the company and to keep them on side. The audit engagement partner has assessed the potential value of the discount to be trivial and inconsequential to any individuals who wish to take advantage of this offer.

During the year, the financial controller of LV Fones Co was ill and hence unable to work. The company had no spare staff able to fulfil the role and hence a qualified audit senior of CL & Co was seconded to the client for three months. The fee income derived from LV Fones Co was boosted by this engagement and along with the audit and tax fee, now accounts for 16% of the firm's total fees.

From a review of the correspondence files you note that the audit engagement partner and the finance director have known each other socially for many years and in fact went on holiday together last summer with their families. As a result of this friendship the audit engagement partner has not yet spoken to the client about the fee for last year's audit, 20% of which is still outstanding.

36   **Which of the following correctly identifies the threats to independence and proposes an appropriate course of action for the firm if any of the audit team takes advantage of the discount?**

	Threats	Course of action
o	Self-interest	Decline the offer
o	Advocacy	The offer can be accepted
o	Familiarity	Consider whether the discount is given to employees
o	Intimidation	Continue with appropriate safeguards

(2 marks)

37   **Which of the following actions should CL & Co take to maintain their objectivity in relation to the level of fee income from LV Fones Co?**

1   Perform an independent review of the work

2   Increase the client base

3   Disclose the issue to the audit committee

4   Resign if fees exceed 15% of the firm's total income for two consecutive years

o   1, 2, 3 and 4

o   1 and 2 only

o   2 and 3 only

o   1, 3 and 4 only

(2 marks)

38 **Which of the following correctly identifies the threats to independence and proposes an appropriate course of action for the firm in respect of the audit senior's secondment to LV Fones Co?**

	Threats	Course of action
○	Self-interest and self-review	The audit senior should not have been seconded to LV Fones Co
○	Self-interest only	The audit senior should be assigned to the audit team to increase efficiency of the audit
○	Self-review only	Perform an engagement quality review
○	Familiarity and self-review	The audit senior must not be assigned to the audit of LV Fones Co

(2 marks)

39 **Which of the following actions should CL & Co take to maintain their objectivity in relation to the outstanding fees from LV Fones Co?**

1   Ask the client to pay the outstanding amount

2   Have an independent review of the work performed

3   Do not issue the auditor's report for the current year until the fees are paid

○   1 and 3 only

○   2 and 3 only

○   1, 2 and 3

○   1 only

(2 marks)

40 **Select one option from each column which identifies the type of ethical threat arising from the engagement partner's friendship with the finance director, and identifies an appropriate course of action the firm should take to manage the threat to an acceptable level.**

Ethical threat		Course of action
Intimidation		Resign from the audit engagement
Familiarity		Structure the audit partner's responsibilities to reduce the potential impact to the engagement
Self-interest		Remove the audit partner from the audit

(2 marks)

The following scenario relates to questions 41–45

It is 1 July 20X5. You are an audit manager in NAB & Co, a large audit firm which specialises in the audit of retailers.

Mickey Co

Mickey Co, a food retailer, has approached NAB & Co to become its auditor. Mickey Co is looking for a new auditor as the previous firm resigned without prior notice three months ago without having started the audit for the year ended 31 December 20X4. Mickey Co has approached several other audit firms since the previous auditor resigned but all have declined to take the engagement. Mickey Co must file its financial statements by 30 September 20X5 in accordance with local legislation and therefore have stated that the audit must be completed before this date. NAB & Co currently audits Goofy Co, Mickey Co's main competitor.

Goofy Co

The audit engagement partner for Goofy Co has been in place for approximately six years and her son has just accepted a job offer from Goofy Co as a sales manager. This role would entitle him to shares in Goofy Co as part of his remuneration package.

Goofy Co has requested NAB & Co provides tax advice to minimise the company's tax liability. Management has suggested that the fee could be based on the level of tax saving achieved to ensure the payment for the service does not outweigh the benefit obtained. The fee is expected to be significant.

Goofy Co's management has decided to establish an audit committee. The company does not have any independent non-executive directors with recent and relevant financial experience and have therefore requested assistance with this. Management has requested that the audit engagement partner assists by reviewing qualifications and advising on technical, financial competence of applicants.

41 **Match the acceptance considerations with the MOST appropriate reason for why they should be considered by NAB & Co before accepting the audit of Mickey Co.**

Acceptance consideration		Reason	
1	The previous audit firm resigned without notice and several firms have declined the engagement	A	There may be threats to objectivity and confidentiality that cannot be managed to an acceptable level
2	The audit must be completed before 30 September 20X5	B	NAB & Co may not be competent to perform the audit
3	Mickey Co is a main competitor of Goofy Co, an existing audit client of NAB & Co	C	The fee may not be sufficient for the level of work that is required
		D	The firm may not have enough resource to perform the audit at the time required
		E	Management of Mickey Co may lack integrity

(2 marks)

42   **What is the correct order of the steps that NAB & Co should take in respect of the conflict of interest arising?**

1   Perform an engagement quality review

2   Obtain consent to act

3   Implement safeguards

4   Inform Mickey Co and Goofy Co

○   3, 1, 4, 2

○   4, 2, 3, 1

○   2, 4, 3, 1

○   4, 2, 1, 3   **(2 marks)**

43   **Select one option from each column which identifies the SIGNIFICANT ethical threat arising from the audit engagement partner's son working for Goofy Co, and identifies an appropriate course of action the firm should take to manage the threat to an acceptable level.**

Ethical threat	Course of action
Intimidation	Remove the audit engagement partner from the audit
Familiarity	Structure the audit partner's responsibilities to reduce the potential impact to the engagement
Self-interest	Inform Goofy Co that it should not employ the audit engagement partner's son

(2 marks)

44   **Which of the following statements is TRUE in respect of Goofy Co's request for the tax advice fee to be based on the tax saving achieved?**

○   The fee basis is acceptable as it does not relate to the audit fee

○   The fee basis is not acceptable as contingent fee arrangements are not acceptable for any accountancy work

○   The fee basis is acceptable if both NAB & Co and Goofy Co agree to it

○   The fee basis will not be acceptable as the fee is significant to the firm   **(2 marks)**

45   **Which of the following statements is TRUE in respect of the request for assistance with recruitment of independent non-executive directors for Goofy Co?**

○   No threat arises and no safeguards are required

○   The audit engagement partner cannot provide assistance and another partner must provide assistance

○   The audit firm cannot provide assistance and the request must be declined

○   The audit engagement partner can provide the assistance but an engagement quality review must be performed   **(2 marks)**

The following scenario relates to questions 46–50

You are an audit manager in Swift & Co responsible for the audit of Kingfisher Co, a retail company planning to list on a stock exchange within the next six months. The board of directors currently comprises the chair, chief executive, three executive directors and three non-executive directors. Details of the three non-executive directors is given below.

Teri Toucan

Teri was an employee of Kingfisher until retirement six years ago. On retirement, Teri became a non-executive director. Teri currently receives a pension from Kingfisher Co and a fixed salary for being a non-executive director. Teri does not own shares in Kingfisher Co.

Pat Parrot

Pat was an employee until ten years ago and was also a shareholder in Kingfisher Co as part of Pat's remuneration package included share options which had been exercised. Pat became a non-executive director three and a half years ago and on appointment, Pat left the company's pension scheme and sold all shares in Kingfisher Co.

Linda Lorikeet

Linda is an independent non-executive director of Kingfisher Co. Linda has been a member of the board for eight years and has extensive retail experience from previous employments.

Proposed changes

Kingfisher Co's management has been advised by the audit engagement partner about the need for compliance with corporate governance principles once the company is listed. The board of directors have identified two more potential independent non-executive directors to join Kingfisher Co. Once more directors are appointed, Kingfisher Co plans to establish an audit committee and a remuneration committee.

The two potential directors are:

Frances Finch

Frances is currently the finance director of a listed multi-national banking company and is a non-executive director and audit committee member for another company. Frances is agreeable to being a non-executive director for Kingfisher Co and to be paid a fixed fee which is not related to profits. Frances is being considered for the role of board chair as the current chair is due to retire in six months' time.

Mica Macaw

Mica is currently a finance director of a small retail company, which does not compete with Kingfisher Co. Mica has stated that she will only be interested in a role at Kingfisher Co if a contract with a minimum three year term is offered. Mica is the sister of Kingfisher Co's chief executive.

46 **Which of the following recommendations is NOT required to be implemented by Kingfisher Co to bring the company in line with corporate governance best practice?**

- ○ More independent non-executive directors must be appointed to ensure at least half of the board are independent

- ○ The board must appoint a workforce representative

- ○ Linda will need to be replaced as an independent non-executive director next year

- ○ The board chair must be appointed from within the company to ensure they have sufficient knowledge of the company **(2 marks)**

47 **In respect of Frances Finch, which of the following statements is TRUE?**

- ○ Frances could become board chair and sit on the audit committee as the person with recent and relevant financial expertise

- ○ Frances could sit on the remuneration committee but must not be committee chair

- ○ If Frances accepts the role of board chair, remuneration will need to include some performance related pay to align her interests with the company

- ○ Frances must resign from one of her current roles if she is to become chair for Kingfisher Co **(2 marks)**

48 **In respect of Teri Toucan, which of the following will compromise independence?**

- ○ Teri receives a pension from Kingfisher Co

- ○ Teri does not own shares in Kingfisher Co

- ○ Teri receives a fixed salary from Kingfisher Co

- ○ Teri was an employee of Kingfisher Co six years ago **(2 marks)**

49 **Which of the follow are advantages of appointing Mica Macaw as a non-executive director of Kingfisher Co?**

1 Mica has close links to Kingfisher Co's chief executive.

2 Mica's experience in retail will help her understand issues faced by the Kingfisher Co.

3 Mica's financial experience will be useful if she serves on the audit committee.

4 Mica wishes to commit to a three year contract.

- ○ 1, 3 and 4 only

- ○ 2 and 3 only

- ○ 1, 2 and 4 only

- ○ 1, 2, 3 and 4 **(2 marks)**

50 Which of the following correctly explains corporate governance guidelines in respect of succession and evaluation of directors?

○ A succession plan should be maintained for the board chair and chief executive

○ The annual report should explain the work of the nomination committee including the process for making appointments

○ Performance of the board chair, the board, the individual executive and non-executive directors and each committee must be evaluated annually

○ All members of the nomination committee must be independent non-executive directors **(2 marks)**

PLANNING AND RISK ASSESSMENT

The following scenario relates to questions 51 – 55

It is 1 July 20X5. You are planning the audit of Veryan Co for the year ending 31 July 20X5. Veryan Co is a new audit client which operates in the oil & gas exploration industry. Companies wishing to operate in this industry require a licence which is valid for 20 years. Licensing authorities take into account public health and safety, protection of the environment and protection of biological resources when granting licences. Veryan Co's activities are geographically spread across three continents in 35 locations.

Veryan Co has been in existence for 30 years and has grown its revenue at an average of 12% per annum. This is in line with the industry average. During your planning meeting with the finance director you were informed that the forecast profit before tax for this financial year is $9.5 million (20X4: $6 million) based on revenues of $124 million (20X4: $100 million).

You have completed the audit strategy and the risk assessment section identifies the following as areas of significant risk of material misstatement:

- Overstatement of receivables due to long outstanding debts

- Misstatement of intangible assets (licences) due to incorrect amortisation

- Overstatement of non-current assets due to impairment of exploration areas which have been decommissioned

- Overstatement of inventory due to the inherent difficulty of establishing the quantity of oil and gas reserves

51 Which of the following is the LEAST significant audit risk to be considered when planning the audit of Veryan Co?

○ Non-compliance with laws and regulations

○ Understatement of trade payables

○ Adequacy of provisions and contingent liabilities

○ Foreign currency transactions **(2 marks)**

52 Which TWO of the following are appropriate responses to address the increased detection risk due to Veryan Co being a new audit client?

- ○ Extended controls testing should be performed

- ○ Obtain an understanding of Veryan Co

- ○ Consideration should be given to relying on the work of an independent expert

- ○ Reduce reliance on tests of controls

- ○ Contact the previous auditor to request working papers **(2 marks)**

53 Which of the following is the LEAST appropriate materiality level to be used in the audit of Veryan Co?

- ○ $1.5 million

- ○ $1.0 million

- ○ $750,000

- ○ $475,000 **(2 marks)**

54 Select whether the following statements are consistent or not consistent with the movement in revenue.

Cut-off of revenue is an audit risk	**Consistent**	**Not consistent**
Completeness of revenue is an audit risk	**Consistent**	**Not consistent**
Occurrence of revenue is an audit risk	**Consistent**	**Not consistent**

(2 marks)

55 Match the audit risks given with the MOST appropriate response the auditor of Veryan Co should take.

Audit risk		Auditor's response	
1	Receivables	A	Physically inspect a sample of exploration areas
2	Non-current assets	B	Contact a sample of customers to confirm the year-end balance
3	Intangible assets (licences)	C	Ask management to adjust the financial statements
		D	Inspect the licence agreement
		E	Review correspondence with customers
		F	Calculate the expected amortisation
		G	Review the depreciation charge for adequacy

(2 marks)

The following scenario relates to questions 56 – 60

It is 1 July 20X5. You are an audit manager in Woodwind & Co and you are planning the audit of Flute Co, a new audit client for your firm which has a year ended of 30 June 20X5. Flute Co is a large mobile phone company which operates a network of stores in countries across Europe.

You have been provided with planning notes from the audit engagement partner following his meeting with the finance director.

During the year the company introduced a bonus based on sales for its sales team. The bonus target was based on increasing the number of customers signing up for 24-month phone line contracts. This strategy has been successful and revenue has increased by 15% compared with 20X4. In particular, there has been a significant increase in sales in May and June 20X5.

Technology companies which supply Flute Co with mobile phones release new versions with updated features every twelve months. When new phones are released, Flute & Co offers significant discounts on older versions.

You are to undertake a preliminary analytical review of the draft financial statements and have been provided with the following information:

	20X5	20X4
	$	$
Revenue	1,267,000	1,205,000
Cost of sales	1,013,000	965,000
Receivables	121,000	100,000
Payables	87,500	85,000
Inventory	160,000	125,000
Cash	123,000	140,000

Overvaluation of inventory and receivables are considered to be significant risks for this year's audit.

56 **Which of the following statements is TRUE in relation to Flute Co being a new audit client of Woodwind & Co?**

   o   Inherent risk is increased as the firm has no cumulative knowledge or experience of Flute Co

   o   The auditor may not be competent to perform the audit and should consider resigning

   o   The auditor should contact the previous auditor to ask if there are any professional matters of which they should be aware

   o   The auditor will need to increase the quality control procedures performed due to the increased risk

(2 marks)

57 **Which of the following is an appropriate explanation of the audit risk relating to the bonus for Flute Co's sales team?**

- ○ There is an increased risk of a reduction in profit for the company as a result of irrecoverable debts

- ○ There is an increased risk of inappropriate cut-off of revenue

- ○ There is an increased risk of understatement of revenue

- ○ There is an increased risk of non-response from customers following direct confirmation audit testing

(2 marks)

58 **Using the financial information provided, calculate the following ratios for both years. Calculate your answers to the nearest round number and enter the answer into the relevant box.**

	20X5	20X4
Receivables collection period		
Inventory holding period		

(2 marks)

59 **Which of the following is NOT an appropriate audit response to the significant risks relating to inventory and receivables?**

	Inventory	Receivables
○	Extend cut-off testing	Extend cut-off testing
○	Review controls over inventory levels	Review controls over the collection of debts
○	Discuss slow-moving inventory items with the finance director	Discuss long-outstanding receivables with the finance director
○	Perform post year end sales invoice testing	Perform post year-end cash receipts testing

(2 marks)

60 **Which TWO of the following statements BEST describe the purpose of using analytical procedures during the planning stage of Flute Co's audit?**

- ○ To help form an overall conclusion on the financial statements

- ○ To obtain relevant and reliable audit evidence

- ○ To assist with identification of risks of material misstatement

- ○ To assist in identifying unusual transactions and events at Flute Co

(2 marks)

The following scenario relates to questions 61 – 65

It is 1 July 20X5. You are an audit senior in Simone & Co. You are planning the audit of Epica Co for the year ending 31 July 20X5. The audit manager has held a planning meeting with the finance director and has provided you with the following notes of his meeting and financial statement extracts.

Epica Co has experienced difficult trading conditions this year which has resulted in sales prices being reduced. Despite this, revenue has continued to fall. In an attempt to improve profit, Epica Co has switched to a cheaper supplier which has resulted in lower quality goods being purchased and a corresponding increase in returns from customers.

During the year the directors performed a review of asset lives which has resulted in an increase in the useful life of the majority of tangible non-current assets. Accordingly, the depreciation charge has reduced from $1 million in 20X4 to $0.8 million in 20X5.

Financial statement extracts for year ending 31 July

	DRAFT 20X5 $m	ACTUAL 20X4 $m
Revenue	12.5	15.0
Cost of sales	(7.0)	(8.0)
Gross profit	5.5	7.0
Operating expenses	(5.0)	(5.1)
Operating profit	0.5	1.9
Inventory	1.9	1.4
Receivables	3.1	2.0
Cash	0.8	1.9
Trade payables	1.6	1.2
Loan due for payment 31 January 20X6	1.0	1.0

61   Using the financial information provided, calculate the following ratios for both years. Calculate your answers to ONE decimal place and enter the answer into the relevant box.

	20X5	20X4
Gross margin		
Current ratio		

(2 marks)

62   In relation to the movement in the payables payment period, which of the following statements is most relevant to the auditor's consideration of audit risk?

○   The payables payment period has decreased which could indicate understatement of payables

○   The payables payment period has decreased which could indicate Epica Co is taking advantage of early payment discounts

○   The payables payment period has increased which could indicate Epica Co has cash flow problems

○   The payables payment period has increased which could indicate Epica Co has is managing its working capital cycle by delaying payments to suppliers

(2 marks)

63   Which THREE of the following describe audit risks that should be addressed during the audit of Epica Co?

○   Inventory may be overstated if sales prices have fallen below cost

○   Provisions for the return of goods may be understated

○   Epica Co have experienced difficult trading conditions causing revenue to fall

○   Sales prices have been reduced which will impact profitability

○   Lower quality goods have been purchased resulting in complaints from customers

○   Inventory may be misstated if returned goods have not been recorded back into inventory   **(2 marks)**

64   Which TWO of the following describe appropriate auditor responses to the audit risk related to the increase in the useful life of tangible non-current assets of Epica Co?

○   Calculate whether the change in depreciation charge is material. If not material, no further action is necessary.

○   Discuss with the directors the reason for the change in useful life

○   Compare the actual useful life of tangible non-current assets recently disposed of to the new depreciation policy to assess whether this reflects the actual useful economic life

○   Compare the fixtures and fittings depreciation rate this year to last year   **(2 marks)**

65   Which of the following correctly describes the term performance materiality?

○   An amount which, through its omission or misstatement, would affect the economic decisions of the users taken on the basis of the financial statements

○   The maximum amount of misstatement the auditor is willing to accept and still conclude that the financial statements are fairly stated

○   An amount which reduces the probability that the aggregate of uncorrected and undetected misstatements exceeds materiality for the financial statements as a whole

○   An amount below which misstatements of balances and classes of transactions in the financial statements would be clearly trivial   **(2 marks)**

The following scenario relates to questions 66 – 70

It is 1 July 20X5. You are an audit manager in Owl & Co responsible for the audit of Hawk Co. Hawk Co manufacture kites which it sells via its website directly to customers. You are currently planning the audit for the year ending 31 July 20X5.

Two issues have been brought to your attention during a planning meeting with the finance director.

Dismissal of financial controller

The financial controller of Hawk Co was dismissed in May 20X5. He had been employed by the company for over 20 years and he has threatened to sue the company for unfair dismissal. The role of financial controller has not yet been filled and his tasks have been shared between the existing finance department team.

Payables ledger supervisor

The payables ledger supervisor left in March 20X5 and a replacement has only been appointed in the last week. However, for this period no supplier statement reconciliations or payables ledger control account reconciliations were performed.

The finance director has also provided you with the most recent management accounts to enable you to perform preliminary analytical procedures. Using that information you have calculated the following ratios:

	20X5	20X4
Gross profit margin	17%	26%
Payables payment period	40 days	75 days
Receivables collection period	38 days	29 days

66 **Which of the following are appropriate auditor responses to the increased audit risk created by the finance team being allocated the work of the financial controller?**

    1   The audit team should be fully briefed and be alert throughout the audit for additional errors

    2   The auditor should appoint an expert to properly assess the risks of misstatement

    3   The finance director should be requested to provide the audit team with assistance for matters that cannot be addressed by the remaining finance function

    4   The auditor should consider resigning from the engagement as audit risk cannot be managed to an acceptable level

    ○   1, 2 and 3

    ○   2, 3 and 4

    ○   1 and 3 only

    ○   1 and 4   **(2 marks)**

67   Which THREE of the following statements are TRUE in relation to the lack of supplier statement reconciliations?

o   The auditor should perform the supplier statement reconciliations for Hawk Co

o   There is an increased risk of misstatement of trade payables

o   Misstatements in the purchase accrual balance may go undetected

o   The auditor will need to send requests for confirmation of balances to suppliers

o   Increased substantive testing will need to be performed over purchases and payables

(2 marks)

68   In respect of the unfair dismissal claim, which of the following audit procedures is NOT appropriate?

o   Review correspondence between the financial controller and the company

o   Review board meeting minutes

o   Review correspondence between the company and its lawyer

o   Discuss the claim with the financial controller **(2 marks)**

69   Which audit risks can be identified from the preliminary analytical procedures performed?

	Gross profit margin	Payables payment period	Receivables collection period
A	Website sales may not be accurately recorded	Payables may not be accurately recorded	Extended credit terms may have been given to customers
B	Revenue may have been recognised too early	Suppliers may be withdrawing credit terms	Receivables may not be completely recorded
C	Revenue may not have occurred	Purchase invoices may have been recorded twice	Receivables may not exist
D	Website sales may not be completely recorded	Payables may not be completely recorded	Receivables may be overvalued

o   Option A

o   Option B

o   Option C

o   Option D **(2 marks)**

70 **Which of the following are reasons why analytical procedures will be performed during the planning of Hawk Co?**

1   To help identify areas of potential risk

2   To help obtain an understanding of Hawk Co

3   To help detect material misstatements in the financial statement figures

o   1 only

o   1 and 2 only

o   1, 2 and 3

o   2 and 3 only   **(2 marks)**

The following scenario relates to questions 71 – 75

It is 1 July 20X5. You are the audit manager responsible for the audit of Swandive Co, a company with a financial year ending 31 July 20X5. You are planning the audit and payroll has been identified as a significant audit risk this year.

You have designed the following procedures for inclusion in the audit plan.

1   For a sample of employees recalculate the gross and net pay and agree to the payroll records.

2   Perform a proof in total of wages and salaries and compare the expected total to actual wages and salaries in draft financial statements.

3   Select a sample of hourly paid employees and verify hours worked have been authorised by their line manager.

4   Review the payroll report for evidence of authorisation by the financial director before any payments are made to employees.

Payroll fraud

During the year, it was discovered that a payroll clerk had been setting up fictitious employees on the payroll system with the wages being paid into the clerk's own bank account. This clerk has subsequently left the company but you are concerned that additional frauds may have taken place in the wages department due to a lack of adequate and effective internal controls.

---

71 **Which TWO of the procedures included in the audit plan describe substantive procedures to confirm the completeness and accuracy of Swandive Co's payroll expense?**

o   1 and 2

o   2 and 3

o   3 and 4

o   1 and 4   **(2 marks)**

72 Select which section of the audit strategy of Swandive Co the following matters would appear. Audit strategy areas may be selected more than once or not at all.

Matter	
1	Risk of material misstatement including the risk of fraud
2	Use of professional scepticism
3	Selection of the audit team
4	Use of computer-assisted audit techniques

Audit strategy section	
A	Characteristics of the engagement
B	Reporting objectives, timing of the audit and nature of communications
C	Significant factors, preliminary engagement activities, and knowledge gained on other engagements
D	Nature, timing and extent of resources

(2 marks)

73 With respect to the fraud at Swandive Co, which of the following statements is TRUE?

o This fraud is an example of fraudulent financial reporting

o The auditor will need to reduce control risk

o Detection risk will need to increase as a result of the fraud

o The audit team should discuss the susceptibility of Swandive Co to fraud **(2 marks)**

74 Which of the following additional controls is most effective at preventing fraud of this type occurring again?

o An exception report should be generated when standing data is changed in the payroll system which is reviewed by the payroll manager

o On a regular basis department managers should be given a list of employees for their department from the payroll system to check

o The people working in the payroll department should not be related

o The finance director should compare the total payroll cost each month to prior month to identify significant differences **(2 marks)**

75 Which THREE of the following procedures would assist in the detection of further frauds of this type at Swandive Co?

o Discuss with management whether they are aware of further frauds at Swandive Co

o Report the fraud to the police to deter other employees from committing a similar fraud

o Trace the amounts per the payroll records to the bank statements to identify any anomalies

o Analyse the bank details of all employees to identify duplicate bank accounts

o Review HR records for the names of employees and reconcile these to the names on the bank transfer lists **(2 marks)**

INTERNAL CONTROLS

The following scenario relates to questions 76 – 80

You are an audit manager in Sandy & Co and you are responsible for the audit of Coastal Co. The internal control systems in relation to purchases and payroll have recently been documented by the audit junior. Tests of controls have been performed to evaluate the effectiveness of the system. The audit junior has used narrative notes and an internal control questionnaire to document the system. You are reviewing the work performed by the audit junior before assessing the impact on the audit approach to be taken in respect of purchases and payroll.

The following features of the purchases and payroll systems have been noted in the audit junior's documentation:

1   Goods are counted and agreed to the supplier's delivery note before signing the delivery note to accept the goods.

2   The purchase invoice is matched to, and filed with, the related goods received note and purchase order by the purchase ledger team in the finance department.

3   Payroll standing data files are sent to department managers on a monthly basis for review.

4   Hours worked are entered onto a pre-printed payroll sheet by the wages clerk.

5   Before payroll payments are made, the finance director reviews the bank transfer list and signs to authorise the payments to be made.

76   **Select whether the following advantages and disadvantages relate to narrative notes, internal control questionnaires or both.**

	Narrative notes	Internal control questionnaires	Both
Advantages			
Can be prepared in advance			
Easy to understand			
Disadvantages			
May overstate the controls			
Some controls may be missed			

(2 marks)

77   Select whether the features of the purchases and payroll systems described are a strength or deficiency of the internal control system of Coastal Co.

1	**Strength**	**Deficiency**
2	**Strength**	**Deficiency**
3	**Strength**	**Deficiency**
4	**Strength**	**Deficiency**

(2 marks)

78   Which of the following control objectives is addressed by feature number 5?

    o   To ensure payroll is classified correctly

    o   To ensure only valid employees are paid

    o   To ensure employees are paid for the correct hours

    o   To ensure employee's salaries have been calculated correctly   **(2 marks)**

79   You have reviewed the work of the audit junior and concluded that reliance can be placed on the internal controls. What impact will this have on the nature and extent of substantive audit procedures to be performed at the final audit?

    o   Less importance can be placed on written representations from management

    o   Greater use of tests of detail and less use of analytical procedures

    o   Decreased sample sizes when performing substantive testing

    o   Increased use of evidence from outside the entity   **(2 marks)**

80   The payroll section of the audit plan of Coastal Co includes the following procedures. For each procedure select whether it is a test of control or a substantive procedure.

Recalculate the total of the bank transfer list	**Test of control**	**Substantive procedure**
Inspect the bank transfer list for evidence of the finance director's signature	**Test of control**	**Substantive procedure**
For a sample of employees, agree the salary details in the standing data files to the calculation of the employee's monthly salary as per the payslip	**Test of control**	**Substantive procedure**
Review the procedures to ensure payroll files and documents are kept secure and confidential	**Test of control**	**Substantive procedure**

(2 marks)

The following scenario relates to questions 81 – 85

Halestorm Co manufactures snacks such as potato chips which are supplied to large and small food retailers. Halestorm Co has experienced significant growth over recent years and in response to this growth, senior management has established an internal audit department to improve the control environment of the company. You are a member of the recently formed internal audit department.

Senior management of Halestorm Co has concerns about the effectiveness of the company's sales and despatch system and has instructed the internal audit department to perform a review of the system. Any deficiencies identified are to be reported to the finance director who will report the findings back to the board of directors at the next board meeting. Recommendations for improvements are also to be provided.

During the review the following deficiencies were identified:

(i)   Availability of inventory is not checked until at the time of ordering

(ii)   Telephone orders are initially noted on a piece of paper and then transferred to an order form after the call has ended

(iii)   Order forms are not sequentially numbered

(iv)   The online ordering system allows customers to place orders which exceed their credit limit.

81   **Which of the following is NOT an objective of Halestorm Co's sales and despatch system?**

○   To ensure that orders are only accepted if goods are available

○   To ensure that all orders are recorded completely and accurately

○   To ensure discounts received are accounted for completely and accurately

○   To ensure that all goods despatched are correctly invoiced   **(2 marks)**

82   **Match the control deficiencies to an appropriate explanation of the issue.**

Deficiency	Explanation	
(i)	A	Risk of incorrect orders being despatched
(ii)	B	Risk of irrecoverable debts
(iii)	C	Risk of orders not being fulfilled on a timely basis
(iv)	D	Orders may go missing leading to unfulfilled orders

(2 marks)

83   **Which TWO of the following are appropriate recommendations to address the credit limit system deficiency?**

○   Credit limits should be reviewed by a responsible official on a regular basis and amended as appropriate

○   Sales order clerks should be allowed to use discretion to raise credit limits to avoid losing revenue

○   The online ordering system should be programmed to allow orders up to a maximum of 5% in excess of the credit limit

○   Orders which would cause a customer to exceed their credit limit should be sent to a responsible official for approval   **(2 marks)**

84 **Which of the following recommendations should be made to address deficiencies (ii) and (iii)?**

1 Order clerks should have online access to view real-time inventory quantities at the time of ordering.

2 Order forms should be sequentially pre-numbered and a regular sequence check should be performed.

3 All orders should be entered directly into the ordering system as the customer is placing the order

4 Customers should be instructed not to place orders by telephone.

- ○ 1 and 2
- ○ 2 and 3 only
- ○ 2, 3 and 4
- ○ 1, 3 and 4 **(2 marks)**

85 **Which of the following statements is TRUE in respect of the review findings?**

- ○ The findings will be communicated to the shareholders at the annual general meeting
- ○ The recommendations will need to be actioned before the external audit commences
- ○ The findings should be reported directly to the board of directors rather than the finance director
- ○ The findings should be discussed with the external auditor before being communicated to the finance director

(2 marks)

The following scenario relates to questions 86 – 90

Primrose Co has recently upgraded its computer system to enable greater automation of transaction processing. The new system has integrated the sales, inventory and purchasing systems resulting in minimal manual entry.

Sales orders are entered into the system manually. The inventory system is automatically updated to reflect that inventory has been allocated to an order. The system will flag if there is insufficient inventory to fulfil the order. The inventory system is linked to the purchasing system so that when inventory falls to a minimum level a purchase order is automatically created and sent to the purchasing manager for authorisation. Once the manager clicks 'authorised' the order is automatically sent electronically to the approved supplier for that item. The system is backed up daily to ensure minimal loss of data in the event of a system failure.

Primrose Co's internal auditors were present during the implementation of the new system and performed tests during the process to ensure the information transferred into the new system was free from error. The internal audit plan of work has been updated to include regular tests of the system throughout the year to ensure it is working effectively.

The external auditor of Primrose Co is planning to use automated tools and techniques during the audit for the first time this year as a result of the new system and is also planning to use the work of Primrose Co's internal audit department if possible.

---

86 **Which of the following is NOT a test of control in respect of Primrose Co's system?**

    O   Trace a sample of purchase orders through to the approved supplier list to ensure the supplier used is approved

    O   Trace a sales order through to the system and into the sales day book to ensure it is recorded

    O   Review a sample of purchases orders in the system to ensure they are authorised within the system

    O   Inspect copies of the back-ups taken to ensure these are taken on a daily basis

(2 marks)

87 **Select whether the following controls identified in Primrose Co's systems are general or application controls?**

Daily backups of the system	General	Application
Authorisation of purchase orders	General	Application
Minimum order quantities	General	Application
Automatic updating of inventory once goods are sold	General	Application

(2 marks)

88 **Which of the following procedures provides the MOST reliable evidence that the inventory system updates automatically once an order has been received?**

    O   Review the inventory level of an item, enter a sales order into the system and review the inventory level again after the order has been placed

    O   Count a sample of items of inventory in the warehouse and agree the quantities to the quantities stated in the inventory system

    O   Review the inventory report detailing quantities of items to identify unusually high or low quantities

    O   Contact a sample of customers to enquire whether they have experienced delays in orders being processed due to insufficient inventory being held   **(2 marks)**

89 **Which can be tested by placing a dummy sales order for a large quantity of goods into the system? Select all that apply.**

Control	
The inventory system is automatically updated to reflect that inventory has been allocated to a sales order	
The system will flag if there is insufficient inventory to fulfil the order	
When inventory falls to a minimum level a purchase order is automatically created and sent to the purchasing manager for authorisation	
The purchase order is automatically sent electronically to the approved supplier for that item	

(2 marks)

90 **Which TWO of the following procedures should be performed by the external auditor of Primrose Co to identify whether the work of Primrose Co's internal audit department can be relied upon?**

○ Review the internal auditor's working papers to ensure sufficient appropriate evidence has been obtained

○ Engage an independent expert to assess the new system and validate the reliability of the internal audit department's work

○ Re-perform a sample of procedures performed by the internal auditor to ensure the same conclusion is reached

○ Assess whether Primrose Co has an audit committee in place responsible for overseeing the internal audit function. If so, the external auditor can rely on the work performed by the internal auditor without the need for further work **(2 marks)**

The following scenario relates to questions 91 – 95

Shroom Co is a manufacturer of vegetarian food including ready meals and plant-based sausages and burgers which it supplies to large grocery chains across the country. The company has grown significantly over the last five years with revenue increasing by 50%. Its year end is 31 July 20X5. You work in the internal audit department of Shroom Co which performs periodic reviews of internal controls, assesses the risk management processes of the company and performs fraud investigations when applicable. The following areas have been reviewed by the internal audit department over the last three years:

20X5   Non-current assets, revenue

20X4   Purchases, payroll

20X3   Inventory, cash

You are reviewing the internal controls over non-current assets and capital expenditure of the company which were last reviewed in 20X2.

You have been provided with the following information relating to the non-current assets cycle.

Shroom Co prepares a rolling five-year capital expenditure budget which is updated annually by the capital expenditure committee. The committee has three members. Each year the heads of department meet with the committee to discuss capital requirements for the budget period. All capital items purchased must be included in the budget, except in exceptional circumstances for which there is a contingency fund set aside.

When capital expenditure is required, the relevant department head must send a requisition to the committee with quotations from at least two suppliers. The requisition is approved by the committee if the items requested are included in the budget and the quotation is acceptable. The approval is noted in the minutes of the meeting. A copy of the approved requisition form is sent to the purchasing department where a purchase order is completed and a copy of the approved requisition is kept with the order. Before the order is placed, the purchasing director must agree the order details to the approved requisition and sign the purchase order as evidence of the check.

On receipt, a goods received note (GRN) is completed. Each asset is checked to the authorised purchase order and checked for condition and evidence of these checks is noted on the GRN. Each asset is assigned a unique serial number which is recorded on the asset and written on the GRN. The GRN is forwarded to the finance team which maintains the non-current asset register. The asset is added to the register.

The non-current asset register contains a description of the asset, the serial number, the cost to be capitalised, the expected useful life, purchase date, department/location and estimated residual value. The non-current asset register is password protected and only a small number of people in the finance department know the password.

On a quarterly basis the management accounts detail the total capital expenditure incurred and the amount budgeted for the period with explanations of any variances greater than 5%.

Once a year the internal audit department performs a reconciliation of physical assets to the asset register to ensure the register is complete.

91 **Which TWO of the following control objectives are addressed by the work of the capital expenditure committee?**

- ○ To ensure capital items purchased are authorised
- ○ To ensure capital items purchased are for a valid business use
- ○ To ensure the non-current asset register is complete
- ○ To ensure capital items purchased represent value for money
- ○ To ensure all capital items purchased are given a unique serial number

(2 marks)

92 **For each of the controls given below, select the type of control activity described.**

The internal audit department confirms the non-current asset register is complete	Physical control	Performance review	Information processing
Variances between actual and budgeted expenditure are analysed in the quarterly management accounts	Segregation of duties	Performance review	Information processing
The non-current asset register is password protected	Physical control	Performance review	Segregation of duties

(2 marks)

93 **Which THREE of the following documents together provide persuasive evidence that capital items purchased during the year have been authorised?**

1   Requisition

2   Order

3   Goods received note

4   Non-current asset register

5   Minutes of capital expenditure committee meetings

- ○ 1, 2 and 3
- ○ 2, 3 and 4
- ○ 3, 4 and 5
- ○ 1, 2 and 5

(2 marks)

94 **Which of the following is NOT a test of control the external auditor of Shroom Co may perform in relation to non-current assets?**

    O   Inspect a sample of assets purchased during the year for a serial number and trace this to the non-current asset register

    O   Review a sample of goods received notes for evidence of the check against purchase order and condition

    O   Compare actual capital expenditure with budgeted capital expenditure during the year and investigate any variances greater than 5%

    O   Review the internal audit working papers documenting the reconciliation of physical assets with the non-current asset register   **(2 marks)**

95 The external auditor has this year expressed an interest in using some individuals from Shroom Co's internal audit department to provide direct assistance with external audit procedures.

For which of the following areas would it be appropriate for internal audit to provide direct assistance?

    O   Assessing controls over non-current assets

    O   Revenue recognition

    O   Valuation of inventory

    O   Performing cash counts   **(2 marks)**

AUDIT EVIDENCE

The following scenario relates to questions 96 – 100

Chester Co manufactures and sells pet toys to the wholesale market. It has prepared its financial statements to 31 July 20X8. You are an audit assistant with Durham & Co and you have been assigned the current liabilities balances in the audit work plan.

You have calculated the payables payment period to be 66 days in 20X8 (45 days in 20X7) and have asked the directors of Chester Co to provide an explanation for the increase in days.

Chester Co receives monthly statements from its main suppliers and performs regular supplier statement reconciliations. There were inconsistencies noted in respect of the following at 31 July 20X8:

Supplier	Balance per payables ledger	Balance per supplier statement
	$	$
Oxford Co	151,480	296,120
Poole Co	(72,168)	84,235
Bath Co	82,348	92,340

Oxford Co

Chester Co has a credit agreement with Oxford Co under which it receives goods 14 days before the supplier raises the invoice. Chester Co received goods worth $144,640 on 18 July 20X8 for which the invoice was received shortly after the year end in accordance with the agreement. Chester Co entered the transaction into its accounting records at the date of invoice.

Poole Co

The difference on this balance has still to be investigated.

Bath Co

Chester Co's finance director has informed you that there was an error in closing the payables ledger and it was closed three days early. Invoices received 29, 30 and 31 July 20X8 were posted to the 20X9 ledger. The directors of Chester Co have confirmed that following the discovery of this error, a manual adjustment was made using the journal book.

---

96   Which of the following supplier balances would indicate a high risk in relation to the COMPLETENESS of the liability recorded at the year end?

    o   A supplier with a high balance at the year end and with a low volume of transactions during the year

    o   A supplier with a low balance at the year end and with a high volume of transactions during the year

    o   A supplier with a low balance at the year end and with a low volume of transactions during the year

    o   A supplier with a high balance at the year end and with a high volume of transactions during the year

                         (2 marks)

97 **Which of the following would correctly explain why the payables payment period has increased from 45 days in 20X7 to 66 days in 20X8?**

o   Chester Co received a prompt payment discount from one of its suppliers for the first time in 20X8

o   Chester Co obtained a trade discount from one of its biggest suppliers which has reduced the amount owed to that supplier by 10% in the year

o   Chester Co purchased an unusually high level of goods in July 20X8 to satisfy a large order and had not paid for those goods by the year end

o   Chester Co took advantage of extended credit terms offered by a new supplier in respect of a large order which it had fully settled by the year end   **(2 marks)**

98 **Which of the following is an appropriate action in respect of the inconsistency in the balance with Oxford Co?**

o   The auditor should take no further action as this is a timing difference which was resolved upon receipt and posting of the invoice

o   The auditor should request that the payables ledger balance is amended at the reporting date to reflect the recent invoice

o   The auditor should contact the supplier and request a supplier statement as at the current date

o   The auditor should request that an accrual is created in respect of the goods received but not yet invoiced   **(2 marks)**

99 **Which of the following would be a valid explanation for the difference in respect of Poole Co?**

1   An invoice for $156,403 has been paid twice

2   An invoice for $156,403 has been posted as a debit note

3   An invoice for $156,403 has been received and processed prior to receipt of the goods

o   1 only

o   1 and 2 only

o   2 and 3 only

o   1, 2 and 3   **(2 marks)**

100 **Which of the following would NOT provide sufficient and appropriate audit evidence over the COMPLETENESS of the payables ledger balance in respect of Bath Co?**

o   Obtain the journal book and confirm that all invoices recorded as received from Bath Co dated 29–31 July have been manually adjusted

o   Review the accruals listing to ensure goods received from Bath Co post year end for which an invoice has not been received have been recorded in the correct period

o   For post year-end cash book payments to Bath Co, confirm date of matching invoice and if pre year end agree to liability

o   Review a sample of invoices received from Bath Co recorded post year end and match to GRN to determine if they should have been recorded at the year end   **(2 marks)**

The following scenario relates to questions 101 – 105

You are an audit senior in Jones & Co and are currently performing the final audit of Walker Co for the year ended 31 October 20X6. The company is a manufacturer and retailer of shoes and boots. The current audit senior is ill and you have been asked to complete the audit of payroll and revenue in their absence.

Payroll

You determine the following information from a review of the current year and prior year audit files:

- As at 31 October 20X5, Walker Co had 500 employees

- On 1 November 20X5, 10% of staff were made redundant, effective immediately, due to discontinuation of a product line

- On 1 January 20X6, all remaining staff received a 6% pay rise

- Over the course of the year, sales levels met performance targets which resulted in a fixed bonus of $1,500 being paid to each employee on 31 October 20X6

Revenue

The following audit procedures are included in the revenue section of the audit plan:

1   Review the treatment of a sample of post year-end returns

2   Select a sample of goods despatched notes and agree to invoices in the sales day book

3   Select a sample of invoices from the sales day book and agree to goods despatched notes

4   Select a sample of invoices and recalculate the invoiced amount agreeing to price list

---

101   Which of the following statements explains the CUT-OFF assertion for wages and salaries?

  ○   Wages and salaries have been fairly allocated within the statement of profit or loss

  ○   Wages and salaries have been appropriately calculated taking into account all relevant taxation costs and adjustments

  ○   Wages and salaries which have been incurred during the period have been accounted for in respect of all personnel employed by Walker Co

  ○   Wages and salaries accounted for relate to the current year ended 31 October 20X6

(2 marks)

102 **The following audit evidence has been gathered relating to the accuracy of wages and salaries for Walker Co:**

1   Proof in total calculation performed by an audit team member

2   Written representation from the directors of Walker Co confirming the accuracy of wages and salaries

3   Verbal confirmation from the finance director of Walker Co confirming the accuracy of wages and salaries

4   Recalculation of the gross and net pay for a sample of employees by an internal audit team member of Walker Co

What is the order of reliability of the audit evidence starting with the MOST RELIABLE first?

o   1, 2, 3, 4

o   1, 4, 2, 3

o   4, 1, 2, 3

o   4, 1, 3, 2   **(2 marks)**

103 The prior year financial statements for Walker Co included $17 million for wages and salaries in the statement of profit or loss.

What would be the estimated current year wages and salaries expense, ignoring redundancy costs, based on the data gathered from the review of the audit files?

o $16,740,000

o $16,893,000

o $16,815,000

o $18,600,000   **(2 marks)**

104 **Select which TWO of the following are substantive ANALYTICAL PROCEDURES for wages and salaries.**

o   Trace and agree the total wages and salaries expense per the payroll system to the draft financial statements

o   Recalculate the gross and net pay for a sample of employees, agree to payroll records and investigate discrepancies

o   Compare the current year total payroll expense to the prior year and investigate any significant differences

o   Perform a proof in total calculation and compare expected expense to actual expense within the draft financial statements   **(2 marks)**

105 In respect of the revenue procedures included in the audit plan, select the assertion being tested.

1	Accuracy	Completeness	Occurrence
2	Accuracy	Completeness	Occurrence
3	Accuracy	Completeness	Occurrence
4	Accuracy	Completeness	Occurrence

(2 marks)

The following scenario relates to questions 106 – 110

You are an audit senior of Viola & Co and are currently conducting the audit of Poppy Co for the year ended 30 June 20X6.

Materiality has been set at $50,000, and you are carrying out the detailed substantive testing on the year-end payables balance. The audit manager has emphasised that understatement of the trade payables balance is a significant audit risk.

Below is an extract from the list of supplier statements as at 30 June 20X6 held by the company and corresponding payables ledger balances at the same date along with some commentary on the noted differences:

Supplier	Statement balance	Payables ledger balance
	$000	$000
Carnation Co	70	50
Lily Co	175	105

Carnation Co

The difference in the balance is due to an invoice which is under dispute due to faulty goods which were returned on 29 June 20X6.

Lily Co

The difference in the balance is due to the supplier statement showing an invoice dated 28 June 20X6 for $70,000 which was not recorded in the financial statements until after the year-end. The payables clerk has advised the audit team that the invoice was not received until 2 July 20X6.

---

106 The audit manager has asked you to review the full list of trade payables and select balances for which supplier statement reconciliations will be performed.

Which THREE of the following items should you select for testing?

○ Suppliers with material balances at the year-end

○ Suppliers which have a high volume of business with Poppy Co

○ Major suppliers of Poppy Co with nil balances at the year-end

○ Major suppliers of Poppy Co where the statement agrees to the ledger

(2 marks)

107 Which of the following audit procedures should be performed in relation to the balance with Lily Co to determine if the payables balance is understated?

   o   Inspect the goods received note to determine when the goods were received

   o   Inspect the purchase order to confirm it is dated before the year-end

   o   Review the post year-end cashbook for evidence of payment of the invoice

   o   Send a confirmation request to Lily Co to confirm the outstanding balance **(2 marks)**

108 Which of the following audit procedures should be carried out to confirm the balance owing to Carnation Co?

   1   Review post year-end credit notes for evidence of acceptance of return

   2   Inspect pre year-end goods returned note in respect of the items sent back to the supplier

   3   Inspect post year-end cash book for evidence that the amount has been settled

   o   1, 2 and 3

   o   1 and 3 only

   o   1 and 2 only

   o   2 and 3 only **(2 marks)**

109 The audit manager has asked you to review the results of some statistical sampling testing, which resulted in 20% of the payables balance being tested.

The testing results indicate that there is a $45,000 error in the sample: $20,000 which is due to invoices not being recorded in the correct period as a result of weak controls and additionally there is a one-off error of $25,000 which was made by a temporary clerk.

What would be an appropriate course of action on the basis of these results?

   o   The error is immaterial and therefore no further work is required

   o   The effect of the control error should be projected across the whole population

   o   Poppy Co should be asked to adjust the payables figure by $45,000

   o   A different sample should be selected as these results are not reflective of the population **(2 marks)**

110 To help improve audit efficiency, Viola & Co is considering introducing the use of automated tools and techniques for some audits. You have been asked to consider how audit software and test data could be used during the audit of Poppy Co.

Select whether the following are examples of using test data or audit software for trade payables testing.

Selecting a sample of supplier balances for testing using monetary unit sampling	**Test data**	**Audit software**
Recalculating the ageing of trade payables to identify balances which may be in dispute	**Test data**	**Audit software**
Calculation of trade payables payment period to use in analytical procedures	**Test data**	**Audit software**
Inputting dummy purchase invoices into the client system to see if processed correctly	**Test data**	**Audit software**

(2 marks)

The following scenario relates to questions 111 – 115

It is 1 July 20X5. You are an audit supervisor in Seagull & Co and you are currently performing the audit of an existing client, Eagle Heating Co (Eagle), for the year ended 31 May 20X5. Eagle manufactures and sells heating and plumbing equipment to a number of home improvement stores across the country.

The following information has been obtained during discussions with the finance director.

Unpaid receivable

One of Eagle's key customers has been experiencing financial difficulties. Eagle has agreed that the customer can take a six-month payment break, after which payments will resume. The finance director does not believe that any allowance is required against this receivable. Your review of industry journals has identified several articles that suggest the key customer may soon cease trading.

Inventory

Eagle has experienced increased competition. In order to maintain its current levels of sales, it has decreased the selling price of its products significantly. Despite the reduction in selling price, inventory levels are significantly higher this year compared to the prior year. In addition to Eagle's inventory, there is inventory stored on behalf of a third party at the year-end. Audit staff attended the year-end inventory count of Eagle which was held three days before the year end due to staff availability of Eagle. A reconciliation has been performed to determine the year-end inventory quantities.

Lawsuit

A customer has filed a claim against the company regarding a heating system that Eagle installed two months before the year end. The customer claims the installation was not done properly resulting in an explosion which caused damage to his home. The customer is claiming compensation of $50,000 which is material to the financial statements. The finance director believes that the claim is not probable to succeed so has not referred to it in the financial statements.

111 Which of the following substantive procedures will provide the MOST reliable evidence as to the recoverability of the outstanding balance from Eagle's key customer?

    o   Obtain a direct confirmation letter from the key customer

    o   Compare the current outstanding balance from the customer to the prior year

    o   Review the industry journal articles referring to the customer's financial difficulties

    o   Review post year-end cash receipts from the key customer   **(2 marks)**

112 Which TWO of the following substantive procedures will provide evidence over the EXISTENCE of Eagle's other trade receivables?

    o   Calculate the receivables collection period and compare with prior year

    o   Perform a receivables circularisation

    o   Review post year-end cash receipts from customers

    o   Recalculate the allowance for irrecoverable receivables   **(2 marks)**

113 Which TWO of the following factors may indicate overvaluation of inventory at Eagle?

    o   Increased competition resulting in a decrease in selling price

    o   Increased inventory levels

    o   Increased inventory turnover ratio

    o   Inventory consists of heating and plumbing equipment for home improvement stores

    o   Inclusion of the third party inventory within Eagle's inventory balance   **(2 marks)**

114 Select whether the following are tests of control or substantive procedures in relation to Eagle's inventory balance.

Observe the client's staff to ensure they are following the inventory count instructions	Test of control	Substantive procedure
Inspect the inventory for evidence of damage or obsolescence	Test of control	Substantive procedure
Re-perform the reconciliation from the inventory count date to the year-end date for inventory to assess the accuracy of the inventory quantities.	Test of control	Substantive procedure

(2 marks)

115 **Which of the following are appropriate audit responses to the lawsuit?**

    1   Ask the finance director to include a provision in the financial statements

    2   Inspect correspondence between the client and their legal advisers

    3   Review board minutes to understand management's view about the claim

    4   Contact the customer to understand the details of the claim

    ○   2 and 3 only

    ○   2, 3 and 4

    ○   1, 3 and 4

    ○   1 and 4 only

        (2 marks)

The following scenario relates to questions 116 – 120

It is 1 July 20X5. You are an audit senior in Staple and Co and you are preparing the audit procedures in respect of the audit of inventory for Gloss Co for the year ending 31 August 20X5. Gloss Co is a paint manufacturer and has been trading for over 50 years. It operates from one central site, which includes the production facility, warehouse and administration offices.

To avoid the disruption of a year-end inventory count, Gloss Co has this year introduced a continuous/perpetual inventory counting system. A timetable of inventory counts is maintained and regularly reviewed.

The following inventory counting processes have been implemented by Gloss Co:

1   The team prints the inventory quantities and descriptions from the system and these records are then compared to the inventory physically present.

2   Any discrepancies in relation to quantities are noted on the inventory sheets, including any items not listed on the sheets but present in the warehouse area.

3   Any damaged or old items are noted and they are removed from the inventory sheets.

4   During the counts there will continue to be inventory movements with goods arriving and leaving the warehouse.

5   Inventory belonging to third parties is removed from the warehouse before the count commences and kept in a separate location.

---

116   **Which of the following statements are TRUE in respect of inventory counts?**

1   The external auditor will perform the inventory count to ensure the inventory figure is accurate for the financial statements

2   The inventory count is used to ensure inventory is valued appropriately in the financial statements

3   All companies must cease production on days an inventory count is performed

4   The external auditor must attend the inventory count if inventory is a material balance

o   1, 2 and 4 only

o   2 and 3 only

o   4 only

o   1, 2, 3 and 4   **(2 marks)**

117   **What is the primary reason for maintaining an inventory count timetable?**

o   To ensure obsolete inventory is identified on a timely basis

o   To ensure the warehouse staff are not stealing inventory

o   To ensure all areas are counted during the year

o   To ensure damaged inventory is identified on a timely basis   **(2 marks)**

118   **Select whether the following statements are true or false in respect of Gloss Co's perpetual inventory system.**

Staple & Co must attend at least one count to ensure adequate controls are applied	**True**	**False**
Cut-off testing will only need to be performed if a full count is carried out at the year-end	**True**	**False**
All lines of inventory must be counted at least twice during the year	**True**	**False**
Staple & Co should visit the client's premises at least once a year and request a surprise inventory count	**True**	**False**

(2 marks)

119   **Select whether the inventory count processes described represent strengths or deficiencies.**

1	**Strength**	**Deficiency**
2	**Strength**	**Deficiency**
3	**Strength**	**Deficiency**
4	**Strength**	**Deficiency**
5	**Strength**	**Deficiency**

(2 marks)

120 During the inventory count you perform test counts agreeing inventory quantities on the count sheets to the physical inventory present in the warehouse and from the physical inventory to the count sheets.

Which financial statement assertions do these two procedures address?

	Count sheet to inventory	Inventory to count sheet
A	Existence	Completeness
B	Completeness	Existence
C	Accuracy, valuation and allocation	Existence
D	Rights and obligations	Accuracy, valuation and allocation

- ○ Option A
- ○ Option B
- ○ Option C
- ○ Option D

(2 marks)

The following scenario relates to questions 121 – 125

It is 1 July 20X5. You are an audit senior in Thor & Co and you have been assigned to the audit of Hemsworth Co for the year ended 31 May 20X5.

You are due to commence the audit of trade payables and the following procedures are listed in the audit plan:

Procedure		Selection method
1	For 20 invoices listed in the payables ledger trace the amount recorded to the purchase invoice	Start at a random point and test every $100th
2	From the cash book, select 10 payments made to suppliers in the first week of June 20X5 and trace to the related GRN. If the goods were received on or before 31 May 20X5 trace through to the payables ledger or accruals list	Highest value payments during the period specified
3	For 10 suppliers included in the payables ledger re-perform supplier statement reconciliations	Any suppliers that have sent supplier statements at the year end

Sample sizes have been selected based on the results of the risk assessment performed at the planning stage.

---

121 **Which THREE of the following should be considered when deciding whether to use sampling?**

○   The time the auditor has available to perform the procedures

○   Appropriateness of the population

○   The size of the population

○   Completeness of the population

○   The ease with which the information is expected to be available **(2 marks)**

122 **Identify whether the selection methods described represent sampling.**

1	Sampling	Not sampling
2	Sampling	Not sampling
3	Sampling	Not sampling

(2 marks)

123 **In respect of procedure 1, if the method stated to test every 100th item, which method would be described?**

○   Monetary unit selection

○   Random selection

○   Systematic selection

○   Block selection **(2 marks)**

124 **In relation to the procedures described, which of the following statements are TRUE?**

1   Procedure 1 addresses the assertion of occurrence

2   Procedures 2 and 3 address the assertion of completeness

3   Procedure 2 uses the least reliable forms of evidence as compared with procedures 1 and 3

4   In respect of procedure 3, if supplier statements have not been retained by Hemsworth Co the auditor should contact the supplier directly

○   1, 2, 3 and 4

○   2 and 3 only

○   1 only

○   2, 3 and 4 **(2 marks)**

125 During the testing of Hemsworth Co's payables balance, several misstatements were found. Which of the following is the most appropriate initial response your audit firm should take?

    ○   Report the matter to the client

    ○   Increase the amount of testing

    ○   Suggest the audit opinion is modified

    ○   Discuss the issue with the audit manager   **(2 marks)**

The following scenario relates to questions 126 – 130

It is 1 July 20X5. You are an audit senior in Apollo & Co assigned to the audit of Delphic Co for the year ended 31 May 20X5. You are due to commence the audit of trade receivables. For the first time at this client, you have decided to use audit software to assist with the audit of the receivables balance.

Delphic Co is a wholesaler of furniture such as chairs, tables and cupboards. Delphic Co buys the furniture from six major manufacturers and sells them to over 600 different customers ranging from large retail chain stores to smaller owner-controlled businesses.

All financial information is stored on Delphic Co's computer systems, although previous audits have tended to adopt an 'audit around the computer' approach. Computer staff at Delphic Co are happy to help the auditor by providing access to the systems, although they cannot confirm completeness of systems documentation, and have warned that the systems have very old operating systems in place which limits file compatibility with more up-to-date programs. As the system is old, the auditor will be provided with copy files and not be allowed any direct access to Delphic Co's computer system.

---

126 Select whether the following explanations provide a valid explanation why audit risk increases when auditing 'around the computer'.

The actual computer files and programs are not tested therefore the auditor has no direct evidence that the programs are working as expected	**Valid**	**Not valid**
Where errors are found in reconciling inputs to outputs, it may be difficult or even impossible to determine why those errors occurred	**Valid**	**Not valid**

(2 marks)

127 Which of the following is NOT a limitation of using audit software at Delphic Co?

    ○   There may be substantial setup costs to use the software, especially where the computer systems of the client have not been fully documented

    ○   The computer audit department at Delphic Co cannot confirm that all system documentation is available, especially for the older systems currently in use

    ○   There are over 600 customers on the system making the use of audit software inappropriate at Delphic Co

    ○   The auditor will be provided with copy files and not be allowed any direct access to Delphic Co's computer system   **(2 marks)**

---

128 Assuming that audit software can be developed for use on Delphic Co's systems, which of the following procedures could be carried out on the receivables balance?

1 Cast the receivables ledger to ensure it is arithmetically correct

2 Compare the balance on each receivable account with its credit limit to ensure this has not been exceeded

3 Stratify the receivables balances and select an appropriate sample for testing

4 Produce an aged receivables analysis to assist with the identification of irrecoverable receivables

o 1 and 2 only

o 1, 3 and 4 only

o 2, 3 and 4 only

o 1, 2, 3 and 4 **(2 marks)**

129 Which THREE of the following statements are TRUE in relation to audit software?

o As the systems are old the audit software may slow Delphic Co's system down

o The audit software will test the programmed controls of Delphic Co

o The use of audit software may save time resulting in greater efficiency

o Audit staff may need to be trained to use the audit software

o The audit will be more expensive each year audit software is used **(2 marks)**

130 Delphic Co has informed you that they plan to implement a new computerised accounting system within the next year.

Which of the following would represent an appropriate audit response in respect of the new computerised accounting system?

1 The audit firm should delay the use of audit software to ensure it is designed to effectively work with the new system

2 The audit engagement partner should provide advice to Delphic Co on which system to implement

3 The external audit team must be present during the installation and testing of the new system

o 2 and 3 only

o 1 and 3 only

o 1 only

o 1, 2, and 3 **(2 marks)**

The following scenario relates to questions 131 – 135

You are an audit manager who specialises in the audit of not-for-profit (NFP) organisations. You are currently assigned to two clients, Hightown and Stargazer. Both audit teams include audit juniors who have only been involved with audits of companies and have not audited NFP organisations before. As the manager, you will be responsible for explaining the differences between the audits of NFPs and companies. The following information is to be communicated to the audit teams of each client.

Hightown

Hightown is a local government authority which receives an allocation of tax payer money from central government. Hightown has been notified by central government of a significant cut in its funding for the following financial year.

Stargazer

Stargazer is a local charity which operates several charity shops. People make donations of goods which the shop sells to customers. All sales are paid for in cash as transaction amounts are usually small and credit card charges incur too great a cost.

Stargazer employs one administrative assistant. All other staff and trustees are volunteers who commit between 1 and 5 hours per week to the charity. The administrative assistant is responsible for paying the bills, including their own wages, and recording the transactions in a spreadsheet. The administrative assistant is also responsible for preparing the financial statements and charity's tax return. Tax rules for charities are different to those for companies and individuals. Once prepared, they are sent to the trustees for approval. None of the trustees have any specific financial expertise.

131   **Which TWO of the following statements is TRUE in relation to the audit of Hightown?**

A   ○   As Hightown is a local government authority the risk of manipulation of the financial statements is lower

B   ○   Hightown requires an audit as it is funded by taxpayers

C   ○   The auditor's report of Hightown will not be publicly available once issued

D   ○   The audit of Hightown will take longer than the audit of a company

E   ○   The audit team should include staff with experience of public sector audits **(2 marks)**

132   **Which of the following statements is FALSE in respect of the notification regarding the cut in funding for Hightown?**

A   ○   Audit risk will increase due to the threat to the going concern status of the organisation

B   ○   The auditor will need to review plans and forecasts to assess how the organisation will ensure it has sufficient funds to continue

C   ○   The auditor's report for Hightown will not need to refer to going concern uncertainties as it is a local government authority

D   ○   The auditor should review any plans Hightown has to reduce costs in the future to assess whether this could realistically be achieved and therefore indicate the organisation has sufficient funds to pay its liabilities when they fall due   **(2 marks)**

133 Completeness of income has been identified as a significant audit risk for the audit of Stargazers. Select THREE procedures which will help identify if income is understated.

A	Compare income by shop and category to the prior year	
B	Inspect credit notes issued post year-end	
C	Agree totals on till receipts to the sales day book, bank statements and cash book	
D	Obtain the sales day book and cast to confirm accuracy	

(2 marks)

134 Which of the following risks require specific consideration for the audit of Stargazers?

1 Less segregation of duties

2 Uncertainty over future funding

3 Complexity of taxation rules

4 Competence of volunteer staff

A ○ 1 and 4 only

B ○ 1, 3 and 4 only

C ○ 1, 2 and 3 only

D ○ 1, 2, 3 and 4

(2 marks)

135 Select whether the following statements are ALWAYS true, NEVER true or MAY be true in respect of the audit of a charity such as Stargazers.

A	Management will have no financial qualifications therefore there is a greater risk of material misstatement	Always true	May be true	Never true
B	Internal control systems will not be as sophisticated as those for profit making companies	Always true	May be true	Never true
C	There are fewer auditing standards applicable to audits of charities	Always true	May be true	Never true
D	Charities such as Stargazers will have different objectives to a profit making company therefore the auditors' assessment of materiality will consider different factors	Always true	May be true	Never true

(2 marks)

The following scenario relates to questions 136 – 140

It is 1 July 20X5. You are an audit senior in Cork & Co and are currently performing the final audit of Bamboo Co for the year ended 31 May 20X5. The company is a manufacturer of environmentally-friendly packaging. You have performed the audit of share capital and reserves. No misstatements have been identified during audit testing.

An extract from the draft financial statements is given below.

	Notes	20X5	20X4
		$m	$m
Ordinary share capital	1	100	50
Retained earnings	2	123	110
Revaluation reserve	3	100	90
		323	250

Notes:

1   A one for two bonus issue took place on 1 October 20X4. A one for three rights issue took place on 1 January 20X5.

2   Profit for the year ended 31 May 20X5 is $40 million.

A dividend in respect of the year ended 31 May 20X4 which was approved in November 20X4 was paid in December 20X4.

A dividend of $10 million has been proposed in respect of the year ended 31 May 20X5 and this will be put to the shareholders for approval at the AGM which is to be held in November.

3   Bamboo Co adopts a policy of revaluation of its properties. A revaluation of all of Bamboo Co's properties was performed by an independent expert on 20 May 20X5 resulting in a surplus of $12 million.

Excess depreciation transferred to retained earnings is $2 million.

136   **Which of the following provides the MOST reliable evidence in respect of the bonus issue of ordinary share capital?**

     O   Bank statements

     O   Share register

     O   Companies House information (or equivalent)

     O   Notes of discussion with the finance director and chief executive   **(2 marks)**

137   **How much was the dividend paid in December 20X4?**

     O $4 million

     O $17 million

     O $19 million

     O $29 million   **(2 marks)**

138 Select the financial statement assertion tested by the following procedures.

Inspect the independent expert's report	**Completeness**	**Cut-off**	**Valuation**
Match the physical properties to the independent expert's report and non-current asset register	**Existence**	**Completeness**	**Presentation**
Recalculate the depreciation on revalued properties	**Completeness**	**Existence**	**Valuation**
Inspect December 20X4 bank statements for payment of dividend	**Occurrence**	**Cut-off**	**Completeness**

(2 marks)

139 Which TWO of the following statements are FALSE in relation to equity and reserves?

○ Equity and reserves are material by nature

○ The auditor must check that total equity and reserves are the same as total assets on the statement of financial position

○ The auditor will rely mainly on substantive analytical procedures when auditing equity and reserves

○ Movements in equity and reserves must be shown in the statement of changes in equity

○ Dividends proposed must be disclosed in the financial statements   (2 marks)

140 Having completed the audit of share capital and reserves, you are now auditing directors' emoluments.

Which of the following procedures should be performed to test COMPLETENESS of directors' emoluments?

1   Obtain a breakdown of payments made to each director, recalculate the total and agree to the financial statements.

2   Trace amounts included on the breakdown of directors' emoluments to the bank statements and cash book

3   Review board minutes for details of bonuses or additional payments to be made to directors

4   Inspect directors' service contracts for salaries and trace through to payroll reports for the year

○   1, 2, 3 and 4

○   1 and 4 only

○   1, 2 and 3 only

○   1, 3 and 4 only   (2 marks)

REVIEW AND REPORTING

The following scenario relates to questions 141–145

Viola Co is a manufacturer of shoes. You are an audit manager in Cello & Co and you are performing an overall review of the financial statements for the year ended 30 September 20X8 prior to the issue of the auditor's report. Profit before tax for the year was $131.4m (20X7: $120.9m).

Analytical procedures

As part of your overall review, you have performed analytical procedures over the draft financial statements and have noted that the trade receivables collection period is lower than it was during the interim audit performed in July 20X8. You are aware that the credit controller of Viola Co left the company in August 20X8 and that the directors have said that, as a result, the company is experiencing difficulties in debt collection.

Disclosures

During the year, Viola Co revalued its head office and as part of your review, you are considering the detail which is disclosed in the property, plant and equipment note in the draft financial statements.

Uncorrected misstatements

Your review also includes an assessment of uncorrected misstatements. These have been recorded by the audit team as follows:

		$000
1	Interest payable omitted in error	1,942
2	Additional allowance for receivables required	9,198
3	Error in sales invoice processing resulting in understatement of sales	8,541
4	Write off in respect of faulty goods	2,900

Faulty goods

The adjustment for faulty goods listed as an uncorrected misstatement above relates to an entire batch of shoes, which was produced on 12 September 20X8. The audit work concluded that the cost of this inventory exceeded its net realisable value by $2.9m. The directors dispute the audit team's figures and believe that the realisable value of the inventory still exceeds its cost.

141 **Which of the following would form part of the auditor's overall review of the financial statements?**

    1   Establishing whether the pre-conditions for an audit are present

    2   Assessing whether the information and explanations obtained during the audit are adequately reflected

    3   Performing a detailed review of the audit working papers to ensure the work has been properly performed

    4   Reviewing the adequacy of the disclosure of accounting policies

    o   1 and 2

    o   3 and 4

    o   1 and 3

    o   2 and 4   **(2 marks)**

142 **Which of the following is a valid explanation for the INCONSISTENCY between the results of the analytical procedures on trade receivables and the directors' statement regarding debt collection problems?**

    A   A change in sales mix towards high value products

    B   An increase in the proportion of cash sales since August 20X8

    C   An increase in the rate of sales tax in September 20X8

    D   Sales growth of 1% per month over the year   **(2 marks)**

143 **Which of the following details should be disclosed in respect of the revaluation of the head office if the auditor is to conclude that the disclosures are adequate?**

    1   Effective date of the revaluation

    2   Name of the valuer

    3   The amount of the revaluation increase

    4   Carrying amount of the head office under the cost model

    A   1, 2 and 3 only

    B   1, 3 and 4 only

    C   2, 3 and 4 only

    D   1, 2, 3 and 4   **(2 marks)**

144 **Which of the uncorrected misstatements numbered (1), (2) and (3) by the audit team MUST be adjusted for if the auditor is to issue an unmodified audit opinion?**

    A   Misstatements 2 and 3 only

    B   Misstatements 1 and 3 only

    C   Misstatements 1, 2 and 3

    D   Misstatement 2 only   **(2 marks)**

145 All adjustments required by the auditors have been made to the financial statements with the exception of adjustment (4) relating to the faulty goods.

Which of the following correctly describes the effect of this matter on the auditor's report?

A   Unmodified opinion with no further disclosure

B   Unmodified opinion with disclosure in an emphasis of matter paragraph

C   Qualified opinion due to material misstatement

D   Qualified opinion due to inability to obtain sufficient appropriate audit evidence

(2 marks)

The following scenario relates to questions 146 –150

It is 1 July 20X5. You are an audit manager in Spring & Co responsible for the audit of Autumn Co. You are reviewing the audit file of Autumn Co for the year ended 31 March 20X5 which is nearing completion. You have noted several issues during your review:

- Several working papers which were prepared by the audit junior have not been signed as reviewed by the audit senior responsible for supervising the audit junior. You are aware that a review has been performed but this is not documented on the audit file.

- One audit working paper states that a sample of 30 purchase invoices should be tested but the results of the test show that only 15 invoices were tested. Several other areas document that samples sizes were reduced in order to save time.

- In the subsequent events review section of the file, the audit senior has documented that he has enquired of management whether there have been any subsequent events and was told that there have not been any. The audit senior has documented in the working paper that no further work is considered necessary as a result.

---

146 **Which of the following statements are true in respect of the reduction in samples sizes?**

1   The audit plan has not been followed

2   Sufficient appropriate evidence may not have been obtained

3   Material misstatements may go undetected

4   Those sections will need to be reviewed by a manager and the manager will form a conclusion on the balances.

    ○   1, 2 and 3 only

    ○   2 and 4 only

    ○   1, 3 and 4 only

    ○   1, 2, 3 and 4

(2 marks)

147 Select whether the following statements are true or false in respect of the subsequent events review of Autumn Co.

Enquiry does not provide sufficient appropriate evidence on its own	True	False
The auditor has demonstrated a lack of professional scepticism	True	False
A written representation should have been obtained from management confirming that they have disclosed all subsequent events to the auditor	True	False
The auditor only needs to perform procedures if they are made aware of any subsequent events	True	False

(2 marks)

148 As a result of the quality control issues encountered during the audit of Autumn Co, which of the following actions should now be taken?

1　The offending members of staff have demonstrated a lack of competence and due care therefore the firm should report them to the ACCA to be disciplined for failing to comply with ethical requirements

2　More frequent quality control reviews may need to take place

3　Further training should be provided to staff

4　The firm's policies and procedures should be reviewed and updated if applicable

○　2 and 4 only

○　1 and 3 only

○　2, 3 and 4 only

○　1, 2, 3 and 4

(2 marks)

149 ISA 220 *Quality Control for an Audit of Financial Statements* requires the use of pre- and post-issuance reviews as part of the audit firm's quality control procedures to ensure the audit is performed to a high standard. Which of the following statements is TRUE in respect of pre and post-issuance reviews?

○　Pre and post-issuance reviews should be documented in the respective audit files

○　A post-issuance review involves a review of the significant judgments affecting the audit

○　A pre-issuance review is also known as a cold review

○　A post-issuance review may identify the need for revision to the firm's policies

(2 marks)

150 **Select whether the following statements are true or false in respect of review of audit working papers.**

	True	False
The audit engagement partner will review all working papers on the audit file before issuing an opinion	**True**	**False**
If working papers have been reviewed there is no quality control issue arising from the lack of documentation	**True**	**False**
All working papers should be signed by the person who prepared them	**True**	**False**
All team members' work should be reviewed by someone more senior than the preparer	**True**	**False**

(2 marks)

The following scenario relates to questions 151 – 155

It is 1 July 20X5. You are an audit manager in Elm & Co and you are finalising the audit of the financial statements of Oak Co for the year ended 31 March 20X5. You are reviewing the results of the final analytical procedures and other outstanding points on the audit file. The auditor's report is due to be signed in the next two weeks.

The following ratio analysis has been completed as part of the final analytical procedures:

	20X5 Final	20X5 Planning	20X4 Final
Gross profit margin	9%	11%	12%
Quick ratio	0.2	0.6	0.8
Payables payment period	45	40	37
Inventory holding period	50	40	42

Discussions with the finance director have also revealed the following:

1   Oak Co lost a major customer, Beech Co, in March 20X5, but new business has been won post year end which has mitigated the impact of the loss of Beech Co.

2   Oak Co is due to repay a substantial loan on 30 September 20X5. Oak Co is currently negotiating revised terms with the bank but it is unlikely that negotiations will be concluded before the auditor's report is signed. This will be disclosed in the financial statements.

3   A number of personnel in the purchasing department left during the year and have not been replaced.

4   A major supplier to Oak Co has just gone out of business with a number of unfulfilled orders.

5   A new product which was due to account for 30% of revenue in 20X5 has not been successful.

6   A litigation claim was filed against Oak Co in April 20X5 with potential damages totalling 3% of this year's profit.

The financial statements for the year ended 31 March 20X5 have been prepared on a going concern basis. The initial going concern assessment conducted by the management of Oak Co covers the six-month period to 30 September 20X5.

151 **Which THREE of the issues identified could result in significant uncertainty over the going concern status of Oak Co?**

    o   1

    o   2

    o   3

    o   4

    o   5

    o   6   **(2 marks)**

152 **Select whether the following comments are consistent or inconsistent with the results of the final analytical procedures.**

The company has increased the sales prices charged to customers while maintaining costs at a level comparable to 20X4	**Consistent**	**Inconsistent**
The company has become more reliant on its overdraft facility during the year	**Consistent**	**Inconsistent**
Due to cash restrictions, the company has encountered delays in paying suppliers	**Consistent**	**Inconsistent**
At the year-end inventory count, a lower level of slow-moving inventory was noted compared to prior year	**Consistent**	**Inconsistent**

(2 marks)

153 **Which of the following procedures would provide the MOST reliable evidence in relation to the new business won post year-end?**

    o   Review post year-end sales orders from the new customer

    o   Inspect email correspondence between the sales director of Oak Co and the new customer

    o   Obtain a written representation confirming the level of business agreed with the new customer

    o   Review board minutes discussing the contract with the new customer   **(2 marks)**

154 **Which of the following is an appropriate course of action for the auditor to take in respect of management's going concern assessment?**

    o   Request management extend the assessment to the date of the auditor's report

    o   Design and carry out procedures to only assess going concern in the period from 31 March 20X5 to the date of the auditor's report

    o   Request management extend the assessment to cover at least until 31 March 20X6

    o   Accept the timeframe used by management as the going concern review is their responsibility   **(2 marks)**

155 The audit engagement partner has concluded that the disclosure included in the financial statements in relation to the loan negotiations is adequate and commented that this disclosure is fundamental to the users' understanding of the financial statements.

Which of the following correctly identifies the implications for the auditor's opinion and report of Oak Co?

	Opinion	Report
○	Unmodified	No additional communication required
○	Unmodified	Material Uncertainty Related to Going Concern paragraph
○	Modified	Emphasis of Matter paragraph
○	Modified	Key audit matters

(2 marks)

The following scenario relates to questions 156 – 160

It is 1 July 20X5. You are an audit manager in Blenkin & Co responsible for the audit of Sampson Co, a large listed retailer. The audit for the year ended 31 March 20X5 is nearing completion and the auditor's report is due to be signed next week.

You have been informed that the financial controller left Sampson Co on 28 February 20X5. As part of the subsequent events audit procedures, you reviewed post year-end board meeting minutes and discovered that a legal case for unfair dismissal has been brought against Sampson Co by the financial controller. During a discussion with the Human Resources (HR) director of Sampson Co, you established that the company received notice of the proposed legal claim on 10 April 20X5.

The HR director told you that Sampson Co's lawyers believe the financial controller's claim is likely to be successful, but estimate that $150,000 is the maximum amount of compensation which would be paid. However, the directors do not intend to make any adjustment for a provision or to include any disclosures in the financial statements relating to the issue.

The draft financial statements currently show a profit before tax of $6.5 million and revenue of $66 million for the financial year ended 31 March 20X5.

---

156 **Subsequent events procedures should be performed between the date of the financial statements and which date?**

- A ○ The date the audit work for subsequent events is performed
- B ○ The date of approval of the financial statements
- C ○ The date of the auditor's report
- D ○ The date the financial statements are issued

(2 marks)

157 Which of the following audit procedures should be performed to form a conclusion as to whether the financial statements require amendment in relation to the unfair dismissal claim?

1   Inspect relevant correspondence with Sampson Co's lawyers

2   Write to the financial controller to confirm the claim and level of damages

3   Review the post year-end cash book and bank statements for evidence the claim has been settled

4   Request management confirms their views in a written representation letter

o   1, 2 and 3

o   1, 2 and 4

o   1, 3 and 4

o   2, 3 and 4   **(2 marks)**

158 Select the type of opinion that is appropriate and the nature of any additional communications necessary if the unfair dismissal case is **NOT** adjusted for or disclosed within the financial statements.

Opinion	Additional communications
Unmodified	No additional communication
Qualified	Emphasis of Matter paragraph
Adverse	Material Uncertainty Related to Going Concern paragraph
Disclaimer	Other matter paragraph

(2 marks)

159 You are drafting the auditor's report for Sampson Co and the audit engagement partner has reminded you that as Sampson Co is a listed company, the report will need to include a Key Audit Matters section.

According to ISA 701 *Communicating Key Audit Matters in the Independent Auditor's Report*, **which of the following should be included in the Key Audit Matters section of the auditor's report?**

A   o   Matters which required significant auditor attention

B   o   Matters which result in a modification to the audit opinion

C   o   All matters which were communicated to those charged with governance

D   o   All matters which were material to the financial statements   **(2 marks)**

160 One month after the financial statements were issued the legal claim was finalised with the court awarding compensation of $500,000 to the ex-financial controller. The directors of Sampson Co have contacted Blenkin & Co to inform them of the outcome.

Which TWO of the following are appropriate actions for Blenkin & Co to take?

A ○ Discuss the matter with management and, where appropriate, those charged with governance

B ○ Obtain a written representation from management

C ○ Consider whether the firm should resign from the engagement

D ○ Enquire how management intends to address the matter in the financial statements where appropriate

(2 marks)

The following scenario relates to questions 161 – 165

It is 1 July 20X5. You are an audit manager in Colorado & Co. You are responsible for the audit of Mississippi Co for the year ended 31 March 20X5. The audit is nearing completion and the auditor's report is due to be signed next week.

The draft financial statements recognise revenue of $18 million (20X4 – $17 million). The draft annual report of Mississippi Co contains a Chair's statement in which the chair has commented that she is pleased to report an increase in revenue of 20% this year. The report also includes an operating review, corporate social responsibility report, financial statements and notes to the financial statements.

The directors of Mississippi Co have indicated that they intend to distribute the annual report to prospective investors in order to obtain additional finance. The audit engagement partner has informed the directors that the auditor's report is only intended for reliance by the existing shareholders and that no liability will be assumed to any other party. The audit engagement partner has asked you to draft the auditor's report for Mississippi Co and requested that a paragraph referring to this restriction of liability is included.

---

161 **Which of the following statements best describes the auditor's responsibilities in respect of other information?**

○ The auditor provides limited assurance over the completeness and accuracy of the other information

○ The auditor must read the other information to ensure it is consistent with the financial statements and their knowledge of the entity obtained during the audit

○ The auditor must audit the other information and obtain sufficient appropriate evidence that the other information is true and fair

○ Other information only needs to be considered if it is made available at the start of the audit with the draft financial statements

(2 marks)

162 **Which of the following sections of Mississippi Co's annual report would NOT be considered 'Other Information'?**

    o   Chair's statement

    o   Operating review

    o   Corporate social responsibility report

    o   Notes to the financial statements   **(2 marks)**

163 **How should the inconsistency between the Chair's statement and financial statements be referred to in the auditor's report of Mississippi Co?**

    o   Within the Other Information section

    o   Within an Emphasis of Matter paragraph

    o   Within an Other Matter paragraph

    o   Within the Auditor's Opinion section   **(2 marks)**

164 **Select whether the following statements are true or false in relation to referring to the Chair's statement in the auditor's report of Mississippi Co.**

Users may be misled if the other information contains incorrect information or information which contradicts the financial statements such as that in the Chair's statement	**True**	**False**
Users may believe the auditor has not audited the financial statements properly if the inconsistency is not highlighted	**True**	**False**
The auditor must expose management's incompetence	**True**	**False**
The inconsistency may undermine the credibility of your auditor's report if not highlighted	**True**	**False**

          (2 marks)

165 **In respect of the partner's request for restricting liability, how should this be addressed in the auditor's report?**

    o   Within the Auditor's Responsibility section

    o   By including an Emphasis of Matter paragraph

    o   By including an Other Matter paragraph

    o   Within the Basis for Opinion section   **(2 marks)**

The following scenario relates to questions 166 – 170

It is 1 July 20X5. You are an audit manager in Atlantic & Co responsible for the audit of Pacific Co. The audit of the financial statements for the year ended 31 March 20X5 is nearing completion and the auditor's report is due to be signed next week.

Included within receivables in the statement of financial position is a balance of $85,000 owed by Arctic Co, a key customer of Pacific Co. Arctic Co has just notified Pacific Co that it is unlikely to be able to pay the balance due to cash flow problems. The customer has asked for an extension of credit for a further three months as it expects its cash flow situation to improve in July and August. Pacific Co has agreed to this extension.

Due to the uncertainty over the recoverability of the debt, you believe that an allowance for receivables should have been made and you have discussed the issue with the finance director who has informed you that he will make adjustment for the balance in the following year's financial statements if the debt is not paid during the extended credit period agreed with Arctic Co.

Revenue for the year is $2.6 million, profit before tax is $1.4 million and total assets are $7.5 million.

166 **Which of the following statements is correct regarding the materiality of the irrecoverable debt?**

    o   The matter is material by nature

    o   The matter is not material as the debt is less than 5% of revenue

    o   The matter is not material as the debt is less than 10% of profit

    o   The matter is likely to be material as it is over 1% of assets   **(2 marks)**

167 **Which THREE of the following procedures would allow the auditor to form a conclusion as to the level of adjustment required to the receivables balance?**

    o   Review correspondence with the customer indicating when payment will be made

    o   Discuss with management why they feel an adjustment is not required in the current year

    o   Perform a direct confirmation of the balance outstanding at the year-end

    o   Review post year-end bank statements to identify if any payment has been received from the customer

    o   Inspect the sales invoice and GDN relating to the receivable balance   **(2 marks)**

168 **Assuming the matter is considered material and Pacific's directors have refused to adjust the financial statements, what is the appropriate opinion to be issued?**

    o   Unmodified

    o   Qualified

    o   Adverse

    o   Disclaimer   **(2 marks)**

169 Select whether the following elements should be included in the auditor's report of Pacific Co.

Addressee	Included	Not included
Other Matter paragraph	Included	Not included
Other Information	Included	Not included
Emphasis of Matter paragraph	Included	Not included

(2 marks)

170 Which TWO of the following are reasons why the auditor would need to modify the auditor's opinion?

o   They conclude that there is a material inconsistency between the audited financial statements and the other information contained in the annual report

o   They wish to draw attention to a matter that is fundamental to the users' understanding of the financial statements

o   They conclude that the financial statements as a whole are not free from material misstatement

o   They have been unable to obtain sufficient appropriate evidence to conclude that the financial statements as a whole are free from material misstatement

o   They wish to restrict reliance on the auditor's report by third parties

(2 marks)

The following scenario relates to questions 171 – 175

It is 1 July 20X5. You are an audit manager in Yellow Submarine & Co responsible for the audit of Magical Mystery Tour (MMT). The audit is nearing completion and the auditor's report is due to be signed next week.

MMT is a travel agency which has been trading for over five years. The company arranges holidays and hotel bookings in remote locations to individual customers and corporate clients. The company is financed partly through overdrafts and loans and also by several large shareholders. The overdraft facility is due for renewal later in July 20X5.

In January 20X5, a new competitor, Pure Shores Co, entered the market. Through competitive pricing, Pure Shores Co has gained considerable market share from MMT, including one of MMT's larger corporate clients which has moved its business to Pure Shores. In addition, a number of MMT's travel agents have left the company and joined Pure Shores. MMT has found it difficult to replace these employees due to the level of skills and knowledge of remote overseas locations required.

The directors have produced a cash flow forecast which shows a significantly worsening position over the coming 12 months. You have been informed that MMT's bankers will not make a decision on the renewal of the overdraft facility until after the auditor's report is issued. The directors have agreed to include brief disclosure of the uncertainty over going concern.

171 Which THREE of the following statements correctly describes the respective responsibilities of directors and auditors in relation to going concern?

A ○ The directors must assess whether the company can continue to trade for the foreseeable future.

B ○ The auditors and the directors must make disclosure of going concern uncertainties in the financial statements

C ○ The auditor will evaluate management's assessment of going concern

D ○ The directors will usually prepare a cash flow forecast to assess whether the company is likely to be able to trade for the foreseeable future

E ○ The directors must assess a period of at least twelve months from the date the financial statements are issued **(2 marks)**

172 Which THREE of the following procedures should be performed to assess the uncertainty arising in relation to the overdraft renewal?

A ○ Calculate key ratios to identify possible financial problems

B ○ Inspect correspondence with the bank to identify any disputes which may indicate the overdraft facility will not be renewed

C ○ Review the level of profit made in previous periods to assess whether the company is likely to continue to trade

D ○ Enquire with management whether any alternative sources of finance have been considered if the bank does not renew the overdraft facility

E ○ Inspect board minutes for discussions of management as to how they plan to improve the financial position of MMT **(2 marks)**

173 What will be the impact on the auditor's report of MMT in the following circumstances?

A	Adequate disclosure of going concern uncertainties is made	**Unmodified opinion with no additional communication**	**Modified opinion**	**Unmodified opinion with Going Concern paragraph**	**Unmodified opinion with Emphasis of Matter**
B	Adequate disclosure of going concern uncertainties is not made	**Unmodified opinion with no additional communication**	**Modified opinion**	**Unmodified opinion with Going Concern paragraph**	**Unmodified opinion with Emphasis of Matter**

(2 marks)

174 In which of the following situations should a company **NOT** prepare financial statements using the break up basis?

A ○ The company has ceased to trade

B ○ A decision has been made to close the company

C ○ There are material uncertainties relating to going concern

D ○ The company has run out of cash and is unable to pay its debts **(2 marks)**

175 What will be the impact on the auditor's report of MMT if the auditor believes the basis of preparation of the financial statements is incorrect?

A   o   Unmodified opinion with no additional communication

B   o   Unmodified opinion with an Emphasis of Matter paragraph

C   o   Qualified opinion with Basis for Qualified Opinion

D   o   Adverse opinion with Basis for Adverse Opinion   **(2 marks)**

The following scenario relates to questions 176 – 180

You are an audit manager in Bond & Co responsible for the audit of Paddington Co which is nearing completion. You are now resolving the last few issues before deciding on the appropriate audit opinion.

During the audit the following issues have been identified:

1   Paddington Co's main competitor filed a lawsuit for $3 million alleging a breach of copyright. This case is ongoing and will not be resolved prior to the auditor's report being signed. Paddington Co's lawyers believe the claim is only possible to succeed. Paddington Co has sufficient cash to make the settlement if it loses the case. The lawsuit has not been mentioned in the financial statements or related disclosures.

2   A warranty provision of $25 million has not been recognised in respect of goods which require repair or replacement within the first twelve months if they do not perform as expected.

3   Depreciation in respect of property, plant and equipment has not been recognised in the financial statements. The auditor has estimated that a depreciation charge of $1 million should be recognised.

4   Intangible assets have been overstated by $12 million due to research costs being capitalised as development costs in the statement of financial position.

Paddington Co's profit before tax is $29 million.

---

176 Which of the issues identified during the audit is likely to lead to an adverse opinion on Paddington Co's financial statements?

o   Lawsuit

o   Warranty provision

o   Depreciation

o   Intangible assets   **(2 marks)**

177 Which of the following statements is TRUE in respect of the lawsuit and its impact on the financial statements and auditor's report thereon?

o   A provision should be recognised in the financial statements of $3 million

o   A contingent liability should be disclosed in the notes to the financial statements

o   The matter is not material as it represents 10.3 % of profit before tax.

o   The lawsuit does not need to be referred to in the financial statements as the case is not settled at the year-end date   **(2 marks)**

178 The audit is now complete and the auditor's report is due to be issued next week. All adjustments requested have been corrected by management.

Which of the following correctly identifies the implications for the audit opinion and report of Paddington Co?

- ○   Unmodified opinion with no additional communication
- ○   Unmodified opinion with an Emphasis of Matter paragraph
- ○   Qualified opinion with Basis for Qualified Opinion
- ○   Disclaimer of opinion with Basis for Disclaimer of Opinion   **(2 marks)**

179 **Match the following auditor's report sections to the appropriate explanation of its purpose.**

Element		Purpose	
1	Title	A	Provides a description of the professional standards applied during the audit to provide confidence to users that the report can be relied upon
2	Addressee	B	Identifies the intended user of the report
3	Basis for opinion	C	Identifies the person responsible for the audit opinion in case of any queries
4	Key audit matters	D	Clearly identifies the report as an Independent Auditor's Report
5	Name of engagement partner	E	Draws attention to any other significant matters of which the users should be aware which have been discussed with those charged with governance

(2 marks)

180 **Which of the following correctly matches the opinion type with the wording for that opinion?**

	Opinion	Wording
○	Unmodified	Except for
○	Disclaimer	Do not express an opinion
○	Adverse	True and fair view
○	Qualified	Do not give a true and fair view

(2 marks)

The following scenario relates to questions 181 – 185

It is 1 July 20X5. You are an audit manager in Grace & Co responsible for the audit of Humphries Co, a chain of food wholesalers. The audit of the financial statements for the year ended 31 March 20X5 is nearing completion and the auditor's report is due to be signed next week.

Revenue for the year is $78 million and profit before taxation is $7.5 million. The following events have occurred subsequent to the year-end.

Receivable

Humphries Co has just become aware that one of its customers is experiencing significant going concern difficulties. There is a receivables balance in respect of this customer at the year-end of $0.3 million. Humphries Co believe that as the company has been trading for many years, they will receive some, if not full, payment from the customer therefore no adjustment has been made for the balance in the financial statements.

Lawsuit

A key supplier of Humphries Co is suing them for breach of contract. The lawsuit was filed prior to the year-end, and the sum claimed by them is $1 million. This has been disclosed as a contingent liability in the notes to the financial statements. Recent correspondence from the supplier indicates that they are willing to settle the case for $0.6 million. It is likely that Humphries Co will agree to this.

Warehouse

Following significant rain on 20 May 20X5, one of Humphries Co's three warehouses was flooded. All of the inventory stored there was damaged and has been disposed of. The insurance company has already been contacted but no response has been received as of yet. No amendments or disclosures have been made in the financial statements.

181 **Calculate the materiality level of the receivable and settlement figure for the lawsuit by reference to profit before tax and state whether they are material. Answers to calculations should be rounded to the nearest whole number with no decimal places.**

	Calculation		
Receivable		Material	Not material
Lawsuit		Material	Not material

(2 marks)

182 **In respect of the receivable and lawsuit, select the type of event and the appropriate accounting treatment.**

	Type of event		Accounting treatment	
Receivable	Adjusting	Non-adjusting	Recognise	Disclose
Lawsuit	Adjusting	Non-adjusting	Recognise	Disclose

(2 marks)

183 **Which of the following is NOT an appropriate procedure to reach a conclusion on the outstanding receivable?**

○ Contact the customer directly and enquire when they are likely to pay the outstanding balance

○ Review correspondence between the customer and Humphries Co to assess whether there is any likelihood of payment

○ Review the post year-end period to see if any payments have been received from the customer

○ Discuss the outstanding debt with the credit control manager

(2 marks)

184 **Assuming that the receivable and warehouse issues are resolved but the lawsuit issue remains unresolved, which FOUR of the following section titles MUST be included in the auditor's report?**

Auditor Responsibilities for the Audit of the Financial Statements	Included	Not included
Basis for Opinion	Included	Not included
Basis for Qualified Opinion	Included	Not included
Key Audit Matters	Included	Not included
Opinion	Included	Not included
Qualified Opinion	Included	Not included
Responsibilities of Management and Those Charged With Governance	Included	Not included

(2 marks)

185 **Which of the following statements is TRUE in respect of the warehouse?**

○ The value of the assets damaged during the flood should be written down to their realisable values

○ If the impact of the flood is material, the directors should include a disclosure note detailing the impact to the company

○ The insurance claim should be recognised as a contingent asset

○ As the flood occurred after the year end it will have no impact on the auditor's report

(2 marks)

The following scenario relates to questions 186 – 190

You are the manager responsible for the audit of Greenfields Co and you are performing the final review stage of the audit. Greenfields Co specialises in manufacturing equipment which can help to reduce toxic emissions in the production of chemicals. The company has grown rapidly over the past eight years and this is due partly to the warranties that the company gives to its customers. It guarantees its products for five years and if problems arise in this period it undertakes to fix them, or provide a replacement product. The following issues have been left for your attention.

Receivable balance owing from Yellowmix Co

Greenfields Co has a material receivable balance owing from its customer, Yellowmix Co. During the year-end audit, your team reviewed the ageing of this balance and found that no payments had been received from Yellowmix Co for over six months, and Greenfields Co would not allow this balance to be circularised. Instead management has assured your team that they will provide a written representation confirming that the balance is recoverable.

Warranty provision

The warranty provision included within the statement of financial position is material. The audit team has performed testing over the calculations and assumptions which are consistent with prior years. The team has requested a written representation from management confirming the basis and amount of the provision are reasonable. Management has yet to provide this representation.

186 **Select the appropriate words/phrases from the options to complete the sentences below. Options may be selected more than once.**

A written representation _____ in respect of the receivable balance. This is because _____.

A written representation _____ in respect of the warranty provision. This is because _____.

○ Is appropriate

○ Is not appropriate

○ The matter is not material

○ The matter involves management judgment

○ Other procedures can be performed which provide more reliable evidence

○ An ISA specifically requires a written representation to be obtained for the item

(2 marks)

187 **Assuming that the directors of Greenfields Co refuse to provide a written representation to the auditor, which of the following statements is TRUE?**

○ The refusal to provide a written representation will only be a matter of concern if it relates to a material area of the financial statements

○ The refusal to provide a written representation may cast doubt over management integrity and as such the reliability of other evidence provided by the client may be called into question

○ The refusal to provide a written representation will result in the need for the auditor to report the directors to the industry regulator

○ The auditor will need to notify the shareholders of the issue in person **(2 marks)**

188 Which TWO of the following audit reporting implications could result if Greenfields Co refuse to provide a written representation letter?

○　　Unmodified opinion

○　　Unmodified opinion with Emphasis of Matter paragraph

○　　Qualified opinion due to material misstatement

○　　Qualified opinion due to an inability to obtain sufficient appropriate evidence

○　　Adverse opinion as the financial statements do not show a true and fair view

○　　Disclaimer of opinion as the auditor does not have sufficient appropriate evidence to be able to express an audit opinion　　　　　　　　**(2 marks)**

189 Written representations are required by International Standards on Auditing in respect of subject-specific areas. Which of the following does NOT require a subject-specific written representation to be obtained?

○　　Fraud and error

○　　Laws and regulations

○　　Analytical procedures

○　　Subsequent events　　　　　　　　**(2 marks)**

190 Which THREE of the following MUST be included in every written representation according to ISA 580 *Written Representations*?

Plans or intentions of management that affect carrying values of assets	Required	Not required
Confirmation from management that they have provided the auditor with all information and access to records during the audit	Required	Not required
Confirmation from management that the financial statements are accurate/free from error	Required	Not required
Confirmation from management that all transactions have been reflected in the financial statements	Required	Not required
Confirmation from management that they have prepared the financial statements in accordance with the applicable financial reporting framework	Required	Not required

(2 marks)

The following scenario relates to questions 191 – 195

It is 1 July 20X5. You are an audit manager in Daffy & Co responsible for the audit of Minnie Co. The audit work for the year ended 31 March 20X5 is nearly complete and you are resolving the last few issues before deciding on the appropriate wording for the auditor's report and opinion. Profit before tax is $10 million.

The following matters have been left for your attention.

Property, plant and equipment

During the year, the property balance was revalued by an independent expert valuer at the request of Minnie Co's management.

Depreciation has been calculated on the total of land and buildings. In previous years it has only been charged on buildings. Total depreciation is $2.5 million and the element charged to land only is $0.4 million.

Computerised wages program

Minnie Co's computerised wages program is backed up daily, however for a period of two months the wages records and the back-ups have been corrupted, and therefore cannot be accessed. Wages and salaries for these two months are $1.1 million.

Lawsuit

Minnie Co's main competitor has filed a lawsuit for $5 million against them alleging a breach of copyright; this case is ongoing and will not be resolved prior to the auditor's report being signed. The matter is correctly disclosed as a contingent liability in the financial statements.

Draft extracts for the auditor's report

Extracts for the auditor's report have already been drafted as follows:

1   We conducted our audit in accordance with International Standards on Auditing applicable to this audit.

2   Our objectives are to obtain maximum assurance about whether the financial statements as a whole are free from material misstatements.

3   Misstatements can arise from deliberate manipulation by management or error.

191   **Which TWO of the following statements are TRUE with respect to the work performed by the expert?**

   o   Daffy & Co must consider the competence and objectivity of the expert

   o   Daffy & Co must assess the expert's work to ensure it is appropriate for audit purposes

   o   The following statement must be included in the auditor's report for Minnie Co:

        'In order to confirm property valuations, we relied on the work undertaken by an independent expert.'

   o   The auditor must document in the audit file how they have complied with ISA 620 *Using the Work of an Auditor's Expert*

   o   The audit fee will be higher due to the need for an expert   **(2 marks)**

192 **Which of the following statements is TRUE with respect to the depreciation on land and buildings?**

- The auditor does not need to ask management to adjust the financial statements as the misstatement is not material

- A prior year adjustment will be required as the client's treatment was incorrect in the 20X4 financial statements

- The auditor must ask management to increase property, plant and equipment by $0.4 million

- The auditor must ask management to decrease property, plant and equipment by $0.4 million   **(2 marks)**

193 **In respect of the computerised wages issue only, select one option from each column which provides an appropriate conclusion.**

Materiality		Opinion		Wording
Not material		Adverse		Do not give a true and fair view
Material but not pervasive		Disclaimer		Give a true and fair view
Material and pervasive		Qualified		'Except for'...give a true and fair view
		Unmodified		Do not express an opinion

(2 marks)

194 **In respect of the lawsuit only, which of the following correctly identifies the implications for the auditor's opinion and report?**

- Unmodified opinion with no additional communication

- Unmodified opinion with an Emphasis of Matter paragraph

- Qualified opinion with Basis for Qualified Opinion

- Disclaimer of opinion with Basis for Disclaimer of Opinion   **(2 marks)**

195 **Which of the draft extracts for the auditor's report do not contain the correct wording as per ISA 700** *Forming an Opinion and Reporting on Financial Statements* **and require amendment?**

- 1 only

- 2 and 3 only

- 3 only

- 1, 2 and 3   **(2 marks)**

The following scenario relates to questions 196 – 200

It is 1 July 20X5. You are an audit manager in Shifu & Co responsible for the audit of Panda Co for the year ended 31 March 20X5. The draft financial statements show revenue of $55 million and profit before taxation of $5.6 million. Panda Co manufactures chemicals and has a factory and four offsite storage locations for finished goods. The final audit is almost complete and the financial statements and auditor's report are due to be signed next week.

The following two events have occurred subsequent to the year-end. No amendments or disclosures have been made in the financial statements in respect of the two events.

Event 1 – Defective chemicals

Chemicals are manufactured up to one month before despatch to enable Panda Co to undertake extensive quality control checks prior to despatch. Testing on 3 April 20X5 found that a batch of chemicals produced in March 20X5 was defective. The cost of this batch was $850,000. In its current condition it can be sold at a scrap value of $100,000 with selling costs of $1,000. The costs of correcting the defect are too significant for Panda Co's management to consider this an alternative option.

Event 2 – Explosion

An explosion occurred at the smallest of the four offsite storage locations on 20 April 20X5. This resulted in some damage to inventory and property, plant and equipment. Panda Co's management have investigated the cause of the explosion and believe that they are unlikely to be able to claim on their insurance. Management of Panda Co has estimated that the value of damaged inventory and property, plant and equipment was $900,000 and it now has no scrap value.

196 Select the option which correctly identifies whether the events are adjusting or non-adjusting

	Event 1	Event 2
o	Adjusting	Adjusting
o	Adjusting	Non-adjusting
o	Non-adjusting	Adjusting
o	Non-adjusting	Non-adjusting

(2 marks)

197 At what figure should the defective inventory be valued in the financial statements?

- o $850,000
- o $100,000
- o $99,000
- o $849,000

(2 marks)

198 **Which THREE of the following procedures should now be performed by the auditor of Panda Co?**

- ○ Obtain written representation from management confirming all subsequent events have been communicated to the auditor

- ○ Inspect purchase invoices to confirm the cost of the defective inventory

- ○ Review the most recent quality control reports in to identify other instances of defective inventory included within inventory at 31 March 20X5

- ○ Obtain a schedule of assets damaged in the explosion to determine the amount of loss incurred

- ○ Review correspondence with the insurance company regarding the likelihood of a successful claim **(2 marks)**

199 **Which of the following statements correctly identifies whether or not the events are material and whether the financial statements should be amended?**

	Material	Amendment
○	Event 1 & Event 2	Event 1 only
○	Event 1 only	Event 1 only
○	Event 2 only	Event 2 only
○	Event 1 & Event 2	Event 1 & Event 2

(2 marks)

200 **Assuming no amendments are made to the financial statements, which of the following will be included in the auditor's report for Panda Co?**

- ○ Basis for qualified opinion

- ○ Adverse opinion

- ○ Emphasis of matter paragraph

- ○ Key audit matter paragraph

(2 marks)

Section 2

PRACTICE QUESTIONS

PLANNING AND RISK ASSESSMENT

201 HARLEM *Walk in the footsteps of a top tutor*

This scenario relates to five requirements.

It is 1 July 20X5. You are an audit supervisor of Brooklyn & Co and are planning the audit of Harlem Co for the year ending 30 September 20X5. The company has been a client of your firm for several years and manufactures car tyres, selling its products to wholesalers and retailers. The audit manager attended a planning meeting with the finance director and has provided you with the following notes of the meeting and financial statement extracts:

Planning meeting notes

Harlem Co sells approximately 40% of its tyres to wholesale customers. These customers purchase goods on a sale or return basis. Under the terms of the agreement, wholesale customers have 60 days during which any returns can be made without penalty. The finance director has historically assumed a return rate of 10%, however, he now feels that this is excessive and intends to change this to 5%.

The company purchased a patent on 30 September 20X4 for $800,000, which was capitalised in the prior year as an intangible asset. This patent gives Harlem Co the exclusive right to manufacture specialised wet weather tyres for four years. In preparation for the manufacture of the wet weather tyres, this year the company conducted a review of its plant and machinery. As part of this review, surplus items of plant and machinery were sold, resulting in a loss on disposal of $160,000.

In May 20X5, the financial controller of Harlem Co was dismissed after it was alleged that she had carried out a number of fraudulent transactions against the company. She has threatened to sue the company for unfair dismissal as she disputes the allegations. The company has only recently started to investigate the extent of the fraud in order to quantify the required adjustment.

A problem occurred in June 20X5, during production of a significant batch of tyres, which affected their quality. The issue was identified prior to any goods being dispatched and management is investigating whether the issues can be rectified and the tyres can subsequently be sold.

Harlem Co's finance director has informed you that in March 20X5 a significant customer was granted a payment break of six months, as it has been experiencing financial difficulties. Harlem Co maintains an allowance for trade receivables and it is anticipated that this will remain at the same level as the prior year.

The report to management issued by Brooklyn & Co following last year's audit highlighted significant deficiencies relating to Harlem Co's purchases cycle.

The finance director has informed you that the company intends to restructure its debt finance after the year end and will be looking to consolidate its loans to reduce the overall cost of borrowing. As a result of the planned restructuring of debt, Harlem Co has not paid its shareholders a dividend this year, choosing instead to undertake a bonus issue of its $0.50 equity shares.

You have been asked by the audit manager to complete the preliminary analytical review and she has provided you with the following information:

Financial statement extracts for year ending 30 September

	Forecast 20X5 $000	Actual 20X4 $000
Revenue	23,200	21,900
Cost of sales	18,700	17,300
Gross profit	4,500	4,600
Finance costs	290	250
Profit before tax	450	850
Intangible asset	800	800
Inventory	2,100	1,600
Long and short-term borrowings	13,000	11,000
Total equity	10,000	9,500

The audit assistant has already calculated some key ratios for Harlem Co which you have confirmed as accurate. She has ascertained that the trade receivables collection period has increased from 38 to 51 days.

Required:

(a) Describe the auditor's responsibilities in relation to the prevention and detection of fraud and error. **(4 marks)**

(b) Calculate the FOUR ratios listed in the table below, for BOTH years, to assist you in planning the audit of Harlem Co. **(4 marks)**

Note: Formulas are NOT required to be shown.

Ratio	20X5	20X4
Gross profit margin		
Inventory holding period		
Gearing		
Interest cover		

(c) Using the information provided and the ratios calculated, describe EIGHT audit risks and explain the auditor's response to each risk in planning the audit of Harlem Co. **(16 marks)**

(d)   Describe substantive procedures the auditor should perform to obtain sufficient and appropriate audit evidence in relation to the VALUATION of trade receivables in the current year. (3 marks)

(e)   Describe substantive procedures the auditor should perform to obtain sufficient and appropriate audit evidence in relation to the DISPOSAL of plant and machinery in the current year. (3 marks)

(Total: 30 marks)

202   PEONY *Walk in the footsteps of a top tutor*

This scenario relates to two requirements.

You are an audit supervisor of Daffodil & Co and are planning the audit of Peony Co for the year ending 31 May 20X9. The company is a food retailer with a large network of stores across the country and four warehouses. The company has been a client of your firm for several years and the forecast profit before tax is $28.9m. The audit manager has attended a planning meeting with the finance director and has provided you with the following notes of the meeting.

Planning meeting notes

Peony Co has an internal audit (IA) department which undertakes controls testing across the network of stores. Each store is visited at least once every 18 months. The audit manager has discussed with the finance director that the external audit team may rely on the controls testing which is undertaken by IA.

During the meeting, the finance director provided some forecast financial information. Revenue for the year is expected to increase by 3% as compared to 20X8; the gross margin is expected to increase from 56% to 60%; and the operating margin is predicted to decrease from 21% to 18%.

Peony Co values inventory in line with industry practice, which is to use selling price less average profit margin. The directors consider this to be a close approximation to cost.

The company does not undertake a full year-end inventory count and instead undertakes monthly perpetual inventory counts, each of which covers one-twelfth of all lines in stores and the warehouses. As part of the interim audit which was completed in January, an audit junior attended a perpetual inventory count at one of the warehouses and noted that there were a large number of exceptions where the inventory records showed a higher quantity than the physical inventory which was present in the warehouse. When discussing these exceptions with the financial controller, the audit junior was informed that this had been a recurring issue.

During the year, IA performed a review of the non-current assets physically present in around one-third of the company's stores. A number of assets which had not been fully depreciated were identified as obsolete by this review.

The company launched a significant TV advertising campaign in January 20X9 in order to increase revenue. The directors have indicated that at the year end a current asset of $0.7m will be recognised, as they believe that the advertisements will help to boost future sales in the next 12 months. The last advertisement will be shown on TV in early May 20X9.

Peony Co decided to outsource its payroll function to an external service organisation. This service organisation handles all elements of the payroll cycle and sends monthly reports to Peony Co which detail wages and salaries and statutory obligations.

Peony Co maintained its own payroll records until 31 December 20X8, at which point the records were transferred to the service organisation.

Peony Co is planning to expand the company by opening three new stores during July 20X9 and in order to finance this, in March 20X9 the company obtained a $3m bank loan. This is repayable in arrears over five years in quarterly instalments. In preparation for the expansion, the company is looking to streamline operations in the warehouses and is planning to make approximately 60 employees redundant after the year end. No decision has been made as to when this will be announced, but it is likely to be in May 20X9.

Required:

(a) **Define and explain materiality and performance materiality.**   **(4 marks)**

(b) **Describe EIGHT audit risks and explain the auditor's response to each risk in planning the audit of Peony Co.**

Note: Prepare your answer using two columns headed Audit risk and Auditor's response respectively.   **(16 marks)**

(Total: 20 marks)

203 DARJEELING *Walk in the footsteps of a top tutor*

This scenario relates to five requirements.

You are an audit supervisor of Earl & Co and are planning the audit of Darjeeling Co for the year ending 30 September 20X8. The company develops and manufactures specialist paint products and has been a client of your firm for several years. The audit manager has attended a planning meeting with the finance director and has provided you with the following notes of the meeting and financial statement extracts. You have been asked by the audit manager to undertake preliminary analytical procedures using the financial statement extracts.

Planning meeting notes

During the year Darjeeling Co has spent $0.9m, which is included within intangible assets, on the development of new product lines, some of which are in the early stages of their development cycle. Additionally, as the company is looking to expand production, during the year it purchased and installed a new manufacturing line. All costs, incurred in the purchase and installation of that asset, have been included within property, plant and equipment. These capitalised costs include the purchase price of $2.2m, installation costs of $0.4m and a five-year servicing and maintenance plan costing $0.5m. In order to finance the development projects and the new manufacturing line, the company borrowed $4m from the bank which is to be repaid in instalments over eight years and has an interest rate of 5%. Developing new products and expanding production is important as the company intends to undertake a stock exchange listing in the next 12 months.

The company started a number of initiatives during the year in order to boost revenue. It offered extended credit terms to its customers on the condition that their sales order quantities were increased.

In addition, Darjeeling Co made an announcement in October 20X7 of its 'price promise': that it would match the prices of any competitor for similar products purchased. Customers who are able to prove that they could purchase the products cheaper elsewhere are asked to claim the difference from Darjeeling Co, within one month of the date of purchase of goods, via its website. The company intends to include a refund liability of $0.25m, which is based on the monthly level of claims to date, in the draft financial statements.

The finance director informed the audit manager that a problem arose in June 20X8 in relation to the mixing of materials within the production process for one particular product line. A number of these faulty paint products had already been sold and the issue was identified following a number of complaints from customers about the paint consistency being incorrect. As a precaution, further sales have been stopped and a product recall has been initiated for any of these specific paint products sold since June.

Management is investigating whether the paint consistency of the faulty products can be rectified and subsequently sold.

Financial statement extracts for year ending 30 September

	Forecast 20X8 $000	Actual 20X7 $000
Revenue	19,850	16,990
Cost of sales	(12,440)	(10,800)
Gross profit	7,410	6,190
Inventory	1,850	1,330
Trade receivables	2,750	1,780
Bank	(810)	560
Trade payables	1,970	1,190

Required:

(a) Explain why analytical procedures are used during THREE stages of an audit.

(3 marks)

(b) Calculate THREE ratios, for BOTH years, which would assist you in planning the audit of Darjeeling Co. (3 marks)

(c) Using the information provided and the ratios calculated, describe EIGHT audit risks and explain the auditor's response to each risk in planning the audit of Darjeeling Co.

Note: Prepare your answer using two columns headed Audit risk and Auditor's response respectively. (16 marks)

(d) Describe substantive procedures the auditor should perform in relation to the faulty paint products held in inventory at the year end. (3 marks)

(e) Describe substantive procedures the auditor should perform to obtain sufficient and appropriate evidence in relation to Darjeeling Co's revenue. (5 marks)

(Total: 30 marks)

204 BLACKBERRY *Walk in the footsteps of a top tutor*

This scenario relates to two requirements.

You are an audit senior of Loganberry & Co and are planning the audit of Blackberry Co for the year ending 31 March 20X8. The company is a manufacturer of portable music players and your audit manager has already had a planning meeting with the finance director. Forecast revenue is $68.6m and profit before tax is $4.2m.

She has provided you with the following notes of the meeting:

Planning meeting notes

Inventory is valued at the lower of cost and net realisable value. Cost is made up of the purchase price of raw materials and costs of conversion, including labour, production and general overheads. Inventory is held in three warehouses across the country.

The company plans to conduct full inventory counts at the warehouses on 2, 3 and 4 April, and any necessary adjustments will be made to reflect post year-end movements of inventory. The internal audit team will attend the counts.

During the year, Blackberry Co paid $1.1m to purchase a patent which allows the company the exclusive right for three years to customise their portable music players to gain a competitive advantage in their industry. The $1.1m has been expensed in the current year statement of profit or loss. In order to finance this purchase, Blackberry Co raised $1.2m through issuing shares at a premium.

In November 20X7, it was discovered that a significant teeming and lading fraud had been carried out by four members of the receivables ledger department who had colluded. They had stolen funds from wholesale customer receipts and then to cover this, they allocated later customer receipts against the older receivables. These employees were all reported to the police and subsequently dismissed. As a result of the vacancies in the receivables ledger department, Blackberry Co decided to outsource its receivables ledger processing to an external service organisation. This service organisation handles all elements of the receivables ledger cycle, including sales invoicing and chasing of receivables balances and sends monthly reports to Blackberry Co detailing the sales and receivable amounts. Blackberry Co ran its own receivables ledger until 31 January 20X8, at which point the records were transferred to the service organisation.

In December 20X7, the financial accountant of Blackberry Co was dismissed. He had been employed by the company for nine years, and he has threatened to sue the company for unfair dismissal. As a result of this dismissal, and until his replacement commences work in April, the financial accountant's responsibilities have been adequately allocated to other members of the finance department. However, for this period no supplier statement reconciliations or payables ledger control account reconciliations have been performed.

In January 20X7, a receivable balance of $0.9m was written off by Blackberry Co as it was deemed irrecoverable as the customer had declared itself bankrupt. In February 20X8, the liquidators handling the bankruptcy of the company publicly announced that it was likely that most of its creditors would receive a pay-out of 40% of the balance owed. As a result, Blackberry Co has included a current asset of $360,000 within the statement of financial position and other income in the statement of profit or loss.

Required:

(a) Describe Loganberry & Co's responsibilities in relation to the prevention and detection of fraud and error. **(4 marks)**

(b) Describe EIGHT audit risks and explain the auditor's response to each risk in planning the audit of Blackberry Co.

Note: Prepare your answer using two columns headed Audit risk and Auditor's response respectively. **(16 marks)**

(Total: 20 marks)

205 PRANCER CONSTRUCTION *Walk in the footsteps of a top tutor*

This scenario relates to three requirements.

You are an audit supervisor of Cupid & Co, planning the final audit of a new client, Prancer Construction Co, for the year ending 30 September 20X7. The company specialises in property construction and providing ongoing annual maintenance services for properties previously constructed. Forecast profit before tax is $13.8m and total assets are expected to be $22.3m, both of which are higher than for the year ended 30 September 20X6.

You are required to produce the audit strategy document. The audit manager has met with Prancer Construction Co's finance director and has provided you with the following notes, a copy of the August management accounts and the prior year financial statements.

Meeting notes

The prior year financial statements recognise work in progress of $1.8m, which comprised property construction in progress as well as ongoing maintenance services for finished properties. The August 20X7 management accounts recognise $2.1m inventory of completed properties compared to a balance of $1.4m in September 20X6. A full year-end inventory count will be undertaken on 30 September at all of the 11 building sites where construction is in progress. There is not sufficient audit team resource to attend all inventory counts.

In line with industry practice, Prancer Construction Co offers its customers a five-year building warranty, which covers any construction defects. Customers are not required to pay any additional fees to obtain the warranty. The finance director anticipates this provision will be lower than last year as the company has improved its building practices and therefore the quality of the finished properties.

Customers who wish to purchase a property are required to place an order and pay a 5% non-refundable deposit prior to the completion of the building. When the building is complete, customers pay a further 92.5%, with the final 2.5% due to be paid six months later. The finance director has informed you that although an allowance for receivables has historically been maintained, it is anticipated that this can be significantly reduced.

Information from management accounts

Prancer Construction Co's prior year financial statements and August 20X7 management accounts contain a material overdraft balance. The finance director has confirmed that there are minimum profit and net assets covenants attached to the overdraft.

A review of the management accounts shows the payables period was 56 days for August 20X7, compared to 87 days for September 20X6. The finance director anticipates that the September 20X7 payables days will be even lower than those in August 20X7.

Required:

(a) Describe the process Cupid & Co should have undertaken to assess whether the PRECONDITIONS for an audit were present when accepting the audit of Prancer Construction Co. **(3 marks)**

(b) Identify THREE main areas, other than audit risks, which should be included within the audit strategy document for Prancer Construction Co, and for each area provide an example relevant to the audit. **(3 marks)**

(c) Using all the information provided describe SEVEN audit risks, and explain the auditor's response to each risk, in planning the audit of Prancer Construction Co.

Note: Prepare your answer using two columns headed Audit risk and Auditor's response respectively. **(14 marks)**

(Total: 20 marks)

206 HURLING *Walk in the footsteps of a top tutor*

This scenario relates to three requirements.

You are an audit supervisor of Caving & Co and you are planning the audit of Hurling Co, a listed company, for the year ending 31 March 20X7. The company manufactures computer components and forecast profit before tax is $33.6 million and total assets are $79.3 million.

Hurling Co distributes its products through wholesalers as well as via its own website. The website was upgraded during the year at a cost of $1.1 million. Additionally, the company entered into a transaction in February to purchase a new warehouse which will cost $3.2 million. Hurling Co's legal advisers are working to ensure that the legal process will be completed by the year end. The company issued $5 million of irredeemable preference shares to finance the warehouse purchase.

During the year the finance director has increased the useful economic lives of fixtures and fittings from three to four years as he felt this was a more appropriate period. The finance director has informed the engagement partner that a revised credit period has been agreed with one of its wholesale customers, as they have been experiencing difficulties with repaying the balance of $1.2 million owing to Hurling Co. In January 20X7, Hurling Co introduced a new bonus based on sales targets for its sales staff. This has resulted in a significant number of new wholesale customer accounts being opened by sales staff. The new customers have been given favourable credit terms as an introductory offer, provided goods are purchased within a two-month period. As a result, revenue has increased by 5% on the prior year.

The company has launched several new products this year and all but one of these new launches have been successful. Feedback on product Luge, launched four months ago, has been mixed, and the company has just received notice from one of their customers, Petanque Co, of intended legal action. They are alleging the product sold to them was faulty, resulting in a significant loss of information and an ongoing detrimental impact on profits. As a precaution, sales of the Luge product have been halted and a product recall has been initiated for any Luge products sold in the last four months.

The finance director is keen to announce the company's financial results to the stock market earlier than last year and in order to facilitate this, he has asked if the audit could be completed in a shorter timescale. In addition, the company is intending to propose a final dividend once the financial statements are finalised.

Hurling Co's finance director has informed the audit engagement partner that one of the company's non-executive directors (NEDs) has just resigned, and he has enquired if the partners at Caving & Co can help Hurling Co in recruiting a new NED.

Specifically he has requested the engagement quality control reviewer, who was until last year the audit engagement partner on Hurling Co, assist the company in this recruitment. Caving & Co also provides taxation services for Hurling Co in the form of tax return preparation along with some tax planning advice. The finance director has recommended to the audit committee of Hurling Co that this year's audit fee should be based on the company's profit before tax. At today's date, 20% of last year's audit fee is still outstanding and was due to be paid three months ago.

Required:

(a)   **Define audit risk and the components of audit risk.**   **(4 marks)**

(b)   **Describe EIGHT audit risks, and explain the auditor's response to each risk, in planning the audit of Hurling Co.**   **(16 marks)**

   Note: Prepare your answer using two columns headed Audit risk and Auditor's response respectively.

(c)   (i)   **Identify and explain FIVE ethical threats which may affect the independence of Caving & Co's audit of Hurling Co, and**

   (ii)   **For each threat, suggest a safeguard to reduce the risk to an acceptable level.**

   Note: The total marks will be split equally between each part. Prepare your answer using two columns headed Ethical threat and Possible Safeguard respectively.

   (10 marks)

   (Total: 30 marks)

207   CENTIPEDE *Walk in the footsteps of a top tutor*

This scenario relates to four requirements.

You are an audit supervisor of Ant & Co and are planning the final audit of Centipede Co, which is a listed company, for the year ended 31 December 20X6. The company purchases consumer packaged goods and sells these through its website and to wholesalers. This is a new client for your firm and your audit manager has already had a planning meeting with the finance director and has provided you with the following notes along with financial statement extracts.

Client background and notes from planning meeting

Rather than undertaking a full year-end inventory count, the company undertakes monthly perpetual inventory counts, covering one-twelfth of all lines monthly. As part of the interim audit which was completed earlier in the year, an audit assistant attended a perpetual inventory count in September and noted that there were a large number of exceptions where the inventory records were consistently higher than the physical inventory in the warehouse. When discussing these exceptions with the finance director, the assistant was informed that this had been a recurring issue all year. In addition, the audit assistant noted that there were some lines of inventory which, according to the records, were at least 90 days old.

Centipede Co has a head office where the audit team will be based to conduct the final audit fieldwork. However, there are four additional sites where some accounting records are maintained and these sites were not visited during the interim audit. The records for these sites are incorporated monthly through an interface to the general ledger. A fifth site was closed down in 20X5, however, the building was only sold in 20X6 at a loss of $825,000.

One of Centipede Co's wholesale customers is alleging that the company has consistently failed to deliver goods in a saleable condition and on time, hence it has commenced legal action against Centipede Co for a loss of profits claim.

The directors have disclosed their remuneration details in the financial statements in line with International Financial Reporting Standards, which does not require a separate list of directors' names and payments. However, in the country in which Centipede Co is based, local legislation requires disclosure of the names of the directors and the amount of remuneration payable to each director.

Financial statement extracts for the year ended 31 December:

	Draft 20X6 $000	Final 20X5 $000
Revenue	25,230	21,180
Cost of sales	(15,840)	(14,015)
Gross profit	9,390	7,165
Operating expenses	(4,903)	(3,245)
Operating profit	4,487	3,920
Inventory	2,360	1,800
Trade receivables	1,590	1,250
Cash	–	480
Trade payables	3,500	2,800
Overdraft	580	–

Required:

(a) Describe the matters which Ant & Co should have considered prior to accepting the audit of Centipede Co. **(5 marks)**

(b) Calculate SIX ratios, for BOTH years, which would assist you in planning the audit of Centipede Co. **(6 marks)**

(c) From a review of the above information and the ratios calculated, describe SEVEN audit risks and explain the auditor's response to each risk in planning the audit of Centipede Co.

Note: Prepare your answer using two columns headed Audit risk and Auditor's response respectively. **(14 marks)**

The finance director of Centipede Co informed Ant & Co that one of the reasons they were appointed as auditors was because of their knowledge of the industry. Ant & Co audits a number of other consumer packaged goods companies, including Centipede Co's main rival. The finance director has enquired how Ant & Co will keep information obtained during the audit confidential.

Required:

(d)   **Explain the safeguards which Ant & Co should implement to ensure that this conflict of interest is properly managed.**   **(5 marks)**

(Total: 30 marks)

208   SITIA SPARKLE *Walk in the footsteps of a top tutor*

This scenario relates to three requirements.

You are an audit supervisor of Chania & Co and are planning the audit of your client, Sitia Sparkle Co which manufactures cleaning products. Its year-end was 31 July 20X6 and the draft profit before tax is $33.6 million.

You are supervising a large audit team for the first time and will have specific responsibility for supervising and reviewing the work of the audit assistants in your team.

Sitia Sparkle Co purchases most of its raw materials from suppliers in Africa and these goods are shipped directly to the company's warehouse and the goods are usually in transit for up to three weeks. The company has incurred $1.3 million of expenditure on developing a new range of cleaning products which are due to be launched into the market place in November 20X6. In September 20X5, Sitia Sparkle Co also invested $0.9 million in a complex piece of plant and machinery as part of the development process. The full amount has been capitalised and this cost includes the purchase price, installation costs and training costs.

This year, the bonus scheme for senior management and directors has been changed so that rather than focusing on profits, it is instead based on the value of year-end total assets. In previous years an allowance for receivables, made up of specific balances, which equalled almost 1% of trade receivables was maintained. However, the finance director feels that this is excessive and unnecessary and has therefore not included it for 20X6 and has credited the opening balance to the profit or loss account.

A new general ledger system was introduced in May 20X6; the finance director has stated that the data was transferred and the old and new systems were run in parallel until the end of August 20X6. As a result of the additional workload on the finance team, a number of control account reconciliations were not completed as at 31 July 20X6, including the bank reconciliation. The finance director is comfortable with this as these reconciliations were completed successfully for both June and August 20X6. In addition, the year-end close down of the payables ledger was undertaken on 8 August 20X6.

Required:

(a)   **Explain the benefits of audit planning.**   **(4 marks)**

(b)   **Describe SIX audit risks, and explain the auditor's response to each risk, in planning the audit of Sitia Sparkle Co.**

      Note: Prepare your answer using two columns headed Audit risk and Auditor's response respectively.   **(12 marks)**

(c)   In line with ISA 220 *Quality Control for an Audit of Financial Statements*, **describe the audit supervisor's responsibilities in relation to supervising and reviewing the audit assistants' work during the audit of Sitia Sparkle Co.**   (4 marks)

(Total: 20 marks)

209   AQUAMARINE *Walk in the footsteps of a top tutor*

This scenario relates to three requirements.

You are an audit supervisor of Amethyst & Co and are currently planning the audit of your client, Aquamarine Co (Aquamarine) which manufactures elevators. Its year-end is 31 July 20X6 and the forecast profit before tax is $15.2 million.

The company undertakes continuous production in its factory, therefore at the year-end it is anticipated that work in progress will be approximately $950,000. In order to improve the manufacturing process, Aquamarine placed an order in April for $720,000 of new plant and machinery; one third of this order was received in May with the remainder expected to be delivered by the supplier in late July or early August.

At the beginning of the year, Aquamarine purchased a patent for $1.3 million which gives them the exclusive right to manufacture specialised elevator equipment for five years. In order to finance this purchase, Aquamarine borrowed $1.2 million from the bank which is repayable over five years.

In January 20X6 Aquamarine outsourced its payroll processing to an external service organisation, Coral Payrolls Co (Coral). Coral handles all elements of the payroll cycle and sends monthly reports to Aquamarine detailing the payroll costs. Aquamarine ran its own payroll until 31 December 20X5, at which point the records were transferred over to Coral.

The company has a policy of revaluing land and buildings and the finance director has announced that all land and buildings will be revalued at the year-end. During a review of the management accounts for the month of May 20X6, you have noticed that receivables have increased significantly on the previous year-end and against May 20X5.

The finance director has informed you that the company is planning to make approximately 65 employees redundant after the year-end. No decision has been made as to when this will be announced, but it is likely to be prior to the year-end.

Required:

(a)   **Define audit risk and the components of audit risk.**   (5 marks)

(b)   **Describe SIX audit risks, and explain the auditor's response to each risk, in planning the audit of Aquamarine Co.**   (12 marks)

Note: Prepare your answer using two columns headed Audit risk and Auditor's response respectively.

(c)   **Explain the additional factors Amethyst & Co should consider during the audit in relation to Aquamarine Co's use of the payroll service organisation.**   (3 marks)

(Total: 20 marks)

210 VENUS *Walk in the footsteps of a top tutor*

This scenario relates to four requirements.

ISA 210 *Agreeing the Terms of Audit Engagements* requires auditors to agree the terms of an engagement with those charged with governance and formalise these in an engagement letter.

Required:

(a) **Identify and explain TWO factors which would indicate that an engagement letter for an existing audit client should be revised.** **(2 marks)**

(b) **List SIX matters which should be included within an audit engagement letter.**

  (3 marks)

You have been asked by the audit engagement partner to gain an understanding about the new client as part of the planning process.

Required:

(c) **Identify FIVE sources of information relevant to gaining an understanding and describe how this information will be used by the auditor.** **(5 marks)**

You are an audit supervisor of Pluto & Co and are currently planning the audit of your client, Venus Magnets Co (Venus) which manufactures decorative magnets. Its year-end is 31 December 20X5 and the forecast profit before tax is $9.6 million.

During the year, the directors reviewed the useful lives and depreciation rates of all classes of plant and machinery. This resulted in an overall increase in the asset lives and a reduction in the depreciation charge for the year.

Inventory is held in five warehouses and on 28 and 29 December a full inventory count will be held with adjustments for movements to the year-end. This is due to a lack of available staff on 31 December. In October, there was a fire in one of the warehouses; inventory of $0.9 million was damaged and this has been written down to its scrap value of $0.2 million. An insurance claim has been submitted for the difference of $0.7 million. Venus is still waiting to hear from the insurance company with regards to this claim, but has included the insurance proceeds within the statement of profit or loss and the statement of financial position.

The finance director has informed the audit manager that the October and November bank reconciliations each contained unreconciled differences; however, he considers the overall differences involved to be immaterial.

A directors' bonus scheme was introduced during the year which is based on achieving a target profit before tax. In order to finalise the bonus figures, the finance director of Venus would like the audit to commence earlier so that the final results are available earlier this year.

Required:

(d) **Describe FIVE audit risks, and explain the auditor's response to each risk, in planning the audit of Venus Magnets Co.** **(10 marks)**

Note: Prepare your answer using two columns headed Audit risk and Auditor's response respectively.

  (Total: 20 marks)

211 SYCAMORE *Walk in the footsteps of a top tutor*

 Question debrief

This scenario relates to four requirements.

You are the audit supervisor of Maple & Co and are currently planning the audit of an existing client, Sycamore Science Co (Sycamore), whose year-end was 30 April 20X5. Sycamore is a pharmaceutical company, which manufactures and supplies a wide range of medical supplies. The draft financial statements show revenue of $35.6 million and profit before tax of $5.9 million.

Sycamore's previous finance director left the company in December 20X4 after it was discovered that he had been claiming fraudulent expenses from the company for a significant period of time. A new finance director was appointed in January 20X5 who was previously a financial controller of a bank, and she has expressed surprise that Maple & Co had not uncovered the fraud during last year's audit.

During the year Sycamore has spent $1.8 million on developing several new products. These projects are at different stages of development and the draft financial statements show the full amount of $1.8 million within intangible assets. In order to fund this development, $2.0 million was borrowed from the bank and is due for repayment over a ten-year period. The bank has attached minimum profit targets as part of the loan covenants.

The new finance director has informed the audit partner that since the year-end there has been an increased number of sales returns and that in the month of May over $0.5 million of goods sold in April were returned.

Maple & Co attended the year-end inventory count at Sycamore's warehouse. The auditor present raised concerns that during the count there were movements of goods in and out the warehouse and this process did not seem well controlled.

During the year, a review of plant and equipment in the factory was undertaken and surplus plant was sold, resulting in a profit on disposal of $210,000.

Required:

(a)   State Maples & Co's responsibilities in relation to the prevention and detection of fraud and error. **(5 marks)**

(b)   Describe EIGHT audit risks, and explain the auditor's response to each risk, in planning the audit of Sycamore Science Co. **(16 marks)**

Note: Prepare your answer using two columns headed Audit risk and Auditor's response respectively.

(c)   Explain the quality control procedures that Maple & Co should have in place during the engagement performance. **(5 marks)**

(d)   Sycamore's new finance director has read about review engagements and is interested in the possibility of Maple & Co undertaking these in the future. However, she is unsure how these engagements differ from an external audit and how much assurance would be gained from this type of engagement.

Required:

(i)   Explain the purpose of review engagements and how these differ from external audits; and   **(2 marks)**

(ii)   Describe the level of assurance provided by external audits and review engagements.   **(2 marks)**

(Total: 30 marks)

 Calculate your allowed time, allocate the time to the separate parts...............

212   RECORDER COMMUNICATIONS *Walk in the footsteps of a top tutor*

This scenario relates to five requirements.

(a)   ISA 300 *Planning an Audit of Financial Statements* provides guidance to auditors. Planning an audit involves establishing the overall audit strategy for the engagement and developing an audit plan. Adequate planning benefits the audit of financial statements in several ways.

Required:

Explain the importance of audit planning.   **(5 marks)**

Recorder Communications Co (Recorder) is a large mobile phone company which operates a network of stores in countries across Europe. The company's year-end is 30 June. You are the audit senior of Piano & Co. Recorder is a new client and you are currently planning the audit with the audit manager. You have been provided with the following planning notes from the audit partner following his meeting with the finance director.

Recorder purchases goods from a supplier in South Asia and these goods are shipped to the company's central warehouse. The goods are usually in transit for two weeks and the company correctly records the goods when received. Recorder does not undertake a year-end inventory count, but carries out monthly continuous (perpetual) inventory counts and any errors identified are adjusted in the inventory system for that month. Manufacturers regularly bring out new models of mobile phones. When this happens, the old models have to be sold at a significant discount as customers usually want the latest model. Recorder has a number of older models in inventory.

During the year the company introduced a bonus based on sales for its sales persons. The bonus target was based on increasing the number of customers signing up for 24-month phone line contracts. This has been successful and revenue has increased by 15%, especially in the last few months of the year. The level of receivables is considerably higher than last year and there are concerns about the creditworthiness of some customers.

Recorder has a policy of revaluing its land and buildings and this year has updated the valuations of all land and buildings.

During the year the directors have each been paid a significant bonus, and they have included this within wages and salaries. Separate disclosure of the bonus is required by local legislation.

Required:

(b)   Describe SEVEN audit risks, and explain the auditor's response to each risk, in planning the audit of Recorder Communications Co.   **(14 marks)**

Note: Prepare your answer using two columns headed Audit risk and Auditor's response respectively.

(c)   Explain the audit procedures you should perform in order to place reliance on the continuous (perpetual) counts for year-end inventory.   **(3 marks)**

(d)   Describe substantive procedures you should perform to confirm the directors' bonus payments included in the financial statements.   **(4 marks)**

The audit of Recorder is nearly complete and the auditor's report is due to be signed next week. The directors are refusing to adjust the valuation of inventory to the lower of cost and net realisable value. The difference is considered to have a material effect on the financial statements.

(e)   Describe the impact on the auditor's report if the issue remains unresolved.

(4 marks)

(Total: 30 marks)

213   KANGAROO CONSTRUCTION *Walk in the footsteps of a top tutor*

This scenario relates to four requirements.

You are the audit senior of Rhino & Co and you are planning the audit of Kangaroo Construction Co (Kangaroo) for the year ended 31 March 20X3. Kangaroo specialises in building houses and provides a five-year building warranty to its customers. Your audit manager has held a planning meeting with the finance director. He has provided you with the following notes of his meeting and financial statement extracts:

Kangaroo has had a difficult year; house prices have fallen and, as a result, revenue has dropped. In order to address this, management has offered significantly extended credit terms to their customers. However, demand has fallen such that there are still some completed houses in inventory where the selling price may be below cost. Cash flow issues have been alleviated partly due to the requirement for customers to pay a deposit of $5,000 to secure the house they wish to buy. The deposit is refundable until the house is 75% complete. At this stage the house is deemed to be built to the customer's specification and the deposit becomes non-refundable.

During the year, whilst calculating depreciation, the directors extended the useful lives of plant and machinery from three years to five years. This reduced the annual depreciation charge.

The directors need to meet a target profit before interest and taxation of $0.5 million in order to be paid their annual bonus. In addition, to try and improve profits, Kangaroo changed their main material supplier to a cheaper alternative. This has resulted in some customers claiming on their building warranties for extensive repairs. To help with operating cash flow, the directors borrowed $1 million from the bank during the year. This is due for repayment at the end of 20X3.

Financial statement extracts for year ended 31 March

	DRAFT 20X3 $m	ACTUAL 20X2 $m
Revenue	12.5	15.0
Cost of sales	(7.0)	(8.0)
Gross profit	5.5	7.0
Operating expenses	(5.0)	(5.1)
Profit before interest and taxation	0.5	1.9
Inventory	1.9	1.4
Receivables	3.1	2.0
Cash	0.8	1.9
Trade payables	1.6	1.2
Loan	1.0	–

Required:

(a)   Explain the concepts of materiality and performance materiality in accordance with ISA 320 *Materiality in Planning and Performing an Audit*.   **(5 marks)**

(b)   Calculate SIX ratios, for BOTH years, which would assist the audit senior in planning the audit of Kangaroo Construction Co.   **(6 marks)**

(c)   Using the information provided and the ratios calculated, identify and describe SEVEN audit risks and explain the auditor's response to each risk in planning the audit of Kangaroo Construction Co.   **(14 marks)**

Note: Prepare your answer using two columns headed Audit risk and Auditor's response respectively.

The audit of Kangaroo Construction is nearly complete and the auditor's report is due to be signed next week. Your audit work discovered that the warranty provision of $0.6m should be increased to $0.9m as a result of the increase in claims. The directors are refusing to make this adjustment.

Required:

(d)   Discuss the issue and describe the impact on the auditor's report if the issue remains unresolved.   **(5 marks)**

(Total: 30 marks)

214 REDSMITH *Walk in the footsteps of a top tutor*

This scenario relates to four requirements.

(a) In agreeing the terms of an audit engagement, the auditor is required to agree the basis on which the audit is to be carried out. This involves establishing whether the preconditions for an audit are present and confirming that there is a common understanding between the auditor and management of the terms of the engagement.

Required:

Describe the process the auditor should undertake to assess whether the PRECONDITIONS for an audit are present. **(3 marks)**

(b) **List FOUR examples of matters the auditor may consider when obtaining an understanding of the entity.** **(2 marks)**

You are the audit senior of White & Co and are planning the audit of Redsmith Co for the year ended 30 September 20X5. The company produces printers and has been a client of your firm for two years. Your audit manager has already had a planning meeting with the finance director. He has provided you with the following notes of his meeting and financial statement extracts.

Redsmith's management were disappointed with the 20X4 results and so in 20X5 undertook a number of strategies to improve the trading results. This included the introduction of a generous sales-related bonus scheme for their salesmen and a high profile advertising campaign. In addition, as market conditions are difficult for their customers, they have extended the credit period given to them.

The finance director of Redsmith has reviewed the inventory valuation policy and has included additional overheads incurred this year as he considers them to be production related. He is happy with the 20X5 results and feels that they are a good reflection of the improved trading levels.

Financial statement extracts for year ended 30 September

	DRAFT 20X5 $m	ACTUAL 20X4 $m
Revenue	23.0	18.0
Cost of Sales	(11.0)	(10.0)
Gross profit	12.0	8.0
Operating expenses	(7.5)	(4.0)
Profit before interest and taxation	4.5	4.0
Inventory	2.1	1.6
Receivables	4.5	3.0
Cash	–	2.3
Trade payables	1.6	1.2
Overdraft	0.9	–

Required:

(c)   Calculate FIVE ratios, for BOTH years, which would assist the audit senior in planning the audit of Redsmith Co.   **(5 marks)**

(d)   Using the information provided and the ratios calculated, describe FIVE audit risks and explain the auditor's response to each risk in planning the audit of Redsmith Co.   **(10 marks)**

Note: Prepare your answer using two columns headed Audit risk and Auditor's response respectively.

(Total: 20 marks)

INTERNAL CONTROLS

215   AMBERJACK *Walk in the footsteps of a top tutor*

This scenario relates to two requirements.

Amberjack Co manufactures and distributes car tyres to a wide customer base both in its country and across the rest of the continent. Its year end was 30 April 20X5. It is 1 July 20X5. You are an audit manager of Pinfish & Co and you are reviewing extracts of the documentation describing Amberjack Co's sales and dispatch system following completion of the interim audit.

Amberjack Co has grown in size over the previous 18 months. All new customers undergo credit checks prior to being accepted and credit limits are subsequently set by the receivables ledger clerks who record the new customer details, assign a unique customer number and set credit limits in the master data file. The company's credit controller is currently on secondment to the internal audit department for six months and no replacement has been appointed.

Customers wishing to order goods, telephone the company's sales order department and provide their unique account details. Sequentially numbered four-part sales orders are generated for all orders, after checking available inventory levels. One copy is retained by the sales ordering team to enable them to monitor progress of the sales orders, one copy is sent to the customer, one copy is sent to one of the company's warehouses for dispatch and the final copy is sent to the finance department. Upon dispatch, a three-part goods dispatch note (GDN) is completed which is assigned the same sequential number as the order number; one copy is sent with the goods, one remains with the warehouse and one is sent to the finance department.

Due to the recent growth of the company, and as there are a large number of sales invoices, additional temporary staff members have been appointed to help the sales clerks to produce the sales invoices. The sales invoices are prepared using quantities from the GDNs and prices from the authorised sales prices list, which is updated every six months. This year, in line with its main competitors, the company offered a 10% discount on all orders placed during one weekend in late November. Where a discount has been given, this has to be manually entered by the sales clerks onto the sequentially numbered invoice.

Customer statements are no longer being generated and sent out. The company only reconciles the receivables ledger control account at the end of April in order to verify the year-end balance.

Required:

(a)   List FOUR control objectives of Amberjack Co's sales and dispatch system. **(4 marks)**

(b)   As the external auditor of Amberjack Co, write a report to management in respect of the sales and dispatch system described which:

(i)   Identifies and explains SEVEN deficiencies in the sales and dispatch system and recommends a control to address each of these deficiencies; and

(ii)   Includes a covering letter

Note: Prepare your answer using two columns headed Control deficiency and Control recommendation respectively. The total marks will be split equally between each part.

Two marks will be awarded within this requirement for the covering letter.

(16 marks)

(Total: 20 marks)

216   FREESIA *Walk in the footsteps of a top tutor*

This scenario relates to four requirements.

(a)   Auditors are required to document a company's accounting and internal control systems as part of their audit process. Two methods available for documenting internal control systems are narrative notes and questionnaires.

Required:

For each of the two methods, NARRATIVE NOTES and QUESTIONNAIRES:

(i)   Describe the method for documenting internal control systems; and

(ii)   Explain an ADVANTAGE of using this method.

Note: The total marks will be split equally between each part.   **(4 marks)**

Freesia Co is a company listed on a stock exchange. It manufactures furniture which it supplies to a wide range of retailers across the region. The company has an internal audit (IA) department and the company's year end is 30 June 20X9. You are an audit supervisor with Zinnia & Co, preparing the draft audit programmes and reviewing extracts from the internal controls documentation in preparation for the interim audit.

Sales

Freesia Co generates revenue through visits by its sales staff to customers' premises. Sales ledger clerks, who work at head office, carry out credit checks on new customers prior to being accepted and then set their credit limits. Sales staff visit retail customers' sites personally and orders are completed using a four-part pre-printed order form. One copy is left with the customer, a second copy is returned to the sales ordering department, the third is sent to the warehouse and the fourth to the finance department at head office. Each sales order number is based on the sales person's own identification number in order to facilitate monitoring of sales staff performance.

Retail customers are given payment terms of 30 days and most customers choose to pay their invoices by bank transfer. Each day Lily Shah, a finance clerk, posts the bank transfer receipts from the bank statements to the cash book and updates the sales ledger. On a monthly basis, she performs the bank reconciliation.

Purchases and inventory

Receipts of raw materials and goods from suppliers are processed by the warehouse team at head office, who agree the delivery to the purchase order, check the quantity and quality of goods and complete a sequentially numbered goods received note (GRN). The GRNs are sent to the finance department daily. On receipt of the purchase invoice from the supplier, Camilla Brown, the purchase ledger clerk, matches it to the GRN and order and the three documents are sent for authorisation by the appropriate individual. Once authorised, the purchase invoices are logged into the purchase ledger by Camilla, who utilises document count controls to ensure the correct number of invoices has been input.

The company values its inventory using standard costs, both for internal management reporting and for inclusion in the year-end financial statements. The basis of the standard costs was reviewed approximately 18 months ago.

Payroll

Freesia Co employs a mixture of factory staff, who work a standard shift of eight hours a day, and administration and sales staff who are salaried. All staff are paid monthly by bank transfer. Occasionally, overtime is required of factory staff. Where this occurs, details of overtime worked per employee is collated and submitted to the payroll department by a production clerk. The payroll department pays this overtime in the month it occurs. At the end of each quarter, the company's payroll department sends overtime reports which detail the amount of overtime worked to the production director for their review.

Freesia Co's payroll package produces a list of payments per employee which links into the bank system to produce a list of automatic bank transfer payments. The finance director reviews the total to be paid on the list of automatic payments and compares this to the total payroll amount to be paid for the month per the payroll records. If any issues arise, then the automatic bank transfer can be manually changed by the finance director.

Required:

(b)   In respect of the internal controls of Freesia Co:

  (i)   Identify and explain SIX deficiencies

  (ii)   Recommend a control to address each of these deficiencies, and

  (iii)   Describe a TEST OF CONTROL the external auditors should perform to assess if each of these controls, if implemented, is operating effectively to reduce the identified deficiency.

  Note: Prepare your answer using three columns headed Control deficiency, Control recommendation and Test of control respectively. The total marks will be split equally between each part.   **(18 marks)**

Freesia Co deducts employment taxes from its employees' wages and salaries on a monthly basis and pays these to the local taxation authorities in the following month. At the year end, the financial statements will contain an accrual for employment tax payable.

Required:

(c)   **Describe the substantive procedures the auditor should perform to obtain sufficient and appropriate audit evidence in respect of Freesia Co's year-end accrual for employment tax payable.**   **(4 marks)**

The listing rules of the stock exchange require compliance with corporate governance principles and the directors of Freesia Co are confident that they are following best practice in relation to this. However, the chair recently received correspondence from a shareholder, who is concerned that the company is not fully compliant. The company's finance director has therefore requested a review of the company's compliance with corporate governance principles.

Freesia Co has been listed for over eight years and its board comprises four executive and four independent non-executive directors (NEDs), excluding the chair. An audit committee comprised of the NEDs and the finance director meets each quarter to review the company's internal controls.

The directors' remuneration is set by the finance director. NEDs are paid a fixed fee for their services and executive directors are paid an annual salary as well as a significant annual bonus based on Freesia Co's profits. The company's chair does not have an executive role and so she has sole responsibility for liaising with the shareholders and answering any of their questions.

Required:

(d)   **Describe TWO corporate governance weaknesses faced by Freesia Co and provide a recommendation to address each weakness to ensure compliance with corporate governance principles.**

Note: Prepare your answer using two columns headed Weakness and Recommendation respectively.   **(4 marks)**

(Total: 30 marks)

217   CAMOMILE *Walk in the footsteps of a top tutor*

This scenario relates to two requirements.

(a)   ISA 260 *Communication with Those Charged with Governance* provides guidance to auditors in relation to communicating with those charged with governance on matters arising from the audit of an entity's financial statements.

        Required:

        (i)   **Explain why it is important for auditors to communicate throughout the audit with those charged with governance; and**

        (ii)   **Identify TWO examples of matters which the auditor may communicate to those charged with governance.**

        Note: The total marks will be split equally between each part.   **(4 marks)**

(b) Camomile Co operates six restaurant and bar venues which are open seven days a week. The company's year end is 31 December 20X8. You are the audit supervisor reviewing the internal controls documentation in relation to the cash receipts and payments system in preparation for the interim audit, which will involve visiting a number of the venues as well as the head office. The company has a small internal audit (IA) department based at head office.

The purchasing department based at the company's head office is responsible for ordering food and beverages for all six venues. In addition, each venue has a petty cash float of $400, held in the safe, which is used for the purchase of sundry items. When making purchases of sundries, employees are required to obtain the funds from the restaurant manager, purchase the sundries and return any excess money and the receipt to the manager. At any time the petty cash sum held and receipts should equal the float of $400 but it has been noted by the company's IA department that on some occasions this has not been the case.

Each venue has five cash tills (cash registers) to take payments from customers. Three are located in the bar area and two in the restaurant area. Customers can pay using either cash or a credit card and for any transaction either the credit card vouchers or cash are placed in the till by the employee operating the till. To speed up the payment process, each venue has a specific log on code which can be used to access all five tills and is changed every two weeks.

At each venue at the end of the day, the tills are closed down by the restaurant manager who counts the total cash in all five tills and the sum of the credit card vouchers and these totals are reconciled with the aggregated daily readings of sales taken from each till. Any discrepancies are noted on the daily sales sheet. The daily sales sheet records the sales per the tills, the cash counted and the total credit card vouchers as well as any discrepancies. These sheets are scanned and emailed to the cashier at head office at the end of each week.

Approximately 30% of Camomile Co's customers pay in cash for their restaurant or bar bills. Cash is stored in the safe at each venue on a daily basis after the sales reconciliation has been undertaken. Each safe is accessed via a key which the restaurant manager has responsibility for. Each key is stored in a drawer of the manager's desk when not being used. Cash is transferred to the bank via daily collection by a security company.

The security company provides a receipt for the sums collected, and these receipts are immediately forwarded to head office. The credit card company remits the amounts due directly into Camomile Co's bank account within two days of the transaction.

At head office, on receipt of the daily sales sheets and security company receipts, the cashier agrees the cash transferred by the security company has been banked for all venues. She agrees the cash per the daily sales sheets to bank deposit slips and to the bank statements. The cashier updates the cash book with the cash banked and details of the credit card vouchers from the daily sales sheets. On a monthly basis, the credit card company sends a statement of all credit card receipts from the six venues which is filed by the cashier.

Every two months, the cashier reconciles the bank statements to the cash book. The reconciliations are reviewed by the financial controller who evidences her review by signature and these are filed in the accounts department. All purchases of food and beverages for the venues are paid by bank transfer. At the relevant payment dates, the finance director is given the total amount of the payments list which he authorises.

Required:

Identify and explain EIGHT DEFICIENCIES in Camomile Co's cash receipts and payments system and provide a recommendation to address each of these deficiencies.

Note: Prepare your answer using two columns headed Control deficiencies and Control recommendation respectively.

(16 marks)

(Total: 20 marks)

218 RASPBERRY *Walk in the footsteps of a top tutor*

This scenario relates to four requirements.

Raspberry Co operates an electric power station, which produces electricity 24 hours a day, seven days a week. The company's year end is 30 June 20X8. You are an audit manager of Grapefruit & Co, the auditor of Raspberry Co. The interim audit has been completed and you are reviewing the documentation describing Raspberry Co's payroll system.

Systems notes – payroll

Raspberry Co employs over 250 people and approximately 70% of the employees work in production at the power station. There are three shifts every day with employees working eight hours each. The production employees are paid weekly in cash. The remaining 30% of employees work at the head office in non-production roles and are paid monthly by bank transfer.

The company has a human resources (HR) department, responsible for setting up all new joiners. Pre-printed forms are completed by HR for all new employees and, once verified, a copy is sent to the payroll department for the employee to be set up for payment. This form includes the staff member's employee number and payroll cannot set up new joiners without this information.

To encourage staff to attend work on time for all shifts, Raspberry Co introduced a discretionary bonus, paid every three months, for production staff. The production supervisors determine the amounts to be paid and notify the payroll department. This quarterly bonus is entered into the system by a clerk and each entry is checked by a senior clerk for input errors prior to processing. The senior clerk signs the bonus listing as evidence of undertaking this review.

Production employees are issued with clock cards and are required to swipe their cards at the beginning and end of their shift. This process is supervised by security staff 24 hours a day. Each card identifies the employee number and links into the hours worked report produced by the payroll system, which automatically calculates the gross and net pay along with relevant deductions. These calculations are not checked.

In addition to tax deductions from pay, some employees' wages are reduced for such items as repayments of student loans owed to the central government. All employers have a statutory obligation to remit funds on a timely basis and to maintain accounting records which reconcile with annual loan statements sent by the government to employers. At Raspberry Co student loan deduction forms are completed by the relevant employee and payments are made directly to the government until the employee notifies HR that the loan has been repaid in full.

On a quarterly basis, exception reports relating to changes to the payroll standing data are produced and reviewed by the payroll director.

No overtime is worked by employees. Employees are entitled to take 28 holiday days annually. Holiday request forms are required to be completed and authorised by relevant line managers, however, this does not always occur.

On a monthly basis, for employees paid by bank transfer, the senior payroll manager reviews the list of bank payments and agrees this to the payroll records prior to authorising the payment. If any errors are noted, the payroll senior manager amends the records.

For production employees paid in cash, the necessary amount of cash is delivered weekly from the bank by a security company. Two members of the payroll department produce the pay packets, one is responsible for preparing them and the other checks the finished pay packets. Both members of staff are required to sign the weekly payroll listing on completion of this task. The pay packets are then delivered to the production supervisors, who distribute them to employees at the end of the employees' shift, as they know each member of their production team.

Monthly management accounts are produced which detail variances between budgeted amounts and actual. Revenue and key production costs are detailed, however, as there are no overtime costs, wages and salaries are not analysed.

Required:

(a)   **In respect of the payroll system of Raspberry Co:**

(i)   **Identify and explain FIVE KEY CONTROLS which the auditor may seek to place reliance on; and**

(ii)   **Describe a TEST OF CONTROL the auditor should perform to assess if each of these key controls is operating effectively.**

Note: Prepare your answer using two columns headed Key control and Test of control respectively. The total marks will be split equally between each part.

(10 marks)

(b)   **Identify and explain FIVE DEFICIENCIES in Raspberry Co's payroll system and provide a recommendation to address each of these deficiencies.**

Note: Prepare your answer using two columns headed Control deficiency and Control recommendation respectively.   (10 marks)

The finance director is interested in establishing an internal audit department (IAD). In the company she previously worked for the IAD carried out inventory counts, however, as this is not relevant for Raspberry Co, she has asked for guidance on what other assignments an IAD could be asked to perform.

Required:

(c)   **Describe assignments the internal audit department of Raspberry Co could carry out.**
(5 marks)

Raspberry Co deducts employment taxes from its employees' wages on a weekly/monthly basis and pays these to the local taxation authorities in the following month. At the year end the financial statements will contain an accrual for income tax payable on employment income.

Required:

(d)   **Describe the substantive procedures the auditor should perform to confirm the year-end accrual for tax payable on employment income.**   (5 marks)

(Total: 30 marks)

219 COMET PUBLISHING *Walk in the footsteps of a top tutor*

This scenario relates to four requirements.

You are an audit supervisor of Halley & Co and you are reviewing the documentation describing Comet Publishing Co's purchases and payables system in preparation for the interim and final audit for the year ending 30 September 20X7. The company is a retailer of books and has ten stores and a central warehouse, which holds the majority of the company's inventory.

Your firm has audited Comet Publishing Co for a number of years and as such, audit documentation is available from the previous year's file, including internal control flowcharts and detailed purchases and payables system notes. As far as you are aware, Comet Publishing Co's system of internal control has not changed in the last year. The audit manager is keen for the team to utilise existing systems documentation in order to ensure audit efficiency. An extract from the existing systems notes is provided below.

Extract of purchases and payables system

Store managers are responsible for ordering books for their shop. It is not currently possible for store managers to request books from any of the other nine stores. Customers who wish to order books, which are not in stock at the branch visited, are told to contact the other stores directly or visit the company website. As the inventory levels fall in a store, the store manager raises a purchase requisition form, which is sent to the central warehouse. If there is insufficient inventory held, a supplier requisition form is completed and sent to the purchase order clerk, Oliver Dancer, for processing. He sends any orders above $1,000 for authorisation from the purchasing director.

Receipts of goods from suppliers are processed by the warehouse team, who agree the delivery to the purchase order, checking quantity and quality of goods and complete a sequentially numbered goods received note (GRN). The GRNs are sent to the accounts department every two weeks for processing.

On receipt of the purchase invoice from the supplier, an accounts clerk matches it to the GRN. The invoice is then sent to the purchase ordering clerk, Oliver, who processes it for payment. The finance director is given the total amount of the payments list, which she authorises and then processes the bank payments. Due to staff shortages in the accounts department, supplier statement reconciliations are no longer performed.

Other information – conflict of interest

Halley & Co has recently accepted the audit engagement of a new client, Edmond Co, who is the main competitor of Comet Publishing Co. The finance director of Comet Publishing Co has enquired how Halley & Co will keep information obtained during the audit confidential.

Required:

(a) **Explain the safeguards which Halley & Co should implement to ensure that the identified conflict of interest is properly managed.**   **(5 marks)**

(b) **Explain the steps the auditor should take to confirm the accuracy of the purchases and payables flowcharts and systems notes currently held on file.**   **(5 marks)**

(c)   In respect of the purchases and payables system of Comet Publishing Co:

   (i)   Identify and explain FIVE deficiencies

   (ii)   Recommend a control to address each of these deficiencies, and

   (iii)   Describe a TEST OF CONTROL the auditor should perform to assess if each of these controls, if implemented, is operating effectively to reduce the identified deficiency.

   Note: Prepare your answer using three columns headed Control deficiency, Control recommendation, and Test of control respectively. The total marks will be split equally between each part.   **(15 marks)**

(d)   Describe substantive procedures the auditor should perform to obtain sufficient and appropriate evidence in relation to Comet Publishing Co's purchases and other expenses.   **(5 marks)**

                                                                                          (Total: 30 marks)

220 EQUESTRIAN *Walk in the footsteps of a top tutor*

This scenario relates to three requirements.

(a)   *ISA 315 Identifying and Assessing the Risks of Material Misstatement through Understanding the Entity and Its Environment* requires auditors to obtain an understanding of control activities relevant to the audit.

Control activities are the policies and procedures which help ensure that management directives are carried out.

Required:

Describe FOUR different types of control activities and, for each type, provide an example control a company may implement.   **(4 marks)**

Equestrian Co manufactures smartphones and tablets. Its main customers are retailers who then sell to the general public. The company's manufacturing is spread across five sites and goods are stored in its nine warehouses located across the country.

You are an audit supervisor of Baseball & Co and in preparation for the forthcoming audit for the year ending 30 June 20X7, you are reviewing the following notes your audit manager has provided you with in relation to the company's internal controls.

Equestrian Co has a small internal audit (IA) department. During the year, IA started a programme of physically verifying the company's assets and comparing the results to the non-current assets register, as this type of reconciliation had not occurred for some time. To date only 15% of assets have had their existence confirmed as IA has experienced significant staff shortages.

During the year, Equestrian Co conducted an extensive reorganisation of its manufacturing process to improve efficiency. Due to the significant number of employee changes required, the human resources department (HR) has been very busy and to ease their workload during this period, the payroll department has assisted by setting up any new employees who have joined the company. In January 20X7, the wage rate paid to employees was increased by the HR director and he notified payroll by emailing the payroll supervisor.

A new receivables ledger system was introduced in May 20X6 and will continue to be run in parallel with the old system until IA has completed its checks between the two systems. New customers obtained by the sales team are required to undergo a full credit check. On the basis of this, a credit limit is proposed by sales staff and approved by the sales director and these credit limits remain static in the sales system.

Monthly perpetual inventory counts are undertaken at each of the nine warehouses, as a full year-end inventory count is too disruptive for the company. High value items are stored in a secure area in each warehouse. Access is via a four digit code, which for convenience is the same across all sites. Due to the company's reorganisation programme, some of the monthly inventory counts were not performed.

Bank reconciliations are undertaken monthly by an accounts clerk and details of all reconciling items are included. Where the sum of the reconciling items is significant, the reconciliation is sent to the financial controller for review. In order to maximise cash balances, the finance director approves all purchase invoices for payment 75 days after receipt of the invoice.

Required:

(b) **Identify and explain EIGHT deficiencies in Equestrian Co's internal controls and provide a recommendation to address each of these deficiencies.** **(16 marks)**

Note: Prepare your answer using two columns headed Control deficiency and Control recommendation respectively.

The directors feel that the internal audit team needs to increase in size and specialist skills are required, but they are unsure whether to recruit more internal auditors, or to outsource the whole function to their external auditors, Baseball & Co.

(c) **Explain the advantages and disadvantages for each of Equestrian Co AND Baseball & Co of outsourcing the internal audit department.**

Note: The total marks will be split as follows:

Equestrian Co	**(8 marks)**
Baseball & Co	**(2 marks)**
	(Total: 30 marks)

221 CATERPILLAR *Walk in the footsteps of a top tutor*

This scenario relates to three requirements.

Caterpillar Co is a clothing retailer which operates 45 stores throughout the country. The company's year end is 31 March 20X7. Caterpillar Co has an internal audit department which has undertaken a number of internal control reviews specifically focusing on cash controls at stores during the year. The reviews have taken place in the largest 20 stores as this is where most issues arise. You are an audit supervisor of Woodlouse & Co and are reviewing the internal controls documentation in relation to the cash receipts system in preparation for the interim audit which will involve visiting a number of stores and the head office.

Each of Caterpillar Co's stores has on average three or four cash tills to take customer payments. All employees based at the store are able to use each till and individuals do not have their own log on codes, although employees tend to use the same till each day. Customers can pay using either cash or a credit card and for any transaction either the credit card payment slips or cash are placed in the till by the cashier. Where employees' friends or family members purchase clothes in store, the employee is able to serve them at the till point.

At the end of each day, the tills are closed down with daily readings of sales taken from each till. These are reconciled to the total of the cash in the tills and the credit card payment slips and any discrepancies are noted. To save time, this reconciliation is done by the store's assistant manager in aggregate for all of the store tills together. Once this reconciliation has taken place, the cash is stored in the shop's small safe overnight and in the morning it is transferred to the bank via collection by a security company. If the store is low on change for cash payments, a junior sales clerk is sent by a till operator to the bank with money from the till and asked to change it into smaller denominations.

The daily sales readings from the tills along with the cash data and credit card payment data are transferred daily to head office through an interface with the sales and cash receipts records. A clerk oversees that this transfer has occurred for all stores. On a daily basis, he also agrees the cash transferred by the security company has been banked in full by agreeing the cash deposit slips to the bank statements, and that the credit card receipts have been received from the credit card company. On a monthly basis, the same clerk reconciles the bank statements to the cash book. The reconciliations are reviewed by the financial controller if there are any unreconciled amounts.

Required:

(a)   State TWO control objectives of Caterpillar Co's cash receipts system.   **(2 marks)**

(b)   Identify and explain THREE KEY CONTROLS in Caterpillar Co's cash receipts system which the auditor may seek to place reliance on and describe a TEST OF CONTROL the auditor should perform to assess if each of these controls is operating effectively.

   Note: Prepare your answer using two columns headed Key control and Test of control respectively.   **(6 marks)**

(c)   Identify and explain SIX DEFICIENCIES in Caterpillar Co's cash receipts system and provide a recommendation to address each of these deficiencies.

   Note: Prepare your answer using two columns headed Control deficiency and Control recommendation respectively.   **(12 marks)**

   (Total: 20 marks)

222 HERAKLION *Walk in the footsteps of a top tutor*

 Question debrief

This scenario relates to four requirements.

Heraklion Co is a manufacturer of footballs and is a new audit client for your firm. You are an audit supervisor of Spinalonga & Co and are currently preparing for the forthcoming interim and final audit for the year ending 31 October 20X6.

You are required to document and assess the sales system, recommend control improvements to deal with a specific fraud issue as well as undertake substantive testing of revenue.

Sales ordering, goods despatched and invoicing

Heraklion Co sells footballs to a range of large and small sports equipment retailers in several countries. Sales are made through a network of sales staff employed by Heraklion Co, but new customer leads are generated through a third party company. Sales staff are responsible for assessing new customers' creditworthiness and proposing a credit limit which is then authorised by the sales director. The sales staff have monthly sales targets and are able to use their discretion in granting sales discounts up to a maximum of 10%. They then record any discount granted in the customer master data file.

The sales staff visit customer sites personally and orders are completed using a two-part pre-printed order form. One copy is left with the customer and the other copy is retained by the sales person. The sales order number is based on the sales person's own identification (ID) number.

The company markets itself on being able to despatch all orders within three working days. Once the order is taken, the sales person emails the finance department and warehouse despatch team with the customer ID and the sales order details and from this a pick list is generated. Sequentially numbered goods despatched notes are completed and filed in the warehouse.

Sequentially numbered invoices are generated using the pick lists for quantities and the customer master data file for prices. Standard credit terms for customers are 30 days and on a monthly basis sales invoices which are over 90 days outstanding are notified to the relevant sales person to chase payment directly with the customer.

Payroll fraud

The finance director, Montse Mirabelle, has informed you that a significant fraud took place during the year in the payroll department. A number of fictitious employees were set up on the payroll and wages were paid into one bank account. This bank account belonged to two supervisors, who were married, and were employed by Heraklion Co. One had sole responsibility for setting up new joiners in the payroll system and the other processed and authorised bank transfer requests for wages and supplier payments. These employees no longer work for the company and Montse has asked the audit firm for recommendations on how to improve controls in this area to prevent this type of fraud occurring again. Heraklion Co operates a Human Resources department.

Required:

(a) Describe TWO methods for documenting the sales system, and for each explain ONE advantage and ONE disadvantage of using this method. **(6 marks)**

(b) Identify and explain SEVEN deficiencies in the sales system of Heraklion Co and provide a recommendation to address each of these deficiencies.

   Note: Prepare your answer using two columns headed Control deficiency and Control recommendation respectively. **(14 marks)**

(c) In relation to the payroll fraud, identify and explain THREE controls Heraklion Co should implement to reduce the risk of this type of fraud occurring again and, for each control, describe how it would mitigate the risk. **(6 marks)**

(d) Describe substantive procedures the auditor should perform to obtain sufficient and appropriate audit evidence in relation to Heraklion Co's revenue. **(4 marks)**

(Total: 30 marks)

 Calculate your allowed time, allocate the time to the separate parts...............

223 LEMON QUARTZ *Walk in the footsteps of a top tutor*

This scenario relates to two requirements.

You are an audit senior of Hessonite & Co and are in the process of reviewing the inventory system documentation for your audit client, Lemon Quartz Co (Quartz) which manufactures computer equipment. The company's factory and warehouse are based on one large site, and their year-end is 30 June 20X6. Quartz is planning to undertake a full inventory count at the year-end of its raw materials, work in progress and finished goods and you will be attending this count. In preparation you have been reviewing the inventory count instructions for finished goods provided by Quartz.

The count will be undertaken by 15 teams of two counters from the warehouse department with Quartz's financial controller providing overall supervision. Each team of two is allocated a number of bays within the warehouse to count and they are provided with sequentially numbered inventory sheets which contain product codes and quantities extracted from the inventory records. The counters move through each allocated bay counting the inventory and confirming that it agrees with the inventory sheets. Where a discrepancy is found, they note this on the sheet.

The warehouse is large and approximately 10% of the bays have been rented out to third parties with similar operations; these are scattered throughout the warehouse. For completeness, the counters have been asked to count the inventory for all bays noting the third party inventories on separate blank inventory sheets, and the finance department will make any necessary adjustments.

Some of Quartz's finished goods are high in value and are stored in a locked area of the warehouse and all the counting teams will be given the code to access this area. There will be no despatches of inventory during the count and it is not anticipated that there will be any deliveries from suppliers.

Each area is counted once by the allocated team; the sheets are completed in ink, signed by the team and returned after each bay is counted. As no two teams are allocated the same bays, there will be no need to flag that an area has been counted. On completion of the count, the financial controller will confirm with each team that they have returned their inventory sheets.

Required:

(a) **In respect of the inventory count procedures for Lemon Quartz Co:**

    (i) **Identify and explain FIVE deficiencies**

    (ii) **Recommend a control to address each of these deficiencies, and**

    (iii) **Describe a TEST OF CONTROL the external auditors would perform to assess if each of these controls, if implemented, is operating effectively.**

Note: Prepare your answer using three columns headed Control deficiency, Control recommendation and Test of control respectively. The total marks will be split equally between each part. **(15 marks)**

(b) Quartz's finance director has asked your firm to undertake a non-audit assurance engagement later in the year. The audit junior has not been involved in such an assignment before and has asked you to explain what an assurance engagement involves.

Required:

Explain the five elements of an assurance engagement. **(5 marks)**

(Total: 20 marks)

224 BRONZE *Walk in the footsteps of a top tutor*

This scenario relates to four requirements.

You are an audit senior in Scarlet & Co and you are in the process of reviewing the systems testing completed on the payroll cycle of Bronze Industries Co (Bronze), as well as preparing the audit programmes for the final audit.

Bronze operate several chemical processing factories across the country, it manufactures 24 hours a day, seven days a week and employees work a standard shift of eight hours and are paid for hours worked at an hourly rate. Factory employees are paid weekly, with approximately 80% being paid by bank transfer and 20% in cash; the different payment methods are due to employee preferences and Bronze has no plans to change these methods. The administration and sales teams are paid monthly by bank transfer.

Factory staff are each issued a sequentially numbered clock card which details their employee number and name. Employees swipe their cards at the beginning and end of the eight-hour shift and this process is not supervised. During the shift employees are entitled to a 30-minute paid break and employees do not need to clock out to access the dining area. Clock card data links into the payroll system, which automatically calculates gross and net pay along with any statutory deductions. The payroll supervisor for each payment run checks on a sample basis some of these calculations to ensure the system is operating effectively.

Bronze has a human resources department which is responsible for setting up new permanent employees and leavers. Appointments of temporary staff are made by factory production supervisors. Occasionally overtime is required of factory staff, usually to fill gaps caused by staff holidays. Overtime reports which detail the amount of overtime worked are sent out quarterly by the payroll department to production supervisors for their review.

To encourage staff to attend work on time for all shifts Bronze pays a discretionary bonus every six months to factory staff; the production supervisors determine the amounts to be paid. This is communicated in writing by the production supervisors to the payroll department and the bonus is input by a clerk into the system.

For employees paid by bank transfer, the payroll manager reviews the list of the payments and agrees to the payroll records prior to authorising the bank payment. If any changes are required, the payroll manager amends the records. For employees paid in cash, the pay packets are prepared in the payroll department and a clerk distributes them to employees; as she knows most of these individuals she does not require proof of identity.

Required:

(a)   **Explain examples of matters the auditor should consider in determining whether a deficiency in internal controls is significant.**   **(3 marks)**

(b)   **In respect of the payroll system of Bronze Industries Co:**

   (i)   **Identify and explain FIVE internal control deficiencies**

   (ii)   **Recommend a control to address each of these deficiencies, and**

   (iii) **Describe a test of control Scarlet & Co should perform to assess if each of these controls is operating effectively.**   **(15 marks)**

Note: Prepare your answer using three columns headed Control deficiency, Control recommendation and Test of control respectively. The total marks will be split equally between each part.

(c)   **Describe substantive ANALYTICAL PROCEDURES you should perform to confirm Bronze Industries Co's payroll expense.**   **(4 marks)**

(d)   **Explain the factors to be considered in determining the suitability of using analytical procedures as a substantive procedure.**   **(4 marks)**

The directors of Bronze Industries Co are considering establishing an internal audit department next year, and the finance director has asked what impact, if any, establishing an internal audit department would have on future external audits performed by Scarlet & Co.

Required:

(e)   **Explain the potential impact on the work performed by Scarlet & Co during the interim and final audits, if Bronze Industries Co was to establish an internal audit department.**   **(4 marks)**

                                                                           (Total: 30 marks)

225 TROMBONE *Walk in the footsteps of a top tutor*

This scenario relates to four requirements.

(a) ISA 315 *Identifying and Assessing the Risks of Material Misstatement through Understanding the Entity and Its Environment* describes the five components of an entity's internal control.

Required:

Identify and briefly explain the FIVE components of an entity's internal control.

(5 marks)

Trombone Co (Trombone) operates a chain of hotels across the country. Trombone employs in excess of 250 permanent employees and its year-end is 31 August. You are the audit supervisor of Viola & Co and are currently reviewing the documentation of Trombone's payroll system, detailed below, in preparation for the interim audit.

Trombone's payroll system

Permanent employees work a standard number of hours per week as specified in their employment contract. However, when the hotels are busy, staff can be requested by management to work additional shifts as overtime. This can either be paid on a monthly basis or taken as days off.

Employees record any overtime worked and days taken off on weekly overtime sheets which are sent to the payroll department. The standard hours per employee are automatically set up in the system and the overtime sheets are entered by clerks into the payroll package, which automatically calculates the gross and net pay along with relevant deductions. These calculations are not checked at all. Wages are increased by the rate of inflation each year and the clerks are responsible for updating the standing data in the payroll system.

Employees are paid on a monthly basis by bank transfer for their contracted weekly hours and for any overtime worked in the previous month. If employees choose to be paid for overtime, authorisation is required by department heads of any overtime in excess of 30% of standard hours. If employees choose instead to take days off, the payroll clerks should check back to the 'overtime worked' report; however, this report is not always checked.

The 'overtime worked' report, which details any overtime recorded by employees, is run by the payroll department weekly and emailed to department heads for authorisation. The payroll department asks department heads to only report if there are any errors recorded. Department heads are required to arrange for overtime sheets to be authorised by an alternative responsible official if they are away on annual leave; however, there are instances where this arrangement has not occurred.

The payroll package produces a list of payments per employee; this links into the bank system to produce a list of automatic payments. The finance director reviews the total list of bank transfers and compares this to the total amount to be paid per the payroll records; if any issues arise then the automatic bank transfer can be manually changed by the finance director.

Required:

(b) In respect of the payroll system of Trombone Co:

    (i) Identify and explain FIVE deficiencies

    (ii) Recommend a control to address each of these deficiencies, and

    (iii) Describe a test of control Viola & Co should perform to assess if each of these controls is operating effectively. **(15 marks)**

Note: Prepare your answer using three columns headed Control deficiency, Control recommendation and Test of control respectively. The total marks will be split equally between each part.

(c) Describe substantive procedures the auditor should perform at the final audit to obtain sufficient and appropriate evidence in relation to COMPLETENESS and ACCURACY of Trombone Co's payroll expense. **(6 marks)**

Trombone deducts employment taxes from its employees' wages on a monthly basis and pays these to the local taxation authorities in the following month. At the year-end the financial statements will contain an accrual for income tax payable on employment income. You will be in charge of auditing this accrual.

Required:

(d) Describe the audit procedures required in respect of the year-end accrual for tax payable on employment income. **(4 marks)**

(Total: 30 marks)

226 OREGANO *Walk in the footsteps of a top tutor*

This scenario relates to three requirements.

You are a member of the recently formed internal audit department of Oregano Co (Oregano). The company manufactures tinned fruit and vegetables which are supplied to large and small food retailers. Management and those charged with governance of Oregano have concerns about the effectiveness of their sales and despatch system and have asked internal audit to document and review the system.

Sales and despatch system

Sales orders are mainly placed through Oregano's website but some are made via telephone. Online orders are automatically checked against inventory records for availability; telephone orders, however, are checked manually by order clerks after the call.

A follow-up call is usually made to customers if there is insufficient inventory. When taking telephone orders, clerks note down the details on plain paper and afterwards they complete a three part pre-printed order form. These order forms are not sequentially numbered and are sent manually to both despatch and the accounts department.

As the company is expanding, customers are able to place online orders which will exceed their agreed credit limit by 10%. Online orders are automatically forwarded to the despatch and accounts department.

A daily pick list is printed by the despatch department and this is used by the warehouse team to despatch goods. The goods are accompanied by a despatch note and all customers are required to sign a copy of this. On return, the signed despatch notes are given to the warehouse team to file.

The sales quantities are entered from the despatch notes and the authorised sales prices are generated by the invoicing system. If a discount has been given, this has to be manually entered by the sales clerk onto the invoice. Due to the expansion of the company, and as there is a large number of sale invoices, extra accounts staff have been asked to help out temporarily with producing the sales invoices. Normally it is only two sales clerks who produce the sales invoices.

Required:

(a)   **Describe TWO methods for documenting the sales and despatch system; and for each explain an advantage and a disadvantage of using this method.**   **(6 marks)**

(b)   **List TWO control objectives of Oregano Co's sales and despatch system.**   **(2 marks)**

(c)   **Identify and explain SIX deficiencies in Oregano Co's sales and despatch system and provide a recommendation to address each of these deficiencies.**   **(12 marks)**

Note: Prepare your answer using two columns headed Control deficiency and Control recommendation respectively.

(Total: 20 marks)

227   FOX INDUSTRIES *Walk in the footsteps of a top tutor*

This scenario relates to three requirements.

Fox Industries Co (Fox) manufactures engineering parts. It has one operating site and a customer base spread across Europe. The company's year-end was 30 April 20X3. Below is a description of the purchasing and payments system.

Purchasing system

Whenever production materials are required, the relevant department sends a requisition form to the ordering department. An order clerk raises a purchase order and contacts a number of suppliers to see which can despatch the goods first. This supplier is then chosen. The order clerk sends out the purchase order. This is not sequentially numbered and only orders above $5,000 require authorisation.

Purchase invoices are input daily by the purchase ledger clerk, who has been in the role for many years and, as an experienced team member, he does not apply any application controls over the input process. Every week the purchase day book automatically updates the purchase ledger, the purchase ledger is then posted manually to the general ledger by the purchase ledger clerk.

Payments system

Fox maintains a current account and a number of saving (deposit) accounts. The current account is reconciled weekly but the saving (deposit) accounts are only reconciled every two months.

In order to maximise their cash and bank balance, Fox has a policy of delaying payments to all suppliers for as long as possible. Suppliers are paid by a bank transfer. The finance director is given the total amount of the payments list, which he authorises and then processes the bank payments.

Required:

(a)   As the external auditor of Fox Industries Co, write a report to management in respect of the purchasing and payments system described which:

   (i)   Identifies and explains FIVE deficiencies in the system and recommends a control to address each of these deficiencies; and

   (ii)   Includes a covering letter

   Note: Up to two marks will be awarded within this requirement for presentation and the remaining marks will be split equally between each part.   **(12 marks)**

(b)   Identify and explain THREE application controls that should be adopted by Fox Industries Co to ensure the COMPLETENESS and ACCURACY of the input of purchase invoices.   **(3 marks)**

(c)   Describe substantive procedures the auditor should perform at the final audit to obtain sufficient and appropriate evidence in relation to the bank and cash balances of Fox Industries Co at the year-end.   **(5 marks)**

(Total: 20 marks)

228   LILY WINDOW GLASS *Walk in the footsteps of a top tutor*

This scenario relates to three requirements.

You are an audit senior in Daffodil & Co and you are responsible for the audit of inventory for Lily Window Glass Co (Lily), including attending the year end inventory count.

Lily is a glass manufacturer, which operates from a large production facility, where it undertakes continuous production 24 hours a day, seven days a week. Also on this site are two warehouses, where the company's raw materials and finished goods are stored. Lily's year-end is 31 December.

Lily is finalising the arrangements for the year-end inventory count, which is to be undertaken on 31 December 20X2. The finished windows are stored within 20 aisles of the first warehouse. The second warehouse is for large piles of raw materials, such as sand, used in the manufacture of glass. The following arrangements have been made for the inventory count:

The warehouse manager will supervise the count as he is most familiar with the inventory. There will be ten teams of counters and each team will contain two members of staff, one from the finance and one from the manufacturing department. None of the warehouse staff, other than the manager, will be involved in the count.

Each team will count an aisle of finished goods by counting up and then down each aisle. As this process is systematic, it is not felt that the team will need to flag areas once counted.

Once the team has finished counting an aisle, they will hand in their sheets and be given a set for another aisle of the warehouse. In addition to the above, to assist with the inventory counting, there will be two teams of counters from the internal audit department and they will perform inventory counts.

The count sheets are sequentially numbered, and the product codes and descriptions are printed on them but no quantities. If the counters identify any inventory which is not on their sheets, then they are to enter the item on a separate sheet, which is not numbered. Once all counting is complete, the sequence of the sheets is checked and any additional sheets are also handed in at this stage. All sheets are completed in ink.

Any damaged goods identified by the counters will be too heavy to move to a central location, hence they are to be left where they are but the counter is to make a note on the inventory sheets detailing the level of damage.

As Lily undertakes continuous production, there will continue to be movements of raw materials and finished goods in and out of the warehouse during the count. These will be kept to a minimum where possible.

The level of work-in-progress in the manufacturing plant is to be assessed by the warehouse manager. It is likely that this will be an immaterial balance. In addition, the raw materials quantities are to be approximated by measuring the height and width of the raw material piles. In the past this task has been undertaken by a specialist; however, the warehouse manager feels confident that he can perform this task.

Required:

(a) **Identify and explain SIX DEFICIENCIES in Lily Window Glass Co's inventory count arrangements and provide a recommendation to address each of these deficiencies**

Note: Prepare your answer using two columns headed Deficiency and Recommendation respectively. **(12 marks)**

(b) **Describe the procedures to be undertaken by the auditor DURING the inventory count of Lily Window Glass Co in order to gain sufficient appropriate audit evidence.** **(6 marks)**

Your manager wishes to utilise automated tools and techniques for the first time for controls and substantive testing in auditing Lily Window Glass Co's inventory.

(c) **For the audit of the inventory cycle and year-end inventory balance of Lily Window Glass Co:**

(i) **Describe FOUR audit procedures that could be carried out using automated tools and techniques.**

(ii) **Explain the potential advantages of using automated tools and techniques, including data analytics.**

(iii) **Explain the potential disadvantages of using automated tools and techniques and data analytics.**

The total marks will be split equally between each part **(12 marks)**

(Total: 30 marks)

229 PEAR INTERNATIONAL *Walk in the footsteps of a top tutor*

Pear International Co (Pear) is a manufacturer of electrical equipment. It has factories across the country and its customer base includes retailers as well as individuals, to whom direct sales are made through their website. The company's year-end is 30 September 20X2. You are an audit supervisor of Apple & Co and are currently reviewing documentation of Pear's internal control in preparation for the interim audit.

Pear's website allows individuals to order goods directly, and full payment is taken in advance. Currently the website is not integrated into the inventory system and inventory levels are not checked at the time when orders are placed.

Goods are despatched via local couriers; however, they do not always record customer signatures as proof that the customer has received the goods. Over the past 12 months there have been customer complaints about the delay between sales orders and receipt of goods. Pear has investigated these and found that, in each case, the sales order had been entered into the sales system correctly but was not forwarded to the despatch department for fulfilling.

Pear's retail customers undergo credit checks prior to being accepted and credit limits are set accordingly by receivables ledger clerks. These customers place their orders through one of the sales team, who decides on sales discount levels.

Raw materials used in the manufacturing process are purchased from a wide range of suppliers. As a result of staff changes in the payables ledger department, supplier statement reconciliations are no longer performed. Additionally, changes to supplier details in the payables ledger master file can be undertaken by payables ledger clerks as well as supervisors.

In the past six months Pear has changed part of its manufacturing process and as a result some new equipment has been purchased, however, there are considerable levels of plant and equipment which are now surplus to requirement. Purchase requisitions for all new equipment have been authorised by production supervisors and little has been done to reduce the surplus of old equipment.

Required:

(a)   **In respect of the internal control of Pear International Co:**

   (i)   **Identify and explain FIVE deficiencies**

   (ii)   **Recommend a control to address each of these deficiencies, and**

   (iii)   **Describe a test of control Apple & Co would perform to assess if each of these controls is operating effectively.   (15 marks)**

   Note: Prepare your answer using three columns headed Control deficiency, Control recommendation and Test of control respectively.

(b)   **Describe substantive procedures the auditor should perform to obtain sufficient and appropriate audit evidence in respect of additions and disposals of plant and equipment.   (5 marks)**

(Total: 20 marks)

SUBSTANTIVE PROCEDURES, COMPLETION AND REPORTING

230 SPADEFISH *Walk in the footsteps of a top tutor*

This scenario relates to four requirements.

It is 1 July 20X5 and you are an audit manager of Spadefish & Co and you are currently responsible for the audits of two existing clients:

Triggerfish Co manufactures hair products and its year ended on 31 May 20X5. You are finalising the audit programmes for the forthcoming year-end audit.

Marlin Co is a distributor of electronic goods and its year ended on 30 April 20X5. The audit is almost complete and the auditor's report is due to be signed shortly.

The following matters have been brought to your attention for each company.

Triggerfish Co – Receivables

Triggerfish Co's draft year-end trade receivables are $3.85m (20X4: $2.45m) and revenue for the year is slightly increased on 20X4. Triggerfish Co has a large number of customers with balances ranging from $5,000 to $45,000. A positive receivables circularisation has been undertaken based on the year-end balances. The majority of responses from customers agreed to the balances as per Triggerfish Co's receivables ledger, however, the following exceptions were noted:

	Balance per Triggerfish	Response from customer
Albacore Co	$36,558	Nil response
Flounder Co	$24,115	$18,265
Menhaden Co	-$5,360 (Credit)	$3,450

Due to the increase in receivables, Triggerfish Co has recently recruited an additional credit controller to chase outstanding receivables. As a result of the additional focus on chasing outstanding receivables the finance director thinks it is not necessary to continue to maintain a significant allowance for receivables and has reduced the closing allowance from $125,000 to $5,000.

Marlin Co – Going concern

During the year under audit Marlin Co has consistently paid a number of its suppliers significantly later than usual and only after several reminders. As a result some of its suppliers have withdrawn credit terms meaning the company must pay cash on delivery. The company has also just received notification that its main supplier who provides the company with over 60% of its specialist electrical equipment has ceased to trade.

The overdraft has increased significantly over the year and the directors have informed you that the overdraft facility is due for renewal next month, and they are confident it will be renewed. The directors have decided that in order to conserve cash, no final dividend will be paid in 20X5.

Required:

(a) Describe the procedures the auditor should perform to resolve the exceptions noted for each customer during the positive receivables circularisation for Triggerfish Co.

(8 marks)

(b) Describe substantive procedures the auditor should perform to obtain sufficient and appropriate audit evidence in relation to the allowance for receivables in the current year. **(4 marks)**

(c) Identify and explain THREE potential indicators that Marlin Co is NOT a going concern. **(3 marks)**

(d) Describe the audit procedures the auditor should perform in assessing whether or not Marlin Co is a going concern. **(5 marks)**

(Total: 20 marks)

231 HYACINTH *Walk in the footsteps of a top tutor*

This scenario relates to four requirements.

Hyacinth Co develops and manufactures computer components and its year end was 31 December 20X8. The company has a large factory, and two warehouses, one of which is off-site. You are an audit supervisor of Tulip & Co and the final audit is due to commence shortly. Draft financial statements show total assets of $23.2m and profit before tax of $6.4m. The following three matters have been brought to your attention:

Inventory valuation

Your firm attended the year-end inventory count for Hyacinth Co and confirmed that the controls and processes for recording work in progress (WIP) and finished goods were acceptable. WIP and finished goods are both material to the financial statements and the audit team was able to confirm both the quantity and stage of completion of WIP.

Before goods are dispatched, they are inspected by the company's quality control department. Just prior to the inventory count, it was noted that a batch of product line 'Crocus', which had been produced to meet a customer's specific technical requirements, did not meet that customer's quality and technical standards. This inventory had a production cost of $450,000. Upon discussions with the production supervisor, the finance director believes that the inventory can still be sold to alternative customers at a discounted price of $90,000.

Research and development

Hyacinth Co includes expenditure incurred in developing new products within intangible assets once the recognition criteria under IAS® 38 *Intangible Assets* have been met. Intangible assets are amortised on a straight line basis over four years once production commences. The amortisation policy is based on past experience of the likely useful lives of the products. The opening balance of intangible assets is $1.9m.

In the current year, Hyacinth Co spent $0.8m developing three new products which are all at different stages of development.

Sales tax liability

Hyacinth Co is required by the relevant tax authority in the country in which it operates to charge sales tax at 15% on all products which it sells. This sales tax is payable to the tax authority. When purchasing raw materials and incurring expenses in the manufacturing process, the company pays 15% sales tax on any items purchased and this can be reclaimed from the tax authority.

The company is required to report the taxes charged and incurred by completing a tax return on a quarterly basis, and the net amount owing to the tax authority must be remitted within four weeks of the quarter end. The draft financial statements contain a $1.1m liability for sales tax for the quarter ended 31 December 20X8.

Required:

(a)   Describe substantive procedures the auditor should perform to obtain sufficient and appropriate audit evidence in relation to the VALUATION of Hyacinth Co's inventory.
(6 marks)

(b)   Describe substantive procedures the auditor should perform to obtain sufficient and appropriate audit evidence in relation to Hyacinth Co's research and development expenditure.
(4 marks)

(c)   Describe substantive procedures the auditor should perform to obtain sufficient and appropriate audit evidence in relation to Hyacinth Co's year-end sales tax liability.
(4 marks)

The audit is now almost complete and the auditor's report is due to be signed shortly. The following matter has been brought to your attention:

On 3 February 20X9, a flood occurred at the off-site warehouse. This resulted in some damage to inventory and property, plant and equipment. However, there have been no significant delays to customer deliveries or complaints from customers. Hyacinth Co's management has investigated the cause of the flooding and believes that the company is unlikely to be able to claim on its insurance. The finance director of Hyacinth Co has estimated that the value of damaged inventory and property, plant and equipment was $0.7m and that it now has no scrap value.

Required:

(d)   (i)   Explain whether the 20X8 financial statements of Hyacinth Co require amendment in relation to the flood; and

(ii)   Describe audit procedures which should be performed in order to form a conclusion on any required amendment.

Note: The total marks will be split equally between each part.   (6 marks)

(Total: 20 marks)

232 JASMINE *Walk in the footsteps of a top tutor*

This scenario relates to four requirements.

Jasmine Co manufactures motor vehicle components and its year end was 30 June 20X8. You are an audit supervisor of Peppermint & Co and the final audit is due to commence shortly. Total assets are $43.2m and profit before tax is $7.2m. The following matters have been brought to your attention:

Trade receivables

Jasmine Co's trade receivables ledger is comprised of a large number of customers. In previous years, the audit team has undertaken a positive trade receivables circularisation to confirm year-end balances. However, the customer response rate has historically been low and so alternative audit procedures have been undertaken. A decision has been made that for the current year audit a circularisation will not be performed.

The year-end trade receivables balance is $3.9m (20X7: $2.8m) and the allowance for trade receivables is $410,000 (20X7: $300,000).

Bank balances

The bank and cash figure included in Jasmine Co's draft financial statements is comprised of a number of bank account balances: an overdraft of $5.1m which is the company's main current account and $0.2m relating to several savings accounts. The finance director has informed the audit manager that all accounts have been reconciled as at the year end.

The overdraft of $5.1m has increased significantly since the prior year (20X7: $1.2m). The directors have informed you that the overdraft facility, which the company requires in order to operate on a daily basis, is due for renewal in October 20X8 and that they are confident it will be renewed.

Required:

(a)   Describe substantive procedures the auditor should perform to obtain sufficient and appropriate audit evidence in relation to Jasmine Co's trade receivables.   **(5 marks)**

(b)   Describe substantive procedures the auditor should perform to obtain sufficient and appropriate audit evidence in relation to Jasmine Co's bank balances.   **(5 marks)**

(c)   Describe the audit procedures the auditor should perform in assessing whether or not Jasmine Co is a going concern.   **(5 marks)**

During the final audit, the finance director has informed the audit team that Jasmine Co's bankers will not make a decision on the renewal of the overdraft facility until after the auditor's report is signed. The audit engagement partner is satisfied that the use of the going concern basis is appropriate.

The directors have agreed to include some brief going concern disclosures in the draft financial statements and the audit team still have to assess the adequacy of these disclosures.

Required:

(d)   Discuss the issue and describe the impact on the auditor's report of Jasmine Co of adequate AND inadequate going concern disclosure.   **(5 marks)**

(Total: 20 marks)

233 GOOSEBERRY *Walk in the footsteps of a top tutor*

This scenario relates to four requirements.

You are an audit manager of Cranberry & Co and you are currently responsible for the audit of Gooseberry Co, a company which develops and manufactures health and beauty products and distributes these to wholesale customers. Its draft profit before tax is $6.4m and total assets are $37.2m for the financial year ended 31 January 20X8. The final audit is due to commence shortly and the following matters have been brought to your attention:

Research and development

Gooseberry Co spent $1.9m in the current year developing nine new health and beauty products, all of which are at different stages of development. Once they meet the recognition criteria under IAS® 38 Intangible Assets for development expenditure, Gooseberry Co includes the costs incurred within intangible assets. Once production commences, the intangible assets are amortised on a straight line basis over three years.

Management believes that this amortisation policy is a reasonable approximation of the assets' useful lives, as in this industry there is constant demand for innovative new products.

Depreciation

Gooseberry Co has a large portfolio of property, plant and equipment (PPE). In March 20X7, the company carried out a full review of all its PPE and updated the useful lives, residual values, depreciation rates and methods for many categories of asset. The finance director felt the changes were necessary to better reflect the use of the assets. This resulted in the depreciation charge of some assets changing significantly for this year.

Bonus

The company's board is comprised of seven directors. They are each entitled to a bonus based on the draft year-end net assets, excluding intangible assets. Details of the bonus entitlement are included in the directors' service contracts.

The bonus, which related to the 20X8 year end, was paid to each director in February 20X8 and the costs were accrued and recognised within wages and salaries for the year ended 31 January 20X8. Separate disclosure of the bonus, by director, is required by local legislation.

Required:

(a)   Describe substantive procedures the auditor should perform to obtain sufficient and appropriate audit evidence in relation to Gooseberry Co's research and development expenditure. **(5 marks)**

(b)   Describe substantive procedures the auditor should perform to obtain sufficient and appropriate audit evidence in relation to the matters identified regarding depreciation of property, plant and equipment. **(5 marks)**

(c)   Describe substantive procedures the auditor should perform to obtain sufficient and appropriate audit evidence in relation to the directors' bonuses. **(5 marks)**

During the audit, the team discovers that the intangible assets balance includes $440,000 related to one of the nine new health and beauty products development projects, which does not meet the criteria for capitalisation. As this project is ongoing, the finance director has suggested that no adjustment is made in the 20X8 financial statements. She is confident that the project will meet the criteria for capitalisation in 20X9.

Required:

(d)   Discuss the issue and describe the impact on the auditor's report, if any, should this issue remain unresolved.   **(5 marks)**

(Total: 20 marks)

234   DASHING *Walk in the footsteps of a top tutor*

This scenario relates to four requirements.

Dashing Co manufactures women's clothing and its year end was 31 July 20X7. You are an audit supervisor of Jaunty & Co and the year-end audit for Dashing Co is due to commence shortly.

The draft financial statements recognise profit before tax of $2.6m and total assets of $18m. You have been given responsibility for auditing receivables, which is a material balance, and as part of the audit approach, a positive receivables circularisation is to be undertaken.

At the planning meeting, the finance director of Dashing Co informed the audit engagement partner that the company was closing one of its smaller production sites and as a result, a number of employees would be made redundant. A redundancy provision of $110,000 is included in the draft financial statements.

Required:

(a)   Describe the steps the auditor should perform in undertaking a positive receivables circularisation for Dashing Co.   **(4 marks)**

(b)   Describe substantive procedures, other than a receivables circularisation, the auditor should perform to obtain sufficient and appropriate audit evidence to verify EACH of the following assertions in relation to Dashing Co's receivables:

   (i)   Accuracy, valuation and allocation

   (ii)   Completeness, and

   (iii)   Rights and obligations.

   Note: The total marks will be split equally between each part.   **(6 marks)**

(c)   Describe substantive procedures the auditor should perform to obtain sufficient and appropriate audit evidence in relation to the redundancy provision at the year end.   **(5 marks)**

(d)   A few months have now passed and the audit team is performing the audit fieldwork including the audit procedures which you recommended over the redundancy provision. The team has calculated that the necessary provision should amount to $305,000. The finance director is not willing to adjust the draft financial statements.

   Required:

   Discuss the issue and describe the impact on the auditor's report, if any, should this issue remain unresolved.   **(5 marks)**

(Total: 20 marks)

235 AIRSOFT *Walk in the footsteps of a top tutor*

 Question debrief

This scenario relates to five requirements.

Airsoft Co is a listed company which manufactures stationery products. The company's profit before tax for the year ended 31 December 20X6 is $16.3 million and total assets as at that date are $66.8 million. You are an audit supervisor of Biathlon & Co and you are currently finalising the audit programmes for the year-end audit of your existing client Airsoft Co. You attended a meeting with your audit manager where the following matters were discussed:

Trade payables and accruals

Airsoft Co purchases its raw materials from a large number of suppliers. The company's policy is to close the payables ledger just after the year end and the financial controller is responsible for identifying goods which were received pre year-end but for which no invoice has yet been received. An accrual is calculated for goods received but not yet invoiced (GRNI) and is included within trade payables and accruals.

The audit strategy has identified a risk over the completeness of trade payables and accruals. The audit team will utilise automated tools and techniques, in the form of audit software while auditing trade payables and accruals.

Bank overdraft and savings accounts

Airsoft Co's draft financial statements include a bank overdraft of $2.6 million, which relates to the company's main current account. In addition Airsoft Co maintains a number of savings accounts. The savings account balances are classified as cash and cash equivalents and are included in current assets. All accounts have been reconciled at the year end.

Directors' remuneration

Airsoft Co's board comprises eight directors. Their overall remuneration consists of two elements: an annual salary, paid monthly and a significant annual discretionary bonus, which is paid in a separate payment run on 20 December. All remuneration paid to directors is included within wages and salaries. Local legislation requires disclosure of the overall total of directors' remuneration broken down by element and by director.

Required:

(a) Describe substantive procedures the auditor should perform to obtain sufficient and appropriate audit evidence in relation to the COMPLETENESS of Airsoft Co's trade payables and accruals. **(4 marks)**

Excluding procedures included in part (a):

(b) Describe audit software procedures which could be carried out during the audit of Airsoft Co's trade payables and accruals. **(3 marks)**

(c) Describe substantive procedures the auditor should perform to obtain sufficient and appropriate audit evidence in relation to Airsoft Co's year-end bank balances. **(5 marks)**

(d) Describe substantive procedures the auditor should perform to confirm the directors' remuneration included in the financial statements at the year end. **(3 marks)**

A member of your audit team has asked for information on ISA 701 *Communicating Key Audit Matters in the Independent Auditor's Report* as she has heard this standard is applicable to listed clients such as Airsoft Co.

Required:

(e) **Identify what a key audit matter (KAM) is and explain how the auditor determines and communicates KAM.** **(5 marks)**

(Total: 20 marks)

 Calculate your allowed time, allocate the time to the separate parts...............

236 INSECTS4U *Walk in the footsteps of a top tutor*

This scenario relates to four requirements.

You are an audit manager of Snail & Co and you are in charge of two audits which are due to commence shortly. Insects4U Co is a registered charity which promotes insect conservation and has been an audit client for several years. Spider Spirals Co, also an existing audit client, manufactures stationery products and its draft total liabilities are $8.1 million. Both clients' financial year ended on 31 October 20X6. The following matters have been brought to your attention for each company.

Insects4U Co

Insects4U Co is a not-for-profit organisation which generates income in a number of ways. It receives monthly donations from its many subscribers and these are paid by bank transfer to the charity.

In addition, a large number of donations are sent through the post to the charity. Insects4U Co also sells tickets for their three charity events held annually. During the audit planning, completeness of income was flagged as a key risk.

Note: Assume that the charity adopts International Financial Reporting Standards.

Spider Spirals Co

Trade payables

The finance director of Spider Spirals Co has informed you that at the year end the payables ledger was kept open for one week longer than normal as a large bank transfer and cheque payment run was made on 3 November 20X6. Some purchase invoices were received in this week and were recorded in the 20X6 payables ledger as well as the payment run made on 3 November.

Trade receivables

Spider Spirals Co has a large number of small customers; the normal credit terms offered to them is 30 days. However, the finance director has informed you that the average trade receivables days have increased quite significantly this year from 34 days to 55 days. This is partly due to difficult trading conditions and also because for six months of the year the role of credit controller was vacant. The company has historically maintained on average an allowance for trade receivables of 1.5% of gross trade receivables.

Required:

(a)   Describe substantive procedures the auditor should perform to obtain sufficient and appropriate audit evidence in relation to the COMPLETENESS of Insect4U Co's income.   **(4 marks)**

(b)   Describe substantive procedures the auditor should perform to obtain sufficient and appropriate audit evidence in relation to Spider Spiral Co's trade payables.

                                                                                                                   (6 marks)

(c)   Describe substantive procedures the auditor should perform to obtain sufficient and appropriate audit evidence in relation to Spider Spiral Co's trade receivables.

                                                                                                                   (5 marks)

The finance director of Spider Spirals Co has informed you that he is not proposing to make an adjustment for the trade payables payment run made on 3 November, as the total payment of $490,000 would only require a change to trade payables and the bank overdraft, both of which are current liabilities.

Required:

(d)   Discuss the issue and describe the impact on the auditor's report, if any, should this issue remain unresolved.   **(5 marks)**

                                                                                                   (Total: 20 marks)

237   ELOUNDA   *Walk in the footsteps of a top tutor*

This scenario relates to four requirements.

Elounda Co manufactures chemical compounds using a continuous production process. Its year-end was 31 July 20X6 and the draft profit before tax is $13.6 million. You are the audit supervisor and the year-end audit is due to commence shortly. The following matters have been brought to your attention.

Revaluation of property, plant and equipment (PPE)

At the beginning of the year, management undertook an extensive review of Elounda Co's non-current asset valuations and as a result decided to update the carrying value of all PPE. The finance director, Peter Dullman, contacted his brother, Martin, who is a valuer and requested that Martin's firm undertake the valuation, which took place in August 20X5.

Inventory valuation

Your firm attended the year-end inventory count for Elounda Co and ascertained that the process for recording work in progress (WIP) and finished goods was acceptable. Both WIP and finished goods are material to the financial statements and the quantity and stage of completion of all ongoing production was recorded accurately during the count.

During the inventory count, the count supervisor noted that a consignment of finished goods, compound E243, with a value of $720,000, was defective in that the chemical mix was incorrect. The finance director believes that compound E243 can still be sold at a discounted sum of $400,000.

Bank loan

Elounda Co secured a bank loan of $2.6 million on 1 October 20X4. Repayments of $200,000 are due quarterly, with a lump sum of $800,000 due for repayment in January 20X7. The company met all loan payments in 20X5 on time, but was late in paying the April and July 20X6 repayments.

Required:

(a) Describe substantive procedures the auditor should perform to obtain sufficient and appropriate audit evidence in relation to the revaluation of Elounda Co's property, plant and equipment. **(5 marks)**

(b) Describe substantive procedures the auditor should perform to obtain sufficient and appropriate audit evidence in relation to the VALUATION of Elounda Co's inventory. **(6 marks)**

(c) Describe substantive procedures the auditor should perform to obtain sufficient and appropriate audit evidence in relation to Elounda Co's bank loan. **(4 marks)**

(d) Describe the procedures which the auditor of Elounda Co should perform in assessing whether or not the company is a going concern. **(5 marks)**

(Total: 20 marks)

238 ANDROMEDA *Walk in the footsteps of a top tutor*

This scenario relates to four requirements.

Andromeda Industries Co (Andromeda) develops and manufactures a wide range of fast moving consumer goods. The company's year-end is 31 December 20X5 and the forecast profit before tax is $8.3 million. You are the audit manager of Neptune & Co and the year-end audit is due to commence in January. The following information has been gathered during the planning process:

Inventory count

Andromeda's raw materials and finished goods inventory are stored in 12 warehouses across the country. Each of these warehouses is expected to contain material levels of inventory at the year-end. It is expected that there will be no significant work in progress held at any of the sites. Each count will be supervised by a member of Andromeda's internal audit department and the counts will all take place on 31 December, when all movements of goods in and out of the warehouses will cease.

Research and development

Andromeda spends over $2 million annually on developing new product lines. This year it incurred expenditure on five projects, all of which are at different stages of development. Once they meet the recognition criteria under IAS 38 *Intangible Assets* for development expenditure, Andromeda includes the costs incurred within intangible assets. Once production commences, the intangible assets are amortised on a straight line basis over five years.

Required:

(a) Explain FOUR factors which influence the reliability of audit evidence. **(4 marks)**

(b) Describe the procedures to be undertaken by the auditor BEFORE and DURING the inventory count of Andromeda Industries Co in order to gain sufficient appropriate audit evidence. **(8 marks)**

(c) Describe substantive procedures the auditor should perform to obtain sufficient and appropriate audit evidence in relation to Andromeda Co's research and development expenditure. **(4 marks)**

During the audit, the team discovers that one of the five development projects, valued at $980,000 and included within intangible assets, does not meet the criteria for capitalisation. The finance director does not intend to change the accounting treatment adopted as she considers this an immaterial amount.

Required:

(d) Discuss the issue and describe the impact on the auditor's report, if any, if the issue remains unresolved. **(4 marks)**

(Total: 20 marks)

239 HAWTHORN *Walk in the footsteps of a top tutor*

 Question debrief

This scenario relates to four requirements.

Hawthorn Enterprises Co manufactures and distributes fashion clothing to retail stores. Its year-end was 31 March 20X5. You are the audit manager and the year-end audit is due to commence shortly. The following three matters have been brought to your attention.

Supplier statement reconciliations

Hawthorn Enterprises Co receives monthly statements from its main suppliers and although these have been retained, none have been reconciled to the payables ledger as at 31 March 20X5. The engagement partner has asked the audit senior to recommend the procedures to be performed on supplier statements.

Bank reconciliation

During last year's audit of Hawthorn Enterprises Co's bank and cash, significant cut off errors were discovered with a number of post year-end cheques being processed prior to the year-end to reduce payables. The finance director has assured the audit engagement partner that this error has not occurred again this year and that the bank reconciliation has been carefully prepared. The audit engagement partner has asked that the bank reconciliation is comprehensively audited.

Receivables

Hawthorn Enterprises Co's receivables ledger has increased considerably during the year, and the year-end balance is $2.3 million compared to $1.4 million last year. The finance director has requested that a receivables circularisation is not carried out as a number of their customers complained last year about the inconvenience involved in responding. The engagement partner has agreed to this request, and tasked you with identifying alternative procedures to confirm the existence and valuation of receivables.

Required:

(a)   (i)   Identify and explain FOUR financial statement assertions relevant to classes of transactions and events for the year under audit; and

     (ii)   For each identified assertion, describe a substantive procedure relevant to the audit of REVENUE.   **(8 marks)**

(b)   Describe substantive procedures the auditor should perform to obtain sufficient and appropriate audit evidence in relation to the supplier statement reconciliations of Hawthorn Enterprises Co.   — not payables procedures   **(3 marks)**

(c)   Describe substantive procedures the auditor should perform to obtain sufficient and appropriate audit evidence in relation to the bank reconciliation of Hawthorn Enterprises Co.   — not bank/cash procedures   **(4 marks)**

(d)   Describe substantive procedures the auditor should perform to obtain sufficient and appropriate audit evidence in relation to the EXISTENCE and VALUATION of Hawthorn Enterprises Co's receivables.   **(5 marks)**

(Total: 20 marks)

 Calculate your allowed time, allocate the time to the separate parts...............

240   PINEAPPLE BEACH HOTEL *Walk in the footsteps of a top tutor*

This scenario relates to four requirements.

Pineapple Beach Hotel Co operates a hotel providing accommodation, leisure facilities and restaurants. Its year-end was 30 April 20X2. You are the audit senior of Berry & Co and are currently preparing the audit programmes for the year-end audit of Pineapple Beach Hotel Co. You are reviewing the notes of last week's meeting between the audit manager and finance director where two material issues were discussed.

Depreciation

Pineapple Beach Hotel Co incurred significant capital expenditure during the year on updating the leisure facilities for the hotel. The finance director has proposed that the new leisure equipment should be depreciated over 10 years using the straight-line method.

Food poisoning

Pineapple Beach Hotel Co's directors received correspondence in March from a group of customers who attended a wedding at the hotel. They have alleged that they suffered severe food poisoning from food eaten at the hotel and are claiming substantial damages. The company's lawyers have received the claim and believe that the lawsuit against the company is unlikely to be successful.

Required:

(a) (i) Identify and explain FOUR financial statement assertions relevant to account balances at the year-end; and

  (ii) For each identified assertion, describe a substantive procedure relevant to the audit of year-end inventory.   **(8 marks)**

(b) Describe substantive procedures the auditor should perform to obtain sufficient and appropriate audit evidence in relation to Pineapple Beach Hotel Co's depreciation.   **(4 marks)**

(c) Describe substantive procedures the auditor should perform to obtain sufficient and appropriate audit evidence in relation to the food poisoning claim.   **(4 marks)**

(d) List and explain the purpose of FOUR items that should be included on every working paper prepared by the audit team.   **(4 marks)**

(Total: 20 marks)

(D) ½ mark for stating item.
½ marks for explaination of the purpose.

ADDITIONAL QUESTIONS

THE FOLLOWING QUESTIONS ARE EXAM STANDARD BUT DO NOT REFLECT THE CURRENT EXAM FORMAT. THESE QUESTIONS PROVIDE VALUABLE PRACTICE FOR STUDENTS NEVERTHELESS.

241 SAXOPHONE ENTERPRISES *Walk in the footsteps of a top tutor*

Saxophone Enterprises Co (Saxophone) has been trading for 15 years selling insurance and has recently become a listed company. Saxophone is required to comply with corporate governance principles in order to maintain its listed status and the finance director has undertaken a review of whether or not the company complies.

Bill Bassoon is the chair of Saxophone, until last year he was the chief executive. Bill is unsure if Saxophone needs more non-executive directors as there are currently three non-executive directors out of the eight board members. He is considering appointing one of his close friends, who is a retired chief executive of a manufacturing company, as a non-executive director.

The finance director, Jessie Oboe, decides on the amount of remuneration each director is paid. Currently all remuneration is in the form of an annual bonus based on profits. Jessie is considering setting up an audit committee, but has not undertaken this task yet as she is very busy. A new sales director was appointed nine months ago. He has yet to undertake his board training as this is normally provided by the chief executive and this role is currently vacant.

There are a large number of shareholders and therefore the directors believe that it is impractical and too costly to hold an annual general meeting of shareholders. Instead, the board has suggested sending out the financial statements and any voting resolutions by email; shareholders can then vote on the resolutions via email.

Required:

Describe TWO corporate governance weaknesses faced by Saxophone Enterprises Co and provide a recommendation to address each weakness to ensure compliance with corporate governance principles.

Note: Prepare your answer using two columns headed Weakness and Recommendation respectively.

(10 marks)

242 **ORANGE FINANCIALS** *Walk in the footsteps of a top tutor*

You are the audit manager of Currant & Co and you are planning the audit of Orange Financials Co (Orange), who specialise in the provision of loans and financial advice to individuals and companies. Currant & Co has audited Orange for many years.

The directors are planning to list Orange on a stock exchange within the next few months and have asked if the engagement partner can attend the meetings with potential investors. In addition, as the finance director of Orange is likely to be quite busy with the listing, he has asked if Currant & Co can produce the financial statements for the current year.

During the year, the assistant finance director of Orange left and joined Currant & Co as a partner. It has been suggested that due to his familiarity with Orange, he should be appointed to provide an independent partner review for the audit.

Once Orange obtains its stock exchange listing it will require several assignments to be undertaken, for example, obtaining advice about corporate governance best practice. Currant & Co is very keen to be appointed to these engagements, however, Orange has implied that in order to gain this work Currant & Co needs to complete the external audit quickly and with minimal questions/issues.

The finance director has informed you that once the stock exchange listing has been completed, he would like the engagement team to attend a weekend away at a luxury hotel with his team, as a thank you for all their hard work. In addition, he has offered a senior member of the engagement team a short-term loan at a significantly reduced interest rate.

Required:

(i)   **Identify and explain FIVE ethical threats which may affect the independence of Currant & Co's audit of Orange Financials Co, and**

(ii)   **For each threat, suggest a safeguard to reduce the risk to an acceptable level.**

Note: The total marks will be split equally between each part. Prepare your answer using two columns headed Ethical threat and Possible Safeguard respectively.

(10 marks)

243 VIOLET & CO *Walk in the footsteps of a top tutor*

You are the audit manager of Violet & Co and you are currently reviewing the audit files for two of your clients for which the audit fieldwork is complete. The audit senior has raised the following issues:

Daisy Co

Daisy Co's year-end is 30 September, however, subsequent to the year-end the company's sales ledger has been corrupted by a computer virus. Daisy Co's finance director was able to produce the financial statements prior to this occurring; however, the audit team has been unable to access the sales ledger to undertake detailed testing of revenue or year-end receivables. All other accounting records are unaffected and there are no backups available for the sales ledger. Daisy Co's revenue is $15.6m, its receivables are $3.4m and profit before tax is $2m.

Fuchsia Co

Fuchsia Co has experienced difficult trading conditions and as a result it has lost significant market share. The cash flow forecast has been reviewed during the audit fieldwork and it shows a significant net cash outflow. Management are confident that further funding can be obtained and so have prepared the financial statements using the going concern basis with no additional disclosures; the audit senior is highly sceptical about this.

The prior year financial statements showed a profit before tax of $1.2m; however, the current year loss before tax is $4.4m and the forecast net cash outflow for the next 12 months is $3.2m.

Required:

For each of the two issues:

(i)   **Discuss the issue, including an assessment of whether it is material;**

(ii)   **Recommend procedures the audit team should undertake at the completion stage to try to resolve the issue; and**

(iii) **Describe the impact on the auditor's report if the issue remains unresolved.**

Notes: 1   The total marks will be split equally between each issue.

2   Report extracts are NOT required.

(10 marks)

Section 3

ANSWERS TO OBJECTIVE TEST CASE QUESTIONS

AUDIT FRAMEWORK

1   OPTION 2

The annual report should describe the work of the audit committee including:

- Significant issues considered relating to the financial statements.
- How it has assessed the independence and effectiveness of the external audit process.
- Where there is no internal audit function, an explanation for the absence and how internal assurance is achieved.
- An explanation of how auditor independence and objectivity are safeguarded, if the external auditor provides non-audit services.

The other options would be included in the annual report but are not related to the work of the audit committee. Options 1 relates to the directors. Option 3 relates to the board. Option 4 relates to the nomination committee.

2   OPTION 3

NEDs' remuneration should not be tied to the performance of Sistar Co as this can compromise their independence. NEDs' remuneration should be based on the time committed to carry out the role.

3

Reports to	Head of IA	Remaining staff members
Finance director	Maria Marquez	Appoint more senior staff with audit experience
Audit committee	Paul Belling	No changes needed
Chief executive		All staff should be new to the company

To ensure effectiveness of the internal audit function they should report into the audit committee. Maria Marquez should be appointed Head Internal Auditor as she has audit experience and is independent of the company. Paul Belling helped design and implement the current control system which creates a self-review threat. Only one of the remaining internal audit staff members has audit experience therefore more staff should be appointed with audit experience.

4   OPTION 1

The assignment described represents a value for money audit as it is focused on assessing the economy, efficiency and effectiveness of Sistar Co's capital expenditure.

5   OPTIONS 3 AND 5

Authorisation of transactions and performing reconciliations are types of control procedures. Internal audit should not design and implement internal control procedures as this will create a self-review threat when they subsequently test the effectiveness of the controls implemented. Internal audit should report any deficiencies identified and provide recommendations for improvement. Management is responsible for implementing the recommendations.

6   OPTION 3

As Foliage Co is a listed company, Jane Leaf should not serve as the Engagement Quality Control Reviewer until a cooling-off period of five years has passed.

7   OPTION 2

Bark & Co should assess whether audit and non-audit fees would represent more than 15% of gross practice income for two consecutive years. If the recurring fees are likely to exceed 15% of annual practice income this year, additional consideration should be given as to whether the taxation and audit-related services should be undertaken by the firm. This is particularly important as the client is listed and many additional services are prohibited. In addition, if the fees do exceed 15% then this should be disclosed to those charged with governance at Foliage. It is highly unlikely Bark will need to resign as auditor.

8   OPTION 1

The ACCA Code of Ethics and Conduct requires individuals to notify the firm of the possibility of employment with an audit client so they can be removed from the audit team.

9   OPTION B

There will be a familiarity threat because of Kim Baum's relationship with the audit team. The audit team may be too trusting of their previous colleague. A self-review threat would be created if an employee of the client joined the audit firm and was assigned to the audit of their previous employer. A self-interest threat would have arisen during the recruitment process as the judgment of the audit manager may have been affected by the desire to be appointed financial controller.

10

	Rule book approach	Conceptual framework approach
Clearly defined laws for the auditor to follow	✓	
Useful in a dynamic environment		✓
A set of guidelines with which the auditor uses judgment to apply to specific circumstances		✓
Easy to know what is allowed and not allowed	✓	

The conceptual framework provides guidelines with the objective that the auditor chooses the most appropriate course of action in the circumstances. This allows flexibility to deal with all possible situations which is useful in a dynamic environment. The guidelines followed are professional guidance but are not law. Laws clearly outline what is acceptable and not acceptable in specific circumstances.

11

	Advocacy	Familiarity	Self-interest
The partner and the finance director have known each other socially for many years		✓	
20% of the fee for last year's audit is still outstanding			✓

The social relationship gives rise to a familiarity threat. Outstanding fees can create self-interest and intimidation threats.

12   OPTION 4

The audit firm should request that the fees are paid. The audit firm must not issue this year's auditor's report until the fees have been paid.

13   OPTION 1

The audit will need to be planned carefully to ensure that the work is not predictable, especially as the new financial controller is an ex-employee of the firm and will know the firm's procedures.

The composition of the audit team should be considered and anyone who has remained in close contact with the new financial controller should be removed from the team to avoid a familiarity threat.

It is unlikely that a significant familiarity threat would arise from an audit senior joining the audit client. The significance of the threat increases with the seniority of the person, e.g. an audit partner, therefore the audit firm would not need to resign. It is the audit firm's responsibility to manage any ethical threats and take appropriate action. They cannot stop someone from taking a job with another organisation.

14   OPTION 2

A discount of 40% is unlikely to be a trivial sum and therefore the most appropriate option is to reject the discount. The ACCA Code of Ethics and Conduct allows acceptance of goods and hospitality that are considered trivial and inconsequential. Approval would be sought from the audit engagement partner not the audit manager.

15   OPTION D

The ACCA Code of Ethics and Conduct states that preparation of tax returns does not generally create a self-review threat. This is because the audit firm would not be calculating the figures to include in the return. The procedure of preparing the tax return is mechanical in nature. Provision of tax advice could create a significant self-review threat as it may be discovered at a later date that the advice was not appropriate and the firm may be reluctant to admit this to the client.

16   OPTIONS 2 AND 4

The audit firm must obtain consent from both firms. If consent is not given, the firm must decide which client to keep. The firm does not have to choose its current audit client. It could decide to resign from the audit of Winnie Co and accept the audit of Piglet Co. There is no requirement for an audit firm to consult with ACCA and request permission when a conflict of interest such as the one described arises.

17   OPTION 2

The audit teams of each client would sign a confidentiality agreement but it would not be necessary to have all employees of the firm sign confidentiality agreements.

18   OPTION 4

Partner rotation is only a requirement for listed companies and only once the partner has been in place for seven years. Self-review is the main threat created when additional services such as payroll and bookkeeping are provided to an audit client. Confidentiality is not an issue as the information obtained relates to the same client and is not being provided to any other parties. Payroll and bookkeeping services can be provided to a non-listed audit client if they are routine and mechanical in nature. Advice on accounting policies is also acceptable as long as the client is responsible for making decisions on which accounting policies to use.

19   OPTION 3

A contingent fee arrangement such as the one described creates a self-interest threat. The auditor would have a financial interest in the client achieving a higher profit and may ignore misstatements which would reduce profit if adjusted. The proposal must be rejected as the ACCA Code of Ethics and Conduct does not allow contingent fee arrangements for assurance work.

20

Senior management is correct that reporting the company will constitute a breach of confidentiality	True	**False**
Tigger & Co must report the breach of laws and regulations to the appropriate authority if the client refuses	**True**	False
Tigger & Co must report the breach of laws and regulations as it is a public interest matter	**True**	False
Tigger & Co must report the matter to the parent company and the audit firm responsible for the parent company audit	**True**	False

In accordance with *Responding to Non-Compliance with Laws and Regulations* and ISA 250 (Revised) *Consideration of Laws and Regulations in an Audit of Financial Statements*, the auditor has increased responsibility when non-compliance by a client is identified. The auditor must try and get the client to report the matter themselves in the first instance. If the client refuses and the breach is likely to be in the public interest, the auditor must report the matter to the appropriate authority.

As Eeyore Co is a global company and the issue relates to environmental pollution, it is highly likely to be considered a public interest matter. As Eeyore Co is a subsidiary, the matter must also be reported to the parent company and any other auditors involved such as the parent company auditor.

21

Ola Osbourne is the chair and chief executive	Strength	**Deficiency**
All of the current NEDs are independent	**Strength**	Deficiency
Ola Osbourne is considering appointing her friend as a non-executive director	Strength	**Deficiency**

The chair and chief executive roles should be performed by different people to avoid too much power being held by one person. In addition, the chair should be independent on appointment and this is not the case with Ola Osbourne who has only recently been appointed chair after being chief executive for five years.

Independent non-executive directors are more likely to ensure the company takes decisions which are in the best interests of the shareholders.

Directors, both executive and non-executive, should be appointed based on merit, relevant skills and experience.

22   OPTION 4

The audit committee must comprise independent NEDs. In addition, the board chair cannot be a member of the audit committee. Therefore neither can be members of the audit committee.

23   1D, 2C

To balance the board of directors, two more non-executive directors need to be appointed. This will create a board of eight directors in total, four of which will be independent non-executive directors. It is unlikely that a company would reduce the number of directors to achieve a balance.

Executive directors' remuneration should include performance related pay linked with the long-term sustainable success of the company, such as share options.

24   OPTION 1

The chair must be independent on appointment. Jules Jardine has been a member of the board for ten years. Independence is deemed to be compromised if a director has served on the board for more than nine years. Options 2, 3 and 4 are all provisions of the Corporate Governance Code.

25

Remuneration of directors should be set by the Nomination Committee	True	**False**
Workforce remuneration should be taken into consideration when setting the remuneration of executive directors	**True**	False
The company should be able to withhold bonuses and share awards from directors whose performance is not acceptable	**True**	False

Remuneration should be set by the remuneration committee to ensure a fair and transparent process. Remuneration of executive directors should be determined using formal and transparent procedures. Executive directors should receive performance related pay linked with sustainable long-term success of the company to incentivise the executive directors to grow the business and maximise shareholder wealth. This should be related to the long term performance of the company rather than short term profits which could provide incentive to manipulate results. Non-executive directors should be paid a fixed salary which represents the time and commitment to the role, in order to improve their independence.

Workforce remuneration and related policies should be taken into account when setting executive directors' remuneration.

Remuneration schemes should include provisions that enable the company to recover or withhold amounts or share awards to reduce the risk of directors being rewarded when the company is under-performing.

26   2D

The fundamental principle at risk is professional competence and due care as many of the audit team are new and do not have relevant experience in relation to the specialised industry in which Fir Co operates. It is not appropriate to reinstate the previous partner as in line with the ACCA *Code of Ethics and Conduct*, the previous partner has been rotated after seven years to prevent a familiarity threat. The audit firm should offer appropriate training for the audit team to ensure they have the necessary knowledge to carry out the work.

27   2C

As the previous audit manager has taken up employment with the client as the finance director, there is a familiarity threat due to the ongoing relationship between the old and new audit manager. The familiarity threat is not so severe that the firm would need to resign. It is not practical to prevent the audit manager speaking to the finance director during an audit as this will reduce the efficiency and effectiveness of the audit. A new audit manager should be appointed.

28

	Self-review	Self-interest	Advocacy
Routine maintenance of payroll records	✓		
Assistance with the selection of a new non-executive director		✓	
Tax services whereby Sycamore & Co would liaise with the tax authority on Fir Co's behalf			✓

As per the ACCA *Code of Ethics and Conduct*, the following threats would be created from carrying out the non-audit services requested by Fir Co:

Payroll – Self-review as the auditor will also be involved in auditing the figures included in the financial statements in relation to wages and salaries.

Recruitment – Self-interest as the auditor would be involved in selecting an officer of the company who has significant influence over the financial statements and audit.

Tax – Advocacy as the auditor may be perceived to be representing and promoting Fir Co's interest in liaising with the tax authority.

29   OPTION 3

Using separate teams will not address the self-interest threat from the fee levels as separating the teams will not alleviate the firm's potential financial dependence on Fir Co.

30   OPTION 2

As per ACCA *Code of Ethics and Conduct*, confidential information may be disclosed when such disclosure is required by law.

31   OPTION 4

In line with ACCA's *Code of Ethics and Conduct*, a self-interest threat would arise due to the personal relationship between the audit engagement partner and finance director.

A self-interest threat, not intimidation threat, would arise as a result of the overdue fee and due to the nature of the non-audit work, it is unlikely that a self-review threat would arise.

32   OPTION 3

In order to maintain independence, Cassie Dixon would be the most appropriate replacement as audit engagement partner as she has no ongoing relationship with Bush Co. Appointing any of the other potential replacements would give rise to self-review or familiarity threats to independence.

33   OPTION 2

If Alan Marshlow accepts the position as a non-executive director for Plant Co, self-interest and self-review threats are created which are so significant that no safeguards can be implemented. Further as per ACCA's *Code of Ethics and Conduct*, no partner of the firm should serve as a director of an audit client and as such, Horti & Co would need to resign as auditor.

34   OPTION 3

Assuming a management responsibility is when the auditor is involved in leading or directing the company or making decisions which are the remit of management.

Designing and maintaining internal controls, determining which recommendations to implement and setting the scope of work are all decisions which should be taken by management.

35   OPTION 1

Weed Co is a listed company and the fees received by Horti & Co from the company have exceeded 15% of the firm's total fees for two years. As per ACCA's *Code of Ethics and Conduct*, this should be disclosed to those charged with governance and an appropriate safeguard should be implemented. In this case, it would be appropriate to have a pre-issuance review carried out prior to issuing the audit opinion for the current year.

36   OPTION 1

The offer of gifts from an audit client can create a threats of self-interest and familiarity. The ACCA Code of Ethics and Conduct states that gifts must be declined if they are offered as an inducement to influence the auditor's behaviour, even if they are trivial and inconsequential. As the finance director has commented that the offer is intended to make the audit team more favourable toward the client, the offer is an inducement and must be declined.

37   OPTION 2

The ACCA Code of Ethics and Conduct states that when fees from a non-listed client represent a large proportion of the firm's total fees, the firm must implement safeguards such as increasing the client base to reduce dependency and having an independent review of the work. Options 3 and 4 are actions that would need to be taken if LV Fones Co was a listed company.

38   OPTION 4

The audit senior must not be assigned to the audit of LV Fones Co as a self-review threat will be created. The audit senior may be responsible for auditing areas which he or she was responsible for when on secondment and may not detect misstatements or may not wish to admit to misstatements if detected. A familiarity threat may also be created because the audit senior may have developed friendships with client staff whilst on secondment.

39   OPTION 3

All three actions should be taken by the audit firm if fees remain outstanding.

40

Ethical threat	Course of action
Intimidation	Resign from the audit engagement
Familiarity	Structure the audit partner's responsibilities to reduce the potential impact to the engagement
Self-interest	Remove the audit partner from the audit

Friendships between the auditor and client create a familiarity threat as the auditor may be too trusting of people they know well, and may therefore exercise less professional scepticism. The audit firm would only need to resign from the engagement if there was no alternative engagement partner that could be assigned to the audit of LV Fones Co. The audit engagement partner has the most influence over the audit and it would be impossible to structure the partner's responsibilities to reduce the potential impact whilst keeping him or her in charge of the engagement. The only way this can be achieved is to remove the partner from the audit and replace with a different partner.

41   1E, 2D, 3A

Difficulties retaining or obtaining an audit firm may indicate that management of Mickey Co lack integrity and audit firms are not willing to take on the engagement. As the audit is required to be completed within a tight deadline, the firm will need to go through the acceptance process, obtain an understanding of the client, plan and perform the audit and issue the auditor's report within three months. This will require sufficient resources to ensure the work can be completed to a high standard and the form may not have sufficient resource to achieve this. As Mickey Co is a main competitor of Goofy Co, another audit client of the firm, a conflict of interest arises which creates a threat to objectivity and confidentiality.

42   OPTION 2

To manage the conflict of interest the firm must: 1. Inform Mickey Co and Goofy Co. 2. Obtain consent to act. 3. Implement safeguards. 4. Perform an engagement quality review.

43   OPTION 3

Ethical threat	Course of action
Intimidation	Remove the audit engagement partner from the audit
Familiarity	Structure the audit partner's responsibilities to reduce the potential impact to the engagement
Self-interest	Inform Goofy Co that it should not employ the audit engagement partner's son

As the son works as a sales manager, he is not in a position to influence the financial statements and therefore this does not create significant familiarity or intimidation threats.

A significant self-interest threat is created by the son receiving shares as part of his remuneration. The ACCA Code of Ethics and Conduct states that a direct, or material indirect financial interest must not be held by the audit team or an immediate family member of the audit team. The partner will need to be removed from the audit.

44   OPTION 4

The ACCA Code of Ethics and Conduct states that contingent fee arrangements are not allowed for non-assurance services provided to audit clients if the fee will be significant to the firm, therefore option 4 is the most appropriate answer.

45   OPTION 1

The ACCA Code of Ethics and Conduct states that reviewing qualifications and assessing competence of applicants does not generally create a threat to objectivity as the auditor is not making any management decisions that could cause a threat to objectivity. Goofy Co can provide this service provided a management responsibility is not assumed.

46   OPTION 4

In accordance with the Corporate Governance Code 2018, the board chair must be independent on appointment and must therefore be appointed externally.

At least half of the board, excluding the chair, must be independent non-executive directors. There should be workforce representation on the board. Independence is deemed to be compromised when a director has served for nine years, therefore Linda must be replaced next year as an independent non-executive director. She can continue to be a member of the board if re-elected but she will not be independent.

47   OPTION 2

The board chair must be independent on appointment. The board chair cannot sit on the audit committee but can be a member of the remuneration committee provided they are not the committee chair. Remuneration of non-executive directors must be a fixed salary. Restrictions on the number of directorships a person can take are only applicable to the largest 100 listed companies (e.g. FTSE 100).

48   OPTION 1

Independence is compromised if a non-executive director was employed by the company less than five years ago, has owned shares in the company within the last three years, or receives remuneration from the company other than a fixed salary for the role of non-executive director, such as a pension.

49   OPTION 2

The lack of independence due to the relationship with the chief executive along with the request for a fixed three year contract when all directors must stand for re-election annually are both disadvantages to Mica taking a non-executive director position.

50   OPTIONS 2 AND 3

In accordance with the Corporate Governance Code 2018, there should be a formal and rigorous annual evaluation of the performance of the board, its committees, the chair and the individual directors. The annual report should describe how the nomination committee has ensured appropriate appointments have been made including gender balance and diversity. A succession plan should be in place for the board and senior management, not just the chair and chief executive. The nomination committee must comprise a majority independent non-executive directors but does not require all members to be INEDs.

PLANNING AND RISK ASSESSMENT

51 OPTION 2

Oil and gas companies are heavily regulated therefore the effect of non-compliance is likely to be a significant audit risk. Provisions and contingent liabilities may arise if there are issues such as oil spills or injury to employees in the workplace given the hazardous nature of the industry. As the company operates in three continents, foreign currency transactions are likely to be significant. Trade payables may be a risk for certain clients but in relation to the other risks stated, is unlikely to be a significant risk.

52 OPTIONS 2 AND 5

Detection risk is greater due to the lack of knowledge and experience of the client. In order to address this, the auditor must spend time obtaining an understanding of the client. The auditor can request copies of working papers from the previous auditor to help with this.

53 OPTION 1

Materiality ranges using traditional benchmarks:

| Revenue (½% – 1%) | $620,000 – $1,240,000 |
| Profit before tax (5% – 10%) | $475,000 – $950,000 |

As Veryan Co is a new audit client it is likely that materiality will be set at the lower end of the materiality scale to reflect the increased detection risk. Option 1 is 16% of profit and 1.2% of revenue and is therefore too high based on the traditional benchmark calculations. Options 2, 3 and 4 all sit within the ranges calculated above.

54

Cut-off of revenue is an audit risk	**Consistent**	**Not consistent**
Completeness of revenue is an audit risk	Consistent	**Not consistent**
Occurrence of revenue is an audit risk	**Consistent**	Not consistent

Revenue has increased by 24% compared with 12% in previous years. Revenue may be overstated due to cut-off errors where sales relating to next year have been included in this year. Revenue may be overstated if sales have not occurred and are fictitious. Completeness would be a risk if revenue was lower than expected, however, as the profit margin has increased from 6% (6/100 × 100) to 7.7% (9.5/124 × 100) revenue appears to be overstated rather than understated.

55 1E, 2G, 3F

Receivables

To assess the recoverability of receivables, reviewing correspondence with customers may highlight any disputes which indicate that payment will not be made. Direct confirmation of a customer balance confirms existence of the debt but does not provide evidence that it will be paid.

Non-current assets

Impairment of non-current assets would necessitate an increased depreciation charge. Reviewing the depreciation charge for adequacy would enable the auditor to assess whether an impairment charge has been made. Inspection of the exploration sites is not a practical or effective audit procedure.

Intangible assets (licences)

Amortisation of intangible assets can be checked by calculating the expected amortisation charge and comparing it with management's figure. Inspecting the licence agreement will only confirm the terms of the licence but will not state the amortisation charge that should be made each year.

56   OPTION 4

Increased audit risk arising from increased detection risk will result in increased quality control procedures such as the need for an engagement quality control review. The auditor's lack of cumulative knowledge and experience of a client is a detection risk. Competence should have been considered **before** accepting. It is not professional to resign immediately after accepting an engagement. The audit firm should have contacted the outgoing auditor **before** accepting to enquire about any professional matters which would affect the acceptance decision.

57   OPTION 2

The risk of revenue cut-off errors increases with employees aiming to maximise their current year bonus. The increased risk of a reduction in profits as a result of irrecoverable debts is a business risk. Revenue is more likely to be overstated in order to achieve a higher bonus. The bonus would have no impact on the customer response level to direct confirmation requests.

58

	20X5	20X4
Receivables collection period	35 (121/1267) × 365	30 (100/1205) × 365
Inventory holding period	58 (160/1013) × 365	47 (125/965) × 365

Formulae:

Receivables collection period = receivables/revenue × 365

Inventory holding period = inventory/cost of sales × 365

59   OPTION 1

Cut-off testing would not provide relevant evidence to the potential valuation issues.

60   OPTIONS 3 AND 4

Option 1 refers to final analytical procedures performed at the completion stage of the audit. Option 2 refers to substantive analytical procedures performed during the fieldwork stage of the audit.

61

	20X5	**20X4**
Gross margin	44.0% (5.5/12.5 × 100)	46.7% (7/15 × 100)
Current ratio	2.2 (1.9 + 3.1 + 0.8)/(1.6 + 1.0)	4.4 (1.4 + 2.0 + 1.9)/1.2

Formulae:

Gross margin = gross profit/revenue × 100

Current ratio = current assets / current liabilities

As the loan is due for payment on 31 January 20X6, this is a current liability in 20X5 but not 20X4.

62   OPTION 3

	20X5	**20X4**
Payables payment period	83 (1.6/7 × 365)	55 (1.2/8 × 365)

Payables payment period = payables/cost of sales × 365

The payables payment period has increased by 28 days. This could indicate cash flow problems which the auditor will need to consider as part of its going concern assessment. If there are uncertainties over the company's ability to continue as a going concern, disclosure will be required in the notes to the financial statements and the auditor's report will need to reference the client's disclosure.

Options 1 and 2 are not correct as the payables payment period has increased not decreased. Option 4 would not need to be considered by the auditor as there is no indication of cash flow problems affecting going concern.

63   OPTIONS 1, 2 AND 6

Options 1, 2 and 6 are audit risks as they clearly describe how the financial statements may be materially misstated. Options 3, 4 and 5 are business risks as they describe issues the directors would be concerned about but which would not necessarily result in the financial statements being materially misstated.

64   OPTIONS 2 AND 3

Options 2 and 3 will allow the auditor to make an assessment of the appropriateness of the change. Option 4 is of no audit value as it is known the policy has changed during the year. In relation to option 1, the auditor will still need to assess the appropriateness of the change in useful life and discuss the matter with management if it is not appropriate. Whilst the change may not have a material impact this year, it may become material in subsequent years therefore the issue should be addressed as soon as it is identified.

65   OPTION 3

Option 1 describes materiality. Option 2 describes tolerable misstatement. Option 4 describes a clearly trivial threshold.

66 OPTION 3

There is no suggestion of any issue that would cause the auditor to consider resigning. The audit team should be fully briefed and advised to be vigilant. The finance director should also be advised that their assistance is likely to be requested by the audit team in the absence of a financial controller.

67 OPTIONS 2, 3 AND 5

Lack of supplier statement reconciliations can mean misstatements within payables and accruals go undetected. As controls are not effective in this area, increased substantive testing will need to be performed. The auditor should not perform the reconciliations as this is the responsibility of Hawk. There is no need to send requests for confirmations if the client has received a supplier statement. The issue relates to the client not reconciling the statement to their own ledgers.

68 OPTION 4

It would not be appropriate or professional for the auditor to discuss the claim with the financial controller, especially when legal proceedings are ongoing.

69 OPTION D

Gross profit margin

The ratio has decreased from 26% to 17% which indicates that website sales may not be completely recorded.

If sales had not occurred, the revenue balance would be overstated and the gross profit margin would increase.

If revenue had been recognised too early, the revenue balance would be overstated and the gross profit margin would increase.

Payables payment period

The ratio has decreased from 75 to 40 days which indicates understatement of payables i.e. payables may not be completely recorded.

Suppliers withdrawing credit terms is a business risk, not an audit risk.

If purchase invoices have been recorded twice, the payables balance would be overstated and the payables payment period would increase.

Receivables collection period

The ratio has increased from 29 to 38 days which indicates that receivables may be overvalued.

Extended credit terms may have been given to customers is not an audit risk.

If receivables are not completely recorded, the receivables balance would be understated and the receivables collection period would decrease.

70   OPTION 2

As the analytical procedures are being performed at the planning stage using the most recent management accounts of Hawk Co, the financial statement figures are not being tested. Analytical procedures at the planning stage are performed to help identify areas of potential risk and to obtain an understanding of the client. When the draft financial statement figures are available, **substantive** analytical procedures can be used to help detect material misstatements.

71   OPTION 1

Procedures 3 and 4 are tests of control not substantive procedures.

72   1C, 2C, 3D, 4A

Matter		Audit strategy section	
1	Risk of material misstatement including the risk of fraud	C	Significant factors, preliminary engagement activities, and knowledge gained on other engagements
2	Use of professional scepticism	C	Significant factors, preliminary engagement activities, and knowledge gained on other engagements
3	Selection of the audit team	D	Nature, timing and extent of resources
4	Use of computer-assisted audit techniques	A	Characteristics of the engagement

73   OPTION 4

The fraud involves an employee stealing money from the company therefore is an example of misappropriation of assets. Detection risk will need to decrease as control risk is higher. For the employee to be able to commit this type of fraud, internal controls must not be working effectively therefore control risk is higher. The auditor can only assess control risk, they cannot influence it. Detection risk is the only component of audit risk the auditor can change. The risk of fraud must always be discussed with the audit team in accordance with ISA 240 *The Auditor's Responsibilities Relating to Fraud in an Audit of Financial Statements*.

74   OPTION 3

If employees working within the same department are related there is an increased risk of collusion which would circumvent any segregation of duties control. Therefore, to prevent frauds occurring in the payroll department, the people working together should not be related. Exception reports and review of employee lists by department managers would detect if fictitious employees had been set up on the payroll system. However, this would be after the fraud had occurred. Comparison of the monthly payroll cost with the prior month may detect fraud if the fraud is of sufficient scale to cause a significant variance but will not prevent fraud.

75 OPTIONS 1, 4 AND 5

A discussion with management would be useful to identify any other suspected frauds. Searching for duplicate bank account numbers would identify possible other frauds that are occurring. Reconciling the number of employees to the number of people being paid will identify fictitious employees on the payroll system.

Reporting the matter to the police is a management function and therefore not an audit procedure to detect further frauds.

As the employee had created fictitious employees to be paid in the payroll system, the details on the payroll records will match the payments in the bank statements therefore further fraud would not be detected.

INTERNAL CONTROLS

76

	Narrative notes	Internal control questionnaires	Both
Advantages			
Can be prepared in advance		✓	
Easy to understand			✓
Disadvantages			
May overstate the controls		✓	
Some controls may be missed			✓

Narrative notes are simple to record and easy to understand. However, controls may be difficult to pick out from the detail.

Internal control questionnaires are prepared in advance which can ensure that all typical controls are covered. However, the ICQ may not identify unusual controls. Clients may overstate the controls by stating that they have the controls listed when in fact they don't. As the questionnaire is standardised it is easy to understand.

77

			Explanation
1	Strength	Deficiency	The goods received should be agreed to the authorised purchase order before signing the delivery note to ensure that only goods actually ordered are accepted. The supplier's delivery note will record what has been sent which may not be the same as the purchase order.
2	Strength	Deficiency	Matching the purchase invoice to the GRN ensures the goods being paid for have been received. Matching the GRN to the order ensures the goods received were ordered. Keeping the documents filed together provides a complete audit trail to support the transaction.

			Explanation
3	Strength	Deficiency	Monthly reviews of standing data by the department manager ensures that the correct details are held on a regular basis. Any employees who have left the company would be identified and could be removed from the payroll records before an invalid payment is made.
4	Strength	Deficiency	Pre-printed payroll sheets ensure that only genuine employees are paid. If any names are added to the sheets this will highlight a potential fraud or error which can be investigated before payment is made.

78 OPTION 2

By reviewing the payment list the finance director will be able to identify any unusual names or duplicate names. This control will ensure only valid employees are paid. The bank transfer list will only show details of names and net pay therefore will not identify incorrect classification of costs, incorrect hours, or incorrect calculations unless a significant error was made.

79 OPTION 3

If reliance can be placed on the internal controls, reduced substantive testing can be performed. If the controls are working effectively it is likely that written representations from management will be more reliable rather than less reliable. Similarly, if controls are effective, the information used for analytical procedures is likely to be more reliable and therefore more reliance can be placed on analytical procedures as compared with tests of detail. Effective controls are unlikely to influence the amount of evidence obtained from a third party (although ineffective controls would influence the auditor to obtain more evidence from third parties as client generated evidence will be less reliable).

80

Recalculate the total of the bank transfer list	Test of control	Substantive procedure
Inspect the bank transfer list for evidence of the finance director's signature	Test of control	Substantive procedure
For a sample of employees, agree the salary details in the standing data files to the calculation of the employee's monthly salary as per the payslip	Test of control	Substantive procedure
Review the procedures to ensure payroll files and documents are kept secure and confidential	Test of control	Substantive procedure

A substantive procedure is used to test the payroll figure in the financial statements.

A test of control is used to test the effectiveness of controls over payroll processing.

81 OPTION 3

Discounts received relate to the purchases system.

82 1C, 2A, 3D, 4B

Deficiency		Explanation	
(i)	Availability of inventory is not checked at the time of ordering	C	Risk of orders not being fulfilled on a timely basis
(ii)	Telephone orders are not recorded immediately	A	Risk of incorrect orders being despatched
(iii)	Order forms are not sequentially numbered	D	Orders may go missing leading to unfulfilled orders
(iv)	The online ordering system allows customers to exceed their credit limit	B	Risk of irrecoverable debts

83 OPTIONS 1 AND 4

The system should not allow credit limits to be exceeded by any amount. Changes to credit limits should only be performed by a responsible senior official.

84 OPTION 2

Orders should be sequentially pre-numbered and a regular sequence check performed to ensure the sequence is complete. Instructing customers not to place orders by telephone may result in sales being lost. A better system would be to enter the orders into the system immediately whilst the customer is placing the order. Option 1 is a recommendation for deficiency (i).

85 OPTION 3

To increase independence of the internal auditors, the findings should be communicated to those charged with governance. If the findings are reported directly to the finance director there is a risk that the finance director perceives any deficiencies as a criticism and may not report the findings to the board of directors.

An internal audit assignment is performed for the company. There is no requirement for findings to be communicated to the external auditor or the shareholders.

86 OPTION 2

Tracing a transaction through the system to ensure it is recorded in the sales day book is a substantive procedure testing the assertion of completeness.

87

	General	Application
Daily backups of the system	**General**	Application
Authorisation of purchase orders	General	**Application**
Minimum order quantities	General	**Application**
Automatic updating of inventory once goods are sold	General	**Application**

Backups relates to the whole computer system therefore are a general control. Authorisation, minimum order quantities and automatic updating of inventory relate to individual aspects of the purchasing and inventory systems therefore are application controls.

88   OPTION 1

Reviewing inventory levels immediately before and after a sales order has been processed enables the auditor to ensure the inventory level is updated automatically. Counting a sample of items to agree the quantities in the system does not prove the system updates automatically. The quantities may agree because that type of inventory may not have been sold recently and the quantities reflect the results of the last inventory count. Reviewing the inventory quantities in the system does not confirm the quantities held in the warehouse or that the system updates automatically. The auditor would not contact a customer to make an enquiry such as the one described.

89

Control	
The inventory system is automatically updated to reflect that inventory has been allocated to a sales order	✓
The system will flag if there is insufficient inventory to fulfil the order	✓
When inventory falls to a minimum level a purchase order is automatically created and sent to the purchasing manager for authorisation	✓
The purchase order is automatically sent electronically to the approved supplier for that item	✓

As all of the controls stated are computerised controls, a dummy order can be used to test them.

90   OPTIONS 1 AND 3

To rely on the internal auditor's work, the external auditor should review the internal auditor's working papers and re-perform a sample of the tests again. An expert would not need to be used in this situation as the auditor can easily see if the internal auditor has performed the work properly by re-performing a sample of tests. The auditor cannot simply assume that the presence of an audit committee means the work of the internal auditor will be reliable, they must assess the work to ensure it is appropriate for audit purposes.

91   OPTIONS 2 AND 4

A control objective should describe a risk to be mitigated by an internal control. Options 1 and 5 describe the internal control but not the risk. Option 3 is a control objective relating to the recording of capital expenditure items but maintenance of the register is not the responsibility of the capital expenditure committee therefore is not a control objective addressed by their work.

92

The internal audit department confirms the non-current asset register is complete	Physical control	Performance review	Information processing
Variances between actual and budgeted expenditure are analysed in the quarterly management accounts	Segregation of duties	Performance review	Information processing
The non-current asset register is password protected	Physical control	Performance review	Segregation of duties

93   OPTION 4

The requisition is approved (authorised) by the capital expenditure committee. The purchase order is authorised by the purchasing director once checked against the approved requisition. Both of these documents contain signatures confirming authorisation/approval. The meeting minutes also contain evidence of the approval of the capital expenditure committee.

The GRN is not authorised although it should be matched to a copy of the authorised purchase order. This is not as persuasive as the signed requisition and order.

It will be assumed that if the controls have worked throughout the cycle, assets should not be able to be purchased and recorded in the non-current asset register unless they have been authorised. This is not as persuasive as the signed requisition and order.

94   OPTION 3

When an external auditor performs a comparison of actual to budget, this is a substantive analytical procedure. The other three procedures provide evidence that a control has operated effectively and are therefore tests of control.

95   OPTION 4

According to ISA 610 *Using the Work of Internal Auditors*, the external auditor must not assign work to the internal auditor which involves significant judgment, a high risk of material misstatement or with which the internal auditor has been involved. Cash counts will be the most appropriate as they do not involve significant judgment and there is nothing to indicate that the petty cash balance is material. The internal audit department is currently assessing internal controls over non-current assets therefore is work with which the internal auditor has recently been involved and may create a self-review threat. Revenue recognition is likely to involve significant judgment and possibly a high risk of material misstatement. Valuation of inventory for a manufacturer is likely to include significant work-in-progress which also involves significant judgment and a high risk of material misstatement.

AUDIT EVIDENCE

96   OPTION 2

A supplier with a low balance at the year end but with a high volume of transactions during the year may indicate that not all liabilities have been recorded at the year-end date.

97   OPTION 3

A purchase of a large volume of goods close to the year end would increase the payables payment period.

The prompt payment and trade discounts would both decrease the payables payment period, and the extended credit terms in this instance would have no impact as there is no closing balance with the new supplier.

98   OPTION 4

The difference of $144,640 with Oxford Co relates to goods which were received by Chester Co prior to the year end but were not recorded in the accounting records until after the year-end date. As Chester Co had a liability to pay for the goods at the date of receipt, an accrual should be created for the goods received not yet invoiced.

99   OPTION 1

The difference in respect of Poole Co may have arisen if the invoice had been paid twice in error as an additional $156,403 will have been debited to the supplier account.

100   OPTION 2

Reviewing the accruals listing would not help the auditor confirm the payables ledger balance with Bath Co as accruals are recorded separately from the payables ledger balance.

101   OPTION 4

The cut-off assertion relates to transactions being recorded in the correct accounting period. In this case, payroll costs reflect payroll transactions for the period to 31 October 20X6. Options 1, 2 and 3 relate to the assertions of classification, accuracy and completeness.

102   OPTION 2

The most reliable evidence will be the work performed by the audit team member as auditor generated evidence is the most reliable. Verbal confirmation is the least reliable form of evidence as it can be disputed or retracted. Written confirmation is the next least reliable form of evidence as it is client generated.

103 OPTION 1

Prior year expense: $17,000,000

Employee numbers reduce from 500 to 450, a decrease of 10%.

Effect of redundancies: $17,000,000 × 90% = $15,300,000.

Effect of pay rise: ($15,300,000 × 2/12) + ($15,300,000 × 106/100 × 10/12) = $16,065,000

Effect of bonus: $16,065,000 + (450 × $1,500) = $16,740,000.

Alternatively, the calculation can be done as follows:

Prior year salaries adjusted for redundancies	= $17m × 0.9	= $15.3m
Adjust for wage rise for remaining staff	= $15.3m × 6% × 10/12	= $0.765m
Include bonus	= $1,500 × 450	= $0.675m
Total		= $16.74m

104 OPTIONS 3 AND 4

Analytical procedures evaluate trends and relationships between data. The auditor should investigate any unusual relationships which don't fit in with their expectation as it may indicate misstatement. A comparison to the prior year with an investigation of differences and a proof in total calculations are both examples of substantive analytical procedures. Recalculation is a simple arithmetical check. Agreeing the wages expense per the payroll system to the draft financial statements involves inspection.

105

1	Review the treatment of a sample of post year-end returns	Accuracy	Completeness	**Occurrence**
2	Select a sample of goods despatched notes and agree to invoices in the sales day book	Accuracy	**Completeness**	Occurrence
3	Select a sample of invoices from the sales day book and agree to goods despatched notes	Accuracy	Completeness	**Occurrence**
4	Select a sample of invoices and recalculate the invoiced amount agreeing to price list	**Accuracy**	Completeness	Occurrence

The occurrence assertion means transactions have occurred and pertain to the entity, i.e. the sale is a genuine transaction of the business. Post year-end returns would mean the transaction had not really occurred and should be removed from sales. Agreeing a sample of invoices to GDNs allows the auditor to confirm the sale is genuine. Selecting items from outside of the accounting records and tracing them into the records is a test for completeness. Recalculating invoices and confirming prices enables the auditor to test accuracy.

106 OPTIONS 1, 2 AND 3

Where completeness is the key assertion, the sample should be selected to verify where the balance may be understated and therefore should include suppliers with material balances, suppliers with a high volume of business with Poppy Co and major suppliers with no outstanding balance at the year-end.

107 OPTION 1

In order to determine if the balance with Lily Co is understated, the auditor should determine if the goods should be included in payables at the year-end by inspecting the goods received note. There is no need to send a confirmation request to Lily Co as a supplier statement has been obtained.

108 OPTION 3

To confirm the balance with Carnation Co, the auditor must determine if the liability exists for the disputed items at the year-end by reviewing pre year-end goods returned notes and post year-end credit notes to verify that the goods have been returned and the order cancelled by the supplier.

109 OPTION 2

Although the control error is immaterial, the auditor must reach a conclusion on the population, based on the sample selected. In order to do so the effect of the error must be considered in relation to the whole population. It is not appropriate to project a one-off error across the population as by its nature it is not representative of the population.

110

Selecting a sample of supplier balances for testing using monetary unit sampling	**Test data**	**Audit software**
Recalculating the ageing of trade payables to identify balances which may be in dispute	**Test data**	**Audit software**
Calculation of trade payables payment period to use in analytical procedures	**Test data**	**Audit software**
Inputting dummy purchase invoices into the client system to see if processed correctly	**Test data**	**Audit software**

Test data involves inputting dummy transactions into the client's system to test how the transactions are processed. The other options are examples of audit software.

111 OPTION 4

A direct confirmation will confirm the amount outstanding but not the intention of the customer to pay this amount. The industry journal articles are unlikely to provide specific detail regarding a company's ability to pay specific debts. Reviewing post year-end receipts will confirm actual recoverability of the outstanding balance therefore provides the most reliable evidence.

112 OPTIONS 2 AND 3

Options 1 and 4 relate to valuation.

113 OPTIONS 1 AND 2

A decrease in selling price may result in the cost of inventory being higher than net realisable value (NRV). Increased inventory levels for a company experiencing a reduction in sales may result in inventory not being sold and therefore NRV may be lower than cost. Inventory turnover would need to decrease to indicate valuation issues. There is nothing to indicate that the nature of the inventory would result in valuation issues. Eagle does not have the right to include third party inventory in their financial statements. Inclusion would overstate inventory quantities but would not represent overvaluation.

114

Observe the client's staff to ensure they are following the inventory count instructions	**Test of control**	**Substantive procedure**
Inspect the inventory for evidence of damage or obsolescence	Test of control	**Substantive procedure**
Re-perform the reconciliation from the inventory count date to the year-end date for inventory to assess the accuracy of the inventory quantities.	Test of control	**Substantive procedure**

Observing the count to ensure the count instructions are followed will provide the auditor with evidence that the controls over the inventory count are operating effectively. The other two tests are substantive in nature providing evidence over the accuracy, valuation and allocation assertion.

115 OPTION 1

The auditor needs to establish whether the claim is probable to succeed before they can ask the client to recognise a provision. If the claim is not probable to succeed it should not be recognised. If it is possible to succeed it should be disclosed as a contingent liability. This evidence should be obtained from the legal adviser as they are an independent expert. The auditor would review board minutes to ascertain the view of the board as a whole in respect of the claim. It would not be appropriate for the auditor to contact the customer making the claim against the client.

116 OPTION 3

The client performs the inventory count. The external auditor will perform a sample of test counts to ensure the count is accurate. The primary objective of the count is to ascertain accurate quantities. Some companies will produce items 24 hours a day. Provided the count is properly organised to ensure goods are not moved in and out of the counting area during the count the company does not need to cease production. ISA 501 *Audit Evidence – Specific Considerations for Selected Items* requires the auditor to attend the inventory count if inventory is a material balance.

117 OPTION 3

If the timetable is not monitored, some areas could be missed and all inventory may not be counted at least once a year.

118

Staple & Co must attend at least one count to ensure adequate controls are applied	True	False
Cut-off testing will only need to be performed if a full count is carried out at the year-end	True	False
All lines of inventory must be counted at least twice during the year	True	False
Staple & Co should visit the client's premises at least once a year and request a surprise inventory count	True	False

119

1	Strength	Deficiency
2	Strength	Deficiency
3	Strength	Deficiency
4	Strength	Deficiency
5	Strength	Deficiency

Process 1 is a deficiency as counters may just agree with the quantity on the sheet and not actually count the goods.

Process 2 ensures discrepancies are highlighted for further investigation.

Process 3 will lead to understatement of inventory. Old or damaged items should be included until they are sold or scrapped.

Process 4 could result in cut-off errors as it will be difficult to identify goods already counted or not counted if movements are happening during the counting process.

Process 5 ensures inventory belonging to third parties is not recorded in Gloss Co's inventory records.

120 OPTION A

Agreeing the items listed on the count sheets to the physical inventory confirms existence. Agreeing the physical inventory quantities to the count sheet confirms completeness.

121 OPTIONS 2, 3 AND 4

When deciding whether to use sampling the population must be complete, accurate and appropriate for the purpose of the test. If the size of the population is small, sampling may not provide the most efficient method of obtaining evidence. Therefore the size of the population would need to be considered. The time the auditor has available and the ease of obtaining evidence should not influence their audit procedures.

122

1	Sampling	Not sampling
2	Sampling	Not sampling
3	Sampling	Not sampling

Sampling involves selecting items for testing where all items have a chance of selection.

Procedure 1 describes monetary unit selection (MUS) which is a sampling method given in ISA 530 *Audit Sampling*.

Procedures 2 and 3 describe **selection** methods, not sampling methods. These procedures require items with specific characteristics to be tested, therefore all items will not have a chance of selection and as a result do not constitute sampling methods.

123 OPTION 3

Systematic sampling is where a sample is chosen with a constant interval. The starting point is chosen randomly.

124 OPTION 4

Procedure 1

This procedure will test the accuracy of the recorded amount.

The assertion of occurrence is not relevant to the audit of payables. Occurrence is relevant to purchases.

Tutorial note

To test occurrence of purchases, the GRN should be inspected and the invoice should be inspected for the name of the client in order to ensure the goods pertain to the Hemsworth Co.

Procedure 2

This procedure will test completeness of payables as it may identify invoices not included within payables or accruals at the year-end.

The payables ledger, cash book and GRNs are client generated evidence, therefore less reliable than third party generated evidence.

Procedure 3

This procedure will test completeness of payables as well as rights and obligations and existence.

A payables circularisation would be performed if a supplier statement has not been retained or received.

Purchase invoices and supplier statements are third party generated evidence, therefore more reliable than client generated evidence.

125 OPTION 2

The amount of testing should be increased before any further action is taken. The issue should then be discussed with the audit manager before discussing with the client. The audit opinion will only be modified if the errors are material and if they are not corrected by the client. This is the final action to be taken rather than the initial course of action.

126

The actual computer files and programs are not tested therefore the auditor has no direct evidence that the programs are working as expected	Valid	Not valid
Where errors are found in reconciling inputs to outputs, it may be difficult or even impossible to determine why those errors occurred	Valid	Not valid

As the system within the computer is not audited, the audit trail can be difficult to follow. This will mean direct evidence that the programs are working as expected cannot be obtained and it will be difficult to determine why the errors occurred.

127 OPTION 3

As there are 600 customers within the receivables listing, this makes the use of audit software much more beneficial to an auditor.

128 OPTION 4

All are procedures that could be performed using audit software.

129 OPTIONS 1, 3 AND 4

Audit software may slow Delphic Co's systems down. Test data is used to test the programmed controls. Audit software enables calculations and data sorting to be performed more quickly resulting in greater efficiency. Audit staff may need to be trained to use the software. Once the audit software has been designed there are no further costs (unless the client changes its systems). Therefore the audit will only be more costly in the year of set up.

130 OPTION 3

If the partner advises Delphic Co which accounting system to choose, a self-review threat will be created. The external audit team does not need to be present during the implementation and testing. This may be impractical in terms of time and resource required. To save unnecessary time and expense, the audit firm should delay the use of audit software to ensure it is designed to effectively work with the new system.

131 OPTIONS 2 AND 5

The financial statements may still be manipulated to show a break even position or to meet a specific target or objective imposed on the organisation. The auditor's report will be publicly available as taxpayers have a right to see the financial statements and associated auditor's report. The time required for the audit will depend on many factors such as complexity of the organisation and its transactions, the volume of transactions, etc., as is the case with company audits. An audit team should always be competent therefore the team should include people with public sector experience.

132 OPTION 3

An auditor's report for a local government authority will need to refer to going concern uncertainties in the same way as for a company.

133

Compare income by shop and category to the prior year	✓
Inspect credit notes issued post year-end	
Agree totals on till receipts to the sales day book, bank statements and cash book	✓
Obtain the sales day book and cast to confirm accuracy	✓

Inspection of credit notes issued post year-end would identify possible overstatement of income rather than understatement.

134 OPTION 4

All risks given are relevant to Stargazers.

135

Management will have no financial qualifications therefore there is a greater risk of material misstatement	Always true	**May be true**	Never true
Internal control systems will not be as sophisticated as those for profit making companies	Always true	**May be true**	Never true
There are fewer auditing standards applicable to audits of charities	Always true	May be true	**Never true**
Charities such as Stargazers will have different objectives to a profit making company therefore the auditors' assessment of materiality will consider different factors	**Always true**	May be true	Never true

Some charities, particularly larger charities may have good internal control systems and predominantly qualified, paid staff responsible for the financial statements. Smaller charities may not have sufficient income to pay staff and may rely heavily on volunteers. Therefore options (1) and (2) MAY be true. Although ISAs are developed for audits of companies, they should still be followed in an audit of a charity or other NFP.

136 OPTION 3

Companies House (or equivalent) information provides independent evidence of the number of shares in issue. Option 1 is not relevant as a bonus issue does not generate cash. The bonus issue is debited against retained earnings in this case as there is no share premium account to utilise. Option 2 is client generated documentary evidence which is less reliable than third party evidence. Option 4 is client generated verbal confirmation which is less reliable than documentary evidence or evidence from third parties.

137 OPTION 1

Retained earnings	$ million
Brought forward	110
Add profit for the year	40
Add transfer of excess depreciation	2
Less bonus issue	(25)
Less dividend paid (β)	(4)
Carried forward	123

The proposed dividend will not be recognised in retained earnings until it is approved by the shareholders therefore does not form part of the calculation.

The bonus issue has increased share capital by $25 million (50 / 2) with a corresponding reduction to retained earnings.

The transfer of excess depreciation increases retained earnings and reduces the revaluation reserve.

138

Inspect the independent expert's report	**Completeness**	**Cut-off**	**Valuation**
Match the physical properties to the independent expert's report and non-current asset register	**Existence**	**Completeness**	**Presentation**
Recalculate the depreciation on revalued properties	**Completeness**	**Existence**	**Valuation**
Inspect December 20X4 bank statements for payment of dividend	**Occurrence**	**Cut-off**	**Completeness**

The independent expert's report will show up-to-date values of the properties. This will only show the property values for those the client has requested and therefore does not confirm completeness. Cut-off is not a relevant assertion for non-current assets.

Matching the physical assets to the expert's report ensures that all properties have been revalued which is a requirement of IAS 16 *Property, Plant and Equipment* and matching into the non-current asset register confirms completeness of the assets in the financial statements.

Depreciation is used to reflect usage of an asset and affects the value of assets. Existence of assets is usually confirmed by physical inspection. Completeness relates to whether all assets have been recorded therefore not related to depreciation.

Inspection of bank statements specifically for December 20X4 will confirm the dividend paid in that month but will not confirm completeness as other dividends may have been paid at other times during the year. Cut-off would require procedures to be focused around the year end to ensure they have been recorded in the correct accounting period.

139 OPTIONS 2 AND 3

Total assets should equal total equity and liabilities on the statement of financial position.

The auditor will perform substantive tests of detail when auditing these equity and reserves as they are material by nature and any movements will be one-off items which are not consistent year on year.

140 OPTION 4

Procedure 2 tests the occurrence assertion as the procedure starts with the amount included in the financial statements and is agreed to supporting documentation. To test completeness, the procedure must start from outside of the accounting records and agreed into the accounting records.

REVIEW AND REPORTING

141 OPTION 4

As part of the overall review of the financial statements, the auditor should assess whether the information and explanations gathered during the audit and accounting policies are adequately reflected and disclosed.

Pre-conditions should be considered as part of the auditor's acceptance procedures and a detailed review of the audit working papers is conducted as part of the firm's quality control procedures.

142 OPTION 2

An increase in the proportion of cash sales since the interim audit would increase sales but not trade receivables resulting in a decreased trade receivables collection period.

143 OPTION 2

The effective date of the revaluation, the amount of the revaluation increase and the carrying amount of the head office under the cost model are disclosures required by IAS® 16 *Property, Plant and Equipment*.

144 OPTION 1

Misstatements (2) and (3) are individually material and would require adjustment for an unmodified opinion to be issued. Misstatement (1) is immaterial and if Viola Co did not make this adjustment, an unmodified opinion could still be issued.

145 OPTION 1

Misstatement (4) is immaterial at 2.2% of profit before tax ($2.9m/$131.4m) and would not require further disclosure. Therefore as all other adjustments have been made, no material misstatement exists and an unmodified opinion can be issued.

146 OPTION 1

By not testing the sample sizes documented in the audit plan the audit plan has not been followed. Sample sizes will have been chosen based on the judgment of the auditor responsible for planning taking into consideration the requirement to obtain sufficient appropriate evidence. It is not acceptable to defer conclusions to the audit manager. If the sample sizes are considered acceptable at the lower quantities, the audit plan should be updated to reflect this. However, sample sizes should not be reduced simply to save time. If sufficient appropriate evidence is not obtained, material misstatements may go undetected and an inappropriate audit opinion could be issued.

147

Enquiry does not provide sufficient appropriate evidence on its own	**True**	False
The auditor has demonstrated a lack of professional scepticism	**True**	False
A written representation should have been obtained from management confirming that they have disclosed all subsequent events to the auditor	**True**	False
The auditor only needs to perform procedures if they are made aware of any subsequent events	True	**False**

Up to the date of the auditor's report the auditor must perform procedures to identify subsequent events and ensure they have been appropriately reflected in the financial statements. It is only after the auditor's report has been signed that they only need to take action if they become aware of any subsequent events. Enquiry alone is not sufficient. Choosing to rely only on enquiry of management demonstrates a lack of professional scepticism.

148 OPTION 3

The firm would not report their staff to the ACCA. The matter will be dealt with internally through communication and training. Disciplinary measures may be taken by the firm if they consider it necessary to do so.

149 OPTION 4

Post-issuance reviews are performed after the file has been archived and as such no further amendments should be made. A review of significant judgments affecting the audit is performed in a pre-issuance review. A pre-issuance review is also known as a 'hot' review. A post-issuance review is known as a cold review. A post-issuance review is part of the firm's monitoring procedures. If issues are identified it may result in the firm's policies and procedures being revised.

150

The audit engagement partner will review all working papers on the audit file before issuing an opinion	True	**False**
If working papers have been reviewed there is no quality control issue arising from the lack of documentation	True	**False**
All working papers should be signed by the person who prepared them	**True**	False
All team members' work should be reviewed by someone more senior than the preparer	**True**	False

151   OPTIONS 2, 4 AND 5

If the loan is not renegotiated the company may experience cash flow difficulties. The loss of a major supplier could have a serious impact on Oak Co if no alternative can be found. Poor results in a product line expected to account for 30% of revenue could also have a significant impact on the company going forward.

152

			Explanation
The company has increased the sales prices charged to customers while maintaining costs at a level comparable to 20X4	Consistent	**Inconsistent**	The gross profit margin would improve if sales prices charged to customers had increased while costs were maintained. Gross margin has decreased which implies that the company is not making as much return as in the prior year. This would most likely be due to an increase in cost of sales or reduction in sales price. Therefore the comment regarding an increase in sales price contradicts the results of the analytical review.
The company has become more reliant on its overdraft facility during the year	**Consistent**	Inconsistent	The deterioration in the quick ratio from 0.8 in 20X5 to 0.2 in 20X6 is consistent with increased reliance on an overdraft facility.
Due to cash restrictions, the company has encountered delays in paying suppliers	**Consistent**	Inconsistent	The increase in the payables payment period is consistent with delays in paying suppliers.
At the year-end inventory count, a lower level of slow-moving inventory was noted compared to prior year	Consistent	**Inconsistent**	The gross profit margin would improve if sales prices charged to customers had increased while costs were maintained. Gross margin has decreased which implies that the company is not making as much return as in the prior year. This would most likely be due to an increase in cost of sales or reduction in sales price. Therefore the comment regarding an increase in sales price contradicts the results of the analytical review.

153 OPTION 1

The review of post year-end sales orders provides the best evidence that the new customer is genuine and is ordering goods. This will allow the auditor to assess the level of sales being made to the new customer and to determine whether this does mitigate the loss of Beech Co. Email correspondence will give an indication of the nature of the relationship between the company and customer but this is not as persuasive as actual sales orders being received.

154 OPTION 3

Management should perform a going concern assessment up to the date of the financial statements, in this case, 31 May 20X7. If management assesses a period of less than twelve months from the date of the financial statements, the auditor must request them to extend the assessment to this date.

155 OPTION 2

The client has made adequate disclosure uncertainty related to going concern therefore the opinion will be unmodified. As per ISA 570 *Going Concern*, where there is a matter of fundamental importance to the users' understanding regarding an uncertainty related to going concern the auditor should include a Material Uncertainty Related to Going Concern paragraph. The inclusion of this paragraph does not modify the opinion.

156 OPTION 3

As per ISA 560 *Subsequent Events*, the auditor has an active responsibility to carry out subsequent events procedures between the date of the financial statements and the date of the auditor's report.

157 OPTION 3

The auditor should not contact the financial controller who is no longer an officer of the company, and the party involved in the claim, to confirm the level of damages payable. All other procedures would be appropriate.

158

Opinion		Additional communications
Unmodified		No additional communication
Qualified		Emphasis of Matter paragraph
Adverse		Material Uncertainty Related to Going Concern paragraph
Disclaimer		Other matter paragraph

The maximum damages of $150,000 is not material to the financial statements at 2.3% of profit before tax and 0.2% of revenue. Therefore no modification to the audit opinion is required.

159 OPTION 1

As per paragraph 9 of ISA 701 *Communicating Key Audit Matters in the Independent Auditor's Report*, in determining key audit matters, the auditor shall determine from the matters communicated to those charged with governance, those which required significant auditor attention.

160 OPTIONS 1 AND 4

$500,000 represents 7.7% of profit before tax and 0.8% of revenue, therefore is material. Had this outcome been known before the financial statements were issued, they would have required adjustment. As per ISA 560 paragraph 15, in the circumstances described, the auditor should initially discuss the matter with management and understand how management intends to address the matter in the financial statements.

161 OPTION 2

The auditor must read the other information to ensure it is consistent with the financial statements and their knowledge of the entity obtained during the audit. They do not audit the other information. No assurance conclusion is expressed on the other information. Other information needs to be considered by the auditor if it is made available before the auditor's report is signed. The client may not have this information prepared at the start of the audit but may provide it to the auditor during the audit.

162 OPTION 4

Notes to the financial statements form part of the financial statements and are subject to audit.

163 OPTION 1

The auditor's report will include a section headed 'Other Information' which describes the auditor's responsibilities in respect of the other information, such as the Chair's statement. The inconsistency between the Chair's statement and the financial statements should be described in this section. The auditor's opinion does not cover the Chair's statement therefore will not need to be modified.

164

Users may be misled if the other information contains incorrect information or information which contradicts the financial statements such as that in the Chair's statement	**True**	**False**
Users may believe the auditor has not audited the financial statements properly if the inconsistency is not highlighted	**True**	**False**
The auditor must expose management's incompetence	**True**	**False**
The inconsistency may undermine the credibility of your auditor's report if not highlighted	**True**	**False**

Inconsistencies between the other information and the financial statements may undermine the credibility of the auditor's report as it may be perceived that the auditor has not identified the inconsistencies and therefore the audit was not performed properly. If the inconsistencies are not brought to the attention of the user they may be misled by the incorrect or inconsistent information.

165 OPTION 3

An Other Matter paragraph can be used to refer to matters concerning the auditor's responsibility. Any restriction of liability should be included in that paragraph.

166 OPTION 4

Materiality is calculated using the following benchmarks: ½ – 1% of revenue, 5 – 10% of profit before tax and 1 – 2% of total assets. The receivable is 3.3% revenue, 6.1% of profit before tax and 1.1% of assets. The irrecoverable debt is material by size. An irrecoverable debt is unlikely to be material by nature unless the effect of the adjustment was so significant it would change a profit to a loss.

167 OPTIONS 1, 2 AND 4

From the scenario the customer has agreed the balance is outstanding but is struggling to make any payments. Confirming an already confirmed balance will not provide evidence over the level of adjustment required. Inspecting the sales invoice and GDN does not provide evidence of when the balance will be received.

168 OPTION 2

The issue is only 6.1% of profit and 1.1% of assets and only affects receivables therefore is material but not pervasive. A qualified opinion is appropriate.

169

Addressee	Included	Not included
Other Matter paragraph	Included	Not included
Other Information	Included	Not included
Emphasis of Matter paragraph	Included	Not included

An Emphasis of Matter paragraph is only required if there is a matter disclosed adequately in the financial statements which the auditor considers to be fundamentally important and wishes to bring to the attention of the user. An Other Matter paragraph is only required if there is a matter not related to the financial statements that the auditor wishes to bring to the attention of the user such as further explanation of the auditor's responsibilities.

170 OPTIONS 3 AND 4

Option 1 would require the other information section of the report to provide a description of the inconsistency. Option 2 would require the inclusion of an Emphasis of Matter paragraph. Option 5 would be included in an Other Matter paragraph. These would not affect the audit opinion.

171 OPTIONS 1, 3 AND 4

The directors will assess whether the company can continue to trade for the foreseeable future. They will prepare forecasts to help with this assessment. The auditor will evaluate the directors' assessment to ensure that it is reasonable. The directors must make disclosure of going concern uncertainties in the financial statements. The auditor will highlight that disclosure in their auditor's report. The auditor does not make disclosure in the financial statements. The directors must consider a period of twelve months from the reporting date.

172 OPTIONS 2, 4 AND 5

Calculation of key ratios may identify indicators of going concern issues which need to be investigated further through audit procedures. However, the ratios do not provide evidence that the company is or is not a going concern. Ratios are calculated using historical information and the client may have already taken action to improve their financial position since that information was created. Reviewing the level of profit made in the past does not provide reliable evidence that the company will be able to trade in the future as the financial circumstances of the company may be different.

173

Adequate disclosure of going concern uncertainties is made	Unmodified opinion with no additional communication	Modified opinion	Unmodified opinion with Going Concern paragraph	Unmodified opinion with Emphasis of Matter
Adequate disclosure of going concern uncertainties is not made	Unmodified opinion with no additional communication	Modified opinion	Unmodified opinion with Going Concern paragraph	Unmodified opinion with Emphasis of Matter

The opinion will not be modified if the disclosures are adequate. The report will need to include a section referring to the Material Uncertainty Related to Going Concern. If the company does not make adequate disclosure the financial statements will be materially misstated which will require a modified opinion.

174 OPTION 3

The financial statements should be prepared on the break up basis if the company has ceased trading, intends to cease trading or has no realistic alternative but to cease trading. If a company cannot pay its debts when they fall due the company will have no alternative but to cease trading. If there are material uncertainties relating to going concern the financial statements will still be prepared on a going concern basis but disclosure of the uncertainties should be included in the notes.

175 OPTION 4

If the basis of preparation is incorrect the financial statements will be materially misstated to such an extent they do not give a true and fair view. This is material and pervasive which would require an adverse opinion. The basis for opinion will change to a basis for adverse opinion and will include an explanation as to why the adverse opinion has been given.

176 OPTION 2

Failure to recognise the warranty provision is likely to require an adverse opinion as the misstatement represents a substantial proportion of Paddington's profit. An adverse opinion is issued when the financial statements are pervasively misstated. This will mean they are unreliable as a whole.

Lawsuit	10% of profit	Material
Provision	86% of profit	Material and pervasive
Depreciation	3% of profit	Not material
Intangible assets	41% of profit	Material

177 OPTION 2

As the claim is only possible to succeed a contingent liability disclosure is required. A provision would only be required if the claim was probable to succeed. At 10.3% of PBT, the claim is material being greater than 5% of PBT.

178 OPTION 1

The matter is correctly treated in the financial statements therefore the opinion should be unmodified. Paddington Co has sufficient cash to make the settlement therefore there is no uncertainty facing the company and hence an emphasis of matter paragraph is not necessary.

179 1D, 2B, 3A, 4E, 5C

Element		Purpose
1	Title	Clearly identifies the report as an Independent Auditor's Report (D)
2	Addressee	Identifies the intended user of the report (B)
3	Basis for opinion	Provides a description of the professional standards applied during the audit to provide confidence to users that the report can be relied upon (A)
4	Key audit matters	Draws attention to any other significant matters of which the users should be aware which have been discussed with those charged with governance (E)
5	Name of engagement partner	To identify the person responsible for the audit opinion in case of any queries (C)

180 OPTION 2

A disclaimer of opinion states the auditor does not express an opinion.

An unmodified opinion means the financial statements give a true and fair view.

An adverse opinion means the financial statements do not give a true and fair view.

A qualified opinion states 'except for' the issue described, the financial statements give a true and fair view.

181

	Calculation	Material	
		Yes	**No**
Receivable	4% PBT (0.3/7.5 × 100)		✓
Lawsuit	8% PBT (0.6/7.5 × 100)	✓	

182

	Type of event		Accounting treatment	
Receivable	**Adjusting**	Non-adjusting	**Recognise**	Disclose
Lawsuit	**Adjusting**	Non-adjusting	**Recognise**	Disclose

The receivable and lawsuit are both issues that were in existence at the year-end therefore are adjusting events. Adjusting events must be adjusted or recognised in the financial statements.

183 OPTION 1

It would not be appropriate to contact the customer directly to enquire about payment of the outstanding balance.

184

Auditor Responsibilities for the Audit of the Financial Statements	Included	Not included
Basis for Opinion	Included	Not included
Basis for Qualified Opinion	Included	Not included
Key Audit Matters	Included	Not included
Opinion	Included	Not included
Qualified Opinion	Included	Not included
Responsibilities of Management and Those Charged With Governance	Included	Not included

As the adjustment is material, the opinion will need to be modified. The issue is material but not pervasive therefore a qualified opinion will be required. The section will be titled 'Qualified Opinion' and will be followed by a 'Basis for Qualified Opinion' section. Responsibilities of both management and auditors are included in every auditor's report. Key audit matters are only compulsory for listed companies. As the scenario does not specify that Humphries Co is a listed client, it cannot be assumed that a Key Audit Matters section must be included in the auditor's report.

185   OPTION 2

The condition causing the damage occurred after the year-end therefore the event is non-adjusting. A non-adjusting event must be disclosed if it is material. If disclosure is required but not made the financial statements will be materially misstated which will impact the auditor's report. The amount claimed from the insurance company could only be recognised in the financial statements if the event was an adjusting event and if it was virtually certain the claim would be paid.

186   OPTIONS 2, 5, 1, 4

A written representation **is not appropriate** in respect of the receivable balance. This is because **other procedures can be performed which provide more reliable evidence**.

A written representation **is appropriate** in respect of the warranty provision. This is because **the matter involves management judgment**.

The client cannot confirm with confidence that the customer will pay their outstanding balance. Therefore a written representation is not appropriate. Other procedures provide more reliable evidence such as after date cash testing. The warranty provision is decided by management based on their experience and judgment. As a result there are limited other procedures that can be performed that would provide sufficient appropriate evidence. Therefore a written representation is appropriate.

187   OPTION 2

The refusal to provide a written representation may cast doubt over the reliability of any other evidence provided by the client which means it will have a material effect. The shareholders will be made aware of the issue if the audit opinion is modified as the auditor will need to provide an explanation of the circumstances giving rise to the modification. The auditor will not need to specifically notify the shareholders of the issue in person. There is no requirement to notify an industry regulator in this situation.

188   OPTIONS 4 AND 6

Written representations are required by ISA 580. Therefore without a written representation the auditor does not have sufficient appropriate evidence. If the auditor considers this to be material but not pervasive a qualified opinion will be issued. If it is deemed pervasive a disclaimer of opinion will be issued.

189   OPTION 3

ISA 580 *Written Representations* Appendix 1 identifies other auditing standards that require subject specific written representations. These include ISA 240 *The Auditor's Responsibilities Relating to Fraud in an Audit of Financial Statements*, ISA 250 *Consideration of Laws and Regulations in an Audit of Financial Statements* and ISA 560 *Subsequent Events*.

190

Plans or intentions of management that affect carrying values of assets	Required	Not required
Confirmation from management that they have provided the auditor with all information and access to records during the audit	Required	Not required
Confirmation from management that the financial statements are accurate/free from error	Required	Not required
Confirmation from management that all transactions have been reflected in the financial statements	Required	Not required
Confirmation from management that they have prepared the financial statements in accordance with the applicable financial reporting framework	Required	Not required

Plans or intentions of management will be specific to the entity therefore only included if relevant but not included in every written representation letter. Management cannot confirm the financial statements are accurate or free from error due to estimates and areas of management judgment affecting the financial statements.

191 OPTIONS 1 AND 2

The expert was arranged by Minnie Co (the audit client) therefore is a management's expert. The auditor must follow the requirements of ISA 500 *Audit Evidence* when relying on the work of a management's expert. This requires consideration of the competence and objectivity of the expert and making sure the work is appropriate for audit purposes. Management will have paid for the work therefore there is no impact on the audit fee. The auditor cannot reduce their responsibility for this area in the auditor's report, therefore a statement such as that given in Option 3 is not appropriate.

192 OPTION 3

Minnie Co has depreciated land which is not in accordance with IAS 16 *Property, Plant and Equipment.* The PPE balance in the financial statements will be understated and the depreciation charge overstated. The misstatement to depreciation and property, plant and equipment is 4% of profit before tax which is not material. However, ISA 450 *Evaluation of Misstatements Identified During the Audit* requires the auditor to request management to correct all identified misstatements therefore Daffy & Co must request that management increases the value of PPE by $0.4 million. The prior year accounting treatment was correct as only buildings were depreciated, therefore there is no reason for a prior year adjustment to be made.

193

Materiality		Opinion		Wording
Not material		Adverse		Do not give a true and fair view
Material but not pervasive		Disclaimer		Give a true and fair view
Material and pervasive		Qualified		'Except for'...give a true and fair view
		Unmodified		Do not express an opinion

The wages system issue means the auditor is unable to obtain sufficient and appropriate evidence in respect of wages. The amount that cannot be confirmed is $1.1 million which represents 11% of profit before tax which is material but not pervasive. A qualified opinion with the 'except for' wording is appropriate.

194 OPTION 2

The lawsuit is a material uncertainty. The matter has been correctly disclosed as a contingent liability, therefore the financial statements give a true and fair view and an unmodified opinion can be issued. An Emphasis of Matter paragraph will be required to draw the user's attention to the contingent liability disclosure made by Minnie Co.

195 OPTION 4

All three extracts require amendment. The correct wording for the extracts should be:

1   We conducted our audit in accordance with **International Standards on Auditing**.

2   Our objectives are to obtain **reasonable assurance** about whether the financial statements as a whole are free from material misstatements.

3   Misstatements can arise from **fraud or error**.

196 OPTION 2

The defective inventory is included in the financial statements as at 31 March 20X5. The quality control checks performed after the year end provide evidence of a condition in existence at the year end. This is an **adjusting event**.

The explosion occurred after the year and the damage caused was therefore not a condition in existence at the year end. This is a **non-adjusting event**.

197 OPTION 3

In accordance with IAS 2 *Inventories*, inventory must be valued at the lower of cost and net realisable value (NRV). NRV is the selling price less any costs that must be incurred to make the sale. Cost is $850,000. NRV is $100,000 − 1,000 = $99,000. Therefore the defective inventory should be valued at $99,000.

198 OPTIONS 1, 4 AND 5

A written representation must be obtained in respect of subsequent events. A breakdown of the damaged items would be obtained to determine the value of assets damaged in the explosion. A review of correspondence with the insurance company will be required to determine the value of any possible reimbursement as this will affect the amount of loss incurred which will need to be disclosed. The auditor will have performed cost and net realisable value testing during the final audit. These procedures would not need to be repeated. Reviewing the most recent quality control reports would not identify defects in inventory held at 31 March 20X5 as they will relate to inventory due to be despatched in July as quality control checks are performed one month prior to despatch.

199 OPTION 4

Event 1: The write down of $751,000 (850k – 99k) is **material** as it represents 13.4% (751/5,600) of profit before tax and 1.4% (751/55,000) of revenue. The directors should **amend** the financial statements by writing down the inventory.

Event 2: The damaged assets of $900,000 are **material** as they represent 16.1% (900/5,600) of profit before tax and 1.6% (900/55,000) of revenue. The directors should **amend** the financial statements by including a disclosure note detailing the explosion and the value of the assets impacted.

200 OPTION 1

Both events are material and require amendment. The misstatements are not pervasive as they do not represent a substantial proportion of the financial statements. A qualified opinion is appropriate. The **basis for qualified opinion** will explain the reason for the qualified opinion and quantify the financial effects of the misstatements on the financial statements.

As the misstatements are not pervasive an adverse opinion is not appropriate. As Panda Co is not listed a key audit matter paragraph is not appropriate. An emphasis of matter paragraph is not appropriate as this is used to draw the user's attention to a matter correctly disclosed in the financial statements which is not the case here.

Section 4

ANSWERS TO PRACTICE QUESTIONS

PLANNING AND RISK ASSESSMENT

201   HARLEM *Walk in the footsteps of a top tutor*

Key answer tips

Part (a) asks for the auditor's responsibility in relation to prevention and detection of fraud and error. A good answer needs to refer to the requirements of the relevant auditing standard, ISA 240. If you can't remember the main points of the ISA, take a common sense approach and think about a logical answer to score at least some marks.

Part (b) asks for specific ratios to be calculated from the information provided. The question specifically states that formulas are not required, therefore, do not waste time typing these out as no marks will be awarded.

Part (c) asks for audit risks and responses. This requirement is examined every sitting. You must make sure the risk relates to either a risk of material misstatement or a detection risk. Read through the scenario to identify information which refers to something that will appear in the financial statements, e.g. intangible assets, property, loans and briefly explain the accounting treatment that should be applied. Think about common mistakes that the client could make either deliberately to manipulate the financial statements or unintentionally. State whether the item in financial statements is as risk of under or overstatement. The response must be a response of the auditor, not the client and must directly relate to the risk you have given. The response may be a procedure or may be an approach that the auditor will take.

Part (d) asks for substantive procedures in respect of the valuation of trade receivables. You must give answers which focus on valuation, as marks will not be awarded for procedures which test any of the other financial statement assertions.

Part (e) asks for substantive procedures in respect of the disposal of plant and machinery. Again, you must focus on the requirement. Any procedures which relate to plant and equipment in general will not earn marks.

(a) Fraud responsibility

Auditors conduct an audit in accordance with ISA 240 *The Auditor's Responsibilities Relating to Fraud in an Audit of Financial Statements* and are responsible for obtaining reasonable assurance that the financial statements taken as a whole are free from material misstatement, whether caused by fraud or error.

In order to fulfil this responsibility, the auditor is required to identify and assess the risks of material misstatement of the financial statements due to fraud.

The auditor needs to obtain sufficient appropriate audit evidence regarding the assessed risks of material misstatement due to fraud through designing and implementing appropriate responses. In addition, the auditor must respond appropriately to fraud or suspected fraud identified during the audit.

When obtaining reasonable assurance, the auditor is responsible for maintaining professional scepticism throughout the audit, considering the potential for management override of controls and recognising the fact that audit procedures which are effective in detecting error may not be effective in detecting fraud.

To ensure that the whole engagement team is aware of the risks and responsibilities for fraud and error, ISA 240 requires that a discussion is held within the team. For members not present at the meeting, the audit engagement partner should determine which matters should be communicated to them.

(b) Ratios to assist in planning the audit:

	20X5	20X4
Gross margin	4,500/23,200 × 100 = **19.4%**	4,600/21,900 × 100 = **21%**
Inventory holding period	2,100/18,700 × 365 = **41 days**	1,600/17,300 × 365 = **34 days**
Gearing	13,000/(10,000 + 13,000) × 100 = **56.5%**	11,000/(9,500 + 11,000) × 100 = **53.7%**
OR	13,000/10,000 × 100 = **130%**	11,000/9,500 × 100 = **116%**
Interest cover	(450 + 290)/290 = **2.6**	(850 + 250)/250 = **4.4**

(c) Audit risk and auditor's response

Audit risk	Auditor's response
The finance director is planning on reducing the estimated return rate for goods sold on a sale or return basis to wholesale customers from 10% to 5%. IFRS® 15 *Revenue from Contracts with Customers* provides that revenue and cost of sales should only be accounted for to the extent that the company foresees that the goods will not be returned.	Discuss the basis of the revised assumption of a 5% return rate with the finance director. Review a period of 60 days to quantify the levels of return in the specified period and compare this to the assumed rate of 5%. Discuss any significant variations with the finance director.

Audit risk	Auditor's response
For the goods which may be returned, the company should recognise a refund liability. If, after 60 days, the goods are not returned, then this liability is reversed and revenue is recognised. By reducing the return rate, there is a risk that revenue and cost of sales may be overstated and liabilities understated.	
The company purchased a patent for $800,000 at the end of the prior year which has a useful life of four years. The carrying amount in the forecast financial statements is $800,000 which is the same as the prior year. In accordance with IAS® 38 *Intangible Assets*, this intangible asset should be amortised over its four-year life. It does not appear that management has correctly accounted for the amortisation. Intangible assets and profits are overstated.	Agree the useful life of the patent is four years to supporting documentation. The amortisation charge should be calculated and the appropriate journal adjustment discussed with management, in order to ensure the accuracy of the charge and that the intangible is correctly valued at the year end.
Surplus plant and machinery was sold during the year, resulting in a loss on disposal of $160,000. Significant profits or losses on disposal are an indication that the depreciation policy of plant and machinery may not be appropriate. Therefore depreciation may be understated and profit and assets overstated.	Recalculate the loss on disposal calculations and agree all items to supporting documentation. Discuss the depreciation policy for plant and machinery with the finance director to assess its reasonableness. Review for other significant gains or losses on disposal of property, plant and equipment to assess the reasonableness of the company's depreciation policies.
Harlem Co's financial controller has allegedly carried out a number of fraudulent transactions at the company. The investigation into the extent of the fraud has only recently commenced. There is a risk that she may have undertaken a significant level of fraudulent transactions leading to an increased control risk which has not yet been identified. These would need to be written off to the statement of profit or loss.	Discuss with the finance director the details of the fraud perpetrated by the financial controller and what procedures have been adopted to date to identify any adjustments which are needed in the financial statements. Additional substantive testing should be conducted over the affected areas of the accounting records. In addition, the team should maintain their professional scepticism and be

Audit risk	Auditor's response
If these have not been uncovered by the year end, the financial statements could include errors resulting in the misstatement of profits.	alert to the risk of further fraud and errors.
In May 20X5, the financial controller was dismissed and is threatening to sue the company for unfair dismissal. If it is probable that Harlem Co will make payment to the financial controller, a provision for unfair dismissal is required to comply with IAS 37 *Provisions, Contingent Liabilities and Contingent Assets*. If the payment is possible rather than probable, a contingent liability disclosure would be necessary. If Harlem Co has not done this, there is a risk over the completeness of any provisions or contingent liabilities disclosures.	The audit team should discuss with management and request confirmation from the company's lawyers of the existence and likelihood of success of any claim from the former financial controller.
Harlem Co has had production problems which have affected the quality of a significant batch of tyres. In addition, the inventory holding period has increased from 34 to 41 days. Inventory may be overvalued as its net realisable value (NRV) may be below its cost. If the tyres can be rectified, the rectification costs may mean that cost exceeds net realisable value. If the tyres cannot be rectified, the inventory may need to be written off completely. There is a risk of overstatement of inventory.	Discuss with the finance director whether any write downs will be made to the affected tyres, and what, if any, modifications may be required with regards to the quality. Testing should be undertaken to confirm cost and NRV of the affected products in inventory and that all inventory on a line-by-line basis is valued correctly.
A significant customer has been granted a six-month payment break and the receivables collection period has increased from 38 to 51 days. An allowance for receivables has historically been maintained, and it is anticipated that it will remain at the prior year level.	Review and test the controls surrounding how the finance director identifies old or potentially irrecoverable receivables balances and credit control to ensure that they are operating effectively.

Audit risk	Auditor's response
There is a risk that receivables will be overvalued as some balances may not be recoverable and so will be overstated if adequate allowance is not made.	Discuss with the director the rationale for maintaining the allowance for receivables at the same level as the prior year, despite the increase in receivables collection period and the payment break granted to a large customer. Extended post year-end cash receipts testing and a review of the aged receivables ledger to be performed to assess valuation and the need for an increased level of allowance for receivables.
The report to management issued after the prior year audit highlighted significant deficiencies relating to the purchases cycle. If these deficiencies have not been rectified, the controls over purchases and payables may continue to be weak leading to increased control risk and risk of misstatements arising. Cost of sales, expenses and trade payables may not be complete or accurate.	Discuss with management whether the purchases cycle recommendations suggested by Brooklyn & Co were implemented successfully this year. If so, undertake tests of these controls to assess if they are operating efficiently. If the controls are not in place or operating efficiently, adopt a fully substantive approach for confirming the completeness and accuracy of cost of sales and other expenses and trade payables.
Harlem Co intends to restructure its debt finance after the year end. However, the interest cover has declined from 4·4 to 2·6 and the level of gearing has increased from 53·7% to 56·5%. In order to maximise the chances of securing the debt finance restructure, Harlem Co will need to present financial statements which show the best possible position and performance. The worsening interest cover and gearing ratio increases the risk that the directors may manipulate the financial statements, by overstating profits and assets and understating debt liabilities.	Brooklyn & Co should ensure that there is a suitably experienced audit team. Also, adequate time should be allocated for team members to obtain an understanding of the company and the significant risks of overstatement of profits and assets and understatement of debt, including attendance at an audit team briefing. The team needs to maintain professional scepticism and be alert to the increased risk of manipulation. Significant estimates and judgements should be carefully reviewed in light of the misstatement risk.

Audit risk	Auditor's response
Harlem Co has issued shares during the year via a bonus issue. Share capital within equity should increase by the value of the shares and a reserve should decrease accordingly. If the company has not accounted for a bonus issue before, there is a risk that it could have been incorrectly treated with equity being under or overstated. In addition, legal issues may arise if the shares have not been issued in accordance with the company's statutory constitution. Additionally, bonus issues require disclosure in the financial statements and there is a risk that these may be incomplete or inaccurate.	Review the treatment of the bonus issue and agree the increase in shares to the share register and share certificates, and agree that the corresponding reduction in reserves is correct. Review board minutes for authorisation and terms of the bonus issue and review if the transaction has been conducted in line with this approval. Review the statutory constitution documents to confirm the legality of the share issue. Review the adequacy of the bonus issue disclosures in the financial statements.

(d) Valuation of trade receivables

- Discuss with the finance director the rationale for not increasing the allowance for trade receivables and review its overall adequacy.

- Obtain a breakdown of the opening allowance and consider if the receivables provided for in the prior year have been recovered to assess the reasonableness of the prior levels of allowances.

- Review the aged trade receivables ledger to identify any slow moving or old receivable balances and discuss the status of these balances with the credit controllers to assess whether they are likely to be received.

- Review whether there are any after-date cash receipts for slow moving/old receivable balances.

- Review customer correspondence with the significant customer and others to identify any balances which are in dispute or are unlikely to be paid.

- Review board minutes to identify whether there are any significant concerns in relation to payments by customers.

- Calculate the potential level of trade receivables which are not recoverable and assess whether this is material or not and discuss with management.

(e) Disposals of plant and machinery

- Obtain a breakdown of disposals, cast the list and review the non-current assets register to confirm that all assets have been removed.

- Select a sample of disposals and agree sale proceeds to supporting documentation such as sundry sales invoices.

- Recalculate the profit/loss on disposal and agree to the trial balance and statement of profit or loss.

- Recalculate the depreciation charge for a sample of disposals to confirm the calculations are correctly applied as per the company policy of a pro rata basis or a full year in the year of acquisition and none in the year of disposal.

- Review the disclosure of the disposals in the draft financial statements and ensure it is in line with IAS 16 *Property, Plant and Equipment*.

Marking guide		
		Marks
(a)	**Auditor's responsibility for fraud**	
	• Obtain reasonable assurance that financial statements are free from material misstatement	1
	• Identify and assess risk of misstatement due to fraud	1
	• Obtain sufficient and appropriate evidence	1
	• Respond appropriately to fraud or suspected fraud	1
	• Maintain professional scepticism	1
	• Discuss risk of fraud with engagement team	1
	Restricted to	4
(b)	**Ratios**	
	• Gross profit margin	1
	• Inventory holding period	1
	• Gearing	1
	• Interest cover	1
		4
(c)	**Audit risks and responses (only 8 required)**	
	• Sale or return assumption	2
	• Intangible asset amortisation	2
	• Significant losses on disposal	2
	• Financial controller dismissal	2
	• Unfair dismissal claim	2
	• Inventory valuation	2
	• Recoverability of receivables	2
	• Purchases cycle control deficiencies	2
	• Intention to restructure finance	2
	• Bonus issue of shares	2
	Max 8 issues, 2 marks each	16
(d)	**Substantive procedures – Valuation of trade receivables**	
	• Discuss with management adequacy of trade receivables allowance	1
	• Outcome of prior year allowance	1
	• Review aged trade receivables listing to identify old balances	1
	• After date cash testing	1
	• Review customer correspondence for evidence of disputes	1
	• Recalculate potential irrecoverable balances and assess adequacy of allowance	1
	Restricted to	3

Marking guide		Marks
(e)	**Substantive procedures – Disposal of plant and machinery**	*Marks*
	• Obtain breakdown of disposals, cast and agree removal to non-current asset register	1
	• Select sample of disposals and agree sales proceeds to invoice	1
	• Recalculate the profit/loss on disposal and agree to trial balance	1
	• Recalculate depreciation to confirm applied on a pro rata basis	1
	• Review disclosures and confirm in line with accounting standards	1
	Restricted to	**3**
Total		**30**

Examiner's comments

This 30-mark question was based on Harlem Co, a car tyre manufacturer. This question tested candidates' knowledge of responsibilities for fraud and error, calculation of ratios, audit risks and responses and substantive procedures. Performance was satisfactory.

Part (a) for four marks required candidates to describe the auditor's responsibilities for fraud and error. One mark was available for each well described point. This is a knowledge area that has been tested in previous diets. Performance was satisfactory. A significant number of candidates were able to detail in sufficient depth the auditor's responsibilities, however some candidates did not fully relate the responsibilities back to fraud and error. In addition, some candidates described management's responsibilities and no credit was awarded for these points.

Part (b) for four marks required a calculation of four specified ratios for both the current and prior year. Most candidates were able to generate enough marks to pass this part of the requirement, however few received full marks. Candidates were able to confidently calculate the gross profit margin and inventory holding period. However, candidates struggled in particular to calculate interest cover and some miscalculated the gearing ratio. The calculation of interest cover required candidates to add back finance costs to the profit before tax. Many failed to do this correctly and this may explain the weaker performance on this ratio. Candidates must ensure that they are able to calculate a range of key ratios used in analytical procedures.

Part (c) for 16 marks required candidates to identify and describe eight audit risks and to explain the auditor's response to each in planning the audit of Harlem Co. Performance was satisfactory. Marks were awarded for the identification of an audit risk (½ mark each), explanation of the audit risks (½ mark each) and an appropriate auditor's responses to each risk (1 mark each). The scenario contained more than eight risks so it was pleasing that most candidates planned their time carefully and generally only attempted to list the required number of points. Candidates generally identified the risks well. However, having correctly identified the relevant fact from the scenario a significant number did not understand the associated audit risk. For example, the company's intention to restructure the debt finance post year end gave rise to a manipulation risk in the current year financial statements. Many candidates incorrectly stated that the company had taken out a new loan and therefore the risk of classification needed to be addressed. This was incorrect, as Harlem Co had not taken out any loans in the current year. In addition, the risk arising on the amortisation of the intangible asset was poorly answered by candidates. Many failed to appreciate that the asset was purchased in the prior year, therefore audit work confirming the cost would have been undertaken in the prior year.

For the current year the auditor needed to focus on whether the amortisation had been appropriately charged. Candidates must take the time to carefully read the scenario, noting dates and other relevant information, to ensure that they correctly understand the audit risks arising.

As in previous diets, many candidates did not adequately explain the risk. To explain the risk candidates need to state the specific area of the financial statements impacted with an assertion (for example cut off, valuation etc), or, a reference to over/under/misstated, or a reference to inherent/ control/ detection risk. A reference to a balance being misstated was only awarded credit if it was clear the balance could be either over/understated. A significant minority of candidates did not clearly state the specific area of the financial statement impacted. For example, for the issue relating to the loss on disposal of surplus plant and machinery, answers which noted 'assets could be overstated' were not awarded credit. Candidates must clearly state the specific area of the financial statements, for example 'property plant and equipment could be overstated' to be awarded the ½ implication mark. Candidates' performance in relation to auditor's responses continues to be mixed. While an auditor's response does not have to be a detailed procedure, rather an approach the audit team will take to address the identified risk, the responses given were often too weak or not related to the actual audit risk. For example, in response to the quality control issue with inventory, the response 'inspect the tyres' was not sufficient to gather evidence over the NRV of these tyres. Candidates needed to explain how they would confirm the valuation, for example by 'discussing with management whether the tyres will be written down'. Future candidates are advised that audit risk is and will continue to be an important element in the syllabus and must be understood. Candidates must ensure that they include adequate question practice as part of their revision on this key topic.

Part (d) for three marks required candidates to describe substantive procedures the auditor should perform in relation to the valuation of trade receivables. One mark was available for each well-described procedure. Performance on this requirement was satisfactory. Many candidates were able to provide an appropriate number of well described audit procedures such as after date cash receipts testing and analytical review procedures. Some candidates suggested procedures which would not address the risk of valuation such as, undertaking a receivables circularisation or agreeing the receivables balance to the financial statements. Procedures unrelated to valuation were not awarded credit.

Part (e) for three marks required candidates to describe substantive procedures the auditor should perform in relation to the disposal of plant and machinery. One mark was available for each well-described procedure. Performance on this requirement was disappointing. Many candidates failed to provide procedures focused on disposals, instead they gave a list of generic property, plant and equipment procedures. This wasted time and often meant that candidates only scored one to two marks at best. Candidates who scored well focused on recalculation of the loss on disposal, confirming the plant and machinery had been removed from the asset register and calculation of depreciation to the point of sale. Candidates are reminded they must take the time to read the question requirements carefully and spend time thinking about what is needed prior to writing their answers rather than listing out generic tests.

202 PEONY *Walk in the footsteps of a top tutor*

Key answer tips

Part (a) asks for a definition and explanation of materiality and performance materiality. This requires knowledge from the text book and the relevant auditing standard. Each constructed response question is likely to have one requirement which is knowledge based and therefore you must take time to learn key definitions and be able to provide an explanation.

Part (b) asks for audit risks and responses. This requirement is examined every sitting. You must make sure the risk relates to either a risk of material misstatement or a detection risk. Read through the scenario to identify information which refers to something that will appear in the financial statements, e.g. intangible assets, property, loans and briefly explain the accounting treatment that should be applied. Think about common mistakes that the client could make either deliberately to manipulate the financial statements or unintentionally. State whether the item in financial statements is as risk of under or overstatement. The response must be a response of the auditor, not the client and must directly relate to the risk you have given. The response may be a procedure or may be an approach that the auditor will take.

(a)   Materiality and performance materiality

Materiality and performance materiality are dealt with under ISA 320 *Materiality in Planning and Performing an Audit*. Auditors need to establish the materiality level for the financial statements as a whole, as well as assess performance materiality levels, which are lower than the overall materiality for the financial statements as a whole.

Materiality

Materiality is defined in ISA 320 as follows: 'Misstatements, including omissions, are considered to be material if they, individually or in the aggregate, could reasonably be expected to influence the economic decisions of users taken on the basis of the financial statements.'

If the financial statements include a material misstatement, then they will not present fairly (give a true and fair view) the position, performance and cash flows of the entity.

A misstatement may be considered material due to its size (quantitative) and/or due to its nature (qualitative) or a combination of both. The quantitative nature of a misstatement refers to its relative size. A misstatement which is material due to its nature refers to an amount which might be low in value but due to its prominence and relevance could influence the user's decision, for example, directors' transactions.

As per ISA 320, materiality is often calculated using benchmarks such as 5% of profit before tax or 1% of total revenue or total assets. These values are useful as a starting point for assessing materiality, however, the assessment of what is material is ultimately a matter of the auditor's professional judgement. It is affected by the auditor's perception of the financial information, the needs of the users of the financial statements and the perceived level of risk; the higher the risk, the lower the level of overall materiality.

In assessing materiality, the auditor must consider that a number of errors each with a low value may, when aggregated, amount to a material misstatement.

Performance materiality

Performance materiality is defined in ISA 320 as follows: 'The amount set by the auditor at less than materiality for the financial statements as a whole to reduce to an appropriately low level the probability that the aggregate of uncorrected and undetected misstatements exceeds materiality for the financial statements as a whole.'

Hence performance materiality is set at a level lower than overall materiality for the financial statements as a whole. It is used for testing individual transactions, account balances and disclosures. The aim of performance materiality is to reduce the risk that the total of all of the errors in balances, transactions and disclosures exceeds overall materiality.

(b) **Audit risk and auditor's response**

Audit risk	Auditor's response
The external audit team may place reliance on the controls testing work undertaken by the IA department. If reliance is placed on irrelevant or poorly performed testing, then the external audit team may form an incorrect conclusion on the strength of the internal controls at Peony Co. This could result in them performing insufficient levels of substantive testing, thereby increasing detection risk.	The external audit team should meet with IA staff, read their reports and review their files relating to store visits to ascertain the nature of the work undertaken. Before using the work of IA, the audit team will need to evaluate and perform audit procedures on the entirety of the work which they plan to use, in order to determine its adequacy for the purposes of the audit. In addition, the team will need to re-perform some of the testing carried out by IA to assess its adequacy.
Forecast ratios from the finance director show that the gross margin is expected to increase from 56% to 60% and the operating margin is expected to decrease from 21% to 18%. This movement in gross margin is significant and inconsistent with the fall in operating margin. There is a risk that costs may have been omitted or included in operating expenses rather than cost of sales. Misclassification of expenses would result in understatement of cost of sales and overstatement of operating expenses.	The classification of costs between cost of sales and operating expenses should be reviewed in comparison to the prior year and any inconsistencies investigated.

Audit risk	Auditor's response
Peony Co's inventory valuation policy is selling price less average profit margin, as this is industry practice. Inventory should be valued at the lower of cost and net realisable value (NRV). IAS 2 *Inventories* allows this as a cost calculation method as long as it is a close approximation to cost. If this is not the case, then inventory could be under or overvalued.	Testing should be undertaken to confirm cost and NRV of inventory and that on a line-by-line basis the goods are valued correctly. In addition, valuation testing should focus on comparing the cost of inventory to the selling price less margin for a sample of items to confirm whether this method is actually a close approximation to cost.
The company utilises a perpetual inventory system at its warehouse rather than a full year-end count. Under such a system, all inventory must be counted at least once a year with adjustments made to the inventory records on a timely basis. Inventory could be under or overstated if the perpetual inventory counts are not all completed, such that some inventory lines are not counted in the year.	The timetable of the perpetual inventory counts should be reviewed and the controls over the counts and adjustments to records should be tested.
During the interim audit, it was noted that there were significant exceptions with the inventory records being higher than the inventory in the warehouse. As the year-end quantities will be based on the records, this is likely to result in overstated inventory.	The level of adjustments made to inventory should be considered to assess their significance. This should be discussed with management as soon as possible as it may not be possible to place reliance on the inventory records at the year end, which could result in the requirement for a full year-end inventory count.
A number of assets which had not been fully depreciated were identified as being obsolete. This is an indication that the company's depreciation policy of non-current assets may not be appropriate, as depreciation in the past appears to have been understated. If an asset is obsolete, it should be written off to the statement of profit or loss. Therefore depreciation may be understated and profit and assets overstated.	Discuss the depreciation policy for non-current assets with the finance director and assess its reasonableness. Enquire of the finance director if the obsolete assets have been written off. If so, review the adjustment for completeness.

Audit risk	Auditor's response
Peony Co is planning to include a current asset of $0.7m, which relates to advertising costs incurred and adverts shown on TV before the year end. The costs were incurred and adverts shown in the year ending 20X9 and there is no basis for including them as a current asset at the year end. The costs should be recognised in operating expenses in the current year financial statements. If these costs are not expensed, current assets and profits will be overstated.	Discuss with management the rationale for including the advertising as a current asset. Request evidence to support the assessment of probable future cash flows, and review for reasonableness. Review supporting documentation for the advertisements to confirm that all were shown before the 20X9 year end. Request that management remove the current asset and record the amount as an expense in the statement of profit or loss.
During the year, Peony Co outsourced its payroll function to an external service organisation. A detection risk arises as to whether sufficient and appropriate evidence is available at Peony Co to confirm the completeness and accuracy of controls over the payroll cycle and liabilities at the year end.	Discuss with management the extent of records maintained at Peony Co for the period since January 20X9 and any monitoring of controls which has been undertaken by management over payroll. Consideration should be given to contacting the service organisation's auditor to confirm the level of controls in place. A type 1 or type 2 report could be requested.
The payroll function was transferred to the service organisation from 1 January 20X9, which is five months prior to the year end. If any errors occurred during the transfer process, these could result in wages and salaries being under/overstated.	Discuss with management the transfer process undertaken and any controls which were put in place to ensure the completeness and accuracy of the data. Where possible, undertake tests of controls to confirm the effectiveness of the transfer controls. In addition, perform substantive testing on the transfer of information from the old to the new system.
A $3m loan was obtained in March 20X9. This finance needs to be accounted for correctly, with adequate disclosure made. The loan needs to be allocated between non-current and current liabilities. Failure to classify the loan correctly could result in misclassified liabilities.	Re-perform the company's calculations to confirm that the split of the loan note is correct between non-current and current liabilities and that total financing proceeds of $3m were received. In addition, the disclosures for this loan note should be reviewed in detail to ensure compliance with relevant accounting standards.

Audit risk	Auditor's response
Peony Co is planning to make approximately 60 employees redundant after the year end.	Discuss with management the status of the redundancy announcement; if before the year end, review supporting documentation to confirm the timing. In addition, review the basis of and recalculate the redundancy provision.
The timing of this announcement has not been confirmed; if it is announced to the staff before the year end, then under IAS 37 *Provisions, Contingent Liabilities and Contingent Assets*, a redundancy provision will be required at the year end as a constructive obligation will have been created.	
Failure to provide or to provide an appropriate amount will result in an understatement of provisions and expenses.	

Marking guide		
		Marks
(a)	**Materiality and performance materiality**	
	• Materiality definition	1
	• Material due to size or nature	1
	• Materiality benchmarks	1
	• Depends on judgement and risk	1
	• Performance materiality definition	1
	• Used for testing individual balances	1
	• Set at lower level than materiality	1
		―――
	Restricted to	4
		―――
(b)	**Audit risks and responses (only 8 required)**	
	• Reliance on internal audit –– increased detection risk	2
	• Unusual movement in margins	2
	• Inventory valuation policy	2
	• Perpetual inventory system	2
	• Obsolete PPE	2
	• Advertising expenditure	2
	• Use of payroll service organisation	2
	• Transfer of data to service organisation	2
	• Bank loan	2
	• Redundancy plan	2
		―――
	Max 8 issues, 2 marks each	16
		―――
Total		**20**
		―――

Examiner's comments

This 20-mark question was based on Peony Co, a food retailer. This question tested candidates' knowledge of materiality and audit risks and responses. Candidates' overall performance was satisfactory.

Part (a) for four marks required candidates to define and explain materiality and performance materiality. One mark was available for each well-explained point. This is a knowledge area which has been tested in previous exam sessions. Performance was mixed. A significant number of candidates correctly described performance materiality as 'being lower than materiality' (1 mark) and 'comprised of small aggregated errors' (1 mark). However, it was disappointing that a number of candidates were not familiar with the commonly used benchmarks for quantitative materiality.

Part (b) for 16 marks required candidates to identify and describe eight audit risks and to explain the auditor's response to each in planning the audit of Peony Co. Performance was satisfactory.

Marks were awarded for identification of audit risk (½ mark each), explanation of audit risks (½ mark each) and an appropriate auditor's response to each risk (1 mark each). The scenario contained more than eight risks so it was pleasing that most candidates planned their time carefully and generally only attempted to list the required number of points.

Candidates identified the risks well. However, a significant minority of candidates noted 'the client had been an audit client for a number of years and hence the auditor would be too familiar with the client'. This was not awarded any credit, as this is a risk to the auditor's independence which should be considered prior to continuing with the engagement. As in previous exam sessions, many candidates did not adequately explain the risk. To explain the risk, candidates need to state the specific area of the financial statements impacted with an assertion (for example, cut-off, valuation etc), or a reference to over/under/misstated, or a reference to inherent/control/detection risk. Misstated was only awarded credit if it was clear the balance could be either over or understated. A significant minority of candidates stated 'inventory could be misstated due to the inventory records being higher than physical counts'. This was not awarded credit as the balance could clearly only be 'overstated'. A significant minority of candidates did not clearly state the specific area of the financial statement impacted. For the above example stating 'current assets could be overstated' without any reference to inventory was not awarded credit. Candidates must clearly demonstrate that they understand the specific area of the financial statements impacted, to be awarded the ½ implication mark.

Candidates' performance in relation to auditor's responses continues to be mixed. While an auditor's response does not have to be a detailed procedure, rather an approach the audit team will take to address the identified risk, the responses given were often too weak. For example, in response to the possible errors in the transfer of data to the service organisation, the response 'check the transfers' was not sufficient, candidates needed to explain how, for example, by 'performing substantive testing on the transfer of information from the old to the new system or performing tests of controls to confirm the effectiveness of the transfer controls'. A significant number of candidates gave management rather than auditor's response. For example, when discussing the redundancy plan a number of candidates noted 'there may be a lack of staff for future expansion'. This was not awarded credit.

Future candidates are advised that audit risk is and will continue to be an important element in the syllabus and must be understood. Candidates must ensure that they include adequate question practice as part of their revision on this key topic.

Key answer tips

Part (a) asks for an explanation of why analytical procedures are used during three stages of an audit. This is knowledge that you should have learned from the text book. Think about what an analytical procedure is – evaluation of plausible relationships between information. Think about the three stages of an audit – planning, final audit and completion. Then link them together – why is it useful to identify inconsistent relationships when planning, when performing the final audit and when completing the audit.

Part (b) asks for ratios to be calculated from the information provided. Remember that the ratios are to help you identify audit risks. You are not evaluating the financial performance of the company.

Part (c) asks for audit risks and responses. This requirement is examined every sitting. You must make sure the risk relates to either a risk of material misstatement or a detection risk. Read through the scenario to identify information which refers to something that will appear in the financial statements, e.g. revenue, property, inventory and briefly explain the accounting treatment that should be applied. Think about common mistakes that the client could make either deliberately to manipulate the financial statements or unintentionally. State whether the item in financial statements is as risk of under or overstatement. The response must be a response of the auditor, not the client and must directly relate to the risk you have given.

Part (d) asks for substantive procedures in respect of the faulty inventory. You must describe procedures that will help you evaluate whether the faulty inventory has been correctly accounted for in the financial statements. Make sure your procedures relate to the faulty inventory as there will be no marks for general audit procedures in relation to inventory.

Part (e) requires substantive procedures in relation to revenue. There should be some marks available here for general revenue procedures. However, there is information in the scenario which should be used to provide procedures specific to Darjeeling Co.

(a)   Analytical procedures

Analytical procedures can be used at all stages of an audit, however, ISA 315 *Identifying and Assessing the Risks of Material Misstatement through Understanding the Entity and Its Environment* and ISA 520 *Analytical Procedures* identify three particular stages.

During the planning stage, analytical procedures must be used as risk assessment procedures in order to help the auditor to obtain an understanding of the entity and assess the risk of material misstatement.

During the final audit, analytical procedures can be used to obtain sufficient appropriate evidence. Substantive procedures can either be tests of detail or substantive analytical procedures.

At the final review stage, the auditor must design and perform analytical procedures which assist them when forming an overall conclusion as to whether the financial statements are consistent with the auditor's understanding of the entity.

(b)   Ratios to assist in planning the audit:

	20X8	20X7
Gross margin	7,410/19,850 = **37.3%**	6,190/16,990 = **36.4%**
Inventory holding period	1,850/12,440 × 365 = **54 days**	1,330/10,800 × 365 = **45 days**
OR		
Inventory turnover	12,440/1,850 = **6.7**	10,800/1,330 = **8.1**
Receivables collection period	2,750/19,850 × 365 = **51 days**	1,780/16,990 × 365 = **38 days**
Payables payment period	1,970/12,440 × 365 = **58 days**	1,190/10,800 × 365 = **40 days**
Current ratio	4,600/(1,970 + 810) = **1.65**	3,670/1,190 = **3.08**
Quick ratio	2,750/(1,970 + 810) = **0.99**	(3,670 − 1,330)/1,190 = **1.97**

(c)   **Audit risks and auditor's response**

Audit risk	Auditor's response
During the year, Darjeeling Co has spent $0.9m on developing new product lines, some of which are in the early stages of their development cycle. This expenditure is classed as research and development under IAS 38 *Intangible Assets*. The standard requires research costs to be expensed to profit or loss and only development costs to be capitalised as an intangible asset. The company has included all of this expenditure as an intangible asset. If research costs have been incorrectly classified as development expenditure, there is a risk that intangible assets could be overstated and expenses understated.	Obtain a breakdown of the expenditure and verify that it relates to the development of the new products. Review expenditure documentation to determine whether the costs relate to the research or development stage. Discuss the accounting treatment with the finance director and ensure it is in accordance with IAS 38.
Darjeeling Co purchased and installed a new manufacturing line. The costs include purchase price ($2.2m), installation costs ($0.4m) and a five-year servicing and maintenance plan ($0.5m). As per IAS 16 *Property, Plant and Equipment*, the cost of an asset includes its purchase price and directly attributable costs only. IAS 16 does not allow servicing and maintenance costs to be capitalised as part of the cost of a non-current asset, as they are not directly related to the cost of bringing the asset to its working condition.	Review the purchase documentation for the new manufacturing line to confirm the exact cost of the servicing and that it does relate to a five-year period. Discuss the accounting treatment with the finance director and the level of any necessary adjustment to ensure treatment is in accordance with IAS 16.

Audit risk	Auditor's response
The servicing costs relate to a five-year period and so should be charged to profit or loss over this time. The upfront payment represents a prepayment for five years; as the services are received, the relevant proportion of the cost should be charged to profit or loss. If the service for 20X8 has been carried out, then $0.1m ($0.5m/5) should be charged to profit or loss. Therefore property, plant and equipment (PPE) and profits are overstated and prepayments are understated.	
The company has borrowed $4m from the bank via an eight-year loan. This loan needs to be correctly split between current and non-current liabilities in order to ensure correct disclosure. Current and non-current liabilities will be misstated if the split is incorrect.	During the audit, the team would need to confirm that the $4 million loan finance was received. In addition, the split between current and non-current liabilities and the disclosures for this loan should be reviewed in detail to ensure compliance with relevant accounting standards and local legislation. Details of security should be agreed to the bank confirmation letter.
As the level of debt has increased, there should be additional finance costs as the loan has an interest rate of 5%. There is a risk that this has been omitted from the statement of profit or loss leading to understated finance costs and overstated profit.	The finance costs should be recalculated and any increase agreed to the loan documentation for confirmation of the 5% interest rate. Interest payments should be agreed to the cash book and bank statements to confirm the amount was paid and is not therefore a year-end payable.
Darjeeling Co intends to undertake a stock exchange listing in the next 12 months. In order to maximise the success of the potential listing, Darjeeling Co will need to present financial statements which show the best possible position and performance. The directors therefore have an incentive to manipulate the financial statements, by overstating revenue, profits and assets.	Earl & Co should ensure that there is a suitably experienced audit team. Also, adequate time should be allocated for team members to obtain an understanding of the company and the significant risks of overstatement of revenue, profits and assets, including attendance at an audit team briefing. The team needs to maintain professional scepticism and be alert to the increased risk of manipulation. Significant estimates and judgments should be carefully reviewed in light of the misstatement risk.

Audit risk	Auditor's response
The receivables collection period has increased from 38 to 51 days and management has extended the credit terms given to customers on the condition that sales order quantities were increased. The increase in the receivables collection period could be solely due to these increased credit terms. However, it could also be due to an increased risk over the recoverability of receivables. Receivables may be overvalued and expenses understated.	Review and test the controls surrounding how Darjeeling Co identifies receivables balances which may not be recoverable and procedures around credit control to ensure that they are operating effectively. Extended post year-end cash receipts testing and a review of the aged receivables ledger to be performed to assess valuation. Also consider the adequacy of any allowance for receivables.
This year the company made a 'price promise' to match the price of its competitors for similar products. Customers are able to claim the difference from the company for one month after the date of purchase of goods. The company should account for the price promise in accordance with IFRS 15 *Revenue from Contracts with Customers*. As the company may be required to provide a refund, the anticipated refund amount should not be initially recognised as revenue but instead as a refund liability until the one-month price promise period has ended. This is a highly subjective area, with many judgments required with regards to the level of likely refund due. As this is a new liability, the directors may not have correctly accounted for this sum resulting in overstated revenue, under/overstated profits and liabilities.	Discuss with management the basis of the refund liability of $0.25m and obtain supporting documentation to confirm the reasonableness of the assumptions and calculations.
Darjeeling Co has stopped further sales of one of its paint products and a product recall has been initiated for any goods sold since June. This product recall will result in Darjeeling Co paying refunds to customers. The sales will need to be removed from the 20X8 financial statements and a refund liability recognised. Also inventory will need to be reinstated, albeit at a possibly written down value.	Review the list of sales of the paint product made between June and the date of the recall, agree that the sales have been removed from revenue and the inventory included. If the refunds have not been paid before the year end, review the draft financial statements to confirm that it is included within current liabilities.

Audit risk	Auditor's response
Failing to account for this correctly could result in overstated revenue, understated liabilities and misstated inventory.	
The company is holding a number of damaged paint products in inventory and overall the inventory holding period has increased from 45 days to 54 days. Due to the issue with the paint consistency, the quality of these products is questionable and management is investigating whether these products can be rectified. There is a risk that this inventory may be overvalued as its net realisable value may be below cost.	Discuss with the finance director whether any write downs will be made to this product, and what, if any, modifications will be required to rectify the quality of the product. Testing should be undertaken to confirm cost and NRV of the affected paint products held in inventory and that on a line by line basis the goods are valued correctly.
Revenue has increased by 16.8% in the year; and the gross margin has increased slightly from 36.4% to 37.3%. This is a significant increase in revenue.	During the audit a detailed breakdown of sales will be obtained, discussed with management and tested in order to understand the sales increase.
Along with the increase in gross margin, may be related to the increased credit period and price promise promotion or could be due to an overstatement of revenue.	Also increased cut-off testing should be undertaken to verify that revenue is recorded in the right period and is not overstated.
The payables payment period has increased from 40 to 58 days. The current ratio has decreased from 3.08 to 1.65. The quick ratio has also decreased from 1.97 to 0.99. In addition, the bank balance has moved from $0.56m to an overdraft of $0.81m. These are all indicators that the company could be experiencing a reduction in its cash flow which could result in going concern difficulties or uncertainties. These uncertainties may not be adequately disclosed in the financial statements.	Detailed going concern testing to be performed during the audit, including the review of cash flow forecasts and the underlying assumptions. These should be discussed with management to ensure that the going concern basis is reasonable.

(d) **Faulty inventory**

- Obtain a breakdown of the damaged goods held in inventory and returned from customers and cast to confirm its accuracy.

- From the breakdown, agree the damaged goods quantities manufactured since June to production records; and agree to sales records the quantities sold.

- Agree on a sample basis the returns from customers as per the breakdown back to sales returns documentation to confirm the existence of the returns quantities.

- Discuss with management the current status of their plans for this product line and whether they are able to rectify the damage and then sell the goods on. If so, agree the costs of rectification to supporting documentation.

- If the damaged inventory has been rectified and sold post year end, agree to the sales invoice to assess NRV in line with the new cost of the product.

- Agree the cost of damaged goods to supporting documentation to confirm the raw material cost, labour cost and any overheads attributed to the cost.

- Discuss with management if the goods have been written down; if so, follow through the write down to the inventory valuation to confirm.

- Inspect monthly board meeting minutes from June 20X8 onwards to obtain further information regarding the faulty paint and its possible resale value.

(e) **Revenue**

- Compare the overall level of revenue against prior years and budget for the year and investigate any significant fluctuations.

- Perform a proof in total calculation for revenue, creating an expectation of the average price for the main paint products multiplied by the increased sales volumes for this year. This expectation should be compared to actual revenue and any significant fluctuations should be investigated.

- Obtain a schedule of sales for the year broken down into the main product categories and compare this to the prior year breakdown and for any unusual movements, discuss with management.

- Calculate the final gross profit margin for Darjeeling Co and compare this to the prior year and investigate any significant fluctuations.

- Select a sample of sales invoices for customers and agree the sales prices back to the price list or customer master data information to ensure the accuracy of invoices.

- For a sample of invoices, recalculate invoice totals including discounts and sales tax.

- Select a sample of credit notes raised, trace through to the original invoice and ensure the invoice has been correctly removed from sales.

- Select a sample of customer orders and agree these to the despatch notes and sales invoices through to inclusion in the sales day book and revenue general ledger accounts to ensure completeness of revenue.

- Select a sample of despatch notes both pre and post year end and follow these through to sales invoices in the correct accounting period to ensure that cut-off has been correctly applied.

- For sales made under the price promise, compare the level of claims made to date with the refund liability recognised and assess whether it is reasonable.

- For a sample of sales invoices issued between June and the product recall, trace to subsequent credit notes to confirm that the sale has been removed from revenue.

<table>
<tr><td colspan="4" align="center">**Marking guide**</td></tr>
<tr><td></td><td></td><td></td><td align="right">*Marks*</td></tr>
<tr><td>(a)</td><td colspan="2">**Analytical procedures**</td><td></td></tr>
<tr><td></td><td>•</td><td>Must be used at planning as risk assessment tool</td><td align="center">1</td></tr>
<tr><td></td><td>•</td><td>Can be used to gather evidence during fieldwork</td><td align="center">1</td></tr>
<tr><td></td><td>•</td><td>Must be used at completion to confirm overall conclusion</td><td align="center">1</td></tr>
<tr><td></td><td></td><td></td><td align="center">___
3
___</td></tr>
<tr><td>(b)</td><td colspan="2">**Ratios**</td><td></td></tr>
<tr><td></td><td>•</td><td>Gross profit margin</td><td align="center">1</td></tr>
<tr><td></td><td>•</td><td>Inventory holding period</td><td align="center">1</td></tr>
<tr><td></td><td>•</td><td>Receivables collection period</td><td align="center">1</td></tr>
<tr><td></td><td>•</td><td>Payables payment period</td><td align="center">1</td></tr>
<tr><td></td><td>•</td><td>Current ratio</td><td align="center">1</td></tr>
<tr><td></td><td>•</td><td>Quick ratio</td><td align="center">1</td></tr>
<tr><td></td><td colspan="2" align="right">**Max 3 ratios, ½ for each calculation**</td><td align="center">___
3
___</td></tr>
<tr><td>(c)</td><td colspan="2">**Audit risks and responses (only 8 risks required)**</td><td></td></tr>
<tr><td></td><td>•</td><td>Treatment of research and development costs</td><td align="center">2</td></tr>
<tr><td></td><td>•</td><td>Incorrect capitalisation of PPE costs</td><td align="center">2</td></tr>
<tr><td></td><td>•</td><td>New significant loan finance</td><td align="center">2</td></tr>
<tr><td></td><td>•</td><td>Finance costs</td><td align="center">2</td></tr>
<tr><td></td><td>•</td><td>Risk of manipulation due to potential listing</td><td align="center">2</td></tr>
<tr><td></td><td>•</td><td>Recoverability of receivables</td><td align="center">2</td></tr>
<tr><td></td><td>•</td><td>Accounting for 'price promise'</td><td align="center">2</td></tr>
<tr><td></td><td colspan="2">*Product recall*</td><td align="center">2</td></tr>
<tr><td></td><td>•</td><td>Inventory valuation</td><td align="center">2</td></tr>
<tr><td></td><td>•</td><td>Significant increase in revenue and gross margin</td><td align="center">2</td></tr>
<tr><td></td><td>•</td><td>Cash flow difficulties</td><td align="center">2</td></tr>
<tr><td></td><td colspan="2" align="right">**Max 8 issues, 2 marks each**</td><td align="center">___
16
___</td></tr>
<tr><td>(d)</td><td colspan="2">**Substantive procedures – faulty inventory**</td><td></td></tr>
<tr><td></td><td>•</td><td>Obtain schedule of faulty inventory, cast and agree to inventory listing</td><td align="center">1</td></tr>
<tr><td></td><td>•</td><td>Agree quantities affected to manufacturing and sales records</td><td align="center">1</td></tr>
<tr><td></td><td>•</td><td>Agree a sample of returns to relevant documentation</td><td align="center">1</td></tr>
<tr><td></td><td>•</td><td>Discuss issue with management and likelihood of subsequent sale</td><td align="center">1</td></tr>
<tr><td></td><td>•</td><td>Agree any post year-end sales to invoice and assess NRV</td><td align="center">1</td></tr>
<tr><td></td><td>•</td><td>Agree costs of faulty goods to supporting documentation</td><td align="center">1</td></tr>
<tr><td></td><td>•</td><td>Discuss any write down with management</td><td align="center">1</td></tr>
<tr><td></td><td>•</td><td>Inspect board minutes for evidence of resale or additional costs</td><td align="center">1</td></tr>
<tr><td></td><td colspan="2" align="right">**Restricted to**</td><td align="center">___
3
___</td></tr>
</table>

	Marking guide		Marks
(e)	**Substantive procedures – revenue**		
	• Compare to prior year and investigate differences		1
	• Perform a proof in total and investigate differences		1
	• Obtain a schedule of revenue by product line and compare to prior year and investigate differences		1
	• Calculate final gross margin and investigate differences		1
	• Agree a sample of orders to GDN, invoice and GL		1
	• Select GDNs from before and after the year end and perform cut-off testing		1
	• For sales made under the price promise, compare level of claims to refund liability		1
	• For a sample of June invoices in relation to the faulty goods, trace to subsequent credit notes		1
		Restricted to	5
Total			**30**

Examiner's comments

This 30-mark question was based on Darjeeling Co, which develops and manufactures specialist paint products. This question tested candidates' knowledge of analytical procedures, ratios, audit risks and responses and substantive procedures for inventory and revenue. Overall candidates' performance was satisfactory.

Part (a) required candidates to explain why analytical procedures are used during the three stages of an audit. One mark was awarded for each well explained point. It was pleasing to see that many candidates were able to clearly explain WHY analytical review procedures were used at three distinct stages in the audit process. However, a number of candidates spent time detailing what analytical procedures were and gave examples, rather than why they were used. This is a knowledge area, which has been tested in previous diets. Candidates are again reminded to read the question requirement carefully and to ensure that they are only answering the question set.

Part (b) required candidates to calculate ratios for the current and prior year. Candidates performed well, with many scoring full marks. However, a significant minority of candidates provided more than the three required ratios. Additionally, some candidates simply stated the ratio formula. However, marks were only awarded (½ mark) for each year's calculation. Therefore no credit was available for workings or stating of ratio formulae. Some candidates simply provided the formula or working but not the final calculation.

Part (c) required candidates to identify and describe eight audit risks and to explain the auditor's response to each in planning the audit of Darjeeling Co. Performance on this question was satisfactory. Marks were awarded for identification of an audit risk (½ mark each), explanation of the audit risk (½ mark each) and an appropriate auditor's response to each risk (1 mark each). The scenario contained more than eight risks so it was pleasing that most candidates planned their time carefully and generally only attempted to list the required number of points. As in previous diets, although candidates identified the risks, many candidates did not adequately explain the risk. To explain the risk, candidates need to state the area of the financial statements impacted with an assertion (for example cut-off/valuation etc), or a reference to over/under/misstated, or a reference to inherent/control/detection risk.

For example, candidates often correctly identified that the company had made a price promise to customers and therefore recognised a refund liability, this was awarded ½ mark for identification, however, no further credit was awarded for explanations relating to the business implications of false claims. To be awarded the ½ explanation mark candidates need to clearly state the audit implication, for example, that 'profit and the liability may be misstated'. Candidates should ensure that when identifying audit risks they use the scenario fully and rather than listing generic risks they use the detail provided. For example, service and maintenance costs had been included within the cost of a new manufacturing line capitalised into property, plant and equipment. The audit risk therefore related to the incorrect capitalisation of the service and maintenance costs and answers should have focused on this specific issue. However, a significant number of candidates provided generic risks and responses relating to capital vs revenue expenditure. Candidate performance in relation to auditor's responses continues to be mixed. While an auditor's response does not have to be a detailed audit procedure, rather an approach the audit team will take to address the identified risk, the responses given were often too weak such as 'discuss with management'. This is not a sufficient response to deal with any identified audit risk and candidates need to be able to use their knowledge of audit procedures to provide a valid response which would adequately address the risk identified.

Future candidates must take note that audit risk is and will continue to be an important element of the syllabus and must be understood. Candidates must also ensure that they include adequate question practice as part of their revision of this key topic.

Part (d) required candidates to describe substantive procedures the auditor should perform in relation to faulty products held within year-end inventory. One mark was awarded for each well described procedure. Performance on this requirement was disappointing. Many candidates failed to provide three procedures, and those listed often focused on the wrong areas. Unfortunately, many answers focused on standard inventory count procedures rather than focusing on the key issue of valuation. It can only be assumed that candidates saw the words 'inventory' and 'at the year end' in the requirement and launched into year-end inventory count procedures without further thought. Again, candidates must take the time to read the question requirements carefully and spend time thinking about what is needed prior to writing their answers. Where valuation was considered many answers were vague such as 'recalculate net realisable value' without any detail of how this should be performed. Some procedures such as 'discuss with management' were provided but without any detail as to what exactly should be discussed.

As addressed in previous examiner's reports, candidates must strive to understand substantive procedures. Learning a generic list of tests will not translate to exam success, as they must be applied to the question requirement.

Part (e) required candidates to describe substantive procedures the auditor should perform in relation to revenue. One mark was awarded for each well described procedure. Performance on this requirement was satisfactory. The most common procedures provided by candidates were analytical review procedures, cut-off tests and tests of detail tracing to goods received notes, invoices and the ledger. Many provided a sufficient number of procedures to pass this requirement. However, some substantive procedures were often vague, for example, 'review transactions to ensure cut-off is appropriate'. Other examples of procedures which were not adequately described such as 'compare revenue to the prior year' (awarded ½ mark), for the full 1 mark candidates needed to also state 'and investigate any significant differences'. Also cut-off procedures were sometimes recommended to be undertaken using sales invoices rather than goods received notes, which would only have scored ½ mark.

204 BLACKBERRY *Walk in the footsteps of a top tutor*

Key answer tips

Part (a) asks for the auditor's responsibility in relation to prevention and detection of fraud and error. A good answer needs to refer to the requirements of the relevant auditing standard, ISA 240. If you can't remember the main points of the ISA, take a common sense approach and think about a logical answer to score at least some marks.

Part (b) asks for audit risks and responses. This requirement is examined every sitting. You must make sure the risk relates to either a risk of material misstatement or a detection risk. Read through the scenario to identify information which refers to something that will appear in the financial statements, e.g. revenue, property, inventory and briefly explain the accounting treatment that should be applied. Think about common mistakes that the client could make either deliberately to manipulate the financial statements or unintentionally. State whether the item in financial statements is at risk of under or overstatement. The response must be a response of the auditor, not the client and must directly relate to the risk you have given.

(a) Fraud responsibility

Loganberry & Co must conduct an audit in accordance with ISA 240 *The Auditor's Responsibilities Relating to Fraud in an Audit of Financial Statements* and is responsible for obtaining reasonable assurance that the financial statements taken as a whole are free from material misstatement, whether caused by fraud or error.

In order to fulfil this responsibility, Loganberry & Co is required to identify and assess the risks of material misstatement of the financial statements due to fraud.

They need to obtain sufficient appropriate audit evidence regarding the assessed risks of material misstatement due to fraud through designing and implementing appropriate responses. In addition, Loganberry & Co must respond appropriately to fraud or suspected fraud identified during the audit.

When obtaining reasonable assurance, Loganberry & Co is responsible for maintaining professional scepticism throughout the audit, considering the potential for management override of controls and recognising the fact that audit procedures which are effective in detecting error may not be effective in detecting fraud.

To ensure that the whole engagement team is aware of the risks and responsibilities for fraud and error, ISA 240 requires that a discussion is held within the team. For members not present at the meeting, Blackberry Co's audit engagement partner should determine which matters should be communicated to them.

(b) **Audit risks and auditor's responses**

Audit risk	Auditor's response
Blackberry Co values its inventory at the lower of cost and net realisable value. Cost includes both production and general overheads. IAS 2 *Inventories* requires that costs included in valuing goods and services should only be those incurred in bringing inventory to its present location and condition. Although production overheads meet these criteria, general overheads do not. If these are included in inventory cost, then this will result in over-valued inventory.	Discuss with management the nature of the overheads included in inventory valuation. If general overheads are included, request management remove them from the valuation to be included in the draft financial statements. Review supporting documentation to verify those overheads deemed to be of a production nature are valid
The company is planning to undertake the full year-end inventory counts after the year end and then adjust for movements from the year end. If the adjustments are not completed accurately, then the year-end inventory could be under or overstated.	The auditor should attend the inventory count held after the year end and note details of goods received and despatched post year end, in order to agree to the reconciliation. During the final audit, the year-end inventory adjustments schedule should be reviewed in detail and agreed to supporting documentation obtained during the inventory count for all adjusting items.
A patent has been purchased for $1.1m and this grants Blackberry Co the exclusive right for three years to customise their portable music players to gain a competitive advantage in their industry. Management has expensed the full amount paid to the current year statement of profit or loss. In accordance with IAS 38 *Intangible Assets*, this should have been included as an intangible asset and amortised over its three-year life. As the sum has been fully expensed and not treated in accordance with IAS 38, intangible assets and profits are understated.	The audit team will need to agree the purchase price to supporting documentation and confirm the useful life is three years as per the contract. Discuss with management the reason for fully expensing the $1.1m paid, and request they correct the treatment. The correcting journal should be reviewed and the amortisation charge recalculated in order to ensure the accuracy of the charge and that the intangible is correctly valued.

Audit risk	Auditor's response
During the year Blackberry Co has raised new finance through issuing $1.2m of shares at a premium. This needs to be accounted for correctly, with adequate disclosure made and the equity finance needs to be allocated correctly between share capital and share premium. If this is not done, then the accounts may be misstated due to a lack of disclosure or share capital and share premium may be misstated.	The audit team should confirm that proceeds of $1.2m were received and that the split of share capital and share premium is correct and appropriately recorded. In addition, the disclosures for this finance should be reviewed in detail to ensure compliance with relevant accounting standards and local legislation.
In November 20X7, it was discovered that a significant teeming and lading fraud had been carried out by four members of the receivables ledger department. There is a risk that the full impact of the fraud has not been quantified and any additional fraudulent transactions would need to be written off in the statement of profit or loss. If these have not been uncovered, the financial statements could be misstated. In addition, individual receivable balances may be under/overstated as customer receipts have been misallocated to other receivable balances.	Discuss with the finance director what procedures they have adopted to fully identify and quantify the impact of the teeming and lading fraud. In addition, discuss with the finance director, what controls have been put in place to identify any similar frauds. Review the receivables listing to identify any unusual postings to individual receivable balances as this could be further evidence of fraudulent transactions. In addition, the team should maintain their professional scepticism and be alert to the risk of further fraud and errors.
During the year Blackberry Co outsourced its receivables ledger processing to an external service organisation. A detection risk arises as to whether sufficient and appropriate evidence is available at Blackberry Co to confirm the completeness and accuracy of controls over the sales and receivables cycle and balances at the year end.	Discuss with management the extent of records maintained at Blackberry Co for the period since February 20X8 and any monitoring of controls undertaken by management over sales and receivables. Consideration should be given to contacting the service organisation's auditor to confirm the level of controls in place.

Audit risk	Auditor's response
The receivables ledger processing transferred to the service organisation from 1 February 20X8. If any errors occurred during the transfer process, these could result in sales and receivables being under/overstated.	Discuss with management the transfer process undertaken and any controls put in place to ensure the completeness and accuracy of the data. Where possible, undertake tests of controls to confirm the effectiveness of the transfer controls. In addition, perform substantive testing on the transfer of information from the old to the new system.
No supplier statement or payables ledger control account reconciliations have been performed in the period from December 20X7 to the year end. This a key control which is being overridden and as such there is an increased risk of errors within trade payables and the year-end payables balance may be under or overstated.	The audit team should increase their testing on trade payables at the year end, including performing supplier statement reconciliations, with a particular focus on completeness of trade payables. Request management prepare a year-end payables ledger control account reconciliation. The audit team should undertake a detailed review of this reconciliation with a focus on any unusual reconciling items.
A current asset of $360,000 has been included within the statement of profit or loss and assets. It represents an anticipated pay out from liquidators handling the bankruptcy of a customer who owed Blackberry Co $0.9m. The sum of $0.9m was written off in the prior year accounts. However, the company has not received a formal notification from the liquidators confirming the payment and this would therefore represent a possible contingent asset. To comply with IAS 37 *Provisions, Contingent Liabilities and Contingent Assets*, this should not be recognised until the receipt is virtually certain. With no firm response to date, the inclusion of this sum overstates profit and current assets.	Discuss with management whether any notification of payment has been received from the liquidators and review the related correspondence. If virtually certain, the treatment adopted is correct. If payment has been received, agree to post-year end cash book. If receipt is not virtually certain, management should be requested to remove it from profit and receivables. If the receipt is probable, the auditor should request management include a contingent asset disclosure note.

	Marking guide		
			Marks
(a)	**Fraud responsibilities**		
	• ISA 240 responsibilities		2
	• Respond appropriately		2
			4
(b)	**Audit risks and responses (only 8 risks required)**		
	• Inventory valuation		2
	• Inventory count after year-end date		2
	• Accounting treatment of patent		2
	• Share issue		2
	• Receivables ledger fraud		2
	• Use of service organisation		2
	• Transfer of data to service organisation		2
	• Claim for unfair dismissal		2
	• Key controls not performed		2
	• Contingent asset		2
		Max 8 issues, 2 marks each	16
Total			20

Examiner's comments

This question was based on Blackberry Co, a manufacturer of portable music players. This question tested the areas of fraud and error, and audit risks and responses. Candidates' performance was mixed.

Part (a) required candidates to describe the auditor's responsibilities in relation to the prevention and detection of fraud and error. One mark was awarded for each well described point. Some candidates performed very well on this requirement and clearly had an excellent understanding of the requirements of ISA 240 *The Auditor's Responsibilities Relating to Fraud in an Audit of Financial Statements*, however, a number of candidates described management's responsibilities rather than auditor's responsibilities and therefore did not answer the requirement of the question. In addition, although many candidates understood that the auditors are not responsible for preventing fraud, some candidates were not clear that the auditor is also not responsible for detecting all errors due to fraud/error. A number of candidates described substantive procedures to detect fraud/error, and again these were not awarded credit as the question asked for 'the responsibilities' of the auditors. This is a knowledge area, which has been tested in previous diets. Candidates are again reminded to read the question requirement carefully and to ensure that they are only answering the question set.

Part (b) required candidates to describe eight audit risks and to explain the auditor's response to each in planning the audit of Blackberry Co. Performance on this question was mixed. Marks were awarded for identification of each audit risk (½ mark each), explanation of each risk (½ mark each) and an appropriate auditor's response to each risk (1 mark each). The scenario contained more than eight risks so it was pleasing that most candidates planned their time carefully and generally only attempted to list the required number of points. As in previous diets, although candidates identified the risks, many of them did not adequately explain the risk. To explain the audit risk candidates need to state the area of the financial statements impacted with an assertion (for example, cut-off/valuation, etc), or a reference to over/under/misstated, or a reference to inherent/control/detection risk.

For example, candidates often correctly identified the financial accountant suing for unfair dismissal, this was awarded ½ mark for identification, however no further credit was awarded for the explanation that 'costs may not be included'. To be awarded the ½ explanation mark candidates need to clearly state the implication, for example, that 'provisions may be understated', or 'provisions may not be complete'. Candidate performance in relation to auditor's responses continues to be mixed. While an auditor's response does not have to be a detailed audit procedure, rather an approach the audit team will take to address the identified risk, the responses given were often too weak such as 'discuss with management'. This is not a sufficient response to deal with any identified audit risk and candidates need to be able to use their knowledge of audit procedures to provide a valid response which would adequately address the risk identified. Future candidates must take note audit risk is and will continue to be an important element of the syllabus and must be understood. Candidates must also ensure that they include adequate question practice as part of their revision of this key topic.

205 PRANCER CONSTRUCTION *Walk in the footsteps of a top tutor*

Key answer tips

Part (a) asks for the preconditions of an audit. This is knowledge you either know don't know. If you don't know it move on and try to compensate by scoring well on other requirements.

Part (b) asks for areas to be included in the audit strategy for Prancer Construction. This requires you to identify the main areas of an audit strategy and apply that knowledge to the specific details of the client in the scenario. Easy marks can be earned here for referring to obtaining an understanding of the internal controls, calculating preliminary materiality and selecting the audit team. These are all things that are done at the planning stage and would be included in the audit strategy.

Part (c) asks for audit risks and responses. This requirement is examined every sitting. You must make sure the risk relates to either a risk of material misstatement or a detection risk. The response must be a response of the auditor, not the client.

(a)   **Preconditions for the audit**

ISA 210 *Agreeing the Terms of Audit Engagements* states that auditors should only accept a new audit engagement when it has been confirmed that the preconditions for an audit are present.

To assess whether the preconditions for an audit are present, Cupid & Co should have determined whether the financial reporting framework to be applied in the preparation of Prancer Construction Co's financial statements is acceptable. In considering this, the auditor should have assessed the nature of the entity, the nature and purpose of the financial statements and whether law or regulation prescribes the applicable reporting framework.

In addition, the firm should have obtained the agreement of Prancer Construction Co's management that it acknowledges and understands its responsibility for the following:

- Preparation of the financial statements in accordance with the applicable financial reporting framework, including where relevant their fair presentation.

- For such internal control as management determines is necessary to enable the preparation of financial statements which are free from material misstatement, whether due to fraud or error.

- To provide Cupid & Co with access to all relevant information for the preparation of the financial statements, any additional information which the auditor may request from management and unrestricted access to personnel within Prancer Construction Co from whom the auditor determines it necessary to obtain audit evidence.

(b) **Areas to be included in the audit strategy document**

The audit strategy sets out the scope, timing and direction of the audit and helps the development of the audit plan. ISA 300 *Planning an Audit of Financial Statements* sets out areas which should be considered and documented as part of the audit strategy document and are as follows:

Main characteristics of the engagement

The audit strategy should consider the main characteristics of the engagement, which define its scope. For Prancer Construction Co, the following are examples of things which should be included:

- Whether the financial information to be audited has been prepared in accordance with the relevant financial reporting framework.

- Whether computer-assisted audit techniques will be used and the effect of IT on audit procedures.

- The availability of key personnel at Prancer Construction Co.

Reporting objectives, timing and nature of communication

It should ascertain the reporting objectives of the engagement to plan the timing of the audit and the nature of the communications required, such as:

- The audit timetable for reporting including the timing of interim and final stages.

- Organisation of meetings with Prancer Construction Co's management to discuss any audit issues arising.

- Any discussions with management regarding the reports to be issued.

- The timings of the audit team meetings and review of work performed.

Significant factors affecting the audit

The strategy should consider the factors which, in the auditor's professional judgement, are significant in directing Prancer Construction Co's audit team's efforts, such as:

- The determination of materiality for the audit.

- The need to maintain a questioning mind and to exercise professional scepticism in gathering and evaluating audit evidence.

Preliminary engagement activities and knowledge from previous engagements

It should consider the results of preliminary audit planning activities and, where applicable, whether knowledge gained on other engagements for Prancer Construction Co is relevant, such as:

– Results of any tests over the effectiveness of internal controls.

– Evidence of management's commitment to the design, implementation and maintenance of sound internal controls.

– Volume of transactions, which may determine whether it is more efficient for the audit team to rely on internal controls.

– Significant business developments affecting Prancer Construction Co, such as the improvement in building practices and construction quality.

Nature, timing and extent of resources

The audit strategy should ascertain the nature, timing and extent of resources necessary to perform the audit, such as:

– The selection of the audit team with experience of this type of industry.

– Assignment of audit work to the team members.

– Setting the audit budget.

(c) **Audit risks and auditor's responses**

Audit risk	Auditor's response
Prancer Construction Co is a new client for Cupid & Co. As the team is not familiar with the accounting policies, transactions and balances of the company, there will be an increased detection risk on the audit.	Cupid & Co should ensure they have a suitably experienced team. In addition, adequate time should be allocated for team members to obtain an understanding of the company and the risks of material misstatement including a detailed team briefing to cover the key areas of risk.
Prancer Construction Co is likely to have a material level of work in progress at the year end, being construction work in progress as well as ongoing maintenance services, as Prancer Construction Co has annual contracts for many of the buildings constructed. The level of work in progress will need to be assessed at the year end. Assessing the percentage completion for partially constructed buildings is likely to be quite subjective, and the team should consider if they have the required expertise to undertake this. If the percentage completion is not correctly calculated, the inventory valuation may be under or overstated.	The auditor should discuss with management the process they will undertake to assess the percentage completion for work in progress at the year end. This process should be reviewed by the auditor while attending the year-end inventory counts. In addition, consideration should be given as to whether an independent expert is required to value the work in progress or if a management expert has been used. If the work of an expert is to be used, then the audit team will need to assess the competence, capabilities and objectivity of the expert.

Audit risk	Auditor's response
The August 20X7 management accounts contain $2.1 million of completed properties; this balance was $1.4 million in September 20X6. IAS 2 *Inventories* requires that inventory should be stated at the lower of cost and NRV. The increase in inventory may be due to an increased level of pre year-end orders. Alternatively, it may be that Prancer Construction Co is struggling to sell completed properties. This may indicate that they are overvalued.	Detailed cost and net realisable value (NRV) testing to be performed at the year end and the aged inventory report to be reviewed to assess whether inventory requires to be written down.
At the year end there will be inventory counts undertaken at all 11 of the building sites in progress. It is unlikely that the auditor will be able to attend all of these inventory counts, increasing detection risk, and therefore they need to ensure that they obtain sufficient evidence over the inventory counting controls, and completeness and existence of inventory for any sites not visited.	The auditor should assess for which of the building sites they will attend the counts. This will be those with the most material inventory or which according to management have the most significant risk of misstatement. For those not visited, the auditor will need to review the level of exceptions noted during the count and discuss with management any issues, which arose during the count.
Prancer Construction Co offers its customers a building warranty of five years, which covers any construction defects. A warranty provision will be required under IAS 37 *Provisions, Contingent Liabilities and Contingent Assets*. Calculating warranty provisions requires judgement as it is an uncertain amount. The finance director anticipates this provision will be lower than last year as the company has improved its building practices and the quality of its finished properties. However, there is a risk that this provision could be understated, especially in light of the overdraft covenant relating to a minimum level of net assets and is being used as a mechanism to manipulate profit and asset levels.	Discuss with management the basis of the provision calculation, and compare this to the level of post year-end claims, if any, made by customers. In particular, discuss the rationale behind reducing the level of provision this year. Compare the prior year provision with the actual level of claims in the year, to assess the reasonableness of the judgements made by management.

Audit risk	Auditor's response
Customers who wish to purchase a property are required to place an order and a 5% non-refundable deposit prior to the completion of the building. These deposits should not be recognised as revenue in the statement of profit or loss until the performance obligations as per the contracts have been satisfied. This is likely to be when the building is finished and the sale process is complete. Instead, they should be recognised as deferred income within current liabilities. Management may have incorrectly treated the deferred income as revenue, resulting in overstated revenue and understated liabilities.	Discuss with management the treatment of deposits received in advance, to ensure it is appropriate. During the final audit, undertake increased testing over the cut-off of revenue and completeness of deferred income.
An allowance for receivables has historically been maintained, but it is anticipated that this will be reduced. There is a risk that receivables will be overvalued; some balances may not be recoverable and so will be overstated if not provided for. In addition, reducing the allowance for receivables will increase asset values and would improve the covenant compliance, which increases the manipulation risk further.	Review and test the controls surrounding how the finance director identifies old or potentially irrecoverable receivables balances and credit control to ensure that they are operating effectively. Discuss with the director the rationale for reducing the allowance for receivables. Extended post year-end cash receipts testing and a review of the aged receivables ledger to be performed to assess valuation and the need for an allowance for receivables.
Prancer Construction Co has a material overdraft which has minimum profit and net assets covenants attached to it. If these covenants were to be breached, the overdraft balance would become instantly repayable. If the company does not have sufficient cash to meet this repayment, then there could be going concern implications. In addition, there is a risk of manipulation of profit and net assets to ensure that covenants are met.	Review the covenant calculations prepared by the company at the year end and identify whether any defaults have occurred; if so, determine the effect on the company. The team should maintain their professional scepticism and be alert to the risk that profit and/or net assets have been overstated to ensure compliance with the covenants.

Audit risk	Auditor's response
Preliminary analytical review of the August management accounts shows a payables payment period of 56 for August 20X7, compared to 87 days for September 20X6. It is anticipated that the year-end payables payment period will be even lower.	The audit team should increase their testing on trade payables at the year end, with a particular focus on completeness of payables. A payables circularisation or review of supplier statement reconciliations should be undertaken.
The forecast profit is higher than last year, indicating an increase in trade, also the company's cash position has continued to deteriorate and therefore, it is unusual for payables payment period to have decreased.	
There is an increased risk of errors within trade payables and the year-end payables may be understated.	

Marking guide			Marks
(a)	**Preconditions for the audit**		
	• Determination of acceptable framework		1
	• Agreement of management responsibilities		1
	• Preparation of financial statements		1
	• Internal control		1
	• Access to information		1
		Restricted to	3
(b)	**Audit strategy document**		
	• Main characteristics of the audit		1
	• Reporting objectives		1
	• Significant factors affecting the audit		1
	• Preliminary engagement activities		1
	• Nature, timing and extent of resources		1
		Restricted to	3
(c)	**Audit risks and responses (only 7 risks required)**		
	• New client, increased detection risk		2
	• Work in progress		2
	• Increased inventory		2
	• Warranty provision		2
	• Attendance at inventory counts		2
	• Deferred income not correctly recognised		2
	• Receivables allowance and valuation		2
	• Overdraft covenants		2
	• Trade payables		2
		Max 7 issues, 2 marks each	14
Total			20

Examiner's comments

This question was based on a property construction company, Prancer Construction Co. This question tested the areas of preconditions, the audit strategy document and audit risks and responses.

Part (a) required the steps the firm should take to confirm whether the preconditions for the audit were in place. Where it was answered, candidates performed unsatisfactorily on this question, which is disappointing as candidates did not perform well the last time this area was tested. It was clear from candidate answers that those who had studied preconditions were able to score all three marks and those who had not studied it failed to score any marks. Those candidates who did not score well tended to focus on ethical threats or pre-acceptance procedures such as gaining professional clearance from the previous auditors, checking the audit firm had adequate resources and competence to undertake the audit. This is a knowledge area and has been tested in previous diets. Candidates must practise past exam questions and ensure they study the breadth of the syllabus.

Part (b) required an identification of three main areas, other than audit risks, to be included within Prancer Construction Co's audit strategy document and an example for each area. This question, where attempted, was poorly answered by most candidates. Most candidates did not answer both parts of the requirement, failing to identify the areas of an audit strategy. This is a knowledge area and demonstrated a gap in candidates' technical knowledge. Where candidates did score marks this was for providing examples, the most common answers given were around materiality, timetable and audit team. Those candidates who did not score well either did not attempt the question or focused on audit risks, despite the question requirement clearly stating "other than audit risks" and then explained inherent, control and detection risks.

Part (c) required an identification and description of seven audit risks from the scenario and the auditor's response for each. Performance on this question was mixed. Marks were awarded for identification of audit risk (½ mark each), explanation of audit risk by referring to the assertion and account balance impacted (½ mark each) and an appropriate auditor's response to each risk. (1 mark each). The scenario contained more than seven risks so it was pleasing that most candidates planned their time carefully and generally only attempted to list the required number of points. As in previous diets, a significant number of candidates tended to only identify facts from the scenario such as "inventory has increased significantly on the prior year"; this would only have scored a maximum of ½ mark. This point did not explain the impact on the financial statements or why this was an audit risk and therefore cannot be awarded the ½ mark for explanation.

To adequately explain audit risk, candidates need to state the area of the accounts impacted with either an assertion (e.g. cut off, valuation etc.), a reference to under/over/misstated, or a reference to inherent, control or detection risk. In addition many candidates incorrectly explained the audit risk. For example they correctly identified that the auditor was not able to attend all the year-end inventory counts, this would have gained ½ mark but incorrectly stated that this would then lead to inventory being misstated. The issue is that if the auditor does not attend all counts this results in an increased detection risk. Also weaker candidates argued that the decrease in trade payable days led to a going concern risk, this was not the case, as with trade payables decreasing there was a completeness of payables risk. Many candidates incorrectly assumed the fact the company had a material overdraft was an audit risk and so focused on going concern procedures, rather than recognising that the risk actually related to the covenants attached to the overdraft and the possible manipulation of profit or assets in order to meet these.

Candidate performance in relation to auditor's responses continues to be mixed. While an auditor's response does not have to be a detailed audit procedure, rather an approach the audit team will take to address the identified risk, the responses given were often too weak such as 'discuss with management'. This is not a sufficient response to deal with any identified audit risk and candidates need to be able to use their knowledge of audit procedures to provide a valid response which would adequately address the risk identified. A minority of candidates continue to give business advice, such as recommending management charge for the free five year warranty provided or implementing improved credit control procedures to address the receivables valuation risk. In addition some responses were impractical, for example suggesting that the audit firm recruit more staff in order to attend all inventory counts. Future candidates must take note audit risk is and will continue to be an important element of the syllabus and must be understood, and candidates must ensure that they include adequate question practice as part of their revision of this key topic.

206 HURLING *Walk in the footsteps of a top tutor*

Key answer tips

Part (a) is a frequently examined requirement asking for definitions of audit risk and the components of audit risk. Take time to learn definitions of common auditing terms such as these.

Part (b) asks for audit risks and responses. This requirement is examined every sitting. You must make sure the risk relates to either a risk of material misstatement or a detection risk. The response must be a response of the auditor, not the client.

Part (c) asks for ethical threats and safeguards from the scenario. To earn a full mark for each threat you must explain how the auditor's objectivity could be impaired i.e. how their behaviour could be affected by the situation which would result in them being biased towards the client.

(a)   Audit risk and the components of audit risk

Audit risk is the risk that the auditor expresses an inappropriate audit opinion when the financial statements are materially misstated. Audit risk is a function of two main components, being the risk of material misstatement and detection risk. Risk of material misstatement is made up of a further two components, inherent risk and control risk.

Inherent risk is the susceptibility of an assertion about a class of transaction, account balance or disclosure to a misstatement which could be material, either individually or when aggregated with other misstatements, before consideration of any related controls.

Control risk is the risk that a misstatement which could occur in an assertion about a class of transaction, account balance or disclosure and which could be material, either individually or when aggregated with other misstatements, will not be prevented, or detected and corrected, on a timely basis by the entity's internal control.

Detection risk is the risk that the procedures performed by the auditor to reduce audit risk to an acceptably low level will not detect a misstatement which exists and which could be material, either individually or when aggregated with other misstatements. Detection risk is affected by sampling and non-sampling risk.

(b) **Audit risks and auditor's responses**

Audit risk	Auditor's response
Hurling Co upgraded their website during the year at a cost of $1.1m. The costs incurred should be correctly allocated between revenue and capital expenditure. Intangible assets and expenses will be misstated if expenditure has been treated incorrectly.	Review a breakdown of the costs and agree to invoices to assess the nature of the expenditure and if capital, agree to inclusion within the asset register or agree to the statement of profit or loss.
As the website has been upgraded, there is a possibility that the new processes and systems may not record data reliably and accurately. This may lead to a risk over completeness and accuracy of data in the underlying accounting records.	The audit team should document the revised system and undertake tests over the completeness and accuracy of data recorded from the website to the accounting records.
Hurling Co has entered into a transaction to purchase a new warehouse for $3.2m and it is anticipated that the legal process will be completed by the year end. Only assets which physically exist at the year-end should be included in property, plant and equipment. If the transaction has not been completed by the year end, there is a risk that assets are overstated if the company incorrectly includes the warehouse at the year end.	Discuss with management as to whether the warehouse purchase was completed by the year end. If so, inspect legal documents of ownership, such as title deeds ensuring these are dated prior to 1 April 20X7 and are in the company name.
Significant finance has been obtained in the year, as the company has issued $5m of irredeemable preference shares. This finance needs to be accounted for correctly, with adequate disclosure made. As the preference shares are irredeemable, they should be classified as equity rather than non-current liabilities. Failing to correctly classify the shares could result in understated equity and overstated non-current liabilities.	Review share issue documentation to confirm that the preference shares are irredeemable. Confirm that they have been correctly classified as equity within the accounting records and that total financing proceeds of $5m were received. In addition, the disclosures for this share issue should be reviewed in detail to ensure compliance with relevant accounting standards.

Audit risk	Auditor's response
The finance director has extended the useful lives of fixtures and fittings from three to four years, resulting in the depreciation charge reducing. Under IAS 16 *Property, Plant and Equipment*, useful lives are to be reviewed annually, and if asset lives have genuinely increased, then this change is reasonable. However, there is a risk that this reduction has occurred in order to boost profits. If this is the case, then fixtures and fittings are overvalued and profit overstated.	Discuss with the directors the rationale for any extensions of asset lives and reduction of depreciation rates. Also, the four-year life should be compared to how often these assets are replaced, to assess the useful life of assets.
A customer of Hurling Co has been encountering difficulties paying their outstanding balance of $1.2m and Hurling Co has agreed to a revised credit period. If the customer is experiencing difficulties, there is an increased risk that the receivable is not recoverable and hence is overvalued.	Review the revised credit terms and identify if any after date cash receipts for this customer have been made. Discuss with the finance director whether he intends to make an allowance for this receivable. If not, review whether any existing allowance for uncollectable accounts is sufficient to cover the amount of this receivable.
A sales-related bonus scheme has been introduced in the year for sales staff, with a significant number of new customer accounts on favourable credit terms being opened pre year end. This has resulted in a 5% increase in revenue. Sales staff seeking to maximise their current year bonus may result in new accounts being opened from poor credit risks leading to irrecoverable receivables.	Increased after date cash receipts testing to be undertaken for new customer account receivables.
In addition, there is a risk of sales cut-off errors as new customers could place orders within the two-month introductory period and subsequently return these goods post year end.	Increased sales cut-off testing will be performed along with a review of any post year-end returns as they may indicate cut-off errors.

Audit risk	Auditor's response
Hurling Co has halted further sales of its new product Luge and a product recall has been initiated for any goods sold in the last four months. If there are issues with the quality of the Luge product, inventory may be overvalued as its NRV may be below its cost.	Discuss with the finance director whether any write downs will be made to this product, and what, if any, modifications may be required with regards the quality. Testing should be undertaken to confirm cost and NRV of the Luge products in inventory and that on a line-by-line basis the goods are valued correctly.
Additionally, products of Luge sold within the last four months are being recalled, this will result in Hurling Co paying customer refunds. The sale will need to be removed and a refund liability should be recognised along with the reinstatement of inventory, although the NRV of this inventory could be of a minimal value. Failing to account for this correctly could result in overstated revenue and understated liabilities and inventory.	Review the list of sales made of product Luge prior to the recall, agree that the sale has been removed from revenue and the inventory included. If the refund has not been paid pre year-end, agree it is included within current liabilities.
Petanque Co, a customer of Hurling Co, has announced that they intend to commence legal action for a loss of information and profits as a result of the Luge product sold to them. If it is probable that the company will make payment to the customer, a legal provision is required. If the payment is possible rather than probable, a contingent liability disclosure would be necessary. If Hurling Co has not done this, there is a risk over the completeness of any provisions or the necessary disclosure of contingent liabilities.	Caving & Co should write to the company's lawyers to enquire of the existence and likelihood of success of any claim from Petanque Co. The results of this should be used to assess the level of provision or disclosure included in the financial statements.
The finance director has requested that the audit completes one week earlier than normal as he wishes to report results earlier. A reduction in the audit timetable will increase detection risk and place additional pressure on the team in obtaining sufficient and appropriate evidence.	The timetable should be confirmed with the finance director. If it is to be reduced, then consideration should be given to performing an interim audit in late March or early April. This would then reduce the pressure on the final audit.

Audit risk	Auditor's response
In addition, the finance team of Hurling Co will have less time to prepare the financial information leading to an increased risk of errors arising in the financial statements.	The team needs to maintain professional scepticism and be alert to the increased risk of errors occurring.
The company is intending to propose a final dividend once the financial statements are finalised. This amount should not be provided for in the 20X7 financial statements as the obligation only arises once the dividend is announced, which is post year end. In line with IAS 10 *Events After the Reporting Date* the dividend should only be disclosed. If the dividend is included, this will result in an overstatement of liabilities and understatement of equity.	Discuss the issue with management and confirm that the dividend will not be included within liabilities in the 20X7 financial statements. The financial statements need to be reviewed to ensure that adequate disclosure of the proposed dividend is included.

(c)   **Ethical threats and safeguards**

Ethical threat	Possible safeguard
The finance director is keen to report Hurling Co's financial results earlier than normal and has asked if the audit can be completed in a shorter time frame. This may create an intimidation threat on the team as they may feel under pressure to cut corners and not raise issues in order to satisfy the deadlines and this could compromise the objectivity of the audit team and quality of audit performed.	The engagement partner should discuss the timing of the audit with the finance director to understand if the audit can commence earlier, so as to ensure adequate time for the team to gather evidence. If this is not possible, the partner should politely inform the finance director that the team will undertake the audit in accordance with all relevant ISAs and quality control procedures. Therefore the audit is unlikely to be completed earlier. If any residual concerns remain or the intimidation threat continues, then Caving & Co may need to consider resigning from the engagement.
A non-executive director (NED) of Hurling Co has just resigned and the directors have asked whether the partners of Caving & Co can assist them in recruiting to fill this vacancy. This represents a self-interest threat as the audit firm cannot undertake the recruitment of members of the board of Hurling Co, especially a NED who will have a key role in overseeing the audit process and audit firm.	Caving & Co is able to assist Hurling Co in that they can undertake roles s~ reviewing a shortlist of c~ reviewing qualif~ Howeve~ they are r~ manageme~ seek out ca~ make the fin~ appointed.

Ethical threat	Possible safeguard
The engagement quality control reviewer (ECQR) assigned to Hurling Co was until last year the audit engagement partner. This represents a familiarity threat as the partner will have been associated with Hurling Co for a long period of time and so may not retain professional scepticism and objectivity.	As Hurling Co is a listed company, then the previous audit engagement partner should not be involved in the audit for at least a period of five years. An alternative ECQR should be appointed instead.
Caving & Co provides taxation services, the audit engagement and possibly services related to the recruitment of the NED. There is a potential self-interest or intimidation threat as the total fees could represent a significant proportion of Caving & Co's income and the firm could become overly reliant on Hurling Co. This could result in the firm being less challenging or objective due to fear of losing such a significant client.	Caving & Co should assess whether audit, recruitment and taxation fees would represent more than 15% of gross practice income for two consecutive years. If the recurring fees are likely to exceed 15% of annual practice income this year, additional consideration should be given as to whether the recruitment and taxation services should be undertaken by the firm. In addition, if the fees do exceed 15%, then this should be disclosed to those charged with governance at Hurling Co. If the firm retains all work, it should arrange for a pre-issuance (before the audit opinion is issued) or post-issuance (after the opinion has been issued) review to be undertaken by an external accountant or by a regulatory body.
The finance director has suggested that the audit fee is based on the profit before tax of Hurling Co which constitutes a contingent fee. Contingent fees give rise to a self-interest threat and are prohibited under ACCA's *Code of Ethics and Conduct*. If the audit fee is based on profit, the team may be inclined to ignore audit adjustments which could lead to a reduction in profit.	Caving & Co will not be able to accept contingent fees and should communicate to those charged with governance at Hurling Co that the external audit fee needs to be based on the time spent and levels of skill and experience of the required audit team members.

Ethical threat	Possible safeguard
At today's date, 20% of last year's audit fee is still outstanding and was due for payment three months ago. A self-interest threat can arise if the fees remain outstanding, as Caving & Co may feel pressure to agree to certain accounting adjustments in order to have the previous year and this year's audit fee paid. In addition, outstanding fees could be perceived as a loan to a client which is strictly prohibited.	Caving & Co should discuss with those charged with governance the reasons why the final 20% of last year's fee has not been paid. They should agree a revised payment schedule which will result in the fees being settled before any more work is performed for the current year audit. The auditor's report for this year must not be issued until the fees from last year have been paid.

	Marking guide	Marks
(a)	**Define audit risk and its components**	
	• Audit risk	2
	• Inherent risk	1
	• Control risk	1
	• Detection risk	1
		4
(b)	**Audit risks and responses (only 8 risks required)**	
	• Capitalisation of website costs	2
	• Completeness and accuracy of data due to new website	2
	• Warehouse acquisition	2
	• Classification of preference shares	2
	• Appropriateness of asset useful lives	2
	• Irrecoverable receivable	2
	• Sales staff bonus scheme	2
	• Product recall – inventory valuation	2
	• Product recall – provision for refunds	2
	• Legal action	2
	• Audit timetable, increased detection risk	2
	• Accounting for proposed dividend	2
	Max 8 issues, 2 marks each	16
(c)	**Ethical threats and safeguards (only 5 threats required)**	
	• Intimidation threat – audit timetable	2
	• Self-interest threat – recruitment	2
	• Familiarity threat – EQCR	2
	• Self-interest/intimidation threat – fees	2
	• Self-interest threat – contingent fee	2
	• Self-interest threat – outstanding fees	2
	Max 5 issues, 2 marks each	10
Total		30

Examiner's comments

This question was based on a listed company, Hurling Co, a manufacturer of computer components. This question tested the areas of audit risks and responses, and ethical threats and safeguards.

Part (a) required candidates to define audit risk and the components of audit risk. This question was generally well answered with the majority of candidates demonstrating a reasonably good knowledge of the area tested. Up to 1 mark was awarded for each definition of audit risk and its components. Most candidates correctly identified the three components of audit risk, however, some candidates did not describe the components correctly. For example inherent risk was often described only as 'the risk due to the nature of the business', rather than 'the susceptibility of an account balance or class of transaction to misstatement before related controls'. In key knowledge areas such as this, candidates must ensure that they are technically accurate in order to score full marks.

Part (b) required identification and description of eight audit risks from the scenario and the auditor's response to each. Performance on this question was mixed. Marks were awarded for identification of audit risk (½ marks each), explanation of audit risk (½ marks each) and an appropriate auditor's response to each risk (1 mark each). The scenario contained more than eight risks so it was pleasing that most candidates planned their time carefully and generally only attempted to list the required number of issues. Some candidates however included ethical issues from part (c) of the question in their answer to part (b). For example incorrectly stating that the outstanding prior year audit fee was an audit risk rather than recognising that this is an ethical issue which can threaten auditor independence but does not influence the risk of material misstatement in the financial statements. A number of candidates did not clearly identify and explain certain audit risks from the scenario. For example, some candidates incorrectly noted the issue of a 'new warehouse' could result in 'incorrect allocation of capital and expenses'. However the issue was that the acquisition of the new warehouse may not have been completed by the year end so there is a risk of existence / rights and obligations not transferred. A large number of candidates are still not explaining how each issue could impact on audit risk and therefore were not awarded the ½ mark for explanation. To adequately explain audit risk, candidates need to state the area of the accounts impacted with either an assertion (e.g. cut off, valuation etc.), a reference to under/over/misstated, or a reference to inherent, control or detection risk. For example, many candidates correctly identified the legal action raised by the customer as an issue (½ mark) but then incorrectly stated the explanation of the risk as this could lead to a loss of customer goodwill / reputational damage for the company. This is an explanation of the risk from the company's perspective and does not explain how the financial statements are impacted. To gain the second ½ mark candidates need to refer to either that liabilities may be understated if a provision is needed but not included or that the financial statements may be misstated as contingent liability disclosure is required.

Candidate performance in relation to auditor's responses continues to be mixed. While an auditor's response does not have to be a detailed audit procedure, rather an approach the audit team will take to address the identified risk, the responses given were often too weak such as 'discuss with management'. This is not a sufficient response to deal with any identified audit risk and candidates need to be able to use their knowledge of audit procedures to provide a valid response which would adequately address the risk identified. A minority of candidates discussed business risks and therefore concentrated their responses on what management should do rather than the auditor. For example advising management not to issue irredeemable preference shares and instead to consider alternative forms of finance.

This is not a valid response as it does not address the audit risk identified and it is not within the remit of the auditor to provide this type of guidance.

An assessment of audit risk, is a fundamental factor in planning and assessing the risks of an audit of an entity, and this remains a highly examinable area and candidates must ensure that they include adequate question practice as part of their revision of this key topic.

Part (c) required an identification and explanation of five ethical threats faced by the auditor and how these threats should be reduced. Performance in this question was satisfactory. Marks were awarded for identification of the issue and type of threat (½ marks each), explanation of the threat (½ marks each) and a safeguard to reduce this threat (1 mark each). Most candidates were able to identify relevant issues from the scenario, however some candidates did not provide the correct category of threat. For example, some candidates incorrectly categorised the contingent audit fee and the outstanding prior year audit fees as intimidation threats rather than self-interest threats. Candidates are reminded that they must be comfortable with the categories of threats and how they arise in line with ACCA's Code of Ethics and Conduct. Some candidates identified threats where there was not an issue. A frequent misunderstanding being that the tax work resulted in a self-review threat. This was not correct as the tax work undertaken related to tax returns so would not have had an effect on the tax balance in the audited financial statements. Candidates often did not explain the issues correctly, or in sufficient detail. For example explaining the threat of self-interest resulting from contingent audit fees, as simply that the auditor will not be independent is not sufficient. Candidates needed to comment on the possibility of the auditor ignoring audit adjustments which reduce profits in order to maintain the fee level in order to obtain the explanation ½ mark. Some candidates thought an issue had to be identified for each of the categories of ethical threats of self-review, self-interest etc. This resulted in them trying to identify a situation from the scenario to fit each of the types of threats. This is not the correct approach to take as it is unlikely that the scenario will be based around one of each of the five ethical threats. The second part of the question required safeguards to reduce the risks to an acceptable level. A safeguard should be an action not just a statement of the rules. For example to simply state that contingent audit fees should never be accepted is a statement rather than an action and therefore cannot constitute a safeguard. To obtain the 1 mark for a safeguard candidates should have recommended that the firm decline this fee structure and to explain to the client that the audit fee is based on time and risk. Some responses were too brief or impractical. For example for the threat of outstanding prior year fees, the response given by some candidates was that the auditor should resign. Resignation is an option for auditors, but it is the last resort and was not appropriate for this threat. To obtain the 1 mark for a safeguard, candidates should have recommended that either a revised payment schedule be arranged with the client and or that further work on this year's audit should be delayed until the outstanding audit fee is paid.

207 CENTIPEDE *Walk in the footsteps of a top tutor*

Key answer tips

In part (a), the matters to consider before accepting the audit should include the matters that might prevent the auditor from being able to accept the engagement such as ethical issues which cannot be safeguarded or other risks mentioned in the scenario.

Part (b) asks for ratios to be calculated from the information provided. Remember that the ratios are to help you identify audit risks. You are not evaluating the financial performance of the company.

Part (c) Audit risk and response is examined every sitting. You must make sure the risk relates to either a risk of material misstatement or a detection risk. Risks can be identified from the ratios you have calculated or from the scenario information. The response must be a response of the auditor, not the client.

Part (d) requires knowledge from the text book on how to manage conflicts of interest.

(a)   Matters to be considered prior to accepting the audit of Centipede Co

ISA 220 *Quality Control for an Audit of Financial Statements* provides guidance to Ant & Co on the steps they should have taken in accepting the new audit client, Centipede Co. It sets out a number of processes which the auditor should perform prior to accepting a new engagement.

Ant & Co should have considered any issues which might arise which could threaten compliance with ACCA's Code of Ethics and Conduct or any local legislation, such as the level of fees from Centipede Co, to ensure they are not unduly reliant on these fees, as well as considering whether any conflicts of interest arise with existing clients. If issues arise, then their significance must be considered.

In addition, they should have considered whether they were competent to perform the work and whether they would have appropriate resources available, as well as any specialist skills or knowledge required for the audit of Centipede Co.

Ant & Co should have considered what they already know about the directors of Centipede Co; they needed to consider the reputation and integrity of the directors. If necessary, the firm may have wanted to obtain references if they do not formally know the directors.

Additionally, Ant & Co should have considered the level of risk attached to the audit of Centipede Co and whether this was acceptable to the firm. As part of this, they should have considered whether the expected audit fee was adequate in relation to the risk of auditing Centipede Co.

Ant & Co should have communicated with the outgoing auditor of Centipede Co to assess if there were any ethical or professional reasons why they should not have accepted appointment. They should have obtained permission from Centipede Co's management to contact the previous auditor; if this was not given, then the engagement should have been refused. Once received, the response from the previous auditor should have been carefully reviewed for any issues which could affect acceptance.

(b) **Ratios to assist the audit supervisor in planning the audit:**

	20X6	*20X5*
Gross margin	9,390/25,230 = **37.2%**	7,165/21,180 = **33.8%**
Operating margin	4,487/25,230 = **17.8%**	3,920/21,180 = **18.5%**
Inventory holding period	2,360/15,840 × 365 = **54 days**	1,800/14,015 × 365 = **47 days**
OR		
Inventory turnover	15,840/2,360 = **6.7**	14,015/1,800 = **7.8**
Receivables collection period	1,590/25,230 × 365 = **23 days**	1,250/21,180 × 365 = **22 days**
Payables payment period	3,500/15,840 × 365 = **81 days**	2,800/14,015 × 365 = **73 days**
Current ratio	3,950/4,080 = **0.97**	3,530/2,800 = **1.26**
Quick ratio	(3,950 – 2,360)/4,080 = **0.39**	(3,530 – 1,800)/2,800 = **0.62**

(c) **Audit risks and auditor's responses**

Audit risk	Auditor's response
Centipede Co is a new client for Ant & Co and is a listed company. As the team is not familiar with the accounting policies, transactions and balances of the company, there will be an increased detection risk on the audit.	Ant & Co should ensure they have a suitably experienced team. Also, adequate time should be allocated for team members to obtain an understanding of the company and the risks of material misstatement, including attendance at an audit team briefing.
The company utilises a perpetual inventory system at its warehouse rather than a full year-end count. Under such a system, all inventory must be counted at least once a year with adjustments made to the inventory records on a timely basis. Inventory could be under or overstated if the perpetual inventory counts are not complete.	The completeness of the perpetual inventory counts should be reviewed and the controls over the counts and adjustments to records should be tested.

Audit risk	Auditor's response
During the interim audit, it was noted that there were significant exceptions with the inventory records being higher than the inventory in the warehouse. As the year-end quantities will be based on the records, this is likely to result in overstated inventory.	The level of adjustments made to inventory should be considered to assess their significance. This should be discussed with management as soon as possible as it may not be possible to place reliance on the inventory records at the year end, which could result in the requirement for a full year-end inventory count.
During the interim audit, it was noted that there were some lines of inventory which according to the records were at least 90 days old. In addition, the inventory holding period has increased from 47 to 54 days. It would appear that there may be an increase in slow-moving inventory. The valuation of inventory as per IAS 2 *Inventories* should be at the lower of cost and net realisable value. There is a risk that obsolete inventory has not been appropriately written down and inventory is overvalued.	The aged inventory report should be reviewed and discussed with management to assess if certain lines of products are slow-moving. Detailed cost and net realisable value testing to be performed to assess whether an allowance or write down of inventory is required.
Centipede Co maintains accounting records at four additional sites which were not visited during the interim audit, and the records from these sites are incorporated monthly into the general ledger. Ant & Co need to ensure that they have obtained sufficient appropriate audit evidence over all the accounting records of the company, not just for those at head office. There is a detection risk if the team does not visit or undertake testing of the records at these sites. Further, if the interface does not occur appropriately, there is a risk that accounting records are incomplete.	Discuss with management the significance and materiality of the records maintained at the four sites. The team should visit some of these sites during the final audit to undertake testing of the records held there. In addition, computer-assisted audit techniques could be utilised by the team to sample test the monthly interface of data from each site to head office to identify any errors.
During 20X6 a building was disposed of with a loss on disposal of $825,000. There is a risk that the disposal has not been removed appropriately from the accounting records or that the loss on disposal calculation is incorrect.	Agree that the asset has been removed from the non-current assets register, recalculate the loss on disposal calculation and agree all items to supporting documentation.

Audit risk	Auditor's response
In addition, significant profits or losses on disposal are an indication that the depreciation policy for land and buildings may not be appropriate. Therefore depreciation may be understated and consequently assets overstated.	Discuss the depreciation policy for land and buildings with the finance director to assess its reasonableness. Review the level of losses on disposal generated from other asset sales to ascertain if this is a more widespread issue.
A customer of Centipede Co has commenced legal action against Centipede Co for a loss of profits claim. If it is probable that the company will make payment to the customer, a legal provision is required. If the payment is possible rather than probable, a contingent liability disclosure would be necessary. If Centipede Co has not done this, there is a risk over the completeness of any provisions and the necessary disclosure of contingent liabilities.	Ant & Co should write to the company's lawyers to enquire of the existence and likelihood of success of any claim from the wholesale customer. The results of this should be used to assess the level of provision or disclosure included in the financial statements
The directors have not disclosed the individual names and payments for each of the directors' remuneration. This is in line with IFRS Standards but disclosure of this is required by local legislation. In cases where the local legislation is more comprehensive than IFRS Standards, it is likely the company must comply with the local legislation. The directors' remuneration disclosure will not be complete and accurate if the names and individual payments are not disclosed in accordance with the relevant local legislation and hence the financial statements will be misstated as a result of the non-compliance.	Discuss this matter with management and review the requirements of the local legislation to determine if the disclosure in the financial statements is appropriate.
Revenue has grown by 19% in the year; however, cost of sales has only increased by 13%. This is a significant increase in revenue and along with the increase in gross margin may be due to an overstatement of revenue.	During the audit a detailed breakdown of sales will be obtained, discussed with management and tested in order to understand the sales increase. Also increased cut-off testing should be undertaken to verify that revenue is recorded in the right period and is not overstated.

Audit risk	Auditor's response
Gross margin has increased from 33.8% to 37.2%. Operating margin has decreased from 18.5% to 17.8%. This movement in gross margin is significant and there is a risk that costs may have been omitted or included in operating expenses rather than cost of sales.	The classification of costs between cost of sales and operating expenses will be compared with the prior year to ensure consistency. Also increased cut-off testing should be performed at the year end to ensure that costs are complete.
The overall liquidity of the company is in decline with the current and quick ratios decreasing from 1.26 to 0.97 and 0.62 to 0.39 respectively. In addition, the cash balances have decreased significantly over the year, and the company now has an overdraft of $580,000 at the end of the year. Further, the trade payables payment period has increased from 73 to 81 days, implying the company is struggling to meet their liabilities as they fall due. All of these changes in key ratios could signal going concern difficulties.	Detailed going concern testing to be performed during the audit as there may be a doubt over going concern and the basis of accounting should be discussed with management to ensure that the going concern basis is reasonable.

(d) **Safeguards to deal with conflict of interest**

- Both Centipede Co and its rival competitor should be notified that Ant & Co would be acting as auditors for each company and, if necessary, consent obtained.

- Advise one or both clients to seek additional independent advice.

- Use separate engagement teams, with different engagement partners and team members. Once an employee has worked on one audit, such as Centipede Co, then they should be prevented from being on the audit of the competitor for a period of time.

- Implement procedures to prevent access to information, for example, strict physical separation of both teams, confidential and secure data filing.

- Communicate clear guidelines for members of each engagement team on issues of security and confidentiality. These guidelines could be included within the audit engagement letters.

- Use confidentiality agreements signed by employees and partners of the firm.

- A senior individual in Ant & Co not involved in either audit should regularly monitor the application of the above safeguards.

Marking guide

		Marks
(a)	**Matters to be considered prior to accepting the audit of Centipede Co**	
	• Compliance with ACCA's Code of Ethics and Conduct	1
	• Competent	1
	• Reputation and integrity of directors	1
	• Level of risk of Centipede Co audit	1
	• Fee adequate to compensate for risk	1
	• Write to outgoing auditor after obtaining permission to contact	1
	• Previous auditor permission to respond	1
	• Review response for any issues	1
	Restricted to	**5**
(b)	**Ratio calculations (½ mark for each year)**	
	• Gross margin	1
	• Operating margin	1
	• Inventory holding period/Inventory turnover	1
	• Receivables collection period	1
	• Payables payment period	1
	• Current ratio	1
	• Quick ratio	1
	Max 6 ratios	**6**
(c)	**Audit risks and responses (only 7 risks required)**	
	• New client, increased detection risk	2
	• Perpetual inventory count adjustments	2
	• Valuation of inventory	2
	• Branch records	2
	• Disposal of building	2
	• Legal case	2
	• Directors remuneration disclosure	2
	• Revenue growth	2
	• Misclassification of costs between cost of sales and operating	2
	• Going concern	2
	Max 7 issues, 2 marks each	**14**
(d)	**Safeguards to deal with conflict of interest**	
	• Notify Centipede Co and its competitor	1
	• Advise seek independent advice	1
	• Separate engagement teams	1
	• Procedures prevent access to information	1
	• Clear guidelines on security and confidentiality	1
	• Confidentiality agreements	1
	• Monitoring of safeguards	1
	Restricted to	**5**
Total		**30**

Examiner's comments

Candidates generally performed well in this question.

Part (a) required candidates to discuss matters to consider before accepting an audit. Candidates who scored well discussed the competence /resources available of the audit firm, the contact with previous auditors, ethical considerations and the preconditions of an audit. Some candidates focused on one area in too much detail, for example, only describing the various ethical considerations that could arise. Some candidates incorrectly focussed on the removal of the prior year auditor. Few candidates discussed money laundering or risk considerations

Part (b) tested candidates' ability to calculate ratios which would assist in the planning of an audit. This question was generally well answered. Some candidates however only wrote the ratio formula and did not actually calculate the ratio. Some candidates calculated movements from one year to the next, but this was not asked for in the question. The current and quick ratios were also sometimes either confused between the two or miscalculated. Some candidates incorrectly calculated inventory days using revenue rather than cost of sales.

Part (c) required candidates to identify and explain the risks from a scenario and give an auditor's response to address the risks. As noted in previous Examiner's Reports a fundamental factor in planning and assessing the risks of an audit of an entity is an assessment of audit risk, and this remains a highly examinable area. Audit risk questions typically require a number of audit risks to be identified (½ marks each), explained (½ marks each) and an auditor's response to each risk (1 mark each). Performance in the audit risk question in December 2016 was mixed. The scenario contained a significant number of issues, and most candidates were able to identify the required number of issues. A significant number of candidates did not explain how each issue could impact on the audit risk and therefore were not awarded the second ½ mark. To explain audit risk candidates need to state the area of the accounts impacted with an assertion (e.g. cut-off, valuation etc.), or, a reference to under/over/misstated, or, a reference to inherent, control or detection risk. Misstated was only awarded if it was clear that the balance could be either over or understated. For example, when explaining the risk of inventory days increasing (½ marks for the issue), credit was only awarded for the audit risk of inventory being overstated (½ marks for the explanation). Auditor's responses were mixed. While an auditor's response does not have to be a detailed audit procedure, rather an approach the audit team will take to address the identified risk, the responses given were sometimes either too weak e.g. 'discuss with management' or, did not address the issue due to a failure to understand the risk. In comparison to recent exam sessions, it was pleasing that fewer candidates discussed business risks in December 2016. However, a minority of candidates continued to concentrate their responses on what management should do rather than the auditor. For example, in relation to inventory, an inappropriate response was to 'put in a FIFO system for inventory'.

Part (d) covered safeguards an audit firm should implement to ensure that a conflict of interest is properly managed. Candidates who scored well discussed a range of safeguards such as the audit team configuration, procedures to prevent access to information, notifying the client to obtain consent, and, obtaining confidentiality agreements. However some candidates concentrated too much on just one area. For example, listing as different points, separate teams, restriction on reassignment of audit team members, and, different engagement partners – when all three are examples of team configuration. Some candidates focused on ethical issues, such as ensuring the auditor has no shares in the client, which was not relevant for this question. Candidates need to be clear when describing the safeguards, for example candidates often mentioned that confidentiality agreements were required but often were unclear who the agreement should be with, occasionally incorrectly noting that the agreement should be with the client.

208 SITIA SPARKLE *Walk in the footsteps of a top tutor*

Key answer tips

Knowledge questions such as part (a) can be examined in section B, and you must take time to learn key definitions and requirements of the auditing standards from text book.

In part (b) make sure you describe audit risks and not business risks. Make sure the response is the response of the auditor and not the client.

Part (c) is trickier as this is a requirement that is relatively new to the syllabus. Make sure you revise all areas of the syllabus to ensure you can attempt to answer all parts of the paper.

(a) **Benefits of audit planning**

Audit planning is addressed by ISA 300 *Planning an Audit of Financial Statements*. It states that adequate planning benefits the audit of financial statements in several ways:

- Helping the auditor to devote appropriate attention to important areas of the audit.

- Helping the auditor to identify and resolve potential problems on a timely basis.

- Helping the auditor to properly organise and manage the audit engagement so that it is performed in an effective and efficient manner.

- Assisting in the selection of engagement team members with appropriate levels of capabilities and competence to respond to anticipated risks and the proper assignment of work to them.

- Facilitating the direction and supervision of engagement team members and the review of their work.

- Assisting, where applicable, in coordination of work done by experts.

(b) **Audit risk and auditors responses**

Audit risk	Auditor's response
Sitia Sparkle Co purchases their goods from suppliers in Africa and the goods are in transit for up to three weeks. At the year-end, there is a risk that the cut-off of inventory, purchases and payables may not be accurate and may be under/overstated.	The audit team should undertake detailed cut-off testing of purchases of goods at the year-end and the sample of GRNs from before and after the year-end relating to goods from suppliers in Africa should be increased to ensure that cut-off is complete and accurate.
Sitia Sparkle Co has incurred expenditure of $1.3 million in developing a new range of cleaning products.	Obtain a breakdown of the expenditure and verify that it relates to the development of the new products. Undertake testing to determine whether the costs relate to the research or development stage.

Audit risk	Auditor's response
This expenditure is classed as research and development under IAS 38 *Intangible Assets.* IAS 38 requires research costs to be expensed to profit or loss and development costs to be capitalised as an intangible asset. If the company has incorrectly classified research costs as development expenditure, there is a risk the intangible asset could be overstated and expenses understated. In addition, as the senior management bonus is based on year-end asset values, this increases this risk further as management may have a reason to overstate assets at the year-end.	Discuss the accounting treatment with the finance director and ensure it is in accordance with IAS 38.
In September 20X5, the company invested $0.9 million in a complex piece of plant and machinery. The costs include purchase price, installation and training costs. As per IAS 16 *Property, Plant and Equipment*, the cost of an asset incudes its purchase price and directly attributable costs only. Training costs are not permitted. Plant and machinery and profits are overstated.	Obtain a breakdown of the $0.9 million expenditure and undertake testing to confirm the level of training costs which have been included within non-current assets. Discuss the accounting treatment with the finance director and the level of any necessary adjustment to ensure treatment is in accordance with IAS 16.
The bonus scheme for senior management and directors of Sitia Sparkle Co has been changed and is now based on the value of year-end total assets. There is a risk that management might be motivated to overstate the value of assets through the judgments taken or through the use of releasing provisions or capitalisation policy.	Throughout the audit, the team will need to be alert to this risk and maintain professional scepticism. Detailed review and testing on judgmental decisions, including treatment of provisions, and compare treatment against prior years. Any manual journal adjustments affecting assets should be tested in detail. In addition, a written representation should be obtained from management confirming the basis of any significant judgments.

Audit risk	Auditor's response
The finance director of Sitia Sparkle Co believes that an allowance for receivables is excessive and unnecessary and therefore has not provided for it at the year-end and has credited the opening balance to profit or loss. There is a risk that receivables will be overvalued; some balances may be irrecoverable and so will be overstated if not written down. In addition, releasing the allowance for receivables will increase asset values and hence the senior management bonus which increases the risk further.	Extended post year-end cash receipts testing and a review of the aged receivables ledger to be performed to assess valuation and the need for an allowance for receivables. Review and test the controls surrounding how Sitia Sparkle Co identifies receivables balances which may require an allowance to ensure that they are operating effectively in the current year. Discuss with the finance director the rationale for not maintaining an allowance for receivables and releasing the opening balance.
A new general ledger system was introduced in May 20X6 and the old and new systems were run in parallel until August 20X6. There is a risk of the balances in May being misstated and loss of data if they have not been transferred from the old system completely and accurately. If this is not done, this could result in the auditor not identifying a significant control risk.	The auditor should undertake detailed testing to confirm that all of the balances at the transfer date have been correctly recorded in the new general ledger system. The auditor should document and test the new system. They should review any management reports run comparing the old and new system during the parallel run to identify any issues with the processing of accounting information.
A number of reconciliations, including the bank reconciliation, were not performed at the year-end, however, they were undertaken in June and August. Control account reconciliations provide comfort that accounting records are being maintained completely and accurately. This is an example of a control procedure being overridden by management and raises concerns over the overall emphasis placed on internal control. There is a risk that balances including bank balances are under or overstated.	Discuss this issue with the finance director and request that the July control account reconciliations are undertaken. All reconciling items should be tested in detail and agreed to supporting documentation.

Audit risk	Auditor's response
The payables ledger of Sitia Sparkle Co was closed down on 8 August, rather than at the year-end 31 July. There is a risk that the cut-off may be incorrect with purchases and payables over or understated.	The audit team should undertake testing of transactions posted to the payables ledger between 1 and 8 August to identify whether any transactions relating to the 20X7 year-end have been included or any 20X6 balances removed.

(c) **Supervision and review of the assistants' work**

Supervision

During the audit of Sitia Sparkle Co, the supervisor should keep track of the progress of the audit engagement to ensure that the audit timetable is met and should ensure that the audit manager and partner are kept updated of progress.

The competence and capabilities of individual members of the engagement team should be considered, including whether they have sufficient time to carry out their work, whether they understand their instructions and whether the work is being carried out in accordance with the planned approach to the audit.

In addition, part of the supervision process should involve addressing any significant matters arising during the audit of Sitia Sparkle Co, considering their significance and modifying the planned approach appropriately.

The supervisor would also be responsible for identifying matters for consultation or consideration by the audit manager or engagement partner of Sitia Sparkle Co.

Review

The supervisor would be required to review the work completed by the assistants and consider whether this work has been performed in accordance with professional standards and other regulatory requirements and if the work performed supports the conclusions reached and has been properly documented.

The supervisor should also consider whether all significant matters have been raised for partner attention or for further consideration and where appropriate consultations have taken place, whether appropriate conclusions have been documented.

	Marking guide	
		Marks
(a)	**Benefits of audit planning**	
	• Important areas of the audit	1
	• Potential problems	1
	• Effective and efficient audit	1
	• Selection of engagement team members and assignment of work	1
	• Direction, supervision and review	1
	• Coordination of work	1
	Restricted to	4
(b)	**Audit risks and responses (only 6 risks required)**	
	• Goods in transit from Africa	2
	• Research and development expenditure	2
	• Capitalisation of costs of plant and machinery	2
	• Senior management bonus scheme	2
	• Allowance for receivables	2
	• Introduction of new general ledger system	2
	• July 20X6 control account reconciliations not undertaken	2
	• Payables ledger closed down on 8 August	2
	Max 6 issues, 2 marks each	12
(c)	**Supervising and reviewing audit assistants' work**	
	• Monitor the progress of the audit engagement to ensure the audit timetable was met	1
	• Consider the competence and capabilities of team members re sufficient available time, understanding of instructions and if work in accordance with planned approach	1
	• Address any significant matters arising, consider their significance and modifying the approach	1
	• Responsible for identifying matters for consultation/consideration by senior team members	1
	• Work performed in line with professional standards and other requirements	1
	• Work supports conclusions reached and properly documented	1
	• Significant matters raised for partner attention or further consideration	1
	• Appropriate consultations have taken place with conclusions documented	1
	Restricted to	4
Total		**20**

Examiner's comments

This question covered audit planning, audit risks and responses and quality control. Performance was mixed across this question.

Part (a) was a knowledge based requirement on the benefits of planning and candidates performed well. Most were able to identify and explain a sufficient number of points. A minority of candidates focused on tasks performed at the planning stage, such as setting the budget, rather than the overall benefits of planning.

Part (b) required candidates to identify and explain the risks from a scenario and give an auditor's response to address the risks. As noted in previous Examiner's Reports a fundamental activity in planning is the assessment of audit risk, and this remains a highly examinable area. Audit risk questions typically require a number of audit risks to be identified (½ marks each), explained (½ marks each) and an auditor's response to each risk (1 mark each). Performance in the audit risk question was mixed. The scenario contained a significant number of issues, and most candidates were able to identify the required number of issues. However many candidates incorrectly identified issues such as the supervisor having responsibility for a large audit team for the first time, or failed to understand the accounting issue such as the incorrect capitalisation of training costs within plant and machinery. In addition, a large number of candidates often did not explain how each issue could impact on the financial statements and therefore were not awarded the explanation mark. To explain audit risk candidates need to state the area of the accounts impacted with an assertion (e.g. cut-off, valuation etc.), a reference to under/ over/misstated, or, a reference to inherent, control or detection risk. Misstated was only awarded if it was clear that the balance could be either over or understated. Auditor's responses were mixed. While an auditor's response does not have to be a detailed audit procedure, rather it is the approach the audit team will take to address the identified risk, the responses given were sometimes either too weak e.g. 'discuss with management' or, did not address the issue due to a failure to comprehensively understand the risk. In comparison to recent exam sessions, it was disappointing that a significant minority of candidates discussed business risks and therefore concentrated their responses on what management should do rather than the auditor (e.g. in relation to the change in the bonus scheme, an inappropriate response was that the bonus should be changed back to being based on profits).

Part (c) on quality control responsibilities, where attempted, was disappointing. A significant proportion of candidates did not even attempt this question. For those who did, general audit objectives or ethical points were given, rather than those for quality control.

209 AQUAMARINE *Walk in the footsteps of a top tutor*

Key answer tips

Requirements (a) and (b) cover frequently examined areas of the syllabus. Knowledge questions such as part (a) can be examined in section B, and you must take time to learn key definitions and requirements of the auditing standards.

In part (b) make sure you describe audit risks and not business risks. Make sure the response is the response of the auditor and not the client.

Part (c) is trickier. This highlights the importance of revising all areas of the syllabus as any area can be tested. If you can't answer the requirement don't waste time, move onto a different question.

(a)   Audit risk and its components

Audit risk is the risk that the auditor expresses an inappropriate audit opinion when the financial statements are materially misstated.

Audit risk is a function of two main components, being the risk of material misstatement and detection risk.

Risk of material misstatement is made up of a further two components, inherent risk and control risk.

Inherent risk is the susceptibility of an assertion about a class of transaction, account balance or disclosure to a misstatement which could be material, either individually or when aggregated with other misstatements, before consideration of any related controls.

Control risk is the risk that a misstatement which could occur in an assertion about a class of transaction, account balance or disclosure and which could be material, either individually or when aggregated with other misstatements, will not be prevented, or detected and corrected, on a timely basis by the entity's internal control.

Detection risk is the risk that the procedures performed by the auditor to reduce audit risk to an acceptably low level will not detect a misstatement which exists and which could be material, either individually or when aggregated with other misstatements. Detection risk is affected by sampling and non-sampling risk.

(b) **Audit risks and auditors' responses**

Audit risks	Auditors' responses
Aquamarine Co (Aquamarine) undertakes continuous production and the work in progress balance at the year-end is likely to be material. As production will not cease, the exact cut-off of the work in progress will need to be assessed. If the cut-off is not correctly calculated, the inventory valuation may be under or overstated.	The auditor should discuss with management the process they will undertake to assess the cut-off point for work in progress at the year-end. This process should be reviewed by the auditor while attending the year-end inventory count. In addition, consideration should be given as to whether an independent expert is required to value the work in progress. If so, this will need to be arranged with consent from management and in time for the year-end count.
Aquamarine has ordered $720,000 of plant and machinery, two-thirds of which may not have been received by the year-end. Only assets which physically exist at the year-end should be included in property, plant and equipment. If items not yet delivered have been capitalised, PPE will be overstated. Consideration will also need to be given to depreciation and when this should commence. If depreciation is not appropriately charged when the asset is available for use, this may result in assets and profit being over or understated.	Discuss with management as to whether the remaining plant and machinery ordered have arrived; if so, physically verify a sample of these assets to ensure existence and ensure only appropriate assets are recorded in the non-current asset register at the year-end. Determine if the asset received is in use at the year-end by physical observation and if so, if depreciation has commenced at an appropriate point.
A patent has been purchased for $1.3 million, and this enables Aquamarine to manufacture specialised elevator equipment for the next five years. In accordance with IAS 38 *Intangible Assets*, this should be included as an intangible asset and amortised over its five-year life. If management has not correctly accounted for the patent, intangible assets and profits could be overstated.	The audit team will need to agree the purchase price to supporting documentation and to confirm the useful life is five years. The amortisation charge should be recalculated in order to ensure the accuracy of the charge and that the intangible is correctly valued at the year-end.

Audit risks	Auditors' responses
The company has borrowed $1.2 million from the bank via a five-year loan. This loan needs to be correctly split between current and non-current liabilities. There is a risk of incorrect disclosure if the loan is not correctly split between current and non-current liabilities.	During the audit, the team would need to confirm that the $1.2 million loan finance was received. In addition, the split between current and non-current liabilities and the disclosures for this loan should be reviewed in detail to ensure compliance with relevant accounting standards. Details of security should be agreed to the bank confirmation letter.
As the level of debt has increased, there should be additional finance costs. There is a risk that this has been omitted from the statement of profit or loss. Finance costs may be understated and profit overstated.	The finance costs should be recalculated and any increase agreed to the loan documentation for confirmation of interest rates. Interest payments should be agreed to the cash book and bank statements to confirm the amount was paid and is not therefore a year-end payable.
During the year Aquamarine outsourced its payroll processing to an external service organisation. The audit team will need to verify controls at the third party. A detection risk arises as to whether sufficient and appropriate evidence is available at Aquamarine to confirm the completeness and accuracy of controls over payroll. If not, another auditor may be required to undertake testing at the service organisation.	Discuss with management the extent of records maintained at Aquamarine and any monitoring of controls undertaken by management over the payroll charge. Consideration should be given to contacting the service organisation's auditor to confirm the level of controls in place.
The payroll processing transferred to Coral Payrolls Co from 1 January. Errors may have occurred during the transfer process. There is a risk that the payroll charge and related employment tax liabilities are under/overstated.	Discuss with management the transfer process undertaken and any controls put in place to ensure the completeness and accuracy of the data. Where possible, undertake tests of controls to confirm the effectiveness of the transfer controls. In addition, perform substantive testing on the transfer of information from the old to the new system.
The land and buildings are to be revalued at the year-end; it is likely that the revaluation surplus/deficit will be material.	Discuss with management the process adopted for undertaking the valuation, including whether the whole class of assets was revalued and if the valuation was undertaken by an expert. This process should be reviewed for compliance with IAS 16.

Audit risks	Auditors' responses
The revaluation needs to be carried out and recorded in accordance with IAS 16 *Property, Plant and Equipment*. Non-current assets may be incorrectly valued.	
Receivables for the year to date are considerably higher than the prior year. The receivables may not be recoverable. There is a risk that receivables may be overvalued.	Discuss with management the reasons for the increase in receivables and management's process for identifying potential irrecoverable debt. Test controls surrounding management's credit control processes. Extended post year-end cash receipts testing and a review of the aged receivables ledger to be performed to assess valuation. Also consider the adequacy of any allowance for receivables.
Aquamarine is planning to make approximately 65 employees redundant after the year-end. The timing of this announcement has not been confirmed; if it is announced to the staff before the year-end, then under IAS 37 *Provisions, Contingent Liabilities and Contingent Assets* a redundancy provision will be required at the year-end. Failure to provide will result in an understatement of provisions and expenses.	Discuss with management the status of the redundancy announcement; if before the year-end, review supporting documentation to confirm the timing. In addition, review the basis of and recalculate the redundancy provision.

(c)   **Payroll service organisations**

Additional factors Amethyst & Co should consider in relation to Aquamarine's use of the service organisation, Coral Payrolls Co (Coral) include:

- The audit team should gain an understanding of the services being provided by Coral, including the materiality of payroll and the basis of the outsourcing contract.

- They will need to assess the design and implementation of internal controls over Aquamarine's payroll at Coral.

- The team may wish to visit Coral and undertake tests of controls to confirm the operating effectiveness of the controls.

- If this is not possible, Amethyst & Co should contact Coral's auditors to request either a type 1 (report on description and design of controls) or type 2 report (on description, design and operating effectiveness of controls).

- Amethyst & Co is responsible for obtaining sufficient and appropriate evidence, therefore no reference may be made in the auditor's report regarding the use of information from Coral's auditors.

		Marks
	Marking guide	
(a)	**Audit risk and its components**	*Marks*
	• Audit risk	2
	• Inherent risk	1
	• Control risk	1
	• Detection risk	1
		———
		5
		———
(b)	**Audit risks and responses (only 6 risks required)**	
	• Work in progress	2
	• Existence of plant and machinery ordered	2
	• Valuation of intangible asset	2
	• New loan finance obtained	2
	• Completeness of finance costs	2
	• Use of service organisation	2
	• Transfer of data to service organisation	2
	• Valuation of land and buildings	2
	• Overvaluation of receivables	2
	• Redundancy provision	2
	Max 6 issues, 2 marks each	———
		12
		———
(c)	**Payroll service organisations**	
	• Gain an understanding of the services being provided	1
	• Assess the design and implementation of internal controls over Aquamarine's payroll at Coral	1
	• Visit Coral and undertake tests of controls	1
	• Contact Coral's auditors to request either a type 1 or type 2 report	1
	• No reference in auditor's report of use of information from Coral's auditors	1
	Restricted to	———
		3
		———
Total		**20**

Examiner's comments

Performance in the audit risk question, as in many previous exams continues to be mixed. The scenario contained more issues than were required to be discussed. A significant minority identified more issues than necessary, often combining risks into one point. This approach sometimes resulted in a lack of detail in the risk and also led to unfocused auditor responses. In addition, a large number of candidates often did not explain how each issue could result in an audit risk or impact on the financial statements and therefore were not awarded the explanation ½ mark. To explain audit risk candidates need to state the area of the financial statements impacted with an assertion (e.g. cut-off, valuation etc.), or, a reference to under/over/misstated, or, a reference to inherent, control or detection risk. Misstated was only awarded if it was clear that the balance could be either over or understated. In addition, many candidates misunderstood the implication of payroll being outsourced, failing to understand that there was an increased detection risk with regards to access to outsourced records and the risk of data being incorrectly transferred to the service organisation.

The provision of relevant auditor responses continues to be a poorly attempted area and candidates are once again reminded to ensure that this area of the syllabus is adequately studied and practised. While an auditor's response does not have to be a detailed audit procedure, rather an approach the audit team will take to address the identified risk, the responses given were sometimes either too weak e.g. "discuss with management" or, did not address the issue due to a failure to understand the risk (e.g. in response to a possible understated provision, an incorrect response was to "undertake going concern testing'). In comparison to recent exam sessions, it was disappointing that a significant minority of candidates discussed business risks and therefore concentrated their responses on what management should do rather than the auditor (e.g. in relation to the plant and machinery ordered pre year-end, an inappropriate response was that the auditor should contact the supplier to ensure the delivery was on time). Further it was pleasing to note that many candidates presented their answers well using a two-column approach with audit risk in one column and the related response in the other column.

In addition there was a knowledge-based question which required a definition of audit risk and its components. This question was generally well answered with candidates demonstrating reasonable knowledge of the area tested. Some candidates failed to maximise their marks as their explanation of inherent risk was incomplete. In key knowledge areas such as this, candidates must be technically correct in order to score full marks.

210 VENUS *Walk in the footsteps of a top tutor*

Key answer tips

Requirements (a) and (b) cover knowledge of engagement letters. For part (a) think of sensible reasons why a contract with a client may need to be amended. Part (b) has been examined many times before and students should be able to score reasonably well on this.

In part (c) you are asked for sources of information, i.e. where the auditor can obtain information to help plan the audit. Make sure you include an explanation of how the information will be used to score the full mark.

Part (d) asks for audit risks which are examined at every sitting. Audit risks need to relate to either a risk of material misstatement or a detection risk. For risk of material misstatement, identify a balance in the scenario that is at risk of misstatement and explain why you believe it could be misstated. This is usually because the client has failed to apply the relevant accounting standards correctly. The accounting standards examinable for ACCA Financial Accounting are examinable for this exam.

Detection risks are the risks the auditor does not detect material misstatements in the financial statements e.g. when it is a new audit client or if there is a tight reporting deadline.

For the response, make sure it relates to the risk, not the balance in general. Try and be as specific as possible, simply saying more testing is required will not be sufficient. State the nature of the tests that should be performed.

A 2 column table should be used to keep the risks in line with the responses and to make sure you address both parts of the requirement.

(a) **Engagement letters**

Engagement letters for recurring/existing clients should be revised if any of the following factors are present:

- Any indication that the entity misunderstands the objective and scope of the audit, as this misunderstanding would need to be clarified.

- Any revised or special terms of the audit engagement, as these would require inclusion in the engagement letter.

- A recent change of senior management or significant change in ownership. The letter is signed by a director on behalf of those charged with governance. If there have been significant changes in management they need to be made aware of what the audit engagement letter includes.

- A significant change in nature or size of the entity's business. The approach taken by the auditor may need to change to reflect the change in the entity and this should be clarified in the engagement letter.

- A change in legal or regulatory requirements. The engagement letter is a contract; hence if legal or regulatory changes occur, then the contract could be out of date.

- A change in the financial reporting framework adopted in the preparation of the financial statements. The engagement letter clarifies the role of auditors and those charged with governance, it identifies the reporting framework of the financial statements and if this changes, then the letter requires updating.

- A change in other reporting requirements. Other reporting requirements may be stipulated in the engagement letter; hence if these change, the letter should be updated.

(b) **Matters to be included in an audit engagement letter**

- The objective and scope of the audit

- The responsibilities of the auditor

- The responsibilities of management

- Identification of the financial reporting framework for the preparation of the financial statements

- Expected form and content of any reports to be issued

- Elaboration of the scope of the audit with reference to legislation

- The form of any other communication of results of the audit engagement

- The fact that some material misstatements may not be detected

- Arrangements regarding the planning and performance of the audit, including the composition of the audit team

- The expectation that management will provide written representations

- The basis on which fees are computed and any billing arrangements

- A request for management to acknowledge receipt of the audit engagement letter and to agree to the terms of the engagement

- Arrangements concerning the involvement of internal auditors and other staff of the entity

- Any obligations to provide audit working papers to other parties

- Any restriction on the auditor's liability

- Arrangements to make available draft financial statements and any other information

- Arrangements to inform the auditor of facts which might affect the financial statements, of which management may become aware during the period from the date of the auditor's report to the date the financial statements are issued.

(c)   Understanding an entity

Prior year financial statements

Provides information in relation to the size of a company as well as the key accounting policies, disclosure notes and whether the audit opinion was modified or not.

Discussions with the previous auditors/access to their files

Provides information on key issues identified during the prior year audit as well as the audit approach adopted.

Prior year report to management

If this can be obtained from the previous auditors or from management, it can provide information on the internal control deficiencies noted last year. If these have not been rectified by management, then they could arise in the current year audit as well and may impact the audit approach.

Accounting systems notes/procedural manuals

Provides information on how each of the key accounting systems operates and this will be used to identify areas of potential control risk and help determine the audit approach.

Discussions with management

Provides information in relation to the business, any important issues which have arisen or changes to accounting policies from the prior year.

Review of board minutes

Provides an overview of key issues which have arisen during the year and how those charged with governance have addressed them.

Current year budgets and management accounts

Provides relevant financial information for the year to date. It will help the auditor during the planning stage for preliminary analytical review and risk identification.

Company website

Recent press releases from the company may provide background on the business during the year as this will help in identifying the key audit risks.

Financial statements of competitors

This will provide information about the company's competitors, in relation to their financial results and their accounting policies. This will be important in assessing the performance in the year and also when undertaking the going concern review.

(d) **Audit risk and auditor's responses**

Audit risk	Auditor's response
The directors have reviewed the asset lives and depreciation rates of plant and machinery, resulting in the depreciation charge reducing. Under IAS 16 *Property, Plant and Equipment*, asset lives should be reviewed annually, and if the asset lives have increased as a result of this review such that the depreciation decreases, then this change may be reasonable. This reduction may have occurred in order to achieve profit targets, due to the introduction of the bonus system. There is a risk that plant and machinery is overvalued and profit overstated if this is the case.	Discuss with the directors the rationale for any extensions of asset lives and reduction of depreciation rates. The revised useful life of a sample of assets should be compared to how often these assets are replaced, as this provides evidence of the useful life of assets.
Due to staff availability, the company is planning to undertake a full year-end inventory count days before the year-end and then adjust for movements to the year-end. The adjustments may not be made accurately or completely. There is a risk that inventory could be under or overstated.	During the final audit the year-end inventory adjustments schedule should be reviewed in detail and supporting documentation obtained for all adjusting items. The audit team should increase the extent of inventory cut-off testing at the year-end.
In October, a fire damaged inventory such that it has been written down from $0.9 million to $0.2 million which is its scrap value. This write down should have been charged to profit or loss. If the goods remain unsold after the year-end the scrap value may be overstated. There is a risk of inventory being overvalued.	Discuss with management the basis of the $0.2 million scrap value attributed. Review whether any of the goods were sold pre or post year-end and at what value; this should assess whether the attributed scrap value is reasonable. If none have been sold, discuss with management the possibility of further write downs.

Audit risk	Auditor's response
An insurance claim for $0.7 million has been submitted and the proceeds included within profit or loss. The company has not received a reply from the insurance company and this would therefore represent a possible contingent asset. To comply with IAS 37 *Provisions, Contingent Liabilities and Contingent Assets*, this should not be recognised until the receipt is virtually certain. With no response to date, the inclusion of this sum overstates profit and receivables.	Discuss with management whether any response has been received from the insurance company and review the related correspondence. If virtually certain, the treatment adopted is correct. If not, management should be requested to remove it from profit and receivables. If the receipt is probable, the auditor should request management include a contingent asset disclosure note.
The bank reconciliations for October and November both contain unreconciled amounts, and the finance director believes the overall differences to be immaterial. Errors in bank reconciliations could represent large errors which net off to a small amount. If the differences are not fully reconciled, it could result in bank balances being under or overstated. Unreconciled amounts in the bank could have arisen due to fraud.	Discuss this issue with the finance director and request that the December reconciliation is fully reconciled. The reconciling items should be tested in detail and agreed to supporting documentation. Throughout the audit, the team should be alert to the risk of fraud and maintain professional scepticism.
A directors' bonus scheme was introduced which is based on achieving a target profit before tax. There is a risk the directors might feel under pressure to manipulate the results through the judgments taken or through the use of provisions. There is a risk of material misstatement of the financial statements in general to increase the bonus payment.	Throughout the audit, the team will need to be alert to this risk and maintain professional scepticism. Detailed review and testing on judgmental decisions, including treatment of provisions, and compare treatment against prior years. Any journal adjustments affecting profit should be tested in detail. In addition, a written representation should be obtained from management confirming the basis of any significant judgments.

Audit risk	Auditor's response
The finance director has requested that the audit commence earlier than normal as he wishes to report results earlier. The audit may be rushed in order to complete by the deadline. There will also be a shorter subsequent events period to obtain evidence. A reduction in the audit timetable will increase detection risk and place additional pressure on the team in obtaining sufficient and appropriate evidence.	The timetable should be confirmed with the finance director. If it is to be reduced, then consideration should be given to performing an interim audit in late December or early January to reduce the pressure on the final audit.
The finance director has requested that the audit commence earlier than normal as he wishes to report results earlier. The finance team will have less time to prepare the financial information. There is an increased risk of errors arising in the financial statements.	The team needs to maintain professional scepticism and be alert to the increased risk of errors occurring.

	Marking guide		
			Marks
(a)	**Changes to engagement letter**		
	• Entity misunderstands the objective and scope of the audit		1
	• Revised or special terms of the audit		1
	• Recent change of senior management/change in ownership		1
	• Change in nature or size of the entity's business		1
	• Change in legal or regulatory requirements		1
	• Change in the financial reporting framework		1
	• Change in other reporting requirements		1
			–––
		Max	2
			–––
(b)	**Engagement letter contents**		
	• Objective/scope		½
	• Responsibilities of auditor		½
	• Responsibilities of management		½
	• Identification of framework for financial statements		½
	• Form/content reports		½
	• Elaboration of scope		½
	• Form of communications		½
	• Some misstatements may be missed		½
	• Arrangement for audit		½
	• Written representations required		½
	• Basis of fees/billing		½
	• Management acknowledge letter		½
	• Internal auditor arrangements		½
	• Obligations to provide working papers to others		½
	• Restriction on auditor's liability		½
	• Arrangements to make draft financial statements available		½
	• Arrangements to inform auditors of subsequent events		½
			–––
		Max	3
			–––

Marking guide		
		Marks
(c)	**Understanding an entity**	
	• Prior year financial statements	1
	• Previous auditor/access to their files	1
	• Prior year report to management	1
	• Accounting systems notes	1
	• Discussions with management	1
	• Review of board minutes	1
	• Current year budgets and management accounts	1
	• Company website	1
	• Financial statements of competitors	1
	Restricted to	5
(d)	**Audit risks and responses (only 5 risks required)**	
	• Depreciation rates and asset lives	2
	• Adjustments for movements in inventory to the year-end date	2
	• Write down of inventory	2
	• Contingent asset	2
	• Unreconciled differences on bank reconciliations	2
	• Manipulation of profit due to directors' bonus	2
	• Reporting timetable shortened	2
	Max 5 issues, 2 marks each	10
Total		20

Examiner's comments

Candidates were presented with a question at this sitting based on a manufacturing company and asked to assess audit risk and responses. As noted in previous Examiner's reports; a fundamental factor in planning and assessing the risks of an audit of an entity is an assessment of audit risk, and this remains a highly examinable area. Audit risk questions typically require a number of audit risks to be identified (½ marks each), explained (½ marks each) and an auditor's response to each risk (1 mark each). Performance was mixed. It was encouraging that candidates generally identified the issues correctly from the scenario. However, candidates sometimes did not explain how each issue could impact on the audit risk and therefore were not awarded the full mark. To explain the audit risk candidates need to state for each issue if this could result in a balance being over stated, under stated, misstated, misclassified, a going concern problem or refer to a relevant assertion. In addition, many candidates misunderstood the implication of the inventory being counted before the year-end and thought the problem was the lack of staff for the count as opposed to the roll forward adjustments which would be necessary. The provision of relevant auditor's responses continues to be a poorly attempted area and candidates are once again reminded to ensure that this area of the syllabus is adequately studied and practised. While an auditor's response does not have to be a detailed audit procedure, rather it should set out an approach the audit team will take to address the identified risk, the responses given were sometimes either too weak (e.g. in response to the directors' bonus being based on profits a weak response was to 'audit the profit or loss account') or, did not address the issue (e.g. in response to the un-reconciled differences on the bank reconciliation, a weak response was to 'obtain a bank confirmation') It was pleasing to note that few candidates discussed business risks. A minority of candidates however did propose, in relation to the director's bonus being based on profits, the inappropriate response that the auditor should inform management not to base bonuses on profit levels in the future.

211 SYCAMORE *Walk in the footsteps of a top tutor*

Key answer tips

Requirements (a) (c) and (d) require repetition of information from the text book – responsibilities of the auditor in respect of fraud and error, quality control procedures and the difference between an audit and a review engagement.

In part (b) audit risks need to relate to either a risk of material misstatement or a detection risk. For risk of material misstatement, identify a balance in the scenario that is at risk of misstatement and explain why you believe it could be misstated. This is usually because the client has failed to apply the relevant accounting standard correctly. The accounting standards examinable for ACCA Financial Accounting are examinable for this exam.

Detection risks are the risks the auditor does not detect material misstatements in the financial statements e.g. when it is a new audit client or if there is a tight reporting deadline.

For the response, make sure it relates to the risk, not the balance in general. Try and be as specific as possible, simply saying more testing is required will not be sufficient. State the nature of the tests that should be performed.

A 2 column table should be used to keep the risks in line with the responses and to make sure you address both parts of the requirement.

(a)   Fraud responsibility

Maple & Co must conduct an audit in accordance with ISA 240 *The Auditor's Responsibilities Relating to Fraud in an Audit of Financial Statements* and are responsible for obtaining reasonable assurance that the financial statements taken as a whole are free from material misstatement, whether caused by fraud or error.

In order to fulfil this responsibility, Maple & Co is required to identify and assess the risks of material misstatement of the financial statements due to fraud.

They need to obtain sufficient appropriate audit evidence regarding the assessed risks of material misstatement due to fraud, through designing and implementing appropriate responses. In addition, Maple & Co must respond appropriately to fraud or suspected fraud identified during the audit.

When obtaining reasonable assurance, Maple & Co is responsible for maintaining professional scepticism throughout the audit, considering the potential for management override of controls and recognising the fact that audit procedures which are effective in detecting error may not be effective in detecting fraud.

To ensure that the whole engagement team is aware of the risks and responsibilities for fraud and error, ISAs require that a discussion is held within the team. For members not present at the meeting, Sycamore's audit engagement partner should determine which matters are to be communicated to them.

If fraud is detected, the auditor must report this to management and those charged with governance.

(b) **Audit risks and auditors' responses**

Audit risks	Auditor's responses
Sycamore's previous finance director left in December after it was discovered that he had been committing fraud with regards to expenses claimed. There is a risk that he may have undertaken other fraudulent transactions; these would need to be written off in the statement of profit or loss. If these have not been uncovered, the financial statements could include errors.	Discuss with the new finance director what procedures they have adopted to identify any further frauds by the previous finance director. In addition, the team should maintain their professional scepticism and be alert to the risk of further fraud and errors.
The new finance director was appointed in January 20X5 and was previously a financial controller of a bank. Sycamore is a pharmaceutical company which is very different to a bank. There is a risk that the new finance director is not sufficiently competent to prepare the financial statements. The financial statements could contain errors.	During the audit, careful attention should be applied to any changes in accounting policies and in particular any key judgmental decisions made by the finance director.
During the year, Sycamore has spent $1.8 million on developing new products; these are at different stages and the total amount has been capitalised as an intangible asset. In order to be capitalised it must meet all of the criteria under IAS 38 *Intangible Assets*. There is a risk that some projects may not reach final development stage and hence should be expensed rather than capitalised. Intangible assets and profit could be overstated.	A breakdown of the development expenditure should be reviewed and tested in detail to ensure that only projects which meet the capitalisation criteria are included as an intangible asset, with the balance being expensed.
Sycamore has borrowed $2.0 million from the bank via a ten-year loan. There is a risk that the loan is not split between current and non-current liabilities correctly resulting in incorrect disclosure.	During the audit, the team would need to confirm that the $2.0 million loan finance was received. In addition, the split between current and non-current liabilities and the disclosures for this loan should be reviewed in detail to ensure compliance with relevant accounting standards.

Audit risks	Auditor's responses
Also as the level of debt has increased, there should be additional finance costs. There is a risk that this has been omitted from the statement of profit or loss, leading to understated finance costs and overstated profit.	The finance costs should be recalculated and any increase agreed to the loan documentation for confirmation of interest rates and cashbook and bank statements to confirm the amount was paid and is not therefore a year-end payable.
The loan has a minimum profit target covenant. If this is breached, the loan would be instantly repayable. There is a risk the liability is incorrectly allocated as a non-current liability rather than a current liability if the covenant is breached. If the company does not have sufficient cash flow to meet this loan repayment, then there could be going concern implications. There is a risk of inadequate disclosure of going concern issues.	Review the covenant calculations prepared by Sycamore and identify whether any defaults have occurred; if so, determine the effect on the company. Review the disclosure of the loan as a current liability. Review cash flow forecasts and enquire of management how they will deal with any need to make the loan repayment.
In addition, there is a risk of manipulation of profit to ensure that covenants are met.	The team should maintain their professional scepticism and be alert to the risk that profit has been overstated to ensure compliance with the covenant.
There have been a significant number of sales returns made subsequent to the year-end. As these relate to pre year-end sales, they should be removed from revenue in the draft financial statements and the inventory reinstated. If the sales returns have not been correctly recorded, then revenue will be overstated and inventory understated.	Review a sample of the post year-end sales returns and confirm if they relate to pre year-end sales, that the revenue has been reversed and the inventory included in the year-end ledgers. In addition, the reason for the increased level of returns should be discussed with management. This will help to assess if there are underlying issues with the net realisable value of inventory.
During Sycamore's year-end inventory count there were movements of goods in and out. If these goods in transit were not carefully controlled, then goods could have been omitted or counted twice. This would result in inventory being under or overstated.	During the final audit, the goods received notes and goods despatch notes received during the inventory count should be reviewed and followed through into the inventory count records as correctly included or not.

Audit risks	Auditor's responses
Surplus plant and equipment was sold during the year, resulting in a profit on disposal of $210,000. As there is a minimum profit loan covenant, there is a risk that this profit on disposal may not have been correctly calculated, resulting in overstated profits.	Recalculate the profit and loss on disposal calculations and agree all items to supporting documentation.
Significant profits or losses on disposal are an indication that the depreciation policy of plant and equipment may not be appropriate. Depreciation may be overstated as a result.	Discuss the depreciation policy for plant and equipment with the finance director to assess its reasonableness.

(c) **Quality control**

Briefing/direction of the team

The audit team should be informed of their responsibilities, the objectives of their work, the nature of the client's business and any other relevant information to enable them to perform their work efficiently and effectively. This will enable them to identify material misstatements and know which areas require greater attention.

Supervision – tracking the progress of the audit

The audit supervisor should keep track of the progress of the audit in order to ensure the work is being completed on time or whether action needs to be taken such as bringing in additional staff to help complete the work or whether to agree an extended deadline with the client.

Supervision – addressing significant matters

The audit supervisor will also ensure that significant matters are being dealt with promptly. If issues are resolved as soon as they are identified the audit is more likely to be completed within the agreed timeframe.

Supervision – considering competence of team

The audit supervisor will consider the competence of the audit team and will provide additional coaching if required. The supervisor should be available for the team members to refer to in case of any queries.

Consultation

Consultation will be required where the team does not have the necessary expertise. The audit supervisor should identify any areas where consultation with an expert is required and make arrangements for such consultation whether this is referring the matter to another person within the audit firm or using an external expert.

Review of work

Each team member's work should be reviewed by someone more senior. This is to ensure the work has been to the required standard. The reviewer may identify additional work that needs to be performed before a conclusion can be drawn reducing the risk that material misstatements go undetected.

EQCR

An engagement quality control review will be necessary for listed clients and other high risk clients, for example to provide an additional safeguard for clients where independence issues have been identified. The engagement quality control reviewer should be someone independent of the audit team who has no prior knowledge of the client and is able to assess the judgmental areas of the audit with an objective mind. The EQCR will review the proposed audit opinion and assess whether there is sufficient appropriate evidence to support that opinion before it is issued.

Documentation

Audit work must be documented to provide evidence that the work was performed in accordance with professional standards and provides a basis for the audit opinion issued. Documentation should enable an experienced auditor to understand the nature, timing and extent of the procedures performed, the results of those procedures and any significant judgments formed. If the auditor's report is called into question at a later date, the audit documentation should be able to prove that the auditor had performed the audit to the required level of quality. Documentation therefore provides protection in the event of a negligence claim.

(d)   (i)   Review engagements

Review engagements are often undertaken as an alternative to an audit, and involve a practitioner reviewing financial data, such as six-monthly figures. This would involve the practitioner undertaking procedures to state whether anything has come to their attention which causes the practitioner to believe that the financial data is not in accordance with the financial reporting framework.

A review engagement differs to an external audit in that the procedures undertaken are not nearly as comprehensive as those in an audit, with procedures such as analytical review and enquiry used extensively. In addition, the practitioner does not need to comply with ISAs as these only relate to external audits.

(ii)   Levels of assurance

The level of assurance provided by audit and review engagements is as follows:

External audit

This provides comfort that the financial statements present fairly in all material respects (or are true and fair) and are free of material misstatements.

A high but not absolute level of assurance is provided. This is known as reasonable assurance.

Review engagements

The practitioner gathers sufficient evidence to be satisfied that the subject matter is plausible.

In this case negative assurance is given whereby the practitioner confirms that nothing has come to their attention which indicates that the subject matter contains material misstatements.

			Marks
		Marking guide	*Marks*
(a)		**Fraud responsibility**	
	•	Reasonable assurance FS free from material misstatement, whether caused by fraud or error	1
	•	Identify and assess the risks of material misstatement due to fraud	1
	•	Obtain sufficient appropriate audit evidence	1
	•	Respond appropriately to fraud identified during the audit	1
	•	Maintain professional scepticism throughout the audit	1
	•	Discussion within the engagement team	1
	•	Report fraud to management and those charged with governance	1
		Restricted to	5
(b)		**Audit risks and responses (only 8 risks required)**	
	•	Fraud of previous finance director	2
	•	Competence of new finance director	2
	•	Treatment of capitalised development expenditure	2
	•	New loan finance – split between current and non-current	2
	•	Completeness of finance costs	2
	•	Loan covenants – risk of incorrect disclosure of loan as non-current liability if covenant is breached and loan is repayable	2
	•	Loan covenants – going concern risk if breached	2
	•	Loan covenants – risk of manipulation to show compliance	2
	•	Post year-end sales returns	2
	•	Goods in and out during the inventory count	2
	•	Profit on disposal – incorrect calculation	2
	•	Profit on disposal – inappropriate depreciation rate	2
		Max 8 issues, 2 marks each	16
(c)		**Quality control**	
	•	Briefing/direction of the team	1
	•	Supervision – tracking the progress of the audit	1
	•	Supervision – addressing significant matters	1
	•	Supervision – considering competence of team	1
	•	Consultation	1
	•	Review of work	1
	•	EQCR	1
	•	Documentation	1
		Restricted to	5
(d)	(i)	**Purpose of review engagements and difference from an audit**	
	•	Description of review engagements	1
	•	Difference to external audit	1
			2
	(ii)	**Level of assurance provided by audit and reviews**	
	•	Level of assurance of external audit	1
	•	Level of assurance of review engagements	1
			2
Total			30

Examiner's comments

Part (a) required an explanation of auditor's responsibilities in relation to the prevention and detection of fraud and error. This question was answered unsatisfactorily and candidates need to be better prepared to tackle questions on core auditor responsibilities. The question required candidates to discuss the auditor's responsibilities in this area; it did not require an explanation of directors' responsibilities. Unfortunately many candidates wasted time providing this and there were no marks available for this. In addition some answers strayed into providing procedures for detecting fraud and error rather than just addressing responsibilities. Candidates are again reminded to read the question carefully and to ensure that they are answering the question that has been set. The majority of candidates were able to gain marks for reporting fraud to management or those charged with governance, for the auditors' general responsibility to detect material misstatements caused by fraud or error or that the auditors are not responsible for preventing fraud or error.

Part (b) required an identification and description of audit risks from the scenario and the relevant auditor's response for each. Performance on this question was mixed and performance in relation to this core area of the syllabus remains overall disappointing. Candidates who scored well in this question went on to describe how the point identified from the scenario was an audit risk by referring to the assertion and the account balance impacted. As in previous diets, a significant number of candidates tended to only identify facts from the scenario such as 'the previous finance director had been claiming fraudulent expenses from the company' but failed to describe how this results in an audit risk, thus limiting the marks that can be scored to ½ marks. To gain the full 1 mark candidates needed to refer to the risk of other fraudulent expenses being claimed resulting in an impact on profit, as the financial statement impact must be referred to. Only by connecting the fact from the scenario to the relevant assertion and area of the financial statements will the candidate have adequately explained the audit risk. Unfortunately many candidates yet again focused on business risks rather than audit risks, and explained the risk in terms of the impact on Sycamore rather than the financial statements risk and hence how it affects the auditor. As in previous sittings, many candidates performed poorly with regards to the auditor's responses. Many candidates gave business advice, such as undertaking quality control procedures over inventory to prevent the increased level of sales returns. In addition a significant proportion of candidates failed to appreciate that the inventory count had already occurred, hence auditor responses focused on procedures to adopt at the count were not relevant in the circumstances. Audit responses need to be practical and should relate to the approach (i.e. what testing) the auditor will adopt to assess whether the balance is materially misstated or not. Once again this was due to a failure to read the scenario carefully. Candidates should read the questions carefully and plan an appropriate response. Future candidates must take note audit risk is and will continue to be an important element of the syllabus and must be understood, and they would benefit from practising audit risk questions.

Part (di) required an explanation of the purpose of review engagements and how they differed to an external audit and (dii) tested the levels of assurance for audits and review engagements. Overall this question was answered unsatisfactorily. Few candidates were able to explain the purpose of a review engagement and many candidates failed to score any marks for (di). Where the question was attempted many candidates repeated points that were then given in (dii). Candidates performed better in (dii) and many produced clear and concise answers which addressed the levels of assurance for each specified type of engagements. A minority of candidates however just referred to positive and negative assurance without linking them back to the two types of engagements.

212 RECORDER COMMUNICATIONS *Walk in the footsteps of a top tutor*

Key answer tips

Part (a) is a straightforward knowledge question. Notice that the question asks for the importance of planning. Answers which just state what activities are performed at the planning stage will not score marks. As planning is the most important stage of the process, students should be aware of the reasons why it is important to plan the audit.

In part (b) audit risks need to relate to either a risk of material misstatement or a detection risk. For risk of material misstatement, identify a balance in the scenario that is at risk of misstatement and explain why you believe it could be misstated. This is usually because the client has failed to apply the relevant accounting standard correctly. Detection risks are the risks the auditor does not detect material misstatements in the financial statements e.g. when it is a new audit client or if there is a tight reporting deadline. For the response, make sure it relates to the risk, not the balance in general. Try and be as specific as possible, simply saying more testing is required will not be sufficient. State the nature of the tests that should be performed.

A 2 column table should be used to keep the risks in line with the responses and to make sure you address both parts of the requirement.

Parts (c) and (d) require procedures over two very specific areas. Make sure you give specific answers that address the requirement.

Part (e) asks for reporting implications of an unresolved issue. To earn the marks you have to state your justification for the audit opinion you are suggesting. You should also consider any other impact to the auditor's report that might be required such as a 'basis for' paragraph.

(a)   Importance of audit planning

- It helps the auditor to devote appropriate attention to important areas of the audit.

- It helps the auditor to identify and resolve potential problems on a timely basis.

- It helps the auditor to properly organise and manage the audit engagement so that it is performed in an effective and efficient manner.

- It assists in the selection of engagement team members with appropriate levels of capabilities and competence to respond to anticipated risks and the proper assignment of work to them.

- It facilitates the direction and supervision of engagement team members and the review of their work.

- It assists, where applicable, in the coordination of work done by experts.

(b) **Audit risks and responses**

Audit risk	Auditor's response
Recorder Communications Co (Recorder) is a new client for Piano & Co. As the team is not so familiar with the accounting policies, transactions and balances of Recorder, there will be an increased detection risk on the audit.	Piano & Co should ensure they have a suitably experienced team. Also, adequate time should be allocated for team members to obtain an understanding of the company and the risks of material misstatement.
Recorder purchases their goods from South Asia and the goods are in transit for two weeks. Therefore at the year-end only goods which have been received into the warehouse should be included in the inventory balance and a respective payables balance recognised. At the year-end there is a risk that the cut-off of inventory, purchases and payables may not be accurate.	The audit team should undertake detailed cut-off testing of goods in transit from the suppliers in South Asia to ensure that the cut-off is complete and accurate.
The company undertakes continuous (perpetual) inventory counts at its central warehouse. Under such a system all inventory must be counted at least once a year with adjustments made to the inventory records. Inventory could be under or overstated if the continuous (perpetual) inventory counts are not complete and the inventory records accurately updated for adjustments.	The completeness of the continuous (perpetual) inventory counts should be reviewed. In addition, the level of adjustments made to inventory should be considered to assess whether reliance on the inventory records at the year-end will be acceptable.
A number of older models of mobile phones are included within inventory which will be sold at a significantly discount. Inventory will be overstated if these have not been written down to the lower of cost and net realisable value.	Review the aged inventory listing to identify items which need to be discounted and compare with the inventory allowance made, if any. Perform detailed NRV and cost testing to ensure the old items are valued appropriately.
A sales-related bonus scheme has been introduced in the year. This may lead to sales cut-off errors with employees aiming to maximise their current year bonus.	Increased sales cut-off testing will be performed along with a review of any post year-end cancellations of contracts as they may indicate cut-off errors.
Receivables are considerably higher than the prior year and there are concerns about the creditworthiness of some customers.	Extended post year-end cash receipts testing and a review of the aged receivables ledger to be performed to assess valuation. Also consider the adequacy of any allowance for receivables.

Audit risk	Auditor's response
There is a risk that some receivables may be overvalued as they are not recoverable.	
In addition, receivables could be overstated as a result of the bonus scheme; some of the customers signed up for contracts may not actually exist.	External confirmation of receivables to confirm that customers exist and represent valid amounts due.
Recorder has a policy of revaluing its land and buildings and these valuations have been updated during the year. Property, plant and equipment could be under or overvalued if the recent valuation has not been carried out in accordance with IAS 16 *Property, Plant and Equipment* and adequate disclosures may not have been made in the financial statements.	Discuss with management the process adopted for undertaking the valuation, including whether the whole class of assets was revalued and if the valuation was undertaken by an expert. This process should be reviewed for compliance with IAS 16. Review the disclosures of the revaluation in the financial statements for compliance with IAS 16.
The directors have each been paid a significant bonus and separate disclosure of this in the financial statements is required by local legislation. The directors' remuneration disclosure will not be complete and accurate if the bonus paid is not disclosed in accordance with the relevant local legislation.	Discuss this matter with management and review the disclosure in the financial statements to ensure compliance with local legislation.

(c) **Audit procedures for continuous (perpetual) inventory counts**

- Attend at least one of the continuous (perpetual) inventory counts to review whether the controls over the inventory count are adequate.

- Confirm that all of the inventory lines have been counted or are due to be counted at least once a year by reviewing the schedules of counts undertaken/due to be undertaken.

- Review the adjustments made to the inventory records on a monthly basis to gain an understanding of the level of differences arising on a month by month basis.

- Discuss with management how they will ensure that year-end inventory will not be under or overstated. If significant differences consistently arise, this could indicate that the inventory records are not adequately maintained.

- Consider attending the inventory count at the year-end to undertake test counts of inventory from records to floor and from floor to records in order to confirm the existence and completeness of inventory.

(d)   Substantive procedures for directors' bonus and remuneration

- Obtain a schedule of the directors' remuneration including the bonus paid and cast the addition of the schedule to confirm arithmetical accuracy.

- Agree the individual bonus payments to the payroll records.

- Inspect the cash book and bank statements to confirm the amount of each bonus paid.

- Review the board minutes to confirm whether any additional bonus payments relating to this year have been agreed.

- Obtain a written representation from management confirming the completeness of directors' remuneration including the bonus.

- Review any disclosures made of the bonus and assess whether these are in compliance with local legislation.

(e)   Reporting implications

- Failure to value inventory at the lower of cost and net realisable value will mean Recorder has not complied with the requirements of IAS 2 *Inventories.*

- The financial statements will be materially misstated due to overstatement of inventory, although the issue is unlikely to be pervasive.

- The audit opinion will be modified with a qualified 'except for' opinion.

- A basis for qualified opinion will be required to explain the material misstatement to the users of the financial statements and quantify the financial effect of the misstatement on the financial statements.

- The basis for paragraph should be positioned below the opinion section within the auditor's report.

Marking guide		Marks
(a)	**Importance of planning**	
	• Important areas of the audit	1
	• Identify potential problems	1
	• Effective and efficient audit	1
	• Selection of engagement team members and assignment of work	1
	• Direction, supervision and review	1
	• Coordination of work	1
	Restricted to	**5**
(b)	**Audit risks and responses (only 7 risks required)**	
	• New client leading to increased detection risk	2
	• Cut-off of goods in transit	2
	• Continuous (perpetual) inventory counts	2
	• Inventory valuation	2
	• Sales cut-off	2
	• Receivables – overvaluation	2
	• Receivables – existence	2
	• Valuation of land and buildings	2
	• Directors' bonus remuneration	2
	Max 7 issues, 2 marks each	**14**

		Marking guide	Marks
(c)		**Perpetual inventory count procedures**	
	•	Attend one of the continuous (perpetual) inventory counts to review whether the controls are adequate	1
	•	Review the schedule of counts to confirm completeness of all inventory lines	1
	•	Review the adjustments made to the inventory records	1
	•	If significant differences, discuss with management how they will ensure that year-end inventory will not be under or overstated	1
	•	Attend the inventory count at the year-end to undertake test counts to confirm the completeness and existence of inventory	1
		Restricted to	**3**
(d)		**Substantive procedures**	
	•	Cast schedule of directors' remuneration including the bonus paid	1
	•	Agree the individual bonus payments to the payroll records	1
	•	Agree bonus paid to the cash book and bank statements	1
	•	Review the board minutes to confirm any additional bonus payments	1
	•	Obtain written representation from management	1
	•	Review disclosures to assess compliance with local legislation	1
		Restricted to	**4**
(e)		**Reporting implications**	
	•	Failure to comply with IAS 2 – inventory overstated	1
	•	Material misstatement – not pervasive	1
	•	Qualified opinion – except for	1
	•	Basis for qualified opinion	1
			4
Total			**30**

Examiner's comments

Part (a) required candidates to explain the importance of audit planning. Candidates' performance was satisfactory on this question. Many candidates were able to confidently identify that planning resulted in sufficient attention being devoted to important areas/audit risks, selection of an appropriate audit team, an efficient and effective audit and resolution of issues in a timely manner. Where candidates did not score enough marks to pass, this tended to be because they focused on the contents of an audit strategy and plan, which was not the specific focus of the question. Often candidates identified the procedures which would be considered prior to planning, such as confirming the independence of auditors or used to obtain an understanding of the entity resulting in some candidates focusing on what was done at the planning stage rather than explaining the importance of planning.

Part (b) required identification and description of audit risks from the scenario and the auditor's response for each. Performance on this question was mixed. The scenario contained significantly more than the number of risks required and so candidates were able to easily identify enough risks, and strong answers went on to describe how the point identified from the scenario was an audit risk by referring to the assertion and the account balance impacted.

As in previous diets, some candidates tended to only identify facts from the scenario such as 'Recorder purchases goods from a supplier in South Asia and the goods are in transit for two weeks' but failed to describe how this could impact audit risk; this would only have scored ½ marks.

To gain 1 mark the point needed to be developed to also explain that this could result in issues over the completeness of inventory. More so than in previous diets, candidates disappointingly provided business risks rather than audit risks with answers such as stock outs due to the two week transit period and possible damage to inventory during transit. As a result these candidates then provided responses related to how management should address these business risks rather than how the auditor should respond. This meant that out of a potential 2 marks per risk, candidates would only score ½ marks for the identification of the issue from the scenario. Some candidates also identified irrelevant risks such as Recorder undertaking continuous inventory counts. While an audit risk was present around inventory in relation to the effectiveness of the perpetual inventory system, very few candidates explained the risk in this manner instead focusing on the lack of a full year-end count. This demonstrated a lack of understanding of continuous inventory counts. Additionally, many candidates performed poorly with regards to the auditor's responses. Many candidates gave business advice, such as changing the salesmen's bonus structure or provided vague responses such as perform detailed substantive testing or maintain professional scepticism. Responses which start with 'ensure that......' are unlikely to score marks as they usually fail to explain exactly how the auditor will address the audit risk. Audit responses need to be practical and should relate to the approach (i.e. what testing) the auditor will adopt to assess whether the balance is materially misstated or not. Most candidates presented their answers well, adopting a two column approach with audit risk in one column and the related response next to it. This helps candidates to ensure that for every risk identified there is a related response and candidates are encouraged to continue to use this approach where appropriate.

Part (c) required procedures the auditor should perform in order to place reliance on the continuous counts for inventory. Candidates' performance was disappointing. Many candidates provided lengthy answers on procedures to be carried out when attending a year-end inventory count or procedures to verify valuation or completeness/existence of inventory, suggesting that a significant proportion of candidates do not understand continuous inventory counts, the risks associated with this and therefore the areas the auditor needs to focus on. A small proportion of candidates correctly identified that it was important to confirm if all inventory items were counted at least once a year and also to assess the level of adjustments made during these counts. Inventory is a key element of the financial statements and candidates need to be able to provide relevant procedures for both full year-end counts as well as continuous counting.

Part (d) required substantive procedures for confirming the directors' bonus payment made during the year. Candidates' performance was disappointing. Unfortunately, many candidates focused on the authorisation of the bonus; this is not a substantive procedure and would not have scored any marks. A significant minority thought that the directors' bonus was based on sales which was not the case. The scenario stated that salesmen's bonuses were based on sales, hence candidates either confused these two items or failed to read the scenario properly. They then looked to recalculate the bonus based on sales levels which was not appropriate in the circumstances. A number of vague procedures were suggested such as obtaining written representations or reading board minutes without explaining what for. Analytical procedures were suggested; however they were unlikely to be valid procedures as bonuses by their nature tend to vary each year.

213 KANGAROO CONSTRUCTION *Walk in the footsteps of a top tutor*

Key answer tips

Part (a) asks for a definition and explanation of materiality and performance materiality. This requires knowledge from the text book and the relevant auditing standard. Each constructed response question is likely to have one requirement which is knowledge based and therefore you must take time to learn key definitions and be able to provide an explanation.

Part (b) asks for ratios to be calculated from the information provided. Remember that the ratios are to help you identify audit risks. You are not evaluating the financial performance of the company.

In part (c) audit risks need to relate to either a risk of material misstatement or a detection risk. For risk of material misstatement, identify a balance in the scenario that is at risk of misstatement and explain why you believe it could be misstated. Detection risks are the risks the auditor does not detect material misstatements in the financial statements e.g. when it is a new audit client or if there is a tight reporting deadline.

For the response, make sure it relates to the risk, not the balance in general. Try and be as specific as possible, simply saying more testing is required will not be sufficient. State the nature of the tests that should be performed.

A 2 column table should be used to keep the risks in line with the responses and to make sure you address both parts of the requirement.

Part (d) asks for the audit reporting implications if the issue is unresolved. First you should discuss what the issue is i.e. what the client has done wrong. Calculate whether the adjustment required is material. If the issue is not material it won't impact the auditor's report. If it is material consider whether it is material and pervasive as this will impact the type of opinion that should be given. Remember to include the key wording of the opinion you are suggesting as well as any other impact on the auditor's report.

(a)   **Materiality and performance materiality**

Materiality and performance materiality are dealt with under ISA 320 *Materiality in Planning and Performing an Audit*. Auditors need to establish the materiality level for the financial statements as a whole, as well as assess performance materiality levels, which are lower than the overall materiality.

Materiality is defined in ISA 320 as follows:

'Misstatements, including omissions, are considered to be material if they, individually or in the aggregate, could reasonably be expected to influence the economic decisions of users taken on the basis of the financial statements.'

In assessing the level of materiality, there are a number of areas that should be considered. First the auditor must consider both the amount (quantity) and the nature (quality) of any misstatements, or a combination of both. The quantity of the misstatement refers to the relative size of it and the quality refers to an amount that might be low in value but due to its prominence could influence the user's decision, for example, directors' transactions.

Materiality is often calculated using benchmarks such as 5% of profit before tax or 1% of total revenue or total expenses. These values are useful as a starting point for assessing materiality.

The assessment of what is material is ultimately a matter of the auditor's professional judgment, and it is affected by the auditor's perception of the financial information needs of users of the financial statements and the perceived level of risk; the higher the risk, the lower the level of overall materiality.

In assessing materiality, the auditor must consider that a number of errors each with a low value may, when aggregated, amount to a material misstatement.

In calculating materiality, the auditor should also set the performance materiality level. Performance materiality is normally set at a level lower than overall materiality. It is used for testing individual transactions, account balances and disclosures. The aim of performance materiality is to reduce the risk that the total of errors in balances, transactions and disclosures does not in total exceed overall materiality.

Tutorial note

Award marks for ISA 320 definition of performance materiality below:

'Performance materiality means the amount or amounts set by the auditor at less than materiality for the financial statements as a whole to reduce to an appropriately low level the probability that the aggregate of uncorrected and undetected misstatements exceeds materiality for the financial statements as a whole. If applicable, performance materiality also refers to the amount or amounts set by the auditor at less than the materiality level or levels for particular classes of transactions, account balances or disclosures.'

(b) **Ratios to assist in planning the audit:**

	20X3	*20X2*
Gross margin	5.5/12.5 = **44%**	7/15 = **46.7%**
Operating margin	0.5/12.5 = **4%**	1.9/15 = **12.7%**
Inventory holding period	1.9/7 × 365 = **99 days**	1.4/8 × 365 = **64 days**
Inventory turnover	7/1.9 = **3.7**	8/1.4 = **5.7**
Receivables collection period	3.1/12.5 × 365 = **91 days**	2.0/15 × 365 = **49 days**
Payables payment period	1.6/7 × 365 = **83 days**	1.2/8 × 365 = **55 days**
Current ratio	5.8/2.6 = **2.2**	5.3/1.2 = **4.4**
Quick ratio	(5.8 – 1.9)/2.6 = **1.5**	(5.3 – 1.4)/1.2 = **3.3**

Tutor's top tips

Ratios are relationships between different numbers in the financial statements. Percentage movements year to year are trends. The question asks for ratios therefore there will be no marks for calculating the percentage decrease in revenue/cost of sales.

(c) **Audit risks and responses**

Audit risk	Audit response
The receivables collection period has increased from 49 to 91 days and management has significantly extended the credit terms given to customers. This leads to an increased risk of recoverability of receivables as they may be overvalued.	Extended post year-end cash receipts testing and a review of the aged receivables ledger to be performed to assess valuation.
Due to the fall in demand for Kangaroo Construction Co's (Kangaroo) houses, there are some houses where the selling price may be below cost. IAS 2 *Inventories* requires that inventory should be stated at the lower of cost and NRV. In addition, the inventory holding period has increased from 64 to 99 days and inventory turnover has fallen from 5.7 in 20X2 to 3.7 in the current year. There is a risk that inventory is overvalued.	Detailed cost and net realisable value (NVR) testing to be performed and the aged inventory report to be reviewed to assess whether inventory requires writing down.
A deposit of $5,000 is paid by customers and is refundable until the house reaches 75% completion. There is a risk that the deposit is recognised as revenue when it is paid instead of when the revenue is earned. Revenue could be overstated as a result.	A schedule of houses which have been reserved but not completed should be obtained and the sales day book reviewed to ensure the $5,000 deposit has only been recognised for houses that have reached a 75% stage of completion.
The directors have extended the useful lives of plant and machinery from three to five years, resulting in the depreciation charge reducing. Under IAS 16 *Property, Plant and Equipment*, useful lives are to be reviewed annually, and if asset lives have genuinely increased, then this change is reasonable.	Discuss with the directors the rationale for extending the useful lives. Also, the five year life should be compared to how often these assets are replaced, as this provides evidence of the useful life of assets.

Audit risk	Audit response
However, there is a risk that this reduction has occurred in order to achieve profit targets. If this is the case, then plant and machinery is overvalued and profit overstated.	
The directors need to reach a profit level of $0.5 million in order to receive their annual bonus. There is a risk that they might feel under pressure to manipulate the results through the judgments taken or through the use of provisions.	Throughout the audit, the team will need to be alert to this risk and maintain professional scepticism. They will need to carefully review judgmental decisions and compare treatment against prior years. In addition, a written representation should be obtained from management confirming the basis of any significant judgments.
Due to a change in material supplier, the quality of products used has deteriorated and this has led to customers claiming on their five-year building warranty. If the overall number of people claiming on the warranty is likely to increase, then the warranty provision should possibly be higher. If the directors have not increased the level of the provision, then there is a risk the provision is understated.	Review the level of the warranty provision in light of the increased level of claims to confirm completeness of the provision.
Kangaroo has borrowed $1.0 million from the bank via a short-term loan. This loan needs to be repaid in 20X3 and so should be disclosed as a current liability. There is a risk of incorrect disclosure if the loan is not classified as a current liability.	During the audit, the team would need to check that the $1.0m loan finance was received. In addition, the disclosures for this loan should be reviewed in detail to ensure compliance with relevant accounting standards and legislation.
In addition, Kangaroo may have given the bank a charge over its assets as security for the loan. There is a risk that the disclosure of any security given is not complete.	The loan correspondence should be reviewed to ascertain whether any security has been given, and this bank should be circularised as part of the bank confirmation process.
The current and quick ratios have decreased from 4.4 to 2.2 and 3.3 to 1.5 respectively. In addition, the cash balances have decreased over the year, there is a fall in demand and Kangaroo have taken out a short-term loan of $1 million, which needs to be repaid in 20X3.	Detailed going concern testing to be performed during the audit and discussed with the directors to ensure that the going concern basis is reasonable.

Audit risk	Audit response
Although all ratios are above the minimum levels, this is still a significant decrease and along with the fall in both operating and gross profit margins, as well as the significant increase in the payables payment period could be evidence of going concern difficulties. There is a risk that going concern uncertainties are not adequately disclosed in the notes to the financial statement.	The team should discuss with the directors how the short-term loan of $1.0 million will be repaid later in 20X3.

(d)   **Reporting implications**

The increase in warranty provision required of $0.3 million represents 60% of profit before tax (0.3/0.5 × 100) which is material to the financial statements.

The financial statements are materially misstated due to understatement of the warranty provision. This may be considered material or material and pervasive.

If considered material, the audit opinion should be qualified with the 'except for' wording.

If deemed material and pervasive the audit opinion should be adverse with the wording stating that the financial statements do not show a true and fair view.

A basis for qualified opinion or basis for adverse opinion would be required to explain the misstatement arising due to understatement of the warranty provision. The basis for paragraph would explain the financial effect of the issue on the financial statement.

The basis for paragraph should be positioned below the opinion section within the auditor's report.

		Marks
(a)	**Materiality and performance materiality**	
	• Materiality for financial statements as a whole and also performance materiality levels	1
	• Definition of materiality	1
	• Amount or nature of misstatements, or both	1
	• 5% profit before tax or 1% revenue or total expenses	1
	• Judgment, needs of users and level of risk	1
	• Small errors aggregated	1
	• Performance materiality	1
	Restricted to	5
(b)	**Ratio calculations**	
	• Gross margin	1
	• Operating margin	1
	• Inventory holding period / inventory turnover	1
	• Receivables collection period	1
	• Payables payment period	1
	• Current ratio	1
	• Quick ratio	1
	Restricted to	6
(c)	**Audit risks and responses (only 7 risks required)**	
	• Receivables valuation	2
	• Inventory valuation	2
	• Revenue recognition – deposit	2
	• Depreciation of plant and machinery	2
	• Management manipulation of profit to reach bonus targets	2
	• Completeness of warranty provision	2
	• Disclosure of bank loan – split between current and non-current	2
	• Disclosure of bank loan – security	2
	• Going concern risk	2
	Max 7 issues, 2 marks each	14
(d)	**Reporting implications**	
	• Materiality calculation	1
	• Misstatement may be material or material and pervasive	1
	• If material – qualified 'except for'	1
	• If pervasive – adverse 'FS do not show TFV'	1
	• Basis for paragraph	1
	• Position of Basis for paragraph	1
	Restricted to	5
Total		**30**

Marking guide

Examiner's comments

Part (a) required an explanation of the concepts of materiality and performance materiality. Candidates' performed well on this question. The vast majority of candidates were able to score marks on the definition of materiality, provision of some benchmarks for the calculations and a reference to performance materiality being at a lower level. These points would have achieved a pass for this part of the question. An adequate level of detail was provided for this 'explain' requirement by the majority of candidates. Some candidates just gave a definition of materiality and nothing else; this would have gained a maximum of 1 mark.

Part (b) required candidates to calculate ratios to assist in planning the audit. This question was answered very well by the vast majority of candidates with many scoring full marks. Some candidates attempted to calculate ratios despite there being inadequate data available, namely return on capital employed and gearing. Candidates need to think about the information provided in the scenario prior to calculating ratios. In order to gain the ½ mark available for each year a relevant ratio had to be calculated.

Part (c) required a description of audit risks from the scenario and ratios calculated and the auditor's response for each. Performance on this question was once again unsatisfactory. The scenario contained more than the required number of risks and so candidates were able to easily identify enough risks. They then went on to describe how the point identified from the scenario or movement in a ratio was an audit risk by referring to the assertion and the account balances impacted. The improvement in this area noted in December 2012 has been reversed and the proportion of candidates who described the audit risk adequately has declined in this session. Some candidates tended to only identify facts from the scenario such as 'Kangaroo has completed houses in inventory where selling price may be below cost' but failed to explain how this could impact audit risk; this would only have scored ½ marks. To gain a full 1 mark they needed to refer to the risk of the inventory being overvalued. Where candidates did attempt to cover the assertion it was often vague; for example stating that 'inventory may be misstated', this is not sufficient to gain the ½ mark available. Additionally, many candidates used the ratios calculated in part (bi) and then gave a detailed analytical review of the ratio movements, commenting on ratio increases and decreases, but with no link at all to the audit risks. It was not uncommon to see very lengthy answers with no audit risks; this just puts the candidate under time pressure. Many candidates focused on business risks rather than audit risks and hence provided responses related to how management should address these business risks. For example, the scenario stated that 'Kangaroo had changed their main supplier to a cheaper alternative and as a result warranty claims had increased'.

Some candidates answered 'this would lead to the company's reputation suffering as the quality of their buildings would decline'. The suggested auditor's response was 'to change back to a more expensive supplier'. Neither the risk nor the response has been related to the financial statements and hence would only gain a ½ mark being the identification of the fact from the scenario. Additionally, candidates performed inadequately with regards to the auditor's responses. As detailed above some candidates gave business advice, other responses focused more on repeating what the appropriate accounting treatment should be, therefore for the risk of inventory valuation due to number of houses where selling price was below cost, the response given was 'inventory should be valued at the lower of cost and NRV', this is not a valid audit response. Responses which start with 'ensure that......' are unlikely to score marks as they usually fail to explain exactly how the auditor will address the audit risk. Also some responses were weak such as 'discuss with the directors' without making it clear what would be discussed and how this would gather evidence. Audit responses need to be practical and should relate to the approach the auditor will adopt to assess whether the balance is materially misstated or not.

Most candidates presented their answers well as they adopted a two column approach with audit risk in one column and the related auditor's response next to it.

214 REDSMITH *Walk in the footsteps of a top tutor*

Key answer tips

Part (a) is a difficult requirement – you either know the answer or you don't. A common sense approach will not help you here. If you don't have the knowledge, move on and try to compensate by scoring well on other requirements.

Part (b) is another purely knowledge based requirement, but a common sense approach will score well here. If you don't know the requirements of ISA 315 you can still score well by thinking generally about the areas/matters that of which the auditor should obtain an understanding.

Part (c) asks for ratios to be calculated from the information provided. Remember that the ratios are to help you identify audit risks. You are not evaluating the financial performance of the company.

Part (d) is a core topic in this syllabus – audit risk and the auditor's response. The auditor's response should be directly linked to the audit risks explained and therefore a columnar approach is appropriate. This is a skills based question – the answers must relate to the issues presented in the scenario or the ratios calculated. Each sufficiently explained audit risk will be awarded 1 mark and each appropriate response a further mark.

(a)   Preconditions for an audit

ISA 210 *Agreeing the Terms of Audit Engagements* provides guidance to auditors on the steps they should take in accepting a new audit or continuing on an existing audit engagement. It sets out a number of processes that the auditor should perform including agreeing whether the preconditions are present, agreement of audit terms in an engagement letter, recurring audits and changes in engagement terms.

To assess whether the preconditions for an audit are present the auditor must determine whether the financial reporting framework to be applied in the preparation of the financial statements is acceptable. In considering this the auditor should assess the nature of the entity, the nature and purpose of the financial statements and whether law or regulations prescribes the applicable reporting framework.

In addition they must obtain the agreement of management that it acknowledges and understands its responsibility for the following:

- Preparation of the financial statements in accordance with the applicable financial reporting framework, including where relevant their fair presentation.

- For such internal control as management determines is necessary to enable the preparation of financial statements that are free from material misstatement, whether due to fraud or error; and

- To provide the auditor with access to all relevant information for the preparation of the financial statements, any additional information that the auditor may request from management and unrestricted access to persons within the entity from whom the auditor determines it necessary to obtain audit evidence.

If the preconditions for an audit are not present, the auditor shall discuss the matter with management. Unless required by law or regulation to do so, the auditor shall not accept the proposed audit engagement:

- If the auditor has determined that the financial reporting framework to be applied in the preparation of the financial statements is unacceptable; or

- If management agreement of their responsibilities has not been obtained.

(b) **Matters to consider in obtaining an understanding of the entity:**

- The market and its competition

- Legislation and regulation

- Regulatory framework

- Ownership of the entity

- Nature of products/services and markets

- Location of production facilities and factories

- Key customers and suppliers

- Capital investment activities

- Accounting policies and industry specific guidance

- Financing structure

- Significant changes in the entity on prior years.

Tutor's top tips

Note the requirement asks for matters to consider in obtaining an understanding of the entity. Procedures that the auditor should perform or sources from which they would obtain this understanding will not score any marks. Also note the verb requirement 'list' and the number of marks available. With a 'list' requirement, each appropriate matter listed will be awarded ½ mark. The length of points provided in the model answer is appropriate for ½ mark.

(c) **Ratios to assist in planning the audit:**

	20X5	20X4
Gross margin	12/23 × 100 = **52.2%**	8/18 × 100 = **44.4%**
Operating margin	4.5/23 × 100 = **19.6%**	4/18 × 100 = **22.2%**
Inventory holding period	2.1/11 × 365 = **70 days**	1.6/10 × 365 = **58 days**
Receivables collection period	4.5/23 × 365 = **71 days**	3.0/18 × 365 = **61 days**

	20X5	*20X4*
Payables payment period	1.6/11 × 365 = **53 days**	1.2/10 × 365 = **44 days**
Current ratio	6.6/2.5 = **2.6**	6.9/1.2 = **5.8**
Quick ratio	(6.6 – 2.1)/2.5 = **1.8**	(6.9 – 1.6)/1.2 = **4.4**

Tutor's top tips

Be sure to calculate ratios and not trends in order to score well in part (i). Simple % increases will not be awarded marks. The auditor will calculate ratios as part of the analytical review required at the planning stage. You should expect to be examined on the practical application of skills required during the audit process.

(d) **Audit risks and responses**

Audit risk	Response to risk
Management was disappointed with 20X4 results and hence undertook strategies to improve the 20X5 trading results. There is a risk that management might feel under pressure to manipulate the results through the judgments taken or through the use of provisions.	Throughout the audit the team will need to be alert to this risk and increase professional scepticism. They will need to carefully review judgmental decisions and compare treatment against prior years.
A generous sales-related bonus scheme has been introduced in the year. This may lead to sales cut-off errors with employees aiming to maximise their current year bonus. There is a risk that sales are overstated.	Increased sales cut-off testing will be performed along with a review of post year-end sales returns as they may indicate cut-off errors.
Revenue has grown by 28% in the year however, cost of sales has only increased by 10%. This increase in sales may be due to the bonus scheme and the advertising however, this does not explain the increase in gross margin. There is a risk that sales may be overstated.	During the audit a detailed breakdown of sales will be obtained, discussed with management and tested in order to understand the sales increase.

Audit risk	Response to risk
Gross margin has increased from 44.4% to 52.2%. Operating margin has decreased from 22.2% to 19.6%. This movement in gross margin is significant and there is a risk that costs may have been omitted or included in operating expenses rather than cost of sales. There has been a significant increase in operating expenses which may be due to the bonus and the advertising campaign but could be related to the misclassification of costs.	The classification of costs between cost of sales and operating expenses will be compared with the prior year to ensure consistency.
The finance director has made a change to the inventory valuation in the year with additional overheads being included. In addition, the inventory holding period has increased from 58 to 70 days. The additional overheads may not be production related and therefore should not be included in inventory. There is a risk that inventory is overvalued.	The change in the inventory policy will be discussed with management and a review of the additional overheads included performed to ensure that these are of a production nature. Detailed cost and net realisable value testing to be performed and the aged inventory report to be reviewed to assess whether inventory requires writing down.
The receivables collection period has increased from 61 to 71 days and management have extended the credit period given to customers. Receivables may not be recoverable. There is a risk that receivables are overstated.	Extended post year-end cash receipts testing and a review of the aged receivables ledger to be performed to assess valuation.
The current and quick ratios have decreased from 5.8 to 2.6 and 4.4 to 1.8 respectively. In addition the cash balances have decreased significantly over the year. Although all ratios are above the minimum levels, this is still a significant decrease and along with the increase of sales could be evidence of overtrading which could result in going concern difficulties. There is a risk of inadequate disclosure of going concern uncertainties in the financial statements.	Detailed going concern testing to be performed during the audit and discussed with management to ensure that the going concern basis is reasonable.

Tutor's top tips

Take care to describe audit risks in part (c) and not business risks or interpretations of the ratios. Audit risk is the risk of giving an inappropriate opinion – you should describe the potential for misstatement in the financial statements or explain how detection risk is increased – be specific. Link the ratios you calculate in part (i) to the information given about the entity described when explaining the audit risk. The auditor's response must directly relate to the risk described – describe a procedure that would help the auditor detect any misstatement that may exist.

Marking guide		
		Marks
(a)	**Preconditions for an audit**	
	• ISA 210 provides guidance	1
	• Determination of acceptable framework	1
	• Agreement of management responsibilities	1
	• Preparation of financial statements with applicable framework	1
	• Internal controls	1
	• Provide auditor with relevant information and access	1
	• If preconditions are not present discuss with management	1
	• Decline if framework unacceptable	1
	• Decline if agreement of responsibilities not obtained	1
	Max	**3**
(b)	**Understanding an entity**	
	½ mark per example	
	Max	**2**
(c)	**Ratio calculations**	
	• Gross margin	1
	• Operating margin	1
	• Inventory holding period / inventory turnover	1
	• Receivables collection period	1
	• Payables payment period	1
	• Current ratio	1
	• Quick ratio	1
	Max 5 ratios	**5**
(d)	**Audit risks and responses (only 5 risks required)**	
	• Management manipulation of results	2
	• Sales cut-off	2
	• Revenue growth	2
	• Misclassification between cost of sales and operating	2
	• Inventory valuation	2
	• Receivables valuation	2
	• Going concern risk	2
	Max 5 issues, 2 marks each	**10**
Total		**20**

INTERNAL CONTROLS

215 AMBERJACK *Walk in the footsteps of a top tutor*

Key answer tips

Part (a) requires control objectives for a sales and dispatch system. Control objectives are the reasons why controls are put in place. They address the risks that could happen in the system. You need to give the reason why the control should be in place.

Part (b) asks for control deficiencies and recommendations in respect of a cash system. This is examined every sitting and with plenty of past papers to practise, this type of question should be straightforward. Fully explain the deficiency in terms of the effect on the company. If management are to take action, they must be concerned about the potential consequences of the deficiency. When providing recommendations for improvement, be as specific as possible.

(a) **Control objectives for sales and dispatch system**

- To ensure that orders are only accepted if goods are available to be processed for customers.

- To ensure that all orders are recorded completely and accurately.

- To ensure that goods are not supplied to poor credit risks.

- To ensure that goods are dispatched for all orders on a timely basis.

- To ensure that the correct quantity of goods are dispatched and they are of an adequate quality.

- To ensure that all goods dispatched are correctly invoiced at authorised prices.

- To ensure completeness of income for goods dispatched.

- To ensure that sales discounts are only provided during the valid period.

(b) **Report to management**

Board of directors
Amberjack Co
21 Under the Sea
Shorelife City
Shark Country

1 July 20X5

Dear Sirs,

Audit of Amberjack Co for the year ended 30 April 20X5

Please find enclosed the report to management on deficiencies in internal controls identified during the audit for the year ended 30 April 20X5. The appendix to this report considers deficiencies in the sales and dispatch system and recommendations to address those deficiencies.

Please note that this report only addresses the deficiencies identified during the audit and if further testing had been performed, then more deficiencies may have been reported.

This report is solely for the use of management and if you have any further questions, then please do not hesitate to contact us.

Yours faithfully

An audit firm

Appendix

Control deficiency	Control recommendation
Customer credit limits are set by receivables ledger clerks. Receivables ledger clerks are not sufficiently senior and so may set limits too high, leading to irrecoverable debts, or too low, leading to a loss of sales.	Credit limits should be set by a senior member of the receivables ledger department and not by receivables ledger clerks. These limits should be regularly reviewed by a responsible official.
Receivables ledger clerks record new customer details and credit limits in the customer master data file and these changes are not reviewed. There is a risk that customers could be set up incorrectly resulting in a loss of customer goodwill and sales revenue. In addition, the receivables ledger clerks are not senior enough to be given access to making changes to master file data as this could increase the risk of fraud.	Receivables ledger clerks should not be able to access the master data file to add new customers or make amendments. Any such additions/amendments to master file data should be restricted so that only supervisors and above can make changes. An exception report of changes made should be generated and reviewed by a responsible official.
Amberjack Co's credit controller is currently on secondment for six months to the internal audit department and has not been replaced. During this period, it does not appear that anyone else has been responsible for monitoring ageing receivables. This could result in an increased risk of irrecoverable debts and lead to customers not paying their outstanding balances on time, or at all, leading to reduced cash flows.	During the period of the secondment, an alternative member of the finance department should be trained in the credit control role and assigned responsibility for reviewing the aged receivables listing and following up on any overdue customers.

Control deficiency	Control recommendation
Goods dispatch notes (GDN) are given the same number as the order number to which they relate. The sales invoices are only raised on receipt of a GDN, and without separate sequential numbers, it is difficult for Amberjack Co to identify if any GDNs are missing as they are not likely to be raised in the same sequence as the sales orders. If GDNs are missing and the company fails to raise invoices in a timely manner, this could lead to a loss of revenue.	GDNs should all be sequentially numbered using a sequence which is different to the order number. On a regular basis, a sequence check of GDNs should be undertaken to identify any missing dispatch notes.
Once orders are processed, copies of GDNs are sent to the finance department, customer and remain in the warehouse. However, the sales order department of Amberjack Co does not receive a copy of the GDN. If the sales order department does not receive a copy of the completed GDNs, they are not able to monitor if orders are being fulfilled on a timely basis. This could result in a loss of revenue and customer goodwill.	The GDN should be amended to be at least four-part. One copy should be sent to the sales order department. Once the copy of the GDN has been received by the order department, it should be matched to the order. A regular review of unmatched orders should be undertaken by the sales order department to identify any unfulfilled orders.
Additional staff has been drafted in to help the sales clerks produce the sales invoices. As the extra staff will not be as experienced as the sales clerks, there is an increased risk of mistakes being made in the sales invoices. This could result in customers being under or overcharged leading to misstated revenue or dissatisfied customers.	Only the sales clerks should be able to raise sales invoices. As Amberjack Co is expanding, consideration should be given to recruiting and training more permanent sales clerks who can produce sales invoices. If this is not currently possible, temporary staff should be adequately trained and additional input checks on invoices should be introduced.
Discounts given to customers who purchased goods during the 10% off weekend are manually entered onto the sales invoices by sales clerks. This could result in unauthorised sales discounts being given as there does not seem to be any authorisation required. In addition, a clerk could forget to manually enter the discount or enter an incorrect level of discount for a customer, leading to the sales invoice being overstated and a loss of customer goodwill.	During the period of any special offers, such as the 10% off weekend, the authorised sales prices file should be updated by a responsible official. These changes should be reviewed for any input errors, this review should be evidenced. The invoicing system should confirm that orders were placed during the discount weekend. Hence the sales invoices for these periods should automatically contain the reduced prices.

Control deficiency	Control recommendation
Unauthorised discounts in excess of 10% would result in a loss of revenue, either due to error or fraud.	The invoicing system should be amended to prevent sales clerks from being able to manually enter sales discounts onto invoices.
Customer statements are no longer being generated and sent to customers. If statements are not sent regularly, this increases the likelihood of errors and any disputed invoices not being quickly identified and resolved by Amberjack Co. This could lead to cash flow issues.	Amberjack Co should produce monthly customer statements for all customers and send them out promptly.
The receivables ledger control account is only reconciled at the end of April in order to verify the year-end balance. If the receivables ledger is only reconciled annually, there is a risk that errors will not be spotted promptly. Receivables may be misstated.	The receivables ledger control account should be reconciled on a monthly basis to identify any errors which should be investigated and corrected. The reconciliations should be reviewed by a responsible official and they should evidence their review by way of signature.

Marking guide		
		Marks
(a)	**Control objectives for sales and dispatch system**	
	• Orders only accepted if goods are available	1
	• All orders are recorded completely and accurately	1
	• Goods are not supplied to poor credit risks	1
	• Goods are dispatched for all orders	1
	• Quantity and quality of goods dispatched appropriate	1
	• All goods dispatched are invoiced for correctly	1
	• Completeness of income for goods dispatched	1
	• Sales discounts are only given during valid period	1
		—
	Restricted to	**4**
		—
(b)	**Control deficiencies and recommendations (only 7 required)**	
	• Customer credit limits	2
	• Customer master data not reviewed	2
	• Credit controller not replaced	2
	• Goods dispatch notes (GDNs) not sequentially numbered	2
	• Insufficient copies of GDN	2
	• Sales invoice processing	2
	• Manual recording of discounts	2
	• Customer statements no longer raised	2
	• Receivables ledger control account only reconciled annually	2
		—
	Max 7 issues, 2 marks each and 2 marks for covering letter	**16**
		—
Total		**20**
		—

Examiner's comments

This 20-mark question was based on Amberjack Co, a manufacturer and distributor of car tyres. This question tested candidates' knowledge of control objectives for the sales cycle and control deficiencies and recommendations. Candidates overall performance was satisfactory.

Part (a) for four marks required candidates to list four control objectives for the sales and dispatch system. Performance, in this knowledge-based question, was mixed. Those candidates who clearly understood what a control objective was often scored full marks. However, in common with previous diets, many candidates provided an example of a control or tests of control rather than an objective. Some simply listed assertions such as completeness and accuracy. Where objectives were given there was often considerable overlap and repetition of points or answers strayed outside the scope of the sales and dispatch system. Candidates are reminded once again that questions in this syllabus area usually contain a knowledge-based requirement. These are straightforward and candidates should be able to score well, provided they spend the necessary time and practise past questions.

Part (b) for 16 marks required candidates to provide a report to management which identified and explained from the scenario seven deficiencies and controls to address each of these deficiencies. Candidates were also required to provide a covering letter. Performance was satisfactory. Internal control deficiency questions such as this typically require internal control deficiencies to be identified (½ mark each), explained (½ mark each) which must cover the implication of the deficiency to the company and a relevant recommendation to address the deficiency (1 mark). The scenario in the exam contained more issues than were required to be discussed. The majority of candidates were able to identify seven deficiencies as required. However, a significant minority of candidates identified irrelevant or incorrect deficiencies. For example, many candidates were concerned about sales prices only being updated every six months or that sales invoices were prepared using quantities from goods dispatch notes. These are not deficiencies and therefore were not awarded any credit. Some candidates did not clearly understand/explain the implication of the deficiency. Candidates are required to explain the implication to the business to be awarded credit. For example, a candidate who correctly identified the deficiency 'discounts are manually entered onto sales invoices' (identification ½ mark awarded), would not have received credit for the explanation 'discounts could be unauthorised'. Candidates must clearly explain the implication to the business, for example that 'this could result in a loss of revenue or loss of customer goodwill', to be awarded the ½ explanation mark. Candidates were able to provide recommendations to address the deficiencies identified however often the recommendations were not described in enough detail. For example, the recommendation that 'credit limits should be set by senior members of the sales department, rather than the clerks' was only awarded ½ mark. Candidates needed to also recommend that 'these limits should be regularly reviewed' to be awarded the full 1 mark. It was disappointing that few candidates provided a covering letter, and of these, few letters contained suitable disclaimer statements. An example disclaimer stating that 'this report only addressed deficiencies identified during the audit and if further testing had been undertaken more deficiencies may have been reported' was required. Internal control questions remain a highly examinable area and future candidates need to ensure that they have undertaken adequate question practice of all examinable control systems.

216 FREESIA *Walk in the footsteps of a top tutor*

Key answer tips

Part (a) requires knowledge from the text book. Use subheadings to make it easy for the marker to see that you have answered both advantages and disadvantages of each type of method.

Part (b) requires the control deficiencies within the sales, purchases and payroll systems to be identified. Use the specific information in scenario rather than giving generic deficiencies. There are always more deficiencies than you need so choose the ones you can write well about. Suggest controls the client can implement to address the control deficiency. Be specific about which member of client staff should be responsible for the control and how frequently they should perform the control. Tests of controls are the audit procedures the auditor will perform to obtain evidence to prove the control suggested is in place and working effectively. Be specific about how they would do this.

Part (c) asks for substantive procedures. A substantive procedure is used to detect material misstatement in the figure. Tests of controls will not score marks. Think about procedures that can be performed to confirm accuracy of the accrual, completeness of the accrual, etc.

Part (d) requires corporate governance weaknesses within the scenario to be explained and a recommendation provided for each. Knowledge of the Corporate Governance Code is required here. Work through on a line by line basis and consider whether the information suggests that the company is compliant with the requirements of the corporate governance best practice.

(a)   Documenting systems

	Description	**Advantage**
Narrative notes	Narrative notes consist of a written description of the system. They detail what occurs in the system at each stage and include any controls which operate at each stage.	They are simple to record; after discussion with staff members, these discussions are easily written up as notes. They can facilitate understanding by all members of the audit team, especially more junior members who might find alternative methods too complex.

Questionnaires	Internal control questionnaires (ICQs) or internal control evaluation questionnaires (ICEQs) contain a list of questions for each major transaction cycle.	Questionnaires are quick to prepare, which means they are a timely method for recording the system.
	ICQs are used to assess whether controls exist whereas ICEQs assess the effectiveness of the controls in place.	They ensure that all controls present within the system are considered and recorded, hence missing controls or deficiencies are clearly highlighted to the audit team.

(b) **Deficiencies, controls and test of controls**

Control deficiency	Control recommendation	Test of control
Customer credit limits are set by sales ledger clerks. Sales ledger clerks are not sufficiently senior. Limits may be set which are too high, leading to irrecoverable debts, or too low, leading to a loss of sales.	Credit limits should be set by a senior member of the sales department and not by sales ledger clerks. These limits should be regularly reviewed by a responsible official.	For a sample of new customers accepted in the year, review the authorisation of the credit limit, and ensure that this was performed by a responsible official. Enquire of sales ledger clerks as to who can set credit limits.
Customer orders are given a number based on the sales person's own identification number. These numbers are not sequential. Without sequential numbers, it is difficult for Freesia Co to identify missing orders and to monitor if all orders are being dispatched in a timely manner. If they are not, this could lead to a loss of customer goodwill.	Sales orders should be sequentially numbered. On a regular basis, a sequence check of orders should be undertaken to identify any missing orders.	Re-perform the control by undertaking a sequence check of sales orders. Discuss any gaps in the sequence with sales ordering staff.

Control deficiency	Control recommendation	Test of control
Lily Shah, a finance clerk, is responsible for several elements of the cash receipts system as she posts the bank transfer receipts from the bank statements to the cash book, updates the sales ledger and performs the bank reconciliations. There is a lack of segregation of duties. Errors will not be identified on a timely basis. There is also an increased risk of fraud.	The key roles of posting bank receipts, updating the sales ledger and performing bank reconciliations should be split between different individuals. If this is not practical, then as a minimum, the bank reconciliations should be undertaken by another member of the finance team.	Review the file of completed bank reconciliations to identify who prepared them. Review the log of IDs of individuals who have posted bank receipts and updated the sales ledger to assess whether these are different individuals. Discuss with the financial controller which members of staff undertake the roles of processing of bank receipts and updating of the cash book and sales ledger.
GRNs are only sent to the finance department. Failing to send a copy to the purchase ordering department means that it is not possible to monitor the level of unfulfilled orders. This could result in a significant level of unfulfilled orders leading to stock-outs and a consequent loss of sales. In addition, if the GRN is lost, then it will not be possible for the finance department to match the invoice to proof of goods being received. This could result in a delay to the invoice being paid and a loss of supplier goodwill.	The GRN should be created in three parts with one copy of the GRN being sent to the ordering department. The second copy should be held at the warehouse and the third sent to the finance department. A purchase ordering clerk should agree their copy of the GRN to the purchase order and change the order status to complete. On a regular basis, a review should be undertaken for all unfulfilled orders and these should be followed up with the relevant supplier.	Review the file of copy GRNs held by the purchase ordering department and review for evidence that these are matched to orders and flagged as complete. Review the file of unfulfilled purchase orders for any overdue items and discuss their status with an ordering clerk.

Control deficiency	Control recommendation	Test of control
Camilla Brown, the purchase ledger clerk, only utilises document count controls when inputting invoices into the purchase ledger. Document count controls can confirm the completeness of input. However, they do not verify the accuracy or validity of input. If the invoices are not input correctly, suppliers may not be paid on time, or paid incorrect amounts leading to an overpayment or loss of supplier goodwill who may withdraw credit facilities.	The purchase ledger clerk should instead input the invoices in batches and apply application controls, such as control totals, rather than just completeness checks to ensure both completeness and accuracy over the input of purchase invoices. In addition, sequence checks should be built into the system to ensure completeness of input.	The audit team should utilise test data procedures to assess whether data can be entered without the use of batch control totals and also whether sequence checks are built into the system. Observe the inputting of purchase invoices and identify what application controls are utilised by the clerk.
The company values its inventory using standard costs, which are not being kept up-to-date. If the standard costs were reviewed 18 months ago, there is the risk that the costs are misstated as changes in raw materials and wages inflation may not have been adjusted for. This could result in inventory being under or overvalued and profits being misstated. In addition for year-end reporting, IAS 2 *Inventories* only allows standard costs to be used for valuation purposes if they are a close approximation to actual costs, which is unlikely if the standard costs remain unchanged for a long period of time. Therefore the valuation may not be in line with IAS 2.	A review of all standard costs currently in use should be undertaken by a senior manager in the production department. Actual costs for materials, labour and overheads should be ascertained and compared to the proposed standard costs to ensure they are a close approximation. The revised standard costs should be reviewed by the production director who should evidence this review. At least annually, a review of the standard costs should be undertaken to ensure they are up-to-date.	Obtain a copy of the standard costs used for inventory valuation, assess when the review was last undertaken and inspect for evidence of review by the production director.

Control deficiency	Control recommendation	Test of control
Overtime worked is not authorised prior to being paid. The information per employee is collated and submitted to payroll by a production clerk, but not authorised. The production director is only informed about overtime levels via quarterly reports. These reports are reviewed sometime after the payments have been made which could result in unauthorised overtime or amounts being paid incorrectly and Freesia Co's payroll cost increasing.	All overtime should be authorised by a responsible official prior to the payment being processed by the payroll department. This authorisation should be evidenced in writing.	Review the overtime report for evidence of authorisation and note the date this occurred to ensure that this was undertaken prior to the payment of the overtime.
The finance director compares the total of the list of bank transfers with the total to be paid per the payroll records. There could be employees omitted or fictitious employees added to the payment listing so that, although the total payments list agrees to payroll totals, there could be fraudulent or erroneous payments being made.	The finance director, when authorising the payments, should on a sample basis perform checks from the human resource department's staff records to payment list and vice versa to confirm that payments are complete and only made to bona fide employees. The finance director should sign the payments list as evidence that these checks have been undertaken.	Obtain a sample of payments lists and review for signature by the finance director as evidence that the control is operating correctly.

(c) **Accrual for employment tax payable**

Substantive procedures the auditor should adopt in respect of auditing this accrual include:

– Compare the accrual for employment tax payable to the prior year, investigate any significant differences.

– Agree the year-end employment tax payable accrual to the payroll records to confirm accuracy.

– Re-perform the calculation of the accrual for a sample of employees to confirm the accuracy.

– Undertake a proof in total test for the employment tax accrual by multiplying the payroll cost for June 20X9 with the appropriate tax rate. Compare this expectation to the actual accrual and investigate any significant differences.

–   Agree the subsequent payment to the post year-end cash book and bank statements to confirm completeness.

–   Review any correspondence with tax authorities to assess whether there are any additional outstanding payments due. If so, confirm they are included in the year-end accrual.

–   Review any disclosures made of the employment tax accrual and assess whether these are in compliance with accounting standards and legislation.

(d)   **Corporate governance weaknesses and recommendations**

Weakness	Recommendation
The finance director is a member of the audit committee. The audit committee should be made up entirely of independent NEDs. The role of the committee is to maintain objectivity with regards to financial reporting; this is difficult if the finance director is a member of the committee as the finance director will be responsible for the preparation of the financial statements.	The audit committee must comprise independent NEDs only, therefore the finance director should resign from the committee.
The remuneration for directors is set by the finance director. However, no director should be involved in setting their own remuneration as this may result in excessive levels of pay being set.	There should be a fair and transparent policy in place for setting remuneration levels. The NEDs should form a remuneration committee to decide on the remuneration of the executives. The board as a whole should decide on the pay of the NEDs.
Executive remuneration includes a significant annual profit related bonus. Remuneration should motivate the directors to focus on the long-term growth of the business, however, annual targets can encourage short-term strategies rather than maximising shareholder wealth.	The remuneration of executives should be restructured to include a significant proportion based on long-term company performance. For example, executives could be granted share options with a minimum vesting and holding period of five years, as this would encourage focus on the longer term position.
The chair has sole responsibility for liaising with the shareholders and answering any of their questions. This is a role which the board as a whole should undertake.	

Weakness	Recommendation
	All members of the board should be involved in ensuring that satisfactory dialogue takes place with shareholders, for example, all should attend meetings with shareholders such as the annual general meeting.
	The board should state in the annual report the steps they have taken to ensure that the members of the board, and in particular the non-executive directors, develop an understanding of the views of major shareholders about the company.

Marking guide		
		Marks
(a)	**Methods of documenting internal control systems**	
	• Narrative notes	2
	• Questionnaires	2
		4
(b)	**Control deficiencies, recommendations and tests of control (only 6 required)**	
	• Credit limits	3
	• No sequential numbering of orders	3
	• Segregation of duties – cash receipts	3
	• Insufficient copies of GRN	3
	• Controls over inputting of invoices	3
	• Out-of-date standard costs	3
	• Overtime not authorised	3
	• Authorisation of bank transfer	3
	Max 6 issues, 3 marks each	18
(c)	**Substantive procedures – accrual for employment tax**	
	• Compare to prior year and investigate differences	1
	• Agree accrual to year-end payroll records	1
	• Recalculate accrual and consider reasonableness	1
	• Perform proof in total and investigate variances	1
	• Confirm post year-end payment	1
	• Review correspondence with tax authorities for any additional liabilities	1
	• Review disclosure and confirm in line with accounting standards	1
	Restricted to	4
(d)	**Corporate governance weakness and recommendations (2 issues required)**	
	• Composition of audit committee	2
	• Finance director sets remuneration	2
	• Executive directors' remuneration	2
	• Only the chair liaises with shareholders	2
	Max 2 issues, 2 marks each	4
Total		30

Examiner's comments

This 30-mark question was based on Freesia Co, a listed furniture manufacturer. This question tested candidates' knowledge of methods of documenting internal control systems, control deficiencies, recommendations and tests of controls, substantive procedures and corporate governance. Performance was mixed.

Part (a) for four marks required candidates to describe documenting internal control systems using narrative notes and questionnaires and explain an advantage of using each method. Performance in this knowledge-based question was satisfactory. There were some good responses, however, a number of candidates were unable to describe each method in enough detail to sufficiently differentiate the two methods of documentation. A number of candidates also discussed the disadvantages of each method, which was not a requirement of the question. In addition, a number of responses described types of questionnaires in too much detail given the marks available. Candidates are reminded to read the question requirement carefully to ensure that they are only answering the question set and to consider the marks available when writing their answers.

Part (b) for 18 marks required candidates to identify and explain from the scenario six deficiencies, recommend a control to address each of these deficiencies, and describe a test of control the external auditors should perform. Performance was satisfactory. Internal control deficiency questions such as this typically require internal control deficiencies to be identified (½ mark each), explained (½ mark each) which must cover the implication of the deficiency to the company, a relevant recommendation to address the deficiency (1 mark), and a test of control the external auditors should perform to assess of the control is operating effectively (1 mark). The scenario in the exam contained more issues than were required to be discussed. It was pleasing that the majority of candidates were able to identify six deficiencies. Very few candidates, however, identified the lack of controls over the accuracy of purchase invoice entry, or the lack of sufficient copies of goods received notes. A minority of candidates identified irrelevant or unrealistic deficiencies. For example, a significant number of candidates were concerned about the range of work performed by the warehouse staff although this was not flagged as an issue in the scenario. Some candidates did not clearly understand/explain the implication of the deficiency. Candidates are required to explain the implication to the business to be awarded credit. For example, a candidate who correctly identified the deficiency 'credit limits are set by the sales ledger clerks' (identification ½ mark awarded), no credit was awarded for the explanation 'the sales ledger clerk is not senior enough'. Candidates must clearly explain the implication to the business that 'this could result in irrecoverable debts if limits set are too high or loss of sales if limits are too low' to be awarded the ½ explanation mark. Candidates were able to provide recommendations to address the deficiencies identified, however, often the recommendations were not described in enough detail. For example, the recommendation that 'sales orders should be sequentially numbered' was awarded only ½ mark, candidates needed to also recommend that 'there should be regular sequence checks' to be awarded the full one mark. Candidates were also able to describe tests of controls the external auditor should perform, however, often they were not described in enough detail. For example, the test of control of 'reviewing the authorised overtime report' was awarded only ½ mark, candidates needed to recommend the auditor also 'notes the date of review to ensure the report is authorised prior to payment' to be awarded the full one mark. It was pleasing that many candidates followed the instructions to set their answer out in three columns, being control deficiency, control recommendation and test of control. Internal control questions remain a highly examinable area and future candidates need to ensure that they have undertaken adequate question practice of all examinable control systems.

Part (c) for four marks required candidates to describe substantive procedures the auditor should perform in relation to a year-end accrual for employment tax payable. One mark was available for each well-described procedure. Performance on this requirement was disappointing. Many candidates failed to provide four procedures, and those listed often focused on payroll expenses and deductions rather than the relevant year-end accrual. Candidates must take the time to read the question requirements carefully and spend time thinking about what is needed prior to writing their answers.

Part (d) for four marks required candidates to describe two corporate governance weaknesses faced by Freesia Co and provide a recommendation to address each weakness to ensure compliance with corporate governance principles. One mark was available per well-explained weakness and one mark per recommendation. Performance was mixed. Candidates generally identified two weaknesses, however, often did not adequately explain why each was a weakness. For example, a significant number of candidates correctly identified the weakness 'the finance director decides on the directors' remuneration' (½ mark), however, only stronger candidates explained 'this could result in setting excessive pay' (½ mark). Weaker candidates simply explained this weakness as being 'against corporate governance rules' and were not awarded the second ½ mark. Recommendations were mixed. A significant number of candidates did not state a clear action as a recommendation. No mark was awarded for giving a statement rather than an action. For example, 'the finance director should not set the remuneration' was not awarded credit. Candidates needed to recommend 'a remuneration committee of non-executive directors should be established to set executives' pay' for one mark.

217 CAMOMILE *Walk in the footsteps of a top tutor*

Key answer tips

Part (a) requires an explanation of the importance of the external auditor communicating with those charged with governance, and asks for two matters which would be communicated. This requires knowledge of ISA 260. Most questions in the constructed response section of the exam will start with a knowledge requirement such as this so make sure you learn the key requirements of the auditing standards as well as being able to tackle the scenario based, application requirements which follow.

Part (b) asks for control deficiencies and recommendations in respect of a cash system. This is examined every sitting and with plenty of past papers to practise, this type of question should be straightforward. Fully explain the deficiency in terms of the effect on the company. If management are to take action, they must be concerned about the potential consequences of the deficiency. When providing recommendations for improvement, be as specific as possible.

(a)   (i)   **Importance of communicating with those charged with governance**

In accordance with ISA 260 *Communication with Those Charged with Governance*, it is important for the auditors to report to those charged with governance as it helps in the following ways:

- It assists the auditor and those charged with governance in understanding matters related to the audit, and in developing a constructive working relationship. This relationship is developed while maintaining the auditor's independence and objectivity.

- It helps the auditor in obtaining, from those charged with governance, information relevant to the audit. For example, those charged with governance may assist the auditor in understanding the entity and its environment, in identifying appropriate sources of audit evidence and in providing information about specific transactions or events.

- It helps those charged with governance in fulfilling their responsibility to oversee the financial reporting process, thereby reducing the risks of material misstatement of the financial statements.

- It promotes effective two-way communication between the auditor and those charged with governance.

(ii)   **Matters to be communicated to those charged with governance**

- The auditor's responsibilities with regards to providing an opinion on the financial statements and that they have carried out their work in accordance with International Standards on Auditing.

- The auditor should explain the planned approach to the audit as well as the audit timetable.

- Any key audit risks identified during the planning stage should be communicated.

- In addition, any significant difficulties encountered during the audit should be communicated.

- Also significant matters arising during the audit, as well as significant accounting adjustments.

- During the audit, any significant deficiencies in the internal control system identified should be communicated in writing or verbally.

- How the external auditor and internal auditor may work together and any planned use of the work of the internal audit function.

- Those charged with governance should be notified of any written representations required by the auditor.

- Other matters arising from the audit which are significant to the oversight of the financial reporting process.

- If any suspected frauds are identified during the audit, these must be communicated.

- If the auditors are intending to make any modifications to the audit opinion, these should be communicated to those charged with governance.

- For listed entities, a confirmation that the auditors have complied with ethical standards and appropriate safeguards have been put in place for any ethical threats identified.

(b) **Control deficiencies and recommendations**

Control deficiency	Control recommendation
Each restaurant maintains a petty cash float of $400, and at any point in time the receipts and funds present should equal the float. It has been noted by the internal audit (IA) department that on occasions there are differences due to the fact that no log is maintained of petty cash requests. This could be as a result of sundry items being purchased without the relevant receipt or voucher being returned. There is also a possibility that the cash is being misappropriated by staff members, or being spent on non-business related items.	A petty cash log should be maintained so the purchase of sundry items is recorded in the log along with the sum borrowed, date and employee. On purchase of the items, the relevant employee should return the relevant receipt or voucher and any funds not spent. The log should be updated to confirm return of funds and receipts. On a weekly basis, the restaurant manager should reconcile the petty cash and if any receipts are missing, these should be followed up with the relevant employee. If it is cash which is missing, then this should be investigated further with the employees who made petty cash purchases during that period.
To speed up the cash payment by customers, for each venue the tills have the same log on code and these codes are changed fortnightly. In the event of cash discrepancies arising in the tills, it would be difficult to ascertain which employees may be responsible as there is no way of tracking who used which till. This could lead to cash being easily misappropriated.	Each employee should be provided with a unique log on code and this is required to be entered when using the tills. In order to facilitate the investigation of till differences, employees should be allocated to a specific till point for their shift. Any discrepancies which arise should initially be double checked to ensure they are not arithmetical errors. If still present, the relevant employees who had access to the till can be identified and further investigations can be undertaken.
The reconciliations of the tills to the daily sales readings are performed in total for all five tills at each venue rather than for each till. This means that when exceptions arise, it will be difficult to identify which till caused the difference. Therefore, employees may require further till training or may have undertaken fraudulent transactions.	The reconciliations should be undertaken on an individual till by till basis rather than in aggregate and any discrepancies noted should be investigated immediately.

Control deficiency	Control recommendation
The cashing up of tills along with the recording of any cash discrepancies is undertaken by just one individual, the restaurant manager. There is a fraud risk as the manager could remove some of the cash and then simply record that there was an exception on the daily sales list. In addition, as there is no segregation of duties, the restaurant manager could, fraudulently or by error, record the total sales as per each till incorrectly leading to incorrect identification of discrepancies.	The cashing up process should be undertaken by two individuals together, ideally an assistant manager and the restaurant manager. One should count the cash and the other record it. Any exceptions to the till reading should be double checked to confirm that they are not simply arithmetical errors. If still present, the relevant employees who had access to the till can be identified and further investigations can be undertaken.
Daily sales sheets are scanned and emailed to head office on a weekly basis. There is a possibility that some sales sheets could be misplaced by the restaurant manager. This will result in incomplete sales and cash receipts data being recorded into the accounting system.	Daily sales sheets for each venue should be sequentially numbered and remitted to head office on a daily basis. At head office, a sequence check should be undertaken on a regular basis to identify any missing sheets and any gaps should be investigated further. Once received, the cashier should post the sales and cash data for all six venues on a daily basis. Once processed, they should then be signed as posted by the cashier and filed away securely.
Cash is stored in a safe at each venue and the restaurant manager stores the safe key in a drawer of their desk when not in use. Although cash is banked on a daily basis, there could still be a significant sum of cash onsite each day. There is a risk of significant cash losses due to theft if access to the safe key is not carefully controlled.	The current key lock safe should be replaced with a safe with a digital code. Only authorised personnel should have the code which should be updated on a regular basis.
The cashier is responsible for several elements of the cash receipts system. She receives the daily sales sheets from restaurants, agrees that cash has cleared into the bank statements, updates the cash book and undertakes the bank reconciliations. There is a lack of segregation of duties and errors will not be identified on a timely basis.	These key roles should be split between different members of the finance team, with ideally the bank reconciliations being undertaken by another member of the team.

Control deficiency	Control recommendation
The cashier is not checking that payments made by credit card have resulted in cash being received by Camomile Co. The credit card statements are not reviewed or reconciled, they are just filed away. There is a risk that receipts of cash by credit card may have been omitted and this would not be identified on a timely basis as the bank is only reconciled every two months. This may result in difficulties in resolving any discrepancies with the credit card company.	The cashier should reconcile the credit card vouchers per restaurant to the monthly statement received from the card company. The daily amounts per the statement should be agreed to the bank statement to ensure that all funds have been received. This reconciliation should be reviewed by a responsible official, such as the financial controller, who should evidence by signature that the review has been undertaken.
The bank reconciliations are only carried out every two months. For a cash-based business, the bank reconciliation is a key control which reduces the risk of fraud and identifies errors. If it is not reconciled regularly enough, then this reduces its effectiveness as fraud and errors may not be identified on a timely basis.	The bank reconciliations should be performed on a monthly basis rather than every two months. The financial controller should continue to review each reconciliation and evidence her review by way of signature on the bank reconciliation.
The finance director only views the total amount of payments to be made rather than the amounts to be paid to each supplier. Without looking at the detail of the payments list, as well as supporting documentation, there is a risk that suppliers could be being paid an incorrect amount, or that sums are being paid to fictitious suppliers. This will cause loss for the company.	The finance director should review the whole payments list prior to authorising. As part of this, he should agree the amounts to be paid to supporting documentation, as well as reviewing the supplier names to identify any duplicates or any unfamiliar names. He should evidence his review by signing the bank transfer list.

Marking guide			
			Marks
(a)	**(i)**	**Importance of communicating with TCWG**	
		• Assists understanding of matters related to the audit	1
		• Obtains information relevant to the audit	1
		• Assists TCWG discharge their responsibilities	1
		• Promotes effective two-way communication	1
			⎯⎯
		Restricted to	**2**
			⎯⎯
	(ii)	**Matters to communicate to TCWG**	
		1 mark for any relevant and well described example	**2**
			⎯⎯

	Marking guide	
		Marks
(b)	**Control deficiencies and recommendations (only 8 issues required)**	
	• Petty cash differences	2
	• Access to tills	2
	• Tills reconciled in total	2
	• Lack of SOD – reconciling cash	2
	• Risk of incomplete daily sales sheets	2
	• Security of cash – access to safes	2
	• Lack of SOD – cashier	2
	• Credit card statements are not reconciled	2
	• Frequency of bank reconciliations	2
	• Payment list not adequately reviewed	2
	Max 8 issues, 2 marks each	**16**
Total		**20**

Examiner's comments

This 20-mark question was based on Camomile Co, which operates a number of restaurant venues. This question tested the areas of communication to those charged with governance and control deficiencies and recommendations. Performance was disappointing.

Part (a) for four marks required candidates to explain why it is important to report to those charged with governance and to then provide two examples of matters which may be communicated. Candidates' performance was disappointing. The majority of candidates were unable to explain why auditors communicate, and instead simply provided examples of matters to report for part (a)(i); these were then repeated for part (a)(ii). Candidates tended to gain the two available example marks for reporting suspected frauds and significant deficiencies or matters. This is a knowledge area, which has been tested in previous diets. Candidates must practise past exam questions, ensure they study the breadth of the syllabus and ensure their responses are relevant to the requirement.

Part (b) for 16 marks required candidates to identify and explain from the scenario eight deficiencies in respect of the cash receipts and payments system and provide a recommendation to address each of these deficiencies. Performance was disappointing.

Internal control deficiency questions such as this typically require internal control deficiencies to be identified (½ mark each), explained (½ mark each) which must cover the implication of the deficiency to the company and a relevant recommendation to address the deficiency (1 mark). The scenario in the exam contained more issues than were required to be discussed, however, unlike previous diets, it was noted that a significant minority of candidates did not identify the required eight points. This is possibly because they were less prepared for a scenario based on the cash receipts and payments system, having only focused on sales, purchases or payroll systems. Internal controls questions remain a highly examinable area and future candidates need to ensure that they have undertaken adequate question practice of all examinable control systems. The deficiencies most candidates were able to identify were the frequency of the bank reconciliation process, access to the safe, the restaurant manager solely cashing up tills and all tills having the same log on code. However, a significant minority of candidates identified irrelevant or unrealistic deficiencies. Some candidates identified that the company's internal audit was too small or that a centralised purchasing department should be implemented. However, the requirement was to focus on the cash system and these points were unrelated to the control system being examined, hence were not awarded any credit. Incorrect answers such as 'employees are not supervised when they enter cash receipts from customers into the tills' were not credited as they were not deficiencies and demonstrated a lack of understanding of a cash system.

In addition, some candidates did not clearly understand/ explain the implication of the deficiency. Candidates are required to explain the implication to the business to be awarded credit. For example, a candidate who correctly identified the deficiency 'cash tills are only cashed up by one individual' (identification ½ mark awarded), no credit was awarded for the explanation 'this could lead to an increased risk of fraud'. Candidates must clearly explain the implication to the business of any system errors not being identified, such as 'the restaurant manager may steal the cash and conceal the error or fraud as no one else is present during the cashing up process' to be awarded the ½ explanation mark. In addition, some candidates correctly identified the deficiency 'bank reconciliations are only performed every two months' but failed to provide any implication at all, thereby restricting marks awarded. Candidates were able to provide some good recommendations to address the deficiencies identified. However, some of the recommendations were not described in enough detail or were auditor responses rather than control recommendations for management.

218 RASPBERRY *Walk in the footsteps of a top tutor*

Key answer tips

Part (a) asks for key controls and tests of controls. Key controls are the actions that management has taken to reduce the risk of fraud and error. Look for evidence of segregation of duties, authorisation, physical controls, etc. For the full mark, explain the risk that the control is designed to mitigate. When describing a test of control you need to say how the auditor will obtain evidence that the control is working effectively. This may come from inspecting a document for evidence of authorisation or observing client staff perform their work to see whether the do what they are supposed to.

Part (b) asks for control deficiencies and recommendations. This is examined every sitting and with plenty of past papers to practise, this type of question should be easy and students should be able to earn most of the marks available. Fully explain the deficiency in terms of the effect on the company. If management are to take action, they must be concerned about the potential consequences of the deficiency. When providing recommendations for improvement, be as specific as possible. For the test of control, describe how the auditor would obtain evidence that the client has implemented the control suggested.

Part (c) asks for assignments that the internal audit department could perform. This is a straightforward knowledge question. If you can't remember the information from the text book think about it logically – the internal audit department perform checks on the company to make sure it is running as efficiently and effectively as possible. This includes making sure the company minimises the risk of fraud and error. By thinking about the purpose of the IAD you may be able to generate ideas.

Part (d) asks for substantive procedures over the tax payable accrual. A substantive procedure tests the number in the financial statements. You must give substantive procedures and not tests of controls for this requirement. Don't make the mistake of testing payroll in general. The question focuses on the tax payable accrual, i.e. the liability at the year-end in respect of employment tax only. Remember that analytical procedures can also be used as substantive procedures so a simple comparison of the accrual this year to last year with investigation of any significant variation is usually an easy one to use to score a mark.

(a) **Key controls and tests of controls**

Key controls	Tests of controls
Raspberry Co has a separate human resources (HR) department which is responsible for setting up all new employees. Having a segregation of roles between human resources and payroll departments reduces the risk of fictitious employees being set up and also being paid.	Review the job descriptions of payroll and HR to confirm the split of responsibilities with regards to setting up new joiners. Discuss with members of the payroll department the process for setting up new joiners and for confirmation that the process is initiated by HR.
Pre-printed forms are completed by HR for all new employees, and includes assignment of a unique employee number, and once verified, a copy is sent to the payroll department. Payroll is unable to set up new joiners without information from these forms. The use of pre-printed forms ensures that all relevant information, such as tax IDs, is obtained about employees prior to set up. This minimises the risk of incorrect wage and tax payments. In addition, as payroll is unable to set up new joiners without the forms and employee number, it reduces the risk of fictitious employees being set up by payroll.	Select a sample of new employees added to the payroll during the year, review the joiner forms for evidence of completion of all parts and that the information was verified as accurate and was received by payroll prior to being added to the system. Select a sample of edit reports for changes to payroll during the year; agree a sample of new employees added to payroll to the joiners forms.
The quarterly production bonus is input by a clerk into the payroll system, each entry is checked by a senior clerk for input errors prior to processing, and they evidence their review via signature. This reduces the risk of input errors resulting in over/underpayment of the bonus to employees.	If attending Raspberry Co at the time of bonus processing, observe the clerk inputting and senior clerk checking the bonus payments into the payroll system. In addition, obtain listings of quarterly bonus payments and review for evidence of signature by the senior clerk who checks for input errors.
Production employees are issued with clock cards and are required to swipe their cards at the beginning and end of their shift, this process is supervised by security staff 24 hours a day. This ensures that genuine employees are only paid for the work actually done, and reduces the risk of employees being paid but not completing their eight-hour shift.	Observe the use of clock cards by employees when entering the power station. Confirm the security team is supervising the process and following up on discrepancies through discussions with the security staff.

Key controls	Tests of controls
In addition, due to the supervision it is unlikely that one employee could swipe in others.	
The clock card information identifies the employee number and links into the hours worked report produced by the payroll system. As the hours worked are automatically transferred into the payroll system, this reduces the risk of input errors in entering hours to be paid in calculating payroll, ensuring that employees are paid the correct amount.	Utilise test data procedures to input dummy clock card information, verify this has been updated into the payroll system.
On a quarterly basis, exception reports of changes to payroll standing data are produced and reviewed by the payroll director. This ensures that any unauthorised amendments to standing data are identified and resolved on a timely basis.	Select a sample of quarterly exception reports and review for evidence of review and follow up of any unexpected changes by the payroll director.
For production employees paid in cash, cash is received weekly from the bank by a security company. It is likely the sum of money required to pay over 175 employees would be considerable. It is important that cash is adequately safeguarded to reduce the risk of misappropriation.	Enquire of payroll clerks how cash is delivered to Raspberry Co for weekly pay packets. Review a sample of invoices from the security company to Raspberry Co for delivery of cash.
The pay packets are prepared by two members of staff with one preparing and one checking the pay packets and this is evidenced by each staff member signing the weekly listing. This ensures there is segregation of duties which prevents fraud and errors not being identified.	Observe the preparation of the pay packets ensuring that two members of staff are involved and that pay packets are checked for accuracy. For a sample of weeks throughout the year, inspect the weekly payroll listing for evidence of signature by the two members of staff involved in the preparation of the pay packets.

(b) **Control deficiencies and recommendations**

Control deficiency	Control recommendation
Production supervisors determine the amount of the discretionary bonus to be paid to employees. Production supervisors should not determine this as they could pay extra bonuses to friends or family members. This will result in additional payroll costs.	The bonus should be determined by a responsible official, such as the production director and should be formulated based on a written policy. If significant in value, the bonus should be formally agreed by the board of directors. The bonus should be communicated in writing to the payroll department.
The wages calculations are generated by the payroll system and there are no checks performed. Therefore, if system errors occur during the payroll processing, this would not be identified. This could result in wages being over or under calculated, leading to an additional payroll cost or loss of employee goodwill.	A senior member of the payroll team should recalculate the gross to net pay workings for a sample of employees and compare their results to the output from the payroll system. These calculations should be signed as approved before payments are made.
Student loan deduction forms are completed by relevant employees and payments are made directly to the third party until the employee notifies HR that the loan has been repaid in full. As the payments continue until the employee notifies HR, and employees are unlikely to be closely monitoring payments. There is the risk that overpayments may be made, which then need to be reclaimed, leading to employee dissatisfaction. In the case of underpayments, Raspberry Co has an obligation to remit funds on time and to reconcile to annual loan statements. If the company does not make payments in full and on time, this could result in non-compliance by both the company and employee, which could result in fines or penalties.	The payroll department should maintain a schedule, by employee, of payments made to third parties, such as the central government as well as the cumulative balance owing. On a regular basis, at least annually, this statement should be reconciled to the loan statement received from the government and sent to the employee for agreement. In accordance with the schedule, payments which are due to cease shortly should be confirmed in writing with the third party, prior to stopping.

Control deficiency	Control recommendation
Holiday request forms are required to be completed and authorised by relevant line managers, however, this does not always occur. This could result in employees taking unauthorised leave, resulting in production difficulties if an insufficient number of employees are present to operate the power plant. In addition, employees taking unauthorised leave could result in an overpayment of wages.	Employees should be informed that they will not be able to take holiday without completion of a holiday request form, with authorisation from the line manager. Payroll clerks should not process holiday payments without agreement to the authorised holiday form.
The senior payroll manager reviews the bank transfer listing prior to authorising the payments and also amends the payroll records for any changes required. There is a lack of segregation of duties as it is the payroll team which processes the amounts and the senior payroll manager who authorises payments. The senior manager could fraudulently increase the amounts to be paid to certain employees, process this payment as well as amend the records.	The senior payroll manager should not be able to process changes to the payroll system as well as authorise payments. The authorisation of the bank transfer listing should be undertaken by an individual outside the payroll department, such as the finance director.
The pay packets are delivered to the production supervisors, who distribute them to employees at the end of their shift. The supervisor is not sufficiently independent to pay wages out. They could adjust pay packets to increase those of close friends whilst reducing others. In addition, although the production supervisors know their team members, payment of wages without proof of identity increases the risk that wages could be paid to incorrect employees.	All pay packets should be distributed by the payroll department, directly to employees, upon sight of the employee's clock card and photographic identification as this confirms proof of identity. Payroll should undertake a reconciliation of pay packets issued to production supervisors, wages distributed with employee signatures to confirm receipt and pay packets returned to payroll due to staff absences. Any differences should be investigated immediately. As employees work eight-hour shifts over 24 hours, consideration should be given to operating a shift system for the payroll department on wages pay out day.

Control deficiency	Control recommendation
	This will ensure that there are sufficient payroll employees to perform the wages pay out for each shift of employees, with the same level of controls in place.
Monthly management accounts do not analyse the variances between actual and budgeted wages and salaries; this is because there are no overtime costs. However, wages and salaries are a significant expense and management needs to understand why variances may have arisen. These could occur due to extra employees being recruited which were not budgeted for, or an increase in wage pay out rates. The board would need to monitor the wages and salaries costs as if they are too high, then this would impact the profitability of the company.	The monthly management accounts should be amended to include an analysis of wages and salaries compared to the budgeted costs. These should be broken down to each relevant department and could also include an analysis of headcount numbers compared to budget.

(c) **Assignments for internal audit department (IAD)**

Value for money review – The IAD could be asked to assess whether Raspberry Co is obtaining value for money in areas such as capital expenditure.

Review of financial/operational controls – The IAD could undertake reviews of controls at head office and the power station and make recommendations to management over such areas as the purchasing process as well as the payroll cycle.

Monitoring asset levels – The IAD could undertake physical verification of property, plant and equipment (PPE) at the production site and head office and compare the assets seen to the PPE register. There is likely to be a significant level of PPE and the asset register must be kept up to date to ensure continuous production. If significant negative differences occur, this may be due to theft or fraud.

Regulatory compliance – Raspberry Co produces electricity and operates a power station, hence it will be subject to a large number of laws and regulations such as health and safety and environmental legislation. The IAD could help to monitor compliance with these regulations.

IT system reviews – Raspberry Co is likely to have a relatively complex computer system linking production data to head office. The IAD could be asked to perform a review over the computer environment and controls.

Cash controls – Raspberry Co's internal auditors could undertake controls testing over cash payments. 70% of employees are paid in cash rather than bank transfer, therefore on a weekly basis cash held is likely to be significant, therefore the cash controls in payroll should be tested to reduce the level of errors.

Fraud investigations – The IAD can be asked to investigate any specific cases of suspected fraud as well as review the controls in place to prevent/detect fraud.

(d) **Substantive procedures – tax payable accrual**

–   Compare the accrual for income tax payable to the prior year, investigate any significant differences.

–   Agree the year-end income tax payable accrual to the general ledger and payroll records to confirm accuracy.

–   Re-perform the calculation of the accrual to confirm accuracy and discuss any unexpected variances with management.

–   Agree the subsequent payment to the post year-end cash book and bank statements to confirm completeness.

–   Review any correspondence with tax authorities to assess whether there are any additional outstanding payments due; if so, agree they are included in the year-end accrual.

–   Review any disclosures made of the income tax accrual and assess whether these are in compliance with accounting standards and legislation.

	Marking guide	Marks
(a)	**Key controls and tests of control (only 5 controls required)**	
	• Separate HR department	2
	• Pre-printed joiners forms	2
	• Data processing checks on bonus information	2
	• Use of clock cards and process supervised	2
	• Direct transfer between clock card and payroll systems	2
	• Exception reports for changes to payroll data	2
	• Security process over cash	2
	• SOD over pay packets	2
	Max 5 key controls, 2 marks each	10
(b)	**Control deficiencies and recommendations (only 5 issues required)**	
	• Production bonus set by supervisor	2
	• No independent checks on wage calculations	2
	• No monitoring of student loan payments	2
	• Holiday requests not always authorised	2
	• Lack of SOD in payroll department	2
	• Pay packets not delivered by independent staff/no evidence of distribution	2
	• Monthly management accounts not analysed	2
	Max 5 issues, 2 marks each	10
(c)	**Internal audit assignments**	
	• Value for money	1
	• Financial/operational review	1
	• Monitoring assets	1
	• Regulatory compliance	1
	• IT systems	1
	• Cash controls	1
	• Fraud investigation	1
	Restricted to	5

	Marking guide	
		Marks
(d)	**Substantive procedures – tax payable accrual**	
	• Compare to prior year and investigate differences	1
	• Agree to TB and payroll records	1
	• Re-perform accrual calculation and discuss with management	1
	• Agree subsequent payment to cash book and bank statement	1
	• Review correspondence with tax authorities	1
	• Review disclosures	1
		___
	Restricted to	5
		___
Total		**30**
		___

Examiner's comments

This question was based on Raspberry Co, a company which operates an electric power station. This question tested candidates' knowledge of key controls and control deficiencies, recommendations and tests of control, internal audit departments, and substantive procedures for accruals.

Part (a) required candidates to identify and explain from the scenario five key controls in respect of the payroll system described which the auditor may seek to place reliance on, and describe a test of control the auditor should perform to assess if each of the key controls is operating effectively. Candidates' performance on this requirement was disappointing. Questions such as this typically require the key control, which has also been examined in the past as a control strength, to be identified (½ mark each), explained as to why it is a key control (½ mark each) and a test of control provided (1 mark). The scenario in the exam contained more key controls than were required to be discussed and it was disappointing that many candidates did not identify the required number of controls noted in the question. Candidates are encouraged to familiarise themselves with the requirements of ISA 330 The Auditor's Responses to Assessed Risks which states that tests of controls should only be performed on controls which are suitably designed to prevent, or detect and correct, a material misstatement, to help them consider what constitutes a key control. Although a number of candidates identified, for ½ mark each, the key controls of separate human resources and payroll departments, supervision of the clocking-in process, and segregation of duties in the preparation of the pay packets, many candidates did not clearly explain the control and so were not awarded the second ½ mark. To explain why the control is key, candidates must explain how the control will prevent or detect and correct a misstatement. For example, to explain the fact that the company operates a separate human resources and payroll department as a key control candidates must state 'it would reduce the risk of fictitious employees being set up' to be awarded the ½ mark, explanations such as 'this is good segregation of duties' was not a sufficient explanation to be awarded credit. A significant number of candidates incorrectly included control deficiencies in part (a). For example, identifying that 'the senior payroll manager agrees BACs payments to the payroll' was not awarded credit as a key control as there was a lack of segregation of duties, as if errors were noted the senior payroll manager also amended the records, which would have prevented the auditor from placing reliance on this control. This point should actually be included as a deficiency in part (b). In common with previous diets, candidates continue to find tests of control challenging. Many candidates confused substantive procedures for tests of control and tests were often vague or incomplete. For example, 'look at the bonus listing' without saying why, i.e. 'for evidence of review', or 'observe the clocking in process' without reference to the overview of the process by the security staff. Tests of control are very commonly tested and future candidates need to ensure that they have undertaken adequate question practice.

Part (b) required candidates to identify and explain from the scenario five deficiencies in respect of the payroll system and provide a recommendation to address each of these deficiencies. Many candidates performed well in this requirement. Internal control deficiency questions such as this typically require internal control deficiencies to be identified (½ mark each), explained (½ mark each) which must cover the implication of the deficiency to the company and a relevant recommendation to address the deficiency (1 mark). The scenario in the exam contained more issues than were required to be discussed and it was pleasing that many candidates identified the required number of issues noted in the question. However, some candidates did not clearly understand/explain the implication of the deficiency. Candidates are required to explain the implication to the business to be awarded credit. For example, a candidate who correctly identified the deficiency 'wage calculations generated by the system are not checked' (identification ½ mark awarded), no credit was awarded for the explanation 'this could lead to errors'. Candidates must clearly explain the implication to the business of any system errors not being identified such as 'wages may be over/under calculated' or 'wages may be overpaid' or 'loss of employee goodwill', to be awarded the ½ explanation mark. Many candidates were able to provide good recommendations to address the deficiencies identified. However, some of the recommendations were not described in enough detail, for example, in relation to management accounts not analysing budget versus actual for wages and salaries, a recommendation 'management accounts should be amended to include an analysis of wages and salaries' was awarded ½ mark, for the full 1 mark candidates needed to go on to say 'and this should be compared to budget' or 'should include a commentary'. It was pleasing that many candidates followed the instructions to set their answer out in two columns being control deficiency and control recommendation. Internal controls questions remain a highly examinable area and future candidates need to ensure that they have undertaken adequate question practice.

Part (c) required candidates to describe assignments the internal audit department of Raspberry Co would carry out. Up to 1 mark was awarded for each well described point. Performance was mixed. Some candidates only listed the assignments rather than describing them and therefore were awarded ½ mark for each. Candidates are again reminded to pay attention to the verb used in the requirement to ensure they are providing sufficiently detailed answers. Common misunderstandings by a number of candidates were 'the internal auditor prepares the financial statements' and 'internal auditors implement the controls'. Some candidates described the differences between internal and external audit, which was not the purpose of the requirement. Further, some candidates included many examples of financial/operational controls which the internal audit department could test, however, this only demonstrated one type of assignment so was awarded only 1 mark overall. In addition, some candidates described assignments, which would not be relevant to an electric power station client, for example 'internal auditors undertaking mystery shopping'. This is principally a knowledge area, which has been tested in previous diets. Candidates must practise past exam questions, ensure they study the breadth of the syllabus and ensure their responses are relevant to the scenario.

Part (d) required candidates to describe substantive procedures the auditor should perform to confirm the year-end accrual for tax payable on employment income. One mark was awarded for each well described procedure. Performance on this requirement was disappointing. The most common procedure provided by candidates was an analytical review against prior year/budget and a review of any significant differences and this was awarded full credit. However, the substantive procedures were often vague, for example, 'agree payment' rather than 'agree to the post year-end cashbook'. Candidates are once again reminded that a well described substantive procedure will clearly detail the source of the evidence.

Other examples of procedures which were not adequately described included: 'review correspondence with tax authorities' (awarded ½ mark), for the full 1 mark candidates needed to also state 'to assess whether there are any outstanding payments due' as a well described procedure must clearly detail the purpose of the test. Similarly, 'review adequacy of disclosures' (awarded ½ mark), for the full 1 mark candidates needed to also state 'for compliance with accounting standards/relevant legislation'. In addition, many candidates did not focus on the year-end accrual and noted general substantive procedures for tax, which did not gain credit. Candidates are reminded to read the question requirement carefully and to ensure that they are not only answering the question set but also fully describing each substantive procedure.

219 COMET PUBLISHING *Walk in the footsteps of a top tutor*

Key answer tips

Part (a) is a regularly seen requirement asking for safeguards to address a conflict of interest. This is rote learned knowledge from the text book and all students should be able to score most, if not all, of the marks available.

Part (b) asks for steps to confirm systems documentation. Again this is straight from the text book knowledge and students should commit this knowledge to memory.

Part (c) asks for control deficiencies, recommendations and tests of controls. This is examined every sitting and with plenty of past papers to practise, this type of question should be easy and students should be able to earn most of the marks available. Fully explain the deficiency in terms of the effect on the company. If management are to take action, they must be concerned about the potential consequences of the deficiency. When providing recommendations for improvement, be as specific as possible. For the test of control, describe how the auditor would obtain evidence that the client has implemented the control suggested.

Part (d) asks for substantive procedures over purchases and expenses. A substantive procedure tests the number in the financial statements. You must give substantive procedures and not tests of controls for this requirement. Don't make the mistake of testing payables. The question asks for purchases. Purchases are the transactions that took place throughout the year. Payables are only the invoices unpaid at the year-end. They are not the same figures. Focus on testing GRNs, purchase invoices and the purchase day book. Analytical procedures can also be used as substantive procedures.

(a) **Safeguards to deal with conflict of interest**

- Both Comet Publishing Co and its rival competitor, Edmond Co, should be notified that Halley & Co would be acting as auditors for each company and, if necessary, consent should be obtained from each.

- Advising one or both clients to seek additional independent advice.

- The use of separate engagement teams, with different engagement partners and team members; once an employee has worked on one audit, such as Comet Publishing Co, then they would be prevented from being on the audit of the competitor for a period of time.

- Procedures to prevent access to information, for example, strict physical separation of both teams, confidential and secure data filing.

- Clear guidelines for members of each engagement team on issues of security and confidentiality. These guidelines could be included within the audit engagement letters.

- Potentially the use of confidentiality agreements signed by employees and partners of the firm.

- Regular monitoring of the application of the above safeguards by a senior individual in Halley & Co not involved in either audit.

(b) **Steps to confirm prior year flowcharts and system notes**

- Obtain the system notes from last year's audit and ensure that the documentation on the purchases and payables system covers all expected stages and is complete.

- Review the audit file for indications of weaknesses in the system and note these for investigation this year.

- Review the prior year report to management to identify any recommendations which were made over controls in this area as this may highlight potential changes which have been made in the current year.

- Obtain system documentation from the client, potentially in the form of a procedure manual. Review this to identify any changes made in the last 12 months.

- Interview client staff to ascertain whether systems and controls have changed including the stores and warehouse to ensure that the flowcharts and notes produced last year is correct.

- Perform walk-through tests by tracing a sample of transactions through the purchases and payables system to ensure that the flowcharts and systems notes contained on the audit file are accurate.

- During the walk-through tests, confirm the systems notes and flowcharts accurately reflect the control procedures which are in place and can be used to identify controls for testing.

(c)   Control deficiencies, control recommendations and tests of control

Control deficiency	Control recommendation	Test of control
It is not possible for a store to order goods from other local stores for customers who request them. Instead, customers are told to contact the other stores or use the company website. Customers are less likely to contact individual stores themselves and this could result in the company losing valuable sales. In addition, some goods which are slow moving in one store may be out of stock at another; if goods could be transferred between stores, then overall sales may be maximised.	An inter-branch transfer system should be established between stores, with inter-branch inventory forms being completed for store transfers. This should help stores whose inventory levels are low but are awaiting their deliveries from the suppliers.	During the interim audit, arrange to visit a number of the stores, discuss with the store manager the process for ordering of inventory items, in particular whether it is possible to order from other branches. At each store, inspect a sample of completed inter-branch inventory forms for confirmation the control is operating.
Purchase orders below $1,000 are not authorised and are processed solely by the purchase order clerk who is also responsible for processing invoices. This could result in non-business related purchases and there is an increased fraud risk as the clerk could place orders for personal goods up to the value of $1,000, which is significant.	All purchase orders should be authorised by a responsible official. Authorised signatories should be established with varying levels of purchase order authorisation.	Select a sample of purchase orders and review for evidence of authorisation, agree this to the appropriate signature on the approved signatories list.
Goods received notes (GRNs) are sent to the accounts department every two weeks. This could result in delays in suppliers being paid as the purchase invoices could not be agreed to a GRN and also recorded liabilities being understated. Additionally, any prompt payment discounts offered by suppliers may be missed due to delayed payments.	A copy of the GRNs should be sent to the accounts department on a more regular basis, such as daily. The accounts department should undertake a sequence check of the GRNs to ensure none are missing for processing.	Enquire of the accounts clerk as to the frequency of when GRNs are received to assess if they are being sent promptly. Undertake a sequence check of GRNs held by the accounts department and discuss any missing items with the accounts clerk.

Control deficiency	Control recommendation	Test of control
GRNs are only sent to the accounts department. Failing to send a copy to the ordering department could result in a significant level of unfulfilled orders leading to a loss of sales and stock-outs.	The GRN should be created in three parts and a copy of the GRN should be sent to the purchase order clerk, Oliver Dancer, who should agree this to the order and change the order status to complete. On a regular basis he should then review for all unfulfilled orders and chase these with the relevant supplier.	Review the file of copy GRNs held by the purchase ordering clerk, Oliver Dancer, and review for evidence that these are matched to orders and flagged as complete. Review the file of unfulfilled purchase orders for any overdue items and discuss their status with Oliver Dancer.
The purchase ordering clerk, Oliver Dancer, has responsibility for ordering goods below $1,000 and for processing all purchase invoices for payment. There is a lack of segregation of duties and this increases the risk of fraud and non-business related purchases being made.	The roles of purchase ordering and processing of the related supplier invoices should be allocated to separate members of staff.	Observe which member of staff undertakes the processing of purchase invoices and confirm this is not the purchase ordering clerk, Oliver Dancer. Inspect a copy of the company's organisation chart to identify if these tasks have now been allocated to different roles.
The finance director authorises the bank transfer payment list for suppliers; however, she only views the total amount of payments to be made. Without looking at the detail of the payments list, as well as supporting documentation, there is a risk that suppliers could be being paid an incorrect amount, or that sums are being paid to fictitious suppliers.	The finance director should review the whole payments list prior to authorising. As part of this, she should agree the amounts to be paid to supporting documentation, as well as reviewing the supplier names to identify any duplicates or any unfamiliar names. She should evidence her review by signing the bank transfer list.	Review the payments list for evidence of review by the finance director. Enquire of accounts staff what supporting documentation the finance director requests when undertaking this review.

Control deficiency	Control recommendation	Test of control
Supplier statement reconciliations are no longer performed. This may result in errors in the recording of purchases and payables not being identified in a timely manner.	Supplier statement reconciliations should be performed on a monthly basis for all suppliers and these should be reviewed by a responsible official.	Review the file of reconciliations to ensure that they are being performed on a regular basis and that they have been reviewed by a responsible official. Re-perform a sample of the reconciliations to ensure that they have been carried out appropriately.

(d) Substantive procedures in relation to purchases and other expenses

– Calculate the operating profit and gross profit margins and compare them to last year and budget and investigate any significant differences.

– Review monthly purchases and other expenses to identify any significant fluctuations and discuss with management.

– Discuss with management whether there have been any changes in the key suppliers used and compare this to the purchase day book to assess completeness and accuracy of purchases.

– Recalculate the accuracy of a sample of purchase invoice totals and related taxes and ensure expense has been included in the correct nominal code.

– Recalculate the prepayments and accruals charged at the year end to ensure the accuracy of the expense charge included in the statement of profit or loss.

– Select a sample of post year-end expense invoices and ensure that any expenses relating to the current year have been included.

– Select a sample of payments from the cash book and trace to expense account to ensure the expense has been included and classified correctly.

– Select a sample of goods received notes (GRNs) from throughout the year; agree them to purchase invoices and the purchase day book to ensure the completeness of purchases.

– Select a sample of GRNs just before and after the year end; agree to the purchase day book to ensure the expense is recorded in the correct accounting period.

	Marking guide	
		Marks
(a)	**Safeguards to deal with conflict of interest**	
	• Notify both parties and obtain consent	1
	• Advise client to seek independent advice	1
	• Separate engagement teams	1
	• Prevent access to information	1
	• Clear guidelines on security and confidentiality provided to client	1
	• Confidentiality agreements	1
	• Monitor safeguards	1
		———
	Max	**5**
		———
(b)	**Steps to confirm prior year flowcharts**	
	• Review PY notes and confirm all stages covered	1
	• Review PY file for weaknesses not actioned	1
	• Review PY report to management	1
	• Review client system documentation for changes	1
	• Interview client staff to confirm client processes	1
	• Walk-through tests to confirm notes	1
	• Walk-through tests to confirm procedures	1
		———
	Restricted to	**5**
		———
(c)	**Control deficiencies, recommendations and tests of control** **(5 issues required)**	
	• No inter-branch transfers	3
	• Not all purchase orders are authorised	3
	• GRNs not processed regularly	3
	• GRNs not send to purchasing department	3
	• Segregation of duties in relation to purchases	3
	• Authorisation of bank payments	3
	• Supplier statement reconciliations not performed	3
		———
	Max 5 issues, 3 marks each	**15**
		———
(d)	**Substantive tests in relation to purchases and other expenses**	
	• Calculate operating and gross margin and compare to PY	1
	• Review monthly purchases and investigate unexpected difference	1
	• Discuss changes in key suppliers and compare to purchase day book	1
	• Recalculate a sample of purchase invoices	1
	• Recalculate prepayments and accruals	1
	• Review post year-end invoices for pre year-end liabilities	1
	• Sample of cash book payments to appropriate expense account	1
	• GRNs to purchase invoice to purchase day book	1
	• Cut-off testing using GRNs	1
		———
	Restricted to	**5**
		———
Total		**30**
		———

Examiner's comments

This question was based on Comet Publishing Co, a book retailer with ten stores. This question tested candidates' knowledge of conflicts of interest, systems documentation, control deficiencies, control recommendations and tests of control as well as substantive procedures for purchases and other expenses.

Part (a) required candidates to explain safeguards the auditor should implement in order to address a potential conflict of interest created by the audit firm which also audited the main competitor of Comet Publishing Co. This question was well answered with the majority of candidates demonstrating a good knowledge of the ethical area tested. Many candidates correctly identified safeguards such as informing both companies, separate engagement teams and keeping information confidential. A number of candidates also included the need for confidentiality agreements. Less commonly suggested safeguards included the need to seek independent advice, and monitoring of safeguards. Also where independent advice was suggested this was in the context of asking for legal advice, which was not relevant. In addition many candidates suggested monitoring of the audit work undertaken by each team rather than the application and monitoring of the ethical safeguards. Some candidates repeated safeguards in slightly different ways, such as having separate audit teams and suggesting separate engagement partners. These are not two points and hence would have only gained one mark in total rather than two. Also some made several suggestions on how information could be kept confidential: separate offices, password protection, storing audit files in different locations. Ultimately these are all examples of the same point and so only received credit once.

Part (b) required candidates to explain the steps the auditor should take to confirm the accuracy of the flowcharts and systems notes held in the prior year audit file for the purchases and payables cycle. Performance on this question, when answered, was very disappointing. Only a minority of candidates understood what flowcharts and system notes were and therefore recommended procedures such as discussions with management on changes to the system; observing the operation of the system or walkthrough tests and updating the systems documentation to reflect any changes. These candidates scored well in this question. Unfortunately, the majority of candidates did not seem to understand what flowcharts and system notes were or simply saw that the question contained the words 'purchases and payables' and hence provided a long list of substantive procedures or compliance tests for auditing purchases and trade payables. This was not what was required and candidates are again reminded that it is imperative that they address the requirement set. In addition a significant minority of candidates demonstrated a fundamental lack of understanding in relation to what a flowchart is or its purpose with suggestions of 'agreeing prior year flowcharts to those of the current year and investigating significant differences', or 'agreeing flowcharts to financial statements' and 'agree flowcharts to purchase invoices'. Internal control is a key part of the syllabus and candidates must be prepared for both knowledge and application questions in this area. There are few knowledge areas in syllabus area C, hence candidates should have learnt these areas and practised past exam questions.

Part (c) required candidates to identify and explain from the scenario five deficiencies in respect of the purchases and payables cycle, provide a recommendation to address each of these deficiencies and a test of control to assess if each control, if implemented, is operating effectively. Candidates' performance was mixed. It was pleasing that many candidates followed the instructions to set their answer out in three columns being deficiency, recommendation and test of control. Internal control questions such as this typically require internal control deficiencies to be identified (½ mark each), explained (½ mark each) which must cover the implication of the deficiency to the company, a relevant recommendation to address the deficiency (1 mark) and a test of control (1 mark).

Internal controls questions remain a highly examinable area. The scenario in the exam contained more issues than were required to be discussed and it was therefore disappointing that some candidates did not identify the required number of issues noted in the question. In addition it was unfortunate that a number of candidates identified facts from the scenario which were not deficiencies, and the related control recommendation and test of control would not have been relevant and therefore did not gain credit. Irrelevant points included 'the store manager raises the requisitions on his own/with no authorisation' this failed to understand that at this point it is just a request (still internal to the company) and not at order stage which is where the authorisation is needed. Also some candidates flagged that the 'warehouse team received goods from suppliers' and that this was somehow problematic as it should be a manager who received goods from suppliers. Candidates were also concerned about overstocking of books and that there was a significant risk of obsolescence or damage which was unlikely in the circumstances. In addition, some candidates did not clearly understand/explain the implication of the deficiency. For example there was concern that the finance director reviewing the payments list resulted in a lack of segregation of duties, rather than a lack of detailed information being given to approve payments, which could result in invalid or fictitious payments. Many candidates were able to provide good recommendations to address the deficiencies. However some of the recommendations were either poorly described, did not clearly address the specific control weakness identified or were impractical suggestions. For example in relation to the lack of supplier statement reconciliations, some recommended that the company simply hire more staff rather than recommending that the company undertake monthly reconciliations and that these should be reviewed by a responsible official. The final part of the requirement was for tests of controls. In common with previous diets, candidates did not perform well. Many candidates confused substantive procedures for tests of control and too often tests were vague or incomplete. For example "review for supplier statement reconciliations" which is not clear about exactly what the reconciliations are being reviewed for. Also "observation" is often suggested as a test of control, while it is a valid audit procedure, it is not always the most appropriate one when testing controls and is rarely sufficient on its own. Tests of control are very commonly tested and future candidates need to ensure that they have undertaken adequate question practice.

Part (d) required candidates to describe substantive procedures the auditor should perform to obtain sufficient and appropriate audit evidence in relation to purchases and other expenses. Performance on this requirement was very disappointing. One mark was awarded for each well described procedure. The most common procedures provided by candidates included analytical review against prior year or budget, detailed tests agreeing to invoices and goods received notes (GRN) or cut-off tests. However, a significant number of candidates provided procedures which were relevant to trade payables rather than purchases and expenses; these would not have gained credit as they did not answer the question asked. For example many candidates described audit procedures such as trade payable circularisations. Candidates are reminded to read the question requirement carefully and to ensure that they are answering the question set. Following on from part (c), candidates also gave tests of control, such as 'review for authorisation of purchase orders' rather than substantive procedures. Further, many candidates provided vague and incomplete tests. For example 'agree purchases to GRNs and invoices' would only be awarded ½ mark as this is an incomplete test of detail as it does not follow the transaction into the books of prime entry. Further cut-off tests were incorrectly described using purchase invoices rather than GRNs, these would have only been awarded ½ mark. Candidates are again reminded to think about the aim of the procedure when they are describing substantive tests.

220 EQUESTRIAN *Walk in the footsteps of a top tutor*

Key answer tips

Part (a) is a straightforward knowledge requirement asking for the control activities as given in ISA 315 and examples of each. This should not cause any problems.

Part (b) asks for control deficiencies and recommendations which is a requirement appearing in every exam. You must fully explain the deficiency in terms of the effect on the company. If management are to take action, they must be concerned about the potential consequences of the deficiency. When providing recommendations for improvement, be as specific as possible.

Part (c) Advantages and disadvantages of outsourcing the internal audit function is a straightforward knowledge requirement.

(a) Control activities

Segregation of duties

Assignment of roles or responsibilities to ensure the tasks of authorising and recording transactions and maintaining custody of assets are carried out by different people, thereby reducing the risk of fraud and error. For example, the payables ledger clerk recording invoices in the payables ledger, and the finance director authorising the payment of those purchase invoices.

Information processing

Controls including application and general IT controls, which ensure the completeness, accuracy and authorisation of information being processed. For example, use of batch control totals when entering transactions into the system.

Authorisation

Approval of transactions by a suitably responsible official to ensure transactions are genuine. For example, authorisation by a responsible official of all purchase orders.

Physical controls

Restricting access to physical assets as well as computer programs and data files, thereby reducing the risk of theft. For example, cash being stored in a safe which only a limited number of employees are able to access.

Performance reviews

Comparison or review of the performance of the business by looking at areas such as budget versus actual results. For example, the review by department heads of monthly results of actual trading to budget and prior year, with analysis of variances.

(b) **Equestrian Co deficiencies and controls**

Control deficiency	Control recommendation
Physical verification of assets within the non-current asset register has not been undertaken for some time. A current programme has started but is only 15% complete, due to staff shortages. If non-current assets are not physically verified on a regular basis, there is an increased risk of assets being misappropriated or misplaced as there is no check that the assets still exist in their correct location.	Additional resources should be devoted to completing the physical verification of all assets within the register. If any assets cannot be located, they should be written off. Following this full review, on a monthly basis a sample of assets at the sites should be agreed back to the register to confirm existence.
Equestrian Co has experienced significant staff shortages within their internal audit (IA) department. Maintaining an IA department is an important control as it enables senior management to test whether controls are operating effectively within the company. If the team has staff shortages or lack of experience, this reduces the effectiveness of this monitoring control.	Senior management should consider recruiting additional employees to join the IA department. If this is not possible, consideration should be given to outsourcing the internal audit function. In the interim, employees from other departments, such as finance, could be seconded to IA to assist them with the internal audits, provided these reviews do not cover controls operating in the department where the employees normally work.
During the year, the human resources (HR) department has been busy, therefore the payroll department has set up new joiners to the company. This is a lack of segregation of duties, as employees are able to set up new joiners in the payroll system and process their pay, this leads to an increased risk of fictitious/duplicate employees being set up.	The HR director should review the workloads of the department as a matter of urgency to assess whether other tasks can be re-prioritised as payroll should cease to set up new joiners. This role must immediately revert back to HR to undertake. Additionally, a review should be undertaken of all new joiners set up by payroll with agreement to employee files to confirm that all new employees are bona fide.
The wage rate has been increased by the HR director and notified to the payroll supervisor by email. As payroll can be a significant expense for a business, any decision to increase this should be made by the board as a whole and not just by the HR director.	All increases of pay should be proposed by the HR department and then formally agreed by the board of directors.

Control deficiency	Control recommendation
In addition, the notification of the payroll increase was via email and the payroll supervisor was able to make changes to the payroll standing data without further authorisation. This increases the risk of fraud or errors arising within payroll.	Upon agreement of the pay rise, a written notification of the board decision should be sent to the payroll supervisor who enters the revised pay rate into the system. This change should trigger an exception report for the payroll director, and the new rate should not go live until the director has signed off the changes.
New customers undergo a credit check, after which a credit limit is proposed by the sales staff and approved by the sales director, these credit limits are not reviewed after this. Over a period of time it may be that the customers' credit limits have been set too high, leading to irrecoverable debts, or too low, leading to a loss of sales.	Credit limits should continue to be approved by the sales director. On a regular basis the sales director should review these limits based on order history and payment record.
High value inventory is stored in a secure location across all nine warehouses and access is via a four digit code, which is common to all sites. A considerable number of people will be aware of the codes and could access inventory at any of the nine sites. This significantly increases the risk of fraud.	The access codes for all of the sites should be changed. Each site should have a unique code, known to a small number of senior warehouse employees. These codes should be changed on a regular basis.
Monthly perpetual inventory counts are supposed to be undertaken at each of the nine warehouses, but some of these are outstanding. In order to rely on inventory records for decision making and the year-end financial statements, all lines of inventory must be counted at least once a year, with high value or high turnover items counted more regularly. If the counts are outstanding, some goods may not be counted, and the inventory records may be incorrect.	The programme of perpetual inventory counts should be reviewed for omissions. Any lines which have been missed out should be included in the remaining counts. At the year end, if any lines are identified as having not been counted, the company should organise an additional count to ensure that all items are confirmed to inventory records.

Control deficiency	Control recommendation
The bank reconciliations are only reviewed by the financial controller if the sum of reconciling items is significant; therefore some reconciliations are not being reviewed. The financial controller relies solely on the accounts clerk's notification that the bank reconciliations require review. The bank reconciliations could contain significant errors, but a low overall amount of reconciling items, as there could be compensating errors which cancel each other out. Bank reconciliations are a key control which reduces the risk of fraud. If they are not reviewed, then this reduces its effectiveness and also results in a lack of assurance that bank reconciliations are being carried out at all or on a timely basis.	The bank reconciliations should be reviewed by the financial controller on a monthly basis, even if the reconciling items are not significant, and he should evidence his review by way of signature on the bank reconciliation.
Invoices are authorised by the finance director, but payment is only made 75 days after receipt of the invoice. There is the risk that Equestrian Co is missing out on early settlement discounts. Also, failing to pay in accordance with the supplier's payment terms can lead to a loss of supplier goodwill as well as the risk that suppliers may refuse to supply goods to the company.	The policy of making payment after 75 days should be reviewed. Consideration should be given to earlier payment if the settlement discounts are sufficient. If not, invoices should be paid in accordance with the supplier's payment terms.

(c)   **Outsourcing internal audit**

Equestrian Co

Advantages

Staffing

Equestrian Co wishes to expand its internal audit department in terms of size and specialist skills. If they outsource, then there will be no need to spend money in recruiting further staff as Baseball & Co will provide the staff members.

Immediate solution

As the current internal audit department is small, then outsourcing can provide the number of staff needed straight away.

Skills and experience

Baseball & Co is likely to have a large pool of staff available to provide the internal audit service to Equestrian Co. In addition, the audit firm is likely to have staff with specialist skills already available.

Cost savings

Outsourcing can be an efficient means to control the costs of internal audit as any associated costs such as training will be eliminated as Baseball & Co will train its own employees. In addition, the costs for the internal audit service will be agreed in advance. This will ensure that Equestrian Co can budget accordingly.

Flexibility

If the internal audit department is outsourced, Equestrian Co will have total flexibility in its internal audit service. Staff can be requested from Baseball & Co to suit the company's workloads and requirements. This will ensure that, when required, extra staff are readily available for as long or short a period as needed.

Disadvantages

Existing internal audit department

Equestrian Co has an existing internal audit department. If they cannot be redeployed elsewhere in the company, then they may need to be made redundant and this could be costly for Equestrian Co. Staff may oppose the outsourcing if it results in redundancies.

Increased costs

As well as the cost of potential redundancies, the internal audit fee charged by Baseball & Co may increase over time, proving to be very expensive.

Knowledge of company

Baseball & Co will allocate available staff members to work on the internal audit assignment. This may mean that each visit the staff members are different and hence they may not fully understand the systems of Equestrian Co. This will decrease the quality of the services provided and increase the time spent by Equestrian Co's employees in explaining the system to the auditors.

Loss of in-house skills

If the current internal audit team is not deployed elsewhere in the company, valuable internal audit knowledge and experience may be lost. If Equestrian Co then decided at a future date to bring the service back in-house, this might prove to be too difficult.

Confidentiality

Knowledge of company systems and confidential data will be available to Baseball & Co. Although the engagement letter would provide confidentiality clauses, this may not stop breaches of confidentiality.

Control

Equestrian Co currently has more control over the activities of its internal audit department. Once outsourced it will need to discuss areas of work and timings well in advance with Baseball & Co.

Baseball & Co Advantages

Additional fees for Baseball & Co

The audit firm will benefit from the internal audit service being outsourced as this will generate additional fee income. However, the firm will need to monitor the fees to ensure that they do not represent too high a percentage of their total fee income. As a public interest company, fee income should not represent more than 15% of gross practice income for two consecutive years.

Disadvantages

Independence

If Baseball & Co provides both external audit and internal audit services, there may be a self-review threat especially where the internal audit work is relied upon by the external auditor team. As a public interest entity, it is probable that internal audit services will not be able to be provided by Baseball & Co due to the restrictions put in place in the ACCA Code of Ethics and Conduct. If internal audit services are likely to relate to the financial reporting systems, Baseball & Co will not be able to provide such services.

Marking guide		Marks
(a) **Control activities**		
• Segregation of duties		1
• Information processing		1
• Authorisation		1
• Physical controls		1
• Performance reviews		1
	Max	4
(b) **Control deficiencies and recommendations (8 required)**		
• Assets not physically verified		2
• Internal audit staff shortages		2
• Payroll setting up new staff		2
• Lack of approval for wage increase		2
• Credit limits not reviewed regularly		2
• Inappropriate access to high value inventory		2
• Perpetual inventory counts not complete		2
• Bank reconciliations not always reviewed		2
• Invoices not paid in line with supplier's terms		2
	Max 8 issues, 2 marks each	16
(c) **Outsourcing internal audit** **Equestrian Co**		
• Staffing gaps addressed		1
• Immediate solution		1
• Skills and experience increased		1
• Costs savings		1
• Flexibility of service		1
• Existing internal audit department staff, cost of potential redundancies		1
• Increased costs as fees may increase over time		1
• Knowledge of company and systems reduced		1
• Loss of in-house skills		1
• Confidentiality issues		1
• Control of department reduced		1
Baseball & Co		
• Additional fees		1
• Independence issues for audit firm		1
	Maximum of 8 marks for Equestrian Co and 2 marks for Baseball & Co	10
Total		30

Examiner's comments

Part (a) was a knowledge-based requirement asking candidates to describe four different types of control activities and for each type to provide an example control a company could implement. Performance was very disappointing. Many candidates did not attempt this requirement. The first ½ mark was awarded for each type of control activity described and the second ½ mark for a relevant control example. Few candidates described the five control activities. Segregation of duties and physical controls were the two most common control activities identified. However, most candidates who did identify these two activities only named and did not describe them so were not awarded the first ½ mark. If a candidate identified a control activity correctly they generally gave a relevant example for the second ½ mark.

Part (b) required candidates to identify and explain from the scenario eight deficiencies in Equestrian Co's internal controls and provide a recommendation to address each of these deficiencies. Candidates' performance was mixed. Internal control questions typically require internal control deficiencies to be identified (½ marks each), explained (½ marks each), and a relevant recommendation to address the control (1 mark). Internal controls questions remain a highly examinable area. The scenario in the exam contained more issues than were required to be discussed and it was therefore disappointing that some candidates did not identify the required number of issues noted in the question. In addition some candidates put more than one deficiency as one point in their answer. For example, some candidates identified 'physical verification of assets had not been completed for some time' due to 'internal audit shortages' and ½ mark was awarded for identifying each of these issues (i.e. 1 mark in total). However when issues are combined in this manner they are often not individually well explained and neither is a separate recommendation noted for each. In addition, some candidates did not clearly explain the implication of the deficiency. For example if PPE is not regularly physically verified some candidates stated that an incorrect carrying value of PPE could arise. This is not fully explaining the implication of the deficiency, i.e. that there may be a possible misappropriation of assets or assets included in the register which cannot be verified. Most candidates were able to provide good recommendations to address the deficiencies. However some of the recommendations were either poorly described, did not clearly address the specific control weakness identified or were impractical suggestions. For example recommending that monthly counts are carried out to address the deficiency that perpetual inventory counts are outstanding for some sites does not remedy the deficiency as monthly counts should already be performed, the issue is that the company is not adhering to their own policy. In addition, many candidates recommended that the company undertake a full year-end count, despite being told in the scenario that this was not an option.

Part (c) required advantages and disadvantages of outsourcing the internal audit department. Candidates performed well on this question. Many candidates were able to identify a good range of points for both companies and the mark allocation was adhered to. Many answers were well structured with a section for each company with sub headings for advantages and disadvantages which facilitated the marking of this question. Those candidates who did not score well tended to provide very little detail in their answers, such as for advantages simply stated 'lower costs' or 'more flexibility' these are far too brief to score the 1 mark available per point. The requirement asked candidates to 'explain' their points and this does not provide adequate explanation. Candidates must pay attention to the requirement verb and provide the required level of detail. In addition some candidates included incorrect points such as for advantages the fact that the internal audit work would be quicker as the external auditors knew the company, or that the audit fee would reduce implying that the same team would be used for both tasks or that the work would automatically be relied on which was not appropriate.

221 CATERPILLAR *Walk in the footsteps of a top tutor*

Key answer tips

Part (a) is a straightforward knowledge requirement. This has been examined many times before so students should be able to answer this part of the question well.

Part (b) asks for key controls and tests of controls. You should describe what the control is designed to achieve. To test the control you need to describe how the auditor would obtain evidence that the control works effectively. Be careful not to suggest performing the control as the auditor requires evidence that the client has implemented the control within their business.

Part (c) is a controls deficiency question which appears in every exam. You must fully explain the deficiency in terms of the effect on the company. If management are to take action, they must be concerned about the potential consequences of the deficiency. When providing recommendations for improvement, be as specific as possible.

(a)   Control objectives – cash receipts system

- To ensure that all valid cash receipts are received and deposited promptly in the bank.

- To ensure all cash receipts are recorded in the cash book.

- To ensure that all receipts are recorded at the correct amounts in the cash book.

- To ensure that cash receipts are correctly posted to the general ledger.

- To ensure that cash receipts are recorded in the correct accounting period.

- To ensure that cash is safeguarded to prevent theft.

- To ensure that management has accurate and timely information regarding the cash position.

(b)   Caterpillar Co's cash cycle key controls and tests of control

Key controls	Test of control
Caterpillar Co has an internal audit (IA) department which has undertaken a number of internal control reviews, which specifically focused on cash controls at stores during the year. This is a strong monitoring control as stores will aim to ensure that company procedures are maintained as they would not wish IA to report any exceptions at their store.	Discuss with IA the programme of their visits to stores and the areas addressed on these visits. This will assess the strength of this monitoring control. In particular, enquire of IA whether over a rolling period all stores will be visited. Review the IA department files for the results of the store visits, to confirm that the 20 stores programmed to be visited did all actually take place and for exceptions noted and actions taken.

Key controls	Test of control
At the end of each day, the tills are closed down with daily readings of sales taken; these are reconciled to the total of the cash in the tills and the credit card payment slips and any discrepancies are noted. Daily cashing up procedures should ensure that the cash is controlled and reduces the risk of fraud as employees are aware that the assistant manager will be looking for cash discrepancies.	For a sample of stores visited, the auditor should review the file of daily reconciliations to ascertain if end of day till reconciliations have taken place on a daily basis. For reconciliations with discrepancies, discuss with the store manager what actions were taken and how these differences were resolved.
Cash received from customers is taken to the bank daily via collection by a security company. This ensures that cash is safeguarded and that the risk of theft when transferring to the bank is minimised.	During the store visits, enquire of staff how the cash is transferred to the bank. A sample of invoices from the collection company should be reviewed and confirmed that they are charging Centipede Co on a daily basis. In addition, during these visits observe the cash collection process carried out by the security company.
The daily sales readings from the tills along with the cash and credit card data are transferred to head office through a daily interface into the sales and cash receipts records. This should ensure that sales and cash records are updated on a prompt basis and are complete and accurate.	During the interim audit at head office, compare the daily sales readings from individual stores, including some visited by the audit team, to the sales and cash receipt records within the general ledger. Review the date on which the sales and cash receipt records were updated to ensure this occurred promptly. Any discrepancies should be discussed with the clerk responsible for overseeing this process.
On a daily basis the clerk agrees that the cash banked and the credit card receipts from the credit card company have been credited to the bank statements in full. This should ensure the completeness of cash receipts, as they are transferred in from two sources, being the security company and the credit card operator.	Discuss with the clerk responsible for reconciling the cash and credit card receipts, the process he undertakes. Review the daily reconciliations he has completed to confirm the process has been undertaken as described.
Bank reconciliations are undertaken on a monthly basis. This should ensure that any discrepancies between the cash book and the bank statements are identified promptly.	Review the file of bank reconciliations to ascertain if there is one for each month and that they are either fully reconciled, or the financial controller has evidenced their review of any unreconciled amounts.

(c) **Caterpillar Co's cash system deficiencies and controls**

Control deficiency	Control recommendation
The IA department only undertakes cash control visits to the 20 largest stores as they feel this is where most issues arise. However, Caterpillar Co has 45 stores in total which means over half of the stores are not being checked. This increases the likelihood of control errors, as these stores may not comply with company procedures. As it is a cash business heightens the chance of frauds occurring.	Caterpillar's IA department should have a rolling programme of visits to all 45 stores. This programme can have a bias to large and high risk stores, but it should ensure that all stores are visited on a cyclical basis.
All store employees are able to use each till and none have an individual log on code when using the tills. Allowing all employees access to the till points increases the risk of fraud and error arising. Also in the event of cash discrepancies arising in the tills, it would be difficult to ascertain which employees may be responsible as there is no way of tracking who used which till.	Only employees for whom criminal record/credit checks have been undertaken should be able to use the tills to take customer payments. Each employee should have a designated till and a log on code, which is required for each payment transaction.
Where employees' friends or family members purchase clothes in store, the employee is able to serve them at the till point. There is a significant fraud risk as employees could fail to put the goods through the till, but retain the cash paid by the friend/family members. Additionally, they could give the goods away for free or undercharge for goods sold, thereby granting unauthorised discounts.	Caterpillar Co should instigate a policy whereby employees are unable to serve friends or family members at the till points. They should be required to request that a manager or supervisor put these goods through the till. In addition, CCTV cameras could be placed in the shops, near to the till points to record the daily till transactions. This would act as a deterrent to employees as well as provide evidence in the case of fraudulent transactions occurring. Also Caterpillar Co should carry out regular inventory counts to identify if goods in the stores are below the levels in the inventory records, as this could identify goods being given away for free.

Control deficiency	Control recommendation
The daily reading of sales and reconciliations to the tills is performed in aggregate rather than for each till. This means if exceptions arise, it will be difficult to identify which till caused the difference and therefore which employees may require further till training or have undertaken fraudulent transactions.	The reconciliations should be undertaken on an individual till by till basis rather than in aggregate.
The cashing up of tills along with the recording of any cash discrepancies is undertaken by just one individual, the assistant store manager. There is a fraud risk as the store manager could remove some of the cash and then simply record that there was an exception on this till.	The cashing up process should be undertaken by two individuals together, ideally the assistant and the store manager. One should count the cash and the other record it. Any exceptions to the till reading should be double checked to confirm that they are not simply addition errors.
The cash is kept at the store overnight in a small safe. Although in a safe, this is not secure as it is likely that the cash sales for one day would be a significant sum. This cash is at risk of being stolen overnight.	The cash should continue to be collected daily by the security company, but rather than in the morning it should be collected as the store closes in the evening so that cash does not have to be stored overnight.
If a store needs change, a junior sales clerk is sent to the bank by a till operator to change it into smaller denominations. There is a risk of the cash being misplaced or stolen on the way to the bank or collusion between the junior clerk and till operator as no record appears to be kept of the money removed from the till in these instances and no confirmation of how much cash is returned is carried out.	Caterpillar's head office should stipulate a float amount per till and how the note denominations should be comprised. When assigning the cash float in the morning, the store manager should ensure that this policy is adhered to. If during the day, further smaller denomination notes are required, the store manager should authorise a member of staff to obtain cash from the bank and should fully record movements in and out of the till.
One clerk is responsible for several elements of the cash receipts system. He oversees the daily interface from stores, agrees that cash has cleared into the bank statements and undertakes the bank reconciliations. There is a lack of segregation of duties and errors will not be identified on a timely basis as well as increasing the risk of fraud.	These key roles should be split between a few individuals, with ideally the bank reconciliations being undertaken by another member of the finance team.

Control deficiency	Control recommendation
The bank reconciliations are only reviewed by the financial controller if there are any unreconciled amounts. The bank reconciliation could reconcile but still contain significant errors as there could be compensating errors which cancel each other out. In addition, for a cash based business, the bank reconciliation is a key control which reduces the risk of fraud. If it is not reviewed, then this reduces its effectiveness.	The bank reconciliations should be reviewed by the financial controller on a monthly basis, even if there are no exceptions, and he should evidence his review by way of signature on the bank reconciliation.

	Marking guide	Marks
(a)	**Control objectives – cash receipts system**	
	• All valid cash receipts are received & deposited promptly in the bank	1
	• All cash receipts are recorded in the cash book	1
	• All receipts are recorded at the correct amounts in the cash books	1
	• Cash receipts are correctly posted to the general ledger	1
	• Cash receipts are recorded in the correct accounting period	1
	• Cash is safeguarded to prevent theft	1
	• Management has accurate and timely information regarding the cash position	1
	Restricted to	2
(b)	**Key controls and tests of control (3 required)**	
	• Internal audit department which undertakes cash control reviews	2
	• Daily sales readings taken from tills and reconciled to cash and credit card payment slips, exceptions noted	2
	• Cash collected daily and taken to the bank by security company	2
	• Daily interface to head office for sales, cash and credit card data into sales and cash receipts books	2
	• Daily agreement of cash banked by security company and cash received from credit card company into bank statements	2
	• Monthly bank reconciliations undertaken	2
	Max 3 issues, 2 marks each	6
(c)	**Control deficiencies and recommendations (only 6 issues required)**	
	• Internal audit only visits 20 largest stores rather than all 45	2
	• All employees able to use tills and no individual log on codes	2
	• Employees can serve friends and family members at the till points	2
	• Daily till reading reconciliations performed in aggregate for all tills	2
	• Cashing up of tills undertaken by just one individual	2
	• Cash stored on site overnight	2
	• Junior sales clerks given cash and sent to the bank	2
	• Lack of segregation of duties in head office	2
	• Bank reconciliations not always reviewed by the financial controller	2
	Max 6 issues, 2 marks each	12
Total		20

Examiner's comments

Performance across this question was mixed.

Part (a) required candidates to state control objectives of a cash receipts system. Candidates' performance was disappointing. A significant number of candidates identified control procedures rather than control objectives. In addition, many candidates did not link objectives specifically to the cash receipts system.

Part (b) required candidates to identify (½ marks each), explain (½ marks each) the key controls from the scenario and describe a test of control that the auditor could perform (1 mark each). Performance was mixed in this question. Candidates often correctly identified key controls from the scenario but few explained why it was a strength i.e. few described the implication for the company. For example, candidates identified the control of 'monthly bank reconciliations' (½ marks) but few candidates noted the implication (½ marks) 'a key control over cash and bank which ensures completeness of cash receipts and transactions'. The scenario in the exam contained more key controls than were required to be discussed and it was therefore pleasing that candidates generally only identified the required number of key controls noted in the question. The tests of controls were of a mixed standard. Some of the tests were poorly described and many described substantive rather than control tests. Candidates are advised that to test a control they need to ensure the client has carried out the control.

Part (c) required candidates to identify (½ marks each), explain (½ marks each) the internal control deficiencies from the scenario and describe a test of control for each deficiency that the auditor could perform (1 mark each). Internal control remains a highly examinable area. It was pleasing to note that candidates generally performed well in this question. Candidates were able to identify the internal control deficiencies from the scenario, however many candidates did not clearly explain the implication of the deficiency. In order to gain the ½ explanation mark for the deficiency, candidates must fully explain the impact on the business. Often the explanation of the deficiency was too vague. For example, the implication of there being no individual logons being described as 'could lead to fraud' was not awarded any credit. Candidates needed to explain the implication for the business that 'they would not be able to determine who was in charge of the till if a discrepancy arose'. The scenario contained a significant number of issues, and it was pleasing to note that most candidates were able to identify the required number of issues Most candidates were able to provide good recommendations to address the deficiencies. However some of the recommendations were either poorly described, did not clearly address the specific control deficiency identified, were impractical suggestions or were incomplete. For example for the deficiency 'all employees can access all tills', a common recommendation was 'to have each employee accessing their own till' which would be impractical with only three or four cash tills per store on average. Candidates are reminded that they should tailor their recommendation to the circumstances presented in the scenario.

222 HERAKLION *Walk in the footsteps of a top tutor*

Key answer tips

Part (a) is a straightforward knowledge requirement. This has been examined many times before so students should be able to answer this part of the question well.

Part (b) is a controls deficiency question which appears on every exam. You must fully explain the deficiency in terms of the effect on the company. If management are to take action, they must be concerned about the potential consequences of the deficiency. When providing recommendations for improvement, be as specific as possible e.g. how frequently should the control be performed, which level of person within the organisation should perform the control.

Part (c) is a more unusual requirement asking for controls to reduce the risk of the payroll fraud occurring again. You need to understand how the fraud was able to occur before thinking of how it could have been prevented. Make sure you explain how the control would mitigate the risk to score the available marks.

Part (d) is a straightforward requirement asking for procedures over revenue. To score the marks make sure you give substantive procedures which test the revenue figure and not tests of controls. Also remember that substantive procedures incorporate analytical procedures as well as tests of detail, therefore calculation of gross profit margin and comparison with prior years will score marks.

(a)   Documenting the sales system

Narrative notes

Narrative notes consist of a written description of the system. They would detail what occurs in the system at each stage and would include any controls which operate at each stage.

Advantages of this method include:

- They are simple to record. After discussion with staff members, these discussions are easily written up as notes.

- They can facilitate understanding by all members of the audit team, especially more junior members who might find alternative methods too complex.

Disadvantages of this method include:

- Narrative notes may prove to be too cumbersome, especially if the system is complex or heavily automated.

- This method can make it more difficult to identify missing internal controls as the notes record the detail but do not identify control exceptions clearly.

Questionnaires

Internal control questionnaires (ICQs) or internal control evaluation questionnaires (ICEQs) contain a list of questions. ICQs are used to assess whether controls exist whereas ICEQs assess the effectiveness of the controls in place.

Advantages of this method include:

- Questionnaires are quick to prepare, which means they are a timely method for recording the system.

- They ensure that all controls present within the system are considered and recorded, hence missing controls or deficiencies are clearly highlighted by the audit team.

Disadvantages of this method include:

- It can be easy for the staff members to overstate the level of the controls present as they are asked a series of questions relating to potential controls.

- A standard list of questions may miss out unusual or more bespoke controls used by the company.

Flowcharts

Flowcharts are a graphic illustration of the internal control system for the sales system. Lines usually demonstrate the sequence of events and standard symbols are used to signify controls or documents.

Advantages of this method include:

- It is easy to view the system in its entirety as it is all presented together in one diagram.

- Due to the use of standard symbols for controls, it can be effective in identifying missing controls.

Disadvantages of this method include:

- They can sometimes be difficult to amend, as any amendments may require the whole flowchart to be redrawn.

- There is still the need for narrative notes to accompany the flowchart and hence it can be a time-consuming method.

Note: Full marks will be awarded for describing TWO methods for documenting the sales system and explaining ONE advantage and ONE disadvantage for each method.

(b)   **Deficiencies and controls over the sales system**

Control deficiency	Control recommendation
New customers' creditworthiness is assessed by a salesperson who sets the credit limit, which is authorised by the sales director. The sales staff have sales targets, and may suggest that new customers are creditworthy simply to meet their targets. This could result in sales being made to poor credit risks.	New customers should complete a credit application which should be checked through a credit agency with a credit limit set. Once authorised by the sales director, the limit should be entered into the system by a credit controller.

Control deficiency	Control recommendation
Sales staff have discretion to grant sales discounts to customers of up to 10%. This could result in a loss of revenue as they may award unrealistic discounts simply to meet sales targets. The discounts granted by sales staff are not being reviewed and could result in unauthorised discounts allowed.	All discounts to be granted to customers should be authorised in advance by a responsible official, such as the sales director. If not practical, then the supervisor of the sales staff should undertake this role.
Sales staff are able to make changes to the customer master data file, in order to record discounts allowed and these changes are not reviewed. There is a risk that these amendments could be made incorrectly. This could result in a loss of sales revenue or overcharging of customers. In addition, the sales staff are not senior enough to be given access to changing master file data as this could increase the risk of fraud.	Sales staff should not be able to access the master data file to make amendments. Any such amendments to master file data should be restricted so that only supervisors and above can make changes. An exception report of changes made should be generated and reviewed by a responsible official.
Inventory availability does not appear to be checked by the sales person at the time the order is placed. In addition, Heraklion Co markets itself on being able to despatch all orders within three working days. There is a risk that where goods are not available, the customer would not be made aware of this prior to placing their order. This could lead to unfulfilled orders and customer dissatisfaction, which would impact the company's reputation.	Prior to the salesperson finalising the order, the inventory system should be checked in order for an accurate assessment of the availability of goods to be notified to customers.

Control deficiency	Control recommendation
Customer orders are recorded on a two-part pre-printed form, one copy is left with the customer and one with the sales person. The sales department of Heraklion Co does not hold these orders centrally and hence would not be able to monitor if orders are being fulfilled on a timely basis. This could result in a loss of revenue and customer goodwill.	The order form should be amended to be at least four-part. The third part of the order should be sent to the warehouse department and the fourth part sent to the finance department. The copy the sales person has should be stored centrally in the sales department. Upon despatch, the goods despatch note should be matched to the order; a regular review of unmatched orders should be undertaken by the sales department to identify any unfulfilled orders.
Customer orders are given a number based on the sales person's own identification (ID) number. These numbers are not sequential. Without sequential numbers, it is difficult for Heraklion Co to identify missing orders and to monitor if all orders are being despatched in a timely manner. This could lead to a loss of customer goodwill.	Sales orders should be sequentially numbered. On a regular basis, a sequence check of orders should be undertaken to identify any missing orders.
The sales person emails the warehouse despatch team with the customer ID and the sales order details, rather than a copy of the sales order itself, and a pick list is generated from this. There is a risk that incorrect or insufficient details may be recorded by the sales person resulting in incorrect orders being despatched, orders being despatched late or orders failing to be despatched at all. This could result in a loss of customer goodwill and revenue.	The third part of the sales order as mentioned previously should be forwarded directly to the warehouse department. The pick list should be generated from the original order form and the warehouse team should check correct quantities and product descriptions are being despatched, as well as checking the quality of goods being despatched to ensure they are not damaged.

Control deficiency	Control recommendation
Sequentially numbered goods despatched notes (GDNs) are completed and filed by the warehouse department. If the finance department does not receive a copy of these GDNs, they will not know when to raise the related sales invoices. This could result in goods being despatched but not being invoiced, leading to a loss of revenue.	Upon despatch of goods, a four-part GDN should be completed, with copies to the customer, warehouse department, sales department to confirm despatch of goods and a copy for the finance department. Upon receipt of the GDN, once matched to the fourth part of the sales order form, a clerk should raise the sales invoices in a timely manner, confirming all details to the GDN and order.
The sales person is given responsibility to chase customers directly for payment once an invoice is outstanding for 90 days. This is considerably in excess of the company's credit terms of 30 days which will lead to poor cash flow. Further, as the sales people have sales targets, they are more likely to focus on generating sales orders rather than chasing payments. This could result in an increase in irrecoverable debts and reduced profit and cash flows.	A credit controller should be appointed and it should be their role, rather than the salesperson, to chase any outstanding sales invoices which are more than 30 days old.

(c) **Controls to reduce risk of payroll fraud**

Control	Mitigate risk
Proof of identity checks should be undertaken by the Human Resources (HR) department and recorded on individuals' personnel files for all new employees set up on the payroll system.	This should reduce the risk of fictitious employees being set up, as in order to be set up on the system a fictitious set of identification would be required which would be an onerous process.
A count should be undertaken of the number of employees in each department of Heraklion Co. This should be reconciled to the number of employees on the payroll system.	This would identify if there are extra employees on the payroll system, which could then be investigated further.
The HR department should initiate the process for setting up new joiners by asking new employees to complete a joiner's form which will be approved by the relevant manager and HR. This request should then be forwarded to the payroll department, who should set up the employee.	This control introduces segregation of duties as in order to set up employees both the HR and payroll departments are involved. Without collusion with an HR employee, the payroll supervisor would be unable to set up fictitious employees.

Control	Mitigate risk
All new joiners should be only be set up by payroll on receipt of a joiner's form and any additions to the system should be authorised by the payroll director. An edit report should be generated and reviewed by HR.	As all new joiners would be authorised by the payroll director, it is unlikely that payroll employees would risk establishing fictitious joiners. A further review by the HR department would also detect any employees without an authorised joiner form.
Where possible, employees who are related should not be allowed to undertake processes which are interrelated whereby they can breach segregation of duty controls for key transaction cycles. A regular review of job descriptions of related employees should be carried out by HR.	This should reduce the risk of related staff colluding and being able to commit a fraud.
The payroll system should be amended to run an exception report which identifies any employees with the same bank account name or number and this should be reviewed by HR.	Identifying the same bank account name or number will prevent multiple fraudulent payments being made to the same employees.
All bank transfer requests should be authorised by a senior responsible official, who is independent of the processing of payments. They should undertake spot checks of payments to supporting documentation, including employee identification cards/records.	This would introduce an additional layer of segregation of duties, which would reduce the risk of fraud occurring. In addition, the spot checks to employee identification cards/records would confirm the validity of payments.

(d) **Substantive procedures in relation to revenue**

- Compare the overall level of revenue against prior years and budgets and investigate any significant fluctuations.

- Obtain a schedule of sales for the year broken down into the main product categories and compare this to the prior year breakdown and for any unusual movements discuss with management.

- Calculate the gross profit margin for Heraklion Co and compare this to the prior year and investigate any significant fluctuations.

- Select a sample of sales invoices for customers and agree the sales prices back to the price list or customer master data information to ensure the accuracy of invoices.

- Select a sample of credit notes raised, trace through to the original invoice and ensure the invoice has been correctly removed from sales.

- Select a sample of customer orders and agree these to the despatch notes and sales invoices through to inclusion in the sales day book and revenue general ledger accounts to ensure completeness of revenue.

- Select a sample of despatch notes both pre and post year-end and follow these through to sales invoices in the correct accounting period to ensure that cut-off has been correctly applied.

	Marking guide	
		Marks
(a)	**Methods for documenting the sales system**	
	• Narrative notes	3
	• Questionnaires	3
	• Flowcharts	3
		———
	Max 2 methods, 1 mark description, 1 mark advantage, 1 mark disadvantage	**6**
		———
(b)	**Control deficiencies and recommendations (only 7 issues required)**	
	• New customers' creditworthiness assessed by sales staff	2
	• Sales staff have discretion to grant discounts up to 10%	2
	• Access to master file data	2
	• Inventory not checked by sales people prior to order being placed	2
	• No copy of order with the sales ordering department, unable to identify unfulfilled orders	2
	• Orders not sequentially numbered	2
	• Warehouse despatch team do not receive a copy of the sales order	2
	• Goods despatch notes filed by warehouse despatch team	2
	• Salesperson responsible for chasing invoices over 90 days old	2
		———
	Max 7 issues, 2 marks each	**14**
		———
(c)	**Controls to reduce risk of payroll fraud**	
	• Proof of identity checks undertaken for all new joiners	2
	• Review of the number of employees per department to the payroll system	2
	• Human resources department initiates request for new joiners	2
	• Authorisation of all new joiners by payroll director	2
	• Relatives not permitted to undertake interrelated processes	2
	• Payroll system reviews same bank account name and number	2
	• Bank transfer requests authorised by senior responsible official, independent of processing of transactions	2
		———
	Max	**6**
		———
(d)	**Substantive procedures in relation to revenue**	
	• Analytical review over revenue compared to budget and prior year	1
	• Analytical review of main product categories of sales compared to prior year	1
	• Gross margin review	1
	• Agree sales prices for customers to price list or master file data	1
	• Review credit notes	1
	• Follow orders to goods despatched note to sales invoice to sales day book	1
	• Sales cut-off	1
		———
	Max	**4**
		———
Total		**30**
		———

Examiner's comments

This question covered the areas of internal controls, documenting systems, fraud and audit procedures for revenue. Candidates' performance was mixed across this question.

Part (a) addressed methods used by the auditor of documenting client accounting systems and advantages and disadvantages for each. This knowledge area has been regularly examined, but it was disappointing to see that a significant minority of candidates did not understand the question requirement. Incorrect answers focused on the two methods being either manual or computerised recording or discussed documents that are used in the sales cycle such as the sales order and invoice. Candidates who scored well tended to describe the methods of narrative notes and flowcharts. Some candidates failed to describe the method and so only gained the ½ identify mark. Additionally some candidates mixed up advantages and disadvantages between the methods hence describing notes as being difficult to amend rather than flowcharts.

Part (b) tested the area of internal controls, these types of questions typically require internal control deficiencies to be identified (½ marks each), explained (½ marks each), a relevant recommendation to address the control deficiency (1 mark). Internal controls questions remain a highly examinable area and in common with prior sittings, performance in the internal control question was mixed. Candidates were able to identify the internal control deficiency from the scenario however many candidates did not clearly explain the implication of the deficiency. In order to gain the ½ explanation mark for the deficiency candidates must fully explain the impact on the company. Additionally some candidates did not understand or incorrectly identified deficiencies, e.g. new customer leads being generated by a third party or sales staff visiting customer sites personally; these were not control deficiencies. The scenario in the exam contained more issues than was required to be discussed and it was therefore pleasing that candidates generally only identified the required number of issues noted in the question. Most candidates were able to provide good recommendations to address the deficiencies. However some of the recommendations were either poorly described, did not clearly address the specific control weakness identified, were impractical suggestions or were incomplete. For example the recommendation for sequentially numbering orders should have also suggested regular sequence checks to be undertaken, however many answers stopped at sequentially numbering the orders.

Part (c) covered controls to prevent a payroll fraud from occurring along with an explanation of how the control would mitigate the risk of the fraud reoccurring. Candidates' performance was unsatisfactory in this question. A significant number of candidates were unable to apply their audit knowledge to this application area. Some just repeated how the fraud had taken place trying to explain the controls that had broken down rather than suggesting preventive controls. Others listed general controls that should be in place over the payroll system or were too generic such as 'establish an internal audit department' or 'set up segregation of duties.' Additionally many candidates didn't describe how the controls would mitigate the fraud risk, or simply stated 'this would mitigate the risk' or 'this will reduce the fraud risk' without explaining how.

Part (d) covered substantive procedures for revenue and candidates' performance was satisfactory. Many candidates provided a range of analytical procedures as well as tests of detail. Some tests lacked sufficient detail such as 'compare revenue to prior year' without discussing investigating significant differences or were vague. In addition a minority of candidates listed receivables procedures rather than revenue.

223 LEMON QUARTZ *Walk in the footsteps of a top tutor*

Key answer tips

Part (a) is a straightforward controls deficiency question which appears on every exam. You must fully explain the deficiency in terms of the effect on the company. If management are to take action, they must be concerned about the potential consequences of the deficiency. Tests of controls are the procedures the auditor will perform to assess whether the controls recommended have been implemented effectively.

Part (b) is a straightforward knowledge question. Make sure you take time to learn key definitions and terms such as the elements of an assurance engagement as they are regularly examined.

(a) Deficiencies, controls and test of controls

Deficiencies	Controls	Tests of controls
The count will be undertaken by teams of warehouse staff. There should be a segregation of roles between those who have day-to-day responsibility for inventory and those who are checking it. If the same team are responsible for maintaining and checking inventory, then errors and fraud could be hidden causing loss for the company.	The counting teams should be independent of the warehouse. Members of alternative departments should undertake the counting rather than the warehouse staff.	Attend the year-end count and enquire of the counting teams which department they normally work in. Inspect the updated inventory count instructions to verify that they have been communicated to members of staff outside the warehouse department.
The inventory sheets contain quantities as per the inventory records. There is a risk that the counting teams may simply agree with the pre-printed quantities rather than counting the balances correctly, resulting in significant errors in inventory.	The count sheets should be sequentially numbered and contain product codes and descriptions but no quantities.	Inspect a sample of the counting sheets being used by the counting teams to verify that only the inventory product codes and description are pre-printed on them.

Deficiencies	Controls	Tests of controls
There are 15 teams of counters, each team having two members of staff. However, there is no clear division of responsibilities within the team. Therefore, both members of staff could count together rather than checking each other's count. Errors in their count may not be identified.	Each team should be informed that both members are required to count their assigned inventory separately. Therefore, one member counts and the second member also undertakes a count and then records the inventory on the count sheets correctly. In addition, the financial controller supervising the count should undertake some sample checks of inventory counted by each team.	Observe the counting teams to assess if they are counting together or if one counts and the other then double checks the quantities counted. Review the records of the sample checks undertaken by the supervisor of the inventory count.
Inventory owned by third parties is also being counted by the teams with adjustments being made by the finance team to split these goods out later. There does not appear to be a method for counters to identify which items are third party inventory. There is a risk that these goods may not be correctly removed from the inventory count sheets, resulting in inventory being overstated.	All inventories belonging to third parties should be moved to one location. This area should be clearly marked and excluded from the counting process.	Enquire of the count supervisor where the third party inventory is to be stored, confirm through inspection of the counting sheets that these bays are not included on any pre-printed forms.
High value inventory which is normally stored in a secure location will be accessible by all team members as they will be given the access code. Any member of the counting team could subsequently access these goods. This significantly increases the risk of theft and loss to the company.	The high value inventory should be kept in the locked area of the warehouse. Senior members of the team should be allocated to count these goods, and they should be given the access code to enter the area. Upon completion of the count the access code should be changed.	Attempt to access the area where the high value inventory is stored, this should not be possible without the access code. At the year-end visit attempt to access with the code which was supplied during the inventory count.

Deficiencies	Controls	Tests of controls
Each bay of the warehouse is counted once only. If inventory is only checked once, then counting errors may arise resulting in under or overstated inventory.	Once all inventories have been counted once, each area should be recounted by a different team. Any differences on the first count should be promptly notified to the count supervisor and a third count undertaken if necessary. If a full second count would be too time-consuming for the company, then sample checks on the inventory counted should be undertaken by a different counting team.	Observe the counting team undertake second counts of all areas to confirm that different teams undertake this process.
Once areas are counted, the teams are not marking the bays as completed. Therefore there is the risk that some areas of the warehouse could be double counted or missed out resulting in errors in the inventory balance.	All bays should be flagged as completed, once the inventory has been counted. In addition, the count supervisor should check at the end of the count that all of the bays with Quartz's inventory have been flagged as completed.	Physically confirm that the completed bays of the warehouse have been flagged to indicate that the goods have been counted. At the end of the count, review any bays containing Quartz's goods which have not been flagged.
The inventory sheets are sequentially numbered and at the end of the count they are given to the count supervisor who confirms with each team that they have returned all sheets. However, no sequence check of the sheets is performed. If sheets are missing, then the inventory records could be understated.	After the counting has finished, each team should return all of their sequentially numbered sheets and the supervisor should check the sequence of all sheets at the end of the count.	Review the sequence of the inventory sheets for any gaps in the sequence and obtain an explanation from the count supervisor.

(b)   Elements of an assurance engagement

In accordance with ISAE 3000 *Assurance Engagements other than Audits or Reviews of Historical Financial Information*, an assurance engagement will require a three-party relationship comprising of:

- The intended user who is the person who requires the assurance report.

- The responsible party, which is the organisation responsible for preparing the subject matter to be reviewed.

- The practitioner (i.e. an accountant) who is the professional who will review the subject matter and provide the assurance.

A second element which is required for an assurance engagement is suitable subject matter. The subject matter is the data which the responsible party has prepared and which requires verification. Thirdly this subject matter is then evaluated or assessed against suitable criteria in order for it to be assessed and an opinion provided.

Fourth, the practitioner must ensure that they have gathered sufficient appropriate evidence in order to give the required level of assurance. Last, an assurance report provides the opinion which is given by the practitioner to the intended user.

Marking guide		*Marks*
(a)	**Control deficiencies, control recommendations and tests of control**	
	• Warehouse employees undertaking the count	3
	• Inventory counting sheets contain quantities per records	3
	• No clear division of roles within counting teams	3
	• Third-party inventory included in the count	3
	• Access to high value finished goods	3
	• Each location counted once only	3
	• No flagging of bays once counted	3
	• No sequence checks of inventory sheets	3
	Max 5 issues, 3 marks each	**15**
(b)	**Elements of an assurance engagement**	
	• Intended user, responsible party, practitioner	1
	• Subject matter	1
	• Suitable criteria	1
	• Appropriate evidence	1
	• Assurance report	1
		5
Total		**20**

Examiner's comments

Performance in this question was mixed. Candidates were able to identify the internal control deficiency from the scenario however some candidates did not clearly explain the implication of the deficiency. Additionally some candidates did not understand or incorrectly identified deficiencies, e.g. renting space in the warehouse to third parties or completing inventory count sheets in ink. The scenario in the exam contained more issues than was required to be discussed and it was therefore pleasing that candidates generally only identified the required number of issues noted in the question. Most candidates were able to provide good recommendations to address the deficiencies. However some of the recommendations were either poorly described, did not clearly address the specific control weakness identified or were impractical suggestions. The tests of controls that the auditor could perform were often not well explained by candidates (e.g. "ensure the bays are flagged" without saying how the auditor would ensure this or just using the word "check" or "observe", did not address the controls identified or were substantive audit procedures rather than tests of control. It was pleasing to note that many candidates presented their answers well using a three-column approach with internal controls deficiencies in one column, the related recommendation in the other and the related test of control in the third column.

224 BRONZE *Walk in the footsteps of a top tutor*

Key answer tips

Part (a) is a tricky knowledge question. This question demonstrates the need for both breadth and depth of knowledge across the syllabus. If you don't know the answer, don't waste time thinking about it, move on to the next part of the question and come back to it later when you have answered the other questions. Take a logical, common sense approach to try and come up with one or two points. Think about which type of deficiencies a client might be more concerned about and therefore more likely to want to do something about because the consequences could be significant, as compared with deficiencies where the consequences might not be so detrimental for the company.

Part (b) requires the control deficiencies within the payroll cycle to be identified. Use the specific information in scenario rather than giving deficiencies that could be present in any payroll system. There are always more deficiencies than you need so choose the ones you can write well about. Suggest controls the client can implement to address the control deficiency. Be specific about which member of client staff should be responsible for the control and how frequently they should perform the control. Tests of controls are the audit procedures the auditor will perform to obtain evidence to prove the control suggested is in place and working effectively. Be specific about how they would do this.

In part (c) you are asked for analytical procedures to confirm payroll. An analytical procedure requires the auditor to form an expectation of the payroll figure to compare with the client's actual figure to assess whether it looks reasonable. Comparisons with prior year, comparison with budget and performing a proof in total would be typical analytical procedures for payroll.

Part (d) requires text book knowledge of analytical procedures and their suitability.

Part (e) covers a small syllabus area. An internal audit function may perform work useful to the external auditor, and depending on the level of assessed competence and objectivity of the internal auditors, the external auditor may be able to place reliance on their work instead of performing those procedures. Before placing reliance, the external auditor will need to assess the internal auditor's work to ensure it is appropriate for audit purposes.

(a) **Examples of matters the external auditor should consider in determining whether a deficiency in internal controls is significant**

- The likelihood of the deficiencies leading to material misstatements in the financial statements in the future.

- The susceptibility to loss or fraud of the related asset or liability.

- The subjectivity and complexity of determining estimated amounts.

- The financial statement amounts exposed to the deficiencies.

- The volume of activity that has occurred or could occur in the account balance or class of transactions exposed to the deficiency or deficiencies.

- The importance of the controls to the financial reporting process.

- The cause and frequency of the exceptions detected as a result of the deficiencies in the controls.

- The interaction of the deficiency with other deficiencies in internal control.

Tutor's top tips

Note that the requirement asks for matters which would mean an internal control deficiency is significant, NOT examples of significant internal control deficiencies. Giving examples of deficiencies will not score any marks.

Tutorial note

ISA 265 Communicating Deficiencies in Internal Control to those charged with Governance and Management states that a significant deficiency in internal control is a deficiency or combination of deficiencies in internal control that, in the auditor's professional judgment, is of sufficient importance to merit the attention of those charged with governance.

(b) **Bronze payroll system deficiencies and controls**

Deficiencies	Controls	Test of control
Employees swipe their cards at the beginning and end of the eight-hour shift. This process is not supervised. This could result in a number of employees being swiped in as present when they are not. This will result in a substantially increased payroll cost for Bronze.	The clocking in and out process should be supervised by a responsible official to prevent one individual clocking in multiple employees. A supervisor should undertake a random check of employees by reviewing who has logged in with a swipe card and confirming visually that the employee is present.	Observe the clocking in and out process to ensure it is supervised by a responsible official. Enquire of the supervisor whether they perform a random check of employees.
Employees are entitled to a 30-minute paid break and do not need to clock out to access the dining area. Employees could be taking excessive breaks. This will result in a decrease in productivity and increased payroll costs.	Employees should be allocated set break times and there should be a supervisor present to ensure that employees only take the breaks they are entitled to.	Review the rota for break-times to ensure break times are formally communicated to staff. Observe the dining area during break times to ensure a supervisor is present.
Although there is a human resources department, appointments of temporary staff are made by factory production supervisors. The supervisor could appoint unsuitable employees and may not carry out all the required procedures for new joiners. This could result in these temporary employees not receiving the correct pay and relevant statutory deductions causing dissatisfaction of employees.	All appointment of staff, whether temporary or permanent, should only be made by the human resources department.	Inspect the HR procedures manual to ensure that appointments of staff are the responsibility of the HR department. For a sample of employees employed by Bronze, inspect the employee's file to ensure the appropriate checks were carried out by the HR department prior to employment.

Deficiencies	Controls	Test of control
Overtime reports which detail the amount of overtime worked are sent out quarterly by the payroll department to production supervisors for review. These reports are reviewed after the payments have been made. This could result in unauthorised overtime or amounts being paid incorrectly and Bronze's payroll cost increasing.	All overtime should be authorised by a responsible official prior to the payment being processed by the payroll department. This authorisation should be evidenced in writing.	Inspect the overtime reports for evidence of a responsible official's signature authorising the overtime prior to the payment being processed.
Production supervisors determine the amount of the discretionary bonus to be paid to employees. Production supervisors are not senior enough to determine bonuses. They could pay extra bonuses to friends or family members causing increased cost for Bronze.	The bonus should be determined by a more senior individual, such as the production director, and this should be communicated in writing to the payroll department.	Inspect the communication of bonuses to the payroll department and ensure it is sent by a senior official.
The bonus is input by a clerk into the payroll system. There is no indication that this input process is reviewed. This could result in input errors or the clerk could fraudulently change the amounts. This could lead to incorrect bonus payments being made and increased payroll costs for Bronze.	Once the clerk has input the bonus amounts, all entries should be double checked against the written confirmation from the production director by another member of the team to identify any amounts entered incorrectly.	Observe the payroll clerk inputting the bonus amounts and subsequent check against the written confirmation from the production director by a different member of the team.

Deficiencies	Controls	Test of control
The payroll manager reviews the bank transfer listing prior to authorising the payments and also amends the payroll records for any changes required. There is a lack of segregation of duties as it is the payroll team which processes the amounts and the payroll manager who authorises payments. The manager could fraudulently increase the amounts to be paid to certain employees, process this payment as well as amend the records causing loss for the company.	The payroll manager should not be able to process changes to the payroll system as well as authorise payments. The authorisation of the bank transfer listing should be undertaken by an individual outside the payroll department, such as the finance director.	Inspect the payroll bank transfer listing for the authorisation signature. Ensure the signature is of a person outside of the payroll department and of suitable authority such as the finance director.
A payroll clerk distributes cash pay packets to employees without requesting proof of identity. Even if most employees are known to the clerk, there is a risk that without identity checks wages could be paid to incorrect employees. This could result in increased payroll costs or dissatisfied employees if incorrect amounts are received.	The payroll clerks should be informed that all cash wages can only be paid upon sight of the employee's clock card and photographic identification as this confirms proof of identity.	Observe the process of wage collection to ensure that employees can only collect their wages on production of their clock card and photographic ID.

(c) **Substantive analytical procedures to confirm payroll expense**

- Compare the total payroll expense to the prior year or budget and investigate any significant differences.

- Review monthly payroll charges, compare this to the prior year and budgets and discuss with management any significant variances.

- Compare overtime pay as a percentage of factory normal hours pay to investigate whether it is at a similar level to the prior year and within an acceptable range. Investigate any significant differences.

- Perform a proof in total of total wages and salaries, incorporating joiners and leavers and any pay increase. Compare this to the actual wages and salaries in the financial statements and investigate any significant differences.

- Calculate statutory deductions as a percentage of gross pay and compare to the prior year to assess the reasonableness of the statutory deductions. Investigate any significant variances.

(d)   Suitability of analytical procedures

- Nature of the balance or class of transactions. Analytical procedures are more suitable to large volume transactions that are predictable over time such as payroll, sales, and expenses.

- Reliability of the information being analysed. If the information being analysed is unreliable, the results of the analytical procedures will be unreliable. Reliability of the information will be affected by source, nature and effectiveness of internal controls.

- Relevance to the assertion being tested. Analytical procedures would usually not be used to test the existence assertion of a tangible asset such as inventory or property, plant and equipment as physical inspection of the asset would provide more reliable evidence.

- Precision of expectation. The auditor should consider whether a sufficiently precise expectation can be developed to be able to identify a material misstatement. If not, there is limited use in using analytical procedures.

- Amount of difference between expected amounts and recorded amounts that is acceptable. This will depend on the level of materiality and the desired level of assurance required by the auditor.

(e)   Impact on interim and final audit

Interim audit

Scarlet & Co could look to rely on any internal control documentation produced by internal audit (IA) as they would need to assess whether the control environment has changed during the year.

If the IA department has performed testing during the year on internal control systems, such as the payroll, sales and purchase systems, then Scarlet & Co could review and possibly place reliance on this work. This may result in the workload reducing and possibly a decrease in the external audit fee.

During the interim audit, Scarlet & Co would need to perform a risk assessment to assist in the planning process. It is possible that the IA department may have conducted a risk assessment and so Scarlet could use this as part of their initial planning process.

Scarlet & Co would need to consider the risk of fraud and error and non-compliance with law and regulations resulting in misstatements in the financial statements. This is also an area for IA to consider, hence there is scope for Scarlet & Co to review the work and testing performed by IA to assist in this risk assessment.

Final audit

It is possible that the IA department may assist with year-end inventory counting and controls and so Scarlet & Co can place some reliance on the work performed by them, however, they would still need to attend the count and perform their own reduced testing.

Marking guide

		Marks
(a)	**Significant deficiencies**	*Marks*
	• Likelihood of deficiencies leading to errors	1
	• Risk of fraud	1
	• Subjectivity and complexity	1
	• Financial statement amounts	1
	• Volume of activity	1
	• Importance of the controls	1
	• Cause and frequency of exceptions	1
	• Interaction with other deficiencies	1
	Maximum	**3**
(b)	**Control deficiencies, control recommendations and tests of control**	
	• Clock in/out process unsupervised	3
	• Employee breaks not monitored	3
	• Temporary staff are not appointed by human resources department	3
	• Overtime report reviewed after payment	3
	• Authorisation of discretionary bonus	3
	• No input checks over entry of bonus into payroll	3
	• Payroll manager reviews the bank transfer listing prior to payment and can change payroll records	3
	• No identity checks prior to cash wages pay out	3
	Max 5 issues, 3 marks each	**15**
(c)	**Substantive analytical procedures**	
	• Compare total payroll expense to the prior year or budget and investigate any significant differences	1
	• Review monthly payroll charges, compare to the prior year, budgets, discuss with management	1
	• Compare overtime pay as a percentage of factory normal hours against prior year, investigate any significant differences	1
	• Perform a proof in total of total wages and salaries, compare to actual, and investigate any significant differences	1
	• Calculate statutory deductions as a percentage of gross pay and compare to the prior year to assess the reasonableness	1
	Maximum	**4**
(d)	**Suitability of analytical procedures**	
	• Nature of the balance or class of transactions	1
	• Reliability of the information being analysed	1
	• Relevance to the assertion being tested	1
	• Precision of expectation	1
	• Amount of difference between expected amounts and recorded amounts that is acceptable	1
	Maximum	**4**
(e)	**Work performed at interim audit**	
	• Systems documentation	1
	• Testing of systems such as payroll, sales, purchases	1
	• Risk assessment	1
	• Fraud and error, non-compliance with law and regulations	1
	Work performed at final audit	
	• Inventory count procedures	1
	Maximum	**4**
Total		**30**

Examiner's comments

Internal control questions typically require internal controls deficiencies to be identified (½ marks each), explained (½ marks each) and, often, to give a relevant recommendation to address the deficiency (1 mark each). Occasionally, candidates may be asked to identify key controls as well as deficiencies. Candidates continue to perform well on internal control questions. Candidates were able to confidently identify internal controls deficiencies from the scenario, however some candidates did not clearly explain the deficiency in terms of how it affects the business. The scenario in the exam will always contain more issues than required to be discussed and it was therefore encouraging that candidates generally applied effective exam technique and focused on providing well explained answers which identified the required number of issues as noted in the question. A minority of candidates, rather than evaluating internal controls just formed a point of view as to how well the company was controlling it's operations, and, also included more 'social' factors such as 'the motivational effect of having/not having a bonus system in force in a company' which was not required and does not answer the question. Recommendations to address control weaknesses were on the whole well explained. Most candidates were able to provide good recommendations to address the deficiencies. However occasionally some of the recommendations did not clearly address the specific control weakness identified and candidates are again reminded to ensure that their recommendation is specifically tailored to the requirements of the scenario.

Part (d) required candidates to explain the impact on the external auditor's work at the interim and final audits if the client was to establish an internal audit department. Performance on this question was unsatisfactory. Where the question was attempted, many candidates failed to score more than 1 mark. What was required was an explanation of tasks that internal audit might perform that the external auditor might then look to rely on in either the interim or final audit. For example, they could utilise systems documentation produced by internal audit during the interim audit. Or they could rely on year-end inventory counts undertaken by internal audit as part of their inventory testing at the final audit. Where candidates achieved 1 mark this was usually for a general comment about relying on the work of internal audit and so reducing substantive procedures.

Mistakes made by candidates were:

- Focusing on the role of internal audit in general.

- Giving lengthy answers on factors to consider when placing reliance on internal audit.

- Providing details of what an external auditor does at the interim and final audit stages.

225 TROMBONE *Walk in the footsteps of a top tutor*

Key answer tips

Part (a) requires repetition of knowledge from the text book of the components of an internal control system. Make sure you explain the components. You do not need to give the full text book definition but make sure some of the key elements are included in your answer.

Part (b) requires the control deficiencies within the payroll cycle to be identified. Use the specific information in scenario rather than giving deficiencies that could be present in any payroll system. There are always more deficiencies than you need so choose the ones you can write well about. Suggest controls the client can implement to address the control deficiency. Be specific about which member of client staff should be responsible for the control and how frequently they should perform the control. Tests of controls are the audit procedures the auditor will perform to obtain evidence to prove the control suggested is in place and working effectively. Be specific about how they would do this.

Parts (c) and (d) ask for substantive procedures. A substantive procedure is used to detect material misstatement in the figure. Tests of controls will not score marks.

(a)   Internal control components

ISA 315 *Identifying and Assessing the Risks of Material Misstatement through Understanding the Entity and Its Environment* considers the components of an entity's internal control. It identifies the following components:

Control environment

The control environment includes the governance and management functions and the attitudes, awareness, and actions of those charged with governance and management concerning the entity's internal control and its importance in the entity. The control environment sets the tone of an organisation, influencing the control consciousness of its people.

The control environment has many elements such as communication and enforcement of integrity and ethical values, commitment to competence, participation of those charged with governance, management's philosophy and operating style, organisational structure, assignment of authority and responsibility and human resource policies and practices.

Entity's risk assessment process

For financial reporting purposes, the entity's risk assessment process includes how management identifies business risks relevant to the preparation of financial statements in accordance with the entity's applicable financial reporting framework. It estimates their significance, assesses the likelihood of their occurrence, and decides upon actions to respond to and manage them and the results thereof.

Information system, including the related business processes, relevant to financial reporting, and communication

The information system relevant to financial reporting objectives, which includes the accounting system, consists of the procedures and records designed and established to initiate, record, process, and report entity transactions (as well as events and conditions) and to maintain accountability for the related assets, liabilities, and equity.

Control activities relevant to the audit

Control activities are the policies and procedures which help ensure that management directives are carried out. Control activities, whether within information technology or manual systems, have various objectives and are applied at various organisational and functional levels.

Monitoring of controls

Monitoring of controls is a process to assess the effectiveness of internal control performance over time. It involves assessing the effectiveness of controls on a timely basis and taking necessary remedial actions. Management accomplishes the monitoring of controls through ongoing activities, separate evaluations, or a combination of the two. Ongoing monitoring activities are often built into the normal recurring activities of an entity and include regular management and supervisory activities.

(b)   **Payroll system deficiencies, controls and test of controls**

Deficiencies	Controls	Test of controls
The wages calculations are generated by the payroll system and there are no checks performed. Therefore, if system errors occur during the payroll processing, this would not be identified. This could result in wages being over or under calculated, leading to an additional payroll cost or loss of employee goodwill.	A senior member of the payroll team should recalculate the gross to net pay workings for a sample of employees and compare their results to the output from the payroll system. These calculations should be signed as approved before payments are made.	Review a sample of the gross to net pay calculations for evidence that they are undertaken and signed as approved.
Annual wages increases are updated in the payroll system standing data by clerks. Payroll clerks are not senior enough to be making changes to standing data as they could make mistakes. This could lead to incorrect payment of wages causing dissatisfied employees. In addition, if they can access standing data, they could make unauthorised changes.	Payroll clerks should not have access to standing data changes within the system. The annual wages increase should be performed by a senior member of the payroll department and this should be checked by another responsible official for errors.	Ask a clerk to attempt to make a change to payroll standing data; the system should reject this attempt. Review the log of standing data amendments to identify whether the wage rate increases were changed by a senior member of payroll.

Deficiencies	Controls	Test of controls
Overtime worked by employees is not all authorised by the relevant department head, as only overtime in excess of 30% of standard hours requires authorisation. This increases the risk that employees will claim for overtime even though they did not work these additional hours. This will result in additional payroll costs for Trombone.	All overtime hours worked should be authorised by the relevant department head. This should be evidenced by signature on the employees' weekly overtime sheets.	Review a sample of employee weekly overtime sheets for evidence of signature by relevant department head.
Time taken off as payment for overtime worked should be agreed by payroll clerks to the overtime worked report; however, this has not always occurred. Employees could be taking unauthorised leave if they take time off but have not worked the required overtime. This will cause loss for the company.	Payroll clerks should be reminded of the procedures to be undertaken when processing the overtime sheets. They should sign as evidence on the overtime sheets that they have agreed any time taken off to the relevant overtime report.	Select a sample of overtime sheets with time taken off and confirm that there is evidence of a check by the payroll clerk to the overtime worked report.
The overtime worked report is emailed to the department heads and they report by exception if there are any errors. If department heads are busy or do not receive the email and do not report to payroll on time, it will be assumed that the overtime report is correct even though there may be errors. This could result in the payroll department making incorrect overtime payments which could cause additional cost for the company or a loss of employee goodwill.	All department heads should report to the payroll department on whether or not the overtime report is correct. The payroll department should follow up on any non-replies and not make payments until agreed by the department head.	For a sample of overtime reports emailed to department heads confirm that a response has been received from each head by reviewing all responses.

Deficiencies	Controls	Test of controls
Department heads are meant to arrange for annual leave cover so that overtime sheets are authorised on a timely basis; however, this has not always happened. If overtime sheets are authorised late, overtime payments will be delayed. This will cause employee dissatisfaction.	Department heads should be reminded of the procedures with regards to annual leave and arrangement of suitable cover. During annual leave periods, payroll clerks should monitor that overtime sheets are being submitted by department heads on a timely basis and follow up any late sheets.	Discuss with payroll clerks the process they follow for obtaining authorisation of overtime sheets, in particular during periods of annual leave. Compare this to the process which they should adopt to identify any control exceptions.
The finance director reviews the total list of bank transfers with the total to be paid per the payroll records. There could be employees omitted along with fictitious employees added to the payment listing, so that the total payments list still agrees to the payroll totals even though it is incorrect. This could mean fraudulent payments are able to be made causing loss for the company.	The finance director when authorising the payments should on a sample basis perform checks from payroll records to payment list and vice versa to confirm that payments are complete and only made to *bona fide* employees. The finance director should sign the payments list as evidence that he has undertaken these checks.	Obtain a sample of payments list and review for signature by the finance director as evidence that the control is operating correctly.

(c) **Substantive procedures in relation to completeness and accuracy of payroll**

- Agree the total wages and salaries expense per the payroll system to the trial balance, investigate any differences.

- Cast a sample of payroll records to confirm completeness and accuracy of the payroll expense.

- For a sample of employees, recalculate the gross and net pay and agree to the payroll records to confirm accuracy.

- Recalculate the statutory deductions to confirm whether correct deductions for this year have been made in the payroll.

- Compare the total payroll expense to the prior year and investigate any significant differences.

- Review monthly payroll charges, compare this to the prior year and budgets and discuss with management for any significant variances.

- Perform a proof in total of total wages and salaries, incorporating joiners and leavers and the annual pay increase. Compare this to the actual wages and salaries in the financial statements and investigate any significant differences.

- Select a sample of joiners and leavers, agree their start/leaving date to supporting documentation, recalculate that their first/last pay packet was accurately calculated and recorded.

- Agree the total net pay per the payroll records to the bank transfer listing of payments and to the cashbook.

- Agree the individual wages and salaries per the payroll to the personnel records for a sample.

- Select a sample of weekly overtime sheets and trace to overtime payment in payroll records to confirm completeness of overtime paid.

(d) **Substantive procedures in relation to income tax payable accrual**

Procedures the auditor should adopt in respect of auditing this accrual include:

- Agree the year-end income tax payable accrual to the payroll records to confirm accuracy.

- Recalculate the accrual to confirm accuracy.

- Agree the subsequent payment to the post year-end cash book and bank statements to confirm completeness.

- Review any correspondence with tax authorities to assess whether there are any additional outstanding payments due; if so, agree they are included in the year-end accrual.

- Review any disclosures made of the income tax accrual and assess whether these are in compliance with accounting standards and legislation.

Marking guide		Marks
(a) **Components of internal control**		
• Control environment – governance and management function, attitudes awareness and actions of management		1
• Control environment – made up of a number of elements (need to list at least 2 to score 1 mark)		1
• Entity's risk assessment – process for identifying risk		1
• Information system relevant to financial reporting – procedures and records to record an entity's transactions, assets and liabilities and to maintain accountability		1
• Control activities – policies and procedures to ensure management directives are carried out		1
• Monitoring controls – assess effectiveness of internal controls		1
Note to markers: Please award credit for reasonable explanations of internal control components.		
Restricted to		5

	Marking guide	Marks

		Marks
(b)	**Control deficiencies, recommendations and tests of control**	
	• Payroll calculations not checked	3
	• Payroll clerks update standing data for wages increases	3
	• Authorisation of overtime sheets only undertaken if overtime exceeds 30% of standard hours	3
	• Time off as payment for overtime not checked to overtime worked report	3
	• Review of overtime worked reports by department heads	3
	• Authorisation of overtime sheets when department heads on annual leave	3
	• Finance director only reviews totals of payroll records and payments list	3
	Max 5 issues, 3 marks each	15
(c)	**Substantive procedures in relation to completeness and accuracy of payroll**	
	• Agree wages and salaries per payroll to trial balance	1
	• Cast payroll records	1
	• Recalculate gross and net pay	1
	• Recalculate statutory deductions	1
	• Compare total payroll to prior year	1
	• Review monthly payroll to prior year and budget	1
	• Proof in total of payroll and agree to the financial statements	1
	• Verify joiners/leavers and recalculate first/last pay	1
	• Agree wages and salaries paid per payroll to bank transfer list and cashbook	1
	• Agree the individual wages and salaries as per the payroll to the personnel records	1
	• Agree sample of weekly overtime sheets to overtime payment in payroll records	1
	Restricted to	6
(d)	**Substantive procedures in relation to accrual for tax payable**	
	• Agree to the payroll records to confirm the accuracy of the accrual	1
	• Recalculate the accrual	1
	• Agree the subsequent payment to the post year-end cash book and bank statements	1
	• Review any correspondence with tax authorities to assess whether there are any additional outstanding payments due, if so, agree they are included in the year-end accrual	1
	• Review disclosures and assess whether these are adequate and in compliance	1
	Restricted to	4
Total		30

Examiner's comments

Part (a) asked candidates to identify and briefly explain the components of an entity's internal control. Candidates' performance was mixed on this question with many not even attempting it. There were some candidates who had clearly revised this area and were able to confidently identify the five components and explain what they related to. Some candidates were confused by 'information systems' and incorrectly related this solely to a computer environment. Many candidates were only able to identify the components and either did not provide an explanation or it was incorrect. Also a significant minority of candidates explained the components from the perspective of what this meant for the audit firm rather than the company. In addition a significant minority of candidates did not understand the question requirement, or did not have sufficient technical knowledge of this area and so instead of providing components, such as, control environment and control activities, focused on providing a list of internal controls such as authorisation or segregation of duties controls.

Part (b) required candidates to identify and explain deficiencies in the payroll system, recommend controls to address these deficiencies, and a test of control for each of these recommendations that could be used to assess if it was operating effectively if implemented. The first two parts of this questions were answered satisfactorily by candidates, however the tests of controls proved challenging for many. Candidates were able to comfortably identify deficiencies from the scenario, although a minority of candidates identified deficiencies which were generic to payroll systems rather than specific to the question, such as references to 'clock cards', which were not a component of the system under review. Also some candidates identified points which were not valid deficiencies, such as employees being able to complete their own overtime sheets, being allowed a choice between days off or payment of overtime and overtime sheets being entered by payroll clerks. Although sufficient deficiencies were identified by many candidates, they did not always adequately explain what the deficiency meant to Trombone. For example, candidates identified the deficiency that 'the overtime worked reports are not always checked,' however some failed to explain the implication of this in that it could lead to employees taking days off when they had not worked the overtime hours required. The requirement to provide controls was answered satisfactorily. Most candidates were able to provide good recommendations to address the deficiencies; however in some instances these recommendations were too brief. Candidates have a tendency to state control objectives rather than valid procedures which can be implemented by the client. In addition some recommendations failed to address the deficiency identified, for example where department heads failed to assign a deputy to authorise overtime whilst on annual leave, many candidates simply recommended that this control already existing control be put in place, rather than addressing how the control should be amended to ensure it was followed at all times. The requirement for tests of controls was answered unsatisfactorily. Many candidates are still confusing substantive procedures and test of controls. A significant number of candidates suggested substantive procedures such as 'recalculating gross and net pay calculations', rather than a test of control which might be to 'review evidence of the recalculation of payroll'. Candidates need to review their understanding of these different types of audit procedures and ensure that they appreciate that substantive tests focus on the number within the financial statements whereas test of controls are verifying if client procedures are operating. In many instances candidates focused on re-performing the control rather than testing it had operated. Observation of a control was commonly suggested by candidates, however in many cases this is not an effective way of testing that a control has operated throughout the year. Most candidates presented their answers well, adopting a three column approach with deficiency, the control recommendation and the test of control in separate columns.

This approach ensured that all elements of the question were addressed and it was easier to see which recommendations and tests related to which deficiencies.

Part (c) required substantive procedures to confirm the completeness and accuracy of the payroll expense. On the whole candidates performed well in this area. A good proportion of candidates were able to suggest practical payroll procedures such as analytical review of prior year and current year charges or undertaking a proof in total calculation. Other common answers included recalculation of a sample of payroll calculations or statutory deductions.

Common mistakes made by candidates were:

- Giving objectives rather than procedures 'ensure that the gross and net pay calculations are correct', this is not a detailed substantive procedure and so would not score any marks.

- Lack of detail in tests such as 'check that the payroll calculations are correct', this would not score any marks as it does not explain what should be checked or how this testing would be carried out.

- Providing tests of controls rather than substantive procedures, such as focusing on authorisation of payroll.

The requirement verb was to 'describe' therefore sufficient detail was required to score the 1 mark available per test. Candidates are reminded yet again that substantive procedures are a core topic area and they must be able to produce relevant detailed procedures and to apply their knowledge to different areas of the financial statements.

Part (d) required substantive procedures in respect of the year-end accrual for tax payable on employment income. Where answered, performance on this requirement was disappointing. Candidates were provided with a short scenario to explain how the employment taxes were remitted to the taxation authorities and that at the year-end there would be an accrual for any outstanding amount. The scenario was provided so that candidates could apply their knowledge of accruals to the specific circumstances; however from the answers provided it seems that some did not take notice of detail provided.

Many answers demonstrated that candidates did not know what a tax accrual was and hence suggested procedures focused on 'discussions with management' or 'obtaining written representations'. This accrual was not judgmental and so the above procedures would not have scored many marks. Those candidates that scored well suggested answers such as 'recalculation of the accrual,' 'comparison with prior year or months' and 'verifying the subsequent payment after the year-end'.

226 OREGANO *Walk in the footsteps of a top tutor*

Tutor's top tips

Part (a) is quite a difficult requirement unless you know the different methods of documenting systems. Therefore if you don't know it, don't waste time in the exam trying to think of something. Move onto the next part of the question and come back to it when you have finished everything you can do on the paper.

Part (b) requires control objectives. A control objective identifies a risk which will be mitigated by a control being in place. Think about the things that could go wrong in a sales and despatch system.

Part (c) is a standard controls deficiency and recommendation requirement. Identify the controls which are missing or ineffective. Explain how that will impact the business. Recommend a good control the company should put in place to overcome the deficiency.

(a)   Documenting the sales and despatch system

Narrative notes

Narrative notes consist of a written description of the system. They would detail what occurs in the system at each stage and would include any controls which operate at each stage.

Advantages of this method include:

- They are simple to record. After discussion with staff members of Oregano, these discussions are easily written up as notes.

- They can facilitate understanding by all members of the internal audit team, especially more junior members who might find alternative methods too complex.

Disadvantages of this method include:

- Narrative notes may prove to be too cumbersome, especially if the sales and distribution system is complex.

- This method can make it more difficult to identify missing internal controls as the notes record the detail but do not identify control exceptions clearly.

Questionnaires

Internal control questionnaires (ICQ) or internal control evaluation questionnaires (ICEQ) contain a list of questions. ICQs are used to assess whether controls exist whereas ICEQs test the effectiveness of the controls.

Advantages of this method include:

- Questionnaires are quick to prepare, which means they are a timely method for recording the system.

- They ensure that all controls present within the system are considered and recorded; hence missing controls or deficiencies are clearly highlighted by the internal audit team.

Disadvantages of this method include:

- It can be easy for the staff members of Oregano to overstate the level of the controls present as they are asked a series of questions relating to potential controls.

- A standard list of questions may miss out unusual controls of Oregano.

Flowcharts

Flowcharts are a graphic illustration of the internal control system for the sales and despatch system. Lines usually demonstrate the sequence of events and standard symbols are used to signify controls or documents.

Advantages of this method include:

- It is easy to view the sales system in its entirety as it is all presented together in one diagram.

- Due to the use of standard symbols for controls, they are easy to spot as are any missing controls.

Disadvantages of this method include:

- They can sometimes be difficult to amend, as any amendments may require the whole flowchart to be redrawn.

- There is still the need for narrative notes to accompany the flowchart and hence it can be a time consuming method.

Note: Full marks will be awarded for describing TWO methods for documenting the sales and despatch system and explaining ONE advantage and ONE disadvantage for each method.

(b) **Control objectives for sales and despatch system**

Tutor's top tips

Control objectives are the reasons why controls are put in place. They address the risks that could happen in the system. Be careful not to suggest that a control objective is to ensure a control is in place. You need to say the reason why the control should be in place.

- To ensure that orders are only accepted if goods are available to be processed for customers.

- To ensure that all orders are recorded completely and accurately.

- To ensure that goods are not supplied to poor credit risks.

- To ensure that goods are despatched for all orders on a timely basis.

- To ensure that goods are despatched correctly to customers and that they are of an adequate quality.

- To ensure that all goods despatched are correctly invoiced.

- To ensure completeness of income for goods despatched.

- To ensure that sales discounts are only provided to valid customers.

(c)   **Deficiencies and controls for Oregano Co's sales and despatch system**

Tutor's top tips

Controls deficiencies and recommendations questions are usually quite straightforward, however, you must explain the deficiencies and controls in sufficient detail to score marks. If you are too brief you will only score ½ marks.

Deficiency	Control
Inventory availability for telephone orders is not checked at the time the order is placed. The order clerks manually check the availability later and only then inform customers if there is insufficient inventory available. There is the risk that where goods are not available, order clerks could forget to contact the customers, leading to unfulfilled orders. This could lead to customer dissatisfaction, and would impact Oregano's reputation.	When telephone orders are placed, the order clerk should check the inventory system whilst the customer is on the phone; they can then give an accurate assessment of the availability of goods and there is no risk of forgetting to inform customers.
Telephone orders are not recorded immediately on the three part pre-printed order forms; these are completed after the telephone call. There is a risk that incorrect or insufficient details may be recorded by the clerk and this could result in incorrect orders being despatched or orders failing to be despatched at all. This will result in a loss of customer goodwill.	All telephone orders should be recorded immediately on the three part pre-printed order forms. The clerk should also double check all the details taken with the customer over the telephone to ensure the accuracy of the order recorded.
Telephone orders are not sequentially numbered. If orders are misplaced whilst in transit to the despatch department, these orders will not be fulfilled. This will result in customer dissatisfaction.	The three part pre-printed orders forms should be sequentially numbered and on a regular basis the despatch department should run a sequence check of orders received. Where there are gaps in the sequence, they should be investigated to identify any missing orders.

Deficiency	Control
Customers are able to place online orders which will exceed their agreed credit limit by 10%. Orders may be accepted from bad credit risks. The company's profit will decrease if irrecoverable debts arise.	Customer credit limits should be reviewed more regularly by a responsible official and should reflect the current spending pattern of customers. If some customers have increased the level of their purchases and are making payments on time, then these customers' credit limits could be increased. The online ordering system should be amended to not allow any orders to be processed which will exceed the customer's credit limit.
A daily pick list is used by the despatch department when sending out customer orders. However, it does not appear that the goods are checked back to the original order. Incorrect goods may be sent out. This will result in a loss of customer goodwill.	In addition to the pick list, copies of all the related orders should be printed on a daily basis. When the goods have been picked ready to be despatched, they should be cross checked back to the original order. They should check correct quantities and product descriptions, as well as checking the quality of goods being despatched to ensure they are not damaged.
Additional staff have been drafted in to help the two sales clerks produce the sales invoices. As the extra staff will not be as experienced as the sales clerks, there is an increased risk of mistakes being made in the sales invoices. This could result in customers being under or overcharged leading to customer dissatisfaction.	Only the sales clerks should be able to raise sales invoices. As Oregano is expanding, consideration should be given to recruiting and training more permanent sales clerks who can produce sales invoices.
Discounts given to customers are manually entered onto the sales invoices by sales clerks. This could result in unauthorised sales discounts being given as there does not seem to be any authorisation required. In addition, a clerk could forget to manually enter the discount or enter an incorrect level of discount for a customer. This could result in the sales invoice being overstated and a loss of customer goodwill.	For customers who are due to receive a discount, the authorised discount levels should be updated to the customer master file. When the sales invoices for these customers are raised, their discounts should automatically appear on the invoice. The invoicing system should be amended to prevent sales clerks from being able to manually enter sales discounts onto invoices.

Marking guide			Marks
(a)	**Methods for documenting the sales and despatch system**		
	• Narrative notes		2
	• Questionnaires		2
	• Flowcharts		2
			———
	Max 2 methods, 1 mark description, 1 mark advantage, 1 mark disadvantage		**6**
			———
(b)	**Control objectives**		
	• To ensure orders are only accepted if goods are available to be processed for customers		1
	• To ensure all orders are recorded completely and accurately		1
	• To ensure goods are not supplied to poor credit risks		1
	• To ensure goods are despatched for all orders on a timely basis		1
	• To ensure goods are despatched correctly to customers and are of an adequate quality		1
	• To ensure all goods despatched are correctly invoiced		1
	• To ensure completeness of income for goods despatched		1
	• To ensure sales discounts are only provided to valid customers		1
			———
		Restricted to	**2**
			———
(c)	**Control deficiencies and recommendations**		
	• Inventory not checked when order taken		2
	• Orders not completed on pre-printed order forms		2
	• Order forms not sequentially numbered		2
	• Credit limits being exceeded		2
	• Goods despatched not agreed to order to check quantity and quality		2
	• Sales invoices being raised by inexperienced staff		2
	• Sales discounts manually entered by sales clerks		2
			———
		Max 6 issues, 2 marks each	**12**
			———
Total			**20**
			———

Examiner's comments

Part (a) required a description of two methods for documenting the sales and despatch system along with an advantage and disadvantage for each method. Candidates' performance was unsatisfactory on this question, with a number of candidates not even attempting it. A significant proportion of candidates did not understand the question requirement fully, and so instead of suggesting methods such as flowcharts, narrative notes or questionnaires they considered manual and automated/electronic methods for a system. In addition some candidates considered online versus telephone methods for recording sales transactions and others interpreted the question as requiring the documents of a sales system and so considered sales invoices and despatch notes. The question requirement was clear, candidates either did not read it carefully or they lacked the technical knowledge on documentation methods. Those candidates who did correctly interpret the requirement often failed to maximise their marks as they identified the methods but did not describe them. In addition, candidates advantages and disadvantages were far too brief, a describe requirement needs more than a few words and 'easy to understand' is not detailed enough to score the 1 mark available.

Part (b) required two controls objectives for the sales and despatch system. Candidates could have used the scenario to help or answered this question using their technical knowledge, however overall performance was unsatisfactory. A significant proportion of candidates provided controls rather than control objectives, this was not what was required and so would not have scored any marks. This indicates a lack of knowledge as to what a control is rather than a control objective. Objectives have been tested in previous diets, and candidates should endeavour to practice past exam questions when preparing for this exam.

Part (c) required an identification and explanation of deficiencies and a recommendation for each of these deficiencies. This part of the question was answered very well and candidates were able to confidently identify six deficiencies from the scenario. However, candidates did not always adequately explain what the deficiency meant to Oregano. For example, candidates easily identified the deficiency that credit limits were being exceeded by 10% for online orders. However some failed to explain that this could lead to an increase in bad debts. The requirement to provide controls was, on the whole, well answered. Most candidates were able to provide good recommendations to address the deficiencies; however some of these recommendations were too brief. In addition some recommendations failed to address the deficiency, for example for the credit limits being exceeded some candidates suggested 'a review of credit limits by a responsible official', this would not prevent orders from exceeding the limits. The main recommendation where candidates failed to maximise their marks was for sequentially numbered orders. Simply recommending 'that sales orders should be sequentially numbered' only scored ½ mark, as the control is to undertake sequence checks, for which the orders need to be sequential. This demonstrated a lack of understanding of this type of control.

227 FOX INDUSTRIES *Walk in the footsteps of a top tutor*

Tutor's top tips

Part (a) When asked for a covering letter, don't ignore this as there are usually presentation marks available. Remember to keep your answer anonymous, don't use your own name in the letter, and make up a name. Don't forget to include the point that the letter is solely for the use of management and don't forget to sign off the letter appropriately.

Controls deficiencies and recommendations questions are usually quite straightforward, however, you must explain the deficiencies and controls in sufficient detail to score marks. If you are too brief you will only score ½ marks.

Part (b) application controls are those controls which apply to a specific application rather than the computer network as a whole. Application controls can help ensure completeness and accuracy of the data entered.

Part (c) asks for substantive procedures. Think about the assertions which need to be tested such as valuation, completeness and existence. Also think about the types of procedure that can be used such as recalculation, external confirmation and inspection.

(a) **Report to management**

Board of directors
Fox Industries Co
15 Dog Street
Cat Town
X Country
6 June 20X3

Dear Sirs,

Audit of Fox Industries Co (Fox) for the year ended 30 April 20X3

Please find enclosed the report to management on deficiencies in internal controls identified during the audit for the year ended 30 April 20X3. The appendix to this report considers deficiencies in the purchasing and payments system, the implications of those deficiencies and recommendations to address those deficiencies.

Please note that this report only addresses the deficiencies identified during the audit and if further testing had been performed, then more deficiencies may have been reported.

This report is solely for the use of management and if you have any further questions, then please do not hesitate to contact us.

Yours faithfully

An audit firm

APPENDIX

Deficiency	Recommendation
When raising purchase orders, the clerks choose whichever supplier can despatch the goods the fastest. Fox may order goods at a much higher price or a lower quality than they would like, as the only factor considered was speed of delivery. This will reduce the company's profit.	An approved supplier list should be compiled; this should take into account the price of goods, their quality and also the speed of delivery. Once the list has been produced, all orders should only be placed with suppliers on the approved list.
Purchase orders are not sequentially numbered. Fox's ordering team is unable to monitor if all orders are being fulfilled in a timely manner; this could result in stock outs. Stocks outs will cause disruption to Fox's operations and customer orders not being fulfilled leading to customer dissatisfaction.	All purchase orders should be sequentially numbered and on a regular basis a sequence check of unfulfilled orders should be performed.

Deficiency	Recommendation
Purchase orders below $5,000 are not authorised and are processed solely by an order clerk. This can result in goods being purchased which are not required by Fox. In addition, there is an increased fraud risk as an order clerk could place orders for personal goods up to the value of $5,000, which is significant. This will result in loss for the company.	All purchase orders should be authorised by a responsible official. Authorised signatories should be established with varying levels of purchase order authorisation.
Purchase invoices are input daily by the purchase ledger clerk and due to his experience, he does not utilise any application controls. Without application controls there is a risk that invoices could be input into the system with inaccuracies or they may be missed out entirely. This could result in suppliers being paid incorrectly or not all, leading to a loss of supplier goodwill.	The purchase ledger clerk should input the invoices in batches and apply application controls, such as control totals, to ensure completeness and accuracy over the input of purchase invoices.
The purchase day book automatically updates with the purchase ledger but this ledger is manually posted to the general ledger. Manually posting the amounts to the general ledger increases the risk of errors occurring. This could result in the payables balance in the financial statements being under or overstated.	The process should be updated so that on a regular basis the purchase ledger automatically updates the general ledger. A responsible official should then confirm through purchase ledger control account reconciliations that the update has occurred correctly.
Fox's saving (deposit) bank accounts are only reconciled every two months. If these accounts are only reconciled periodically, there is the risk that errors will not be spotted promptly. Also, this increases the risk of employees committing fraud. If they are aware that these accounts are not regularly reviewed, then they could use these cash sums fraudulently. This will cause loss for the company.	All bank accounts should be reconciled on a regular basis, and at least monthly, to identify any unusual or missing items. The reconciliations should be reviewed by a responsible official and they should evidence their review.

Deficiency	Recommendation
Fox has a policy of delaying payments to their suppliers for as long as possible. Whilst this maximises Fox's bank balance, there is the risk that Fox is missing out on early settlement discounts. This can lead to a loss of supplier goodwill as well as the risk that suppliers may refuse to supply goods to Fox.	Fox should undertake cash flow forecasting/budgeting to maximise bank balances. The policy of delaying payment should be reviewed, and suppliers should be paid in a systematic way, such that supplier goodwill is not lost.

(b) **Application controls**

Document counts – the number of invoices to be input are counted, the invoices are then entered one by one, at the end the number of invoices input is checked against the document count. This helps to ensure completeness of input.

Control totals – here the total of all the invoices, such as the gross value, is manually calculated. The invoices are input, the system aggregates the total of the input invoices' gross value and this is compared to the control total. This helps to ensure completeness and accuracy of input.

One for one checking – the invoices entered into the system are manually agreed back one by one to the original purchase invoices. This helps to ensure completeness and accuracy of input.

Review of output to expected value – an independent assessment is made of the value of purchase invoices to be input, this is the expected value. The invoices are input and the total value of invoices is compared to the expected value. This helps to ensure completeness of input.

Check digits – this control helps to reduce the risk of transposition errors. Mathematical calculations are performed by the system on a particular data field, such as supplier number, a mathematical formula is run by the system, this checks that the data entered into the system is accurate. This helps to ensure accuracy of input.

Range checks – a pre-determined maximum is input into the system for gross invoice value, for example, $10,000; when invoices are input if the amount keyed in is incorrectly entered as being above $10,000, the system will reject the invoice. This helps to ensure accuracy of input.

Existence checks – the system is set up so that certain key data must be entered, such as supplier name, otherwise the invoice is rejected. This helps to ensure accuracy of input.

Tutor's top tips

Make sure you give 'application' controls, i.e. those that you would perform at the time of entering the data to ensure it is complete and accurate. General controls will not score marks.

(c)   Substantive procedures in relation to bank and cash

- Obtain Fox's current bank account reconciliation and check the additions to ensure arithmetical accuracy.

- Obtain a bank confirmation letter from Fox's bankers for all of its accounts.

- For the current account, agree the balance per the bank statement to an original year-end bank statement and also to the bank confirmation letter.

- Agree the reconciliation's balance per the cash book to the year-end cash book.

- Trace all of the outstanding lodgements to the pre year-end cash book, post year-end bank statement and also to paying-in-book pre year-end.

- Trace all un-presented cheques through to a pre year-end cash book and post year-end statement. For any unusual amounts or significant delays obtain explanations from management.

- Examine any old un-presented cheques to assess if they need to be written back into the payables ledger as they are no longer valid to be presented.

- Agree all balances listed on the bank confirmation letter to Fox's bank reconciliations or the trial balance to ensure completeness of bank balances.

- Review the cash book and bank statements for any unusual items or large transfers around the year-end, as this could be evidence of window dressing.

- Examine the bank confirmation letter for details of any security provided by Fox or any legal right of set-off as this may require disclosure.

- For the saving (deposit) bank accounts, review any reconciling items on the year-end bank reconciliations and agree to supporting documentation.

- In respect of material cash balances, count cash balances at the year-end and agree to petty cash records, such as the petty cash book.

- Review the financial statements to ensure that the disclosure of cash and bank balances are complete and accurate.

Marking guide		Marks
(a) Control deficiencies and recommendations		
- No approved suppliers list		2
- Purchase orders not sequentially numbered		2
- Orders below $5,000 are not authorised by a responsible official		2
- No application controls over input of purchase invoices		2
- Purchase ledger manually posted to general ledger		2
- Saving (deposit) bank accounts only reconciled every two months		2
- Payments to suppliers delayed		2
- Finance director only reviews the total of the payment list prior to payment authorising		2
	Max 5 issues, 2 marks each	10
Presentation		
- Letterhead		½
- Introductory paragraph		½
- Disclaimers		½
- Courteous sign off		½
		2

	Marking guide		
			Marks
(b)	**Application controls**		
	• Document counts		1
	• Control totals		1
	• One for one checking		1
	• Review of output to expected value		1
	• Check digits		1
	• Range checks		1
	• Existence checks		1
		Restricted to	3
(c)	**Substantive procedures in relation to bank and cash**		
	• Check additions of bank reconciliation		1
	• Obtain bank confirmation letter		1
	• Bank balance to statement/bank confirmation		1
	• Cash book balance to cash book		1
	• Outstanding lodgements		1
	• Unpresented cheques review		1
	• Old cheques write back		1
	• Agree all balances on bank confirmation		1
	• Unusual items/window dressing		1
	• Security/legal right set-off		1
	• Review reconciliations for saving (deposit) accounts		1
	• Cash counts for significant cash balances		1
	• Review disclosure of bank and cash in financial statements		1
		Restricted to	5
Total			20

Examiner's comments

Part (a) required a report to management which identifies and explains deficiencies and a recommendation for each of these deficiencies. In addition a covering letter was required. This part of the question was answered very well and candidates were able to confidently identify the deficiencies from the scenario. However, candidates did not always adequately explain the implication of the deficiency to the business. For example, for the deficiency of purchase orders not being sequentially numbered, many candidates focused on the difficulties of agreeing invoices to orders, as opposed to the key issue of unfulfilled orders and hence stock outs. In addition many implications were vague such as 'there will be errors if application controls are not applied by the purchase ledger clerk' this answer does not give any examples of what type of errors and where they may occur. Candidates need to think in a practical manner and apply their knowledge when answering these types of questions. The requirement to provide controls was, on the whole, well answered. Most candidates were able to provide good recommendations to address the deficiencies. However some of these recommendations were too brief, for example simply stating 'apply application controls' to address the deficiency of the purchase ledger clerk. The main recommendation where candidates failed to maximise their marks was for sequentially numbered purchase orders. Simply recommending 'that purchase orders should be sequentially numbered' only scored ½ marks, as the control is to undertake sequence checks, for which the orders need to be sequential. This demonstrated a lack of understanding of this type of control.

A covering letter to the report was required and there were 2 marks available. Despite this specific requirement a significant number of candidates provided their answers as a memo rather than as a letter. Adopting a memo format resulted in a failure to maximise marks. The two marks were allocated as ½ for a letterhead, ½ for an introductory paragraph, ½ for disclaimers and ½ for a courteous sign off of the letter, which requires more than just a signature.

Many candidates set their answer out in columns. However, those who explained all of the deficiencies and then separately provided all of the recommendations tended to repeat themselves and possibly wasted some time. A significant proportion of candidates provided many more than the number of points required. It was not uncommon to see answers with eight deficiencies. Also in many answers deficiencies were combined such as; 'purchase orders are not sequentially numbered and only orders over $5,000 require authorisation', the implications and recommendations would then also be combined. Providing many more points than required and combining answers leads to unstructured answers that are difficult to mark. Spending too much time on this part of the exam also puts candidates under time pressure for the rest of the paper.

Part (b) required application controls to ensure the completeness and accuracy of the input of purchase invoices. Performance on this question was quite unsatisfactory. Many candidates failed to pick up marks for this question; also this question was left unanswered by some candidates. The requirement was for application controls, these could be computerised or manual, but they needed to address the specific area of INPUT of invoices. Many candidates gave general computer controls such as passwords or provided auditor's substantive tests. In addition candidates listed recommendations from the previous requirement such as 'sequentially numbered orders or regular bank reconciliations'; these have nothing to do with input of invoices. Some answers focused on auditing the purchase cycle, agreeing orders to goods received notes and to invoices. Candidates clearly either have a knowledge gap in this area or failed to read the question requirement carefully.

Part (c) required substantive procedures for bank and cash at the year-end. Performance on this question was unsatisfactory. Substantive procedures are a key area of the paper and may feature in each session. Some scripts were with hardly any valid bank and cash procedures. Tests which start with 'to ensure that' are unlikely to gain any marks as these are objectives rather than audit tests. Also some candidates failed to read the question requirement which stated that the audit was of year-end cash and bank. These answers focused more on tests of controls over the whole of the year for cash and bank, these did not gain any credit. Some candidates focused on the bank reconciliation and auditing its detail, such as un-presented cheques and outstanding lodgements. Most candidates were able to suggest obtaining a bank confirmation letter and counting petty cash, however this seemed to be the extent of many answers. It was unsatisfactory to see that many candidates did not understand the purpose of the bank reconciliation as a common answer was 'to agree the bank confirmation letter to the financial statements' as opposed to the bank reconciliation. Many provided vague answers such as 'cast the ledger' and a minority misunderstood the question and focused on auditing payables and receivables.

228 LILY WINDOW GLASS *Walk in the footsteps of a top tutor*

Tutor's top tips

Part (a) Controls deficiencies and recommendations questions are usually quite straight-forward, however, you must explain the deficiencies and controls in sufficient detail to score marks. If you are too brief you will only score ½ marks.

Part (b) Audit procedures performed during the inventory count will include a mixture of tests of controls and substantive procedures. Make sure you give procedures that will be done during the count, which is usually conducted at the year end date, and not procedures that will be performed during the final audit.

Part (c) Automated tools and techniques include audit software, test data and data analytics. Data analytics is an emerging technology in the auditing profession. Look out for examiner articles on the use of data analytics.

(a)   Inventory count arrangements

Deficiencies	Recommendations
The warehouse manager is planning to supervise the inventory count. Whilst he is familiar with the inventory, he has overall responsibility for the inventory and so is not independent. He may want to hide inefficiencies and any issues that arise so that his department is not criticised.	An alternative supervisor who is not normally involved with the inventory, such as an internal audit manager, should supervise the inventory count. The warehouse manager and his team should not be involved in the count at all.
There are ten teams of counters, each team having two members of staff. However, there is no clear division of responsibilities within the team. Therefore, both members of staff could count together rather than checking each other's count. Errors in their count may not be identified.	Each team should be informed that both members are required to count their assigned inventory separately. Therefore, one counts and the second member checks that the inventory has been counted correctly.
The internal audit teams are undertaking inventory counts. Internal audit should review the controls and perform sample test counts to confirm the count is being performed accurately and effectively. Issues with the count may not be identified resulting in an ineffective count.	The internal audit counters should sample check the counting undertaken by the ten teams to provide an extra control over the completeness and accuracy of the count.

Deficiencies	Recommendations
Once areas are counted, the teams are not flagging the aisles as completed.	All aisles should be flagged as completed, once the inventory has been counted. In addition, internal audit or the count supervisor should check at the end of the count that all 20 aisles have been flagged as completed.
Some areas of the warehouse could be double counted or missed out.	
This will increase the risk of the inventory quantities being either under or overstated.	
Inventory not listed on the sheets is to be entered onto separate sheets, which are not sequentially numbered.	Each team should be given a blank sheet for entering any inventory count which is not on their sheets. This blank sheet should be sequentially numbered, any unused sheets should be returned at the end of the count, and the supervisor should check the sequence of all sheets at the end of the count.
The supervisor will be unable to ensure the completeness of all inventory sheets.	
This could result in understatement of inventory.	
There is no indication that the completed count sheets are signed by the counting team.	All inventory sheets should be signed by the relevant team upon completion of an aisle. When the sheets are returned, the supervisor should check that they have been signed.
If any issues arise with the counting in an aisle, it will be difficult to follow up as the identity of the counting team will not be known.	
Damaged goods are not being stored in a central area, and instead the counter is just noting on the inventory sheets the level of damage.	Damaged goods should be clearly flagged by the counting teams and at the end of the count appropriate machinery should be used to move all damaged windows to a central location. This will avoid the risk of selling these goods.
It will be difficult for the finance team to decide on an appropriate level of write down if they are not able to see the damaged goods.	
The inventory value for the damaged items may not be appropriate.	A senior member of the finance team should then inspect these goods to assess the level of any write down or allowance.
In addition, if these goods are left in the aisles, they could be inadvertently sold to customers or moved to another aisle.	
Lily Window Glass Co undertakes continuous production and so there will be movements of goods during the count.	It is not practical to stop all inventory movements as the production needs to continue. However, any raw materials required for 31 December should be estimated and put to one side. These will not be included as raw materials and instead will be work-in-progress.
Goods may be missed or double counted due to movements in the warehouse.	
Inventory records could be under or overstated as a result.	

Deficiencies	Recommendations
	The goods which are manufactured on 31 December should be stored to one side, and at the end of the count should be counted once and included within finished goods.
	Any goods received from suppliers should be stored in one location and counted once at the end and included as part of raw materials. Goods to be despatched to customers should be kept to a minimum for the day of the count.
The warehouse manager is to assess the level of work-in-progress and raw materials. In the past, a specialist has undertaken this role. It is unlikely that the warehouse manager has the experience to assess the level of work-in-progress as this is something that the factory manager would be more familiar with. Work-in-progress may be under or overvalued.	A specialist should be utilised to assess both work-in-progress and the quantities of raw materials.
The warehouse manager will also estimate the quantity of raw materials. He may make a mistake when assessing the quantities. Inventory could be materially misstated.	With regards to the warehouse manager, he could estimate the raw materials and the specialist could check it. This would give an indication as to whether he is able to accurately assess the quantities for subsequent inventory counts.

(b)   Procedures during the inventory count

- Observe the counting teams of Lily Window Glass to confirm whether the inventory count instructions are being followed correctly.

- Select a sample and perform test counts from inventory sheets to warehouse aisle and from warehouse aisle to inventory sheets.

- Confirm the procedures for identifying and segregating damaged goods are operating correctly.

- Select a sample of damaged items as noted on the inventory sheets and inspect these windows to confirm whether the level of damage is correctly noted.

- Observe the procedures for movements of inventory during the count, to confirm that no raw materials or finished goods have been omitted or counted twice.

- Obtain a photocopy of the completed sequentially numbered inventory sheets for follow up testing on the final audit.

- Identify and make a note of the last goods received notes (GRNs) and goods despatched notes (GDNs) for 31 December in order to perform cut-off procedures.

- Observe the procedures carried out by the warehouse manager in assessing the level of work-in-progress and consider the reasonableness of any assumptions used.

- Discuss with the warehouse manager how he has estimated the raw materials quantities. To the extent that it is possible, re-perform the procedures adopted by the warehouse manager.

- Identify and record any inventory held for third parties (if any) and confirm that it is excluded from the count.

(c)   Automated tools and techniques

(i)   Audit procedures using automated tools and techniques

- The audit team can use audit software to calculate the inventory holding period for the year-to-date to compare against the prior year to identify whether inventory is turning over more slowly, as this may be an indication that it is overvalued.

- Audit software can be utilised to produce an aged inventory analysis to identify any slow-moving goods, which may require write down or an allowance.

- Cast the inventory listing to confirm the completeness and accuracy of inventory.

- Audit software can be used to select a representative sample of items for testing to confirm net realisable value and/or cost.

- Audit software can be utilised to recalculate cost and net realisable value for a sample of inventory.

- Verify cut-off by testing whether the dates of the last GRNs and GDNs recorded relate to pre year-end; and that any with a date of 1 January 20X3 onwards have been excluded from the inventory records.

- Use audit software to confirm whether any inventory adjustments noted during the count have been correctly updated into final inventory records.

(ii)   Advantages

- Enables the audit team to test a large volume of inventory data accurately and quickly.

- If audit software is utilised on the audit of Lily, then as long as the company does not change its inventory system, it can be cost effective after setup.

- Test data can test program controls within the inventory system as well as general IT controls, such as passwords.

- Allows the team to obtain information directly from the system and test the actual inventory system and records rather than printouts from the system which could be incorrect.

- Potentially reduces the level of human error in testing and hence provide a better quality of audit evidence.

- Results from the use of automated techniques can be compared with traditional audit testing; if these two sources agree, then overall audit confidence will increase.

- The use of automated tools and techniques frees up audit team members to focus on judgmental and high risk areas, rather than number crunching.

- Enables the auditor to perform audit procedures throughout the year rather than just at the year end.

(iii)   Disadvantages

- The cost in the first year will be high as there will be significant set up costs, it will also be a time-consuming process which increases costs.

- As this is the first time that automated tools and techniques will be used on Lily's audit, then the team may require training.

- If Lily's inventory system is likely to change in the foreseeable future, then costly revisions may be required.

- The inventory system may not be compatible with the audit firm's technology, in which case bespoke software may be required which will increase the audit costs.

- If testing is performed over the live inventory system, then there is a risk that the data could be corrupted or lost.

- If testing is performed using copy files rather than live data, then there is the risk that these files are not genuine copies of the actual files.

- There must be adequate systems documentation available. If this is not the case for Lily, then it will be more difficult to devise appropriate automated procedures due to a lack of understanding of the inventory system.

- The data obtained may not be complete which will limit the assurance that can be obtained.

- The inventory balance is still influenced by subjective estimates and management judgement, e.g. work-in-progress and allowance for slow-moving inventory. Therefore, audit staff with appropriate experience and scepticism will still be required to audit these areas.

			Marking guide	Marks

Marking guide

<table>
<tr><td></td><td colspan="2"></td><td></td><td>Marks</td></tr>
<tr><td>(a)</td><td colspan="3">Control deficiencies and recommendations</td><td></td></tr>
<tr><td></td><td>•</td><td colspan="2">Warehouse manager supervising the count</td><td>2</td></tr>
<tr><td></td><td>•</td><td colspan="2">No division of responsibilities within each counting team</td><td>2</td></tr>
<tr><td></td><td>•</td><td colspan="2">Internal audit teams should be checking controls and performing sample counts</td><td>2</td></tr>
<tr><td></td><td>•</td><td colspan="2">No flagging of aisles once counting complete</td><td>2</td></tr>
<tr><td></td><td>•</td><td colspan="2">Additional inventory listed on sheets which are not sequentially numbered</td><td>2</td></tr>
<tr><td></td><td>•</td><td colspan="2">Inventory sheets not signed by counters</td><td>2</td></tr>
<tr><td></td><td>•</td><td colspan="2">Damaged goods not moved to central location</td><td>2</td></tr>
<tr><td></td><td>•</td><td colspan="2">Movements of inventory during the count</td><td>2</td></tr>
<tr><td></td><td>•</td><td colspan="2">Warehouse manager not qualified to assess the level of work-in-progress</td><td>2</td></tr>
<tr><td></td><td>•</td><td colspan="2">Warehouse manager not experienced enough to assess the quantities of raw materials</td><td>2</td></tr>
<tr><td></td><td colspan="3" align="right">Max 6 issues, 2 marks each</td><td>12</td></tr>
<tr><td>(b)</td><td colspan="3">Audit procedures during the inventory count</td><td></td></tr>
<tr><td></td><td>•</td><td colspan="2">Observe the counters to confirm if inventory count instructions are being followed</td><td>1</td></tr>
<tr><td></td><td>•</td><td colspan="2">Perform test counts inventory to sheets and sheets to inventory</td><td>1</td></tr>
<tr><td></td><td>•</td><td colspan="2">Confirm procedures for damaged goods are operating correctly</td><td>1</td></tr>
<tr><td></td><td>•</td><td colspan="2">Inspect damaged goods to confirm whether the level of damage is correctly noted</td><td>1</td></tr>
<tr><td></td><td>•</td><td colspan="2">Observe procedures for movements of inventory during the count</td><td>1</td></tr>
<tr><td></td><td>•</td><td colspan="2">Obtain a photocopy of the completed inventory sheets</td><td>1</td></tr>
<tr><td></td><td>•</td><td colspan="2">Identify and make a note of the last goods received notes and goods despatched notes</td><td>1</td></tr>
<tr><td></td><td>•</td><td colspan="2">Observe the procedures carried out by warehouse manager in assessing the level of work-in-progress</td><td>1</td></tr>
<tr><td></td><td>•</td><td colspan="2">Discuss with the warehouse manager how he has estimated the raw materials quantities</td><td>1</td></tr>
<tr><td></td><td>•</td><td colspan="2">Identify inventory held for third parties and ensure excluded from count</td><td>1</td></tr>
<tr><td></td><td colspan="3" align="right">Restricted to</td><td>6</td></tr>
<tr><td>(c)</td><td>(i)</td><td colspan="2">Substantive procedures</td><td></td></tr>
<tr><td></td><td></td><td>•</td><td>Calculate the inventory holding period</td><td>1</td></tr>
<tr><td></td><td></td><td>•</td><td>Produce an aged inventory analysis to identify any slow-moving goods</td><td>1</td></tr>
<tr><td></td><td></td><td>•</td><td>Cast the inventory listing</td><td>1</td></tr>
<tr><td></td><td></td><td>•</td><td>Select a sample of items for testing to confirm net realisable value (NRV) and/or cost</td><td>1</td></tr>
<tr><td></td><td></td><td>•</td><td>Recalculate cost and NRV for sample of inventory</td><td>1</td></tr>
<tr><td></td><td></td><td>•</td><td>Confirm cut-off</td><td>1</td></tr>
<tr><td></td><td></td><td>•</td><td>Confirm whether inventory adjustments noted during the count have been updated to inventory records.</td><td>1</td></tr>
<tr><td></td><td colspan="3" align="right">Restricted to</td><td>4</td></tr>
</table>

		Marking guide	
			Marks
(ii)	**Advantages**		
	•	Test a large volume of inventory data accurately and quickly	1
	•	Cost effective after setup	1
	•	Test data can test program controls as well as general IT controls	1
	•	Test the actual inventory system and records rather than printouts from the system	1
	•	Potentially reduces the level of human error in testing	1
	•	Results can be compared with traditional audit testing	1
	•	Free up audit team members to focus on judgmental and high risk areas	1
		Restricted to	4
(iii)	**Disadvantages**		
	•	Costs in the first year will be high	1
	•	Team may require training	1
	•	Changes in the inventory system may require costly revisions	1
	•	The inventory system may not be compatible with the audit firm's software	1
	•	If testing the live system, there is a risk the data could be corrupted or lost	1
	•	If using copy files rather than live data, there is the risk that these files are not genuine copies	1
	•	Adequate systems documentation must be available	1
	•	Data may not be complete	1
	•	Still requires audit staff with appropriate experience and scepticism to audit inventory	1
		Restricted to	4
Total			30

Examiner's comments

Part (a) required candidates to identify and explain, for the inventory count arrangements of Lily, deficiencies and suggest a recommendation for each deficiency. Most candidates performed very well on this part of the question. They were able to confidently identify deficiencies from the scenario. However, some candidates did not address the question requirement fully as they did not 'identify and explain'. Candidates identified, but did not go on to explain why this was a deficiency. For example 'additional inventory sheets are not numbered' would receive ½ mark, however to obtain the other ½ mark they needed to explain how this could cause problems during the inventory count such as 'the additional sheets could be lost resulting in understated inventory quantities'. The requirement to provide controls was also well answered. Most candidates were able to provide practical recommendations to address the deficiencies. The main exception to this was with regards to the issue of continued movements of goods during the count. The scenario stated that Lily undertakes continuous production; therefore to suggest 'that production is halted for the inventory count' demonstrated a failure to read and understand the scenario. The scenario is designed to help candidates and so they should not ignore elements of it. Some candidates incorrectly identified deficiencies from the scenario, demonstrating a fundamental lack of understanding of the purpose of an inventory count. For example, a significant minority believed that inventory sheets should contain inventory quantities when in fact this is incorrect, as this would encourage markers to just agree the stated quantities rather than counting properly.

In addition candidates felt that counters should not use ink on the count sheets as pencil would be easier for adjustments, again this is incorrect, as if the counts are in pencil then the quantities could be erroneously amended after the count. Also candidates felt that there should be more warehouse staff involved in the count, despite the self-review risk. Many candidates set their answer out in two columns being deficiency and recommendation. However, those who explained all of the deficiencies and then separately provided all of the recommendations tended to repeat themselves and possibly wasted some time. In addition, it was not uncommon to see candidates provide many more answers than required.

Part (b) required procedures the auditor should undertake during the inventory count of Lily. Performance was unsatisfactory on this part of the question. The requirement stated in capitals that procedures DURING the count were required; however a significant proportion of candidates ignored this word completely and provided procedures both before and after the count. Many answers actually stated 'before the count...', candidates must read the question requirements properly. Those candidates who had read the question properly often struggled to provide an adequate number of well described points. The common answers given were 'to observe the inventory counters' although candidates did not make it clear what they were observing for; or 'undertake test counts' but with no explanation of the direction of the test and whether it was for completeness or existence. Some candidates provided all possible inventory tests, in particular focusing on NRV testing. This demonstrated that candidates had learnt a standard list of inventory tests and rather than applying these to the question set just proceeded to list them all. This approach wastes time and tends not to score well as of the answers provided very few tended to be relevant.

Part (ci) required a description of four audit procedures that could be carried out for inventory using CAATs. Performance on this question was unsatisfactory. Candidates needed to apply their knowledge of CAATs to inventory procedures, many failed to do this. Again lots of candidates did not read the question properly and so despite the requirement to apply their answer to inventory, they proceeded to refer to tests on receivables and payables. Also many candidates appear not to actually understand what CAATs are, who uses them and how they work. Therefore many answers focused on the company using CAATs rather than the auditor, many procedures given were not related to CAATs for example 'discuss inventory valuation with the directors' or 'agree goods received notes to purchase invoices'. Those candidates who scored well tended to mainly focus on analytical review procedures for inventory that could be undertaken as part of audit software tests.

Part (cii) required an explanation of the advantages of using CAATs. This question was on the whole answered well. Candidates were able to identify an adequate number of advantages to score well on this part of the question. The main advantages given related to saving time; reducing costs; improving the accuracy of testing and the ability to test larger samples. A minority of candidates failed to explain their advantages; answers such as 'saves time' were commonly provided, this is not an explanation and so would not have scored well.

Part (ciii) required an explanation of the disadvantages of using CAATs. Again, this part of the question was answered well. Candidates were able to identify an adequate number of points to score well. The main disadvantages given related to increased costs; training requirements and the corruption of client data. It was apparent that candidates had learnt a standard list of points for CAATs.

229 PEAR INTERNATIONAL *Walk in the footsteps of a top tutor*

Key answer tips

Part (a) Controls deficiencies and recommendations questions are usually quite straight-forward, however, you must explain the deficiencies and controls in sufficient detail to score marks. If you are too brief you will only score ½ marks. When suggesting tests of control remember that you are looking for evidence that the client has implemented the control effectively. Do not suggest the auditor should perform the control as this doesn't prove the client has performed the control. Also be careful not to give substantive procedures as these have a different purpose to a test of control and will not score marks.

Part (b) requires substantive procedures in respect of additions and disposals of plant and equipment. A substantive procedure is used to test the numbers in the financial statements and focus on the financial statement assertions. Think of how you would obtain evidence that the client has correctly included the additions and removed the disposals.

(a)   Pear International's internal control

Deficiency	Control	Test of control
Currently the website is not integrated into inventory system. This can result in Pear accepting customer orders when they do not have the goods in inventory. This can cause them to lose sales and customer goodwill.	The website should be updated to include an interface into the inventory system; this should check inventory levels and only process orders if adequate inventory is held. If inventory is out of stock, this should appear on the website with an approximate waiting time.	Test data could be used to attempt to process orders via the website for items which are not currently held in inventory. The orders should be flagged as being out of stock and indicate an approximate waiting time.
For goods despatched by local couriers, customer signatures are not always obtained. Customers may falsely claim that they have not received their goods. Pear would not be able to prove that they had in fact despatched the goods and may result in goods being despatched twice. This could cause loss for the company.	Pear should remind all local couriers that customer signatures must be obtained as proof of despatch and payment will not be made for any despatches with missing signatures.	Select a sample of despatches by couriers and ask Pear for proof of despatch by viewing customer signatures.

Deficiency	Control	Test of control
There have been a number of situations where sales orders have not been fulfilled in a timely manner.	Once goods are despatched they should be matched to sales orders and flagged as fulfilled.	Review the report of outstanding sales orders. If significant, discuss with a responsible official to understand why there is still a significant time period between sales order and despatch date.
This can lead to a loss of customer goodwill and if it persists will damage the reputation of Pear as a reliable supplier.	The system should automatically flag any outstanding sales orders past a predetermined period, such as five days. This report should be reviewed by a responsible official.	Select a sample of sales orders and compare the date of order to the goods despatch date to ascertain whether this is within the acceptable predetermined period.
Customer credit limits are set by receivables ledger clerks.	Credit limits should be set by a senior member of the receivables ledger department and not by receivables ledger clerks. These limits should be regularly reviewed by a responsible official.	For a sample of new customers accepted in the year, review the authorisation of the credit limit, and ensure that this was performed by a responsible official.
Receivables ledger clerks are not sufficiently senior to perform this task and so may set limits too high, or too low.		Enquire of receivables ledger clerks as to who can set credit limits.
This could lead to a loss of sales if limits are set too low or irrecoverable debts if limits are set too high.		
Sales discounts are set by Pear's sales team.	All members of the sales team should be given authority to grant sales discounts up to a set limit. Any sales discounts above these limits should be authorised by sales area managers or the sales director.	Discuss with members of the sales team the process for setting sales discounts.
In order to boost their sales, members of the sales team may set the discounts too high.		Review the sales discount report for evidence of review by the sales director.
This will lead to a loss of revenue and profit for the company.	Regular review of sales discount levels should be undertaken by the sales director, and this review should be evidenced.	

Deficiency	Control	Test of control
Supplier statement reconciliations are no longer performed. Errors in the recording of purchases and payables may not be identified in a timely manner. This could result in late or incorrect payments to suppliers and a loss of supplier goodwill.	Supplier statement reconciliations should be performed on a monthly basis for all suppliers and these should be reviewed by a responsible official.	Review the file of reconciliations to ensure that they are being performed on a regular basis and that they have been reviewed by a responsible official.
Changes to supplier details in the payables ledger master file can be undertaken by payables ledger clerks. Key supplier data may be accidently amended or fictitious suppliers being set up. This increases the risk of fraud and loss for the company.	Only payables ledger supervisors should have the authority to make changes to master file data. This should be controlled via passwords. Regular review of any changes to master file data by a responsible official and this review should be evidenced.	Request a payables ledger clerk to attempt to access the master file and to make an amendment, the system should not allow this. Review a report of master data changes and review the authority of those making amendments.
Pear has considerable levels of surplus plant and equipment. Surplus unused plant increases storage costs and is at risk of theft. If the surplus plant is not disposed of the company could lose sundry income and incur additional costs which will reduce profit.	Regular review of the plant and equipment on the factory floor by senior factory personnel to identify any old or surplus equipment. As part of the capital expenditure process there should be a requirement to confirm the treatment of the equipment being replaced.	Observe the review process by senior factory personnel, identifying the treatment of any old equipment. Review processed capital expenditure forms to ascertain if the treatment of replaced equipment is stated.
Purchase requisitions are authorised by production supervisors. Production supervisors are not sufficiently independent or senior to authorise capital expenditure. This could lead to unnecessary cost for the company if capital expenditure is not needed by the company or if the best price is not obtained.	Capital expenditure authorisation levels to be established. Production supervisors should only be able to authorise low value items, any high value items should be authorised by the board.	Review a sample of authorised capital expenditure forms and identify if the correct signatory has authorised them.

(b) **Substantive procedures – Additions and disposals**

Additions

- Obtain a breakdown of additions, cast the list and agree to the non-current asset register to confirm completeness of plant & equipment (P&E).

- Select a sample of additions and agree cost to supplier invoice to confirm valuation.

- Verify rights and obligations by agreeing the addition of plant and equipment to a supplier invoice in the name of Pear.

- Review the list of additions and confirm that they relate to capital expenditure items rather than repairs and maintenance.

- For a sample of additions recorded in P&E physically verify them on the factory floor to confirm existence.

Disposals

- Obtain a breakdown of disposals, cast the list and agree all assets removed from the non-current asset register to confirm existence.

- Select a sample of disposals and agree sale proceeds to supporting documentation such as sundry sales invoices.

- Recalculate the profit/loss on disposal and agree to the income statement.

Marking guide		Marks
(a) **Control deficiencies, recommendations and tests of control**		
• Website not integrated into inventory system		3
• Customer signatures		3
• Unfulfilled sales orders		3
• Customer credit limits		3
• Sales discounts		3
• Supplier statement reconciliations		3
• Payables ledger master file		3
• Surplus plant and equipment		3
• Authorisation of capital expenditure		3
	Max 5 issues, 3 marks each	15
(b) **Additions**		
• Cast list of additions and agree to non-current asset register		1
• Vouch cost to recent supplier invoice		1
• Agree addition to a supplier invoice in the name of Pear to confirm rights and obligations		1
• Review additions and confirm capital expenditure items rather than repairs and maintenance		1
• Physically verify them on the factory floor to confirm existence		1
Disposals		
• Cast list of disposals and agree removed from non-current asset register		1
• Vouch sale proceeds to supporting documentation such as sundry sales invoices		1
• Recalculate the profit/loss on disposal		1
	Max	5
Total		20

Examiner's comments

Part (a) required candidates to identify and explain deficiencies, suggest a control for each deficiency and recommend tests of controls to assess if the internal controls of Pear were operating effectively. Most candidates performed well on this part of the question. They were able to confidently identify deficiencies from the scenario. However, many candidates did not address the question requirement fully as they did not 'identify and explain'. Candidates identified, but did not go on to explain why this was a deficiency. For example 'couriers do not always record customer signatures as proof of delivery' would receive ½ mark, however to obtain the other ½ mark they needed to explain how this could cause problems for the company such as customers could dispute receipt of goods and Pear would need to resend them. The requirement to provide controls was generally well answered. Some candidates gave objectives rather than controls for example 'Pear should ensure that all sales are forwarded to the despatch department' without explaining what the control should be to ensure that this happened. In addition some candidates provided controls which were just too vague to attain the 1 mark available per control. The requirement to provide tests of control was not answered well. Many candidates simply repeated their controls and added 'to check that' or 'to make sure'. These are not tests of control. Also many candidates suggested that the control be tested through observation. For example 'observe the process for authorisation of sales discounts'. This is a weak test as it is likely that if the auditor is present that the control will operate effectively; instead a better test would be 'to review sales invoices for evidence of authorisation of discounts by sales manager.' The requirement was for five deficiencies; it was not uncommon to see candidates provide many more than five. Often in one paragraph they would combine two or three points such as authorisation of credit limits and of sales discounts. When points were combined, some candidates did not fully provide controls and tests of controls for each of the given points, therefore failing to maximise their marks.

Part (b) required substantive procedures the auditor should perform on year-end property, plant and equipment (PPE) additions and disposals. Performance was mixed on this part of the question. Candidates who scored well often did so by providing a number of tests for each area, each test was average and so scored ½ mark each and so they managed to attain full marks in this way. However, some candidates provided detailed procedures and so achieved the 1 mark available per test. This is better utilisation of time. The requirement verb was to 'describe' therefore sufficient detail was required to score 1 mark per test. Candidates are reminded that substantive procedures are a core topic area and they must be able to produce relevant detailed procedures. Many tests given were just too brief. Answers such as 'check accounting records to ensure correct treatment of disposals' are far too vague as it does not explain how we gain comfort that disposals have been recorded correctly. In addition answers such as 'ensure that additions are correctly included' are objectives rather than substantive procedures. Other common mistakes made by candidates were:

- Providing general PPE tests such as for depreciation, rather than just focusing on additions and disposals.

- Giving unrealistic tests such as 'to physically verify on the factory floor that an asset has been disposed of' if it's been disposed of then how can it be physically verified!

- Focusing too much on whether the asset has been disposed of for the best possible price; this is a concern of management and not of the auditor.

SUBSTANTIVE PROCEDURES, COMPLETION AND REPORTING

230 SPADEFISH *Walk in the footsteps of a top tutor*

Key answer tips

Part (a) requires audit procedures to investigate exceptions arising from a receivables circularisation. Where differences are found, these must be investigated to understand the reasons for the differences. This may be due to errors, which will need to be corrected, or due to timing differences, which will need to be confirmed.

Part (b) requires audit procedures in relation to the allowance for receivables. The client must make an allowance for expected credit losses. Your procedures should focus on whether the provision is likely to be adequate to cover the credit losses which may occur in the future. Remember that the client is likely to want to make as little allowance as possible as the greater the allowance, the lower the level or reported profits and assets.

Part (c) requires an explanation of the going concern indicators of a client. Your explanation needs to describe the impact to the company of the indicator identified.

Part (d) requires procedures to assess whether the company is a going concern. Some procedures can be general procedures that must always be performed in relation to going concern, such as obtaining a written representation or reviewing and assessing the cash flow forecast. However, you should always try to include some procedures specific to the scenario information.

(a) Exceptions in the receivables circularisation

The following steps should be undertaken in regard to the exceptions arising in the positive receivables circularisation:

Albacore Co

– For the non-response from Albacore Co, with the client's permission, the team should arrange to send a follow-up circularisation.

– If Albacore Co does not respond to the follow up, then with the client's permission, the auditor should telephone the customer and ask whether they are able to respond in writing to the circularisation request.

– If there is still no response, then the auditor should undertake alternative procedures to confirm the balance owing from Albacore Co. Such as detailed testing of the balance by agreeing to sales invoices and goods dispatched notes (GDN).

Flounder Co

– For the response from Flounder Co, with a difference of $5,850 the auditor should identify any disputed amounts, and identify whether these relate to timing differences or whether there are possible errors in the records of Triggerfish.

– If the difference is due to timing, such as cash in transit, this should be agreed to post year-end cash receipts in the cash book.

– If the difference relates to goods in transit, then this should be agreed to a pre year-end GDN.

Menhaden Co

- The reason for the credit balance with Menhaden should be discussed with the credit controller or finance department to understand how a credit balance has arisen.

- Review the payables ledger to identify if Menhaden is a supplier as well as a customer; if so, a purchase invoice may have been posted in error to the receivables rather than payables ledger.

- If the difference is due to credit notes, this should be agreed to pre year-end credit notes dispatched around the year-end date.

- The receivables ledger should be reviewed to identify any possible mis-postings as this could be a reason for the difference with Menhaden Co.

(b)   Allowance for trade receivables

- Discuss with the finance director the rationale for not providing against any receivables and consider the reasonableness of the allowance.

- Obtain a breakdown of the opening allowance of $125,000 and consider if the receivables provided for in the prior year have been fully recovered as a result of the additional credit control procedures or if they have now been fully written off.

- Inspect the aged trade receivables ledger to identify any slow moving or old receivable balances and discuss the status of these balances with the credit controllers to assess whether they are likely to be received.

- Review whether there are any after-date cash receipts for identified slow moving/old receivable balances.

- Review customer correspondence to identify any balances which are in dispute or are unlikely to be paid and confirm if these have been considered when determining the allowance.

- Inspect board minutes to identify whether there are any significant concerns in relation to payments by customers and assess if these have been considered when determining the allowance.

- Recalculate the potential level of trade receivables which are not recoverable and compare to allowance and discuss differences with management.

(c)   Going concern indicators

Marlin Co has paid some of its suppliers considerably later than usual and only after many reminders; hence some of them have withdrawn credit terms meaning the company must pay cash on delivery. This suggests that the company was struggling to meet their liability as they fell due and will also put significant additional pressure on the company's cash flow, because the company will have to pay for goods on delivery but is likely to have to wait for cash from its receivables due to credit terms.

Marlin Co's main supplier who provides over 60% of the company's specialist equipment has just stopped trading. If the equipment is highly specialised, there is a risk that Marlin Co may not be able to obtain these products from other suppliers which would impact on the company's ability to trade. More likely, there are other suppliers available but they may be more expensive or may not offer favourable credit terms which will increase the outflows of Marlin Co and worsen the cash flow position.

Marlin Co's overdraft has grown significantly during the year and is due for renewal within the next month. If the bank does not renew the overdraft and the company is unable to obtain alternative finance, then it may not be able to continue to meet its liabilities as they fall due, especially if suppliers continue to demand cash on delivery, and the company may not be able to continue to trade.

In order to conserve cash, Marlin Co has decided not to pay a final dividend for the year ended 30 April 20X5. This may result in shareholders losing faith in the company and they may attempt to sell their shares; in addition, they are highly unlikely to invest further equity, and Marlin Co may need to raise finance to repay their overdraft.

(d)   Going concern procedures

–   Obtain the company's cash flow forecast and review the cash in and outflows. Assess the assumptions for reasonableness and discuss the findings with management to understand if the company will have sufficient cash flows.

–   Perform a sensitivity analysis on the cash flows to understand the margin of safety the company has in terms of its net cash in/outflow.

–   Evaluate management's plans for future actions, including their contingency plans in relation to ongoing financing and plans for generating revenue, and consider the feasibility of these plans.

–   Review the company's post year-end sales and order book to assess if the levels of trade are likely to increase and if the revenue figures in the cash flow forecast are reasonable.

–   Review any agreements with the bank to determine whether any covenants have been breached, especially in relation to the overdraft.

–   Review any bank correspondence to assess the likelihood of the bank renewing the overdraft facility.

–   Review post year-end correspondence with suppliers to identify if any have threatened legal action or any others have refused to supply goods.

–   Inspect any contracts or correspondence with suppliers to confirm supply of the company's specialist equipment. If no new supplier has been confirmed, discuss with management their plans to ensure the company can continue to meet customer demand.

–   Enquire of the lawyers of Marlin Co as to the existence of any litigation.

–   Perform audit tests in relation to subsequent events to identify any items which might indicate or mitigate the risk of going concern not being appropriate.

–   Review the post year-end board minutes to identify any other issues which might indicate further financial difficulties for the company.

–   Review post year-end management accounts to assess if in line with cash flow forecast.

–   Consider whether any additional disclosures as required by IAS 1 Presentation of Financial Statements in relation to material uncertainties over going concern should be made in the financial statements.

–   Consider whether the going concern basis is appropriate for the preparation of the financial statements.

–   Obtain a written representation confirming the directors' view that Marlin Co is a going concern.

Marking guide

		Marks
(a)	**Audit procedures – trade receivables circularisation**	
	• Albacore Co	3
	• Flounder Co	3
	• Menhaden Co	3
	Restricted to	8
(b)	**Substantive procedures – allowance for trade receivables**	
	• Discuss the rationale and reasonableness with the finance director	1
	• Obtain breakdown of opening allowance and confirm recovered	1
	• Inspect the aged receivables listing and discuss old or slow moving balances	1
	• Perform after-date cash testing on identified slow moving and old balances	1
	• Review customer correspondence for evidence of disputed balances	1
	• Inspect board minutes for balances which may not be recovered	1
	• Recalculate potential level of irrecoverable balance and compare to allowance and discuss differences	1
	Restricted to	4
(c)	**Going concern indicators**	
	• Withdrawal of credit – impact explained	1
	• Loss of main supplier – impact explained	1
	• Overdraft facility due for renewal – impact explained	1
	• No final dividend – impact explained	1
	Restricted to	3
(d)	**Going concern procedures**	
	• Obtain cash flow forecast and assess assumptions	1
	• Perform sensitivity analysis on cash flow forecast	1
	• Evaluate management's plans for future actions	1
	• Review post year-end order book to assess levels of trade	1
	• Review agreements with the bank to determine whether any covenants breached	1
	• Review bank correspondence for evidence of renewal	1
	• Review correspondence with suppliers for dispute/legal action	1
	• Inspect contracts with supplier to confirm supply	1
	• Obtain confirmation from company lawyers about any legal action	1
	• Review post year-end board minutes for any indications of financial difficulties	1
	• Review management accounts to assess if in line with cash flow	1
	• Review financial statement disclosure	1
	• Consider if going concern basis is appropriate	1
	• Obtain a written representation	1
	Restricted to	5
Total		20

Examiner's comments

This 20-mark question was based on Spadefish Co, an audit firm undertaking the audits of Triggerfish Co, a manufacturer of hair products and Marlin Co a distributor of electronic goods. This question tested candidates' knowledge of substantive procedures for receivables. The question also tested candidates' knowledge of going concern indicators and audit procedures. Overall performance was disappointing.

Part (a) for eight marks required candidates to describe procedures the auditor should perform to resolve exceptions noted during a receivables circularisation for Triggerfish Co. Performance on this requirement was very disappointing. One mark was awarded for each well-described audit procedure. Candidates were provided with three customer balances as per Triggerfish's receivables ledger and the response from the receivables circularisation. It was disappointing to see that a significant minority of candidates did not even attempt this requirement or simply provided one very brief procedure for each of the three exceptions. Of the three customer balances, Albacore Co was best attempted by candidates. Well prepared candidates gained marks for procedures such as after date cash receipts testing as an alternative procedure, chasing the customer to request a response or sending a follow up circularisation request. The second balance in respect of Flounder Co related to a potential overstatement or timing difference. The third balance in respect of Menhaden Co was a credit balance in the receivables ledger but a debit balance in the circularisation response. Candidates seemed to really struggle with these exceptions and other than suggesting 'discuss the reason for the difference with management' they could not provide many other relevant procedures. Candidates incorrectly focused on 'agreeing to sales invoices and goods dispatched notes' or trying to understand how the credit balance in Menhaden Co may have occurred, without providing any procedures. For the balance with Flounder Co, candidates needed to focus their tests on items which could have been in transit at the year end to have caused the difference. Procedures around cash in transit or goods in transit were required. For the balance with Menhaden Co, procedures should have focused on credit notes or identifying mis-postings. A significant minority of candidates produced very repetitive responses, providing audit procedures for Albacore Co and then simply copying these tests for each of the other two exceptions. Candidates should note that duplicating tests will not result in credit being awarded more than once. Candidates are reminded that substantive procedures are an important part of the syllabus and it is imperative they are able to attempt different types of question requirements.

Part (b) for four marks required candidates to describe substantive procedures the auditor should perform to obtain sufficient and appropriate evidence in relation to Triggerfish Co's allowance for receivables. Performance on this requirement was also very disappointing. One mark was awarded for each well-described audit procedure. It was disappointing that despite the question requiring procedures for the allowance for receivables, a significant number of candidates listed generic procedures for trade receivables such as receivables circularisation, cut off testing and reviewing disclosure. The majority of these procedures were not awarded any credit as they were not focused on the allowance. Candidates must carefully read the requirement of the question and tailor their answers accordingly.

Where candidates did attempt to audit the allowance, many of the procedures were not relevant. For example, undertaking analytical review of the allowance when the scenario stated it had been significantly reduced in the year, and reviewing board minutes for authorisation of the allowance were not awarded credit as they were not valid. As addressed in previous examiner's reports candidates must strive to understand substantive procedures. Learning a generic list of tests will not translate to exam success, as they must be applied to the question requirements.

Part (c) for four marks required the candidate to identify and explain indicators that Marlin Co was not a going concern. Questions such as this typically require indicators to be identified (½ mark each) and explained (½ mark each). Performance was satisfactory. The scenario contained more issues than were required to be discussed. The majority of students were able to identify three going concern indicators as required. A number of candidates incorrectly identified that 'suppliers being paid later than usual' was a going concern indicator. Many companies choose to pay suppliers late in order to maximise working capital, and on its own this would not be enough to raise concerns over going concern. Instead credit was awarded for 'suppliers having withdrawn credit or requiring cash on delivery.' The explanation of the indicators caused difficulties for some candidates, with generic answers being given such as 'this will cause cash flow problems for the company'. In order to be awarded the second ½ mark, candidates needed to explain how the indicator could cause cash flow issues for Marlin Co. Those candidates who did not score well provided going concern indicators which were not in the scenario such as 'sale of significant assets', these had clearly been learnt as a generic list of indicators of going concern.

Part (d) for five marks required candidates to describe audit procedures to assess whether Marlin Co was a going concern. Performance was satisfactory on this requirement. One mark was awarded for each well described substantive procedure. Those candidates who had practiced past questions scored well, noting procedures such as reviewing the cash flow forecast, discussions with management regarding future plans, reviewing board minutes and obtaining a written representation. Those candidates who did not score well provided procedures which lacked sufficient detail, for example, 'discuss with management' without explaining what was to be discussed. Vague procedures such as this are not awarded any credit. In addition, some candidates provided irrelevant procedures such as undertaking ratio analysis or reviewing bank statements. These procedures would not provide evidence as to whether the company was a going concern or not and so were not awarded any credit.

231 HYACINTH *Walk in the footsteps of a top tutor*

Key answer tips

This question focuses mainly on substantive procedures. A substantive procedure is used to test the figures in the financial statements with the aim of identifying material misstatements. One approach to generating audit procedures is to think about the financial statement assertions which need to be tested and design a procedure which does that. Another approach that can be used is to think about the audit techniques of inspection, enquiry, etc. and design procedures using those techniques. Whilst you may be able to use generic procedures learned from the text book, be careful to make sure the procedures you give address any specific issues mentioned in the scenario. For a balance such as research and development costs, think about how you can confirm whether the criteria from the relevant accounting standard have been met.

Part (d) requires discussion of a subsequent event. First of all discuss whether the event is an adjusting or non-adjusting event. You will need to assess whether the impact of the event is material. Next, suggest procedures that will provide sufficient appropriate evidence as to the level of adjustment if it is an adjusting event or the information that will need to be disclosed if it is a material non-adjusting event.

(a)   Inventory valuation

-   Obtain the breakdown of WIP and agree a sample of WIP assessed during the inventory count to the WIP schedule, agreeing the percentage completion to that recorded at the inventory count.

-   For a sample of inventory items (finished goods and WIP), obtain the relevant cost sheets and agree raw material costs to recent purchase invoices, labour costs to time sheets or payroll records and confirm overheads allocated are of a production related nature.

-   Examine post year-end credit notes to determine whether there have been returns which could signify that a write down is required.

-   Select a sample of year-end finished goods and compare cost with post year-end sales invoices to ascertain if net realisable value (NRV) is above cost or if an adjustment is required.

-   Discuss the basis of WIP valuation with management and assess its reasonableness.

-   Select a sample of items included in WIP at the year end and ascertain the final unit cost price by verifying costs to be incurred to completion to relevant supporting documentation. Compare to the unit sales price included in sales invoices post year-end to assess NRV.

-   Review aged inventory reports and identify any slow moving goods, discuss with management why these items have not been written down or if an allowance is required.

-   For the defective batch of product Crocus, review board minutes and discuss with management their plans for selling these goods, and why they believe these goods have a NRV of $90,000.

-   If any Crocus products have been sold post year end, review the sales invoice to assess NRV.

-   Agree the cost of $450,000 for product Crocus to supporting documentation to confirm the raw material cost, labour cost and any overheads attributed to the cost.

-   Confirm if the final adjustment for the damaged product is $360,000 ($450,000 – $90,000) and discuss with management if this adjustment has been made. If so, follow through the write down to confirm.

(b)   Research and development

-   Obtain and cast a schedule of intangible assets, agree the closing balances to the general ledger, trial balance and draft financial statements.

-   Discuss with the finance director the rationale for the four-year useful life and consider its reasonableness.

-   Recalculate the amortisation charge for a sample of intangible assets which have commenced production and confirm that it is in line with the amortisation policy of straight line over four years and that amortisation only commenced from the point of production.

-   For the three new computing software projects, discuss with management the details of each project along with the stage of development and whether it has been capitalised or expensed.

- For those expensed as research, agree the costs incurred to invoices and supporting documentation and to inclusion in profit or loss.

- For those capitalised as development, agree costs incurred to invoices.

- Confirm technically feasible and intention to complete the project by discussion with development managers or review of feasibility reports.

- Review market research reports to confirm Hyacinth Co has the ability to sell the product once complete and probable future economic benefits will arise.

- Review the costs, projected revenue and cash flow budgets for the each of the three projects to confirm Hyacinth Co has adequate resources to complete the development stage and that probable future economic benefits exist. Agree the budgets to supporting documentation.

- Review the disclosures for intangible assets in the draft financial statements to verify that they are in accordance with IAS 38 *Intangible Assets*.

(c)   Sales tax liability

- Agree the year-end sales tax liability in the trial balance to the tax return/reconciliation submitted to the tax authority and cast the return/reconciliation.

- Agree the quarterly sales tax charged equates to 15% of the last quarter's sales as per the sales day book.

- Recalculate the sales tax incurred as per the reconciliation is equal to 15% of the final quarter's purchases and expenses as per the purchase day book.

- Recalculate the amount payable to the tax authority as being sales tax charged less sales tax incurred.

- Compare the year-end sales tax liability to the prior year balance or budget and investigate any significant differences.

- Agree the subsequent payment to the post year-end cash book and bank statements to confirm completeness and that it has been paid in line with the terms of the tax authority.

- Review any current and post year-end correspondence with the tax authority to assess whether there are any additional outstanding payments due. If so, confirm they are included in the year-end liability.

- Review any disclosures made of the sales tax liability to ensure that it is shown as a current liability and assess whether disclosures are in compliance with accounting standards and legislation.

(d)   Subsequent event

A flood has occurred at the off-site warehouse and property, plant and equipment and inventory valued at $0.7 million have been damaged and now have no scrap value. The directors do not believe they are likely to be able to claim on the company's insurance for the damaged assets. This event occurred after the reporting period and is not an event which provides evidence of a condition at the year end and so this is a non-adjusting event.

The damaged assets of $0.7 million are material as they represent 10.9% ($0.7m/$6.4m) of profit before tax and 3.0% ($0.7m/$23.2m) of total assets. As a material non-adjusting event, the assets do not need to be written down to zero in this financial year. However, the directors should consider including a disclosure note detailing the flood and the value of assets impacted.

The following audit procedures should be applied to form a conclusion on any amendment:

– Obtain a schedule showing the damaged property, plant and equipment and agree the net book value to the non-current assets register to confirm the total value of affected assets.

– Obtain a schedule of the water damaged inventory, visit the off-site warehouse and physically inspect the impacted inventory. Confirm the quantity of goods present in the warehouse to the schedule; agree the original cost to pre year-end production costs.

– Review the condition of other PPE and inventory to confirm all damaged assets identified.

– Review the damaged property, plant and equipment and inventory and discuss with management the basis for the zero scrap value assessment.

– Discuss with management why they do not believe that they are able to claim on their insurance; if a claim were to be made, then only uninsured losses would require disclosure, and this may be an immaterial amount.

– Discuss with management whether they will disclose the effect of the flood, as a non-adjusting event, in the year-end financial statements.

Marking guide		Marks
(a) **Substantive procedures – valuation of inventory**		
• Agree percentage completion recorded at inventory count to final inventory records		1
• Confirm costs to invoice/timesheets		1
• Inspect post year-end sales invoices for finished goods to assess NRV		1
• Discuss basis of WIP valuation with management		1
• Inspect WIP valuation with sales prices less costs to complete		1
• Review aged inventory reports and discuss allowance		1
• Discuss with management basis of valuation for Crocus products		1
• Inspect post year-end sales value of Crocus products		1
• Confirm adjustment regarding Crocus products		1
	Restricted to	6
(b) **Substantive procedures – R&D expenditure**		
• Obtain schedule, cast and agree to trial balance		1
• Review reasonableness of useful lives		1
• Recalculate amortisation and confirm in line with policy		1
• Discuss with management treatment of costs for new products		1
• Agree research costs expensed		1
• For capitalised costs, confirm IAS 38 criteria met		1
• Inspect budgets to confirm adequate resources to complete		1
• Review disclosure and confirm in line with accounting standards		1
	Restricted to	4

		Marks
	Marking guide	
		Marks
(c)	**Substantive procedures – accrual for sales tax liability**	
	• Obtain schedule/return, cast and agree to trial balance	1
	• Recalculate sales tax in relation to sales and agree to return	1
	• Recalculate sales tax in relation to purchases and agree to return	1
	• Recalculate overall amount due to tax authority	1
	• Compare liability to prior year end, investigate differences	1
	• Confirm payment to post year-end cashbook and bank statements	1
	• Review correspondence with the tax authority for evidence of additional liability	1
	• Review disclosure and confirm in line with IAS 37	1
	Restricted to	**4**
(d)	**Subsequent event**	
	• Discussion of amendment	3
	• Audit procedures	3
	Restricted to	**6**
Total		**20**

Examiner's comments

This 20-mark question was based on Hyacinth Co, a manufacturer of computer components. This question tested candidates' knowledge of substantive procedures for inventory, research and development, and the year-end sales tax liability. The question also tested candidates' knowledge of the treatment of subsequent events in the financial statements. Overall performance was mixed.

Part (a) for six marks required candidates to describe substantive procedures the auditor should perform to obtain sufficient and appropriate audit evidence in relation to the valuation of Hyacinth Co's inventory. Performance on this requirement was disappointing. One mark was awarded for each well-described audit procedure. The most common procedures provided by candidates were confirming raw material costs to purchase invoices, and comparing post year-end sales invoices to cost to assess net realisable value. While it was pleasing that a significant number of candidates noted analytical review procedures, these were often not adequately explained for a full one mark. For example, many candidates only noted 'compare year-end inventory days with the prior year' (this was awarded ½ mark), for an additional ½ mark the candidate needed to also state 'and investigate any significant differences'. It was disappointing that despite the requirement stating procedures for the 'valuation' of inventory, a significant number of candidates listed procedures for the existence and completeness of inventory such as 'attending the inventory count'. This was not awarded any credit. Candidates must carefully read the requirement of the question and tailor their answers accordingly. In addition, many candidates did not specifically refer to audit procedures for the Crocus product which had not met customer quality and technical standards. Candidates are advised again to carefully read the scenario and tailor their procedures to address the issues described.

Part (b) for four marks required candidates to describe substantive procedures the auditor should perform to obtain sufficient and appropriate evidence in relation to Hyacinth Co's research and development expenditure. Performance on this requirement was mixed. One mark was awarded for each well-described audit procedure. The most common procedures provided by candidates were to cast the schedule of intangible assets, agree it to the trial balance, and discuss with management if the new projects were capitalised or expensed. In order to score well in this very commonly tested area, candidates needed to explain how a procedure should be performed. For example, 'ensure the four year amortisation policy is reasonable' would not have gained full credit. The candidate needed to explain how the auditor could achieve this. For one mark the candidate needed to state 'discuss with the finance director the rationale for the four-year useful life and consider its reasonableness'.

While it was pleasing that a significant number of candidates noted the auditor should 'review the disclosures of intangibles in the financial statements' (½ mark), it was disappointing that candidates did not also state 'and verify that they are in line with accounting standards' to be credited a further ½ mark. Candidates are reminded that substantive procedures must be well explained to be awarded a full one mark. It was pleasing that candidates noted (for 1 mark) that 'if capitalised, agree compliance with the criteria in IAS 38 for capitalisation'. However it was disappointing that few candidates suggested detailed testing to ensure this compliance. For example, very few candidates noted 'review market research reports to confirm the ability to sell the product'. It was disappointing that many candidates listed generic audit procedures, which were not relevant to the scenario. For example, a significant number of candidates noted analytical review procedures with the prior year, which was not appropriate.

As addressed in previous examiner's reports, candidates must strive to understand substantive procedures. Learning a generic list of tests will not translate to exam success, as they must be applied to the question requirements.

Part (c) for four marks required candidates to describe substantive procedures to obtain sufficient and appropriate audit evidence in relation to Hyacinth Co's year-end sales tax liability. Performance was disappointing. One mark was awarded for each well-described audit procedure. The most common procedures provided by candidates were analytical review procedures and after-date cash payment. A significant minority of candidates disappointingly listed procedures for revenue rather than sales tax, and/or listed procedures to audit the sales tax system throughout the year rather than testing the year-end liability. Candidates again are advised to read the question carefully.

Part (d) for six marks required candidates to (i) explain whether the financial statements required amendment in relation to a flood and (ii) describe audit procedures, which should be performed in order to form a conclusion on any required amendment. One mark was available per valid point and the marks were split equally between each part.

Performance for part (i) was reasonable. A significant number of candidates scored well by calculating materiality, concluding the 'matter was material', and stating that 'the financial statements required amendment'. However, it was disappointing that few candidates stated either that 'a disclosure note was necessary' or specifically stated that 'it was a non-adjusting event'.

Performance for part (ii) was disappointing. Despite the scenario stating that 'the company is unlikely to be able to claim on its insurance', a significant number of candidates inappropriately suggested 'writing to the insurance company'. A significant number of candidates also discussed the potential impact on the auditor's report, but this was not a requirement of the question. Candidates are again reminded to read the question requirement carefully.

232 JASMINE *Walk in the footsteps of a top tutor*

Key answer tips

This question focuses mainly on substantive procedures. A substantive procedure is used to test the figures in the financial statements with the aim of identifying material misstatements. One approach to generating audit procedures is to think about the financial statement assertions which need to be tested and design a procedure which does that. Another approach that can be used is to think about the audit techniques of inspection, enquiry, etc. and design procedures using those techniques. Whilst you may be able to use generic procedures learned from the text book, be careful to make sure the procedures you give address any specific issues mentioned in the scenario. For example, part (a) asks for substantive procedures over receivables excluding performing a circularisation. Part (b) requires procedures over Jasmine's bank balance which include an overdraft and savings accounts. It also states that the accounts are not reconciled and that the overdraft is due for renewal, therefore procedures will need to be performed in respect of these issues.

Part (c) requires procedures over the going concern status of Jasmine. Here you need to perform procedures that will provide sufficient appropriate evidence that the company can afford to pay its liabilities when they fall due. You will need to obtain evidence to assess the likely cash inflows and outflows for the year ahead.

Part (d) asks for the audit reporting implications if adequate and inadequate disclosures regarding going concern are made. Remember that the audit opinion should only be modified if the financial statements are not prepared in accordance with the financial reporting framework. If the financial statements are prepared properly, the auditor may need to include additional communication to the users regarding matters disclosed by the client if they are fundamental to the user's understanding.

(a) Trade receivables

- Obtain the aged receivables listing and agree to the balance on the receivables ledger control account and trial balance.

- Review the aged trade receivables ledger to identify any slow moving or old balances, discuss the status of these balances with the credit controller to assess whether they are likely to pay.

- Select a representative sample of trade receivables and review for any after-date cash receipts. Ensure that a sample of slow moving/old receivable balances is also selected.

- Review customer correspondence to identify any balances which are in dispute or unlikely to be paid and discuss with management.

- Review board minutes to identify whether there are any significant concerns in relation to payments by customers.

- Calculate the average receivables collection period and compare this to the prior year and investigate any significant differences.

- Inspect post year-end sales returns/credit notes and consider whether an additional allowance against receivables is required.

- Obtain a breakdown of the allowance for trade receivables, recalculate and compare to any potentially irrecoverable balances to assess if the allowance is adequate.

- Select a sample of goods despatched notes (GDN) immediately before and after the year end and follow through to the receivables ledger to ensure they are recorded in the correct accounting period.

- Select a sample of year-end receivables balances and agree back to valid supporting documentation of sales invoices, GDNs and sales orders to ensure existence.

(b) **Bank balances**

- Obtain a bank confirmation letter from Jasmine Co's bankers for all of its accounts.

- Agree all accounts listed on the bank confirmation letter to the company's bank reconciliations or the trial balance/general ledger to ensure completeness of bank balances.

- For the current account, obtain Jasmine Co's bank reconciliation and cast to check the additions to ensure arithmetical accuracy.

- Agree the balance per the bank reconciliation to an original year-end bank statement and to the bank confirmation letter.

- Agree the reconciliation's balance per the cash book to the year-end cash book.

- Trace all the outstanding lodgements to the pre year-end cash book, post year-end bank statement and also to the paying-in book pre year end.

- Trace all unpresented cheques through to a pre year-end cash book and post year-end bank statement. For any unusual amounts or significant delays, obtain explanations from management.

- Examine any old unpresented cheques to assess whether they need to be written back.

- Review the cash book and bank statements for any unusual items or large transfers around the year end, as this could be evidence of window dressing.

- Examine the bank confirmation letter for details of any security provided by Jasmine Co, with regards to the bank overdraft or any legal right of set-off as this may require disclosure.

- For the savings bank accounts, review any reconciling items on the year-end bank reconciliations and agree to supporting documentation.

- Review the financial statements to ensure that the disclosure of bank balances is complete and accurate and classified appropriately between current assets and current liabilities.

(c) **Going concern procedures**

- Obtain the company's cash flow forecast and review the cash inflows and outflows. Assess the assumptions for reasonableness and discuss the findings with management to understand if the company will have sufficient cash.

- Perform a sensitivity analysis on the cash flows to understand the margin of safety the company has in terms of its net cash in/outflow.

- Evaluate management's plans for future actions, including their contingency plans in relation to ongoing financing and plans for generating revenue, and consider the feasibility of these plans.

- Review the company's post year-end sales and order book to assess if the levels of trade are likely to increase and if the revenue figures in the cash flow forecast are reasonable.

- Review any agreements with the bank to determine whether any covenants have been breached, especially in relation to the overdraft.

- Review any bank correspondence to assess the likelihood of the bank renewing the overdraft facility.

- Review post year-end correspondence with suppliers to identify if any have threatened legal action or any others have refused to supply goods.

- With the client's permission, enquire of the lawyers of Jasmine Co as to the existence of any litigation and if so, the likely outcome of any litigation.

- Perform audit tests in relation to subsequent events to identify any items which might indicate or mitigate the risk of going concern not being appropriate.

- Review the post year-end board minutes to identify any other issues which might indicate further financial difficulties for the company.

- Review post year-end management accounts to assess if in line with cash flow forecast.

- Consider whether any additional disclosures as required by IAS 1 *Presentation of Financial Statements* in relation to material uncertainties over going concern should be made in the financial statements.

- Consider whether the going concern basis is appropriate for the preparation of the financial statements.

- Obtain a written representation confirming the directors' view that Jasmine Co is a going concern.

(d) **Auditor's report**

As the outcome regarding the negotiations for the overdraft facility renewal will not be known at the time of signing the auditor's report, there is a material uncertainty which may cast significant doubt on the company's ability to continue as a going concern. The impact on the auditor's report depends on whether this uncertainty is deemed to be adequately disclosed in the financial statements.

Disclosure adequate

If the disclosures are adequate, then the auditor's report will need to include a material uncertainty related to going concern section.

The section will state that the audit opinion is not modified, indicate that there is a material uncertainty and will cross reference to the disclosure note made by management.

It would be included after the opinion and basis for opinion paragraph.

Disclosure inadequate

If the disclosures made by management are not adequate, the audit opinion will need to be modified as there is a material misstatement relating to inadequate disclosure.

The failure to adequately disclose is likely to be material but not pervasive due to the ongoing nature of the negotiations and so a qualified opinion will be issued.

The opinion paragraph will state that 'except for' the failure to adequately disclose the uncertainty, the financial statements give a true and fair view.

The report will contain a basis for opinion paragraph, subsequent to the opinion paragraph, explaining that a material uncertainty exists and that the financial statements do not adequately disclose this matter.

	Marking guide	
		Marks
(a)	**Substantive procedures – trade receivables**	
	• Obtain aged receivables listing, cast and agree to TB	1
	• Review listing for old balances and discuss with management	1
	• Perform cash after-date testing	1
	• Inspect customer correspondence for evidence of disputed items and discuss with management	1
	• Calculate receivables collection period, compare to PY and investigate differences	1
	• Inspect post year-end returns and consider need for additional allowance	1
	• Obtain a breakdown of the allowance, recalculate and consider adequacy	1
	• Select sample of GDNs from before and after year end and confirm recorded in correct period	1
	• Select a sample of balances and agree to order, GDN and invoice	1
		–––
	Restricted to	**5**
		–––
(b)	**Substantive procedures – bank balances**	
	• Bank confirmation letter	1
	• Agree to bank reconciliation and TB	1
	• Cast bank reconciliations	1
	• Testing on bank reconciliations (1 mark per relevant procedure)	4
	• Review cash book and bank statements for window dressing	1
	• Examine bank letter for evidence of security granted	1
	• Review financial statement disclosure	1
		–––
	Restricted to	**5**
		–––

	Marking guide		
			Marks
(c)	**Going concern procedures**		
	• Obtain cash flow forecast and assess assumptions		1
	• Perform sensitivity analysis on cash flow forecast		1
	• Evaluate management's plans for future actions		1
	• Review post year-end order book to assess levels of trade		1
	• Review agreements with the bank to determine whether any covenants breached		1
	• Review bank correspondence for evidence of renewal		1
	• Review correspondence with suppliers for dispute/legal action		1
	• Obtain confirmation from company lawyers about any legal action		1
	• Review post year-end board minutes for any indications of financial difficulties		1
	• Review management accounts to assess if in line with cash flow		1
	• Review financial statement disclosure		1
	• Consider if going concern basis is appropriate		1
	• Obtain a written representation		1
		Restricted to	5
(d)	**Impact on auditor's report**		
	• Discussion of issue		1
	• Disclosure adequate		2
	• Disclosure inadequate		2
			5
Total			**20**

Examiner's comment

This 20-mark question was based on Jasmine Co, a company which manufactures motor vehicle components. This question tested candidates' knowledge of substantive procedures for trade receivables and bank, going concern procedures and auditor's reports. Overall performance was mixed.

Part (a) for five marks required candidates to describe substantive procedures the auditor should perform to obtain sufficient and appropriate audit evidence in relation to Jasmine's trade receivables. Performance on this requirement was satisfactory. One mark was awarded for each well described substantive procedure. Those candidates who had practised past questions scored well, noting procedures such as after-date cash receipts testing, analytical review procedures, review of aged receivables reports and discussions with management regarding recoverability and allowances. Although many candidates recommended cut-off testing, candidates once again suggested using invoices rather than goods dispatched notes. Those candidates who did not score well provided procedures which lacked sufficient detail. For example, 'discuss receivables with management' without explaining what was to be discussed. Vague procedures such as this are not awarded any credit. In addition, despite the scenario stating that a trade receivables circularisation was not going to be performed, it was disappointing to see that many candidates still recommended procedures relating to the circularisation. Candidates must carefully read the scenario and tailor their procedures accordingly.

Part (b) for five marks required candidates to describe substantive procedures the auditor should perform to obtain sufficient and appropriate audit evidence in relation to the company's bank balances. Performance on this requirement was disappointing. As in part (a), one mark was awarded for each well described substantive procedure.

Disappointingly, the substantive procedures often lacked detail and failed to focus specifically on auditing the bank balances. Candidates seemed to note that the bank balance was an overdraft and so focused on going concern procedures. Whether the bank balance is a current asset or liability, the principal focus of the procedures should have been to audit the bank reconciliation in detail, however, very few candidates did this. The most common procedures listed included 'obtain a bank letter' which on its own would only have scored ½ mark. To obtain 1 mark the test needed to agree the account names to the trial balance or to agree the balance given to the bank reconciliation. Vague references to auditing the bank reconciliation were given, such as 'ensure the bank statement balance matches the cashbook balance'. In order to score well in this very commonly tested area, candidates needed to focus on each line in the bank reconciliation and provide procedures to confirm that each line represented a valid reconciling item between the bank statement and cash book.

Part (c) for five marks required candidates to describe going concern procedures. Many candidates performed well on this requirement. Again one mark was available for each well described procedure. This area has been tested extensively in previous diets and many candidates were able to provide a sufficient number of valid going concern procedures. A minority of procedures were too brief or vague, often not giving the source for the test, or stating 'ensure' without explaining how the test would achieve this. For example, 'obtain written representations' would not have gained any credit, to obtain the available mark the procedure should be 'obtain a written representation confirming the directors' view that Jasmine Co is a going concern'. In addition, a minority of candidates suggested 'the auditor should call the bank to ask if they will renew the company's bank overdraft'. This is impractical as the bank will not provide such a response to the auditor.

Part (d) for five marks required a discussion of an issue and the impact on the auditor's report of adequate and inadequate disclosure. The issue being brief going concern disclosures made in the financial statements. Auditor's report questions have shown a gradual improvement in recent diets so it is very disappointing that performance for this requirement was poor. Marks were awarded for a discussion of the issue (1 mark), the impact on the auditor's report of adequate disclosure (2 marks) and inadequate disclosure (2 marks). It was disappointing that candidates often do not discuss the issue. In order to be awarded the mark for discussing the issue, candidates should not just re-write the issue from the question. In this case candidates needed to explain that as the outcome of the overdraft renewal would not be known until after the auditor's report was signed, this was a material uncertainty (½ mark) and that the effect on the auditor's report depends on the adequacy of the disclosure (½ mark). The question then required candidates to consider the impact on the auditor's report of adequate and inadequate disclosure. Answers should have addressed each of these outcomes and this was clearly flagged in the requirement. To score well, candidates should have considered whether any additional information would be required in the auditor's report for 'adequate disclosure' and if the opinion would be impacted. Inadequate disclosure resulted in a modification of the opinion and as a result candidates tended to perform better. Many answers were poorly structured as they did not split out the two possible outcomes and it was at times difficult to see which points related to which outcome, resulting in difficulties in allocating marks. Incorrect answers for adequate disclosure focused on the use of emphasis of matter paragraphs. For inadequate disclosure some candidates suggested an adverse opinion, despite the scenario stating that the engagement partner was satisfied with the use of the going concern basis. In addition, many answers failed to consider whether the audit opinion was modified or not. Future candidates should note that credit will only be awarded to a consideration of whether the opinion, rather than the report, requires modification.

233 GOOSEBERRY *Walk in the footsteps of a top tutor*

Key answer tips

Part (a) asks for substantive procedures in relation to research and development. Think about the accounting treatment required by the relevant accounting standard and design procedures to test whether the treatment is appropriate. In the case of R&D there are a number of criteria which must be met in order for the costs to be capitalised. Generate audit procedures around each of these criteria to obtain evidence as to whether the costs should be capitalised or expensed. Don't forget the easy marks such as recalculating the breakdown of costs and agreeing the total to the financial statements.

Part (b) requires substantive procedures depreciation. Depreciation is an estimate and as such is an area of management judgement. Management may use an inappropriate depreciation rate to manipulate the financial statements. Your audit procedures should therefore not just focus on the calculation of depreciation but also whether the rate used by the client is appropriate.

Part (c) requires substantive procedures over director's bonuses. Once again, easy marks can be earned for recalculating the list of bonuses and agreeing to the financial statements. For other procedures think about the supporting documentation that provide evidence as to whether the figures are accurate and complete.

Part (d) asks for the audit reporting implications if the issue is unresolved. First you should discuss what the issue is i.e. what the client has done wrong. Calculate whether the adjustment required is material. If the issue is not material it won't impact the auditor's report. If it is material consider whether it is material and pervasive as this will impact the type of opinion that should be given. Remember to include the key wording of the opinion you are suggesting as well as any other impact on the auditor's report.

(a)   Research and development

–   Obtain and cast a schedule of intangible assets, detailing opening balances, amounts capitalised in the current year, amortisation and closing balances.

–   Agree the closing balances to the general ledger, trial balance and draft financial statements.

–   Discuss with the finance director the rationale for the three-year useful life and consider its reasonableness.

–   Recalculate the amortisation charge for a sample of intangible assets which have commenced production and confirm it is in line with the amortisation policy of straight line over three years and that amortisation only commenced from the point of production.

–   For the nine new projects, discuss with management the details of each project along with the stage of development and whether it has been capitalised or expensed.

–   For those expensed as research, agree the costs incurred to invoices and supporting documentation and to inclusion in profit or loss.

– For those capitalised as development, agree costs incurred to invoices and confirm technically feasible by discussion with development managers or review of feasibility reports.

– Review market research reports to confirm Gooseberry Co has the ability to sell the product once complete and probable future economic benefits will arise.

– Review the disclosures for intangible assets in the draft financial statements to verify that they are in accordance with IAS 38 *Intangible Assets*.

(b)   Depreciation

– Discuss with management the rationale for the changes to property, plant and equipment (PPE) depreciation rates, useful lives, residual values and depreciation methods and ascertain how these changes were arrived at.

– Confirm the reasonableness of these changes, by comparing the revised depreciation rates, useful lives and methods applied to PPE to industry averages and knowledge of the business.

– Review the capital expenditure budgets for the next few years to assess whether the revised asset lives correspond with the planned period until replacement of the relevant asset categories.

– Review the non-current asset register to assess if the revised depreciation rates have been applied.

– Review and recalculate profits and losses on disposal of assets sold/scrapped in the year, to assess the reasonableness of the revised depreciation rates.

– Select a sample of PPE and recalculate the depreciation charge to ensure that the non-current assets register is correct and ensure that new depreciation rates have been appropriately applied.

– Obtain a breakdown of depreciation by asset categories, compare to prior year; where significant changes have occurred, discuss with management and assess whether this change is reasonable.

– For asset categories where there have been a minimal number of additions and disposals, perform a proof in total calculation for the depreciation charged on PPE, discuss with management if significant fluctuations arise.

– Review the disclosure of the depreciation charges and policies in the draft financial statements and ensure it is in line with IAS 16 *Property, Plant and Equipment*.

(c)   Directors' bonuses

– Obtain a schedule of the directors' bonus paid in February 20X8 and cast the schedule to ensure accuracy and agree amount disclosed in the financial statements.

– Review the schedule of current liabilities and confirm the bonus accrual is included as a year-end liability.

– Agree the individual bonus payments to the payroll records.

– Recalculate the bonus payments and agree the criteria, including the exclusion of intangible assets, to supporting documentation and the percentage rates to be paid to the directors' service contracts.

-   Confirm the amount of each bonus paid post year end by agreeing to the cash book and bank statements.

-   Agree the amounts paid per director to board minutes to ensure the sums included in the current year financial statements are fully accrued and disclosed.

-   Review the board minutes to identify whether any additional payments relating to this year have been agreed for any directors.

-   Obtain a written representation from management confirming the completeness of directors' remuneration including the bonus.

-   Review the disclosures made regarding the bonus paid to directors and assess whether these are in compliance with local legislation.

(d)   Impact on auditor's report

One of the new health and beauty products Gooseberry Co has developed in the year does not meet the recognition criteria under IAS 38 *Intangible Assets* for capitalisation but has been included within intangible assets.

This is contrary to IAS 38, as if the criteria are not met, then this project is research expenditure and should be expensed to the statement of profit or loss rather than capitalised.

The error is material as it represents 6.9% of profit before tax (0.44m/6.4m) and 1.2% of net assets (0.44m/37.2m).

Management should adjust the financial statements by removing this amount from intangible assets and charging it to the statement of profit or loss instead. IAS 38 requires costs to date to be expensed; if the project meets the recognition criteria in 20X9, then only from that point can any new costs incurred be capitalised. Any costs already expensed cannot be written back to assets.

If management refuses to amend this error, then the auditor's opinion will need to be modified. As management has not complied with IAS 38 and the error is material but not pervasive, then a qualified opinion would be necessary.

A basis for qualified opinion paragraph would be needed after the opinion paragraph and would explain the material misstatement in relation to the incorrect treatment of research and development and the effect on the financial statements. The opinion paragraph would be qualified 'except for'.

Marking guide		
		Marks
(a) **Substantive procedures – Research & development**		
	• Cast and agree closing balance to TB and draft FS	1
	• Discuss amortisation policy with management and assess reasonableness	1
	• Recalculate amortisation charge/commenced in line with production	1
	• Discuss new projects and stage of development	1
	• For research costs agree invoices and to profit or loss	1
	• For development costs agree to invoices and confirm meets criteria	
	• Review market research to confirm ability to sell	
	• Review disclosures in line with IAS 38	
	Restricted to	

		Marking guide		
				Marks
(b)		**Substantive procedures – depreciation**		
	•	Discuss reasons for change with management		1
	•	Compare to industry averages and knowledge of business		1
	•	Review capex budgets to assess revised lives appropriate		1
	•	Agree new rates to non-current asset register		1
	•	Recalculate profit/loss on disposal and consider new rates		1
	•	Recalculate depreciation charge for a sample of assets		1
	•	Perform a proof-in-total on depreciation charge		1
	•	Review disclosure is in line with IAS 16		1
			Restricted to	**5**
(c)		**Substantive procedures – directors' bonuses**		
	•	Cast schedule of bonuses and agree to TB		1
	•	Confirm bonus accrual as current liability		1
	•	Agree bonus payments to payroll records		1
	•	Recalculate bonus payments in line with contracts		1
	•	Confirm post year-end payment to bank statement		1
	•	Review board minutes for additional sums		1
	•	Obtain written representation confirming completeness		1
	•	Review disclosures in line with local legislation		1
			Restricted to	**5**
(d)		**Impact on auditor's report**		
	•	Discussion of issue		1
	•	Calculation of materiality and conclusion		1
	•	Type of opinion modification required		2
	•	Impact on auditor's report		1
				5
Total				**20**

Examiner's comments

This question was based on Gooseberry Co, a company which develops and manufactures health and beauty products and distributes these to wholesale customers. This question tested candidates' knowledge of substantive procedures for research and development, depreciation and directors' bonuses, and auditor's reports.

Part (a) required candidates to describe substantive procedures the auditor should perform to obtain sufficient and appropriate audit evidence in relation to Gooseberry's research and development expenditure. Performance on this requirement was mixed. One mark was awarded for each well described substantive procedure. Hence for a five mark requirement, candidates should have provided at least five substantive procedures. Disappointingly this was not the case, as some answers only contained one or two procedures for each area and these were often not well described, resulting in a maximum of ½ mark each. Candidates are severely limiting the opportunity to score marks and are reminded to ensure that they employ effective exam technique. Many procedures were vague, often not giving the source for the test, or stating 'ensure' without explaining how the test would achieve this. For example, 'recalculate expenditure' rather than clearly stating 'recalculate the amortisation charge and confirm it is in line with the company's policy'. Only a minority of strong candidates demonstrated an understanding of IAS 38 *Intangible Assets* and tailored their answer around these criteria.

Part (b) required the candidates to describe substantive procedures the auditor should perform to obtain sufficient and appropriate audit evidence in relation to depreciation. Performance on this requirement was disappointing. As in part (a), one mark was awarded for each well described substantive procedure. Disappointingly often the substantive procedures were either not well described, or were not related to depreciation. A significant number of candidates did not clearly answer the specific requirement of the question to describe depreciation substantive procedures. Although many candidates were able to correctly suggest recalculating the depreciation charge, candidates often described more general property, plant and equipment substantive procedures including confirming additions and disposals. In addition, many candidates referred to procedures which were not relevant to the requirement or the scenario, for example, verifying the credentials of the valuer, to audit the revaluation of the property, plant and equipment, suggesting that candidates have rote learned a list of procedures from previous questions. Candidates are advised to read the question scenario and requirements carefully and tailor their answer accordingly. In general, there was clear evidence of a lack of tailoring of knowledge to the specific scenario provided. Candidates have clearly learned that the depreciation charge should be compared to the prior year. However, this substantive procedure is not relevant if there is a change in the useful life of the assets in the year as was detailed in this scenario. As addressed in previous examiner's reports candidates must strive to understand substantive procedures. Learning a generic list of tests will not translate to exam success, as they must be applied to the question requirement.

Part (c) required the candidates to describe substantive procedures the auditor should perform to obtain sufficient and appropriate audit evidence in relation to the directors' bonuses. Performance on this requirement for many candidates was pleasing. As in part (a) and (b), one mark was available for each well described procedure. Many candidates were able to correctly suggest agreeing the bonus payment to the payroll records/payslips, agreeing the bonus criteria to the directors' service contracts, and agreeing the bonus payment to the post year-end cash book/bank statement. A number of candidates also correctly described agreeing the amounts paid for each director to the board minutes.

Some candidates did not describe the substantive procedures in sufficient depth, for example, no credit was awarded for 'ensure the bonus is paid' as this provides no source or clear indication as to how this would be achieved. Candidates are reminded that substantive procedures are a core topic area and they must be able to produce relevant detailed procedures.

Part (d) for five marks required a discussion of an issue and the impact on the auditor's report if the issue remained unresolved. The issue presented related to $440,000 of development costs which had been incorrectly capitalised by the client. Auditor's report questions have shown a gradual improvement in recent diets so it is disappointing that performance for this question was mixed. Marks are awarded for a discussion of the issue (1 mark), assessment of the materiality of the issue (1 mark), a description of the type of modification (up to 2 marks) and the resultant impact on the auditor's report (1 mark). It was disappointing that candidates often do not discuss the issue. In order to be awarded the mark for discussing the issue candidates should not just re-write the fact from the question. Candidates need to explain the effect of the item being incorrectly recorded, i.e. this overcapitalisation results in assets/liabilities/profit being over/understated. Many candidates described the issue as 'development costs are incorrectly capitalised' which was a restatement of fact and were not awarded credit. To be awarded marks candidates should have noted 'the costs should have been expensed to the statement of profit or loss' (½ mark) and therefore 'profit/assets are overstated' (½ mark).

It was pleasing that most candidates correctly calculated materiality (½ mark) and concluded whether this was material (½ mark). Candidates attempted to identify the type of modification and the impact on the report, however, many answers were incomplete, for example, many candidates did not refer to a 'material misstatement' or a 'basis for qualified opinion paragraph'. A number of candidates described the impact on the auditor's report if the issue was resolved and also if the issue remained unresolved. The question clearly asked for the impact if the issue remained unresolved. Once again, candidates are advised to read the question requirements carefully.

234 DASHING *Walk in the footsteps of a top tutor*

Key answer tips

Part (a) asks for the steps to obtain a receivables circularisation. Take a methodical approach and think of each and every step involved in the process.

Part (b) requires substantive procedures over receivables for specific assertions. A substantive procedure tests the balance included in the financial statements. Think carefully about the objective of the procedure you are suggesting to ensure you include it under the appropriate assertion.

Part (c) requires substantive procedures over the redundancy provision. Again, a methodical approach can help. Think of how the balance will have been calculated and design procedures to test the calculation. Think about the accounting treatment required by the relevant accounting standard and design procedures to test whether the treatment is appropriate.

Part (d) asks for the audit reporting implications if the issue is unresolved. First you should discuss what the issue is i.e. what the client has done wrong. Calculate whether the adjustment required is material. If the issue is not material it won't impact the auditor's report. If it is material consider whether it is material and pervasive as this will impact the type of opinion that should be given. Remember to include the key wording of the opinion you are suggesting as well as any other impact on the auditor's report.

(a)   Steps in undertaking a positive receivables circularisation for Dashing Co

- Obtain consent from the finance director of Dashing Co in advance of undertaking the circularisation.

- Obtain a list of trade receivables at the year end, cast this and agree it to the receivables ledger control account total.

- Select a sample from the receivables list ensuring that a number of nil, old, credit and large balances are selected.

- Circularisation letters should be prepared on Dashing Co's letterhead paper, requesting a confirmation of the year-end receivables balance, and for replies to be sent directly to the audit team using a pre-paid envelope.

- The finance director of Dashing Co should be requested to sign all the letters prior to them being sent out by a member of the audit team.

- Where no response is received, follow this up with another letter or a phone call and where necessary alternative procedures should be performed

- When replies are received, they should be reconciled to Dashing Co's receivables records, any differences such as cash or goods in transit should be investigated further.

(b) **Receivables**

Accuracy, valuation and allocation

- Review the after date cash receipts and follow through to pre year-end receivable balances.

- Inspect the aged receivables report to identify any slow-moving balances and discuss these with the credit control manager to assess whether an allowance or write down is necessary.

- For any slow-moving/aged balances review customer correspondence to assess whether there are any invoices in dispute.

- Review board minutes of Dashing Co to assess whether there are any material disputed receivables.

Completeness

- Select a sample of goods despatched notes from before the year end, agree to sales invoices and to inclusion in the year-end receivables ledger.

- Agree the total of individual receivables ledger accounts to the receivables control account and to the trial balance.

- Obtain the prior year aged receivables listing and for significant balances compare to the current year receivables listing for inclusion and amount due. Discuss with management any missing receivables or significantly lower balances.

- Review the receivables ledger for any credit balances and discuss with management whether these should be reclassified as payables.

Rights and obligations

- Review bank confirmations and loan agreements for any evidence that receivables have been assigned as security for amounts owed by Dashing Co.

- Review board minutes for evidence that legal title to receivables has been sold onto a third party such as a factor.

- For a sample of receivables, agree the balance recorded on the receivables ledger to the original name of the customer on a sales order or a contract.

Tutorial note: Marks will be awarded for any other relevant receivables tests.

(c) **Redundancy provision**

- Discuss with the directors of Dashing Co as to whether they have formally announced their intention to close the production site and make their employees redundant, to confirm that a present obligation exists at the year end.

- If announced before the year end, review supporting documentation to verify that the decision has been formally announced.

- Review the board minutes to ascertain whether it is probable that the redundancy payments will be paid.

- Obtain a breakdown of the redundancy calculations by employee and cast it to ensure completeness and agree to trial balance.

- Recalculate the redundancy provision to confirm completeness and agree components of the calculation to supporting documentation such as employee contracts.

- Review the post year-end cash book to identify whether any redundancy payments have been made, compare actual payments to the amounts provided to assess whether the provision is reasonable.

- Obtain a written representation from management to confirm the completeness of the provision.

- Review the disclosure of the redundancy provision to ensure compliance with IAS 37 *Provisions, Contingent Liabilities and Contingent Assets*.

(d)   Impact on auditor's report

The company has included a redundancy provision of $110,000 in the draft financial statements, however, audit fieldwork testing has confirmed that the provision should actually be $305,000. The provision is understated and profit before tax overstated if the finance director does not amend the financial statements.

The provision included is $110,000, it should be $305,000 hence an adjustment of $195,000 is required which represents 7.5% of profit before tax (195/2,600) or 1.1% of total assets (195/18,000) and hence is a material matter.

If management does not adjust the redundancy provision, the audit opinion will need to be modified.

As provisions are understated and profit overstated, there is a material misstatement, which is not pervasive.

Therefore, a qualified opinion would be necessary, stating that the opinion is qualified 'except for'.

A basis for qualified opinion paragraph would also need to be included subsequent to the opinion paragraph. This would explain the material misstatement in relation to the redundancy provision and the effect on the financial statements.

Marking guide		Marks
(a) **Steps for a receivables circularisation**		
• Obtain consent from client		1
• Agree receivables listing to SL		1
• Select sample including nil, credit, old and large balances		1
• Prepare letters on company letterhead		1
• Sent by auditor		1
• Where no response, perform alternative procedures		1
• For replies received, reconcile and investigate differences		1
	Restricted to	4

	Marking guide		Marks
(b)	**Substantive procedures – receivables s**		
	• Accuracy, valuation and allocation tests		2
	• Completeness tests		2
	• Rights and obligations tests		2
		Restricted to	6
(c)	**Substantive procedures – redundancy provision**		
	• Discuss with directors when announcement was made		1
	• If before year end, agree to supporting documentation		1
	• Review board minutes for details of redundancy payments		1
	• Obtain a breakdown of redundancy calculations		1
	• Recalculate the redundancy provision		1
	• Review post y/e cash book for payments		1
	• Obtain written representation		1
	• Review disclosure in FS		1
		Restricted to	5
(d)	**Impact on auditor's report**		
	• Discussion of issue		1
	• Calculation of materiality		1
	• Type of opinion modification required		2
	• Impact on auditor's report		1
			5
Total			**20**

Examiner's comments

This question was based on Dashing Co and tested candidates' knowledge of performing a receivables' circularisation, receivables and redundancy provision substantive procedures and auditor's reports.

Part (a) required the steps the auditor should perform in undertaking a positive receivables circularisation. Performance on this requirement was disappointing. One mark was awarded for each well described step. This was a knowledge area and a straight forward requirement. Candidates should have been able to easily describe enough steps to pass this part of the question. However, a significant minority of candidates did not seem to understand what a receivables circularisation was and so just produced a list of receivables substantive procedures. Other answers incorrectly focused on the differences between positive and negative circularisations which were not requested. Stronger candidates were able to suggest some of the following steps: selecting a sample of receivable balances, sending a letter out, requesting a response, chasing up non-replies, undertaking alternative procedures in the event of no response and reconciling to records for those replies received.

Part (b) required substantive procedures for receivables relating to three specific assertions: (i) accuracy, valuation and allocation, (ii) completeness and (iii) rights and obligations. Candidates' performance was disappointing. One mark was awarded for each well described substantive procedure. Hence for a six-mark requirement, candidates should have provided at least six substantive procedures. Disappointingly this was not the case, as some answers only contained one for each area and these were often not well described, resulting in maximum of ½ mark each.

In order to gain the available one mark each substantive procedure needed to be sufficiently detailed, and be clearly linked to the relevant financial statement assertion. Most candidates either structured their answers into the three sub category headings of (i), (ii) and (iii) or the tests included a reference to which assertion it addressed. Candidates' performance was most disappointing for (iii) rights and obligations, where often no answer was provided. A significant number of candidates provided example procedures which were not related to receivables, but instead focused on revenue or on a receivables circularisation which were specifically excluded from this question requirement. This can only be due to a failure to read the question requirement properly. In addition many procedures were vague, often not giving the source for the test, or stating 'check' or 'ensure' without explaining how the test would achieve this. In addition many tests were incomplete such as agreeing goods despatch notes (GDNs) to sales invoices but not then agreeing the invoices to the year-end receivables ledger, and these GDNs and invoices should have been close to the year-end. Also many of the procedures were tests of control rather than substantive procedures.

Part (c) required substantive procedures for confirming the redundancy provision. Candidates' performance was mixed. Again one mark was awarded for each well described substantive procedure. Many candidates were able to correctly suggest recalculation of the provision, obtaining a written representation confirming the completeness of the provision and agreeing to supporting documentation such as board minutes, employment contracts or payroll records. However there was clear evidence of a lack of tailoring of knowledge to the specific scenario provided. Candidates have clearly learnt that all provisions should be compared to the prior year and that legal advice is required to confirm the amount of the provision. These are not relevant for a redundancy provision as it is unlikely there was a similar provision last year or that the company's lawyers would estimate the costs of redundancy. As addressed in previous examiner's reports candidates must strive to understand substantive procedures. Learning a generic list of tests will not translate to exam success as they must be applied to the question requirement.

The requirement verb for (a), (b) and (c) was to 'describe' therefore sufficient detail was required to score the 1 mark available per procedure. Also candidates must provide enough tests to score the marks and should assume 1 mark per valid procedure. Candidates are reminded that substantive procedures are a core topic area and they must be able to produce relevant detailed procedures.

Part (d) required a discussion of the specific issue detailed in the requirement and the impact on the auditor's report if the issue remained unresolved. The issue being that the redundancy provision was understated by $195,000. Performance was satisfactory on this question, with an improvement by candidates on the last time this style of question was tested. Some candidates launched straight into assessing materiality without discussing the issue, which was that the redundancy provision should be $305,000 rather than $110,000 (½ mark). Therefore the provision was understated (½ mark) and hence missed out on the available 1 mark for this. A further mark was available for the calculation and assessment of materiality. A number of candidates incorrectly used the total provision balance of $305,000 in calculating materiality rather than the under provision of $195,000. However, if they then stated that the balance was material they would have gained ½ mark. Many candidates were able to then correctly identify the type of opinion modification required (2 marks available), and attempt to describe the impact on the auditor's report (1 mark). Candidates answers tended to be more focused this session, rather than adopting a scatter gun approach of all possible auditor's report options.

235 AIRSOFT *Walk in the footsteps of a top tutor*

Key answer tips

Part (a) requires substantive procedures over completeness of payables. Make sure your procedures only focus on this one assertion otherwise you will not score marks. The requirement also specifies substantive procedures, therefore tests of controls will not score marks.

Part (b) asks for audit procedures using audit software. Audit software is used to manipulate data and perform calculations which would be time consuming to perform manually.

Parts (c) and (d) require substantive procedures over bank balances and directors' remuneration. Here you are not limited to a specific assertion so any relevant procedures will score marks.

Part (e) focuses on the key audit matters section of an auditor's report. You should learn the different sections of the auditor's report and their purpose.

(a) **Trade payables and accruals**

- Compare the total trade payables and list of accruals against prior year and investigate any significant differences.

- Select a sample of post year-end payments from the cash book; if they relate to the current year, follow through to the payables ledger or accruals listing to ensure they are recorded in the correct period.

- Obtain supplier statements and reconcile these to the payables ledger balances, and investigate any reconciling items.

- Select a sample of payable balances and perform a trade payables' circularisation, follow up any non-replies and any reconciling items between the balance confirmed and the trade payables' balance.

- Review after date invoices and credit notes to ensure no further items need to be accrued.

- Enquire of management their process for identifying goods received but not invoiced or logged in the payables ledger and ensure that it is reasonable to ensure completeness of payables.

(b) **Audit software procedures**

- The audit team can use audit software to calculate the payables payment period for the year-to-date to compare against the prior year to identify whether payables days have changed in line with trading levels and expectations. If the ratio has decreased, this may be an indication that payables are understated.

- Audit software can be used to cast the payables and accruals listings to confirm the completeness and accuracy of trade payables and accruals.

- Audit software can be used to select a representative sample of items for further testing of payables balances.

- Audit software can be utilised to recalculate the accruals for goods received not invoiced at the year end.

- Undertake cut-off testing by assessing whether the dates of the last GRNs recorded relate to pre year end; and that any with a date of 1 January 20X6 onwards were excluded from trade payables.

(c) **Bank balances**

- Obtain a bank confirmation letter from Airsoft Co's bankers for all of its bank accounts.

- Agree all accounts listed on the bank confirmation letter to Airsoft Co's bank reconciliations and the trial balance to ensure completeness of bank balances.

- For all bank accounts, obtain Airsoft Co's bank account reconciliation and cast to ensure arithmetical accuracy.

- Agree the balance per the bank reconciliation to an original year-end bank statement and to the bank confirmation letter.

- Agree the reconciliations balance per the cash book to the year-end cash book.

- Trace all the outstanding lodgements to the pre year-end cash book, post year-end bank statement and also to the paying-in-book pre year end.

- Trace all unpresented cheques through to a pre year-end cash book and post year-end statement. For any unusual amounts or significant delays, obtain explanations from management.

- Examine any old unpresented cheques to assess if they need to be written back into the payables ledger as they are no longer valid to be presented.

- Review the cash book and bank statements for any unusual items or large transfers around the year end, as this could be evidence of window dressing.

- Examine the bank confirmation letter for details of any security provided by Airsoft Co or any legal right of set-off as this may require disclosure.

- Review the financial statements to ensure that the disclosure of bank balances is complete and accurate.

(d) **Directors' remuneration**

- Obtain a schedule of the directors' remuneration, split by salary and bonus paid in December and cast the schedule to ensure accuracy.

- Agree a sample of the individual monthly salary payments and the bonus payment in December to the payroll records.

- Confirm the amount of each bonus paid by agreeing to the cash book and bank statements.

- Review the board minutes to identify whether any additional payments relating to this year have been agreed for any directors.

- Agree the amounts paid per director to board minutes to ensure the sums included are genuine.

- Obtain a written representation from management confirming the completeness of directors' remuneration including the bonus.

- Review the disclosures made regarding the directors' remuneration and assess whether these are in compliance with local legislation.

(e) Key audit matters

Key audit matters (KAM) are those matters which, in the auditor's professional judgement, were of most significance in the audit of the financial statements of the current period. Key audit matters are selected from matters communicated with those charged with governance.

The purpose of including key audit matters in the auditor's report is to help users in understanding the entity, and to provide a basis for the users to discuss with management and those charged with governance about matters relating to the entity and the financial statements. A key part of the definition is that these are the most significant matters. Identifying the most significant matters involves using the auditor's professional judgement.

ISA 701 *Communicating Key Audit Matters in the Independent Auditor's Report* suggests that in determining key audit matters the auditor should take the following into account:

- Areas of higher assessed risk of material misstatement, or significant risks.

- Significant auditor judgements relating to areas in the financial statements which involved significant management judgement.

- The effect on the audit of significant events or transactions which occurred during the period.

The description of each KAM in the Key Audit Matters section of the auditor's report should include a reference to the related disclosures in the financial statements and covers why the matter was considered to be one of most significance in the audit and therefore determined to be a KAM; and how the matter was addressed in the audit.

Marking guide		Marks
(a) **Substantive procedures for completeness of payables and accruals**		
	Compare to prior year and investigate differences	1
	Post y/e cash book payments to ledger	1
	Supplier statement reconciliations	1
	Trade payables circularisation	1
	Review after date invoices and credit notes	1
	Enquiry of management process for identifying accruals	1
	Restricted to	**4**
(b) **Audit software procedures over trade payables and accruals**		
	Calculate trade payables payment period	1
	Cast the payables and accruals schedule	1
	Select sample for circularisation	1
	Recalculate accruals	1
	Cut-off testing on GRNs	1
	Restricted to	**3**
(c) **Substantive procedures – year-end bank balances**		
	Bank confirmation letter	1
	Agree to bank reconciliation and TB	1
	Cast bank reconciliations	1
	Testing on bank reconciliations (1 mark per relevant procedure)	1
	Review cash book and bank statements for window dressing	1
	Examine bank letter for evidence of security granted	1
	Review financial statement disclosure	1
	Restricted to	**5**

	Marking guide		Marks
(d)	**Substantive procedures – directors' remuneration**		
	• Cast schedule of remuneration		1
	• Agree payments to payroll records		1
	• Confirm bonus payments to cash book		1
	• Review board minutes for additional remuneration		1
	• Obtain written representation confirming completeness		1
	• Review financial statement disclosure		1
		Restricted to	**3**
(e)	**Key audit matters**		
	• Definition of KAM		1
	• Purpose of KAM		1
	• Significant matters and areas of judgement		1
	• Examples of KAM		2
	• KAM disclosure		1
		Restricted to	**5**
Total			**20**

Examiner's comments

This question was based on a listed company, Airsoft Co, a manufacturer of stationery products. This question tested candidates' knowledge of financial statement assertions and substantive procedures.

Part (a) required candidates to describe substantive procedures the auditor should perform to obtain sufficient and appropriate audit evidence in relation to the completeness of Airsoft Co's trade payables and accruals. Performance on this requirement was disappointing. One mark was awarded for each well described procedure. A number of candidates provided procedures which were not relevant to trade payables or accruals. For example many candidates described audit procedures for purchases and inventory. Candidates are reminded to read the question requirement carefully and to ensure that they are answering the question set. Further, many candidates provided incomplete tests. For example 'obtain supplier statements and agree to the payables ledger' would only be awarded ½ mark as without reference to reconciliation and the investigation of reconciling items, this test does not offer much assurance to the auditor. Candidates are again reminded to think about the aim of the procedure when they are describing substantive tests. Some candidates described audit procedures that did not focus on the completeness assertion. For example, agreeing amounts on the goods received not invoiced listing to post year end invoices, will not ensure that all items which should have been accrued at the year-end have been included. Candidates are reminded to think carefully about the direction of their procedure when they are tackling completeness and existence testing, and are reminded that financial statement assertions are a key element of this syllabus.

Part (b) required candidates to describe audit software procedures which could be carried out during the audit of Airsoft Co's trade payables and accruals. Candidates' performance was disappointing. Some candidates did not attempt this question. Again one mark was awarded for each well described procedure. Although specifically advised not to, some candidate repeated their tests from part (a). For example, many candidates repeated the analytical review procedures in (a) in their answer to part (b). Marks were only awarded once. Often candidates did not make it clear the procedure related specifically to payables. For example, using audit software to cast the ledger, without making it clear which ledger exactly did not score the full mark.

Some candidates described control rather than substantive procedures. For example, run dummy data to ensure the payables system is operating correctly, would not be awarded any credit as this is an example of test data and not audit software.

Part (c) candidates to describe substantive procedures the auditor should perform to obtain sufficient and appropriate evidence in relation to Airsoft Co's year-end bank balance. Candidates' performance in this area was mixed. Again, one mark was awarded for each well described procedure. Candidates who suggested a detailed audit procedure for each line of a standard bank reconciliation performed well on this question, however, some candidate descriptions of the tests were unclear, for example 'trace outstanding lodgements to pre and post year end'. This is another example of an incomplete test as there is no reference to what source documentation is being used to perform this test. When writing substantive procedures candidates are reminded that their procedure should make clear where the information is being drawn from as well as what it is being agreed to. The scenario noted that Airsoft Co had a bank overdraft of $2.6m. Some candidates therefore described a number of going concern audit procedures. However, this was not relevant as, not only was it not asked for in the question, but the scenario clearly showed the company was profitable, with profit before tax of $16.3m and total assets of $66.8m and there was no indication in the question that funding was an issue. Candidates must ensure that they read the requirement and answer the question as set.

Part (d) required candidates to describe substantive procedures the auditor should perform to confirm the directors' remuneration included in the financial statements at the year end. The director's remuneration included their salary and a discretionary bonus. Candidates' performance was disappointing. As in parts (a) (b) and (c) tests were often incomplete or were control tests. The most common incomplete test was simply 'review the disclosures' without going on to say 'to ensure compliance with local legislation'. The most common control test being 'review payroll listings to ensure monthly pay is authorised' The requirement verb for (a) (b) (c) and (d) was to 'describe' therefore sufficient detail was required to score the 1 mark available per procedure. Also candidates must provide enough tests to score the marks and should assume 1 mark per valid procedure. Candidates are reminded that substantive procedures are a core topic area and they must be able to produce relevant detailed procedures.

Part (e) required candidates to identify a Key Audit Matter (KAM) and explain how the auditor determines and communicates KAM. This was a knowledge-based requirement based on the relatively new standard, ISA 701 Communicating Key Audit Matters in the Independent Auditor's Report. Candidates' performance was very disappointing with some candidates not attempting this requirement. Candidates often incorrectly described a KAM as an important matter that the auditor would consider at the planning stage of an audit. Candidates are reminded that knowledge of Auditor Reporting and the relevant ISAs is a key area of this syllabus.

Key answer tips

Parts (a) to (c) require substantive procedures over three specific issues. Make sure your procedures address the issue described otherwise you will not score marks. The requirement also specifies substantive procedures, therefore tests of controls will not score marks.

Part (d) asks for the impact on the auditor's report if the issue described remains unresolved. You need to refer to materiality considerations to establish whether or not the opinion needs to be modified. Then consider the type of modification. Finally consider any other impact to the report. If the opinion is to be modified, the basis for opinion section will need to explain the reason for the modification.

(a)   Completeness of Insects4U Co income

- Obtain a schedule of all Insects4U Co's income and cast to confirm completeness and accuracy of the balance.

- Compare the individual categories of income against prior year and investigate any significant differences.

- For monthly donations, trace a sample of donations received in the bank statements to the cash book to ensure that they are recorded completely and accurately.

- For a sample of new subscribers in the year, agree from their completed subscription form the monthly sum and start date, trace to the monthly donations received account and agree to the cash book and bank statements.

- For donations received in the post, review correspondence from donors, agree to the donations account and trace sums received to the cash book and bank statements to ensure all completely recorded.

- For the charity events, undertake a proof in total calculation of the number of tickets sold multiplied by the ticket price, compare this to the income recorded and discuss any significant differences with management.

(b)   Spider Spirals Co trade payables

- Calculate the trade payables payment period for Spider Spirals Co and compare to prior years and investigate any significant difference, in particular any decrease for this year due to the payment run on 3 November.

- Compare the total trade payables and list of accruals against prior year and investigate any significant differences.

- Discuss with management the process they have undertaken to quantify the misstatement of trade payables due to the late payment run and cut-off error of purchase invoices and consider the materiality of the error in isolation as well as with other misstatements found.

- Select a sample of purchase invoices received between the period of 1 and 7 November, ascertain through reviewing goods received notes (GRNs) if the goods were received pre or post year end, if post year end, then confirm that they have been excluded from the ledger or follow through to the correcting journal entry.

- Review after date payments; if they relate to the current year, then follow through to the payables ledger or accrual listing to ensure they are recorded in the correct period.

- Obtain supplier statements and reconcile these to the payables ledger balances, and investigate any reconciling items.

- Select a sample of payables balances and perform a trade payables' circularisation, follow up any non-replies and any reconciling items between the balance confirmed and the trade payables' balance.

- Select a sample of GRNs before the year end and after the year end and follow through to inclusion in the correct period's payables balance, to ensure correct cut-off.

(c)   Spider Spirals Co trade receivables

- Review the aged receivables listing to identify any slow-moving or old receivables balances, discuss the status of these balances with the finance director to assess whether they are likely to pay.

- Review customer correspondence to identify any balances which are in dispute or unlikely to be paid.

- Review whether there are any after date cash receipts for slow-moving/old receivables balances.

- Review board minutes to identify whether there are any significant concerns in relation to payments by customers.

- Calculate the potential level of receivables which are not recoverable and assess whether this is material or not and discuss with management.

- Recalculate the allowance for receivables and compare to the potentially irrecoverable balances to assess if the allowance is adequate.

- Inspect post year-end sales returns/credit notes and consider whether an additional allowance against receivables is required.

(d)   Impact on auditor's report

The company made a payment run of $490,000 for payables on 3 November, which is post year-end. The trade payables which were outstanding at the year end have been understated as they have been recorded as being paid.

In addition, the bank overdraft is overstated as the payments are recorded as coming out of the year-end bank balance. This is evidence of window dressing, as the company has attempted to record a lower level of payable obligations at the year-end.

The finance director's argument that no adjustment is necessary because the balances affected are both current liabilities is irrelevant, as although both balances are liabilities, they should each still be materially correct.

The amount of the payment run is $490,000 which represents 6.0% of total liabilities (490/8,100) and hence is a material matter.

If management refuses to adjust for the post year-end payment run, the audit opinion will need to be modified. As trade payables are understated and the bank overdraft is overstated and there is a material misstatement which is not pervasive, a qualified opinion would be necessary. The opinion paragraph would be qualified 'except for'.

A basis for qualified opinion paragraph would need to be included subsequent to the opinion paragraph. This would explain the material misstatement in relation to the treatment of the trade payables and bank overdraft and the effect on the financial statements.

	Marking guide	Marks
(a)	**Substantive procedures – completeness of income**	
	• Cast schedule of all of the company's income	1
	• Compare individual categories of income to prior year	1
	• Trace monthly donations from bank statements to cash book	1
	• Agree subscription forms to donations received account, cash book and bank statements	1
	• Review correspondence from donors, agree to donations account, cash book and bank statements	1
	• Perform proof in total of tickets sold multiplied by ticket price	1
	Restricted to	**4**
(b)	**Substantive procedures – Spider Spirals Co trade payables**	
	• Calculate the trade payables payment period	1
	• Compare total trade payables and accruals to prior year	1
	• Discuss with management process to quantify misstatement	1
	• Sample invoices received between 1 to 7 November	1
	• Review after date payments	1
	• Review supplier statements reconciliations	1
	• Perform a trade payables' circularisation	1
	• Cut-off testing pre and post year-end GRN	1
	Restricted to	**6**
(c)	**Substantive procedures – Spider Spirals Co trade receivables**	
	• Aged receivables report to identify any slow-moving balances	1
	• Review customer correspondence for disputes	1
	• Review the after date cash receipts	1
	• Review board minutes	1
	• Discuss level of irrecoverable receivables with management	1
	• Recalculate allowance for receivables	1
	• Post year-end sales returns/credit notes	1
	Restricted to	**5**
(d)	**Effect of uncorrected misstatement and impact on auditor's report**	
	• Discussion of issue	1
	• Calculation of materiality	1
	• Type of opinion modification required	2
	• Impact on auditor's report	1
		5
Total		**20**

Examiner's comments

Part (a) required candidates to describe substantive procedures to assess the completeness of income. In this type of question one mark was awarded for each well described procedure. As in previous diets, performance in questions requiring substantive tests to be described continues to be disappointing. Most candidates did not understand the implications of testing for completeness and/or the implication of being a not-for-profit organisation. Many candidates therefore just gave standard tests over income such as agreeing goods despatch notes to invoices. Many candidates also placed too much emphasis to the cash at bank suggesting a bank reconciliation should be performed, with no reference to donations or income. Most candidates were unable to tailor their knowledge of general substantive procedures to the specific issues in the question requirements, or provided vague tests such as 'check' or objectives of 'ensure that....' As addressed in previous Examiner's Reports candidates must strive to understand substantive procedures. Learning a generic list of tests will not translate to exam success – procedures must be tailored to the specific requirements of the question.

Part (b) required candidates to describe substantive procedures for trade payables as the payables ledger was kept open one week longer than normal. One mark was awarded for each well described procedure. Performance in this question was also disappointing. Candidates often listed general trade payable tests and did not relate to the specific requirement of the question. Although many candidates suggested suitable analytical review tests such as compare with prior year figure, few provided a full procedure by ensuring that 'significant differences should be investigated' and hence only scored ½ marks. Many candidates did attempt to explain a cut-off test however often, incorrectly, described sourcing the sample from invoices rather than goods received notes. Many candidates suggested testing purchase orders to goods received notes and invoices, however, this would not verify the year-end trade payable balance.

Part (c) required candidates to describe substantive procedures for trade receivables as the trade receivable days had increased. Again one mark was awarded for each well described procedure. Performance in this question was disappointing. Candidates again generally listed general trade receivable tests and did not relate to the specific requirement of the question. Many candidates incorrectly included substantive tests such as analytical review, receivable circularisation, cut-off testing, reconciling the ledger to the control account etc., which are not relevant to the question. Candidates must read the question carefully and apply their knowledge to the scenario provided.

Part (d) required candidates to describe the impact on the auditor's report if the issues remained unresolved. Performance was mixed across this question, however overall performance on auditor's reports showed an improvement over previous diets. Most candidates correctly calculated materiality and correctly suggested the type of modification. However many candidates repeated the facts from the scenario and/or discussed how to resolve the issue. Few candidates noted that the issue resulted in trade payables being understated and therefore the bank overdraft being overstated. While most candidates correctly stated the impact on the auditor's report would be an 'except for' opinion, few discussed the need to include a 'basis of qualified opinion' paragraph.

237 ELOUNDA *Walk in the footsteps of a top tutor*

Key answer tips

Parts (a) to (c) require substantive procedures over three specific issues. Make sure your procedures address the issue described otherwise you will not score marks. The requirement also specifies substantive procedures, therefore tests of controls will not score marks.

Part (d) asks for procedures to assess whether the company is a going concern. This is a regularly examined topic, therefore students should be able to answer this question well.

(a)   Revaluation of property, plant and equipment (PPE)

- Obtain a schedule of all PPE revalued during the year and cast to confirm completeness and accuracy of the revaluation adjustment and agree to trial balance and financial statements.

- Consider the competence and capability of the valuer, Martin Dullman, by assessing through enquiry his qualification, membership of a professional body and experience in valuing these types of assets.

- Consider whether the valuation undertaken provides sufficiently objective audit evidence. Discuss with management whether Martin Dullman has any financial interest in Elounda Co which along with the family relationship could have had an impact on his independence.

- Agree the revalued amounts to the valuation statement provided by the valuer.

- Review the valuation report and consider if all assets in the same category have been revalued in line with IAS 16 *Property, Plant and Equipment*.

- Agree the revalued amounts for these assets are included correctly in the non-current assets register.

- Recalculate the total revaluation adjustment and agree correctly recorded in the revaluation surplus.

- Recalculate the depreciation charge for the year to ensure that for the assets revalued during the year, the depreciation was based on the correct valuation and was for 12 months.

- Review the financial statements disclosures relating to the revaluation to ensure they comply with IAS 16.

(b)   Inventory valuation

- Obtain a schedule of all raw materials, finished goods and work in progress (WIP) inventory and cast to confirm completeness and accuracy of the balance and agree to trial balance and financial statements.

- Obtain the breakdown of WIP and agree a sample of WIP assessed during the count to the WIP schedule, agreeing the percentage completion as recorded at the inventory count.

- For a sample of inventory items (finished goods and WIP), obtain the relevant cost sheets and confirm raw material costs to recent purchase invoices, labour costs to time sheets or wage records and overheads allocated are of a production nature.

- For a sample of inventory items, review the calculation for equivalent units and associated equivalent unit cost and recalculate the inventory valuation.

- Select a sample of year-end finished goods and review post year-end sales invoices to ascertain if net realisable value (NRV) is above cost or if an adjustment is required.

- Select a sample of items included in WIP at the year-end and ascertain the final unit cost price, verifying to relevant supporting documentation, and compare to the unit sales price included in sales invoices post year-end to assess NRV.

- Review aged inventory reports and identify any slow-moving goods, discuss with management why these items have not been written down or if an allowance is required.

- For the defective chemical compound E243, discuss with management their plans for disposing of these goods, and why they believe these goods have a NRV of $400,000.

- If any E243 has been sold post year-end, agree to the sales invoice to assess NRV.

- Agree the cost of $720,000 for compound E243 to supporting documentation to confirm the raw material cost, labour cost and any overheads attributed to the cost.

- Confirm if the final adjustment for compound E243 is $320,000 (720 – 400) and discuss with management if this adjustment has been made; if so follow through the write down to confirm.

- Review the financial statements disclosures relating to inventory and WIP to ensure they comply with IAS 2 *Inventories*.

(c) Bank loan

- Agree the opening balance of the bank loan to the prior year audit file and financial statements.

- For any loan payments made during the year, agree the cash outflow to the cash book and bank statements.

- Review bank correspondence to identify whether any late payment penalties have been levied and agree these have been charged to profit or loss account as a finance charge.

- Obtain direct confirmation at the year-end from the loan provider of the outstanding balance and any security provided. Agree confirmed amounts to the loan schedule and financial statements.

- Review the loan agreement for details of covenants and recalculate to identify any breaches in these.

- Agree closing balance of the loan to the trial balance and draft financial statements and that the disclosure is adequate, including any security provided, that the loan is disclosed as a current liability and disclosure is in accordance with accounting standards and local legislation.

(d)   Going concern procedures

- Obtain Elounda's cash flow forecast and review the cash in and out flows. Assess the assumptions for reasonableness and discuss the findings with management to understand if the company will have sufficient cash flows to meet liabilities as they fall due.

- Discuss with management their ability to settle the next instalment due for repayment to the bank and the lump sum payment of $800k in January 20X7 and ensure these have been included in the cash flow forecast.

- Review current agreements with the bank to determine whether any key ratios or covenants have been breached with regards to the bank loan or any overdraft.

- Review the company's post year-end sales and order book to assess the levels of trade and if the revenue figures in the cash flow forecast are reasonable.

- Review post year-end correspondence with suppliers to identify whether any restrictions in credit have arisen, and if so, ensure that the cash flow forecast reflects the current credit terms or where necessary an immediate payment for trade payables.

- Enquire of the lawyers of Elounda Co as to the existence of litigation and claims; if any exist, then consider their materiality and impact on the going concern basis.

- Perform audit tests in relation to subsequent events to identify any items which might indicate or mitigate the risk of going concern not being appropriate.

- Review the post year-end board minutes to identify any other issues which might indicate financial difficulties for the company.

- Review post year-end management accounts to assess if in line with cash flow forecast and to identify any issues which may be relevant to the going concern assessment.

- Consider whether any additional disclosures as required by IAS 1 *Presentation of Financial Statements* in relation to material uncertainties over going concern should be made in the financial statements.

- Obtain a written representation confirming the directors' view that Elounda Co is a going concern.

		Marking guide	Marks

Marking guide

			Marks
(a)		**Substantive procedures – revaluation**	*Marks*
	•	Cast schedule of PPE revalued this year and agree to TB/FS	1
	•	Consider reasonableness of the valuer's qualifications, membership of professional body and experience	1
	•	Discuss with management if the valuer has financial interests in the company which may impact his independence	1
	•	Agree the revalued amounts to the valuation statement	1
	•	Consider if all items in the same class of assets have been revalued	1
	•	Agree the revalued amounts included correctly in the non-current assets register	1
	•	Recalculate the total revaluation adjustment and agree recorded in the revaluation surplus	1
	•	Recalculate the depreciation charge for the year	1
	•	Review the financial statements disclosures for compliance with IAS 16	1
		Restricted to	**5**
(b)		**Substantive procedures – inventory valuation**	
	•	Cast a schedule of all raw materials, finished goods and work in progress (WIP) inventory and agree to TB/FS	1
	•	Obtain breakdown and agree sample of WIP from the count to the WIP schedule, agree percentage completion	1
	•	Obtain relevant cost sheets and confirm costs to supporting documentation	1
	•	Review the calculation for equivalent units and associated equivalent unit cost and recalculate the inventory valuation	1
	•	Review post year-end sales invoices to ascertain if net realisable value (NRV) is above cost	1
	•	Ascertain the final unit cost price of WIP and compare to the sales invoices post year-end to assess NRV	1
	•	Review aged inventory reports, identify slow-moving goods, discuss with management	1
	•	Compound E243, discuss with management plans for disposing of goods, why NRV is $400,000	1
	•	If any of defective goods have been sold post year-end, agree to the sales invoice to assess NRV	1
	•	Agree the cost of $720,000 for compound E243 to supporting documentation	1
	•	Confirm the final adjustment for compound E243, discuss with management if adjustment made	1
	•	Review financial statements disclosures for compliance with IAS 2	1
		Restricted to	**6**
(c)		**Substantive procedures – bank loan**	
	•	Agree the opening balance to the prior year audit file and FS	1
	•	For loan payments made, agree to cash book and bank statements	1
	•	Review the bank correspondence for late payment penalties, agree to statement of profit or loss	1
	•	Obtain direct confirmation of year-end balance from bank, agree to the loan schedule	1
	•	Review loan agreement for details of covenants and recalculate to identify any breaches	1
	•	Agree closing balance to the TB and draft FS and review the disclosure of the current liability bank loan	1
		Restricted to	**4**

	Marking guide	Marks
(d)	**Going concern procedures**	
	• Review cash flow forecasts	1
	• Review bank loan agreements, breach of key ratios or covenants	1
	• Review post year-end sales and order book	1
	• Review suppliers correspondence	1
	• Enquire of lawyers for any litigation	1
	• Subsequent events	1
	• Board minutes	1
	• Management accounts	1
	• Consider additional disclosures under IAS 1	1
	• Written representation	1
	Restricted to	**5**
Total		**20**

Examiner's comments

This question covered the area of audit evidence and going concern. Performance across this question was disappointing.

Parts (a) to (c) were scenario based and required substantive procedures for three areas; revaluation of property, plant and equipment (PPE), WIP valuation and bank loans. A key requirement of this part of the syllabus is an ability to describe relevant audit procedures for a particular class of transactions or event. As in previous diets overall performance in this key syllabus area was once again disappointing. Most candidates were unable to tailor their knowledge of general substantive procedures to the specific issues in the question requirements, or provided vague tests such as 'check' or objectives of 'ensure that....' As addressed in previous Examiner's Reports candidates must strive to understand substantive procedures. Learning a generic list of tests will not translate to exam success – procedures must be tailored to the specific requirements of the question. On the revaluation question many candidates provided general PPE tests on areas of title or additions/disposals. Additionally candidates focused on authorisation of capital expenditure or discussing why PPE had been revalued. Answers over auditing the WIP valuation were particularly disappointing. A significant proportion of candidates focused on inventory counts rather than valuation. Candidates must read the question and apply their knowledge to the scenario provided. Substantive procedures provided for the bank loan were stronger, however, again genera bank and cash tests were provided rather than for the bank loans. Additionally some candidates strayed into auditing going concern rather than the liability associated with the bank loan.

Part (d) on going concern procedures was answered satisfactorily. Many candidates were able to generate a sufficient number of points to provide a strong answer. However some candidates failed to understand the question was about procedures rather than going concern indicators. Additionally some procedures lacked detail e.g. 'review board minutes' but the procedure failed to explain what this key source of evidence was being reviewed for.

238 ANDROMEDA *Walk in the footsteps of a top tutor*

Key answer tips

Part (a) is a knowledge question regarding reliability of evidence. This requires text book knowledge. Make sure you provide an explanation.

Parts (b) and (c) ask for audit procedures before and during an inventory count and in relation to R&D expenditure. Your procedures need to be sufficiently detailed to enable another person to understand the procedure to be performed and the reason it should be performed.

Part (d) asks for the reporting implications of an unresolved issue. Work through the information in a logical manner to arrive at the appropriate suggestion. Document each step of the process as this is what earns the marks. You cannot earn all of the marks available if you only state the opinion required.

(a)   Reliability of audit evidence

- The reliability of audit evidence is increased when it is obtained from independent sources outside the entity.

- The reliability of audit evidence which is generated internally is increased when the related controls imposed by the entity, including those over its preparation and maintenance, are effective.

- Audit evidence obtained directly by the auditor is more reliable than audit evidence obtained indirectly or by inference.

- Audit evidence in documentary form, whether paper, electronic or other medium, is more reliable than evidence obtained orally.

- Audit evidence provided by original documents is more reliable than audit evidence provided by photocopies or facsimiles, the reliability of which may depend on the controls over their preparation and maintenance.

(b)   Inventory count procedures

Before the count

- Review the prior year audit files to identify whether there were any particular warehouses where significant inventory issues arose last year.

- Discuss with management whether any of the warehouses this year are new, or have experienced significant control issues.

- Decide which of the 12 warehouses the audit team members will attend, basing this on materiality and risk of each site.

- Obtain a copy of the proposed inventory count instructions, review them to identify any control deficiencies and if any are noted, discuss them with management prior to the counts.

During the count

- Observe the counting teams of Andromeda to confirm whether the inventory count instructions are being followed correctly.

- Select a sample of inventory and perform test counts from inventory sheets to warehouse aisle and from warehouse aisle to inventory sheets.

- Confirm the procedures for identifying and segregating damaged goods are operating correctly, and assess inventory for evidence of any damaged or slow-moving items.

- Observe the procedures for movements of inventory during the count, to confirm that all movements have ceased.

- Obtain a photocopy of the completed sequentially numbered inventory sheets for follow up testing on the final audit.

- Identify and make a note of the last goods received notes and goods despatched notes for 31 December in order to perform cut-off procedures.

- Discuss with the internal audit supervisor how any raw materials quantities have been estimated. Where possible, re-perform the procedures adopted by the supervisor.

(c)   Research and development

- Obtain and cast a schedule of intangible assets, detailing opening balances, amount capitalised in the current year, amortisation and closing balances.

- Agree the opening balances to the prior year financial statements.

- Agree the closing balances to the general ledger, trial balance and draft financial statements.

- Recalculate the amortisation charge for a sample of intangible assets which have commenced production and confirm it is line with the amortisation policy of straight line over five years.

- For the five new projects, discuss with management the details of each project along with the stage of development and whether it has been capitalised or expensed.

- For those expensed as research, agree the costs incurred to invoices and supporting documentation and to inclusion in profit or loss.

- For those capitalised as development, agree costs incurred to invoices and confirm technically feasible by discussion with development managers or review of feasibility reports.

- Review market research reports to confirm Andromeda has the ability to sell the product once complete and probable future economic benefits will arise.

- Review the disclosures for intangible assets in the draft financial statements are in accordance with IAS 38 *Intangible Assets*.

(d) **Auditor's report**

One of the projects Andromeda has developed in the year does not meet the recognition criteria under IAS 38 *Intangible Assets* for capitalisation but has been included within intangible assets. This is contrary to IAS 38, as if the criteria are not met, then this project is research expenditure and should be expensed to profit or loss rather than capitalised.

The error is material as it represents 11.8% of profit before tax (0.98m/8.3m).

Management should adjust the financial statements by removing this project from intangible assets and charging it to profit or loss instead. The finance director's argument that the balance is immaterial is not correct.

If management refuses to amend this error, then the audit opinion will need to be modified as management has not complied with IAS 38.

The error is material but not pervasive, therefore the opinion paragraph would be qualified 'except for'.

A basis for qualified opinion paragraph would be needed and would explain the material misstatement in relation to the incorrect treatment of research and development and the effect on the financial statements.

Marking guide		Marks
(a) **Reliability of evidence**		
• Reliability increased when it is obtained from independent sources		1
• Internally generated evidence more reliable when the controls are effective		1
• Evidence obtained directly by the auditor is more reliable than evidence obtained indirectly or by inference		1
• Evidence in documentary form is more reliable than evidence obtained orally		1
• Evidence provided by original documents is more reliable than evidence provided by copies		1
	Restricted to	**4**
(b) **Inventory count audit procedures**		
Before the count		
• Review the prior year audit files to identify significant inventory issues from last year		1
• Discuss with management if any new warehouses or any sites have significant control issues		1
• Decide which of the 12 warehouses to attend		1
• Review a copy of the proposed inventory count instructions		1
During the count		
• Observe the counters to confirm if inventory count instructions are being followed		1
• Perform 2-way test counts		1
• Confirm procedures for damaged goods		1
• Observe procedures for movements of inventory		
• Obtain a photocopy of the completed inventory sheets		
• Identify and make a note of the last GRNs and GDNs		
• Discuss with the internal audit supervisor how he has estimated the raw materials quantities		
	Restricted to	

Marking guide		Marks
(c)	**Research and development**	
	• Cast the schedule of intangible assets	1
	• Agree the opening balances to the prior year financial statements	1
	• Agree the closing balances to the general ledger, trial balance and draft financial statements	1
	• Recalculate amortisation charged in the year and confirm in line with the policy of straight line over five years	1
	• For new projects, discuss with management the stage of development and if capitalised or expensed	1
	• For those expensed as research, agree costs to invoices, supporting documentation and to inclusion in profit or loss	1
	• Agree development costs to invoice and confirm technically feasible by discussion with development managers	1
	• Review market research reports to confirm Andromeda has the ability to sell the product	1
	• Review the disclosures in the financial statements in accordance with IAS 38	1
	Restricted to	**4**
(d)	**Impact on auditor's report**	
	• Discussion of issue	1
	• Calculation of materiality	1
	• Type of opinion modification required	1
	• Impact on auditor's report	1
		4
Total		**20**

Examiner's comments

Part (a) Candidates were firstly asked to explain factors which influence the reliability of audit evidence. One mark was available for each factor. Candidates were required to either fully explain the factor or compare that factor to another source. This question was generally well answered. A minority of candidates did not fully describe each factor e.g. they noted written evidence was reliable but did not explain why it was reliable, or alternatively, did not make a comparison such as written evidence is stronger than oral evidence. It was pleasing that candidates planned their time carefully and generally only described the required number of factors.

In parts (b) and (c), candidates were further provided with a short scenario based question and were required to describe audit procedures that would be performed before and during an inventory count and audit procedures in relation to research and development costs. As in previous sitting and as noted in previous examiner's reports the provision of audit procedures relevant to particular circumstances was not well attempted by the majority of candidates. Most candidates were able to identify that the count procedures should be obtained before the inventory count, however a significant number did not expand to explain the purpose of obtaining this information or the importance of the auditor reviewing the adequacy of these instructions. Candidates often then listed further details to be obtained e.g. location of count, assembling the audit team, whether to use an expert etc. A number of candidates referred to third party inventory however this was not mentioned in the scenario and therefore any related procedures were not valid. Only the better candidates suggested looking at prior year audit files or, considered the materiality of the sites and control issues at sites. Most candidates did note that during the count the auditor should observe the counters to ensure the instructions were being followed.

However a significant number of candidates then proceeded to list the count procedures that the company's counting team should follow thereby straying into management responsibilities rather than the procedures relevant to the auditor. Some candidates correctly suggested undertaking test counts, while only a minority suggested obtaining copies of the completed count sheets. Overall it was disappointing that candidates did not seem familiar with the auditor's role at an inventory count. In relation to research and development costs, some candidates correctly suggested that the auditor needed to ensure compliance with the capitalisation criteria in IAS 38 and also suggested recalculating the amortisation charge, but few candidates identified any other relevant procedures. Many candidates did not score any marks for this requirement. Although many candidates suggested a review of invoices, the procedure described was most often testing valuation or rights and obligations rather than to ensure correct classification.

Part (d) Candidates were required to discuss the implication on the auditor's report if an issue surrounding research and development costs remained unresolved. This question was well answered. Most candidates stated the issue, being that the project did not meet the capitalisation criteria, however few candidates explained the impact on the financial statements e.g. assets would be overstated and profit understated. The majority of candidates correctly calculated materiality, however a small number of candidates incorrectly calculated materiality based on the size of the project as a percentage of total research and development spend (i.e. 49%), thereby not considering the materiality of the issue to the financial statements as a whole. Overall it was encouraging to note that reporting questions have shown a continued improvement in recent sittings.

239 HAWTHORN *Walk in the footsteps of a top tutor*

Key answer tips

In part (a) make sure you give assertions relevant to transactions and events. Procedures need to be properly described to earn a full mark. Make it clear what the auditor needs to do and what the procedure will achieve.

The scenario for parts (b) to (d) provides details of very specific issues that have occurred during the year. Your procedures need to focus on these issues rather than the balances in general.

(a)   Occurrence

The transactions and events that have been recorded have actually occurred and pertain to the entity.

Substantive procedures

Select a sample of sales transactions recorded in the sales day book; agree the details back to a goods despatched note (GDN) and customer order.

Review the monthly breakdown of sales per key product, compare to the prior year and budget and investigate any significant differences.

Completeness

All transactions and events that should have been recorded have been recorded.

Substantive procedures

Select a sample of GDNs raised during the year; agree to the sales invoice and that they are recorded in the sales day book.

Review the total amount of sales, compare to the prior year and budget and investigate any significant differences.

Accuracy

The amounts and other data relating to recorded transactions and events have been recorded appropriately.

Substantive procedures

Select a sample of sales invoices and recalculate that the totals and calculation of sales tax are correct.

For a sample of sales invoices, confirm the sales price stated agrees to the authorised price list.

Cut-off

Transactions and events have been recorded in the correct accounting period.

Substantive procedures

Select a sample of pre and post year-end GDNs and agree that the sale is recorded in the correct period's sales day books.

Review the post year-end sales returns and agree if they relate to pre year-end sales that the revenue has been correctly removed from the sales day book.

Classification

Transactions and events have been recorded in the proper accounts.

Substantive procedures

Agree for a sample of sales invoices that they have been correctly recorded within revenue nominal account codes and included within revenue in the financial statements.

Presentation

Transactions and events are appropriately aggregated or disaggregated and clearly described, and related disclosures are relevant and understandable in the context of the applicable financial reporting framework.

Substantive procedures

Obtain a breakdown of revenue by account code and cast to ensure accuracy. Agree the breakdown of revenue disclosed in the financial statements to the revenue account codes within the nominal ledger.

(b) **Supplier statement reconciliations**

- Select a representative sample of year-end supplier statements and agree the balance to the payables ledger of Hawthorn. If the balance agrees, then no further work is required.

- Where differences occur due to invoices in transit, confirm from goods received notes (GRN) whether the receipt of goods was pre year-end, if so confirm that this receipt is included in year-end accruals.

- Where differences occur due to cash in transit from Hawthorn to the supplier, confirm from the cashbook and bank statements that the cash was sent pre year-end.

- Discuss any further adjusting items with the payables ledger supervisor to understand the nature of the reconciling item, and whether it has been correctly accounted for.

(c) **Bank reconciliation**

- Obtain Hawthorn's bank account reconciliation and cast to check the additions to ensure arithmetical accuracy.

- Agree the balance per the bank reconciliation to an original year-end bank statement and to the bank confirmation letter.

- Agree the reconciliation's balance per the cash book to the year-end cash book.

- Trace all the outstanding lodgements to the pre year-end cash book, post year-end bank statement and also to paying-in-book pre year-end.

- Trace all un-presented cheques through to a pre year-end cash book and post year-end statement. For any unusual amounts or significant delays, obtain explanations from management.

- Examine any old un-presented cheques to assess if they need to be written back into the payables ledger as they are no longer valid to be presented.

(d) **Receivables**

- Review the aged receivable ledger to identify any slow-moving or old receivable balances, discuss the status of these balances with the credit controller to assess whether they are likely to pay.

- Select a significant sample of receivables and review whether there are any after date cash receipts, ensure that a sample of slow-moving/old receivable balances is also selected.

- Review customer correspondence to identify any balances which are in dispute or unlikely to be paid.

- Review board minutes to identify whether there are any significant concerns in relation to payments by customers.

- Calculate the average receivables collection period and compare this to prior year, investigate any significant differences.

- Inspect post year-end sales returns/credit notes and consider whether an additional allowance against receivables is required.

- Select a sample of goods despatched notes (GDN) before and just after the year-end and follow through to the receivables ledger to ensure they are recorded in the correct accounting period.

- Select a sample of year-end receivable balances and agree back to valid supporting documentation of GDN and sales order to ensure existence.

	Marking guide	Marks
(a)	**Assertions and substantive procedures relevant to revenue**	
	• Occurrence	
	• Completeness	2
	• Accuracy	2
	• Cut-off	2
	• Classification	2
	• Presentation	2
	Restricted to	**8**
(b)	**Supplier statement reconciliations**	
	• Select a sample of supplier statements and agree the balance to the payables ledger	1
	• Invoices in transit, confirm via GRN if receipt of goods was pre year-end, if so confirm included in year-end accruals	1
	• Cash in transit, confirm from cashbook and bank statements the cash was sent pre year-end	1
	• Discuss any further adjusting items with the payables ledger supervisor	1
	Restricted to	**3**
(c)	**Bank reconciliation**	
	• Check additions of bank reconciliation	1
	• Bank balance to statement/bank confirmation	1
	• Cash book balance to cash book	1
	• Outstanding lodgments	1
	• Un-presented cheques review	1
	• Old cheques write back	1
	Restricted to	**4**
(d)	**Receivables**	
	• Aged receivables report to identify any slow-moving balances	1
	• Review the after date cash receipts	1
	• Review customer correspondence to assess whether there are any invoices in dispute	1
	• Review board minutes	1
	• Calculate the average receivables collection period	1
	• Post year-end sales returns/credit notes	1
	• Cut-off testing of GDN	1
	• Agree to GDN and sales order to ensure existence	1
	Restricted to	**5**
Total		**20**

Examiner's comments

Part (a) comprised (ai) which required four financial statement assertions relevant to classes of transactions and events and part (aii) which required an example substantive procedure for each assertion identified which would be relevant to the audit of revenue. This question was unrelated to the scenario and was knowledge based, and candidates' performance was unsatisfactory. Financial statement assertions are a key element of the syllabus and so it was very disappointing to see that a significant minority of candidates do not know the assertions relevant to classes of transactions and events. A significant proportion of candidates provided existence and valuation which were irrelevant as these are assertions relevant to account balances. Where candidates did correctly identify the assertions they often failed to explain them adequately or did so with reference to assets and liabilities rather than transactions. Also many explanations were too brief or simply repeated the assertion, such as, 'accuracy ensures the amounts in the financial statements are accurate'. A number of candidates provided example procedures which were not relevant when testing revenue, but instead focused on receivables or purchases. This can only be due to a failure to read the question requirement properly. In addition many procedures were vague or incomplete, such as agreeing goods despatch notes to sales invoices but not then agreeing the invoices to the sales day book. Also many of the procedures were tests of control rather than substantive procedures. The direction of the occurrence and completeness tests were often confused resulting in incorrect procedures. The direction of occurrence tests should generally start at accounting records, whereas completeness procedures should begin at source documents.

The remainder of the question provided candidates with three short scenarios detailing matters that had been brought to attention prior to the audit fieldwork and candidates were expected to produce appropriate substantive procedures relevant to each matter. Part (b) required substantive procedures in relation to auditing supplier statement reconciliations. Part (c) required substantive procedures over the bank reconciliation and finally part (d) required substantive procedures in relation to the existence and valuation of receivables. Performance on this question was unsatisfactory. A significant minority did not attempt all parts of this question. Most candidates were unable to tailor their knowledge of general substantive procedures to the specific issues in the scenario and question requirements. Many candidates spotted the terms payables, bank and receivables and proceeded to list all possible tests for these areas. This is not what was required and this approach scored few or no marks. The scenario was provided so that candidates could apply their knowledge. However it seems that many candidates did not take any notice of the scenario at all. As addressed in previous examiner's reports candidates must strive to understand substantive procedures, learning a generic list of tests will not translate to exam success as they must be responsive to the scenario.

In part (b) candidates needed to focus on testing supplier statement reconciliations rather than trade payables in general. The most common correct answer awarded credit was 'agree the supplier statements to the payables ledger.' Very few candidates scored more than 1 mark. Incorrect answers focused on calculating trade payables days or undertaking a payables circularisation.

In part (c) many candidates focused on auditing the cash balance rather than the bank reconciliation. Hence answers such as casting the cash book, requesting a bank confirmation letter or counting the petty cash balance were not awarded any credit. Preparation of bank reconciliations is part of the Financial Accounting syllabus and therefore candidates should have considered the items which are included as part of the bank reconciliation and focused on deriving tests to audit each component. In addition to verify if un-presented cheques and outstanding lodgements were valid reconciling items, audit procedures should have focused on inclusion in the pre year-end cashbook and post year-end bank statements. Very few candidates demonstrated an understanding of this point.

In part (d) stronger candidates were able to generate tests focusing on analytical review against prior year balances, review of aged receivables listing or discussions with management about an allowance for receivables. However, a significant proportion of candidates incorrectly suggested undertaking receivables circularisation, including the detailed steps required, this was despite the scenario clearly stating that the finance director had requested that a circularisation not be carried out. The requirement verb was to 'describe' therefore sufficient detail was required to score the 1 mark available per test. Candidates must provide enough tests as they should assume 1 mark per valid procedure. Candidates are reminded yet again that substantive procedures are a core topic area and they must be able to produce relevant detailed procedures.

240 PINEAPPLE BEACH HOTEL *Walk in the footsteps of a top tutor*

Key answer tips

In part (a) make sure you give assertions relevant to account balances. Procedures need to be properly described to earn a full mark. Make it clear what the auditor needs to do and what the procedure will achieve.

Parts (b) and (c) require substantive procedures over two specific issues. Substantive procedures are used to test the amounts included in the financial statements, therefore focus on how to obtain evidence to support the depreciation charge for the new equipment and the claim for food poisoning.

Part (d) is a knowledge requirement covering working paper contents. This is rote-learned knowledge from the text book.

(a) **Financial statement assertions and inventory substantive procedures**

(i) **Existence**

Assets, liabilities and equity interests exist.

Substantive procedures

During the inventory count select a sample of assets recorded in the inventory records and agree to the warehouse to confirm the assets exist.

Obtain a sample of pre year-end goods despatch notes and agree that these finished goods are excluded from the inventory records.

(ii) **Rights and obligations**

The entity holds or controls the rights to assets, and liabilities are the obligations of the entity.

Substantive procedures

Confirm during the inventory count that any goods belonging to third parties are excluded from the inventory records and count.

For year-end raw materials and finished goods confirm title belongs to the company by agreeing goods to a recent purchase invoice in the company name.

(iii) **Completeness**

All assets, liabilities and equity interests that should have been recorded have been recorded.

Substantive procedures

Obtain a copy of the inventory listing and agree the total to the general ledger and the financial statements.

During the inventory count select a sample of goods physically present in the warehouse and confirm recorded in the inventory records.

(iv) **Accuracy, valuation and allocation**

Assets, liabilities and equity interests are included in the financial statements at appropriate amounts and any resulting valuation or allocation adjustments are appropriately recorded.

Substantive procedures

Select a sample of goods in inventory at the year-end, agree the cost per the records to a recent purchase invoice and ensure that the cost is correctly stated.

Select a sample of year-end goods and review post year-end sales invoices to ascertain if net realisable value is above cost or if an adjustment is required.

(v) **Presentation/Classification**

Account balances are appropriately aggregated or disaggregated and clearly described, and related disclosures are relevant and understandable in the context of the applicable financial reporting framework.

Assets, liabilities and equity interests have been recorded in the proper accounts.

Substantive procedures

Agree the breakdown of finished goods, work-in-progress and raw materials disclosed in the financial statements to the account codes within the nominal ledger.

(b) Depreciation

- Review the reasonableness of the depreciation rates applied to the new leisure facilities and compare to industry averages.

- Review the capital expenditure budgets for the next few years to assess whether there are any plans to replace any of the new leisure equipment, as this would indicate that the useful life is less than 10 years.

- Review profits and losses on disposal of assets disposed of in the year to assess the reasonableness of the depreciation policies.

- Select a sample of new leisure equipment and recalculate the depreciation charge to ensure arithmetical accuracy of the charge.

- Perform a proof in total calculation for the depreciation charged on the new equipment, discuss with management if significant fluctuations arise.

- Review the disclosure of the depreciation charges and policies in the draft financial statements.

(c) **Food poisoning claim**

- Review the correspondence from the customers claiming food poisoning to assess whether Pineapple has a present obligation as a result of a past event.

- Send an enquiry letter to the lawyers of Pineapple to obtain their view as to the probability of the claim being successful.

- Review board minutes to understand whether the directors believe that the claim will be successful or not.

- Review the post year-end period to assess whether any payments have been made to any of the claimants.

- Discuss with management as to whether they propose to include a contingent liability disclosure or not, consider the reasonableness of this.

- Obtain a written management representation confirming management's view that the lawsuit is unlikely to be successful and hence no provision is required.

- Review the adequacy of any disclosures made in the financial statements to ensure they are in accordance with IAS 37 *Provisions, Contingent Liabilities and Contingent Assets*.

(d) **Working papers**

- Name of client – identifies the client being audited.

- Year-end date – identifies the year-end to which the audit working papers relate.

- Subject – identifies the area of the financial statements that is being audited, the topic area of the working paper, such as receivables circularisation.

- Working paper reference – provides a clear reference to identify the number of the working paper.

- Preparer – identifies the name of the audit team member who prepared the working paper, so any queries can be directed to the relevant person.

- Date prepared – the date that the audit work was performed by the team member; this helps to identify what was known at the time and what issues may have occurred subsequently.

- Reviewer – the name of the audit team member who reviewed the working paper; this provides evidence that the audit work was reviewed by an appropriate member of the team.

- Date of review – the date the audit work was reviewed by the senior member of the team; this should be prior to the date that the auditor's report was signed.

- Objective of work/test – the aim of the work being performed, could be the related financial statement assertion; this provides the context for why the audit procedure is being performed.

- Details of work performed – the audit tests performed along with sufficient detail of items selected for testing.

- Results of work performed – whether any exceptions arose in the audit work and if any further work is required.

- Conclusion – the overall conclusion on the audit work performed, whether the area is true and fair.

	Marking guide		Marks
(a)	**Assertions and substantive procedures relevant to inventory**		
	• Existence		2
	• Rights and obligations		2
	• Completeness		2
	• Valuation and allocation		2
	• Presentation / Classification		2
			–––
		Restricted to	8
			–––
(b)	**Depreciation**		
	• Review the reasonableness of the depreciation rates		1
	• Review the capital expenditure budgets		1
	• Review profits and losses on disposal for assets disposed of in year		1
	• Recalculate the depreciation charge for a sample of assets		1
	• Perform a proof in total calculation		1
	• Review the disclosure in the draft financial statements		1
			–––
		Restricted to	4
			–––
(c)	**Food poisoning claim**		
	• Review the correspondence from the customers		1
	• Enquire of the lawyers as to the probability of the claim being successful		1
	• Review board minutes		1
	• Review the post year-end period to assess whether any payments have been made		1
	• Discuss with management as to whether they propose to include a contingent liability disclosure		1
	• Obtain a written management representation		1
	• Review any disclosures made in the financial statements		1
			–––
		Restricted to	4
			–––
(d)	**Working paper contents**		
	• Name of client		1
	• Year-end date		1
	• Subject		1
	• Working paper reference		1
	• Preparer		1
	• Date prepared		1
	• Reviewer		1
	• Date of review		1
	• Objective of work/test		1
	• Details of work performed		1
	• Results of work performed		1
	• Conclusion		1
			–––
		Restricted to	4
			–––
Total			20
			–––

Examiner's comments

This question required substantive procedures for depreciation and a contingent liability for a food poisoning case. Performance on this question was unsatisfactory. A significant minority did not even attempt this part of the question. Candidates' answers for depreciation tended to be weaker than for the food poisoning. On the depreciation many candidates did not focus their answer on the issue identified, which related to the depreciation method adopted for the capital expenditure incurred in the year. In the scenario the issue was headed up as depreciation and so this should have given candidates a clue that they needed to focus just on depreciation. However, a significant proportion of answers were on general PPE tests often without any reference at all to depreciation. In addition many felt that generic tests such as 'get an expert's advice' or 'obtain management representation' were appropriate tests; they are not. The food poisoning issue tended to be answered slightly better, however again tests tended to be too brief, 'read board minutes', 'discuss with management' or 'discuss with the lawyer' did not score any marks as they do not explain what is to be discussed or what we are looking for in the board minutes.

In addition a minority of candidates focused on auditing the kitchen and food hygiene procedures with tests such as 'observing the kitchen process' or 'writing to customers to see if they have had food poisoning.' This is not the focus of the auditor and does not provide evidence with regards to the potential contingent liability.

Substantive procedures are a core topic area and future candidates must focus on being able to generate specific and detailed tests.

ADDITIONAL QUESTIONS

241 SAXOPHONE ENTERPRISES *Walk in the footsteps of a top tutor*

Key answer tips

This question requires corporate governance weaknesses within the scenario to be explained and a recommendation provided for each. Knowledge of the Corporate Governance Code is required here. Work through on a line by line basis and consider whether the information suggests that the company is being properly managed and controlled in the best interests of the shareholders.

Corporate governance weaknesses and recommendations

Weakness	Recommendation
Bill Bassoon is now the chair after having been the chief executive until last year. The chair must be an independent non-executive director and hence cannot have previously been the chief executive of the same company. The roles of chair and chief executive are both very important and carry significant responsibilities.	Bill Bassoon should return to his role as chief executive as this will fill the current vacancy and an independent non-executive director should be recruited to fill the role of chair. Open advertising and/or an external search

Weakness	Recommendation
Too much power resides in the hands of one individual.	consultancy should be used for the appointment of the chair.
The board comprises five executives and only three non-executive directors. There should be an appropriate balance of executives and non-executives, to ensure that the board makes the correct objective decisions, which are in the best interest of the stakeholders of the company. The executives can dominate the board's decision-making.	At least half the board, excluding the chair should be independent NEDs. Hence the board of Saxophone should consider recruiting and appointing two additional independent non-executive directors.
Bill Bassoon is considering appointing his close friend as a non-executive director. The friend has experience of running a manufacturing company. If this director is a close friend of Bill Bassoon, then it is possible that he will not be independent. In addition, other than being a former chief executive, he does not have any relevant experience of the insurance industry and so it is questionable what value he will add to Saxophone.	Only independent non-executives with relevant experience and skills should be appointed to the board of Saxophone. Appointments should be based on merit and objective criteria and should promote diversity. The close friend of Bill Bassoon is unlikely to meet these criteria, as he has no experience in the insurance industry, and so should not be appointed. Open advertising and/or an external search consultancy should be used for the appointment of the NEDs.
The remuneration for directors is set by Jessie Oboe, the finance director. However, no director should be involved in setting their own remuneration as this may result in excessive levels of pay being set. Jessie may pay more to directors who are willing to support his agenda in board meetings.	The board should establish formal and transparent procedures for developing the policy for executive directors' remuneration. The remuneration committee should determine the policy for executive director remuneration, as well as set the remuneration for the chair, executive directors and senior management.
All directors' remuneration is in the form of an annual bonus. Pay should motivate the directors to focus on the long-term growth of the business. Annual targets can encourage short-term strategies rather than maximising shareholder wealth.	The remuneration of executives should be restructured to include a significant proportion aimed at long-term, sustainable company performance. Shares awards should be released for sale on a phased basis and be subject to a total vesting and holding period of five years or more.

Weakness	Recommendation
In addition, non-executive directors' pay should not be based on meeting company targets as their pay should be independent of how the company performs.	NED remuneration should be determined by the board. It should reflect time commitment and responsibilities of the role and should not include share options or other performance related elements.
Saxophone does not currently have an audit committee. Audit committees undertake an important role in that they help the directors to satisfy their responsibility of accountability with regards to maintaining an appropriate relationship with the company's auditor. Without an audit committee there is no oversight of the financial reporting processes of the company.	Saxophone should appoint an audit committee as soon as possible. The committee should comprise at least three independent non-executives, one of whom should have relevant financial experience.
A new sales director was appointed nine months ago, however, he has not undergone any board training. All directors should receive induction training when they first join the board so that they are fully aware of their responsibilities. The new sales director may not be fully effective in the role without the relevant training and induction.	The new sales director should immediately receive relevant training from Bill Bassoon to ensure that he has a full understanding of his role and responsibilities.
Saxophone is not planning to hold an annual general meeting (AGM) as the number of shareholders are such that it would be too costly and impractical. However, the AGM is an important meeting in that it gives the shareholders an opportunity to raise any concerns, receive an answer and vote on important resolutions. The proposal to send the financial statements and resolutions by email is not appropriate as it does not allow shareholders an opportunity to raise relevant questions.	The company should continue to hold the AGM. Sending information by email in advance of the meeting may be practical and save some costs; however, this should not be seen as a replacement for the AGM.

Marking guide

	Marks
Corporate governance weaknesses and recommendations	
• Chief executive is now chair	2
• Currently only three of eight directors are non-executive, should be at least half	2
• Chair considering appointing his friend as a non-executive	2
• Finance director decides on the remuneration for the directors	2
• Remuneration for all directors in form of annual bonus	2
• No audit committee at present	2
• No induction training for new sales director	2
• No AGM planned as felt impractical and too costly	2
Max 5 issues, 2 marks each	10
Total	10

Examiner's comments

Candidates performed well on this question. Most candidates were able to confidently identify weaknesses from the scenario. However many could not explain the weakness, relying on explanations such as 'this is not good corporate governance'. This was not sufficient to score the extra ½ marks available for each point. Candidates needed to be able to explain how these weaknesses impacted the company.

In addition a significant proportion of candidates misread the scenario and thought the chair and chief executive was the same person. This was not correct. Bill Bassoon had been the chief executive and was now the chair. Hence answers focused on these key roles being held by the same person rather than the chair not being independent and failed to score marks as a result. Candidates must read the scenario carefully before they start to write.

The recommendations provided were not adequate in many cases and often answers gave corporate governance objectives rather than recommendations, such as, 'the board should be balanced between executive and nonexecutives'. This is an objective; the recommendation should have been to 'appoint additional non-executive directors to ensure a balanced board'.

242 ORANGE FINANCIALS *Walk in the footsteps of a top tutor*

Key answer tips

This is a typical ethical threats question focusing on threats to objectivity. Remember to explain the threat properly, don't just state the name of the threat but explain how it could affect the auditor's behaviour when performing the audit.

For the safeguard, state the relevant guidance from the ACCA Code of Ethics and Conduct.

Ethical threats and managing these risks

Ethical Threat	Managing Risk
Orange Financials Co (Orange) has asked the engagement partner of Currant & Co to attend meetings with potential investors. This represents an advocacy threat. The audit firm may be perceived as promoting investment in Orange and this threatens objectivity.	The engagement partner should politely decline this request from Orange, as it represents too great a threat to independence.
Due to the stock exchange listing, Orange has requested that Currant & Co produce the financial statements. This represents a self-review threat. The auditor may not detect errors in the financial statements they were responsible for preparing, or, may not wish to admit to errors that are detected.	As Orange is currently not a listed company then Currant & Co are permitted to produce the financial statements and also audit them. However, Orange is seeking a listing, therefore, ideally Currant & Co should not undertake the preparation of the financial statements as this would represent too high a risk. If Currant & Co chooses to produce the financial statements then separate teams should undertake each assignment and the audit team should not be part of the accounts preparation process. The preparation must be routine and mechanical in nature, therefore the audit firm must not be responsible for selecting accounting policies or determining accounting estimates.
The assistant finance director of Orange has joined Currant & Co as a partner and has been proposed as the review partner. This represents a self-review threat. The new review partner will not be independent and may not detect errors, or, may not wish to admit to errors that are detected in the financial statements he was responsible for whilst in the position of FD. He will also lack professional scepticism.	This partner must not be involved in the audit of Orange until a cooling-off period has been served. An alternative review partner should be appointed.
Orange has several potential assurance assignments available and Currant & Co wish to be appointed to these. There is a potential self-interest threat as these assurance fees along with the external audit fee could represent a significant proportion of Currant & Co's fee income.	The firm should assess whether these assignments, along with the audit fee, would represent more than 15% of gross practice income for two consecutive years. These assurance assignments will only arise if the company obtains its listing and hence will be a public interest company.

Ethical Threat	Managing Risk
The firm may be reluctant to upset their client for fear of losing the work and associated fees.	If the recurring fees are likely to exceed 15% of annual practice income then additional consideration should be given as to whether these assignments should be sought by the firm. Fees will need to be discussed with the audit committee.
Orange has implied to Currant & Co that they must complete the audit quickly and with minimal questions/issues if they wish to obtain the assurance assignments. This creates an intimidation threat on the team. They may feel pressure to cut corners and not raise issues, and this could compromise the objectivity of the audit team.	The engagement partner should politely inform the finance director that the team will undertake the audit in accordance with all relevant ISAs and their own quality control procedures. This means that the audit will take as long as is necessary to obtain sufficient, appropriate evidence to form an opinion. If any residual concerns remain or the intimidation threat continues then Currant & Co may need to consider resigning from the engagement.
The finance director has offered the team a free weekend away at a luxury hotel. This represents a self-interest threat. The audit team may feel indebted to the client and reluctant to raise issues identified during the audit.	Acceptance of goods and services, unless clearly trivial and inconsequential in value, is not permitted. As it is unlikely that a weekend at a luxury hotel for the whole team has an insignificant value, then this offer should be politely declined.

Marking guide		Marks
Ethical threats and safeguards		
• Engagement partner attending listing meeting		2
• Preparation of financial statements		2
• Assistant finance director as review partner on audit		2
• Total fee income		2
• Pressure to complete audit quickly and with minimal issues		2
• Weekend away at luxury hotel		2
• Provision of loan at preferential rates		2
	Max 5 issues, 2 marks each	10
Total		10

Examiner's comments

This question required an explanation of ethical threats from the scenario and a method for reducing each of these threats. This was very well answered with many candidates scoring full marks. Ethics questions are often answered well by candidates and the scenario provided contained many possible threats. Where candidates did not score well this was usually because they only identified rather than explained the ethical threat. In addition some candidates identified the threat but when explaining them they came up with incorrect examples of the type of threat; such as attending the weekend away at a luxury hotel gave rise to a familiarity threat rather than a self-interest threat. The threat which candidates struggled with the most was the intimidation threat caused by management requesting the audit team ask minimal questions. The response given by many candidates was to decline the assurance engagement which does not address the intimidation threat. Instead candidates needed to stress that this issue needed to be discussed with the finance director and that appropriate audit procedures would be undertaken to ensure the quality of the audit was not compromised. In addition when explaining issues some candidates listed many examples of ethical threats; such as 'the assistant finance director being the review partner gives rise to a familiarity, self-review and self-interest threat.' This scatter gun approach to questions is not recommended as it wastes time.

243 VIOLET & CO *Walk in the footsteps of a top tutor*

Key answer tips

This is a typical completion and reporting question and the requirement gives you an approach to use. Discuss the issue, consider if it is material, recommend further procedures and describe the impact on the auditor's report. When discussing the impact on the auditor's report, remember that the opinion is only one element of the report. Consider whether there is a need for any further impact such as a 'basis for' paragraph if you are suggesting the opinion should be modified.

Daisy Co

(i)   Daisy Co's sales ledger has been corrupted by a computer virus therefore no detailed testing has been performed on revenue and receivables. The audit team will need to see if they can confirm revenue and receivables in an alternative manner. If they are unable to do this, then two significant balances in the financial statements will not have been confirmed.

Revenue and receivables are both higher than the total profit before tax (PBT) of $2 million. Receivables are 170% of PBT and revenue is nearly eight times the PBT, hence this is a very material issue.

(ii)   Procedures to be adopted include:

- Discuss with management whether they have any alternative records which detail revenue and receivables for the year.

- Attempt to perform analytical procedures, such as proof in total or monthly comparison to last year, to gain comfort in total for revenue and for receivables.

(iii)   The auditors will need to modify the opinion as they are unable to obtain sufficient appropriate evidence in relation to two material and pervasive areas, being receivables and revenue.

The opinion paragraph will be a disclaimer of opinion and will state that the auditor does not express an opinion on the financial statements.

A basis for disclaimer of opinion paragraph will explain the limitation in relation to the lack of evidence over revenue and receivables.

Fuchsia Co

(i)   Fuchsia Co is facing going concern problems as it has experienced difficult trading conditions and it has a negative cash outflow. However, the financial statements have been prepared using the going concern basis of accounting, even though it is possible that the company is not a going concern.

The prior year financial statements showed a profit of $1.2 million and the current financial statements show a loss before tax of $4.4 million, the net cash outflow of $3.2 million represents 73% of this loss (3.2/4.4) and hence is a material issue.

(ii)   Management are confident that further funding can be obtained, however the team is sceptical and so the following procedures should be adopted:

- Discuss with management whether any finance has now been secured.

- Review the correspondence with the finance provider to confirm the level of funding that is to be provided and this should be compared to the net cash outflow of $3.2 million.

- Review the most recent board minutes to understand whether management's view on Fuchsia Co's going concern has altered.

- Review the cash flow forecasts for the year and assess the reasonableness of the assumptions adopted.

(iii)   If management refuses to amend the going concern basis, or at the very least make adequate going concern disclosures, the audit opinion will need to be modified.

As the going concern basis is probably incorrect the misstatement is material and pervasive.

The opinion paragraph will be an adverse opinion and will state that the financial statements do not give a true and fair view.

A basis for adverse opinion paragraph will explain the inappropriate use of the going concern basis of accounting.

Marking guide	Marks
Daisy Designs Co	
• Discussion of issue	1
• Calculation of materiality	1
• Procedures at completion stage	2
• Type of audit opinion modification required	1
• Impact on auditor's report	1
Fuchsia Co	
• Discussion of issue	1
• Calculation of materiality	1
• Procedures at completion stage	2
• Type of audit opinion modification required	1
• Impact on auditor's report	1
Max 5 marks per issue	10
Total	**10**

Examiner's comments

This question required a discussion of two issues; an assessment of the materiality of each; procedures to resolve each issue and the impact on the auditor's report if each issue remained unresolved. Performance was mixed on this question. There were a significant minority of candidates who did not devote sufficient time and effort to this question bearing in mind the number of marks available. The requirement to discuss the two issues of Daisy Co's corrupted sales ledger and Fuchsia Co's going concern problem was on whole, answered well by most candidates. In addition many candidates correctly identified that each issue was clearly material. A significant minority seemed to believe the corruption of the sales ledger was an adjusting event and so incorrectly proceeded to focus on subsequent events. With regards to procedures to undertake at the completion stage, candidates seemed to struggle with Daisy. Given that the sales ledger had been corrupted procedures such as 'agree goods despatch notes to sales invoices to the sales ledger' or 'reconcile the sales ledger to the general ledger' were unlikely to be possible. Most candidates correctly identified relevant analytical procedures and a receivables circularisation. Candidates performed better on auditing the going concern of Fuchsia Co, however some candidates wasted time by providing a long list of going concern tests when only one or two were needed. Performance on the impact on the auditor's report if each issue remained unresolved was unsatisfactory. Candidates still continue to recommend an emphasis of matter paragraph for all reporting questions, this is not the case and it was not relevant for either issue. Candidates need to understand what an emphasis of matter paragraph is and why it is used. A significant number of candidates were unable to identify the correct modification, suggesting that Daisy Co's should be qualified or adverse, as opposed to disclaimer of opinion. Also some answers contradicted themselves with answers of 'the issue is not material therefore qualify the opinion'. Additionally many candidates ignored the question requirement to only consider the impact if the issue was unresolved. Lots of answers started with 'if resolved the auditor's report …..' this was not required. In relation to the impact on the auditor's report, many candidates were unable to describe how the opinion paragraph would change and so failed to maximise their marks. Once again future candidates are reminded that the auditor's report is the only output of a statutory audit and hence is considered very important for this exam.

Section 5

SPECIMEN EXAM QUESTIONS

Section A

This section of the exam contains **three OT cases**.

Each OT case contains a scenario which relates to **five OT questions**.

Each question is worth **2 marks** and is compulsory.

This exam section is worth **30 marks** in total.

Select **Next** to continue.

You are an audit manager at Buffon & Co, responsible for the audit of Maldini Co and you have become aware of the following information:

Audit engagement partner
The audit engagement partner for Maldini Co, a listed company, has been in place for approximately eight years and her son has just been offered a role with Maldini Co as a sales manager. This role would entitle him to shares in Maldini Co as part of his remuneration package.

Internal audit function
Maldini Co's board of directors are considering establishing an internal audit function, and the finance director has asked your firm about the differences in the role of internal audit and external audit. If the internal audit function is established, the board has suggested that they may wish to outsource this to Buffon & Co.

Auditor characteristics
Following management's request for information regarding the different roles of internal and external auditors, the audit assistant has collated a list of key characteristics:

(1) Appointed by audit committee
(2) Reports are publicly available to shareholders
(3) Review effectiveness of internal controls to improve operations
(4) Express an opinion on the truth and fairness of the financial statements

Fees
The finance director has suggested to the board that if Buffon & Co are appointed as internal as well as external auditors, then fees should be renegotiated with at least 20% of all internal and external audit fees being based on the profit after tax of the company, as this will align the interests of Buffon & Co and Maldini Co. This fee income would be significant to Buffon & Co.

Q1

Your audit assistant has highlighted a number of potential threats to independence in respect of the audit of Maldini Co.

Identify which of the following represent valid threats to independence, matching each threat to the appropriate category.

Facts	Category of threat

Facts	Category of threat
Length of time the audit engagement partner has been in position	Self-interest
Maldini Co's request for advice regarding internal audit	Self-interest
Potential holding of shares by audit partner's son	Familiarity
Possible provision of internal audit services	Self-review
Basis of fee	

Q2

In relation to the audit engagement partner holding the role for eight years, and her son's offer of employment with Maldini Co:

Which of the following safeguards should be implemented in order to comply with ACCA's Code of Ethics and Conduct?

⊙ The audit partner should be removed from the audit team

⊙ An engagement quality control reviewer should be appointed

⊙ A third party such as a professional body should be consulted on key audit judgments

⊙ Buffon & Co should resign from the audit

Q3

In line with ACCA's Code of Ethics and Conduct, which TWO of the following factors must be considered before the internal audit engagement should be accepted?

☐ Whether the external audit team have the expertise to carry out the internal audit work

☐ If the assignments will relate to the internal controls over financial reporting

☐ If management will accept responsibility for implementing appropriate recommendations

☐ The probable timescale for the outsourcing of the internal audit function

Q4

Match each of the characteristics identified by the audit assistant to the appropriate type of auditor.

Characteristic
1
2
3
4

Type of auditor
Internal auditor
Internal auditor
External auditor
External auditor

Q5

If the internal and external audit assignments are accepted, which of the following statements is TRUE regarding the proposed basis for the fee?

- As long as the total fee received from Maldini Co is less than 15% of the firm's total fee income then no safeguards are needed

- The client should be informed that only the internal audit fee can be based on profit after tax

- The fees should be based on Maldini Co's profit before tax

- No safeguards can be applied and this basis for fee determination should be rejected

It is 1 July 20X5. Balotelli Co operates a number of hotels providing accommodation, leisure facilities and restaurants. You are an audit supervisor of Mario & Co, conducting the audit of Balotelli Co for the year ended 31 December 20X4. The following information has been brought to your attention.

Non-current assets

Balotelli Co incurred significant capital expenditure during the year updating the leisure facilities at several of the company's hotels. Depreciation is charged on all assets monthly on a straight-line basis (SL) and it is company policy to charge a full month's depreciation in the month of acquisition and none in the month of disposal. The audit team has obtained the following extract of the non-current assets register detailing some of the new leisure equipment acquired during the year:

Date	Description	Cost ($)	Depreciation policy	Charge for the year ($)	Carrying amount ($)
01/05/X4	15 treadmills	18,000	36 months SL	4,000	14,000
15/05/X4	20 exercise bikes	17,000	3 years SL	5,667	11,333
17/08/X4	15 rowing machines	9,750	36 months SL	2,167	7,583
19/08/X4	10 cross trainers	11,000	36 months SL	1,528	9,472
		55,750		13,362	42,388

In order to verify the depreciation charge for the year the audit team has been asked to recalculate a sample of the depreciation charges. The audit team has also been asked to carry out detailed testing on the valuation of non-current assets.

Food poisoning - litigation

Balotelli Co's directors received correspondence in November 20X4 from a group of customers who have alleged that they suffered severe food poisoning from food eaten at the hotel and are claiming substantial damages. Management have stated that based on discussions with their lawyers the claim is unlikely to be successful.

Trade receivables circularisation

The audit team has obtained the following results from the receivables circularisation:

Customer	Balance per sales ledger ($)	Balance per customer confirmation ($)	Comment
Willow Co	42,500	42,500	
Cedar Co	35,000	25,000	Invoice raised 28 December 20X4
Maple Co	60,000	45,000	Payment made 30 December 20X4
Laurel Co	55,000	55,000	A balance of $20,000 is currently being disputed by Laurel Co

Q6

Which of the following correctly calculates the depreciation expense for the new assets for the year ended 31 December 20X4 and explains the resultant impact on non-current assets?

○ Depreciation should be $10,660, assets are understated

○ Depreciation should be $18,583, assets are understated

○ Depreciation should be $9,111, assets are overstated

○ Depreciation should be $12,549, assets are overstated

Q7

Which FOUR of the following audit procedures are appropriate to test the VALUATION assertion for non-current assets?

☐ Review board minutes for evidence of disposals during the year and verify that these are appropriately reflected in the non-current asset register

☐ Agree a sample of additions included in the non-current assets register to purchase invoice and cash book

☐ Review the repairs and maintenance expense account for evidence of items of a capital nature

☐ Recalculate the depreciation charge for a sample of assets ensuring that it is being applied consistently and in accordance with IAS 16 Property, Plant and Equipment

☐ Review physical condition of non-current assets for any signs of damage

☐ Ensure disposals are properly accounted for and recalculate gain/loss on disposal

Q8

Which of the following audit procedures would provide the auditor with the MOST reliable audit evidence regarding the likely outcome of the litigation?

◯ Request a written representation from management supporting their assertion that the claim will not be successful

◯ Send a confirmation request to the lawyers of Balotelli Co to obtain their view as to the probability of the claim being successful

◯ Review the correspondence from the customers claiming food poisoning to assess whether Balotelli Co has a present obligation as a result of a past event

◯ Review board minutes to understand why the directors believe that the claim will not be successful

Q9

Which TWO of the following are benefits of carrying out a trade receivables circularisation?

☐ It provides evidence from an independent external source

☐ It provides sufficient appropriate evidence over all balance assertions

☐ It improves audit efficiency as all customers are required to respond

☐ It improves the reliability of audit evidence as the process is under the control of the auditor

Q10

The audit team has been asked to assess whether any additional work is required on receivables.

Based on the results of the circularisation, match each customer to the appropriate audit procedure.

Customer	Audit procedure
Willow Co	Agreed to post year end cash book and bank statement
Cedar Co	Discuss with management and consider whether amount should be included in allowance for receivables
Maple Co	No further audit procedures required
Laurel Co	Agree to pre year end invoice

It is 1 July 20X5. Cannavaro.com is a website design company whose year end was 31 December 20X4. The audit is almost complete and the financial statements are due to be signed shortly. Profit before tax for the year is $3.8m and revenue is $11.2m.

Form and content of auditor's report

The company has only required an audit for the last two years and the board of directors has asked your firm to provide more detail in relation to the form and content of the auditor's report. In particular they have queried why the following elements are included:

(1) Date of report

(2) Addressee

(3) Auditor's responsibilities

(4) Opinion paragraph

Balance due from Pirlo Co

During the audit it has come to light that a key customer, Pirlo Co, with a receivables balance at the year end of $285,000, has just notified Cannavaro.com that they are experiencing cash flow difficulties, meaning they are unable to make any payments for the foreseeable future. The finance directors of Cannavaro.com has notified the auditor that he will write this balance off as an irrecoverable debt in the financial statements for the year ended 31 December 20X5.

Audit work

The audit partner has asked you to perform the following work in respect of the receivables balance due from Pirlo Co:

(1) Make an initial assessment of the materiality of the issue and consider the overall impact on the financial statements.

(2) Perform additional procedures in order to conclude on whether the financial statements require adjustment.

Q11

Match the following elements of the unmodified auditor's report queried by the directors of Cannavaro.com, to the correct explanation for its inclusion.

Element of auditor's report	Reason for inclusion
1	Explains the financial statements are presented fairly
2	Demonstrates the point at which sufficient appropriate evidence has been obtained
3	Clarifies who may rely on the opinion included in the report
4	Explains the role and remit of the audit

Q12

The audit assistant assigned to the audit of Cannavaro.com wants a better understanding of the impact that subsequent events have on the audit and has made the following statements.

Identify, by clicking on the relevant box in the table below, whether each of the following statements is true or false.

	TRUE	FALSE
All material subsequent events require the numbers in the financial statements to be adjusted	TRUE	FALSE
A non-adjusting event is a subsequent event for which NO amendments to the current year financial statements are required	TRUE	FALSE
The auditor's responsibilities for subsequent events which occur prior to the auditor's report being signed are different from their responsibilities after the auditor's report has been issued	TRUE	FALSE
The auditor should request a written representation confirming that all relevant subsequent events have been disclosed	TRUE	FALSE

Q13

In response to the partner's request, which of the following options correctly summarises the effect of the outstanding balance with Pirlo Co?

Option	Material	Impact on financial statements
A	No	Revenue is overstated
B	No	Gross profit is understated
C	Yes	Profit is overstated
D	Yes	Going concern basis is in doubt

○ Option A

○ Option B

○ Option C

○ Option D

Q14

Which TWO of the following audit procedures should be performed to form a conclusion as to whether the financial statements require adjustment?

☐ Discuss with management the reasons for not amending the financial statements

☐ Review the cash book post year end for receipts from Pirlo Co

☐ Send a request to Pirlo Co to confirm the outstanding balance

☐ Agree the outstanding balance to invoices and sales orders

Q15

The finance director has asked you to outline the appropriate audit opinions which will be provided depending on whether the company decides to amend or not amend the 20X4 financial statements for the issue identified regarding the recoverability of the balance with Pirlo Co.

Complete the following sentences by dragging and dropping the appropriate audit opinions.

If the 20X4 financial statements are not amended, our opinion will

be [ ]

If the appropriate adjustment is made to the financial statements, our

opinion will be [ ]

Audit opinions	
adverse	disclaimer
unmodified with emphasis of matter paragraph	qualified 'except for'
unmodified	

Section B

This section of the exam contains **three constructed response questions**.

Each question contains a scenario which relates to one or more requirement(s) which may be split over multiple question screens.

Each question is worth **20 or 30 marks** and is compulsory.

This exam section is worth **70 marks** in total.

Important: In your live exam please show all notes/workings that you want the marker to see within the spreadsheet or word processing answer areas where applicable. Remember, any notes/workings made on the Scratch Pad or on your workings paper will not be marked.

Select **Next** to continue.

Audit and Assurance (AA) - Specimen Exam

🔆 E̲xplain Answer   Æ Sym̲bol   ⊟ Calculator   📝 Scratch Pa̲d

This scenario relates to five requirements.

Milla Co manufactures fizzy drinks such as cola and lemonade as well as other soft drinks and its year end is 30 September 20X5. It is 1 July 20X5. You are an audit manager of Totti & Co and are currently planning the audit of Milla Co. You attended the planning meeting with the audit engagement partner and finance director last week and the minutes from the meeting are shown below. You are reviewing these as part of the process of preparing the audit strategy document.

Minutes of planning meeting for Milla Co

Milla Co's trading results have been strong this year and the company is forecasting revenue of $85m, which is an increase from the previous year. The company has invested significantly in the cola and fizzy drinks production process at the factory. This resulted in expenditure of $5m on updating, repairing and replacing a significant amount of the machinery used in the production process.

As the level of production has increased, the company has expanded the number of warehouses it uses to store inventory. It now utilises 15 warehouses; some are owned by Milla Co and some are rented from third parties. There will be inventory counts taking place at all 15 of these sites at the year end.

A new accounting general ledger has been introduced at the beginning of the year, with the old and new systems being run in parallel for a period of two months. In addition, Milla Co has incurred expenditure of $4.5m on developing a new brand of fizzy soft drinks. The company started this process in July 20X4 and is close to launching their new product into the market place.

As a result of the increase in revenue, Milla Co has recently recruited a new credit controller to chase outstanding receivables. The finance director thinks it is not necessary to continue to maintain an allowance for receivables and so has released the opening allowance of $1.5m.

The finance director stated that there was a problem in April in the mixing of raw materials within the production process which resulted in a large batch of cola products tasting different. A number of these products were sold; however, due to complaints by customers about the flavour, no further sales of these goods have been made. No adjustment has been made to the valuation of the damaged inventory, which will still be held at cost of $1m at the year end.

As in previous years, the management of Milla Co is due to be paid a significant annual bonus based on the value of year-end total assets.

Q16

(a) Explain audit risk and the components of audit risk.

(5 marks)

(b) Using the minutes provided, describe SEVEN audit risks, and explain the auditor's response to each risk, in planning the audit of Milla Co.

(14 marks)

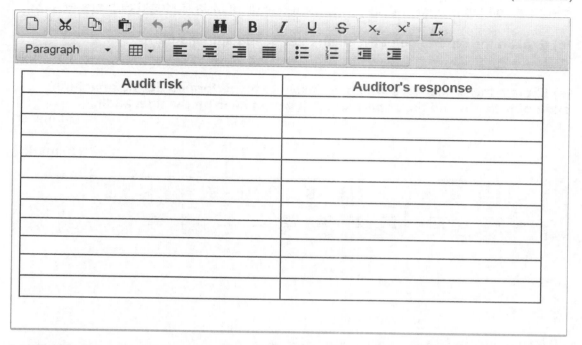

Audit risk	Auditor's response

(c) Identify the main areas, other than audit risks, which should be included within the audit strategy document for Milla Co, and for each area provide an example relevant to the audit.

(4 marks)

The finance director has requested that the deadline for the 20X6 audit be shortened by a month and has asked the audit engagement partner to consider if this will be possible. The partner has suggested that in order to meet this new tighter deadline the firm may carry out both an interim and final audit for the audit of Milla Co to 30 September 20X6.

(d) Explain the difference between an interim and a final audit.

(3 marks)

(e) Explain the procedures which are likely to be performed during an interim audit of Milla Co and the impact which it would have on the final audit.

(4 marks)

(30 marks)

Audit and Assurance (AA) - Specimen Exam

☼ E̲xplain Answer Æ Sym̲bol ⊟ Calculator ▧ Scratch Pa̲d

This scenario relates to four requirements.

It is 1 July 20X5. Baggio Co is a manufacturer of electrical equipment. It has factories across the country and its customer base includes retailers as well as individuals, to whom direct sales are made through their website. The company's year end is 30 September 20X5. You are an audit supervisor of Suarez & Co and are currently reviewing documentation of Baggio Co's internal control in preparation for the interim audit.

Baggio Co's website allows individuals to order goods directly, and full payment is taken in advance. Currently the website is not integrated into the inventory system and inventory levels are not checked at the time when orders are placed. Inventory is valued at the lower of cost and net realisable value.

Goods are dispatched via local couriers; however, they do not always record customer signatures as proof that the customer has received the goods. Over the past 12 months there have been customer complaints about the delay between sales orders and receipt of goods. Baggio Co has investigated these and found that, in each case, the sales order had been entered into the sales system correctly but was not forwarded to the dispatch department for fulfilling.

Baggio Co's retail customers undergo credit checks prior to being accepted and credit limits are set accordingly by sales ledger clerks. These customers place their orders through one of the sales team, who decides on sales discount levels.

Raw materials used in the manufacturing process are purchased from a wide range of suppliers. As a result of staff changes in the purchase ledger department, supplier statement reconciliations are no longer performed. Additionally, changes to supplier details in the purchase ledger master file can be undertaken by purchase ledger clerks as well as supervisors.

In the past six months, Baggio Co has changed part of its manufacturing process and as a result some new equipment has been purchased. However, there are considerable levels of plant and equipment which are now surplus to requirement. Purchase requisitions for all new equipment have been authorised by production supervisors and little has been done to reduce the surplus of old equipment.

Q17

(a) In respect of the internal control of Baggio Co:

(i) Identify and explain SIX deficiencies;
(ii) Recommend a control to address each of these deficiencies; and
(iii) Describe a test of control Suarez & Co would perform to assess whether each of these controls, if implemented, is operating effectively.

Note: The total marks will be split equally between each part.

(18 marks)

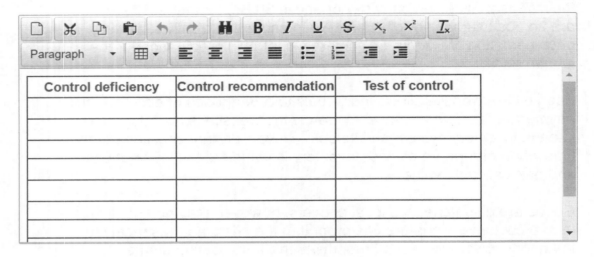

(b) Describe substantive procedures the auditor should perform at the year end to confirm plant and equipment additions.

(2 marks)

(20 marks)

Audit and Assurance (AA) - Specimen Exam

🔆 E**x**plain Answer Æ Sym**b**ol 🗍 Calculator 📝 Scratch Pa**d**

This scenario relates to four requirements.

It is 1 July 20X5. Vieri Co manufactures a range of motor cars. You are an audit supervisor of Rossi & Co and are currently preparing the audit programmes for the audit of Vieri Co for the year ended 31 March 20X5. You have had a meeting with your audit manager and he has notified you of the following issues identified during the audit risk assessment process:

Land and buildings
Vieri Co has a policy of revaluing land and buildings, this is undertaken on a rolling basis over a five-year period. During the year Vieri Co requested an external independent valuer to revalue a number of properties, including a warehouse purchased in October 20X4. Depreciation is charged on a pro rata basis.

Work in progress
Vieri Co undertakes continuous production of cars, 24 hours a day, seven days a week. An inventory count is to be undertaken at the year end and Rossi & Co will attend. You are responsible for the audit of work in progress (WIP) and will be part of the team attending the count as well as the final audit. WIP constitutes the partly assembled cars at the year end and this balance is likely to be material. Vieri Co values WIP according to percentage of completion, and standard costs are then applied to these percentages.

Q18

(a) Explain the factors Rossi & Co should consider when placing reliance on the work of the independent valuer.

(5 marks)

(b) Describe the substantive procedures the auditor should perform to obtain sufficient and appropriate audit evidence in relation to the revaluation of land and buildings and the recently purchased warehouse.

(6 marks)

(c) Describe the substantive procedures the auditor should perform to obtain sufficient and appropriate audit evidence in relation to the valuation of work in progress.

(4 marks)

During the audit, the team has identified an error in the valuation of work in progress, as a number of the assumptions contain out of date information. The directors of Vieri Co have indicated that they do not wish to amend the financial statements.

(d) Explain the steps Rossi & Co should now take and the impact on the auditor's report in relation to the directors' refusal to amend the financial statements.

(5 marks)

(20 marks)

Section 6

ANSWERS TO SPECIMEN EXAM QUESTIONS

SECTION A

1

Fact 1 - Partner has been in role for 8 years which contravenes the code and represents a **familiarity** threat.

Fact 2 - Providing information on internal audit does not give rise to a threat to independence.

Fact 3 - Partner's son holding shares represents a **self-interest** threat as a close family member of the partner holds a financial interest.

Fact 4 - Providing internal audit services raises a **self-review** threat as it is likely that the audit team will be looking to place reliance on the control system reviewed by IA.

Fact 5 - This represents fees on a contingent basis and raises a **self-interest** threat as the audit firm's fee will rise if the company's profit after tax increases.

2

If the engagement partner's son accepts the role and obtains shares in the company it would constitute a self-interest threat BUT as the partner has already exceeded the seven year relationship rule, in line with ACCA's Code of Ethics and Conduct, the partner should be rotated off the audit irrespective of the decision made by her son.

As Maldini Co is a listed company an engagement quality control reviewer should already be in place in line with ISA 220.

Consulting a third party on key audit judgments would be a potential safeguard in respect of overdependence on fees but would not be adequate in the circumstances described.

It is unlikely that the firm needs to resign from the audit (due to the stated circumstances) as the threat to objectivity can be mitigated.

3

Statement 1 is inappropriate as the external and internal audit team should be separate and therefore consideration of the skills of the external team is not appropriate in the circumstances.

Statement 4 does not apply in that the timescale of the work is not relevant to consider the threats to objectivity

Statement 2 and 3 are valid considerations -as per ACCA's Code of Ethics and Conduct providing internal audit services can result in the audit firm assuming a management responsibility. To mitigate for this it is appropriate for the firm to assess whether management will take responsibility for implementing recommendations. Further for a listed company the Code prohibits the provision of internal audit services that reviews a significant proportion of the internal controls over financial reporting as these may be relied upon by the external audit team and the self review threat is too great.

4

Internal audit are appointed by the audit committee (external audit by the shareholders) and it is the role of internal audit to review the effectiveness and efficiency of internal controls to improve operations. External audit looks at the operating effectiveness of internal controls on which they may rely for audit evidence. A by-product may be to comment on any deficiencies they have found.

Therefore characteristics 1 and 3 relate to internal audit

The external auditor's report is publicly available to the shareholders of the company (internal audit reports are addressed to management) and the external auditor provides an opinion on the truth and fairness of the financial statements.

Therefore characteristics 2 and 4 relate to external audit.

5

The proposal in relation to the fees is a contingent fee basis which is expressly prohibited by ACCA's Code of Ethics and Conduct and therefore the only viable option here is to reject the fee basis

6

Depreciation should be calculated as:

Treadmills/exercise bikes = (18,000 + 17,000)/36 x 8 months = 7,778
Rowing machines/cross trainers = (9,750 + 11,000)/36 x 5 months = 2,882

Therefore total depreciation is **$10,660** and assets are currently **understated** as too much depreciation has currently been charged.

7

Reviewing board minutes for disposals and verifying that they have been removed from the asset register is a test for existence

Review the expense accounts for items of a capital nature is a test for completeness

All other tests are relevant for valuation

8

While all procedures would be valid in the circumstances only the written confirmation from the company's lawyers would allow the auditor to obtain an expert, third party confirmation on the likelihood of the case being successful. This would provide the auditor with the most reliable evidence in the circumstances

9

As per ISA 505 External Confirmations, the evidence obtained from a trade receivables circularisation should be reliable as it is from an external source and the risk of management bias and influence is restricted due to the process being under the control of the auditor.

Customers are not obliged to answer and often circularisations have a very low response rate. A circularisation will not provide evidence over the valuation assertion for receivables

10

Willow Co - external confirmation has confirmed the balance and no further work on existence is required.

Cedar Co - Represents an invoice in transit and therefore should be confirmed to a pre year end invoice to verify that it is a legitimate timing difference.

Maple Co - Represents a payment in transit and should be agreed to post year end payment to confirm that it is a legitimate timing difference

Laurel Co- Customer is disputing the balance and therefore the need for an allowance against the balance should be assessed.

11

Addressee - sets out who the report is addressed to - usually the shareholders - and is there to clarify who can place reliance on the audit opinion.

Auditor's responsbilities - this paragraph sets out that the auditor is required to express an opinion on the financial statements and seeks to explain the difference between the role of the auditor and those charged with governance. Thus this paragraph sets out the role and remit of the auditor.

Opinion paragraph - this paragraph sets out the auditors conclusion on the financial statements. In an unmodified report this takes the form of the auditor confirming that the financial statements present a true and fair view or are presented fairly.

Date of report - The auditor's report shall be dated no earlier than the date on which the auditor has obtained sufficient appropriate audit evidence on which to base the auditor's opinion on the financial statements. The date of the audit report is important in the case of subsequent events which impact the financial statements.

12

Statement 1 is false as not all subsequent events will require an adjustment to the numbers within the financial statements. IAS 10 Events after the Reporting Period makes a distinction between an adjusting and non-adjusting event. Only material adjusting events would require an amendment to the figures within the financial statements.

Statement 2 is false as while a non-adjusting event would not require a change to the numbers it may require a disclosure to be made. If this is material, non-disclosure could still result in a modification to the auditor's report.

Statement 3 is true as the auditor is required to carry out procedures up to the date of the auditor's report to gain sufficient appropriate evidence that all relevant subsequent events have been identified and dealt with appropriately. After the auditor's report is issued the auditor does not need to actively look for subsequent events.

Statement 4 is true as per ISA 560 Subsequent Events, the auditor is required to obtain written confirmation from management or those charged with governance that all subsequent events have been identified and dealt with in accordance with the appropriate reporting framework.

13

The outstanding balance with Pirlo Co is likely to be irrecoverable as the customer is experiencing financial difficulties The balance is material at 7.5% of PBT and 2.5% of revenue and therefore would need adjusted as without an adjustment the financial statements would be materially misstated as profit and assets are overstated by $285k.

Therefore Option C is correct

14

After date cash testing is the best way for the auditor to assess if the balance is recoverable wholly or in part and therefore the cashbook should be reviewed for any receipts that will change the assessment of the debt after the year end.

The issue should also be discussed with management to understand their reasons for not wanting to amend the financial statements as this may be due to a change in circumstances.

Writing to the customer/agreeing to invoices, while valid procedures during the audit to verify the existence of an outstanding balance, would not allow the auditor to assess the recoverability of the balance which is the key issue in determining whether an adjsutment is required.

15

The debt with Pirlo Co should be written off or included in the allowance for trade receivables. As the balance is material to the financial statements at 7.5% of PBT and 2.5% of revenue.This represents a material misstatement which is material but not pervasive

As such, if no adjustment is made the auditor will be required to provide a qualified 'except for' opinion.

If the required change is made no material misstatement exists and therefore the auditor will be able to issue an unmodified opinion.

SECTION B

16   Milla Cola Co

Milla Cola Co

Audit risk and its components

Audit risk is the risk that the auditor expresses an inappropriate audit opinion when the financial statements are materially misstated. Audit risk is a function of two main components being the risks of material misstatement and detection risk. Risk of material misstatement is made up of two components, inherent risk and control risk.

Inherent risk is the susceptibility of an assertion about a class of transaction, account balance or disclosure to a misstatement that could be material, either individually or when aggregated with other misstatements, before consideration of any related controls.

Control risk is the risk that a misstatement which could occur in an assertion about a class of transaction, account balance or disclosure and which could be material, either individually or when aggregated with other misstatements, will not be prevented, or detected and corrected, on a timely basis by the entity's internal control.

Detection risk is the risk that the procedures performed by the auditor to reduce audit risk to an acceptably low level will not detect a misstatement which exists and which could be material, either individually or when aggregated with other misstatements. Detection risk is affected by sampling and non-sampling risk.

AA Specimen Exam - Section B Milla Co		
	Marks available	Marks awarded
Requirement – component of audit risk		
Explanation of audit risk	2	
Explanation of components of audit risk: Inherent, control and detection risk	3	
Total marks	**5**	

Milla Co

Audit risks and responses

Audit risk	Auditor's response
Milla Co has incurred $5m on updating, repairing and replacing a significant amount of the production process machinery. If this expenditure is of a capital nature, it should be capitalised as part of property, plant and equipment (PPE) in line with IAS 16 *Property, Plant and Equipment*. However, if it relates more to repairs, then it should be expensed to the statement of profit or loss If the expenditure is not correctly classified, profit and PPE could be under or overstated.	The auditor should review a breakdown of these costs to ascertain the split of capital and revenue expenditure, and further testing should be undertaken to ensure that the classification in the financial statements is correct.
At the year end there will be inventory counts undertaken in all 15 warehouses. It is unlikely that the auditor will be able to attend all 15 inventory counts and therefore they need to ensure that they obtain sufficient appropriate audit evidence over the inventory counting controls, and completeness and existence of inventory for any warehouses not visited.	The auditor should assess which of the inventory sites they will attend the counts for. This will be any with material inventory or which have a history of significant errors. For those not visited, the auditor will need to review the level of exceptions noted during the count and discuss with management any issues which arose during the count.
Inventory is stored within 15 warehouses; some are owned by Milla Co and some rented from third parties. Only warehouses owned by Milla Co should be included within PPE. There is a risk of overstatement of PPE and understatement of rental expenses if Milla Co has capitalised all 15 warehouses.	The auditor should review supporting documentation for all warehouses included within PPE to confirm ownership by Milla Co and to ensure non-current assets are not overstated.
A new accounting general ledger system has been introduced at the beginning of the year and the old system was run in parallel for two months. There is a risk of opening balances being misstated and loss of data if they have not been transferred from the old system correctly. In addition, the new accounting general ledger system will require documenting and the controls over this will need to be tested.	The auditor should undertake detailed testing to confirm that all opening balances have been correctly recorded in the new accounting general ledger system. They should document and test the new system. They should review any management reports run comparing the old and new system during the parallel run to identify any issues with the processing of accounting information.
Milla Co has incurred expenditure of $4·5 million on developing a new brand of fizzy drink. This expenditure is research and development under IAS 38 *Intangible Assets*. The standard requires research costs to be expensed and development costs to be capitalised as an intangible asset. If Milla Co has incorrectly classified research costs as development expenditure, there is a risk the intangible asset could be overstated and expenses understated.	Obtain a breakdown of the expenditure and undertake testing to determine whether the costs relate to the research or development stage. Discuss the accounting treatment with the finance director and ensure it is in accordance with IAS 38.

The finance director of Milla Co has decided to release the opening provision of $1·5 million for allowance for receivables as he feels it is unnecessary. There is a risk that receivables will be overvalued, as despite having a credit controller, some balances will be irrecoverable and so will be overstated if not provided against. In addition, due to the damaged inventory there is an increased risk of customers refusing to make payments in full.	Extended post year-end cash receipts testing and a review of the aged receivables ledger to be performed to assess valuation and the need for an allowance for receivables. Discuss with the director the rationale for releasing the $1.5m opening allowance for receivables.
A large batch of cola products has been damaged in the production process and will be in inventory at the year end. No adjustment has been made by management. The valuation of inventory as per IAS 2 *Inventories* should be at the lower of cost and net realisable value. Hence it is likely that this inventory is overvalued.	Detailed cost and net realisable value testing to be performed to assess how much the inventory requires writing down by.
Due to the damaged cola products, a number of customers have complained. It is likely that for any of the damaged goods sold, Milla Co will need to refund these customers. Revenue is possibly overstated if the sales returns are not completely and accurately recorded.	Review the breakdown of sales of damaged goods, and ensure that they have been accurately removed from revenue.
The management of Milla Co receives a significant annual bonus based on the value of year-end total assets. There is a risk that management might feel under pressure to overstate the value of assets through the judgements taken or through the use of releasing provisions.	Throughout the audit the team will need to be alert to this risk. They will need to maintain professional scepticism and carefully review judgemental decisions and compare treatment against prior years.

AA Specimen Exam - Section B Milla Co	Marks available	Marks awarded
Requirement – Audit risks and responses (only 7 risks required)		
$5 million expenditure on production process	2	
Inventory counts at 15 warehouses at year end	2	
Treatment of owned v third party warehouses	2	
New general ledger system introduced at the beginning of the year	2	
Release of opening provision for allowance for receivables	2	
Research and development expenditure	2	
Damaged inventory	2	
Sales returns	2	
Management bonus based on asset values	2	
Max 7 issues, 2 marks each	14	

Milla Cola Co

Audit strategy document

The audit strategy sets out the scope, timing and direction of the audit and helps the development of the audit plan. It should consider the following main areas:

It should identify the main characteristics of the engagement which define its scope. For Milla it should consider the following:
- Whether the financial information to be audited has been prepared in accordance with IFRS.
- To what extent audit evidence obtained in previous audits for Milla will be utilised.
- Whether computer-assisted audit techniques will be used and the effect of IT on audit procedures.
- The availability of key personnel at Milla.

It should ascertain the reporting objectives of the engagement to plan the timing of the audit and the nature of the communications required, such as:

- The audit timetable for reporting and whether there will be an interim as well as final audit.
- Organisation of meetings with Milla's management to discuss any audit issues arising.
- Location of the 15 inventory counts.
- Any discussions with management regarding the reports to be issued.
- The timings of the audit team meetings and review of work performed.
- If there are any expected communications with third parties.

The strategy should consider the factors that, in the auditor's professional judgement, are significant in directing Milla's audit team's efforts, such as:

- The determination of materiality for the audit.
- The need to maintain a questioning mind and to exercise professional scepticism in gathering and evaluating audit evidence.

It should consider the results of preliminary audit planning activities and, where applicable, whether knowledge gained on other engagements for Milla is relevant, such as:

- Results of previous audits and the results of any tests over the effectiveness of internal controls.
- Evidence of management's commitment to the design, implementation and maintenance of sound internal control.
- Volume of transactions, which may determine whether it is more efficient for the audit team to rely on internal control.
- Significant business developments affecting Milla, such as the change in the accounting system and the significant expenditure on an overhaul of the factory.

The audit strategy should ascertain the nature, timing and extent of resources necessary to perform the audit, such as:

- The selection of the audit team with experience of this type of industry.
- Assignment of audit work to the team members.
- Setting the audit budget.

Tutorial note: *The answer is longer than required for four marks but represents a teaching aid*

AA Specimen Exam - Section B Milla Co		
	Marks available	Marks awarded
Requirement – Audit strategy document		
Main characteristics of the audit	1	
Reporting objectives of the audit and nature of communications required	1	
Factors that are significant in directing the audit team's efforts	1	
Results of preliminary engagement activities and whether knowledge gained on other engagements is relevant	1	
Nature, timing and extent of resources necessary to perform the audit	1	
Restricted to	**4**	

Milla Co

(d) Differences between an interim and a final audit

<u>Interim audit</u>

The interim audit is that part of the audit which takes place before the year end. The auditor uses the interim audit to carry out procedures which would be difficult to perform at the year end because of time pressure. There is no requirement to undertake an interim audit; factors to consider when deciding upon whether to have one include the size and complexity of the company along with the effectiveness of internal controls.

<u>Final audit</u>

The final audit will take place after the year end and concludes with the auditor forming and expressing an opinion on the financial statements for the whole year subject to audit. It is important to note that the final opinion takes account of conclusions formed at both the interim and final audit.

(e) Procedures which could be undertaken during the interim audit include:

– Review and updating of the documentation of accounting systems at Milla Co
– Discussions with management on the recent growth and any other changes within the business which have occurred during the year to date at Milla Co to update the auditor's understanding of the company.
– Assessment of risks which will impact the final audit of Milla Co.
– Undertake tests of controls on Milla Co's key transaction cycles of sales, purchases and inventory, and credit control.
– Perform substantive procedures on profit and loss transactions for the year to date and any other completed material transactions.

Impact of interim audit on final

If an interim audit is undertaken at Milla Co then it will have an impact on the final audit and the extent of work undertaken after the year end. Firstly, as some testing has already been undertaken there will be less work to be performed at the final audit, which may result in a shorter audit and audited financial statements possibly being available earlier.   The outcome of the controls testing undertaken during the interim audit will impact the level of substantive testing to be undertaken. If the controls tested have proven to be operating effectively then the auditor may be able to reduce the level of detailed substantive testing required as they will be able to place reliance on the controls. In addition if substantive procedures were undertaken at the interim audit then only the period from the interim audit to the year end will require to be tested.

AA Specimen Exam - Section B Milla Co	Marks available	Marks awarded
Requirement (d) – Difference between interim and final audit		
Interim audit	2	
Final audit	2	
Restricted to	**3**	
Requirement (e) – Procedures/impact of interim audit on final audit		
Example procedures	3	
Impact on final audit	3	
Restricted to	**4**	

17   Baggio International Co

Baggio Co's internal control assessment

Deficiency	Control recommendations	Test of Control
Currently the website is not integrated into inventory system. This can result in Baggio Co accepting customer orders when they do not have the goods in inventory. This can cause them to lose sales and customer goodwill	The website should be updated to include an interface into the inventory system; this should check inventory levels and only process orders if adequate inventory is held. If inventory is out of stock, this should appear on the website with an approximate waiting time.	Test data could be used to attempt to process orders via the website for items which are not currently held in inventory. The orders should be flagged as being out of stock and indicate an approximate waiting time.
For goods despatched by local couriers, customer signatures are not always obtained. This can lead to customers falsely claiming that they have not received their goods. Baggio Co would not be able to prove that they had in fact despatched the goods and may result in goods being despatched twice.	Baggio Co should remind all local couriers that customer signatures must be obtained as proof of delivery and payment will not be made for any despatches with missing signatures.	Select a sample of despatches by couriers and ask Baggio Co for proof of delivery by viewing customer signatures.
There have been a number of situations where the sales orders have not been fulfilled in a timely manner. This can lead to a loss of customer goodwill and if it persists will damage the reputation of Baggio Co as a reliable supplier.	Once goods are despatched they should be matched to sales orders and flagged as fulfilled. The system should automatically flag any outstanding sales orders past a predetermined period, such as five days. This report should be reviewed by a responsible official.	Review the report of outstanding sales orders. If significant, discuss with a responsible official to understand why there is still a significant time period between sales order and despatch date. Select a sample of sales orders and compare the date of order to the goods despatch date to ascertain whether this is within the acceptable predetermined period.
Customer credit limits are set by sales ledger clerks. Sales ledger clerks are not sufficiently senior and so may set limits too high, leading to irrecoverable debts, or too low, leading to a loss of revenue.	Credit limits should be set by a senior member of the sales ledger department and not by sales ledger clerks. These limits should be regularly reviewed by a responsible official.	For a sample of new customers accepted in the year, review the authorisation of the credit limit, and ensure that this was performed by a responsible official. Enquire of sales ledger clerks as to who can set credit limits.
Sales discounts are set by Baggio Co's sales team. In order to boost their sales, members of the sales team may set the discounts too high, leading to a loss of revenue.	All members of the sales team should be given authority to grant sales discounts up to a set limit. Any sales discounts above these limits should be authorised by sales area managers or the sales director. Regular review of sales	Discuss with members of the sales team the process for setting sales discounts. Review the sales discount report for evidence of review by the sales director.

	discount levels should be undertaken by the sales director, and this review should be evidenced.	
Supplier statement reconciliations are no longer performed. This may result in errors in the recording of purchases and payables not being identified in a timely manner.	Supplier statement reconciliations should be performed on a monthly basis for all suppliers and these should be reviewed by a responsible official.	Review the file of reconciliations to ensure that they are being performed on a regular basis and that they have been reviewed by a responsible official.
Changes to supplier details in the purchase ledger master file can be undertaken by purchase ledger clerks. This could lead to key supplier data being accidently amended or fictitious suppliers being set up, which can increase the risk of fraud.	Only purchase ledger supervisors should have the authority to make changes to master file data. This should be controlled via passwords. Regular review of any changes to master file data by a responsible official and this review should be evidenced.	Request a purchase ledger clerk to attempt to access the master file and to make an amendment, the system should not allow this. Review a report of master data changes and review the authority of those making amendments.
Baggio Co has considerable levels of surplus plant and equipment. Surplus unused plant is at risk of theft. In addition, if the surplus plant is not disposed of then the company could lose sundry income.	Regular review of the plant and equipment on the factory floor by senior factory personnel to identify any old or surplus equipment. As part of the capital expenditure process there should be a requirement to confirm the treatment of the equipment being replaced.	Observe the review process by senior factory personnel, identifying the treatment of any old equipment. Review processed capital expenditure forms to ascertain if the treatment of replaced equipment is stated.
Purchase requisitions are authorised by production supervisors. Production supervisors are not sufficiently independent or senior to authorise capital expenditure.	Capital expenditure authorisation levels to be established. Production supervisors should only be able to authorise low value items, any high value items should be authorised by the board.	Review a sample of authorised capital expenditure forms and identify if the correct signatory has authorised them.

AA Specimen Paper – Section B Baggio Co	Marks available	Marks awarded
Requirement – Control weaknesses, recommendations and tests of controls (only 6 issues required)		
Website not integrated into inventory system	3	
Customer signatures	3	
Unfulfilled sales orders	3	
Customer credit limits	3	
Sales discounts	3	
Supplier statement reconciliations	3	
Purchase ledger master file	3	
Surplus plant and equipment	3	
Authorisation of capital expenditure	3	
6 issues required, 3 marks each	**18**	

Baggio Co

Substantive procedures - additions

- Obtain a breakdown of additions, cast the list and agree to the non-current asset register to confirm completeness of plant and equipment (P&E).
- Select a sample of additions and agree cost to supplier invoice to confirm valuation.
- Verify rights and obligations by agreeing the addition of plant and equipment to a supplier invoice in the name of Baggio Co.
- Review the list of additions and confirm that they relate to capital expenditure items rather than repairs and maintenance.
- Review board minutes to ensure that significant capital expenditure purchases have been authorised by the board.
- For a sample of additions recorded in P&E, physically verify them on the factory floor to confirm existence.

AA Specimen Exam - Section B Baggio Co	Marks available	Marks awarded
Requirement – Substantive procedures for PPE		
Cast list of additions and agree to non-current asset register	1	
Vouch cost to recent supplier invoice	1	
Agree addition to a supplier invoice in the name of Baggio Co to confirm rights and obligations	1	
Review additions and confirm capital expenditure items rather than repairs and maintenance	1	
Review board minutes to ensure authorised by the board	1	
Physically verify them on the factory floor to confirm existence	1	
Other		
Restricted to	**2**	

18 Vieri Motor Cars Co

Vieri Co

Reliance on the work of an independent valuer

ISA 500 *Audit Evidence* requires auditors to evaluate the competence, capabilities including expertise and objectivity of a management expert. This would include consideration of the qualifications of the valuer and assessment of whether they were members of any professional body or industry association.

The expert's independence should be ascertained, with potential threats such as undue reliance on Vieri Co or a self-interest threat such as share ownership considered.

In addition, Rossi & Co should meet with the expert and discuss with them their relevant expertise, in particular whether they have valued similar land and buildings to those of Vieri Co in the past. Rossi & Co should also consider whether the valuer understands the accounting requirements of IAS 16 *Property, Plant and Equipment* in relation to valuations.

The valuation should then be evaluated. The assumptions used should be carefully reviewed and compared to previous revaluations at Vieri Co. These assumptions should be discussed with both management and the valuer to understand the basis of any valuations.

AA Specimen Exam - Section B Vieri Co		
	Marks available	**Marks awarded**
Requirement – Reliance on independent valuer		
ISA 500 requires consideration of competence and capabilities of expert	1	
Consider if member of professional body or industry association	1	
Assess independence	1	
Assess whether relevant expertise of type of properties as Vieri Co	1	
Evaluate assumptions	1	
Total marks	**5**	

Vieri Co

Substantive procedures for revaluation of land and buildings

– Obtain a schedule of land and buildings revalued this year and cast to confirm completeness and accuracy of the revaluation adjustment.

– On a sample basis agree the revalued amounts to the valuation statement provided by the valuer.

– Agree the revalued amounts for these assets are included correctly in the non-current assets register.

– Recalculate the total revaluation adjustment and agree correctly recorded in the revaluation surplus.

– Agree the initial cost for the warehouse addition to supporting documentation such as invoices to confirm cost.

– Confirm through a review of the title deeds that the warehouse is owned by Vieri Co.

– Recalculate the depreciation charge for the year to ensure that for assets revalued during the year, the depreciation was based on the correct valuation and for the warehouse addition that the charge was for six months only.

– Review the financial statements disclosures of the revaluation to ensure they comply with IAS 16 *Property, Plant and Equipment*.

AA Specimen Exam - Section B Vieri Co	Marks available	Marks awarded
Requirement – Substantive procedures for revaluation of land and buildings.		
Cast schedule of land and buildings revalued this year	1	
Agree the revalued amounts to the valuation statement provided by the valuer	1	
Agree the revalued amounts included correctly in the non-current assets register	1	
Recalculate the total revaluation adjustment and agree recorded in the revaluation surplus	1	
Agree the initial cost for the warehouse to invoices to confirm cost	1	
Confirm through title deeds that the warehouse is owned by Vieri Co	1	
Recalculate the depreciation charge for the year	1	
Review the financial statements disclosures for compliance with IAS 16 *Property, Plant and Equipment*	1	
Other		
Restricted to	**6**	

Vieri Co

Substantive procedures for valuation of work in progress (WIP)
- Prior to attending the inventory count, discuss with management how the percentage completions are attributed to the WIP, for example, is this based on motor cars passing certain points in the production process.
- During the count, observe the procedures carried out by Vieri Co staff in assessing the level of WIP and consider the reasonableness of the assumptions used.
- Agree for a sample that the percentage completions assessed during the count are in accordance with Vieri Co's policies communicated prior to the count.
- Discuss with management the basis of the standard costs applied to the percentage completion of WIP, and how often these are reviewed and updated.
- Review the level of variances between standard and actual costs and discuss with management how these are treated.
- Obtain a breakdown of the standard costs and agree a sample of these costs to actual invoices or payroll records to assess their reasonableness.
- Cast the schedule of total WIP and agree to the trial balance and financial statements.
- Agree sample of WIP assessed during the count to the WIP schedule, agree percentage completion is correct and recalculate the inventory valuation.

AA Specimen Exam - Section B Vieri Co		
	Marks available	**Marks awarded**
Requirement – Substantive procedures for work in progress (WIP)		
Discuss with management how the percentage completions are attributed to WIP	1	
Observe the procedures carried out in the count in assessing the level of WIP; consider reasonableness of the assumptions used	1	
During the count, agree a sample of percentage completions are in accordance with Vieri Co's policies	1	
Discuss with management the basis of the standard costs	1	
Review the level of variances between standard and actual costs	1	
Obtain a breakdown of the standard costs and agree a sample of these costs to actual invoices	1	
Cast the schedule of total WIP and agree to the trial balance and financial statements	1	
Agree sample of WIP assessed during the count to the WIP schedule, agree percentage completion is correct and recalculate the inventory valuation	1	
Other		
Restricted to	**4**	

Vieri Co

Impact of misstatement on auditor's report

Discuss with the management of Vieri Co why they are refusing to make the amendment to WIP. Assess the materiality of the error; if immaterial, it should be added to the schedule of uncorrected misstatements. The auditor should then assess whether this error results in the total of uncorrected misstatements becoming material; if so, this should be discussed with management; if not, there would be no impact on the auditor's report.

If the error is material and management refuses to amend the financial statements, then the auditor's report will need to be modified. It is unlikely that any error would be pervasive as although WIP in total is material, it would not have a pervasive effect on the financial statements as a whole. As management has not complied with IAS 2 *Inventories* and if the error is material but not pervasive, then a qualified opinion would be necessary. The opinion paragraph would be qualified 'except for'.

A basis for qualified opinion paragraph would need to be included after the opinion paragraph. This would explain the material misstatement in relation to the valuation of WIP and the effect on the financial statements.

AA Specimen Exam - Section B Vieri Co	Marks available	Marks awarded
Requirement – Impact on auditor's report		
Discuss with management reasons for non-amendment	1	
Assess materiality	1	
Immaterial – schedule of uncorrected adjustments	1	
Material not pervasive – qualified opinion	1	
Opinion paragraph – qualified 'except for'	1	
Basis for qualified opinion paragraph	1	
Restricted to	**5**	